Seminal Contributions to Information Systems Engineering

Janis Bubenko • John Krogstie • Oscar Pastor
Barbara Pernici • Colette Rolland • Arne Sølvberg
Editors

Seminal Contributions to Information Systems Engineering

25 Years of CAiSE

Editors
Janis Bubenko
Royal Institute of Technology
Department of Computer, and Systems Science
Kista, Sweden

Barbara Pernici
Politecnico di Milano
Dipartimento di Elettronica, Informazione e Bioingegneria
Milan, Italy

John Krogstie
Arne Sølvberg
Norwegian University of Science and Technology
Department of Computer and Information Science
Trondheim, Norway

Colette Rolland
Université Paris1
Centre de Recherche en Informatique
Paris, France

Oscar Pastor
Universidad Politecnica de Valencia
Depto. Sistemas Informaticos y, Computacion
Valencia, Spain

ISBN 978-3-642-42662-9 ISBN 978-3-642-36926-1 (eBook)
DOI 10.1007/978-3-642-36926-1
Springer Heidelberg New York Dordrecht London

ACM Computing Classification (1998): H.4, H.3, D.2, J.1

Printed on acid-free paper

Springer is part of Springer Science+Business Media (www.springer.com)

Preface

In 2013, the International Conference on Advance Information Systems Engineering (CAiSE) is turning 25. Started in 1989, in these years, the conference has provided a broad forum for researchers working in the area of Information Systems Engineering. To reflect on the work done so far and to examine perspectives of future work, the CAiSE Steering Committee decided to collect a selection of papers published in the conference proceedings in these years and to ask their authors, well-known researchers in the area, to comment on their work and how it developed during the years. CAiSE Proceedings have been published by Springer in the Lecture Notes in Computer Science Series (LNCS) since 1990. The editors of this book, who are the members of the Conference Advisory Board and the chairs of the Steering Committee, selected papers from CAiSE conferences from 1992 to 2008, to provide a broad overview on the topics that were presented and discussed in the conference and their evolution. The selection phase has not been easy, since many papers were well received in the research community and had a broad impact on future work. In the book, the original paper is reprinted, and after it, a short paper illustrating the evolution of the research related to the paper is included. As editors, we are thankful to the authors who accepted to participate in this adventure.

In addition, the book provides an overview on the conference from different points of view: a historical analysis on how it developed and its goals over the years, a social network analysis of the positioning of CAiSE in the research community, and future perspectives for the conference in an evolving world. As analyzed in these chapters, and as it is evident from the selected papers, the scope of the conference is broad but, at the same time, well positioned in an area which is related to the topics of modeling and designing information systems, collecting their requirements, but also with a special attention on how information systems are engineered, towards their final development as software components. Such focus has been consistently present in the development of the conference and in recent years. As such, the conference attracted over the years a larger and larger number of researchers, participating both in the conference and in its related events, such as workshops, related conferences, tutorials, and the Doctoral Consortium.

We think that as a whole the book provides a comprehensive overview of the research in this area and also provides many inspiring considerations for future work.

A very large number of people have to be thanked for their work in the CAiSE community in the last 25 years. It is impossible to mention everybody, but authors, reviewers, conference organizers and chairs, and organizers of related events all deserve our gratitude for their constant work in the community.

In particular, in the following, we would like to mention the editors of the CAiSE Proceedings, program chairs, and organizers, listing all conferences proceedings and the locations and countries in which the conferences were held:

- Jolita Ralyté, Xavier Franch, Sjaak Brinkkemper, Stanisław Wrycza (Eds.): Advanced Information Systems Engineering – 24th International Conference, CAiSE 2012, Gdansk, Poland, June 25–29, 2012, LNCS 7328, Springer, 2012
- Haralambos Mouratidis, Colette Rolland (Eds.): Advanced Information Systems Engineering – 23rd International Conference, CAiSE 2011, London, UK, June 20–24, 2011, LNCS 6741, Springer, 2011
- Barbara Pernici (Ed.): Advanced Information Systems Engineering, 22nd International Conference, CAiSE 2010, Hammamet, Tunisia, June 7–9, 2010, LNCS 6051, Springer, 2010
- Pascal van Eck, Jaap Gordijn, Roel Wieringa (Eds.): Advanced Information Systems Engineering, 21st International Conference, CAiSE 2009, Amsterdam, The Netherlands, June 8–12, 2009, LNCS 5565, Springer, 2009
- Zohra Bellahsene, Michel Léonard (Eds.): Advanced Information Systems Engineering, 20th International Conference, CAiSE 2008, Montpellier, France, June 16–20, 2008, LNCS 5074, Springer, 2008
- John Krogstie, Andreas L. Opdahl, Guttorm Sindre (Eds.): Advanced Information Systems Engineering, 19th International Conference, CAiSE 2007, Trondheim, Norway, June 11–15, 2007, LNCS 4495, Springer, 2007
- Eric Dubois, Klaus Pohl (Eds.): Advanced Information Systems Engineering, 18th International Conference, CAiSE 2006, Luxembourg, Luxembourg, June 5–9, 2006, LNCS 4001, Springer, 2006
- Oscar Pastor, João Falcão e Cunha (Eds.): Advanced Information Systems Engineering, 17th International Conference, CAiSE 2005, Porto, Portugal, June 13–17, 2005, LNCS 3520, Springer, 2005
- Anne Persson, Janis Stirna (Eds.): Advanced Information Systems Engineering, 16th International Conference, CAiSE 2004, Riga, Latvia, June 7–11, 2004, LNCS 3084, Springer, 2004
- Johann Eder, Michele Missikoff (Eds.): Advanced Information Systems Engineering, 15th International Conference, CAiSE 2003, Klagenfurt, Austria, June 16–18, 2003, LNCS 2681, Springer, 2003
- Anne Banks Pidduck, John Mylopoulos, Carson C. Woo, M. Tamer Özsu (Eds.): Advanced Information Systems Engineering, 14th International Conference, CAiSE 2002, Toronto, Canada, May 27–31, 2002, LNCS 2348, Springer, 2002

- Klaus R. Dittrich, Andreas Geppert, Moira C. Norrie (Eds.): Advanced Information Systems Engineering, 13th International Conference, CAiSE 2001, Interlaken, Switzerland, June 4–8, 2001, LNCS 2068, Springer, 2001
- Benkt Wangler, Lars Bergman (Eds.): Advanced Information Systems Engineering, 12th International Conference CAiSE 2000, Kista, Stockholm, Sweden, June 5–9, 2000, LNCS 1789, Springer, 2000
- Matthias Jarke, Andreas Oberweis (Eds.): Advanced Information Systems Engineering, 11th International Conference CAiSE'99, Heidelberg, Germany, June 14–18, 1999, LNCS 1626, Springer, 1999
- Barbara Pernici, Costantino Thanos (Eds.): Advanced Information Systems Engineering, 10th International Conference CAiSE'98, Pisa, Italy, June 8–12, 1998, LNCS 1413, Springer, 1998
- Antoni Olivé, Joan Antoni Pastor (Eds.): Advanced Information Systems Engineering, 9th International Conference, CAiSE'97, Barcelona, Catalonia, Spain, June 16–20, 1997, LNCS 1250, Springer, 1997
- Panos Constantopoulos, John Mylopoulos, Yannis Vassiliou (Eds.): Advanced Information System Engineering, 8th International Conference, CAiSE'96, Heraklion, Crete, Greece, May 20–24, 1996, LNCS 1080, Springer, 1996
- Juhani Iivari, Kalle Lyytinen, Matti Rossi (Eds.): Advanced Information Systems Engineering, 7th International Conference, CAiSE'95, Jyväskylä, Finland, June 12–16, 1995, LNCS 932, Springer, 1995
- Gerard Wijers, Sjaak Brinkkemper, Anthony I. Wasserman (Eds.): Advanced Information Systems Engineering, CAiSE'94, Utrecht, The Netherlands, June 6–10, 1994, LNCS 811, Springer, 1994
- Colette Rolland, François Bodart, Corine Cauvet (Eds.): Advanced Information Systems Engineering, CAiSE'93, Paris, France, June 8–11, 1993, LNCS 685, Springer, 1993
- Pericles Loucopoulos (Ed.): Advanced Information Systems Engineering, CAiSE'92, Manchester, UK, May 12–15, 1992, LNCS 593, Springer, 1992
- Rudolf Andersen, Janis A. Bubenko Jr., Arne Sølvberg (Eds.): Advanced Information Systems Engineering, CAiSE'91, Trondheim, Norway, May 13–15, 1991, LNCS 498, Springer, 1991
- Bo Steinholtz, Arne Sølvberg, Lars Bergman (Eds.): Advanced Information Systems Engineering, Second Nordic Conference CAiSE'90, Stockholm, Sweden, May 8–10, 1990, LNCS 436, Springer, 1990
- Janis Bubenko, Janis Stirna (Eds.) The First Nordic Conference on Advanced Systems Engineering, CASE89, Kista, Stockholm, Sweden, May 9–11, 1989, CEUR-WS Vol-961, 2013.

Kista, Sweden — Janis Bubenko
Trondheim, Norway — John Krogstie
Valencia, Spain — Oscar Pastor
Milan, Italy — Barbara Pernici
Paris, France — Colette Rolland
Trondheim, Norway — Arne Sølvberg
February 2013

Contents

The CAiSE Adventure

Janis Bubenko, Colette Rolland, and Arne Sølvberg

Abstract What was to become a series of annual international, scientific conferences celebrating its 25th anniversary in 2013 came out of a modest, perhaps even an accidental start. The following gives an account of the early history of the CAiSE conference series, and of the considerations on setting up the organization and the guiding principles of the conferences. The first conference was arranged in Stockholm in May 1989 in Stockholm and was originally intended for a mixed audience of Nordic practitioners and scientists. Soon the conferences developed more into a meeting place for academic researchers, and have stayed as such for the remaining sequence of annual conferences up to this date.

1 Prelude

What was to become a series of annual international, scientific conferences celebrating its 25th anniversary in 2013 came out of a modest, perhaps even an accidental, start. The first conference was arranged in Stockholm in May 1989.

J. Bubenko (✉)
Department of Computer and Systems Science, KTH & Stockholm University, Forum 100, 16440 Kista, Sweden
e-mail: Janis@dsv.su.se

C. Rolland
Université Paris1 Panthéon Sorbonne, 90, rue de Tolbiac, 75013 Paris, France
e-mail: Rolland@univ-paris1.fr

A. Sølvberg
Department of Computer and Information Science, NTNU- The Norwegian University of Science and Technology, Trondheim, Norway
e-mail: asolvber@idi.ntnu.no

J. Bubenko et al. (eds.), *Seminal Contributions to Information Systems Engineering*,
DOI 10.1007/978-3-642-36926-1_1, © Springer-Verlag Berlin Heidelberg 2013

The Swedish Institute for Systems Development[1] (SISU) in co-operation with the Swedish Society for Information Processing SSI) organized it. The conference was called CASE – conference on Computer Aided Systems Engineering. The acronym CAiSE – Conference on Advanced Information Systems Engineering – came later, in 1990. The first conference was originally intended for a mixed audience of Nordic practitioners and scientists. Computer aided information system design was "in" at the time. Sweden was advanced both in practice and theory. Several CASE prototypes had been developed in the Nordic countries and had met with interest by practitioners. The IT department at KTH – The Royal Institute of Technology – was at the center of academic research of information system design theory and of methodological research. The department had educated a large number of students who had found good positions both in industry and in public administration. Janis had got the chair of Information Systems at KTH and had started the SYSLAB research group in the early 1980s. Arne and Colette had been in research cooperation with Janis for years, and were actively supporting this first conference.

The original plan was to create a meeting place for academics and practitioners. Researchers would be encouraged to present their findings to a mixed industrial/academic audience, and practitioners would be encouraged to challenge the research community in order to find solutions to their most pressing problems in designing and using information systems. The aim was to engage the two communities in discussions on practical problems of building real-world information system, from which both parties could emerge wiser. Janis, Colette and Arne were all participating in large international scientific and professional networks. They now called upon their colleagues in the international information systems research community to contribute. Several researchers from the Nordic countries, Europe and USA participated in the first 1989 conference.

2 Considerations in Forming the CAiSE Framework

The evaluation of the first conference indicated that one could hardly expect to have a continuous flow of a sufficient number of high-quality papers from the practical world lasting for many years unless going international on a much larger scale than in the Nordic countries alone. The reward mechanisms in industry for producing research type papers were deemed to be weaker than needed for guaranteeing sufficient local industry participation in such an endeavor. The question was how to achieve a framework that could survive.

The discussion about internationalization started prior to the first "CASE" conference. During the fall of 1989 Janis and Arne engaged in extensive email discussions on how to proceed after the first conference. Arne spent the academic year 1988–1989 on sabbatical leave in California while Janis stayed put in Stockholm

[1] More information about SISU can be found at http://www.sisuportal.se/ partly in Swedish.

building up the research institute SISU. The first CASE conference in 1989 also fitted well into the plans for establishing the research institute as an active player in the European research community. This was before the World Wide Web and Skype. The costs of travelling and telephone usage were high, so email was the preferred mode of communication.

We all had considerable experiences in arranging international conferences and workshops. We participated in extensive international networks of scientists in information systems, databases and software engineering. We had also recently become involved in EU sponsored projects under the Esprit 2 program. So we were fairly well placed to develop a new conference series.

In the following we present some considerations that lay behind establishing the CAiSE conference series.

2.1 Was There a Need for a New Conference Series?

Conferences that covered different parts of the relevant research fields were organized within several existing scientific communities. We were involved with three of them: IFIP Working Group 8.1 (WG8.1) for Information Systems, IFIP WG2.6 for Data Bases, the conference series VLDB (Very Large Data Bases) and to a lesser extent with the Entity-Relationship conference series.

The formal title of IFIP WG8.1 is "Design and evaluation of information systems". It includes many aspects of IS use and design such as requirements analysis, modeling and description of IS, computer aided methods and tools for IS design, human-computer interaction design, as well as aligning information systems to organizations and organizational needs. IFIP Technical Committee TC8 on Information Systems was established in 1977. Arne and Colette were national representatives in TC8 representing Norway and France. The working group WG8.1 was established in 1977. Arne was chair of WG8.1 in the early 1980s (with Janis as secretary). Colette was member of WG8.1 from the start, and served as WG8.1 officer from 1988 to 1999. The essential output of an IFIP working group was working conferences within its scientific field. WG8.1 had a good record on working conferences, in particular the highly successful CRIS (Comparative Review of Information Systems Design Methodologies) that were arranged at Noordwijkerhout in The Netherlands. But IFIP 8.1 lacked an annual "sustainable" conference focusing on the field as a whole, or a subfield of Information Systems.

IFIP WG2.6 was at this time primarily concerned with issues of data semantics. While a useful and interesting topic, data semantics was not considered "central" to the field of Information Systems, at least not by us. Furthermore, a conference on data semantics would not draw many delegates to a conference. The theme was a bit narrow.

The first VLDB conference was arranged in Framingham, Massachusetts, in 1975. The conference may be considered as an academic response to a practical need, as expressed by government, business, and industry, a need to pay more attention to approaches to organize, describe, store and search massive amounts of data, a problem of increasing importance for many practical applications. The "VLDB problem" is, of course, typical and essential for Information Systems, as databases are essential parts of any Information System. But the VLDB topic area seemed a bit too specialized for our purposes. We should also mention that our relationship to VLDB was excellent. All three of us presented papers at the VLDB conference in 1979. Both Arne and Janis were members of the VLDB Endowment. Janis chaired the Endowment 1989–1993. VLDB 1985 was organized in Stockholm and attended by about 800 delegates.

Peter Chen published his Entity-Relationship model in 1976. The first ER-conference was arranged in 1979 in Los Angeles and later developed into a series of conferences. In the beginning these conferences were almost totally focused on Chen's ER model. At this time we thought this narrow focus to be too restricted to base a conference on. Later, of course, the thematic scope of the ER-conferences widened considerably, to the extent that the conference series later on changed name to International Conference on Conceptual Modeling.

Our conclusion about the situation was that none of the four groups could give us what we wanted. VLDB was in its main focus too far off the central issues of the field of Information Systems Engineering, although the main VLDB issues were very important, also for Information Systems Engineering. The Entity-Relationship conference was deemed to be too narrow, and too closely associated to data modeling of the Entity-Relationship variety. The organizational set-up of IFIP was deemed to be too closed, not being open enough to attract the young and up coming. There was no effective organizational mechanism for renewing membership in the governing bodies. The organizational philosophy as well as the bureaucracy of IFIP was simply not well suited to serve the rapidly evolving field of Information Technology.

In the end the choice was not so difficult: we decided to go for a new conference series provided that we could find an organizational set-up that had acceptable chances of success.

2.2 *Was There a Sufficient Strong Research Basis That Could Be Tapped Into?*

A primary concern was the availability of high quality papers. We had to associate the new conference series with major research groups. We had to encourage young PhD students to publish with us. Many of the relevant research groups were already active in IFIP, primarily in WG8.1. The WG8.1 approach was to arrange one or two working conferences each year inviting contributions within special topics within the central theme of information systems. This opened up for us to arrange an annual conference with a wider thematic coverage. We chose Information Systems Engineering to be the wider theme. We invited submissions from all research areas relevant to this theme. By doing this we opened up a publication channel where researchers once a year could publish a continuity of new research results as their research projects matured and their PhD students developed their research from the idea stage to a more mature stage.

The research groups that were associated with WG8.1 and WG2.6 were deemed to be not enough to support a sustainable annual conference. We had to evaluate whether our international contact net could bring more international research groups into "the fold". We found that a number of the research groups affiliated with VLDB also had strong activities in Information Systems Engineering, and were on the fringes of the VLDB central theme of very large data bases. A similar situation was found for the emerging ER-conferences. Many research groups were associated with several of the conference series.

Finally, Norway and Sweden had recently been permitted to participate in EU-sponsored research projects. Together with several other European research groups, we had been awarded a 5-year long ESPRIT II project, the TEMPORA project. This project could provide us with research results that could be published in future CAiSE conferences. The project also provided us with a better economic basis for pursuing the stabilization of a series of annual conferences. Other Esprit European projects of relevance to our planned conference came later, e.g., KIWIS (Advanced Knowledge-Based Environments for Database Systems) and F^3 (F-cube – from Fuzzy to Formal – an endeavor in Requirements Engineering). Some of us were in these projects as well.

Our conclusion was that there was a sufficient strong research basis for supporting a new conference series. Last but not least, we could count on the research institute SISU together with their supporters (about 30 Swedish enterprises) to provide us an economic stability and guarantee for this kind of endeavor.

2.3 Location: Should We Go for a Regional Conference or a Global Conference?

A next issue was location. The four conference organizing communities mentioned above were in principle of a global nature. The Tempora project was strictly European. The two IFIP groups were in practice mostly European. The two conference series VLDB and ER were both initially US based, but expanded rapidly to have a global reach.

After some thinking we decided to go for a European conference. We considered that there were enough global conferences within the topic area. After all there was a limit to how many international travels a normal research group budget could accommodate. We considered it a safer choice to go for a European based conference series, but with a possibility to arrange CAiSE conferences outside of Europe if there were strong arguments for this. We gave ourselves the freedom to elevate non-European countries to a temporary classification of being European.

Because of the starting point of CAiSE being Nordic, we also permitted ourselves to build into the conference charter that future CAiSE conferences should be arranged in the Nordic countries from time to time.

2.4 *Timing: Winter, Spring, Summer or Autumn Conference?*

It was clear that if we were going international we were up for stiff competition on the selection of time slots. So we tried to avoid the times for other conferences with partly overlapping themes. We wanted to be both international and local. We wanted timing, which was suitable for the Nordic countries as well as for the rest of Europe and the USA. The spring or early summer was an obvious choice. Few places on earth are as attractive as the Nordic countries during late spring, late May and June.

2.5 *How to Organize the Continuity of a Conference Series?*

Aiming at creating a series of CAiSE conferences it was clear that we had to associate the conferences to an organizational body, which would exist in between conferences. Each individual conference would be set up with its own organization to prepare and operate the conference, and to be dissolved after the conference was over. But how should we organize the period in-between two conferences? What procedure to follow when choosing new conference sites? And – how should we deal with economical matters?

Most conferences at the time were associated with professional societies like IFIP, ACM and IEEE. A few were independent of the professional societies. They had created their own boards, which took the responsibility in-between conferences, like VLDB and the ER-conference.

Our experience from IFIP and VLDB was that we did not want to create an organization that had to handle money, provide seed money to the next conferences and things like that. Each conference and its economy should be the responsibility of its own organizing body. This meant that the organizer had to be prepared to take a larger risk than if leaning on a central organization. On the other hand, there was a good chance to make a profit because there was no profit sharing required with a central organization. Of course, the profit/loss statement had to be openly presented at each conference.

Initially, the organization and management of CAiSE was simple. There was to be an ever-extending steering expanding each year with two persons from the previous conference. Over time this led to a rather large steering group. There was a need for a smaller body to take day-to-day decisions without having to consult too widely. So Arne, Janis and later also Colette formed an "advisory committee". The advisory committee and the steering group had an informal "non-meeting" at each CAiSE conference. Matters like selecting future conference sites and publicity issues were handled there. This simple, informal scheme worked very well for many years, and was not changed until 2011 (see below).

2.6 How to Publish the Papers?

We were aiming at finding a rock solid publisher. It was very clear that there was no hope of creating a conference series unless we could find a trustworthy publisher. We all had good experience with Springer so this matter was easily decided. The cooperation with Springer went very well during all these years, very efficiently and in a friendly way. We are thankful to Springer for their very positive and reactive attitude to all our demands. We would like to take this opportunity to particularly thank Ralf Gerstner who has been our very supportive contact for many years including setting up this book proposal on a short time notice.

3 The First Conference

The first Conference on "Advanced Systems Engineering", **CASE'89**, was arranged during May 9–11 1989, jointly by SISU (Swedish Institute for Systems Development) and SSI (Swedish Society for Information Processing, a member of IFIP). The conference was also supported by the research laboratory SYSLAB and DSV – the department of computer and systems science at Royal Institute of Technology and University of Stockholm. In fact the conference was called "The First Nordic conference ..." as our initial aim was to anchor this as a Nordic event. The economic risk and also the economic surplus were solely taken by SISU.

The main aim of CASE'89 was to bridge the gap between theory and practice in systems development. Consequently, CASE'89 was organised in two parallel streams, one more theoretical and one more practical. The theoretical track was traditionally organised by submitted, peer-reviewed, and accepted papers, primarily from researchers. The practical track consisted mainly of solicited, in some cases invited, talks from business, industry and the public sector. General conference co-chairpersons were Agneta Qwerin, Swedish Society for Information Processing, and Janis Bubenko Jr, the managing director of SISU. The executive Program Committee consisted of Björn Nilsson, SISU, chairman, Håkan Dahl, Christer Dahlgren, Kurt Gladh, Lars Swärd, and Örjan Odelhög. Lars Bergman, SISU, chaired the Organising Committee. As can be seen, the program committee was dominated by practitioners, all Swedish.

For our first conference we had to have well reputed keynote speakers to set the future direction: the CAiSE conferences were to become a high quality scientific conference series. The obvious choice for keynote speaker was Colette Rolland of Sorbonne. Colette has held the chair of the IFIP WG8.1, and her staff participated also in the Tempora, F3 and other EU projects. The three of us had similar ideas about Information Systems Engineering, and we started to work as a team for arranging the future CAiSE conferences. Colette later arranged the 1993 conference in Paris. The theme of Colette's invited talk was "On the future of modeling – why current CASE-tools insist on supporting 20 years old methods".[2] Indeed an intriguing topic: the idea was to be a bit provocative in addressing the prevalent view of CASE tools' vendors. The ISE community has, already in the 1970s, made the assumption that an information system captures some excerpt of world history and hence has concentrated on modelling information about the Universe of Discourse. This led to the conceptual modelling wave and the creation of a large number of semantically powerful conceptual models. The talk was arguing that CASE tools' editors should implement such rich modelling approaches instead of old-fashion structured analysis and design methods.

CASE'89 turned – a bit unexpectedly – out to be a success. A large number of contributed papers and international delegates could be noted. Forty-three papers were presented. The number of attending delegates was about 180.

The program chair of CASE'89, Dr. Björn Nilsson (deputy managing director of SISU) and the invited speaker, Professor Colette Rolland, University of Paris 1 (Photo by Janis Bubenko at the Riga, Latvia, CAiSE 2004)

[2]The two other invited speakers were Frans van Assche, James Martin Associates Co. amd Simon Holloway, DCE, U.K. Frans's talk was "On the future of CASE tools". Simon's theme was "Organisational implications caused by the fourth generation environment",

4 The Following Conferences

We were now ready to organize our next CAiSE conference. We decided that the 1990 conference should take place in Stockholm, and the 1991 conference in Trondheim.

The success of CASE'89 gave us the courage to continue the CASE conference in a more international setting. The name of the 1990 conference was, however, changed to **CAiSE** (Conference on Advanced information Systems Engineering) in order not to be mixed up with another US-based conference, which had taken the CASE name. CAiSE'90 was also arranged in Stockholm by SISU and was supported by the department of Computer and Systems Science, the Royal Institute of Technology and Stockholm University (DSV). The general chair was Arne Sølvberg, the program chair Bo Steinholtz (DSV), and the organising chair was Lars Bergman (SISU). All three were also co-editors of the first Springer Verlag (Lecture Notes in Computer Science) publication of the CAiSE'90 proceedings. About 200 delegates from more than 20 countries attended CAiSE'90. Our European colleagues expressed considerable interest to continue CAiSE on a European scale. Janis and Arne decided to support this challenge and worked out a few simple rules for CAiSE. Simply speaking, CAiSE was to be a conference with almost no rules. It was to have an expanding steering committee, which essentially consists of chairs of previous conferences. The organizing body of each CAiSE conference is responsible for the finances, profits as well as losses. About every fifth year it is expected that CAiSE returns to a Nordic country. CAiSE is guided by an advisory committee consisting of Colette Rolland, Janis Bubenko jr., and Arne Sölvberg.

Since its start in 1989 and 1990 in Stockholm, CAiSE has been hosted in Norway (1991, 2007), U.K. (1992, 2011), France (1993), the Netherlands (1994, 2009),

The banquet of the 1997 CAiSE was celebrated at the Market Place designed by Gaudi at the Parc GULL in Barcelona. The attendance of CAiSE'97 was exceptionally good so the organisers decided we could afford this elegant setting and the outstanding menu

Finland (1995), Greece (1996), Catalonia (1997), Italy (1998), Germany (1999), Sweden (2000), Switzerland (2001), Canada (2002), Austria (2003), Latvia (2004), Portugal (2005), Luxembourg (2006), Tunisia (2010) and Poland (2012). The 25th event of CAiSE will be held in Valencia, 2013. Springer Verlag, Lecture Notes in Computer Science, has published all CAiSE proceedings, since 1990.

In our opinion the CAiSE series has been quite successful. Each conference has attracted between 200 and 300 submitted papers. About 40 of the submissions have been accepted for inclusion in the conference proceedings, giving an acceptance rate of 13–17 %. The attendance number has been 200 or more delegates. Papers in CAiSE proceedings have in general had good citation ratings.

5 Seminal Contributions of 25 Years of CAiSE

During these last 25 years, the CAiSE community shared the same broad view of information systems and the passion to develop advanced engineering solutions. On one hand, we all place an information system in a big picture in which ICT, socio-economic, organisational and business issues are intertwined. On the other hand, CAiSE research is part of design science but we clearly prefer to focus on the *design* side of it than on its *evaluation* dual part. The 17 seminal papers reedited in this book reflect these two key characteristics of CAiSE contributions.

The first CASE conference was held at the end of the conceptual modelling wave when providing an automated support to modelling became a key concern of CAiSE authors. The three papers on MetaEdit+ (*A fully configurable Multi-User & Multi-tool CASE and CAME environment*), OICSI (*A natural language approach for requirements engineering*) and OO-Method (*An OO software production environment combining conventional and formal methods*) introduced approaches (meta-modelling, natural language processing, and model transformations, respectively) that have still interest today.

This was also the time to go beyond the traditional way of engineering information systems through conceptual modelling. Whereas conceptual modelling allowed our community to understand the semantics of information and led to a large number of semantically powerful conceptual models, experience demonstrated that it failed in supporting the delivery of systems that were accepted by the community of their users. Indeed, a number of studies showed that systems failed due to an inadequate or insufficient understanding of the requirements they seek to address. To correct this situation, it was necessary to address the issue of requirements elicitation, validation, and specification in a relatively more focussed manner. The field of requirements engineering has emerged to meet this expectation. The hope was that as a result of this, more acceptable systems would be developed in the future. Three papers in this book address different aspects of requirements engineering: *The three dimensions of requirements engineering: a framework and its applications; Towards a deeper understanding of quality in requirements engineering; A requirements-driven development methodology.*

Databases have always been part of CAiSE research (*Database schema matching using machine learning with feature selection; Data integration under integrity constraints*).

With time passing, new forms of information systems came into play. The CAiSE community paid a lot of attention in early 2000s to workflows (*Time constraints in workflow systems; Adaptive and dynamic service composition in eFlow; On structured workflow modelling; The P2P approach to inter-organizational workflows*) and to a less extent to data warehouses (*Architecture and quality in data warehouses*).

The CAiSE community has always been involved on the topic of methods, leading to the production of methods on one hand, but also contributing to understanding what a method is. It is thus, not surprising to note that the concept of Method Engineering was introduced by CAiSists (!) and further developed by a few groups in the world deeply involved with CAiSE and the EMMSAD workshop which each year was organized in conjunction with the main conference. Method engineering represents the effort to improve the usefulness of systems development methods by creating an adaptation framework whereby methods are created to match specific organisational situations. There are at least two objectives that can be associated to this adaptation. The first objective is the production of contingency methods, that is, situation-specific methods for certain types of organisational settings. This objective represents method engineering as the creation of a multiple choice setting. The second objective is one in which method engineering is used to produce method "on-the-fly". Situational method engineering is the construction of methods, which are tuned to specific situations of development projects. Each system development starts then, with a method definition phase where the development method is constructed on the spot.

In recent years the CAiSE community has been involved with emerging concepts such as variability (*Automated reasoning on features models*).

Finally, the book reflects the considerable attention received in recent years by Business Process Management (BPM) and its fundamental concept of a business process. Process models may be used to configure information systems, but may also be used to analyze, understand, and improve the processes they describe. Hence, the introduction of BPM technology has both managerial and technical ramifications, and may enable significant productivity improvements, cost savings, and flow-time reductions. The practical relevance of BPM and rapid developments over the last decade justify the large number of highly cited BPM papers in the last CAiSE conferences (*Change patterns and change support features in process-aware information systems; Measuring similarity between process models; How much language is enough: Theoretical and practical use of business process modeling notation*).

6 Other Outcomes of CAiSE

Another interesting effect of CAiSE is its regular set of tutorials and workshops, normally arranged during 2 days preceding the conference itself. Some well-known workshops, such as EMMSAD (Evaluating Modelling Methods for Systems Analysis and Design) have been held every year since the start of CAiSE. EMMSAD was initially organised by Yair Wand of University of British Columbia, Canada. In fact, EMMSAD has evolved into being – informally – the "official" IFIP WG8.1 annual working conference. An official, annual WG8.1 business meeting follows each EMMSAD workshop. Other workshops, such as REFSQ (Requirements Engineering: Foundation for Software Quality) have evolved into independent conferences. Another such activity is POEM – Practice of Enterprise Modelling. One could say that POEM is a "spin-off" from EMMSAD and CAiSE activities and is now running as an independent conference.

Last but not least we should mention the doctoral consortium, which is organized at each CAiSE conference. Here young PhD candidates get the chance to present their early research results to experienced thesis advisors and to discuss their main findings and ideas.

7 The New CAiSE

In 2009 the young generation expressed thought exchanges on the Web, the wish to have a more controlled organisation of CAiSE conferences. Sensitive to this movement we proposed to set up a task force to make propositions about a new and more formalised CAiSE steering committee. Antoni Olivé accepted to chair this task force who presented its conclusions during the non-committee meeting of CAISE 2010 in Tunisia. These were accepted, implemented during the year 2011 and finalized during the last non-committee meeting of CAiSE 2011 in London. The three nominated officers of the new Executive Steering Committee, namely Barbara Pernici, Oscar Pastor and John Krogstie took the lead at that time.

8 Singing at CAiSE

Singing eventually became a tradition at the CAiSE dinner banquets on Thursdays. We are not 100 % sure when it all started but already at CAiSE'92 at UMIST, Manchester, U.K. Keith Jeffery (of Ruherford Appleton Laboratories, RAL) had brought his guitar and accompanied some singing in the conference center bar. This somehow developed into an informal rule that the workshops, taking normally place during Mondays and Tuesdays, should prepare a "show" of singing and dancing to be presented at the workshop dinner. This idea was extremely well appreciated.

At the same time the advisory committee, then Janis and Arne also wanted to make a small contribution. Janis came up with the idea to perform a Danish drinking song (see below). We believe that some CAiSE delegated found it nice while others were more surprised and/or confused. In any case, after a while we found that the advisory committee had to be extended – we needed a "farmer's wife" according to the text of the song. That is how Colette became the farmer's wife in our little "show". Arne played the farmer and Janis was the "young student".

The song goes like this:

Han skulle gaa ud efter öl

(the translation is not guaranteed)
:/: Det var en go' gammel bondemand
han skulde gaa ud efter öl.:/:
Han skulde gaa ud efter öl,
han skulde gaa ud efter öl,
efter öl, efter hoppsansa, trallallala
han skulde gaa ud efter öl.
There was a gentle old farmer
Who wanted to go out for a beer
:/: Till konen kom der en ung student
mens manden var ude efter öl.:/:
Mens manden var ude efter öl,
mens manden var ude efter öl,
efter öl, efter hoppsansa, trallallala
mens manden var ude efter öl.
A young student came to his wife –
while the farmer was out for a beer
:/: Han kyssed henne paa rosenmund
og klapped henne paa kind.:/:
Mens manden var ude efter öl,
mens manden var ude efter öl,
efter öl, efter hoppsansa, trallallala
mens manden var ude efter öl.
He kissed her on her rosy mouth
and cuddled her on her chin
while the farmer was out for a beer
:/: Men manden han stod bagved dören og saa
hvorledes det hele gik til.:/:
De troed' han var ude efter öl,
de troed' han var ude efter öl,
efter öl, efter hoppsansa, trallallala
de troed' han var ude efter öl.
But the farmer had been standing behind the door – he saw all what did happen - while they thought he was out for a beer
:/: Saa sköd han studenten och kaellingen med
og saa gik han ud efter öl.:/:
Og saa gik han ud efter öl,
og saa gik han ud efter öl,
efter öl, efter hoppsansa, trallallala
og saa gik han ud efter öl.
So the farmer took his gun and shot the student as well as his wife – and then he went out for a beer

Og laer her af alle bondemaend
nor I skal gaa ud efter öl.
laas konen inog ta nöglen med
nor I skal gaa ud efter öl.
Nor I skal gaa ud efter öl,
nor I skal gaa ud efter öl,
efter öl, efter hoppsansa, trallallala
nor I skal gaa ud efter öl.

So let this be a lesson to all of you who want to go out for a beer – first lock your wife up and bring the key along – when you go out for a beer

This last verse is perhaps a bit rude. There is another and better last verse:
Moralen er, ta din kone med,
nor I skal gaa ud efter öl.
Etc., etc.

The morale is
Take your wife along
When you go out for a beer
Etc. etc.

Our recommendation is obvious: You should always bring your partner to CAiSE!

Authors of this book chapter performing the drinking song at the 2003 CAiSE in Klagenfurt/Velden, Austria

9 Conclusion

In conclusion we have had fantastic 25 years of CAiSE. We have had great fun not only technically and scientifically but also socially. We all have made many new friends and met dear old friends many times; we are happy CAiSE has managed to keep up its scientific and technical quality during all years. What more can we do than wish our followers at least 25 more years of successful international exchange.

Evolution of the CAiSE Author Community: A Social Network Analysis

Matthias Jarke, Manh Cuong Pham, and Ralf Klamma

Abstract The CAiSE community has always prided itself as more than just a normal conference – a successful social network with a very special culture. In this chapter, we apply formal social network analysis to study this community and its evolution of its first quarter-centennial of existence. Using a methodology and dataset developed for an analysis of Computer Science as a whole, we demonstrate the unusual positioning of CAiSE as a quasi-interdisciplinary conference between several sub-disciplines of Computer Science. We show that under an evolution model developed in our research CAiSE pursues a very successful and promising path, and we identify key topics and key players among the CAiSE authors. As the social network analysis focusses on formal aspects such as co-authorship and citations, we unfortunately must leave out one of the undoubtedly most critical success factors: the fun of being in the CAiSE community.

1 Introduction

The CAiSE community, as the community of other scientific conferences, can be considered as a community of practice (CoP) [13]. A community of practice is defined as "*a group of people who share a concern, a set of problem, or a passion about a topic, and who deepen their knowledge and expertise in this area by interacting on an ongoing basis*" [3]. CAiSE is a community of practice due to several aspects. First, members of CAiSE are working on a common research area, the Information Systems. Second, members are distributed across disciplines, which include information systems, database, requirement engineering, business process management, etc. Members are also distributed across organizations, cultures and

M. Jarke (✉) · M.C. Pham · R. Klamma
Information Systems and Databases, RWTH Aachen University, Ahornstr. 55, D52056, Aachen, Germany
e-mail: jarke@dbis.rwth-aachen.de; pham@dbis.rwth-aachen.de; klamma@dbis.rwth-aachen.de

J. Bubenko et al. (eds.), *Seminal Contributions to Information Systems Engineering*,
DOI 10.1007/978-3-642-36926-1_2, © Springer-Verlag Berlin Heidelberg 2013

geographical regions. Third, members communicate with each other via face-to-face conferences as well as technology-enhanced interaction. Finally, CAiSE attracts not only fundamental research, but also practical systems and architectures. That results in a very heterogeneous community where methods from different disciplines are used and practices are built on the basic and applied research.

In [12], we have developed a framework for analyzing the development of such scientific communities based on Social Network Analysis (SNA). The framework allows us to monitor the status of a community, qualify its development and compare its development pattern with other communities. It also enables the identification of key members and subgroups of the community. Different techniques are employed in this framework, including visualization, SNA ranking measures, and clustering techniques. Using the DBLP and CiteSeer databases as our data set, we applied this framework to the evolution of Computer Science as a whole. Moreover, we were able to show formally that a few leading computer science conferences are indeed equally important in terms of impact as the top journals in the field, which makes Computer Science quite different from many other disciplines where conference publications only play a marginal role.

In this chapter, we apply this framework to analyze the evolution of the CAiSE conference series. In particular, we are interested in the following questions:

- **Relationship with other communities**: what is the relationship between CAiSE and other communities in the field? What is the role of CAiSE to those communities?
- **Membership of CAiSE**: how do members come and stay in CAiSE? How is the community stabilized?
- **Connectivity**: how do members connect to each other? Does the connectivity grow over time? What is the pattern of the connections?
- **Topic analysis**: what topics are addressed by CAiSE community? How do topics connect to each other? who are the key researchers with the highest impact?

The rest of the chapter is organized as follows. In Sect. 2, we describe our analytical framework and the data we used in the analysis. Section 3 presents the results which aim to answer the above questions. The chapter finishes with a discussion and conclusion.

2 Methods and Data

Our general study of the evolution of digital libraries in general, and of computer science in particular [9] has resulted in a model to explain the community-building process, as well as the co-authoring and citation behavior in conferences and journals [12]. For example, a study of Technology Enhanced Learning research communities found interesting development patterns [11]. In this section, we describe this model and its underlying formal metrics as well as the data set we used for the analysis of CAiSE.

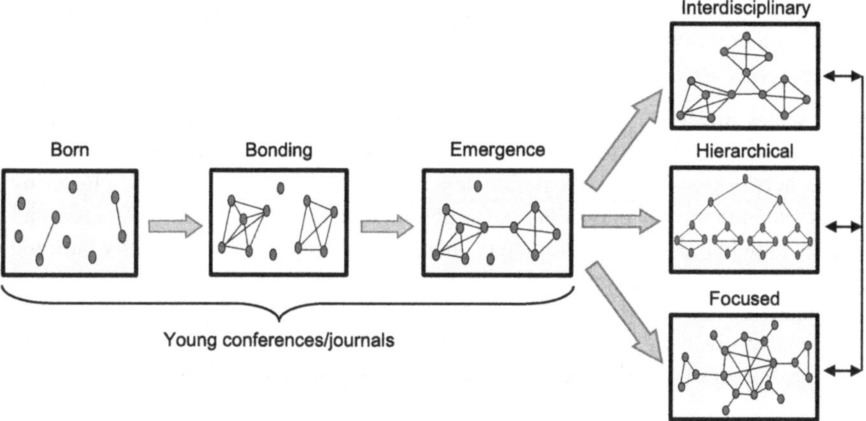

Fig. 1 The development model for scientific communities

Readers with a deeper methodological interest can also consult the Ph.D. thesis [10]. Moreover, an online version of the AERCS[1] analysis system by which the results in the thesis and in this paper were derived, is accessible for experimental use. AERCS does not just support the kind of long-term SNA we show in this paper, but also offers a component for mobile context-dependent advice to attendees of specific conferences.

2.1 The Development Model

Our basic evolution model depicted in Fig. 1 includes four stages: born, bonding, emergence, with the final stage being either interdisciplinary, hierarchical or focussed. Following earlier research in scientific community network analysis, the network employs two types of links: co-authorship and citation. The *co-authorship* subnet of a conference series consists of authors as nodes. There is an edge between two authors if they have co-authored at least one paper published in a conference event in that series. In the born phase, we typically find few connections between authors. After some events, author groups become apparent in the bonding phase. In the best case, they gradually integrated through joint publications from more than one group (emergence phase). Finally, successful conference series typically forms a network topology that features a strongly connected core group of authors that is connected to other smaller groups (*focused* topology). Alternatively, the co-authorship can develop into an interdisciplinary topology where several groups are connected via some gatekeepers, but where there is no core group. Or there

[1] http://bosch.informatik.rwth-aachen.de:5080/AERCS/

might emerge a hierarchical topology which exposes some "super gatekeepers" who connect a hierarchy of groups.

Time series analysis. To quantitatively characterize the development process of a community according to this development model, we apply time series analysis on the networks to reveal six parameters over time: densification law, clustering coefficient, maximum betweenness, largest connected component, diameter, and average path length. These parameters enable us to explain the community building process in Fig. 1. To interpret the shape of the community, one needs to use a combination of all of these parameters.

Formally, given the network $G = (V, E)$, where V is the set of vertices or nodes, and E is the set of edges, these network metrics are defined as follows:

- *Densification law*: [4] discovered that complex networks densify over time, with the number of edges growing super-linearly with the number of nodes, meaning that the average degree (i.e., number of edges) of the nodes is increasing. The densification follows a power-law pattern: $e(t) \propto n(t)^{\alpha}$, where $e(t)$ and $n(t)$ are the number of edges and nodes at time t, respectively, and α is an exponent that lies between 1 and 2 ($\alpha = 1$ corresponds to constant average degree over time, while $\alpha = 2$ corresponds to very dense graph where on average each node has edges to a constant fraction of all nodes). We use this exponent to differentiate the "speed" by which networks are densified.
- The *clustering coefficient* of a network [6] is defined as the total number of pairs of vertices that have a common neighbor and are themselves connected, divided by the total number of pairs of vertices that have a common neighbor:

$$C = \frac{3 \times \textit{ number of triangles in the graph}}{\textit{number of connected triples of vertices in the graph}} \tag{1}$$

  Intuitively, during the born phase, the clustering coefficient is low, since nodes are unconnected with each other. In the bonding phase, the clustering coefficient tends to increase quickly as nodes are clustered into very dense, yet unconnected components. When the unconnected components subsequently start to connect with each other, the clustering coefficient drops and stays relatively stable after some time.
- *Betweenness* measures the extent to which a particular node lies between the other nodes in the network:

$$B(u) \equiv \sum_{u \neq i \neq j} \frac{\sigma^{u}(i, j)}{\sigma(i, j)} \tag{2}$$

  where $\sigma(i, j)$ is the number of shortest-paths between nodes i and j, $\sigma^{u}(i, j)$ is the number of shortest-paths between i and j that pass through u. Nodes with high betweenness have more power to control the information flow in the network, and are normally the gatekeepers who connect several dense groups. For the network, the maximum betweenness of all authors is therefore a good indicator of whether there are strong gatekeepers within the network. Maximum betweenness increases when more components become connected (emergence stage) and continues to increase when the network develops toward a hierarchical or interdisciplinary topology. However, maximum betweenness will achieve a stable value when the network is at focused stage.

- *Largest connected component* (or giant component) measures the fraction of nodes that are connected with each other in the largest sub-network. As observed in Fig. 1, this fraction is small in the first two phases, and gradually increases as authors from different sub-networks connect with each other. It achieves a stable state when the fraction of nodes that connect to the largest component is equal to the fraction of new nodes that stay unconnected from the largest component.
- *Diameter* is the length of the greatest geodesic distance (i.e., the length of the longest shortest path) between any two nodes. Intuitively, in the beginning, the diameter is small, and then it increases. After some time, the diameter starts to shrink as new edges between existing nodes continue to be added. If the network develops toward a tree-like topology (hierarchical stage), the diameter will be larger than in the focused or interdisciplinary topologies.
- *Average path length* is the average length of all the shortest paths in the network. Clearly, during the first two phases, the average path length is small and increases when the network grows. In general, the average path length of a hierarchical network is larger than that of the other two topologies.

In summary, for the co-authorship network, the emergence of the giant component indicates the cohesiveness of collaboration within the community, while the betweenness shows the existence of gatekeepers and their importance. The clustering coefficient measures the extent to which the community is clustered into sub-communities. Other parameters such as diameter and average shortest path length, show whether the community is still developing or whether it is stable. For the citation network, combining these parameters helps to understand the interdisciplinarity of a conference.

2.2 Data: DBLP and CiteSeerX

The data set used in our study integrates the DBLP and CiteSeerX digital libraries. DBLP is a computer science bibliography, which also includes publications in interdisciplinary areas of computer science. We retrieved the publication lists of conferences from DBLP. However, DBLP does not record citations. Therefore, we used CiteSeerX to fill the citation list of publications in DBLP. DBLP data, as downloaded in July 2012, consists of 1,138,661 authors, 1,947,188 publications, 3,217 conference series and 1,193 journals. CiteSeerX data was downloaded in March, 2011, which includes 9,121,166 publications, 22,735,140 references and over 6 million author names. We combined DBLP and CiteSeerX using the canopy clustering technique [5]. Overall, the matching algorithm gave us 864,097 pairs of matched publications. From those data sets, we created the co-authorship and citation networks for our analysis. The co-authorship network is created based on DBLP data and the citation network is formulated by the combined DBLP and CitaSeerX data.

3 Development of CAiSE Community

In this section, we present the analytical results of CAiSE community, concerning the questions we posed in the introduction. We work inside out, starting with the positioning of CAiSE within Computer Science, then proceeding to the evolution pattern of CAiSE with respect to the development model of Sect. 2, and end with the internal structure of CAiSE concerning its main topics and its key players.

3.1 The Position of CAiSE in Computer Science

Our general study of the evolution of the Computer Science community [12] showed how the field has evolved a coherent giant component with clearly demarked subfields that have more or less strong citation interactions with each other (see Fig. 2); for example, Theoretical Computer Science interacts, albeit somewhat loosely, with almost all other areas. An extract from this map (see Fig. 3) shows that CAiSE can be seen as a kind of interdisciplinary gateway between neighboring research areas such as information systems, databases, software engineering, data mining and knowledge management, conceptual modeling, process modeling and world wide web. Overall, 237 conference and journals have at least 50 authors who also published in CAiSE. Table 1 lists the top 10 among them. Many other established conferences/journals also have common authors with CAiSE, such as SIGMOD Record (235 common authors), TKDE (212), TSE (191), ACM SIGMOD (183), CACM (156), VLDB Journal (127) and IJCAI (105). This demonstrates the diversity of CAiSE community membership, and its interdisciplinary nature.

The standing of CAiSE within the computer science community can also be assessed by ranking it in the citation network according to the centrality measures discussed in the previous section. The data set contains a total of 455 conferences in the fields of databases, data mining, and software engineering which are close to CAiSE in the graph. Among these 455 conferences, which include all the traditional top conferences of these fields, CAiSE is among the top 8 % in terms of PageRank [8] and the top 5 % in terms of authority [2], which is already quite good, but among the top 2 % in terms of betweenness. Thus, CAiSE is not just highly interdisciplinary but also an important bridge among the other fields and even a strong authority for its kinds of results.

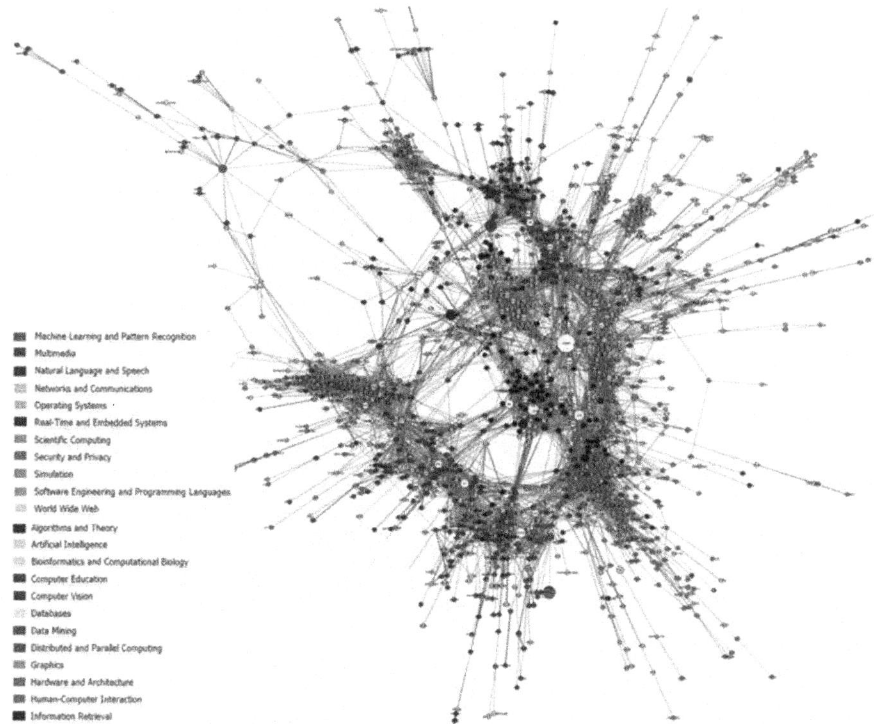

Fig. 2 The map of Computer Science (giant component)

The interdisciplinarity of CAiSE can be shown in more detail by citation data, which indicate the knowledge exchange between publications. In detail, CAiSE publications have been cited by 472 conferences and journals. CAiSE publications have cited publications from 689 conferences and journals. Tables 2 and 3 list top conferences and journals who cited CAiSE or were cited by CAiSE. Note that the citation data we extract from CiteSeerX are incomplete and only cover conferences and journals indexed by DBLP. Therefore, the actual number of conferences and journals referenced to and cited by CAiSE is somewhat bigger.

To summarize, CAiSE is a very interdisciplinary conference, shown by the diversity in its membership as well as the citation data.

3.2 Evolution of Author Community Membership

The next question we want to address is how CAiSE community evolves over time. We apply the model described in Sect. 2 on the co-authorship network to analyze its development pattern. To make our analysis more meaningful, we compare the

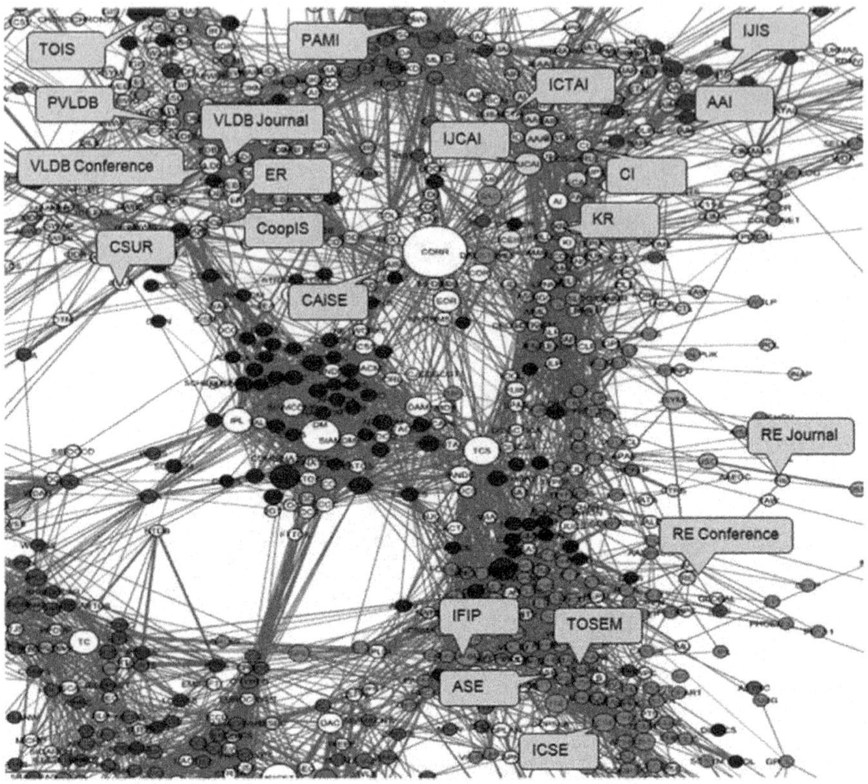

Fig. 3 The position of CAiSE in the map of Computer Science

Table 1 Top overlapping conferences/journals with CAiSE

	Name of conferences/journals	#Common authors
1	International Conference on Conceptual Modeling (ER)	624
2	OTM Conferences/Workshops	435
3	Information Systems	421
4	Data and Knowledge Engineering	358
5	Business Process Management	317
6	International Conference on Data Engineering (ICDE)	305
7	Very Large Data Bases (VLDB) Conference	290
8	International Conference on Information and Knowledge Management(CIKM)	281
9	International World Wide Web Conferences (WWW)	264
10	Information and Software Technology	256

evolution of CAiSE with that of the three well-known conferences at the top of Table 3: ER, VLDB, and ICDE. Some basic authorship data for these conferences is summarized in Table 4.

Table 2 Top conferences/journals who cited CAiSE

	Name of conferences/journals	#
1	International Conference on Conceptual Modeling (ER)	84
2	Business Process Management	52
3	Data and Knowledge Engineering	41
4	OTM Conferences / Workshops	33
5	Information Systems	28
6	Requirements Engineering	26
7	International Conference on Cooperative Information Systems (CoopIS)	22
8	Semantic Web	22
9	International Conference on Service Oriented Computing	22
10	Very Large Data Bases (VLDB) Conference	21

Table 3 Top conferences/journals cited by CAiSE

	Name of conferences/journals	#
1	Very Large Data Bases (VLDB) Conference	142
2	Communications of the ACM (CACM)	139
3	International Conference on Conceptual Modeling (ER)	132
4	IEEE Transactions on Software Engineering (TSE)	107
5	International Conference on Data Engineering (ICDE)	97
6	International Conference on Software Engineering (ICSE)	87
7	ACM SIGMOD Conference	87
8	Information Systems	82
9	Requirements Engineering	80
10	Data and Knowledge Engineering	78

Table 4 Data summary of ER, ICDE, VLDB and CAiSE conferences

Conference series	Events	#Authors	#Papers
International Conference on Conceptual Modeling (ER)	1979–2011	2,997	1,945
International Conference on Data Engineering (ICDE)	1984–2011	5,886	3,683
Very Large Data Bases (VLDB) Conference	1975–2010	3,660	2,397
Conference on Advanced Information Systems Engineering (CAiSE)	1990–2012	3,129	1,876

We begin with a simple analysis of the number of published papers over time. Figure 4a plots the absolute numbers of authors and papers of CAiSE over years. In general, the numbers of authors and papers increase over years, with a significant increase in 2002 and drop in 2007; the latter is obviously due to the decision of the steering committee at that time to reduce the acceptance rate sharply. A view into the individual proceedings shows that the number of submissions continued to increase, such that CAiSE nowadays attracts very high numbers of submissions despite acceptance rates that are among the toughest in the IS area.

Next, we study the distribution of authorship intensity, i.e. the number of CAiSE conferences authors have published in, and the number of papers they have written for CAiSE. Figure 4b plots this distribution in log-log axes. The distribution of

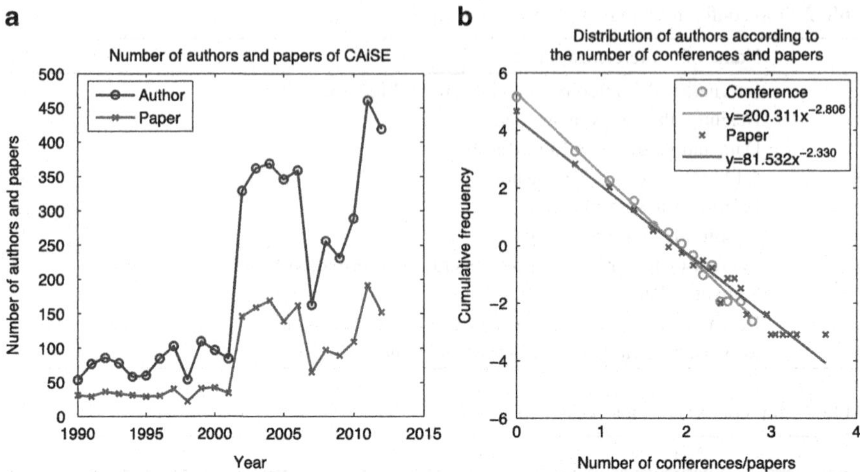

Fig. 4 Number and distribution of authors of CAiSE over years

authors according to the number of conferences and papers follows Power-law distributions with the exponent α equals to 2.806 and 2.33, respectively. This indicates that there is a "tail" of authors who significantly contribute to CAiSE despite appearing there only once. In detail, 79 % of authors contributed only to one conference, while 21 % contributed to at least 2 conferences and 94 authors (3 %) contributed to at least 5 conferences. In term of the number of papers, 76 % of authors contributed only 1 paper and 141 authors (about 4 %) contributed at least 5 papers to CAiSE.

To investigate the contributions of returning authors to CAiSE over the years, we calculated two measures in comparison to our three benchmark conferences: the rate of recurring authors and their publications over years. A paper is published by *recurring authors* if at least one of its authors has published in the previous conference. A high rate of recurring authors, together with a low rate of papers by recurring authors, indicates that recurring authors mainly collaborate with each other (one paper has more recurring authors). On the other hand, a high rate of recurring authors, together with a high rate of papers by recurring authors, indicates that recurring authors collaborate mainly with new authors, which contributes to community development. Those two measures allow us to assess one important principle to cultivate scientific communities [13]. On the one hand, a community needs to retain the authors in order to establish and keep the old ideas. On the other hand, it also needs to attract new authors who probably will bring new ideas.

In Fig. 5, we recognize that the basic trend during the early stage of all conferences is to retain authors. The frequency of papers by recurring authors also increased. In the first 11 years, CAiSE retained the authors at a lower rate (around 25 %) in comparison to VLDB, ER and ICDE. After that, CAiSE managed an author recurring at a similar rate as VLDB (around 38 %). Similar observation can be made for the papers by recurring author rate.

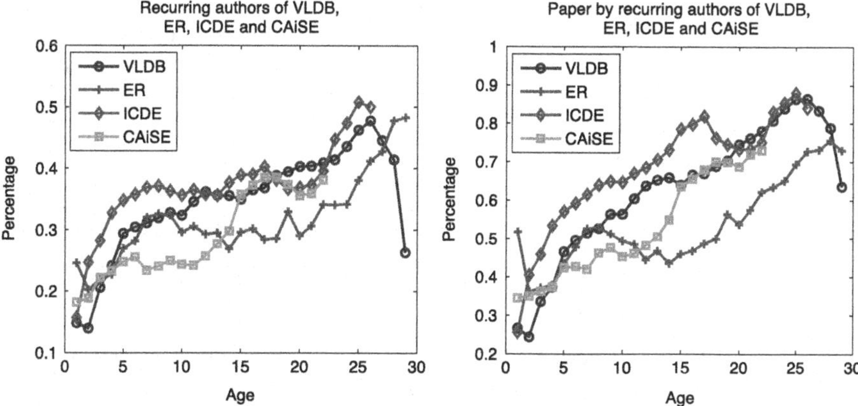

Fig. 5 Recurring authors and papers by recurring authors over years

In summary, CAiSE constantly developed in the last 24 years in term of authors and contribution intensity. There is set of authors who contribute continuously and greatly to CAiSE. Over time, CAiSE manages to not only retain authors who are working on the established ideas of the conference, but also to attract new authors who would bring fresh ideas to the community. A comparison of the returning rating of CAiSE authors and their contributions to other conferences shows that CAiSE now retains a healthy fraction of recurring authors in order to keep the community open.

3.3 *The Evolution of Connectivity in CAiSE*

Having looked at the phenomena of author activity at the individual level, we are now in the position to look at the question what this means for the shape of the CAiSE author community network as a whole. The basis for this are the co-authorship graphs, and the six network metrics we defined in Sect. 2.

The evolution of these six metrics for VLDB, ER, ICDE and CAiSE is shown in Fig. 6. VLDB, ICDE and CAiSE expose the same evolution pattern but with a slight delay for CAiSE. The maximum betweenness and largest connected component of the co-authorships of VLDB and ICDE started increasing after 10 years, while it took CAiSE 15 years. The ER conference faced an even bigger delay (22 years) which can perhaps be explained somewhat by the very late entry of US research into their community. Note that in our earlier studies we also found conferences where this has never happened, which was typically closely correlated with very low impact in terms of citation. In this sense, all four conferences can nowadays be considered successful. However, the decreasing parameters average shortest path length and diameter over long times (VLDB: 10 years, ICDE: 7 years, CAiSE: 5 years) suggest that these communities are now more stable while the ER

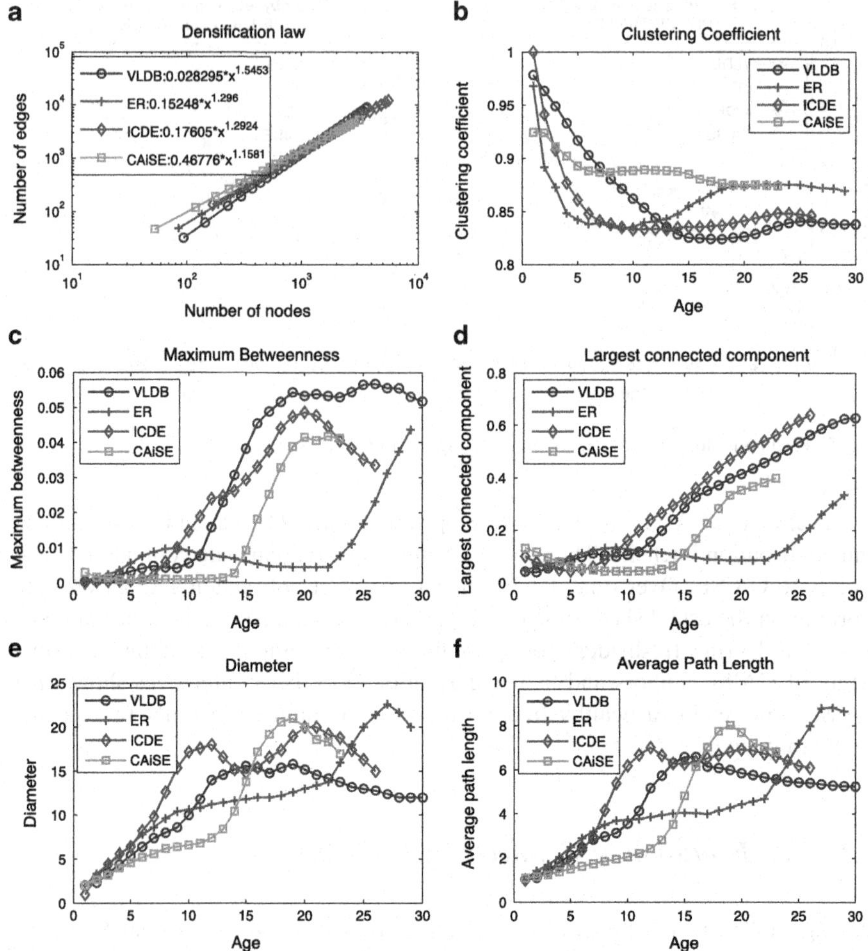

Fig. 6 Co-authorship network parameters of CAiSE and other conferences

community is still developing. Interestingly, the clustering coefficient of CAiSE and ER is higher than for VLDB and ICDE, indicating that CAiSE and ER are clustered in more sub-groups (with many disconnected components).

To summarize, the connectivity of CAiSE community has been increasing significantly over the last 12 years. The community is developing towards a well-connected and cohesive structure. Compared to other established conferences, we see that CAiSE is currently developing as fast as VLDB and ICDE. To illustrate where this might lead in the future, we compare in Figs. 7 and 8 snapshots of the co-authorship networks of CAiSE and VLDB for every fifth year of their respective histories (for CAiSE starting 1989, for VLDB 1975). Obviously, CAiSE and VLDB developed very similarly in the first 25 years, as both of them built their community

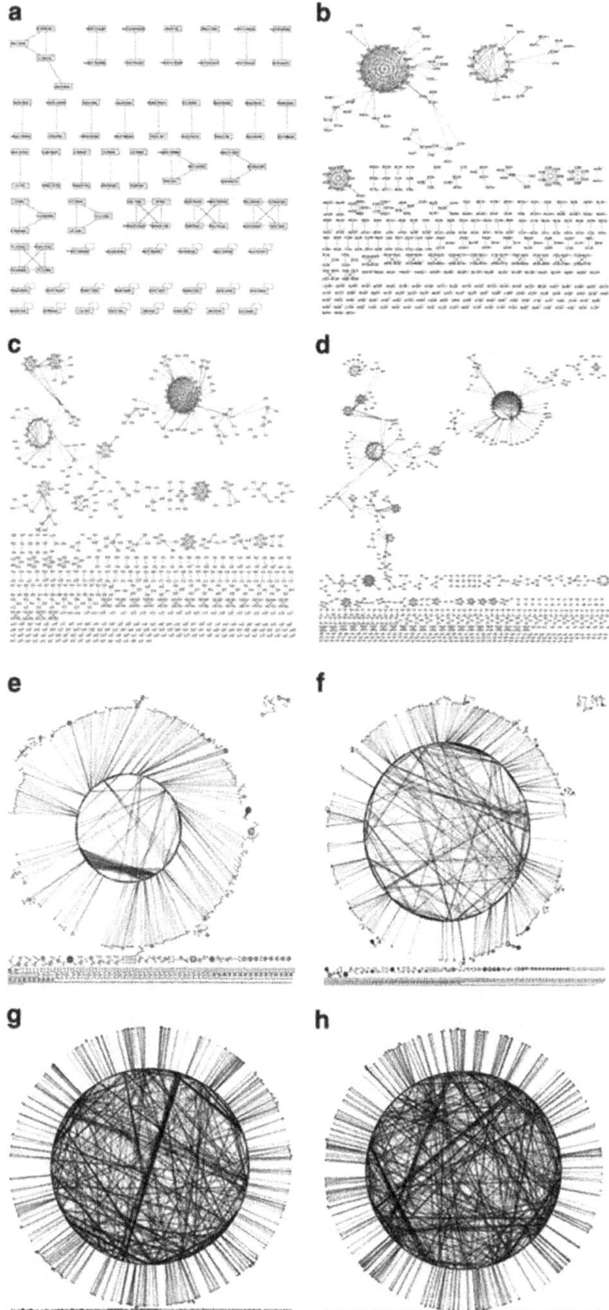

Fig. 7 Development of VLDB co-authorship network. (**a**) VLDB in 1975. (**b**) VLDB in 1980. (**c**) VLDB in 1985. (**d**) VLDB in 1990. (**e**) VLDB in 1995. (**f**) VLDB in 2000. (**g**) VLDB in 2005. (**h**) VLDB in 2010

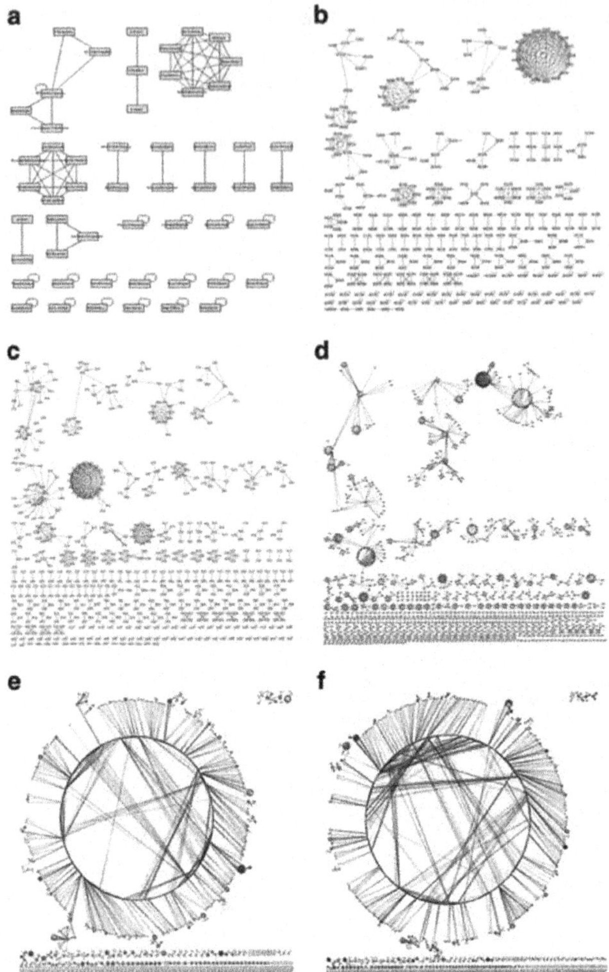

Fig. 8 Development of CAiSE co-authorship network. (**a**) CAiSE in 1990. (**b**) CAiSE in 1995. (**c**) CAiSE in 2000. (**d**) CAiSE in 2005. (**e**) CAiSE in 2010. (**f**) CAiSE in 2012

from a *born* to *bonding*, then *emergence* and finally *focused* topology. However, the last 10 years of VLDB (parts (g) and (h) in Fig. 7) also exhibit a possible danger; they show an ever denser giant component where new authors often can only enter by co-authoring with members of that component. It might then well happen that important new topics are not recognized early enough by the community, a danger that CAiSE has so far well managed to avoid.

The high betweenness centrality and big giant component of the CAiSE co-authorship network suggest that there is an increasing number of active members

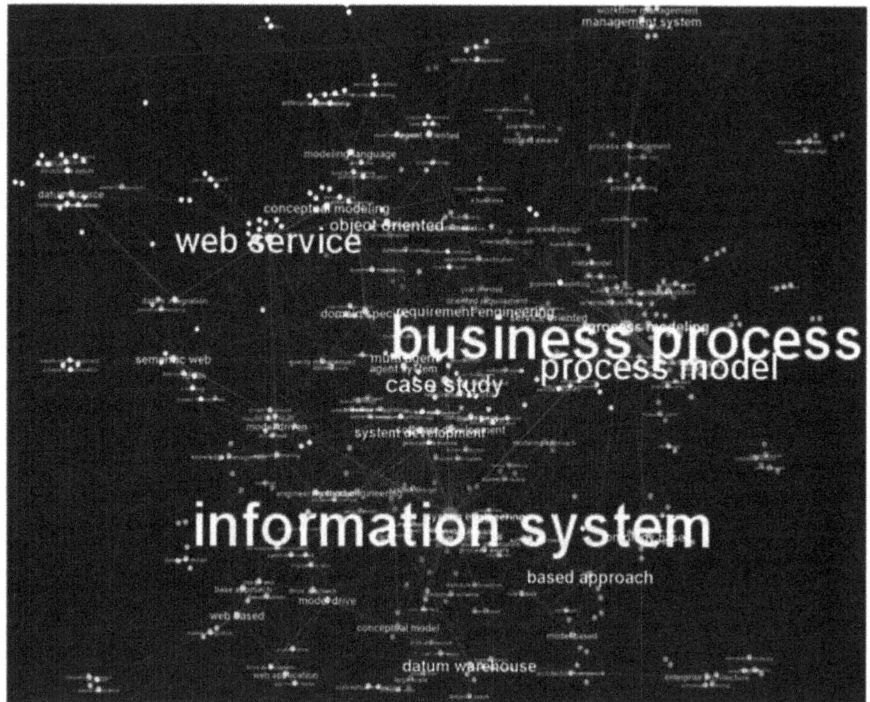

Fig. 9 The visualization of CAiSE keywords

who collaborate across sub-communities. These very active authors form the core of the community which we will identify in the next section.

3.4 *Main Themes and Key Members of the CAiSE Author Community*

It has been mentioned that CAiSE boasts a somewhat richer structure of sub-communities in its giant components than e.g. VLDB. This can likely be linked the diversity themes studied by these sub-communities. One of the simplest and most popular ways to study this phenomenon automatically is simply the generation of keyword networks based on the paper titles. There is a link between two keywords if they co-occur in at least one paper title. The connection is weighted by the number of co-occurences. We visualize this network using the ForceAtlas layout (see Fig. 9), where the size of nodes and labels denotes the PageRank score of keywords. Nodes are colored according to the clusters detected by a modularity-based clustering algorithm [7].

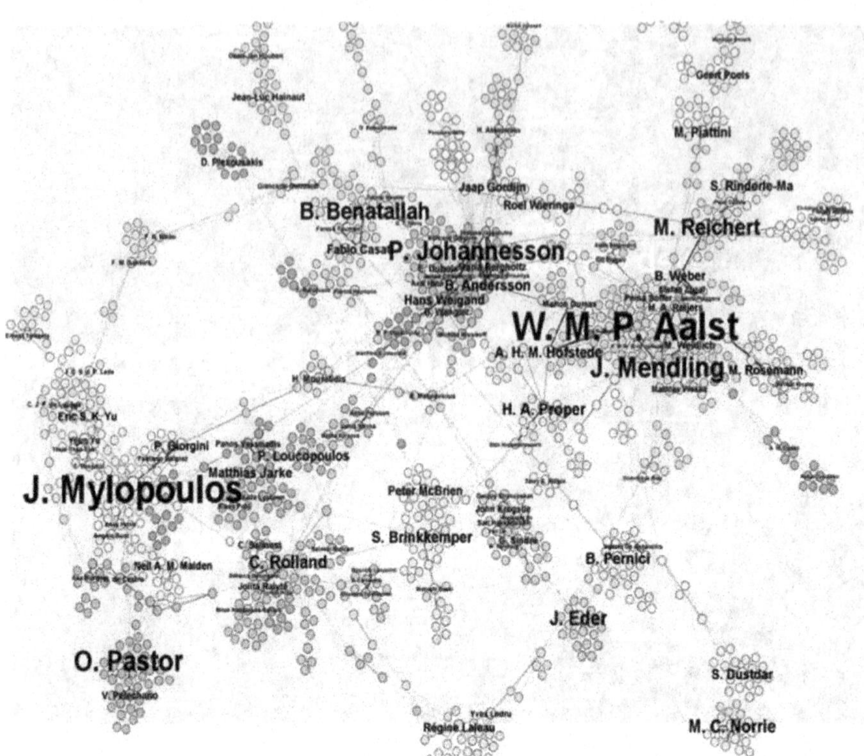

Fig. 10 Co-authorship network (giant component) of CAiSE (as of 2012)

With surprising clarity, the visualization shows two big clusters around the topics of Information System and Bussiness Process. For frequent attendees, it is probably obvious in hindsight that bringing these two themes – one more from Computer Science, the other more from MIS – together is one of the main attractions of CAiSE for members of both communities. Indeed, the other major keywords – Web Service, Process Model, Case Study, Data Warehouse, Object Oriented, Requirement Engineering, Multi Agent, Ontology Based, Conceptual Modeling, Management Systems and Semantic Web – are either closely related to one of these main topics or build some kind of bridge among them.

To investigate the key members in these sub-community and CAiSE as a whole, we applied two SNA ranking measures: the betweenness and the PageRank score of authors in the co-authorship network. The CAiSE co-authorship network in 2012 is given in Fig. 10, using again the ForceAtlas layout [1]. Nodes are colored according to their assignments to sub-communities detected by the modularity-based clustering algorithm [7]. The size of labels and nodes denotes the PageRank [8] score of authors. This visualization shows us the key members not only by their prestige (denoted by PageRank score), but also by their important position in the collaboration network.

Table 5 Top 20 authors by betweenness and PageRank in the co-author network

	Betweenness		PageRank	
1	John Mylopoulos	201,591	John Mylopoulos	0.0035
2	Wil M. P. van der Aalst	183,018	Wil M. P. van der Aalst	0.0034
3	Pericles Loucopoulos	148,551	Oscar Pastor	0.0024
4	Birger Andersson	147,759	Jan Mendling	0.0023
5	Raimundas Matulevicius	145,736	Paul Johannesson	0.0022
6	Benkt Wangler	142,569	Boualem Benatallah	0.0021
7	Marlon Dumas	128,972	Manfred Reichert	0.0020
8	Eric Dubois	97,785	Johann Eder	0.0018
9	Jan Mendling	87,883	Moira C. Norrie	0.0017
10	Paul Johannesson	80,494	Colette Rolland	0.0017
11	Arthur H. M. ter Hofstede	79,558	Henderik Alex Proper	0.0016
12	Haralambos Mouratidis	78,250	Barbara Pernici	0.0016
13	Colette Rolland	76,631	Sjaak Brinkkemper	0.0015
14	Paolo Giorgini	70,613	Birger Andersson	0.0015
15	Guttorm Sindre	69,171	Arthur H. M. ter Hofstede	0.0015
16	Boualem Benatallah	67,998	Schahram Dustdar	0.0015
17	Sjaak Brinkkemper	60,984	Mario Piattini	0.0014
18	Jaap Gordijn	60,481	Stefanie Rinderle-Ma	0.0014
19	Roel Wieringa	59,734	Matthias Jarke	0.0014
20	Manfred Reichert	55,062	Pericles Loucopoulos	0.0014

Interestingly, the topic structure is well reflected in this figure, as each of the themes has a clear "leader", John Mylopoulos in the case of Information Systems, and Wil van der Aalst for Business Process. In addition, the many smaller sub-groups are connected by a set of gatekeepers. For example, Paul Johannesson, Oscar Pastor, Colette Rolland, Jan Mendling, Manfred Reichert, Pericles Loucopoulo, Boualem Benatallah, Johann Eder and Barbara Pernici connect their own sub-groups with many other sub-groups. Those authors together form the core, which ensures the connectivity of the community as a whole. Moreover, it is interesting to note that former students and collaborators of the CAiSE founders and Advisory Committee members Janis Bubenko (most prominently Paul Johannesson), Arne Solvberg (e.g. John Krogstie and Peter McBrien), and more recently Colette Rolland still play important betweenness nodes linking the two main subfields. To provide a bit more detail, Table 5 gives the top 20 authors according to their betweenness and PageRank score in the co-authorship network.

Complementing the co-authorship network, there is of course the citation network which, however, extends far beyond the CAiSE community itself. Indeed, the selection of papers reproduced and commented in this volume was based on such an analysis, taking the ranking of numbers of citations as a starting point. We therefore do not discuss this aspect in this chapter. Suffice it to say that the truly outstanding h indexes of Wil van der Aalst (83) and John Mylopoulos (69) confirm impressively the exceptional role we also saw in the co-authorship network.

4 Conclusion

The Social Network Analysis of the CAiSE Conference author community shows a quite interesting strategic position within the Computer Science discipline, and – after a somewhat slow start – an impressive development towards a conference community that exhibits all the ingredients of success found in earlier success stories such as VLDB: a strong giant component of long-term collaborators with very high impact within and beyond the conference itself, combined with a topical openness and interdisciplinarity that promises sufficient openness for innovation. The long-term visionary but very open and friendly leadership of what is now called the senior Advisory Committee has certainly contributed to this success, as has the small "revolution" of a few junior key players around 2007 that made CAiSE one of the most strictly refereed conference in the field and thus – for the naive perhaps surprisingly – increased not just the prestige and quality, but also the quantity of submissions from several important collaborating sub-areas.

We hasten to admit that our choice of data sources implies some limitations of this study. First, both DBLP and CiteSeer show only author and published paper information about the conference; so our social network is limited to co-authorship, citation, and keywords. It leaves out the very important network of conference organizers but also conference attendees and authors of unsuccessful submissions. Second and perhaps more importantly, especially CiteSeer focuses on Computer Science only, so our analysis of the integrated data set cannot evaluate impact on or by related fields in other disciplines such as Management Information Systems.

Despite these limitations, regular CAiSE participants will find that many of their personal social experiences in CAiSE are reproduced fairly well by even by the co-author and citation analysis we employ. Perhaps – like the first author – they have also faced some interesting surprises in this paper which, however, can be well explained from their deep knowledge of the conference history on second thought. For ourselves, these limitations create the challenge to find and integrate data sources which are less narrow in their view of the IT field, yet – unlike much of the Web of Science – do include information about conferences and their impact. Especially the broad field of Management Information Systems seems in urgent need for such a study, as many of their representatives work in business schools where conference publications are not taken seriously at all.

Acknowledgements This work is supported by the DFG-funded excellence cluster UMIC, the B-IT Research School, and EU Integrated Project Layers.

References

1. Bastian, M., Heymann, S., and Jacomy, M. (2009). Gephi: An open source software for exploring and manipulating networks. In *International AAAI Conference on Weblogs and Social Media*, pages 361–362.

2. Kleinberg, J. M. (1999). Authoritative sources in a hyperlinked environment. *J. ACM*, 46: 604–632.
3. Lave, J. and Wenger, E. (1991). *Situated Learning: Legitimate Peripheral Participation*. Learning in Doing. Cambridge University Press.
4. Leskovec, J., Kleinberg, J., and Faloutsos, C. (2005). Graphs over time: densification laws, shrinking diameters and possible explanations. In *Proceedings of the eleventh ACM SIGKDD international conference on Knowledge discovery in data mining*, KDD '05, pages 177–187, New York, NY, USA. ACM.
5. McCallum, A., Nigam, K., and Ungar, L. H. (2000). Efficient clustering of high-dimensional data sets with application to reference matching. In *KDD '00: Proceedings of the sixth ACM SIGKDD International Conference on Knowledge Discovery and Data Mining*, pages 169–178, New York, NY, USA. ACM.
6. Newman, M. E. J. (2001). The structure of scientific collaboration networks. *Proc.Natl.Acad.Sci.USA*, 98:404.
7. Newman, M. E. J. (2004). Fast algorithm for detecting community structure in networks. *Physical Review E*, 69:066133.
8. Page, L., Brin, S., Motwani, R., and Winograd, T. (1998). The pagerank citation ranking: Bringing order to the web. Technical report;, Stanford University.
9. Pham, M. and Klamma, R. (2010). The structure of the computer science knowledge network. In *2010 International Conference on Advances in Social Networks Analysis and Mining (ASONAM)*, pages 17–24.
10. Pham, M. C. (2013). *Dynamic Social Network Analysis and Recommender Technologies in Scientific Communities: The Case of Computer Science*. PhD thesis, RWTH Aachen University, Aachen – Germany.
11. Pham, M. C., Derntl, M., Klamma, R., and Jarke, M. (2012). Development patterns of scientific communities in technology enhanced learning. *Educational Technology and Society*, 15(3):323–335.
12. Pham, M. C., Klamma, R., and Jarke, M. (2011). Development of computer science disciplines: a social network analysis approach. *Social Netw. Analys. Mining*, 1(4):321–340.
13. Wenger, E., McDermott, R., and Snyder, W. (2002). *Cultivating communities of practice: a guide to managing knowledge*. Harvard Business School Press.

A NATURAL LANGUAGE APPROACH FOR REQUIREMENTS ENGINEERING

C. ROLLAND[1] C. PROIX[2]

ABSTRACT : The term Requirements Engineering refers to this part of a database development cycle that involves investigating the problems and requirements of the users community and developing a conceptual specification of the future system.
Natural language plays an important role during this stage that has proved to be crucial in the development of computerized systems. The required acquisition of application domain knowledge is achieved either through documents and texts analysis or by means of interviews i.e through language manipulation. Similarly validation of the specification is made via oral discussions with users.
The paper proposes that Requirements Engineering (R.E) should be supported by a CASE tool based on a linguistic approach. It presents a R.E support environment that generates the conceptual specification from a description of the problem space provided through natural language statements. Complementary, validation is based on texts generation from the conceptual specification to natural language. The paper focuses on the linguistic approach, demonstrates its generality and overviews its implementation in a CASE tool.

KEY WORDS : Requirements engineering, Natural language analysis, conceptual schema, information system design, text generation

1. Introduction

The need for modelling techniques by which systems may be described in high level conceptual terms has been recognized in the earlier phases of Databases and Information Systems (DB/IS) development in industry, business and administration.

---

[1] Université de Paris 1, 17 rue de la Sorbonne, 75231 Paris cedex 05, France
[2] Société CRIL, 146 Boulevard de Valmy 92707 Colombes cedex, France

This has caused the introduction of various conceptual models that have proved to be extremely useful to build in a high level specification of the future system (the so called conceptual schema) before this system is developed. (see the survey presented by Hull and King [Hull 87] for example).

However, the task of constructing the conceptual schema remains problematical. The route to reach the conceptual schema e.g the conceptual modelling process has the purpose of abstracting and conceptualizing the relevant part of the application domain. This is guided by requirements. The term Requirements Engineering introduced by Dubois [Dubois 89] has been used for this part of the DB/IS development that involves investigating the problems and requirements of the users community and developing a specification of the future system. The succeeding phase, where this specification is realized in a working system which is verified against the specification may be called Design Engineering [Bubenko 90]. Figure 1.1 shows the organization of DB/IS development cycle based upon requirements and system engineering.

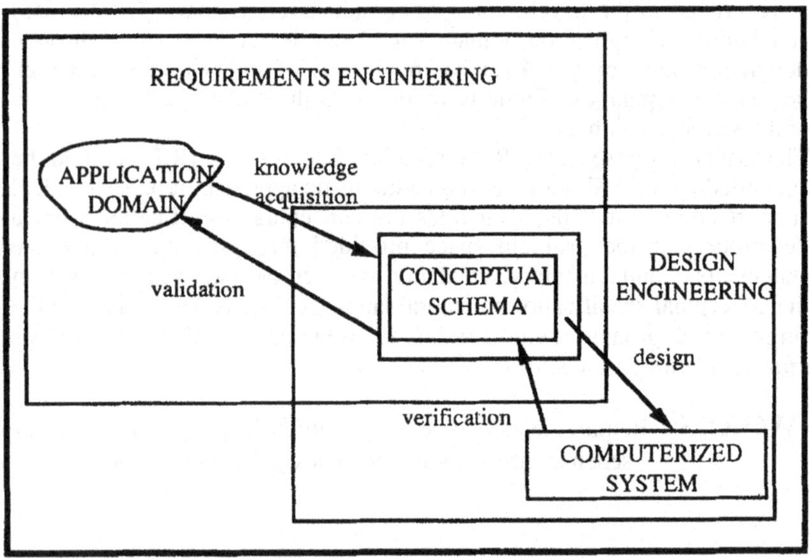

Figure 1.1 : DB/IS development cycle

Requirements Engineering consists of knowledge acquisition and validation.

The **acquisition task** falls into two areas, namely, analysis and modelling. The Requirements Engineering process starts with an observation of the real world, in order to identify pertinent real phenomena, their properties and constraints, and to classify similar phenomena into classes. Then the analyst represents and describes the classes, their properties and constraints through types of a specific conceptual model. Analysis leads to problem-statements, while modelling allows the description of elements of the conceptual schema.

The **validation task** has the objective of checking whether the conceptual schema is consistent and whether it correctly expresses the requirements informally stated by the users.

In many cases, analysts are able to correctly use concepts of a model but have difficulties to abstract reality in order to represent it through these concepts. This is similar to school students who are able to use simple equations but have many difficulties to build in equations from problem-statements. Similarly correcting a conceptual schema is easy while validating its adequacy to requirements is more difficult.

Analysis, modelling and validation are cognitive processes. However, analysis is based on domain-dependent knowledge, modelling requires model-dependent knowledge and validation requires both. More generally, Vitalari has shown, [Vitalari 83], [Vitalari 85], that experienced analysts use different categories of knowledge namely : organization specific knowledge, application domain knowledge, development methodology knowledge and functional domain knowledge.

It is the authors' belief that there is a need for CASE tools that support the Requirements Engineering process in a way that better reflects the problem solving behaviour of experienced analysts. This requires to identify, understand and formalize the cognitive mechanisms that allow the analyst to abstract reality and to represent it through concepts and to diagnose the specification from users points of view.

OICSI[1] (French acronym for intelligent tool for information system design) is a system prototype based on this premise. It exploits knowledge-based paradigms to provide an active aid to DB/IS analysts during the Requirements Engineering process. OICSI supports the analysts in the process of problem-statements acquisition, elicitation, modelling and validation.

In addition, the authors recognize that Requirements Engineering is mainly based on abstraction and have granted a privilege to a natural language approach.

Indeed, psychological research works dealing with the study of abstraction mechanisms show that abstraction is strongly interlocked with language manipulation.

Following this line, problem-statements in OICSI are expressed with the French natural language and automatically interpreted in terms of the OICSI conceptual model. Complementary, OICSI uses a text generation technique to feed back to the user information about the specification (i.e the conceptual schema).

This choice is enhanced by the fact that analysts do not proceed by direct observation of the real world but through a media which is the natural language. Indeed, the two most common ways for acquiring application domain knowledge are interviews and studies of existing documents (forms, legal documents...).

---

[1] OICSI is the name used in the academic area; in the industrial world this case tool is named ALECSI, it is developed by CRIL company.

According to the OICSI paradigm illustrated in figure 1.2, the analysis task refers to the description of the relevant real world phenomena using the French natural language, the modelling task refers to the mapping of problem-statements onto basic concepts of the OICSI underlying DB/IS development methodology and the validation task is based upon a paraphrased description of the conceptual schema in the French natural language.

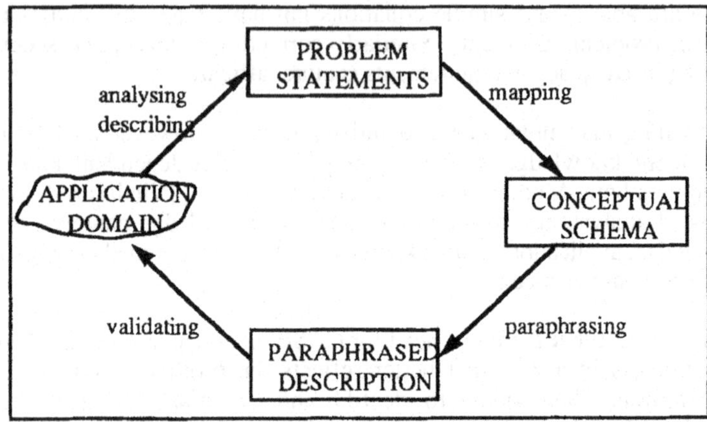

Figure 1.2 : Analysis and Modelling process.

Using OICSI, the conceptual schema is hidden to the future system users. The "system referential", they have to understand, comment upon and validate, is expressed using natural language. Even for the analysts the conceptual model and the conceptual schema are partially hidden since OICSI automatically supports modelling as well as text generation.

However, it must be mentioned that OICSI provides a graphical interface. Depending on their personal abilities to understand conceptual modelling, the analysts will use the most appropriate interface.

Similar approaches to solving Requirements Engineering from the description of the application domain uttered with natural language sentences have been followed for example in the AMADEUS project which aims at combining graphics and natural language [Black 87]. Others examples are SECSI [Bouzegoub 86] and ACME [Kersten 86] which are conceptual modelling expert systems.

Text generation has been used in different areas of databases : it is an important matter in natural language interfaces to databases; it also used for tutorial purposes in learning a query language and for generating readable error messages. Examples of prototype systems are EXPOUND [Chester 76] which translates formal proofs into English, CO-OP [McKeown 86] based upon a syntactic approach, PERFORM [Muckstein 85] and ELFS [Luk 86] which are knowledge based approaches for text generation from SQL to natural language, De Roeck paraphrasing of relational calculus [De Roeck 88] and Grishman paraphrasing of predicate logic [Grishman 79].
The remainder of this paper describes the natural language approach for Requirements Engineering and its implementation in OICSI. Section 2 presents the linguistic approach for requirements acquisition and elicitation. The paraphrasing mechanism for validation is presented in section 3. A brief overview of implementation aspects is given in section 4.

2. The linguistic approach

Conceptual modelling in OICSI is based on a linguistic approach that tries to formalize the linguistic mechanisms through which analysts are able to abstract observed phenomena onto concepts.

The problem-solving behaviour of analysts is first intuitively introduced. The "CASE for CASE" theory (which is the foundation of the formalization of the analyst behaviour) is thus recalled. Finally, our linguistic approach is detailed and the conceptual schema generation is presented.

2.1 Intuitive introduction to analysts problem solving behaviour

This section is an attempt to highlight the linguistic mechanisms used by analysts.

Let us imagine that our favourite analyst *Ado* is used to manipulate the Entity-Relationship (E-R) model [Chen 76]. This means that *Ado* will try, when observing the real world, to identify classes of real world phenomena that can be modelled as entity types, attributes or relationship types.

Thus, during an interview, if *Ado* hears the sentence:

"A subscriber has a name and an address."

He will probably introduces in the conceptual schema an entity type SUBSCRIBER with two attributes NAME and ADDRESS.
Now, in order to understand the analyst behaviour, let us ask the question :"How did *Ado* get this result?".

A first response could be that *Ado* knows the meaning of the words "*subscriber*", "*name*" and "*address*", and how they relate one with others. This means that *Ado* uses a kind of common-sense knowledge to match the sentence onto the E-R schema. This knowledge is based on couples (word, real object) which allow to relate a word to a well known object in the real world.

But assume now that the sentence is :

"The colydrena have a pedistylus and a folicul."

As *Ado* did, many analysts will make the hypothesis that the word "*colydrena*" is a non lexical object type that can be modelled by an entity type and that "*pedistylus*" and "*folicul*" are two attributes related to the entity type. *Ado* is not certain that he did the right interpretation of the sentence but the interpretation is plausible and he can, later, validate its truth discussing with domain specialists.

In this case, *Ado* did not use the same kind of common-sense knowledge as previously. He does not know the meaning of the words (they are imaginary), but, however without any understanding of the words he found a model of the described situation (which is, indeed, correct).

Ado's reasoning is based on the recognition of a particular sentence pattern which is colloquial to him. The knowledge which is used, is a linguistic knowledge related to language manipulation. It allows him to recognize and to interpret the following sentence pattern :

<Subject Group><Verb expressing ownership><Complement Group>

The pre-established interpretation of such pattern allows Ado to associate the subject group of the sentence to a real entity class as the owner of the attributes represented by the complement group's words.

The linguistic knowledge is certainly the most common knowledge within the analysts population. Analysts use it, sometimes explicitly, but most often in an implicit way. Our goal is to make explicit the different types of sentence patterns in order to formalize this kind of linguistic knowledge and to support the process of the problem-statements interpretation and modelling in a computerized way.

The linguistic approach implemented in OICSI is borrowed from the Fillmore's theory "Case for Case" [Fillmore 68].

Section 2.2 summarizes the main points of this theory. Its specialization for OICSI is presented in section 2.3.

2.2 The Fillmore's case system

The main concept of the Fillmore's theory is the notion of case introduced as follows: "*the case notions comprise a set of universal, presumably innate, concepts which identify certain types of judgement human beings are capable of making about the events which are going on around them...*".

Cases are types of relationships that groups of words have with the verb in any clause of a sentence. One of the basic Fillmore's assumption is that it exists a limited number of cases. Fillmore exhibits six major cases: AGENTIVE, INSTRUMENTAL, DATIVE, FACTITIVE, LOCATIVE and OBJECTIVE.

(1) John opens the door.
(2) The door is opened by John.
(3) The key opens the door.
(4) John opens the door by means of the key.
(5) John uses the key in order to open the door.
(6) John believes that he will win.
(7) John is ill.

Figure 2.1 : Examples of sentences

For example in sentences (1) and (2) of the figure 2.1 "*John*" is associated to the case AGENTIVE and "*door*" to the case OBJECTIVE; the word "*key*" in sentences (3), (4), (5) is associated to the INSTRUMENTAL case, while in sentences (6) and (7) "*John*" is associated to the DATIVE case.

Obviously, the same word can correspond to different cases in different sentences.

One complementary assumption of the Fillmore's theory is that the meaning of any clause is derivable from the meaning of the verb and the recognition of embedded cases. This leads to the identification of predefined patterns with associated derivable meanings.

For example, due to the fact that sentence (1) has a structure of the type:

<Verb expressing action, AGENTIVE, OBJECTIVE>

allows to infer that "*John*" is the agent who performs the action on the object "*door*".

Sentences (1) and (2) correspond to the previously mentioned structure; the structure of sentence (3) matches the type :

<Verb expressing action, INSTRUMENTAL, OBJECTIVE>

and finally, sentences (4) and (5) have the following pattern :

<Verb expressing action,OBJECTIVE, AGENTIVE, INSTRUMENTAL>.

The Fillmore's patterns allow to perform a classification of natural language sentences with regards to their structure and, thus, to infer their meaning according to the class they belong to.

2.3 Specialization of the Fillmore's case system

Experimentations of the Fillmore's theory convinced the authors that the theory was applicable and pertinent to support the DB/IS analysis and modelling process. However, we reach the conclusion that the cases might be adapted to the purpose of establishing problem-statements allowing the construction of an DB/IS conceptual schema. Indeed statements about real world phenomena fall into two categories: fact descriptions and rules.

Examples of fact descriptions (we consider a subscription library system) are as follows:

(1) In the library, a book is described by a unique reference number, the authors' names, the publisher name and the year and version of editing.
(2) Last and first names of the subscriber, his address, first year of subscription and last date of subscription fees payment are recorded.
(3) The status of each copy of a book is recorded in real time.

Our understanding of facts is similar to the Nijssen's approach [Nijssen 89].

The following are examples of rules:

(1) Subscription fees are paid every year.
(2) A subscriber, properly registered (i.e who paid the fees) is called an "active" subscriber.
(3) A subscriber cannot borrow more than three books at the same time.
(4) Books are only loaned to active subscribers.
(5) When a loan request cannot be satisfied it becomes a "waiting request".
(6) After 13 months without paying the subscription fees, the subscriber status becomes "inactive".
(7) "Waiting request" are treated in their chronological order.

As just exemplified, rules can express management rules independent or dependent of time, static constraint rules or dynamic constraint rules .

Sentences describing either facts or rules are the problem-statements that OICSI automatically interprets by performing a case approach.

2.3.1 The case classification

The case notion has been extended in two directions: cases are applicable to clauses and the classification of cases has been revised.

. According to the Fillmore's theory, cases relate to words in sentences. It is the authors' belief that the notion of case could be successfully applied not only to words but also to clauses in sentences. This allows to interpret a complex sentence in a top-down fashion. The case approach is first applied to subordinate clauses with regards to the verb of the main clause. Thus, the case approach is again applied to each of the subordinate clause.

. The classification of cases used by OICSI is as follows :
<OWNER, OWNED, ACTOR, TARGET, CONSTRAINED*, CONSTRAINT*, LOCALIZATION* , ACTION* , OBJECT>.

We exemplified the meaning of these cases on the following set of sentences.

(1) A subscriber is described by a name, an address and a number.
(2) A subscriber borrows books.
(3)When a subscriber makes a request of loan, the request is accepted, if a copy of the requested book is available, else the request is delayed.

In sentence (1), "*subscriber*" is associated to the OWNER case and "*name*", "*address*" and "*number*" are associated to the OWNED case.

In sentence (2), "*subscriber*" is associated to the ACTOR case and the OWNER case, while "*books*" is associated to the OWNED case; these two cases express that there is a relationship between "*subscriber*" and "*books*". The entire clause is associated to the ACTION case.

In sentence (3) :

- the clause "*When a subscriber requests for a loan*" is associated to the LOCALIZATION case,
- inside this clause, the phrase "*request of loan*" is associated to OBJECT case,
- the clause "*if a copy of the requested book is available*" is associated to the CONSTRAINT case,
- the clause "*the request is accepted*" is associated to the ACTION and the CONSTRAINED case,
- inside this clause, the word "*request*" is associated to the TARGET case.

---

* denotes cases that may be applied to clauses

Complementary, classes of verbs have been identified. The figure 2.2 shows both the hierarchy of classes and some examples of class instances.

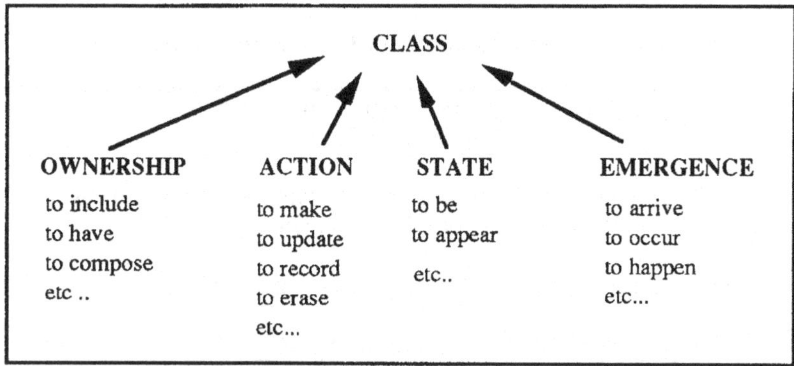

Figure 2.4 : Hierarchy and instances of classes of verbs

2.3.2 The linguistic patterns

A set of patterns that combine cases and classes of verbs previously introduced have been defined. These patterns are of two different types:

- elementary patterns allow to associate cases to syntactic units of a clause,
- sentence patterns allow to associate cases to clauses of a sentence.

Both are introduced and exemplified in turn.

Elementary patterns

They fall again into three different categories:

- structural pattern,
- behavioural pattern,
- constraint pattern.

SP1 and SP2 are examples of simple **structural patterns.**

SP1 : [Ng_subject](OWNER) [verbal form](ownership_subject)
[Ng_complement](OWNED)

SP2 : [Ng_subject](OWNED) [verbal form](ownership_complement)
[Ng_complement](OWNER).

The notation [syntactic unit](case) means that the "syntactic unit" is associated to the case "case". The following abbreviations Ng, Cl, Sub, Mn, are respectively used to refer to a Nominal group, a Clause, a Subordinate clause and a Main clause.

The clause : "*any subscriber has a name and an address*" matches the SP1 pattern and can be interpreted in the following way:

- the clause subject "*any subscriber*" plays the role of OWNER,
- "*has*" is the verb belonging to the ownership class,
- "*a name* " and "*an address*" are subject complements playing the role of OWNED.

It is obvious that patterns of the SP1 family are appropriated to fact sentences.

The sentence " *loan-requests are made by subscribers*" can be unified to pattern SP2.

BP1, BP2, BP3, and BP4 are four examples of **behavioural patterns**.

BP1 : [Ng_subject](ACTOR) [verbal form](action)
[Ng_complement](TARGET)

BP2 : [Conjunction](LOCALIZATION) [Ng_subject](ACTOR)
[verbal form](action) [Ng_complement](OBJECT)

BP3 : [preposition](LOCALIZATION) [Ng](OBJECT)

BP4 : [Ng](TARGET) [verbal form](action)

"*Subscribers borrow books*" is a clause that matches the BP1 pattern :

- "*subscribers*" as the subject of the clause plays the role of ACTOR,
- "*borrow*" is a verb belonging to the action class,
- "*books*" is the subject complement which plays the role of TARGET.

The clause : "*when a subscriber returns a book copy*" can be unified with BP2 pattern with the following interpretation:

- "*when*" is a conjunction that expresses the LOCALIZATION of the action,
- "*a subscriber*" is the subject that plays the role of ACTOR,
- "*returns*" is the verb that belongs to the action class,
- "*a book copy*" is the complement that plays the role of OBJECT of action.

BP3 is a pattern which deals with circumstantial complements and, for this reason, is not organized around the verb but around the preposition.

Within the clause: "*As soon as the receipt of a subscriber's subscription fees, the subscriber's status is updated*", the phrase "*As soon as the receipt of a subscriber's subscription fees*" matches the BP3 pattern with the following interpretation:

- "*As soon as*" is the preposition that describes the LOCALIZATION of action expresses by the clause,
- "*the receipt of a subscriber's subscription fees*" is the phrase that plays the role of OBJECT.

Finally the BP4 pattern allows to interpret a particular type of clauses which describe actions such as "*the loan is agreed upon*".

At last CP1 is an example of **constraint pattern**.

CP1 : [Ng_subject](CONSTRAINED) [verbal form](state)
[Ng_complement](CONSTRAINT)

The clause: "*the number of loans is equal or less than three*", can be unified to the CP1 pattern in such a way that:

- "*the number of loans*" plays the role of CONSTRAINED, and
- "*equal or less than three*" is the predicate group associated to the CONSTRAINT case.

Sentence patterns

The sentence patterns define the cases of embedded clauses in a same sentence. They are constructed combining elementary patterns. Let us consider two examples:

SPT1 : [Main clause]

SPT2 : [Subordinate clause unifying a BP pattern](LOCALIZATION)
[Subordinate clause unifying a BP2 pattern](CONSTRAINT)
[main clause unifying a BP pattern with a verb expressing an action](ACTION + CONSTRAINED)

SPT1 corresponds to sentences composed with only one main clause. This clause must be able to match :

- either a structural pattern; the sentence "*A subscriber is described by his name and his address*" is an example of it,
- or a behavioural pattern with a verb expressing an action; "*Subscribers borrow copies of books*" matches this pattern. The ACTION case is thus affected to the sentence,
- or a constraint pattern; this corresponds to the sentence "*The number of loans is limited to three*". This sentence is associated to the CONSTRAINT case.

The subordinate clause that can be unified to a behavioural pattern determines the spatio-temporal LOCALIZATION of the action described by the main clause.

The sentence: "*When there is a loan request, the loan is agreed only if the subscriber's status is "active" and if a copy of the requested book is available*" corresponds to the SPT2 pattern :

- the clause "*When there is a loan request*" matches the BP2 pattern and is associated to the LOCALIZATION case;
- the clauses "*only if the subscriber's status*" and "*if a copy of the requested book is available*" match the CP1 pattern and are associated to the CONSTRAINT case.
- the clause "*the loan is agreed*" matches the BP4 pattern and corresponds simultaneously to the ACTION and CONSTRAINED cases.

2.4 Conceptual schema generation

We assume that it is possible to simply link cases and concepts. Thus the conceptual schema generation is grounded upon rules that map cases onto concepts. These rules are dependant of the target conceptual model. Conversely the linguistic patterns are independent of a particular modelling technique and can be used within any design methodology.

Figure 2.3 gives a brief overview of the main mapping rules implemented in the OICSI envirronment. We recall that OICSI is based upon the REMORA methodology [Rolland 82] which identifies four basic concepts namely, objects, actions, events and constraints. A detailed description of this aspect can be found in [Rolland 87]. These are the four type of nodes of the semantic net used by OICSI to implement the conceptual schema under construction. Arcs of the net are of five types :

- rl : expresses a relationship between two objects nodes;
- md : expresses that an action modifies an object;
- tr : expresses that an event triggers an action;
- act : expresses that an object has a particular state change which is an event;
- ct : connect a constraint to the node (object, action or event) which is constrained.

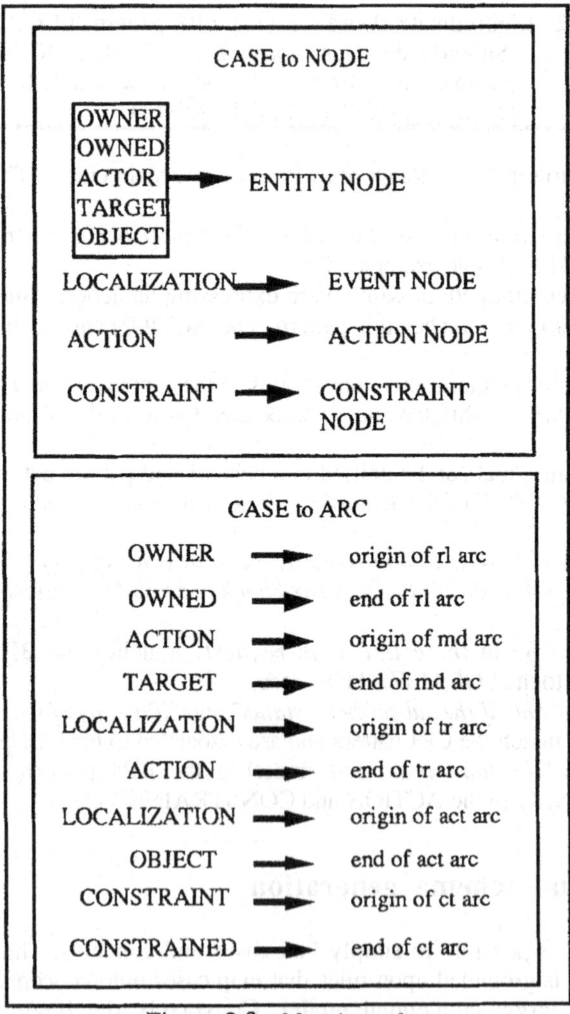

Figure 2.3 : Mapping rules

3. Conceptual schema validation and paraphrasing

The Requirements Engineering process includes also the validation cycle. In order to base the whole Requirements Engineering process on a natural language approach, we propose to feed back to the user information about the conceptual schema using again the French natural language.

The paraphrasing technique we have developed has the scope to generate natural language texts using the words and expressions of the users community and avoiding to describe the conceptual schema contents in technical terms.

We introduce first the main principles of the techniques used for text generation and then we present our solution to conceptual schema validation by paraphrasing.

3.1 Principle of natural language generation

A system for text generation must be able to select information from some knowledge base and to organize it into a natural language text. Several approaches have been proposed for this purpose. Most of them use the distinction between the "what to say" from the "how to say". However, they differ from the degree of overlap of these two aspects.

The "what to say" deals with the determination of informations which are relevant for the purpose of the text, with what the users need to know, and how much detailed an object or event must be described.

The "how to say" deals with the choice of a linear order for the information selected, specifying how to aggregate the information (determination top-form paragraphs and sentence boundaries).

The structuralist approach, which is mainly represented by Bloomfield [Mounin 72], [Harris 85], admits this distinction but concentrates the semantics in the "how to say".

The fonctionnalist approach [Harrys 85] is not aware of this distinction. In this approach the "what to say" and the "how to say" are mixed.The sentences are directly built from the knowledge base.

Finally the third approach admits that the major part of the semantic is included in the "what to say" and the minor part of it is in the "how to say" [Chomsky 57]. Chomsky who has initially followed the structuralist approach is the father of this third approach.

Among the set of possible solutions we have retained the Chomsky approach [Chomsky 65] .
The basic Chomsky assumption is the existence of a underlying structure, namely the deep structure, to any sentence in any human language. In addition, there is an infinite number of ways, namely the surface structures to represent the deep structure in different languages.

The deep structure expresses the semantics of a sentence by means of semantic elements and relationships among them. It corresponds to the "what to say".

Grouped all together, the deep structures corresponding to a knowledge base, allow us to reach a semantic understanding of its contents.

The surface structure represents each sentence of a text by means of a set of phrases. It corresponds to the "how to say". Many sets of surface structures may correspond to the same deep structure. In addition, it is possible to define a set of transformation rules (a generative grammar [Chomsky 69]) which allow to map a deep structure into an infinite set of surface structure.

Based upon this distinction the process of generating natural language texts is summarized in figure 3.1.

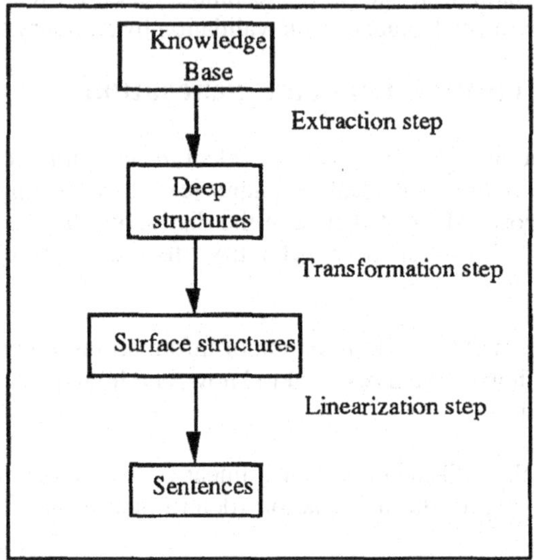

Figure 3.1 : process of generating natural language texts

It is assumed that the knowledge base provides the description of some application domain.

The first step consists of defining the appropriate deep structures for the knowledge base contents. Deep structures are often represented through semantic nets.

The second step maps the deep structure onto a surface structure. This step uses a generative grammar [Chomsky 69] which allows to produce skeletons of sentences in the target natural language. This surface structure includes all the phrases of the future sentence and its grammatical structure.

The last step, so called linearization step, uses the surface structure to produce a readable sentence. This step uses a lexical knowledge base in order to solve problem such as :

- determination of valid articles,
- tacking into account singular, plural, ...
- use of idiomatic forms,
- phonological short-cuts.

It is eventually possible to complete the process by a structuration step which aims at reorganizing the collection of sentences into chapters, sections and paragraphs.

3.2 The OICSI paraphrasing process

Following the Chomsky's guidelines we have organized the process for paraphrasing from the conceptual schema to a French text into a similar way which is shown in figure 3.1.

The knowledge base mentioned in figure 3.1 is the OICSI base of facts i.e. the semantic net which represents the conceptual schema under construction.

The deep structure definition consists of grouping nodes and arcs of the semantic net. As a matter of fact, two rules are used in order to group in a same deep structure :

- all the nodes and arcs describing an entity,
- all the nodes and arcs describing an event and its triggered operations.

We name a situation of the semantic net, a set of nodes and arcs which correspond to a deep structure.

This solution is motivated by the fact that we want to restitute to the users descriptions of their application domain as close as possible to the problem statements they have initially provided to the system. Following our assumption in section 2.3 , we consider that facts and management rules are the two easier entry points for users in the process of developing information systems.

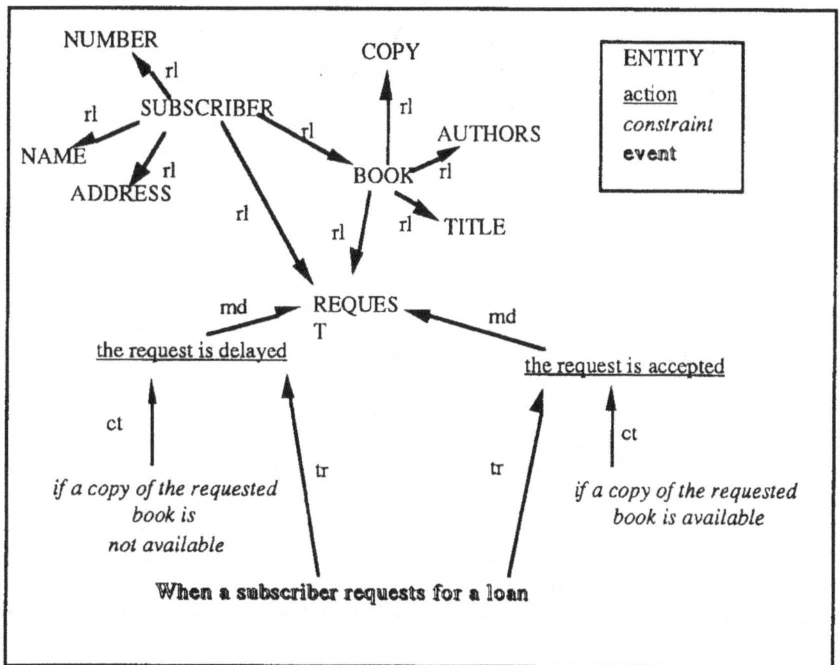

Figure 3.2 : The graphical representation of the conceptual schema

Thus the text generated by the system will describe :
- on one hand, the static aspects of the world through entities, their properties and relationships;
- on the other hand, the behavioural aspects through rules with the standard pattern "*when event, if condition then action*".

For example, from the conceptual schema presented in the figure 3.2, the system recognizes the two deep structures shown in the figure 3.3.

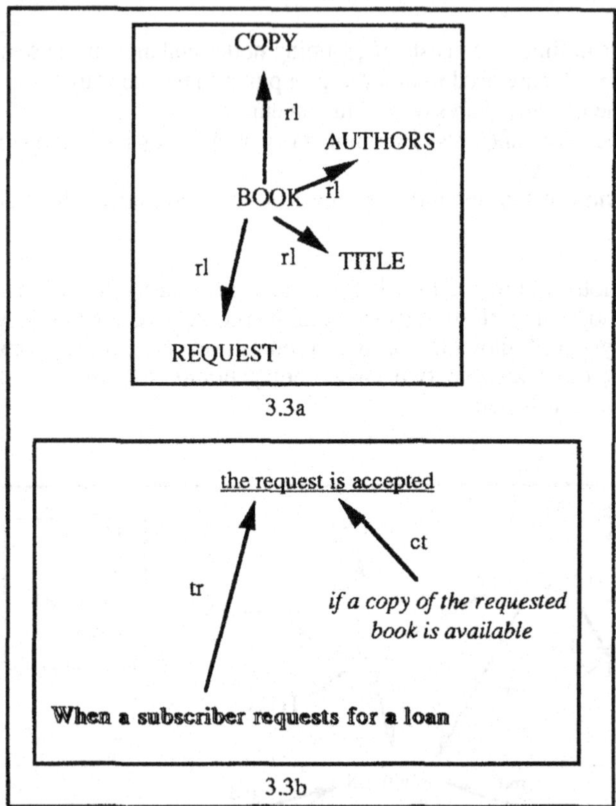

Figure 3.3 : The two deep structures recognized from figure 3.2

The 3.3a deep structure includes all informations about the entity BOOK, and the 3.3b deep structure includes all informations about the event "*a subscriber requests for a loan*".

The second step is the transformation of a deep structure into a surface structure. We make the hypothesis that the number of different types of situations in the conceptual schema is limited and that these situations are well defined. Therefore, the transformation step is based on a set of surface structure patterns which are associated to each type of situation.

For example, the 3.3a deep structure will be associated to the following surface structure:

sentence(verb(*to have***), subject(***book***), complement(***title, many copies, one or many authors, one or many requests***)).**

The 3.3b deep structure corresponds to the following surface structure :

> **sentence(circumstantial proposition(***a subscriber requests for a loan***),**
> **conditional proposition** *(if a copy of the requested book is available)*,
> **main proposition(***the request is accepted***)).**

The last step is the linearization phase. Using lexical knowledge and the surface structure this step produces readable sentences. The main tasks realized here is :

- to conjugate correctly the verbs of the sentence;
- to determine the conjunctions for the subordinate propositions;
- to select the appropriate articles.

For example, the sentences produced from the previously defined surface structure are :

- A book has a title, many copies and one or many authors.
- When a subscriber requests for a loan, if a copy of the requested book is available then the request is accepted.

4. Implementation overview

The two processes, namely the conceptual schema generation process and the paraphrasing process are implemented in an expert system approach. This means that the two processes are performed by an inference engine which uses rules. For modularity and flexibility reasons the rules are Prolog production rules.

We limit ourselves to a brief overview of the two processes mentioning the different classes of rules and their role.

4.1 The conceptual schema generation process

The OICSI inference engine uses three main classes of rules :

- lexical and syntactic rules,
- linguistic rules,
- mapping rules,

in order to progressively transform NL sentences onto nodes and arcs of the semantic net. The process is organized into three steps.

. During the **analysis step** the system builds an internal representation of the initial sentences by means of syntactic trees, with the purpose of decomposing each sentence into grammatical unit.
This part of the process is based on wellknown techniques developed for the general purpose of natural language recognition [Bruce 75], [Cordier 79] and [Kayser 81].

The role of lexical rules is to determine the grammatical nature of each word of any clause of a sentence and to classify the verb clause into the four classes: ownership, action, state, emergence. Lexical rules use a dictionary which contains information about the grammatical nature of words and about the meaning and the classification of verbs. Syntactic rules allow the system, on one hand, to verify that a sentence belongs to the authorized language, and, on the other hand, to build up the syntactic trees. These rules are based on the use of a generative grammar which corresponds to the system's grammatical knowledge.

. During the **linguistic step**, the system makes pattern matching in order to unify each syntactic tree with one of the sentence pattern defined in section 2, and to associate each syntactic unit with a case. Pattern matching and association of cases to the phrases of a sentence is performed simultaneously in the same rule. Basically any linguistic rule as the following form :

- the premise of the rule correspond to the conditions that allow to recognize the sentence (or clause) pattern,
- the conclusions of the rule associate cases to elements of the sentence (or clause).

Patterns recognition is based both on the class of the verb (as identified during step 1 and attached to it in the syntactic tree) and on the grammatical structure of the sentence (or clause). Generally, a pattern is implemented through a set of linguistic rules in order to take into account the variety of grammatical structures. As an illustration, rules RL1 and RL2 are two examples of rules necessary for implementing the pattern SP1.

RL1 :
IF meaning(clause(verbal form)) = ownership_subject
AND gram_structure(Ng_subject) = <article, noun_1>
AND gram_structure(Ng_complement) = <article, noun_2>
THEN case(noun_1) = OWNER
case(noun_2) = OWNED.

RL2 :
IF meaning(clause(verbal form)) = ownership_subject
AND gram_structure(Ng_subject) = <article, noun_1, predicate_1>
AND gram_structure(Ng_complement) = <article, noun_2>
AND gram_structure(predicate_1) = <preposition, article, noun_3>
THEN case(noun_1) = OWNER(verb)* and OWNED(predicate)
case(noun_2) = OWNED.

* the notation OWNER(verb) and OWNED(predicate) mean that the role OWNER is played in regards to the verb and that the role OWNED is played in regards to the predicate. By default, the case meaning is in regards to the verb.

. Finally, the **mapping step** consists of building the semantic net. Each syntactic tree is mapped onto a set of nodes and arcs of the semantic net. Mapping rules implement the relationship summarized in figure 2.3 (see section 2). They allow to automatically build nodes and arcs of the semantic net from cases and patterns determined in the previous step.

4.2 The paraphrasing process

Similarly the OICSI inference engine uses three main classes of rules :

- extraction rules,
- transformation rules,
- linearization rules,

in order to perform the three steps of the paraphrasing process illustrated in figure 3.2.

. **Extraction rules** are used to cluster nodes and arcs related to either an entity or an event type and to construct the corresponding deep structure.

. **Transformation rules** allow to map the deep structures into surface structures. A pattern matching mechanism is used in order to associate to a deep structure the appropriate surface structure.

. **Linearization rules** are used in order to rewrite a surface structure into a readable sentence. They include rules for to conjugate the verbs, to select the article and so on. A major part of these rules use a dictionary which represents the lexical knowledge of the tool.

Obviously, the two processes (conceptual schema generation and paraphrasing) are performed in an interactive way. For example the user's aid may be solicitated during the analysis step to add a new verb in the dictionary. At any time the user can ask for explanation about the system deductions and this can lead to pattern transformation. At last the analyst/user is allowed to directly manipulate the semantic net through a graphical interface in order to add, delete or change any arc or node of the net. In addition, the two processes are fully integrated. This means that the user can ask for paraphrasing from the conceptual schema at any point of its generation process. This allow to constantly keep the equivalence between a set of natural sentences and the formalized conceptual schema. We believe that this is helpful to validate the conformance of the system specifications to the user requirements.

Similar considerations have been discussed as the premise of the RUBRIC [Van Assche 88] and TEMPORA [Loucopoulos 90] projects.

A more detailed description may be found in [Loucopoulos 92].

5. Conclusion

The paper has argued that the natural language plays an important role during the DB/IS development cycle. Therefore, the ideas that Requirements Engineering should be supported by a Case tool based on a linguistic approach and that validation of specifications must be performed by means of text generation technique have been presented.

In a first time, the work reported in this paper is based on the premise that Requirements engineering is strongly interrelated to language manipulation. It represents an attempt at improving problem-statements elicitation, interpretation and modelling through the use of a linguistic approach. It is proposed that the problem-statements for an information system development should be expressed via natural language sentences.

The work reported presents how a linguistic approach based on the Case notion can be used to automatically carry out the IS modelling. The paper details the linguistic approach and its implementation in the expert design system, known as OICSI. The thesis put forward in the paper is that the linguistic approach is general, in the double sense that it can be customized for different modelling techniques and, in addition, it can be applied in a wider sphere of problems. From this point of view the work reported relates to other research works such KOD [Vogel 88] or SECSI [Bouzeghoub86].

In a second time, the paper presents some solutions based on theorical linguistic works in order to validate the conceptual schema by paraphrasing from conceptual schema to natural language texts. This paraphrasing technique has the scope to generate natural language texts with words and expressions of the users community and avoiding description of the conceptual schema contents in technical terms.

References

[Bouzeghoub 86] M. Bouzeghoub and G. Gardarin : "SECSI : an expert system approach for data base design", in Proc. of IFIP world congress, Dublin, Sept 1986.

[Bruce 75] B. Bruce : "Case systems for natural language", Artificial Intelligence Nb 6, 1975.

[Black 87] WJ. Black: "Acquisition of Conceptual data models from natural language descriptions, 3rd Conf. of the European chapter of ACM, Danemark, 1987.

[Bubenko 90] J. Bubenko et all : Syslab/Decode research plan Syslab report 1990.

[Chen 76] P.P.S Chen : "The entity relationship model : toward a unified view" ACM Trans. on data base systems, Vol 1, Nb1, 1976.

[Chester 76] D. Chester : "The translation of formal proofs into English", Artificial Intelligence, vol 7, n°2, 1976.

[Chomsky 57] N. Chomsky : "Syntactic strutures", Mouton Ed, The Hague 1957.

[Chomsky 65] N. Chomsky : "Aspects of the theory of syntax", MIT Press Ed, Cambridge Mass, 1965.

[Chomsky 69] N. Chomsky : "Language and Mind", Payot ed, 1969.

[Cordier 79] M. Cordier: Connaissances sémantiques et pragmatiques en compréhension du langage naturel, 2Çme congrés AFCET-INRIA, Reconnaissances des formes et Intelligence Artificielle, Toulouse 1979.

[De Roeck 88] A.N.D Roeck, B.G.T. Lowden : "Generating English paraphrases from formal relational calculus expressions" Coling (Pub) 1988.

[Dubois 89] E. Dubois, J. Hagelstein, A. Rifaut : "Formal requirements engineering with ERAE", Philips journal of research, vol 43, N) 3/4 1989.

[Grishman 79] R. Grishman : "Response generation in question answering systems" in ACL 1979.

[Fillmore 68] CJ. Fillmore : "The Case for Case", in Universals in linguistics theory; Holt, Rinehart and Winston, Inc., E. Bach/R.T. Harms (eds) 1968.

[Harris 85] M. Dee Harris : "Introduction to Natural Language processing", Reston Publishing company, 1985.

[Hull 87] R. Hull and R. King : Semantic Database Modeling : Survey, Applications and Research issues", ACM computing Surveys, vol 19, n¯3, 1987.

[Kayser 81] D. Kayser : "Les ATN sÇmantiques" 3Çme congräs AFCET-INRIA, Reconnaissances des formes et Intelligence Artificielle, 1981

[Kersten 86] M.L. Kersten, H. Weigand, F. Dignum, J; Proom: "A conceptual modelling expert system", 5th Int. Conf. ont the ER Approach S. Spaccapietra(ed), Dijon, 1986.

[Loucopoulos 90] P. Loucopoulos et all : "From software engineering to business engineering: Esprit projects in information systems engineering", in CAISE'90, Int. Conference on : "Advanced Information System Engineering ", Springer-Verlag, 1990.

[Loucopoulos 92] "Conceptual modelling databases and Case: an integrated view of information systems development", P. Loucopoulos (ed), Mac Grawhill (Pub) 1992 (to be published).
[Luk 86] W.S Luk, S. Kloster : "ELFS: English language from SQL", ACM Trans. on Databases systems, vol 11, n°4, 1986.
[Mc Keown 86] K. Mc Keown : "Paraphrasing questions using given and new information", Am. journal of computational linguistics, vol 9 n°1, 1986.
[Muckstein 87] E.M Muckstein, M.G. Datovsky :" Semantic interpretation of a database query language", Data and Knowledge engineering, vol 1, 1985.
[Maddison 83] R. Maddison : "Information System methodologies", Wiley-Heyden 1983.
[Mounin 72] G. Mounin : "La linguistique du 20ième siècle", Presses Universitaires de France Ed, 1972.
[Nijssen 89] G.M. Nijssen, T.A. Halpin : "Conceptual Schema and relational database design : a fact oriented approach", Prentice-Hall, Englewood Cliffs, New Jersey, 1989.
[Olle 82] T.W. Olle, H.G. Sol and A.A Verrijn Stuart :"Information System design methodologies : a comparative review", (IFIP WG 8.1 CRIS 1) North Holland, Amsterdam , NL, 1982.
[Rolland 82] C. Rolland and C. Richard : "The Remora methodology for information systems design and management" in [Oll 82].
[Rolland 87] C. Rolland, G. Benci and O. Foucault : "Conception des systèmes d'information : la méthode REMORA", Eyrolles (Pub) 1987.
[Van Assche 88] F. Van Assche, P.J. Layzell, P. Loucopoulos and G. Speltinex : "Information Systems development : a rule based approach", in Journal of knowledge based systems, 1988.
[Vit alari 83] N.P. Vitalari and G.W. Dickson : "Problem solving for effective systems analysis : an experimental exploration ", in Comm. ACM Vol 26 N¯11, (November 1983).
[Vitalari 85] N.P. Vitalari : "Knowledge as a basis for expertise in systems analysis : an empirical study", MIS Q, (September 1985).
[Vogel 88] : C. Vogel : "Génie cognitif", Masson collection Sciences cognitives, 1988.

Conceptual Modeling and Natural Language Analysis

Colette Rolland

Abstract The CAiSE'92 paper presented a tool called OICSI that used Natural Language Processing (NLP) techniques to support both the generation of an Information System (IS) conceptual schema from textual requirements and in the reverse way, schema paraphrasing to ease schema understanding and evaluation by stakeholders. Both topics have been of interest during the next 20 years among other new usages of NLP techniques in the context IS development. For sake of space, this paper concentrates on an overview of NLP techniques used as elicitation techniques.

1 The Initial Paper and Related Works

The initial paper was written at a stage of IS engineering maturity at which it was clear that an IS represents some excerpt of the World and that IS engineering shall focus on modeling the concepts of the world on which IS users need information. As a consequence of this assumption, a number of conceptual modeling languages were developed such as [1–4] to name a few. It was also becoming clear that these languages were not understandable by people other than modelers. This evidence raised the issue of how to master the creation of a conceptual model (called schema at that time) as long as the process implies exchanges between domain experts & stakeholders (who know their wishes, needs and requirements) on one hand, and modelers (who master conceptual languages) on the other hand. For the same reason, validation was also an issue as stakeholders can hardly validate whether the conceptual model really reflects their needs. As long as natural language is used during this conceptualization process, the end-users and all stakeholders participating in the IS project have a chance to be involved. Then, the idea to support

C. Rolland (✉)
Université Paris1 Panthéon Sorbonne, 90, rue de Tolbiac, 75013 Paris, France
e-mail: Rolland@univ-paris1.fr

J. Bubenko et al. (eds.), *Seminal Contributions to Information Systems Engineering*, DOI 10.1007/978-3-642-36926-1_4,

NL communication during both phases of model creation and model validation came in mind.

OICSI was developed as a CASE tool that supports conceptual model generation from requirements statements expressed in NL and helps in the validation of this model by paraphrasing it, i.e. reformulating its semantic content as natural language sentences. The generation phase is based on the adaptation of the Fillmore's 'Case to Case' theory [5] whereas the paraphrasing phase uses Chomsky's approach [6].

Whereas OICSI partly automates the generation of a conceptual model, some early attempts to support this task were based on manual guidelines [4, 7–9]. The Functional Grammar [10] was preferred to the Case Grammar used in OICSI in [11] and [12]. Some other few approaches of the same period presented tools, which used parsers to extract model elements from NL sentences [13, 14].

From these beginnings, the ways NLP techniques have been used in IS development and particularly during requirements engineering and conceptual modeling are manifold. The analysis of literature suggests to organize them according to four strategies, which (a) support the generation of models from NL input texts, (b) support model paraphrasing, (c) help in the general understanding of NL input texts and (d) Improve NL texts quality. For space restriction this paper only comments on point (a).

2 Generation of Models from NL Input Texts

Typically, these approaches take as input a document expressed in full or structured Natural Language (most of the time in English) and generate model elements of a given conceptual model formalism. They can be further classified into techniques focusing on (a) structural (static) aspects of an IS conceptual model (e.g. entity-relationship diagrams) or (b) behavioral aspects (e.g. uses cases & scenarios). Some approaches (c) deal with the generation of other types of models such business rule models, ontologies or traceability models or with different activities such as compliance with regulation documents.

Like in OICSI, many researchers have used NLP techniques to generate structured or formal models from requirements documents expressed in NL. NL-OOPS [15] is a Case tool that supports requirements analysis and generates object-oriented models from NL requirements documents. It uses the LOLITA NLP toolkit that linguistically analyze texts. CICO [16] transforms tagged requirements statements into various forms of structured models based on rules. Moreno [17] has developed a method that transforms NL requirement statements into an object model. Her method is based on a grammatical analysis of requirement statements, and initially transforms them into a restricted form of NL. Subsequently, the restricted statements are transformed into object structures; this is based on patterns that transform linguistic structures into conceptual structures. The approach was further developed in [18, 19]. The authors of [20] describe an approach that uses part-of-speech tagging and morphological analysis for the generation of candidate elements of a class diagram. Additionally, an ontology is used to refine the candidates according to the specificity of the real world domain. Finally, classes that do not appear in relationships and relationships which do not involved at least two classes are deleted. In [21] controlled NL is used to express requirements that are automatically transformed into formal specifications.

Approaches concentrating on the extraction of modeling concepts for dynamic models can be found [22–26]. COLOR-X [22] supports non-automatic construction of formal events languages from lists of events described in natural language). In [23] we used a linguistic pattern approach inspired from OICSI to transform a textual scenario of a use case into a so-called conceptualized scenario. The process includes a parsing of the full NL scenario text to identify linguistic structures that allow the identification of linguistic semantic patterns, which in turn, are mapped to scenario conceptual elements. The conceptualized scenario serves as a basis to reason about missing requirements and to suggesting additions in the requirements specification [27]. Extraction of use cases and scenarios are also described in [25, 26]. Vice-versa the approach presented in [24] uses use-cases as inputs to generate behavior specifications. In the LIDA approach [28] candidate objects, attributes and methods as well are extracted from textual requirement statements.

NLP techniques have been also used to generate models other than the typical IS conceptual models. For example, in the area of *ontology engineering*, the Text2Onto approach [29] uses machine-learning techniques together with linguistic processing in order to derive an ontology from a text. A lightweight NLP is used in [30] to automatically generate and maintain *traceability relations* between different types of software requirements artifacts. In the BROCOM approach [31] the targeted output are *business rules*. In the SMART approach [32] NLP techniques are used to automate the generation of a *business process model* from textual requirements. *Requirements specifications* can also be the target of a transformation process, which uses textual requirements as inputs and generates a precise list of requirements expressed in some controlled NL [33]. In the area of *compliance with regulations* [34] presents a technique to check the compliance of requirements with regulations while eliciting requirements. The approach checks compliance by trying to match a newly discovered requirement to regulations represented by combinations of case frames resulting from the Case Grammar technique. In [35] we used the Case Grammar to define a Goal template and to develop a tool supporting *a controlled formulation of a goal*. A similar linguistic approach to goal formulation was used in [36] to reason about *variability in requirements*. The approach considers the goal linguistic frame elements as variability concerns.

To conclude it seems that NLP techniques remain useful in conceptual modeling but only occasionally. The reason might be that requirements/concepts elicitation is part of a decision process that cannot be automated from analysis of NL texts.

Acknowledgements The original paper was co-authored by Christophe Proix, who was my doctoral student at that time. Christophe deserves an equal share of the credit for the work that we have accomplished. Unfortunately, I was unable to contact Christophe for the purpose of this article.

References

1. Chen, P. P. S. (1976) The entity relationship model: toward a unified view. In: ACM Trans. on Data Base Systems (TODS), 1(1), pp. 9–38. ACM
2. Dubois, E., Hagelstein, J., and Rifaut, A. (1989) Formal requirements engineering with ERAE. In: Philips Journal of Research, 43(3). Philips
3. Rolland, C., and Richard, C. (1982) The Remora methodology for information systems design and management. In: Proc. Int'l Conf. on Comparative Review of Information Systems Methodologies. CRIS. IFIP WG8.1. North Holland, 1982
4. Nijssen, G.M, Halpin, T.A. (1989) Conceptual schema and relational database design: a fact oriented approach. Prentice-Hall, Englewood Cliffs, New Jersey
5. Fillmore, C.J. (1968) The Case for Case. In Holt, Rinehart and Winston, Inc., E. Bach/R.T. Harms (eds.) Universals in linguistics theory
6. Chomsky, N. (1965) Aspects of the theory of syntax. MIT, Cambridge Massachusetts
7. Chen, P. (1983) English Sentence Structure and Entity Relationship Diagrams. In: Int'l Journal of Information Sciences. Vol. 29, pp. 127–149
8. Abbott, R.J. (1983) Program Design by Informal English Descriptions. In: Communications of the ACM. 26 (11), pp. 882–894. ACM
9. Saeki, M., Horai, H., Enomoto, H. (1989) Software Development from Natural Language Specification. In: Proc. Int'l Conference on Software Engineering (ICSE), pp. 64–73, IEEE
10. Dik, S. (1980) Studies in Functional Grammar. Academic Press
11. Dignum, F., van de Riet, R.P. (1991) Knowledge base modelling based on linguistic and founded in logic. In: Data & Knowledge Engineering. Vol. 7, pp. 1–34. Elsevier
12. Burg J.F.M. (1997) Linguistic Instruments in Requirements Engineering. IOS Press, Amsterdam
13. Buchholz, E., Cyriaks, H., Düsterhöft, A., Mehlan, H., and Thalheim, B. (1995) Applying a Natural Language Dialogue Tool for Designing Databases. In: Int'l Workshop on Applications of Natural Language to Databases. NLDB'95, pp. 119–133, 1995
14. Tjoa, A.M., Berger, L. (1993) Transformation of Requirement Specification Expressed in Natural Language into an EER Model. In: Proc. 12th Int'l Conf. on Entity Relationship Approach. ER1993, pp. 127–149, Springer, Heidelberg, 1993
15. Mich.: NL-OOPS (1996) From natural language to object oriented requirements using the natural language processing system LOLITA. In: Natural Language Engineering. Cambridge Universal Press
16. Ambriolla V., Gervazi V. (1997) Processing Natural Language Requirements. In: Proc. of Int'l Conf. on Automated Software Engineering. ASE '97, pp. 36–45. IEEE, 1997
17. Moreno A. (1997) Object-Oriented Analysis from Textual Specifications. In: Proc. 9th Int'l Conf. on Software Engineering and Knowledge Engineering. SEKE 97, 1997
18. Juristo, N., Morant, J.L, and Moreno, A., M. (1999) A formal approach for generating OO specifications from natural language. In: Journal of Systems and Software. Elsevier
19. Juristo, N., Moreno, A.M., López, M. (2000) How to use linguistic instruments for object-oriented analysis. Software. IEEE
20. Harmain, H.M., Gaizauskas, R.: CM-Builder (2000) An Automated NL-based Case Tool. In: 15th Int'l Conf. on Automated Software Engineering. ASE'00, pp. 45–54. IEEE, 2000
21. Cabral, C., Sampaio, A. (2008) Formal specification generation from requirement documents. In: Electronic Notes in Theoretical Computer Science. Elsevier
22. Burg J., van de Riet R. (1995) COLOR-X: Linguistically-based Event Modelling: A General Approach to Dynamic Modelling. In: Proc. 17th Int. Conf. on Advanced Information System Engineering. CAiSE1995. LNCS, pp. 26–39, Springer, Heidelberg, 1995
23. Rolland, C., Ben Achour, C. (1998) Guiding the construction of textual use case specifications. In: Data & Knowledge Engineering, Vol.25, pp. 125–160. Elsevier
24. Menck, V. (2004) Deriving behavior specifications from textual use cases. In: Proc. Workshop on Intelligent Technologies. Reference.kfupm.edu.sa, 2004

25. Kof, L. (2007) Scenarios: Identifying Missing Objects and Actions by Means of Computational Linguistics. In: Proc.15th Int'l Requirements Engineering Conference (RE 2007), pp. 211–130. IEEE, 2007
26. Santos, J., Moreira, A., Araujo, J., Amaral, V., Alferez, M., Kulesza, U. (2008) Generating Requirements Analysis Models from Textual Requirements. In: First Int'l Workshop on Managing Requirements Knowledge. MARK2008, pp. 32–41. IEEE, 2008
27. Rolland, C., Souveyet, C., and Ben Achour, C. (1998) Guiding Goal Modelling Using Scenarios. In.: Transactions on Software Engineering (TSE). 24(12), pp. 1055–1071, IEEE
28. Overmyer, S.P. Lavoie, B. Rambow, O. (2001) Conceptual modeling through linguistic analysis using LIDA. In: Proc. 23rd Int'l Conference on Software Engineering. ICSE2001, pp. 401–410. IEEE, 2001
29. Cimiano, P., Völker, J. (2005) Text2Onto: A Framework for Ontology Learning and Data-driven Change Discovery. In: Proc. 10th Int'l Conf. on Applications of Natural Language to Information Systems (NLDB). LNCS, vol. 3513, pp. 227–238. Springer, Heidelberg, 2005
30. Zisman, A., Spanoudakis, G., and Pérez-Miñana, E. (2003) Tracing software requirements artifacts. In: Proc. Int'l Conf. on Software Engineering Research and Practice. SERP, 2003
31. Herbst, H. (1997) Business rule-oriented conceptual modeling. (Physica Verlag). Springer, Heidelberg
32. Rayson, P., Emmet, L., Garside, R., Sawyer, P. (2001) The REVERE Project: Experiments with the application of probabilistic NLP to Systems Engineering. In: M. Bouzeghoub et al (eds.). Natural Language Processing and Information Systems. LNCS, pp. 288–300, Springer, Heidelberg, 2001
33. Gervasi, V., Zowghi, D. (2005) Reasoning about inconsistencies in natural language requirements. In: Transactions on Software Engineering and Methodology. TOSEM 14(3), pp. 277–330. ACM
34. Saeki, M., Kaiya, H. (2008) Supporting the elicitation of requirements compliant with regulations. In: Z. Bellasene, M. Leonard (eds.). CAiSE 2008. LNCS, vol. 5074, pp. 228–242, Springer, Heidelberg, 2008
35. Prat, N. (1997) Goal formalisation and classification for requirements engineering. In: Proc. 3rd Int'l Workshop on Requirements Engineering: Foundations of Software Quality. REFSQ1997. LNCS, pp. 145–156. Springer, Heidelberg, 1997
36. Liaskos, S., Lapouchnian, A., Yu, Y., Mylopoulos, J. (2006) On goal variability acquisition and analysis. In: Proc. Int'l Conf. on 14th Requirements Engineering Conference. RE2006, pp. 79–88. EEE, 2006

The Three Dimensions of Requirements Engineering+

Klaus Pohl

Informatik V, RWTH-Aachen, Ahornstr. 55, 5100 Aachen
pohl@informatik.rwth-aachen.de

Abstract. Requirements engineering (RE) is perceived as an area of growing importance. Due to the increasing effort spent for research in this area many contributions to solve different problems within RE exist. The purpose of this paper is to identify the main goals to be reached during the requirements engineering process in order to develop a framework for RE. This framework consists of the three dimensions:

- the specification dimension
- the representation dimension
- the agreement dimension

Looking at the RE research using this framework, the different approaches can be classified and therefore their interrelationships become much clearer. Additionally the framework offers a first step towards a common understanding of RE.

1 Introduction

There is general agreement among software engineers and researchers that an early stage of the software development life cycle called *requirements engineering* exists. Furthermore requirements engineering (RE) is perceived as an area of growing importance. Due to the increasing effort spent for research in this area many contributions to solve different problems within RE exist. The purpose of this paper is to identify the main goals to be reached during the requirements engineering process in order to develop a framework for RE, the three dimensions of requirements engineering. Looking at the RE research using this framework the different approaches can be classified and therefore their interrelationships become much clearer. Additionally the framework offers a first step towards a common understanding of RE.

A first impression of the research subsumed under the term requirements engineering can be gained by looking at the topics (cf. table 1) of the first major international meeting on RE (International Symposium on RE 1993).

+ This work was supported by ESPRIT Basic Research Action 6353 (NATURE) which is concerned with Novel Approaches to Theories Underlying Requirements Engineering and by the state Nordrhein-Westfalen, Germany.

- formal representation schemes and RE modelling
- descriptions of the RE process
- tools and environments to support RE
- requirements engineering methods;
- requirements analysis and validation;
- requirements elicitation, acquisition and formalization
- establishing traceability to requirements
- reuse and adaptation of requirements;
- intersections with AI, domain modelling and analysis
- intersections with computer-human-interaction and cognitive science;
- intersections with group and cooperative work
- intersections with systems engineering

Tab. 1. Topics of the First International Symposium on Requirements Engineering.

Even to understand the topics, the question *"What is requirements engineering?"* must be answered first. For example, before talking about tools and environments for supporting RE, a clear idea of the aim of RE (e.g., building a requirement specification as defined in IEEE STD 830–1984) and the problems to deal with, must be available. Also before looking at the intersections between RE and other research areas, a common understanding of RE must be gained first. But the topics illustrate, that RE is an interdisciplinary research area.

To get a more detailed view of the ongoing research, we give a brief overview of the RE literature. First, we focus on the research dealing with the *detection of requirements*. This includes the problems of requirements elicitation and capture as well as the problems of validation and verification of requirements (e.g., [11], [29], [30], [84], [64], [87]). To *represent requirements* formal specification languages (e.g., Z [92], VDM [8], [47], PAISLey [100]) and knowledge representation languages (e.g., RML [41], ERAE [45], TELOS [76], [55]) were proposed. They offer the advantage of automatic reasoning (e.g., [9], [73], [65], [62], [96]) but applying them to RE is not straight forward (e.g., [4], [46], [3], [28]). Moreover, they must be generated from, and integrated with, informal RE specifications (e.g., [41], [6], [57], [38], [34], [74], [59]).

During the RE process *different views* of the system to be built exist. Some work concerns view integration and viewpoint resolution (e.g., [63], [64], [31]). Others suggest to focus on the social and cognitive aspects of RE (e.g., [90], [40]), thus gaining a better specification. Methods of AI are also used to support the RE process (e.g., [1], [5], [65], [69], [58], [94], [86], [68]). The advantages of reusing specification for economical reasons as well as for avoiding errors were lined out (e.g., [7], [36], [66], [94], [67], [22], [16], [68]). Other research focuses on the *RE process* (e.g., [43], [17], [44], [53], [18], [80]). It was recognized, that the RE process must be traceable (e.g., [33]) and understandable. Therefore the recording of design rationale (e.g., [83], [88], [53]) and the integration of argumentation concepts into the RE area are proposed (e.g., [15], [85]). Generally speaking it can be said that methodologies for supporting RE that based on different representation formalisms exist, but do not tell the requirements engineer very clearly how to proceed (e.g., ER [13], SA [95], [98], JSD [12], object–oriented analysis [93], [79], [75], [14], conceptual modelling [77], F-ORM [22], PSL/PSA [89], SREM

[2], ASPIS [84], KBSA [19]). Also some classification of the methods were proposed (e.g., [101], [21]).

Even with the coarse classification of the literature made above the *main goals* and the *real problems* of RE are not visible. A first step into getting to the heart of RE is to distinguish between two kinds of problems:

- original requirements engineering problems and
- problems caused by approaches which try to solve the original problems.

Making the original RE problems and the goals to be reached during the process explicit provides the basis for classifying the research of the RE area and for guiding a RE process. In section 2, we consider the RE process at an abstract level. Looking at the *initial input* and the *desired output*, three main characteristics can be identified. These features lead to the three dimensions of requirements engineering which are the main contribution of this paper (section 3). In section 4 we look at the RE process within the three dimensions. Thus the goals to be reached by the RE process are recognized and the problems which occur during the process can be classified. A classification of computer support for requirements engineering is made in section 5. In section 6 our contributions are summarized.

2 The Requirements Engineering Process

McMenamin and Palmer [71] suggest to distinguish between the essence of a system and its incarnation. The essence is defined by all essential activities and data stores whereas the sum of people, phones, computer systems, offices, typewriters, pencils, rubbers and so forth that are used to implement the system are the incarnation (cf. [71], [98]). To get a clear idea of the essence of a system they assume that the system can be implemented using perfect internal technology. This assumption makes it easier to concentrate on the essence of the system instead of getting influenced by unnecessary side aspects. Therefore the essence of a system has to be clearly defined first; aspects which come from the use of imperfect technology are not considered. After this, the so gained *essential model* of the system is extended by actions and data stores based on the use of imperfect technology. In the following we use this approach to look at the RE process.

Looking at a process (e.g., the requirements engineering process) on a abstract level, its essence is transforming an input to a desired output. Assuming that the RE process can make use of perfect technology (perfect tools, no social conflicts, no cognitive limitations etc.) it is insignificant how the transformation is achieved. Let us focus on the output of the RE process first.

2.1 The Desired Output

There is no doubt, that at the end of requirements engineering a specification of the system to be built (at least for the current version of the system) must exist. This specification serves as a basis for the next phase within the software life cycle. Thus, as a first characteristic of the output of the RE process, a specification of the system can be identified. We don't focus on the details of the final specification at this point. It is enough to keep in mind that the **complete specification**, as expected, is the basic result of the RE process.

If the system specification is expressed using e.g. natural language, different people may understand the same specification in different ways. This may lead to unexpected designs and implementations. To avoid different interpretation of a specification, more and more people suggest to use a formal language for representing the specification of the system. Additionally a formal language offers the possibility of reasoning support. So the result of the RE process should be expressed using a **formal language**.

But it is not enough to produce a specification expressed in a formal language. Assume that a functionality called *work control* is well defined and that there exists no problem in mapping this part of the specification into a design and an implementation later on. But within the requirements engineering team only a few people agree on this functionality promoted by the people which are responsible for cost control. The representatives of the users don't like this functionality at all. If no common agreement is reached during the RE phase, the problems caused by this must be solved later on. As experience has shown, more effort is needed to correct errors in the later phases of the software life cycle [11]. To avoid expensive error corrections all people involved in the RE process should end up on a **common agreement** on the final specification.

Summarizing the main characteristics of the *desired output* of the RE process are a complete system specification expressed using a formal language on which all people involved agree.

2.2 The Initial Input of the Process

At the beginning of the RE process the knowledge about the system is coarse. Some features of the system are obvious, whereas about others only vague imaginations exist. Therefore the understanding of the system and the specification which can be gained out of it is very **opaque**. Since people involved in the RE process have various roles (e.g., user representative, system developer, maintenance staff, financial officer) and different skills and knowledge, each of them has his own understanding of the system to be built. Especially at the beginning of the RE process many different visions of the system exist. They may have something in common, but this is not necessarily the case. Hence at the beginning of the RE process many **personal views** on the system exist and no common representation format is used to express the expectations. Each stakeholder uses his preferred representation format for expressing his personal view of the system. Some of them may just think about the system (representing the knowledge in brain-structures), others may make notes using natural language, or may draw pictures or graphics. Hence mainly **informal representations** are used at the beginning of the RE process.

Summarizing, at the beginning of the RE process opaque personal views of the system exist which are recorded using informal languages.

3 The Three Dimensions of Requirements Engineering

Looking at the brief description of the *initial input* and the *desired output*, three main goals of the RE process can be identified:

- improving an opaque system comprehension into a complete system specification;
- transforming informal knowledge into formal representations;
- gaining a common agreement on the specification out of the personal views;

Out of these goals, three dimensions of RE can be gained: **specification, representation** and **agreement** dimension. Within the three dimensions, the *initial input*, as well as the *desired output* can be characterized. This is shown in figure 1, where the *initial input* is characterized by *personal views, opaque system specification* and *informal representation* and the *desired output* by *common agreement, complete system specification* and *formal representation.* In the following the three dimensions are described.

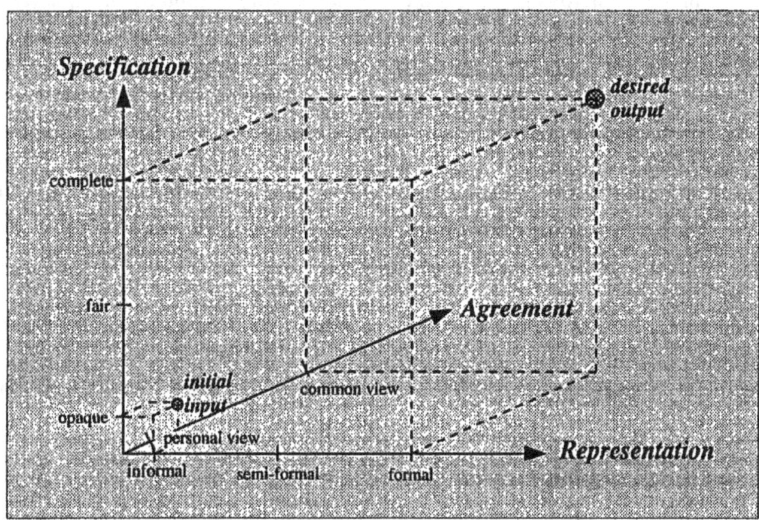

Fig. 1. The Three Dimensions of Requirements Engineering.

3.1 The Specification Dimension

The *specification* dimension deals with the degree of requirements understanding at a given time. At the beginning of the RE process the specification of the system and its environment is more or less opaque. This goes along with the vague imagination of the system at the early stage of the RE process. Focusing on this dimension, the aim of RE is to transform the operational need into a complete system specification through an iterative process of definition and validation (e.g., analysis, trade-off-studies, prototyping).

Several standards and guidelines describe how the final requirements specification should look like (e.g., IEEE Std. 830 [49], British Standard 6719, European Space Agency ESA PSS-05-0 [72]). In the following we briefly describe the properties a requirements specification should have. A more detailed description of the attributes of a requirements specification and an overview of existing standards and guidelines can be found in [25].

First of all, a requirement specification is supposed to state what a system should do and not how (cf. [20]). Additionally, the specification must be unambiguous, complete, verifiable, consistent, modifiable, traceable and usable during operations and maintenance (cf. [49] for a detailed description).

Secondly a differentiation between two kinds of requirements can be made:

- functional requirements
- non-functional requirements

The functional requirements specify what the software must do. According to IEEE 830, non-functional requirements can be further divided into *performance*, *design constraints*, *external interface* and *quality attributes*. Performance requirements deal with the execution time and computational accuracy. Design constraints are predefined designs imposed on the software development by the customer. External interface requirements define everything outside the subject of the system the software must deal with (e.g., constraints from other standards, hardware or people). With quality attributes the quality of the software to be reached is defined (cf. [61] for examples of quality attributes).

Beside this classification of requirements a distinction between *vital* requirements and *desirable* requirements should be made (cf. British Standard 6719 [48]). *Vital* requirements must be completely accomplished by the system, whereas *desirable* requirements may be relaxed and need not be met within the stated limits. Some standards propose to include *costs* and *schedule* information in the requirements specification (e.g., British Standard 6719) whereas other separate them from requirements engineering (e.g., IEEE Statement of Work). Additionally many proposals for validation and verification of system specification were made (e.g., [11], [99], [10], [35], [25], [64]).

Summarizing the first main goal of RE, as identified by many researchers, is to built a requirements specification, according to the standard and/or guideline used. The degree of the specification (opaque to complete) is captured by the *specification* dimension.

3.2 The Representation Dimension

The *representation* dimension copes with the different representations (informal and formal languages, graphics, sounds etc.) used for expressing knowledge about the system. Within RE there are three categories of representations. The first category includes all informal representations, such as arbitrary graphics, natural language, descriptions by examples, sounds and animations. The second category subsumes the semi-formal languages such as SA-diagrams, ER-diagrams, SADT etc. The third category covers formal languages such as specification languages (e.g., VDM [8], Z [92]) or knowledge representation languages (e.g. ERAE [45], Telos [76]).

Each of these categories offers some unique advantages. Informal representations like natural language are user-oriented. They are well known, since they are used in daily life. The expressive power offered by *informal representation* is very high and all kinds of requirements freedom are available (e.g., ambiguity, inconsistency, contradictory; cf. [4], [28] for more detail). *Semi-formal representations* like SA or ER diagrams are based on a structured graphical visualization of the system. The representations are clear and provide a good overview of the system ("one picture says more than a thousand words"). Additionally they are widely used within industry as a quasi-standard. In contrast to informal representation the semi-formal representation come with formally defined semantics, which could be used for reasoning. But the formal defined semantic of semi-formal languages is very poor, so still most of the represented knowledge has no formal meaning. *Formal representation languages* have a richer well defined semantic.

Therefore reasoning about most of the represented knowledge is possible. Even code can be (partially) automatically generated out of a them. So formal representation languages are more system oriented.

The use of a particular representation language has two main reasons. The first reason for using a special language is simply personal preference. Due to the advantages of each representation class, different people prefer different representations. For example the system user may like natural language, whereas the system specialist may prefers formal representation. The second reason for using a particular language is the current state of the specification. At the beginning of the RE process normally informal languages are used, whereas at the end specifications are often represented using formal languages. Hence the RE process must assure, that out of the informal requirements a formal specification is achieved. Since different representation languages are used within the RE process in parallel, they must additionally be kept consistent. Suppose that a requirement was expressed using natural language by the customer. Out of this requirement, a formal specification was built by the system specialist. If, for example, the informal requirement is revised, it must be assured that the formal representation of the specification is modified accordingly.

The representation language used does not imply if a specification is vague or precise. Hence the *representation* dimension is orthogonal to the *specification* dimension. A vague imagination of the system can be expressed using a natural language, but also using a formal representation language. Also concrete (formally defined) ideas can obviously be represented using a formal representation language, but they can also be exactly described using natural language (e.g., lawyers try to do so). Looking at the specification `'the age of Carl is 10 years'` and on a formal specification, e.g., using first order logic, `'age (Carl, 10, years)'` no difference can be recognized. Whereas the vague specification *'Carl is young'* is also vague if it is represented in first order logic `'young (Carl)'`. Hence the difference between the two specifications, vague versus precise, remains the same, independent of the representation language used.

Summarizing, during the RE process different representation languages are used. At the beginning of the process the knowledge about the system is expressed using informal representations, whereas at the end of RE the specification must also be formally represented.

The second main goal of the RE process is threefold. First, different representations must be offered. Second, the transformation between the representations (e.g., informal to semi-formal, informal to formal) must be supported. Third, the different representations must be kept consistent.

3.3 The Agreement Dimension

The third dimension deals with the degree of agreement reached on a specification. At the beginning of the RE process each person involved has its own personal view of the system. Of course few requirements may be shared among the team, but many requirements exist only within personal views of the people, e.g., stemming from the various roles the people have (system analyst, manager, user, developer etc.). In the following the expression *common system specification* is used for the system specification on which the RE team has agreed.

The RE process tries to increase the *common system specification*. But still requirements exist on which none or only partial agreement was reached. Let's focus on a simple example. Assume, that a library system is currently specified by an RE team. An agreement was gained, that data about the real world object `'book'` must be stored. Each stakeholder defines (from his point of view) the properties of the object `'book'`. The user defines the properties `'book-title, author-name, year'` using natural language. The system analyst additionally defines the properties `'book-id, status-of-book (loaned | available | defect | stolen | ordered)'` using a formal representation language and the specification of the librarian consists of the properties `'names of authors, keywords, classification-no., location,...'`. Therefore, the need for storing information about the object book belongs to the *common system specification*, whereas at the same time the properties to be stored are pertained by the personal views. In addition the coexistent specifications are expressed using different representation languages.

Different views of the same system have positive effects on the RE process. First, they provide a good basis for requirements elicitation (e.g., [64]). Second, the examination of the differences resulting from them can be used as a way of assisting in the early validation of requirements. Hence having different views enables the team to detect additional requirements. Moreover, if contrasting requirements were stated, conflicts can be detected and therefore become explicit.

It is important to recognize that the integration of different views at the representation level (e.g., integrating formally represented views into a comprehensive view) and the agreement on the integrated view among the people involved in the process are two separate actions. The fact, that a view was formally integrated has nothing to do with the agreement which exists on this view. A detected conflict must be solved through communication among people. Of course this communication has the aim of attaining an agreement (solving the conflict), but as a side effect additional unknown arguments (requirements) could be detected (cf. [15], [85]). Support for conflict resolution can be found in the area of computer supported cooperative work (e.g., [97], [42], [15]). Additionally support can be offered through different representations, e.g., by providing informal knowledge for explanation of formal representations, by offering graphical representation for overview of the system, or by automated detection of differences between formal specifications.

Summarizing, the *agreement* dimension is as important as the *representation* and *specification* dimension. We have pointed out that several specifications expressed in different representation formats may exist at the same time. Further we showed, that the coexistence of different views has positive effects on the RE process. Thus, allowing different views and supporting the evolution form the personal views to a common agreement on the final specification is the third main goal of RE.

4 The RE Process within the Three Dimensions

Looking at the RE process within the three dimension, the aim of the RE process can be stated as getting from the *initial input* to the *desired output*. So the trace of the RE process is an arbitrary curve within the cube spanned by the three dimensions (cf. figure 2).

The *initial input* is characterized as opaque personal views of the system represented using informal languages, whereas the *desired output* is characterized as formally represented, complete system specification on which agreement was gained (cf. section 2 for details). The main goals of the RE process can be sketched as follow (cf. section 3 for details):

- develop a complete system specification out of a opaque system understanding
- providing integrated representations and support the transformation between them
- accomplish a common agreement on the final specification allowing personal views.

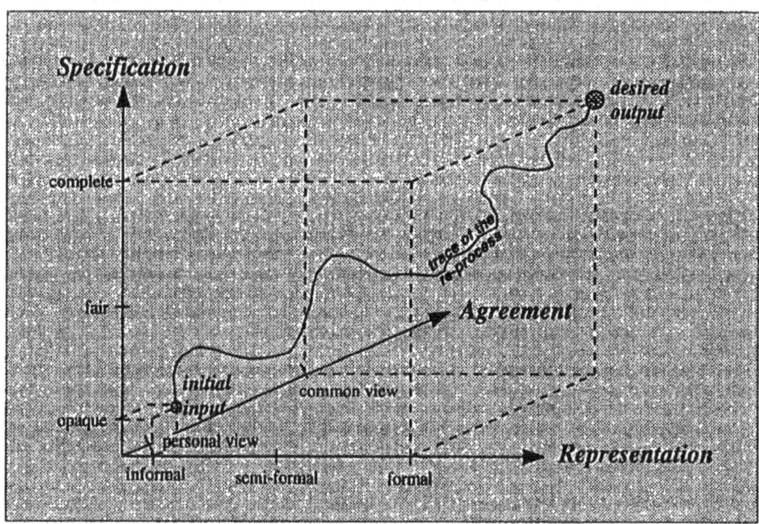

Fig. 2. The RE process within the three dimensions.

Getting from the *initial input* to the *desired output* is an interactive process consisting of different actions. An action can of course affect more than one dimension; improving one dimension often lead to a step back in another dimension.

The transformation of informally represented knowledge into a formal specification is a good example of an action (transformation step) affecting all three dimensions. An improvement within the *representation* dimension is gained, since informal knowledge is transformed into a formal representation. But during the formalization a contradiction within the formal representation may be detected by automated reasoning. This leads to a communication within the RE team to gain an agreement about the conflict (improvement of the *agreement* dimension), but additionally as a side effect a new requirement was noticed. The integration of the requirement as well as the agreement about the contradiction lead to an improvement of the *specification* dimension. The original action, transforming informally represented knowledge into a formal representation causes the execution of other actions and therefore affects all three dimensions.

This view of the RE process can not only be applied for the overall system specification. Also the evolution of each individual requirement can be covered by the three dimensions. A specific requirement can be represented within different specifications (personal views), each of these views can be represented using different representations and the specific requirement can be well understood by a part of the RE team, whereas the other part may have still only vague ideas about it. Hence, the three dimensions and the view of the RE process as an interactive transformation process consisting of actions also helps to understand the RE process at a microscopic level.

Since the RE process takes place in the *'normal'* world, the result of the RE process is influenced by various factors. All of them can have both positive and negative influence on the RE process. We identified five main factors influencing the RE process:

- *Methods and Methodologies:* The process is influenced by the methods and methodologies used for guiding the process. Of course using another method during the process can lead to different results, since they focus on different things. If e.g., structured analysis was used, the final formal specification can be totally different in comparison to a specification gained by using object oriented analysis.
- *Tools:* The final specification depends on the tools used during the process. If e.g., a reasoning tool for formal representations was used, inconsistencies can be detected, which otherwise could be still in the final specification.
- *Social Aspects:* The social environment of the RE team affects their working results. If e.g., there are conflicts between the different persons, they work more ineffectively; if the people feel fine at work, the output of the work is much better.
- *Cognitive Skills:* People have different cognitive skills. If very bright people are involved in the RE process, the final specification is usually better.
- *Economical constraints:* Economical constraints limit the resources (people, money, tools, etc.) which can be used during the RE process. It's not always true, that with more resources a better result can be gained, but if the available resources are low a certain limit, the output of the process gets less quality.

Discussing these influences in detail is beyond the scope of this paper. But it should be clear, that these are not unique to the RE process. Most of the existing processes, e.g., the production processes, are influenced by these factors.

For these reasons it is necessary to distinguish between problems which are *original* RE problems and those problems which are caused by one of the five influences mentioned above. The problem of keeping SA-diagrams, ER-diagrams as well as the data-dictionary consistent is an example for a problem caused by one of the five influences mentioned above (methods). Another example is the problem of motivating people (social aspects). *Original* RE problems are all the problems which are caused by the three dimensions. Hence requirements capture, elicitation of requirements, transformations between different representations, integration of different views are examples for *original* RE problems.

5 Computer Support for Requirements Engineering

Traditional CAD/CASE systems have often neglected that computer support for any engineering activity must be based on an understanding of the process. In this section we use the framework presented is this paper to characterize the kinds of computer support that could be useful for RE. We distinguish between computer support for improving the result of the RE process in one of the three RE dimensions, for guiding the process of RE and for easing the influences on the process.

5.1 Specification Dimension

Getting to a deeper understanding of the system and therefore to a better system specification can mainly be supported by three different kind of approaches.

First, generic knowledge (domain knowledge) can be used to improve the specification of the system. There exist generic knowledge which is valid within a particular domain, e.g., banking systems, but also domain knowledge which is valid within many domains, e.g., stock control. It was demonstrated by many research contributions that the use of *domain knowledge* has positive effects on the RE task (e.g., [5], [1], [36], [84], [65], [86], [68], [51]).

Second, the reuse of specific knowledge can lead to a better system specification. Reusing requirements specification of already existing systems leads to better insight of the systems behavior and avoids misspecifications. If the requirements specification of an existing system is not available it can be gained through reverse engineering (e.g., [36], [7], [56], [16]). For both using generic and specific knowledge during the RE process, support for retrieving suitable knowledge must be offered, e.g. using similarity based search approaches (e.g., [39], [16], [91]).

Third, the current specification of the system can be improved by applying techniques for requirements validation. Validating a software specification was characterized by Boehm as *"Am I building the right product"* [11]. During the validation errors and gaps within the current specification can be detected. This leads to a correct specification of already known requirements (correcting the errors) or the detection of new requirements (filling the gaps, e.g.,[11], [30], [87]).

5.2 Representation Dimension

Within the *representation* dimensions the support which can be offered is twofold.

First, due to certain strengths and weaknesses of the different representation formats the use of informal representation (e.g., natural language, graphics), semi-formal (e.g., ER, SA) and formal representation languages (e.g., VDM, Z, TELOS, ERAE) must be possible. For keeping the knowledge, expressed in the different representation formats, consistent, the different representations must be integrated. The relationship between formal and informal representations is much less understood. But hypertext offers a opportunity to structure informal requirements and to relate them to formal approaches (e.g., [60], [15], [85], [59]).

Second, the transformation between informal, semi-formal and formal representations must be supported. On one side, support for automated derivation of formal specifications out of informal descriptions has to be offered (e.g., [41], [57], [74], [34], [87]). On the other side, the transformation process must be supported by offering requirements freedom within the formal representation language. Formally specifications have traditionally been expected to be complete, consistent and unambiguous. However, during the initial definition and revision of formal requirements, they are typically fragmented, contradictory, incomplete, inconsistent and ambiguous. Furthermore the expressions may include various levels of abstractions (concrete, examples, general properties etc.). Since formal requirements are built out of non-formal, the acquisition process must allow many freedoms (cf. [3], [28], [51]).

5.3 Agreement Dimension

There was not much research done in supporting the *agreement* dimension within the area of requirements engineering. Nevertheless, three kinds of essential assistance for the *agreement* dimension can be identified.

First, as pointed out in section 3.3, different views of the system exist during the RE process. Even within formal languages it must be possible, that different views and different specifications exist in parallel. Also the different views and specifications must be maintained during the RE process.

Second, support for detecting dissimilarities and inconsistencies between the different views must be offered. Additionally the integration of different views must be supported by appropriated tools. Contradictions for example can be made explicit through automatic reasoning and of course the work out of a solution can be supported. Viewpoint resolution and view integration are two good examples for such support (e.g., [64], [31]).

Third, as mentioned in section 3.3, an agreement can only be gained through communication among the involved people. Hence supporting the communications, conversations, coordination and collaboration between people as well as decision support leads to better and possibly faster agreements. Research done in the CSCW area can contribute basic solutions for this (e.g., [97], [42], [32], [27], [70]).

5.4 Process Modeling

To support the overall RE process a suitable process model must be developed for guiding the RE process within the three dimensions.

According to Dowson [26], process models can be classified in three categories: activity-oriented, product-oriented and decision-oriented models. From the viewpoint of requirements engineering, only the last category appears to be partially appropriate. It is probably difficult to impossible to write down a realistic state-transition diagram (to cite a popular activity-oriented model) that adequately describes what has to happen or actually happens in RE. But relying on the pure object history is also insufficient. Even the decision-based approach (e.g., [52], [88], [82]) offer only limited hints when and how to decide on what. The central aspect of the process model for RE is therefore that it makes the notion of situation (in which to decide) explicit and relates it to the broader question of context handling (e.g., [80]).

Using the three dimensions, for each action a prediction, how the specification will change after the actions was applied, can be made. For example for validation at least a prediction can be made, that after the validation, the *specification* dimension will be improved. Within the NATURE [50] project it is assumed, that the basic building block of any process can be modelled as a triplet <*situation, decision, action*> [43]. A process model based on this assumption for supporting the RE process within the three dimensions is currently under development.

The last two feature, to be mentioned here, is the importance of quality orientation and process improvement (cf. [53], [80] for more information about quality and improvement oriented process models). It was recognized within the mechanical engineering community, that it is insufficient to correct the missing quality of a product after the fact it was produced. Quality must be produced in the first place. Therefore quality oriented process models are necessary. Especially in rapidly changing areas, like software production, it is very important to have evolving and quality oriented process models.

5.5 Easing the Influences on RE

As identified in section 4 five main influences on RE exist. *Social aspects, cognitive skills* and *economical constraints* are basic influences on the process. In contrast, *methods and methodologies* as well as *tools* are designed to support the process within the three dimensions, but also to ease the basic influences on the process (social aspects, cognitive skills and economical constraints). For designing appropriate methods, methodologies or tools knowledge gained within other research area can be used, e.g., management methods (e.g., TQM [23], [78]), organizational measures (e.g. value-added chains [81]).

Beside the task of building suitable methods and tools the need for recording of process knowledge was recognized to make the development process of software and specifications traceable (e.g., [24], [88], [54], [53]). Informal, semi-formal as well as formal knowledge must be recorded, and therefore interrelated. Hypertext is supposed to offer a solution for the integration of different representation (e.g., [37], [6], [38]).

6 Conclusions

In this paper we introduced a framework for requirements engineering (RE). First we focused on the essence of the RE process. We characterized the *'initial input'* of the RE process as opaque personal views at the system expressed using informal representation languages. The *'desired output'* was sketched as a complete system specification expressed using formal languages on which an agreement was reached. Based on this characterization the three main goals of RE were identified:

- gaining a complete system specification out of the opaque views available at the beginning of the process, according to the standard and/or guideline used,
- offering different representation formats, supporting the transformation between the representation (e.g., informal to semi-formal, informal to formal) and keeping the various representations consistent,
- allowing various views and supporting the evolution form personal views to common agreement on the finial specification.

Out of these, the three dimensions of RE were gained:

- *specification,*
- *representation and*
- *agreement dimension*

Looking at RE using these three dimensions we identified the main tasks and goals to be reached within each dimension during the RE process. But RE is not only driven by its goals, it is also influenced by the environment. We identified five main factors influencing requirements engineering: methods and methodologies, tools, social aspects, cognitive skills and economical constraints. Accordingly existing research and computer support was briefly sketched by distinguishing between computer support for improving the specification in one of the three RE dimension, for guiding the process of RE and for easing the influences on RE.

Within the NATURE project this framework is used for classifying RE problems and for making process guidance possible. The framework itself should be seen as a first attempt to accomplish a common understanding of RE within the community. It should serve as a basis for discussing research topics and identifying the main problems of RE.

Acknowledgments

I am indebted to Stephan Jacobs and Matthias Jarke for many fruitful comments on an earlier version of this paper. Additionally I am grateful to John Mylopolous and many colleagues within the NATURE project for discussions which have positively influenced this paper.

References

1. B. Adelson and E. Soloway. The Role of Domain Experience in Software Design. *IEEE Transaction on Software Engineering*, 11(11), 1985.
2. Mack W. Alford. Software Requirements Engineering Methodology (SREM) at the age of two. In *4th Int. Computer Software & Applications Conference, New York*, pages 866–874. IEEE, 1980.
3. R. Balzer. Tolerating Inconsistency. In *Int. Conference on Software Engineering*, pages 158–165, Austin, Texas, 1991.
4. R. Balzer, N. Goldman, and D. Wile. Informality in program specifications. *IEEE Transactions on Software Engineering*, 4(2):94–103, 1978.
5. D.R. Barstow. Domain Specific Automatic Programming. *IEEE Transaction on Software Engineering*, 11(11), 1985.
6. James Bigelow. Hypertext and CASE. *IEEE Software*, pages 23–27, March 1988.
7. T. Biggerstaff and R. Richter. Reusability Framework, Assesment and Directions. *IEEE Transaction on Software Engineering*, 13(2), 1987.
8. D. Bjoerner and C.B. Jones. *VDM'87 VDM-A Formal Method at Work*. LNCS 252, Springer Verlag, 1988.
9. Alexander Borgida, Sol Greenspan, and John Mylopoulos. Knowledge Representation as the Basis for Requirements Specifications. *Computer*, 18(4):82–91, April 1985.
10. Marilyn Bush. Improving Software Quality: The use of Formal Inspections at the Jet Propulsion Laboratory . In *Proc. of the 12th Int. Conf. on Software Engineering, March 26–30, Nice, France*, pages 196–199, 1990.
11. B.W.Boehm. Verifying and Validating Software Requirements and Design Specifications. *IEEE Software*, 1(1):75–88, January 1984.
12. John R. Camaron. An Overview of JSD. *IEEE Transaction on Software Engineering*, 12(2):222–240, February 1986.
13. P.P.S. Chen. The Entity-Relationship Approach: Towards a Unified View of Data. *ACM Transactions on Database Systems*, 1(1), 1976.
14. Peter Coad and Edward Yourdon. *Object Oriented Analysis*. Prentice-Hall, Englewood Cliffs, New Jersey, 1990.

15. J. Conklin and M. J. Begeman. gIBIS: A Hypertext Tool for Exploratory Policy Discussion. *ACM Transaction on Office Information Systems*, 6(4):303–331, 1988.
16. P. Constantopoulos, M. Jarke, J. Mylopoulos, and Y. Vassiliou. Software Information Base: A server for reuse. ESPRIT project ITHACA, Heraklion, Crete, ICS-FORTH, 1991.
17. B. Curtis, H Krasner, and N. Iscoe. Field Study of the Software Design Process for Large Systems. *Communication of the ACM*, 33(11):1268–1287, 1988.
18. Bill Curtis, Marc I. Kellner, and Jim Over. Process Modelling. *Communications of the ACM*, 35(9):75–90, September 1992.
19. A. Czuchry and D. Harris. KBSA: A New Paradigm for Requirements Engineering. *IEEE Expert*, 3(4):21–35, 1988.
20. Alan M. David. The Analysis and Specification of Systems and Software Requirements. In Thayer R.H. and M. Dorfman, editors, *Systems and Software Requirements Engineering*, pages 119–134. IEEE Computer Society Press — Tutorial, 1990.
21. Alan M. Davids. A Comparison of Techniques for the Specification of External System Behavior. *Communications of the ACM*, 31(9):1098–1115, 1988.
22. V. de Antonellis, B. Pernici, and P. Samarati. F-ORM Method: Methodology for reusing Specifications. *ITHACA Journal*, (14):1–24, 1991.
23. W. E. Deming. *Out of the Crisis*. Massachusetts Institiute of Technology, Center for Advanced Engineering Study, Cambridge, 1986.
24. V. Dhar and M. Jarke. Dependency Directed Reasoning and Learning in System Maintenance Support. *IEEE Transactions on Software Engineering*, 14(2):211–228, 1988.
25. Merlin Dorfman and Richard H. Thayer. *Standards, Guidelines and Examples on System and Software Requirements Engineering*. IEEE Computer Society Press – Tutorial, 1990.
26. M. Dowson. Iteration in the Software Process. In *Proceedings 9th Int. Conf. on Software Engineering*, April 1987.
27. C. A. Ellis, S. J. Gibbs, and G. L. Rein. Groupware: Some Issues and Experience. *Communication of the ACM*, 34(1):38–58, 1991.
28. M. S. Feather and S. Fickas. Coping with Requirements Freedom. In *Proceedings of the International Workshop on the Development of Intelligent Information Systems*, pages 42–46, Niagara-on-the-Lake, Ontario, Canada, April 1991.
29. S. Fickas. Automating analysis: An example. In *Proceedings of the 4th International Workshop Software Specification and Design*, pages 58–67, Washington, DC, April 1987.
30. S. Fickas and P. Nagarajan. Critiquing Software Specifications. *IEEE Software*, pages 37–47, November 1988.
31. A. Finkelstein, J. Kramer, B. Nuseibeh, L. Finkelstein, and M. Goedicke. Viewpoints: A Framework for Integration Multiple Perspectives in System Development. *International Journal of Software Engineering and Knowledge Engineering*, 1(2), May 1992.
32. Gerhard Fischer, Raymond McCall, and Anders Morch. JANUS: Integrating Hypertext with a Knowledge-based Design Environment. In *Proceedings of Hypertext '89, November 5–8, Pittsburgh, Pennsylvania*, pages 105–117, 1989.
33. R.F. Flynn and D. Dorfmann. The Automated Requirements Traceability System (ARTS): An Experience of Eight Year. In Thayer R.H. and M. Dorfman, editors, *Systems and Software Requirements Engineering*, pages 423–438. IEEE Computer Society Press — Tutorial, 1990.
34. Martin D. Fraser, Kuldeep Kumar, and Vijay K. Vaishnavi. Informal and Formal Requirements Specification Languages Bridging the Gap. *IEEE Transactions on Software Engineering*, 17(5):454–466, May 1991.
35. Daniel P. Freeman and Gerald M. Weinberg. *Handbook of Walkthroughs, Inspections and Technical Reviews*. Dorset House Publishing, New York, 1990.
36. P. Freemann, editor. *Software reusability*. IEEE Press – Tutorial, 1987.

37. Pankaj K. Garg and Walt Scacchi. On Designing Intelligent Hypertext Systems for Information Management in Software Engineering. In *Proceedings of Hypertext '87, November 13–15, Chapel Hill, North Carolina*, pages 409–432, 1987.
38. Pankaj K. Garg and Walt Scacchi. A Hypertext System to Manage Software Life-Cycle Documents. *IEEE Software*, pages 90–98, May 1990.
39. D. Gentner. Structure Mapping: A Theoretical Framework for Analogy. *Cognitive Science*, 5:121–152, 1983.
40. Joseph A. Goguen, Marina Jirotka, and Matthew J. Bickerton. Research on Requirements Capture and Analysis. Technical report, Oxford University Computing Laboratory, Centre for Requirements and Foundations, December 1991.
41. S.J. Greenspan. *Requirements Modeling: A Knowledge Representation Approach to Software Requirements Definition*. PhD thesis, Dept. of Computer Science, University of Toronto, 1984.
42. I. Greif, editor. *Readings in Computer-Supported Cooperative Work*. Morgan Kaufmann, 1988.
43. George Grosz and Colette Roland. Using artificial intelligence techniques to formalize the information system design process. In *Proc. Int. Conf. Databases and expert Systems Applications*, pages 374–380, 1990.
44. R. Guidon and B. Curtis. Control of cognitive process during software design: What tools are needed? In E. Soloway, D. Frye, and S.B. Sheppard, editors, *Proc. of CHI '88 Conference: Human Factors in Computer Systems*, pages 263–269. ACM Press NY, 1991.
45. J. Hagelstein. Declarative Approach to Information Systems Requirements. *Knowledge Base Systems*, 1(4):211–220, 1988.
46. Anthony Hall. Seven Myths of Formal Methods. *IEEE Software*, (9):11–19, September 1990.
47. C.A.R. Hoare. International Conference on VDM and Z. LNCS 428, Springer Verlag, 1990.
48. IEEE. *Standards, Guidelines, and Examples on System and Software Requirements Engineering*. IEEE Computer Society Press – Tutorial, 1990.
49. IEEE. IEEE Std. 830–1984. In *IEEE Software Engineering Standards Collection*. IEEE, New York, 1991.
50. Matthias Jarke, Janis Bubenko, Colette Rolland, Allistair Sutcliffe, and Yannis Vassiliou. Theories Underlying Requirements Engineering: An Overview of NATURE at Genesis. In *Proceedings of the 1th Int. Symposium of Requirements Engineering*, San Diego, CA, 1993. to appear.
51. Matthias Jarke, Stephan Jacobs, and Klaus Pohl et. al. Requirements Engineering: An Integrated View of Representation, Process and Domain. In *submitted to: ECSE '93*, 1993.
52. Matthias Jarke, Manfred Jeusfeld, and Thomas Rose. A Software Process Data Model for Knowledge Engineering in Information Systems. *Information Systems*, 15(1):85–116, 1990.
53. Matthias Jarke and Klaus Pohl. Information System Quality and Quality Information Systems. In *Proceedings of the IFIP 8.2 Working Conference on the Impact of Computer-Supported Techniques on Information Systems Development*, 1992.
54. Matthias Jarke and T. Rose. Specification Management with CAD^0. In P. Loucopoulos and R. Zicari, editors, *Conceptual Modeling Databases, and CASE*, 1991.
55. Manfred Jeusfeld. *Änderungskontrolle in deduktiven Objektbanken*. INFIX Pub, Bad Honnef, Germany, 1992.
56. P. Johannesson and K. Kalman. A Method for Translating Relational Schemas into Conceptual Schemas. In *8th Int. Conf. on Entity-Relationship Approach*, pages 279–294, 1989.
57. W. Lewis Johnson. Deriving Specifications from Requirements. In *Proceedings of the 10th International Conference on Software Engineering*, pages 428–438, Singapore, April 1988.
58. W. Lewis Johnson and Martin Feather. Building An Evolution Transformation Library. In *Proceedings of the 12th International Conference on Software Engineering*, pages 428–438, Nice, France, March 1990.

59. W. Lewis Johnson, Martin. S. Feather, and David. R. Harris. Representation and Presentation of Requirements Knowledge. *IEEE Transactions on Software Engineering*, 18(10), October 1992.

60. W. Lewis Johnson and David R. Harris. The ARIES Project. In *Proceedings 5th KBSA Conference*, pages 121–131, Liverpool, N.Y., 1990.

61. S. E. Keller, L. G. Kahn, and R. B.Panara. Specifying Software Quality Requirements with Metric. In Thayer R.H. and M. Dorfman, editors, *Systems and Software Requirements Engineering*, pages 145–163. IEEE Computer Society Press — Tutorial, 1990.

62. Manolis Koubarakis, John Mylopoulos, Martin Stanley, and Matthias Jarke. Telos: A Knowledge Representation Language for Requirements Modelling. Technical Report KRR-TR-89–1, Department of Computer Science, University of Toronto, 1989.

63. Julio Cesar S. P. Leite. Viewpoint Analysis: A Case Study. In *Proceedings of the 5th International Workshop on Software and Design*, pages 111–119, Pittsburgh, PA, 1989.

64. Julio Cesar S. P. Leite and Peter A. Freeman. Requirements Validation Through Viewpoint Resolution. *IEEE Transactions on Software Engineering*, 17(12):1253–1269, December 1991.

65. P. Loucopoulos and R. Champion. Knowledge-Based Approach to Requirements Engineering Using Method and Domain Knowledge. *Knowledge-Based Systems*, 1(3), 1988.

66. M.D. Lubars and M.T. Harandi. Knowledge-Based Software Design Using Design Schemas. In *Proceedings 9th Int. Conf. on Software Engineering*, April 1987.

67. Neil Maiden. Analogy as a Paradigm for Specification Reuse. *Software Engineering Journal*, 1991.

68. Neil Maiden. *Analogical specification Reuse during Requirements Analysis*. PhD thesis, City University London, 1992.

69. M. Mannino and V. Tseng. Inferring Database Requirements from Examples in Forms. In *Int. Conf. on Entity-Relationship Approach*, pages 391–405. Elsevier Publishers B.V. (North-Holland), 1989.

70. David Marca and Geoffrey Bock. *Groupware: Software for Computer-Supported Cooperative Work*. IEEE Computer Society Press, Los Alamitos, CA, 1992.

71. Stephen M. McMenamin and John F. Palmer. *Essential System Analysis*. Yourdon Press, Prentice Hall, Englewood Cliffs, NJ 07632, 1984.

72. Richard H. Thayer Merlin Dorfman, editor. *Standards, Guidelines, and Examples on System and Software Requirements Engineering*, chapter ESA Software Engineering Standards, pages 101–120. IEEE Computer Society Press Tutorial, 1990.

73. Bertrand Meyer. On Formalism in Specifications. *IEEE Software*, pages 6–26, January 1985.

74. Kanth Miriyala and Mehdi T. Harandi. Automatic Derivation of Formal Software Specifications Form Informal Descriptions. *IEEE Transactions on Software Engineering*, 17(10):1126–1142, October 1991.

75. David E. Monarchi and Gretchen I. Puhr. A Research Typology for Object-Oriented Analysis and Design. *Communications of the ACM*, 35(9):35–47, September 1992.

76. John Mylopoulos, Alex Borgida, Matthias Jarke, and Manolis Koubarakis. Telos: Representing Knowledge about Information Systems. *Transactions on Information Systems*, 8(4):325–362, 1990.

77. John Mylopoulos and Hector J. Levesque. *On Conceptual Modelling*. Springer Verlag, 1986.

78. J. S. Oakland. Total Quality Management. In *Proceedings 2nd Int. Conf. on Total Quality Management*, pages 3–17. Cotswold Press Ltd., 1989.

79. Barbara Pernici. Requirements Specifications for Object Oriented Systems. *ITHACA Journal*, (8):43–63, January 1991.

80. Klaus Pohl and Matthias Jarke. Quality Information Systems: Repository Support for Evolving Process Models. Technical report, RWTH Aachen, Informatik-Berichte 37–92, 1992.

81. M. Porter. *Competitive Advantage*. Free Press, New York, 1985.
82. C. Potts. A Generic Model for Representing Design Methods. In *Proceedings 11th International Conference on Software Engineering*, 1989.
83. C. Potts and G. Bruns. Recording the Reasons for Design Decisions. In *Proceedings 10th International Conference on Software Engineering*, 1988.
84. P. Paolo Puncello, Piero Torrigiani, Francesco Pietri, Riccardo Burlon, Bruno Cardile, and Mirella Conti. ASPIS: A Knowledge-Based CASE Environment. *IEEE Software*, pages 58–65, March 1988.
85. B. Ramesh and V. Dhar. Process-Knowledge Based Group Support in Requirements Engineering. *IEEE Transactions on Software Engineering*, 18(6), 1992.
86. Howard B. Reubenstein and Richard C. Waters. The Requirements Apprentice: Automated Assistance for Requirements Acquisition. *IEEE Transactions on Software Engineering*, 17(3):226–240, March 1991.
87. C. Rolland and C. Proix. A Natural Language Approach for Requirements Engineering. In *Proceedings of the 4th International Conference on Advanced Information Systems Engineering*, LNCS 593, 1992.
88. T. Rose, M. Jarke, M. Gocek, C.G. Maltzahn, and H.W. Nissen. A Decision-based Configuration Process Environment. *Special Issue on Software Process Support, IEE Software Engineering Journal*, 6(5):332–346, 1991.
89. H.H. Sayani. PSL/PSA at the Age of Fifteen. In Thayer R.H. and M. Dorfman, editors, *Systems and Software Requirements Engineering*, pages 403–417. IEEE Computer Society Press — Tutorial, 1990.
90. Walt Scacchi. Managing Software Engineering Projects: A Social Analysis. *IEEE Transaction on Software Engineering*, 10(1):49–59, 1984.
91. G. Spanoudakis and P. Constantopoulos. Similarity for Analogical Software Reuse. In *Proc. ERCIM Workshop on Methods and Tools for Software Reuse*, Heraklion, Crete, 1992.
92. J.M. Spivey. An introduction to Z and formal specifications. *Software Engineering Journal*, 4(1):40–50, 1990.
93. Alistair Sutcliffe. Object Oriented Systems Analysis: The Abstract Question. In *Proc. IFIP WG 8.1 Conf. The Object Oriented Approach in Information Systems*, Quebec City, Canada, 1991.
94. Alistair Sutcliffe and Neil Maiden. Software reuseability: Delivering Productivity gains or short cuts. In *Proceedings INTERACT*, pages 948–956. North-Holland, 1990.
95. C.P. Svoboda. Structured Analysis. In Thayer R.H. and M. Dorfman, editors, *Systems and Software Requirements Engineering*, pages 218–227. IEEE Computer Society Press — Tutorial, 1990.
96. Jeanette M. Wing. A Specifier's Introduction to Formal Methods. *Computer*, (9):8–24, September 1990.
97. T. Winograd and F. Flores. *Understanding Computers and Cognition: A New Foundation for Design*. Ablex Norwood, NJ, 1986.
98. Edward Yourdon. *Modern Structured Analysis*. Prentice-Hall, Englewood Cliffs, NJ, 1989.
99. Edward Yourdon. *Structured Walkthroughs*. Prentice-Hall, Englewood Cliffs, NJ, 1989.
100. Pamala Zave. An Insider's Evaluation of PAISLey. *IEEE Transaction on Software Engineering*, 17(3):212–225, March 1991.
101. Pamela Zave. A Comparison of the Major Approaches to Software Specification and Design. In Thayer R.H. and M. Dorfman, editors, *Systems and Software Requirements Engineering*, pages 197–199. IEEE Computer Society Press — Tutorial, 1990.

The Three Dimensions of Requirements Engineering: 20 Years Later

Klaus Pohl and Nelufar Ulfat-Bunyadi

Abstract Requirements engineering is the process of eliciting stakeholder needs and desires and developing them into an agreed set of detailed requirements that can serve as a basis for all other subsequent development activities. In order to structure this field, we identified in 1993 three key dimensions which drive the requirements engineering (RE) process, namely, the specification, the representation, and the agreement dimension. In this chapter, we revisit the three dimensions of RE and sketch their evolution into our comprehensive RE framework in the past 20 years.

1 The Three Dimensions of Requirements Engineering (1993)

In the original CAiSE paper from 1993 [3], we identified the three dimensions of RE as depicted in Fig. 1.

The goal within the specification dimension is to arrive at a preferably complete requirements specification. At the beginning of the RE process, the understanding of the system and its requirements is typically opaque. At the end, the understanding about the requirements should be as complete as possible. In other words, all functional requirements, quality requirements, and constraints should be known at the required level of detail.

The goal within the representation dimension is to document all requirements as formally as possible to avoid misinterpretations. At the beginning of the RE process, mainly natural language (informal representations) is used to document the requirements for the system. At the end of the RE process, all requirements should be documented using a formal language. Key reason for the documentation using

K. Pohl (✉) • N. Ulfat-Bunyadi
paluno, The Ruhr Institute for Software Technology, University of Duisburg-Essen, Essen, Germany
e-mail: klaus.pohl@paluno.uni-due.de; nelufar.ulfat-bunyadi@paluno.uni-due.de

J. Bubenko et al. (eds.), *Seminal Contributions to Information Systems Engineering*,
DOI 10.1007/978-3-642-36926-1_6, © Springer-Verlag Berlin Heidelberg 2013

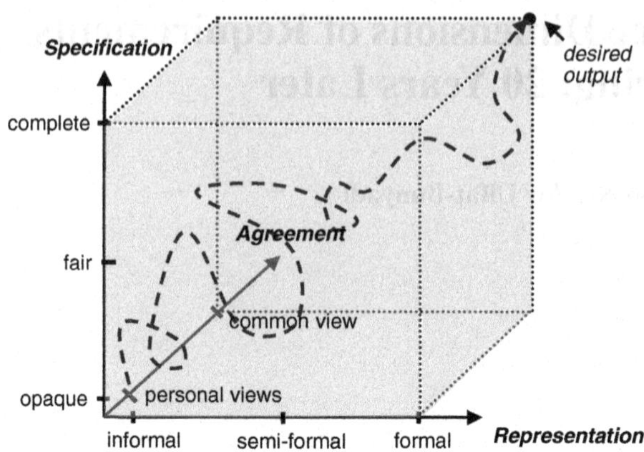

Fig. 1 The three dimensions of RE in 1993 [3]

a formal language is the precise semantics of formal languages which restricts the interpretation of the requirements and thus avoids some typical misinterpretations.

The goal within the agreement dimension is to reach an agreement on the requirements among all the stakeholders involved in the RE process. At the beginning of the RE process, the stakeholders typically have different views with regard to the goals and the requirements of the system. At the end, these different views should have converged. In other words, conflicts should have been detected and resolved and a common, integrated view about the goals and the requirements the system should fulfill should have been established.

Progress in one dimension can impact progress in the other two dimensions both, in a positive but also in a negative way. For example, the elicitation of new requirements may lead to new conflicts among stakeholders or may uncover existing conflicts. In this case, the progress in the specification dimension leads to a drawback in the agreement dimension. Or, the formalization of a requirement may reveal some gaps within the specification which leads to a drawback in the specification dimension.

2 The Three Dimensions and Their Application (1994)

In the 1994 Information Systems paper [4] (a selected best paper of CAiSE'93), we outlined various ways of applying the three dimensions including:

- The categorization of existing RE methods and tools by analyzing the support they provide with regard to the three dimensions and uncovering gaps in the support;
- The classification of RE problems (e.g. technical, social, and cognitive problems) by identifying the cause of the problem based on the three dimensions;

- The analysis of RE practice by identifying problems within industrial RE processes based on the three dimensions and solving them;
- The description of specific situations of an RE process within the three dimensions which are used as guidance for the engineers and for decisions to be made by the requirements engineer;
- The support for establishing pre-traceability of requirements by defining the information to be recorded during the RE process based on the three dimensions.

All these applications have been researched more deeply in the subsequent years and led to several publications. Our comprehensive textbook "Requirements Engineering: Fundamentals, Principles, and Techniques" [5] describes most of those findings and integrates most of these results into a holistic RE framework (see below).

3 Evolution of the Three Dimensions (2012)

From 1993 till today, various industrial cooperations as well as further research led to a deeper understanding of RE and in turn to an adaptation of the three dimensions. The key adaptations are:

- ***Content dimension*** (previously specification dimension): We renamed the specification dimension into content dimension. The reasons for this renaming are mainly twofold. First, the term 'specification dimension' led to various misunderstandings. Most notably, people mixed it up with the requirements specification itself. Second, as already described in 1993 [3], the goal of this dimension is to arrive at a "complete system specification" meaning that all relevant requirements are known and each requirement is understood at the required level of detail. Thus, this dimension actually deals with the knowledge gained during RE about the requirements and the constraints (independently of how this knowledge is represented). Therefore, 'content dimension' is a much better term for this dimension.
- ***Documentation dimension*** (previously representation dimension): We renamed the representation dimension into documentation dimension. This renaming reflects the need for documenting different types of information during the RE process including decisions, rationales, change requests, priorities, risks. Consequently, we refined and adjusted the goal to be achieved within this dimension. The goal is to document the content gained during RE using appropriate documentation languages (e.g. text-based use-case templates, decision tables, formal RE languages, structured text, graphical languages, pictures and the like) and to establish, at the end of the RE process, a requirements specification, which complies with the specification rules defined for the development project (see [5] for details). The final requirements specification does not necessarily have to be formal. In general, the choice of the language used to document particular

requirements information during the whole RE process depends on the usage of the information and the stakeholders using the documentation of the information. For example, the language used to document the requirements to support a proper validation could be totally different than, for example, the language used to document the same content to support design or test activities.

4 Comprehensive Framework for Requirements Engineering

The three dimensions served as a basis for developing our comprehensive RE framework, which comprises the following main building blocks (see Fig. 2):

- ***Three Core RE Activities***: There are three core RE activities, namely elicitation, documentation, and negotiation. The three core activities are directly derived from the three dimensions and are performed iteratively during the RE process depending on the progress made in each dimension.
- ***Four System Context Facets***: Each system is embedded into a context in which it is going to operate and for which it has to provide an added value. Among others, the context comprises the sources for requirements elicitation as well as the users of the system (people and other systems). The context does not only strongly influence the elicitation and definition of the requirements and the constraints about the system, but also the understanding and interpretation of this information. Since the system context is typically very complex, our framework structures the context into four facets: the subject, the usage, the IT system, and the development facet (cf. [1, 2]). Among others, the four facets support a systematic elicitation of information, stakeholder identification, and validation during requirements engineering (cf. [5]).
- ***Three Types of Requirements Artifacts***: The requirements artifacts are the main outcomes of the RE process and are used to drive the RE process itself, e.g. to decide what to do next. Over the years, the use of goals and scenarios has proven to be very beneficial for RE as well as subsequent system development. Thus, goals and scenarios should be used during RE in addition to the traditional solution-oriented requirements (see [5] for a detailed description). There are many key reasons for using goals and scenarios during RE. For example, conflicts among stakeholders can be identified and resolved more easily on a goal level than on the level of detailed solution-oriented requirements. Or, a scenario typically describes a concrete, envisioned system usage which provides a clear business or customer value. Therefore, our framework differentiates between three key requirements artifacts: goals, scenarios, and solution-oriented requirements. The latter comprise the traditional functional, data, and behavioral perspectives on requirements used in system development. In [5], we elaborate on the three key RE artifacts as well as their usage within the RE process.

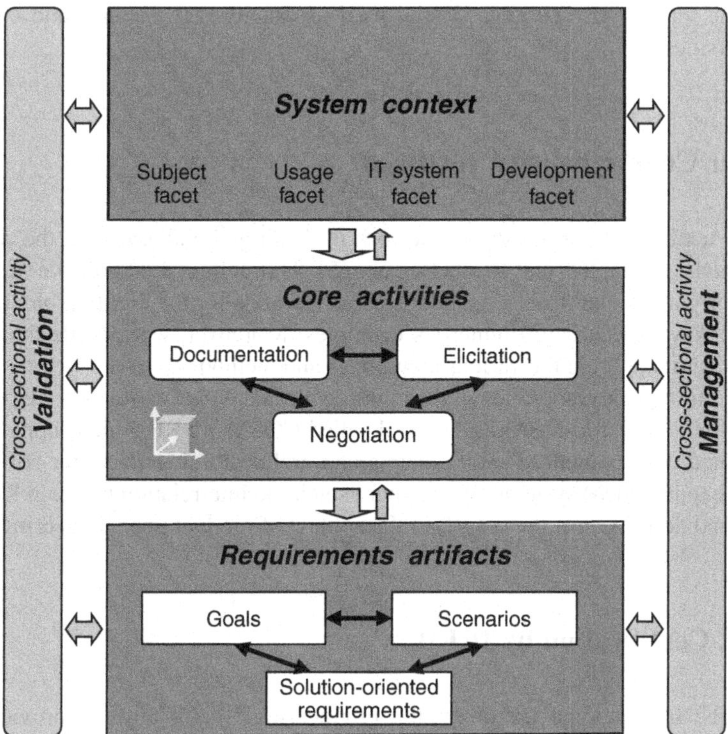

Fig. 2 Our comprehensive RE framework [5]

- ***Two Cross-sectional Activities***: Two cross-sectional activities, namely validation and management, complete our comprehensive RE framework:
  - ***Validation:*** Validation ensures proper quality assurance during the whole RE process. According to our framework, validation not only comprises the validation of the three key requirements artifacts but also the validation of the consideration of the four context facets as well as the validation of a proper execution of the three core activities (cf. [5]).
  - ***Management:*** Similar to validation, the cross-sectional management activity is not restricted to the management of the three key requirements artifacts but includes the management of the system context (e.g. to identify contextual changes) and the management of the execution and scheduling of the three core activities (cf. [5]).

Our comprehensive RE framework is widely used in industry and education. For example, the framework is used as reference model for structuring RE and RE processes within organizations, for determining weaknesses and improvement potentials of RE within the organizations, and as reference structure for trainings provided to managers, requirements engineers, developers, etc. Moreover it is the backbone for our RE textbook [5] and used to structure RE lectures and courses at universities.

5 Our Comprehensive Textbook

Our RE textbook describes the framework in detail and elaborates on the related foundations, principles, and RE techniques [5]. Throughout the book, we describe the underlying fundamentals, techniques, and methods for the building blocks and illustrate key aspects with numerous examples. Moreover, we provide hints and guidelines for applying the various techniques and methods.

In addition to the elaboration of the building blocks of our framework, we present our goal- and scenario-based RE method called COSMOD-RE which supports the intertwined development of requirements and architectural artifacts for software-intensive (embedded) systems. We further sketch the interrelation between RE and testing and describe specifics of RE in the context of product line engineering.

6 RE Certification by IREB

IREB (the International Requirements Engineering Board) aims at providing a certification model and fostering further education in the field of RE. Members of the board are independent, internationally recognized experts from industry, research, consulting, and education. The 'Certified Professional for Requirements Engineering' (CPRE) certification model currently offers two qualification levels: foundation and advanced level.

Our comprehensive RE framework served as a basis for defining the syllabus and the exams for the foundation level. The foundation level requires being familiar with the terminology of RE, understanding the basic techniques and methods of RE and their application, and being familiar with well-known notations for requirements. To support people in preparing for the CPRE foundation level certificate, we have published the "Requirements Engineering Fundamentals" book [6]. This textbook is (will be) available in different languages including English, German, Portuguese, Spanish, and French. More than 10,000 requirements engineers world-wide have already passed successfully the certification of the IREB CPRE foundation level.

References

1. M. Jarke, K. Pohl: Establishing Visions in Context – Towards a Model of Requirements Processes. In: Proceedings of the 14th International Conference on Information Systems, 1993, pp. 23–34.

2. J. Mylopoulos, A. Borgida, M. Jarke, M. Koubarakis: Telos – Representing Knowledge about Information Systems. ACM Transactions on Information Systems, Vol. 8, No. 4, 1990, pp. 325–362.
3. K. Pohl: The Three Dimensions of Requirements Engineering. In: Proceedings of the 5th Conference on Advanced Information Systems Engineering (CAiSE'93), Springer, LNCS, Vol. 22, 1993.
4. K. Pohl: The Three Dimensions of Requirements Engineering – A Framework and its Applications. In: Information Systems, Special Issue on Computer Supported Information System Development, Vol. 19, No. 3, 1994.
5. K. Pohl: Requirements Engineering – Fundamentals, Principles, and Techniques. 1st ed., Springer, 2010. (also appeared in German: Requirements Engineering – Grundlagen, Prinzipien, Techniken, 2. ed., dpunkt, 2008)
6. K. Pohl, C. Rupp: Requirements Engineering Fundamentals: A Study Guide for the Certified Professional for Requirements Engineering Exam. 1st ed., Rocky Nook, 2011. (also appeared in German: Basiswissen Requirements Engineering, 3. ed., dpunkt, 2011, and in Portuguese)

Towards a Deeper Understanding of Quality in Requirements Engineering

John Krogstie Odd Ivar Lindland Guttorm Sindre

Faculty of Electrical Engineering and Computer Science
University of Trondheim, Norway

Abstract. The notion of quality in requirements specifications is poorly understood, and in most literature only bread and butter lists of useful properties have been provided. However, the recent frameworks of Lindland et al. and Pohl have tried to take a more systematic approach. In this paper, these two frameworks are reviewed and compared. Although they have different outlook, their deeper structures are not contradictory.

The paper also discusses shortcomings of the two frameworks and proposes extensions to the framework of Lindland et al. The extensions build on social construction theory and the resulting framework should contribute to understanding quality in requirements engineering and conceptual modelling.

Keywords: **Requirements engineering, conceptual modelling, quality, social construction**

1 Introduction

The notion of quality in requirements specifications is so far poorly understood. Software metrics [7] have mostly concentrated on the deliverables of the later phases, such as design and coding, or on detailed process metrics. Moreover, these efforts have concentrated far more on the issue of 'building the product right' than 'building the right product', whereas both should be covered to ensure quality from the user's point of view [2]. Previously proposed quality goals for conceptual models [6, 14, 22, 25] have included many useful aspects, but unfortunately in the form of unsystematic bread and butter lists. Two recent frameworks [17, 20] have attempted to take a more structured approach to understanding the problem. Still, both these need more development before they can result in concrete guidelines for the requirements engineering process. A useful first iteration is to compare the two frameworks and see if they fit together, and possibly unite and extend them.

The rest of the paper is structured as follows: Section 2 reviews and compares the two frameworks. Then, section 3 establishes an extended framework based on the comparison. Section 4 concludes the paper. The terminology used in the papers follows the one usually used in the areas of conceptual modelling and requirements engineering. One should be aware of that the use of many terms in these areas differs significantly from their use in for instance logic programming.

2 Review and Comparison

We will briefly present the main parts of the two frameworks, before performing a comparison between them.

2.1 Lindland/Sindre/Sølvberg's Framework

The main structure of this framework is illustrated in Figure 1. The basic idea is to evaluate the quality of models along three dimensions — syntax, semantics, and pragmatics — by comparing sets of statements. These sets are:

- $\mathcal{M}$, the model, i.e., the set of all the statements explicitly or implicitly made in the model. The explicit model $\mathcal{M}_E$, consists of the statements explicitly made, whereas the implicit model, $\mathcal{M}_I$, consist of the statements not made, but implied by the explicit ones.
- $\mathcal{L}$, the language, i.e., the set of all statements which are possible to make according to the vocabulary and grammar of the modelling languages used.
- $\mathcal{D}$, the domain, i.e., the set of all statements which would be correct and relevant about the problem at hand. Hence, notice that the term domain is used somewhat differently from the usual. Here, it means the 'ideal' model/solution to the problem.
- $\mathcal{I}$, the audience interpretation, i.e., the set of all statements which the audience (i.e., various actors in the modeling process) think that the model consists of.

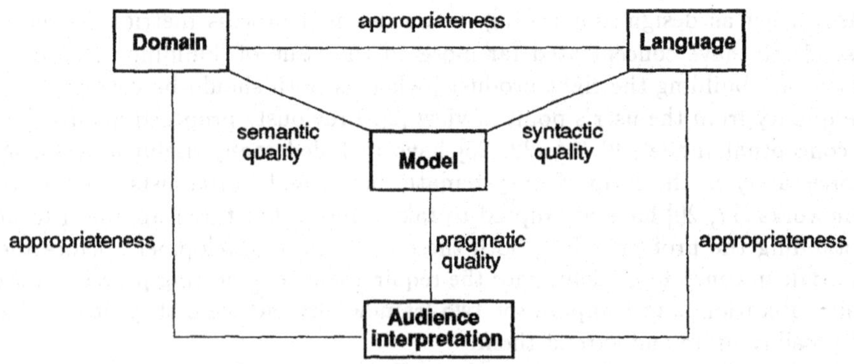

Fig. 1.: The framework by Lindland et al. (From [17])

The primary sources for model quality are defined using the relationships between the model and the three other sets:

- *syntactic quality* is the degree of correspondence between model and language, i.e., the set of syntactic errors is $\mathcal{M} \setminus \mathcal{L}$.
- *semantic quality* is the degree of correspondence between model and domain. If $\mathcal{M} \setminus \mathcal{D} \neq \emptyset$ the model contains invalid statements; if $\mathcal{D} \setminus \mathcal{M} \neq \emptyset$ the model is incomplete. Since total validity and completeness are generally impossible, the notions of *feasible validity* and *feasible completeness* were introduced. Feasible validity is reached when the benefits of removing invalid statement from $\mathcal{M}$ are less than the drawbacks, whereas feasible completeness is reached when the benefits of adding new statements to $\mathcal{M}$ is less than the drawbacks. The term drawback is used instead of the more familiar term cost in an effort to cover both purely economic issues and factors like user preferences and ethics.
- *pragmatic quality* is the degree of correspondence between model and audience interpretation (i.e., the degree to which the model has been understood). If $\mathcal{I} \neq \mathcal{M}$, the comprehension of the model is not completely correct. Usually, it is neither necessary nor possible that the whole audience understand the entire conceptual model — instead each group in the audience should understand the part of the model which is relevant to them. *Feasible comprehension* was defined along the same lines as feasibility for validity and completeness.

In addition to these primary quality concerns, it is pointed out that correspondence between domain and language, between domain and audience interpretation, and between language and audience interpretation may affect the model quality indirectly. These relationships are all denoted *appropriateness* as shown in Figure 1.

It is also argued that previously proposed quality goals such as minimality, traceability, consistency, and unambiguity are subsumed by the four goals of syntactic correctness, validity, completeness, and comprehension, and a distinction is made between goals and means to reach these goals. For more details on this framework, the reader should consult [17]. The parts of the framework dealing with fault detection have been applied in connection with integrating the development and testing of object-oriented software [18].

2.2 Pohl's Framework

Pohl's framework [20] which is one of the results of the NATURE-project [12] defines three dimensions of requirements engineering:

- *the specification dimension* deals with the degree of requirements understanding. At the beginning of the process, this understanding is opaque. The desired output of the RE process is a complete system specification, where completeness is measured against some standard, guideline, or model.
- *the representation dimension* deals with the degree of formality. Various languages can be used in the process; informal ones such as natural language,

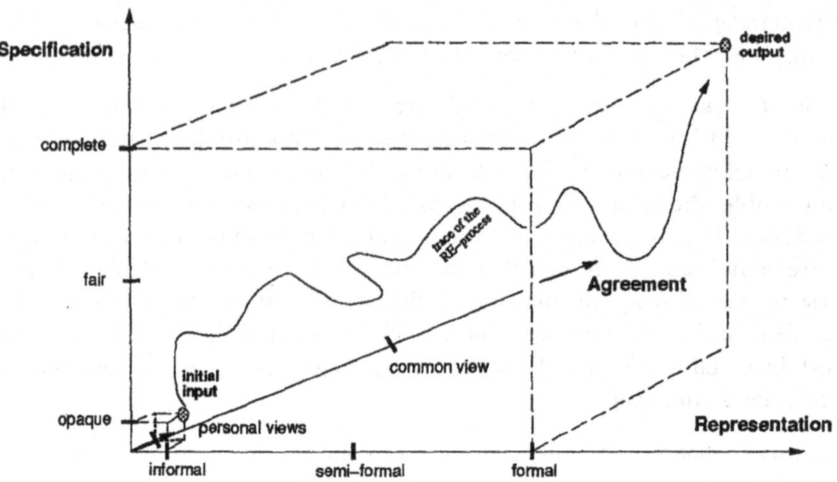

Fig. 2.: Pohl's framework (From [20])

semi-formal ones such as many graphical modelling languages, and formal ones (e.g., logic). At the beginning of the process, statements will usually be informal. Since formal representations allow reasoning and partial code-generation, these are more system-oriented. Hence, a transformation of informal requirements to a formal representation is desirable.

- *the agreement dimension* deals with the degree of agreement. The RE process has many stakeholders, and in the beginning each of these will have their personal views concerning the requirements to be made. The goal of the process is to reach agreement on the requirements. Detected conflicts must be solved through discussions among those affected.

The RE process can be characterized as an arbitrary curve within the cube spanned by these three dimensions, as illustrated in Figure 2. Pohl distinguishes between *original* RE problems, which are those caused by the three dimensions, and problems caused by approaches to solve the original problems, i.e., those related to methods, tools, social aspects, cognitive skills and economical constraints. Furthermore, the article discusses the computer support for RE in light of the three dimensions and discusses how the framework can be applied in analyzing RE methods, practise, problems, and process situations.

2.3 Overall comparison and critique

At first sight, the two frameworks may seem completely different. The terminology used is different. Lindland et al. [17] defines the quality of models (e.g., requirements specifications) according to the linguistic dimensions of syntax, semantics, and pragmatics, Pohl's framework [20] identifies the goals of requirements engineering along the three dimensions of completeness, formality, and agreement.

Although the two frameworks have a quite different appearance, they are rather similar in their deeper structure. The following observations can be made:

- the *representation* dimension corresponds to the *syntactic* dimension, since both these deal with the relationship between the specification and the language(s) used. The main differences in this respect is that Pohl's framework discusses several languages, whereas Lindland's framework sees the language as one and just considers whether the specification is correct according to the rules of that language (which may be a union of several languages, formal and informal). It should also be noted that Pohl's framework regards a formal specification as a *goal*. Lindland's framework states that formality is a *mean* to reach a syntacticly correct specification, as well as higher semantic and pragmatic quality through consistency checking and model executions of different kinds.
- the *specification* dimension corresponds to the *semantic* dimension, since both these deal with the goal of completeness. A notable difference here is that Pohl sees completeness as the sole goal (possibly including validity?), whereas Lindland's framework also identifies the notions of validity and feasibility. The reason for this discrepancy seems to be a somewhat different use of the term completeness, where Pohl uses the term relative to some standard, whereas Lindland et al. uses it relative to the the set of all statements which would be correct and relevant about the problem at hand.
- the *agreement* dimension is related to the *pragmatic* dimension, since both these deal with the specification's relationship to the audience involved. The difference is that Pohl states the goal that the specification should be agreed upon, whereas Lindland et al. aim at letting the model be understood. In a way these goals are partly overlapping. Agreement without understanding is not very useful in a democratic process. On the other hand, using the semiotic levels described in the FRISCO-report [16], it seems more appropriate to put agreement into the social realm, thus going beyond the framework of Lindland et al.

Although both frameworks contribute to improving the understanding of quality issues in requirements engineering, they still have several shortcomings. For instance, in Pohl's framework it appears that a formal, agreed, and complete specification is the goal of the requirements engineering phase. Although we support this as desirable, we — as argued in [17] feel that such goals are unrealistic and we need mechanisms for discussing when the specification/model is *good enough*. The notion of feasibility that is included in Lindland's framework addresses this aspect. In Pohl's framework such mechanisms are only implicitly included through the adherence to standards which potentially include them.

We also feel it is problematic that a completely formal representation is a goal of the RE process. It is not always desirable that all the products of a requirement specification process are formal. For instance, when developing a goal-hierarchy as used in, e.g., TEMPORA [23], it is not meaningful to formalise the high-level business goals, even if these are an important result of requirements engineering in order for the participants to understand and agree about the requirements to the information system. This kind of information is also of vital importance when the requirements to the information systems must be reevaluated during maintenance.

In Lindland's framework, on the other hand, the social aspect of agreement is currently not handled in a satisfactory way. Even if people understand the requirements, this does not mean that they will agree to them. When discussing agreement, the concept of domain as currently defined is also insufficient, since it represents some ideal knowledge about a particular problem, a knowledge not obtainable for the actors that are to agree.

3 Framework extensions

This section aims at extending Lindland et al.'s framework in order to include some of the good aspects of Pohl's framework and also hopefully eliminate the inherent shortcomings of the current version of Lindland's framework.

The key area for improvement is related to the relationships between the domain, model, and audience interpretations and the introduction of the social goal of agreement.

3.1 Background on social construction

Since 'agreement' was not thoroughly discussed in [17], we will first introduce our ontological position for discussing the concept. This will also influence some of the other relationships in the framework.

We base our treatment of agreement on the idea that 'reality' is socially constructed [1], an idea which is the foundation of most of the current theoretical discussion within social sciences [5], and which has received increased attention in the information systems community [8, 16, 24]. For a constructivist, the relationship between 'reality' and models of this reality are subject to negotiation among the audience, and may be adapted from time to time. This is in contrast to a more traditional objectivistic ontology, where the relationship between 'reality' and models thereof is obvious.

The mechanisms of social construction in an organization can briefly be described as follows [9]: An organization consists of individual social actors that perceive the world in a way specific to them. The *local reality* is the way the individual perceives the world that s/he acts in. Whereas some of this local reality may be made explicit and talked about, a lot of what we know about the world is tacit. The term 'individual knowledge' is below restricted to the *explicit* local reality of an individual actor.

When social actors act, they *externalise* their local reality. The most important ways the social actors of an organization externalise their reality, are to speak and to construct languages, artifacts, and institutions. What they do is to construct *organizational reality*: To make something that other actors have to relate to in their work. Finally, *internalisation* is the process of making sense of the institutions, artifacts, technology etc. in the organization, and making this organizational reality part of the individual local reality.

Whereas the development of a requirements specification based on a social actor's local reality is partly a process of externalisation of her/his reality, the process of developing conceptual models can also be looked upon as part of a sense-making process. The views of several actors are collected in a conceptual model and agreement about the validity of this is reached. It should also be noted that the ability and possibility for the different stakeholders to externalise their local reality will differ. Thus, in the words of Goguen one should think about requirements as " ...emergent, in the sense that they do not already exist, but rather emerge from interactions between the analyst and the client organization" [10].

In the framework of Lindland et al, 'reality' is represented by the domain, $\mathcal{D}$. The domain represents the perfect understanding of the problem. From the viewpoint of social construction, as well as the view of information systems engineering as a wicked problem [21], it can be questioned whether a perfect solution at all exists. This is not an important point, however, since the perfect solution is anyway stated to be unachievable. Hence, the domain $\mathcal{D}$ serves only as a useful conceptual fixpoint to make it easier to define quality terminology. To discuss the social aspects, the actors' understanding of the domain must be added to the framework, in the same sense as their understanding of the model was already introduced in the previous version of the framework.

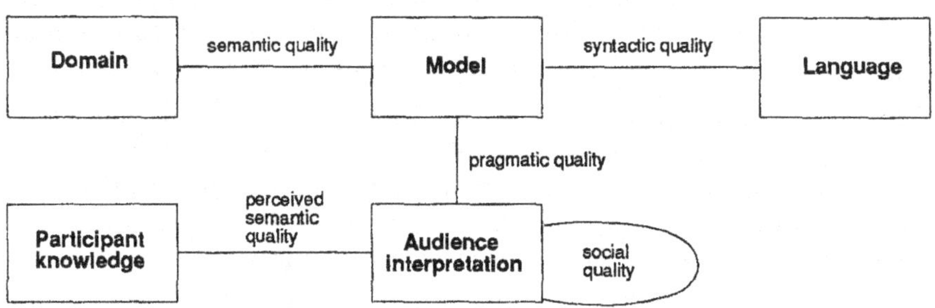

Fig. 3.: Extended framework

3.2 Extended framework

We are now ready to extend the framework of Lindland et al. The main concepts and their relationships are shown in Figure 3. The following sets are defined:

- $\mathcal{A}$, the audience, i.e., the union of the set of individual actors $A_1,...,A_k$ the set of organizational social actors $A_{k+1},...,A_n$ and the set of technical actors $A_{n+1},...,A_m$ who needs to relate to the model. The individual social actors being members of the audience is called the ***participants*** of the modelling process. An organizational social actor is made up of several individuals. The audience consists of all who need to understand the model during the RE process. The participants are a subset of the stakeholders of the process of developing the new or improved information system, a stakeholder being someone who potentially stands to gain or lose in the process. Stakeholders typically include project managers, system developers and analysts, financers, maintainers, and future users.

  A technical actor is typically a computer or computer program, which must "understand" part of the specification to automatically manipulate it. $\mathcal{A}$ is often evolving during the process of requirements engineering.

- $\mathcal{M}$, the model, i.e., the set of all statements explicitly or implicitly made in the model. At an early point of requirements engineering there may be one model for each participant, but usually fewer models which are the joint models of organizational actors exists. For each participant, the part of the model which is considered relevant for the actor can be seen as a projection of the total model, hence $\mathcal{M}$ can be divided into projections $\mathcal{M}^1,...,\mathcal{M}^k$ corresponding to the involved participants $A_1,...,A_k$. Generally, these projections will not be disjoint, but their union cover $\mathcal{M}$. The complete model will be evolving during the process of requirements engineering.

- $\mathcal{L}$, the language, i.e., the set of all statements that are possible to make according to the vocabulary and grammar of the modelling languages used. Several languages can be in use at the same time, corresponding to the sets $\mathcal{L}_1,...,\mathcal{L}_j$. A sub-language is related to the complete language by limitations on the vocabulary or on the set of allowed grammar rules or both.

  The set $\mathcal{L}$ can be divided into several subsets, e.g., $\mathcal{L}_I$, $\mathcal{L}_S$, and $\mathcal{L}_F$ for the informal, semi-formal and formal parts of the language, respectively. A language with formal syntax is termed semi-formal, whereas a language which also has formal semantics, is termed formal. Note that this does not imply that the language has a semantics based on formal logic.

- $\mathcal{D}$, the domain, i.e., the set of all statements which would be correct and relevant about the problem at hand. $\mathcal{D}$ denotes the ideal knowledge about the problem. The domain evolves during the requirements engineering process.

- $\mathcal{I}$, the audience interpretation, i.e., the set of all statements which the audience thinks that a model consists of. Various parts of the model will be of interest to various participants. Just like the model is projected into $calM^1,...,\mathcal{M}_k$ above, its interpretation can be projected into $\mathcal{I}_1,...,\mathcal{I}_k$ according to the interests of the participants.

- $\mathcal{K}$, the knowledge of the participants, i.e., the union of the sets of statements $\mathcal{K}_1,\ldots,\mathcal{K}_k$, one for each individual social actor in the audience. The set $\mathcal{K}_i$ contains all possible statements that would be correct and relevant for addressing the problem at hand according to the knowledge of the actor A_i. $\mathcal{K}_i$ is a subset of the explicit internal reality of the social actor $\mathcal{K}^i$. $\mathcal{K}^i$ is also evolving during requirements engineering. $\mathcal{M}_i$ is an externalisation of $\mathcal{K}_i$ and is a model made on the basis of the knowledge of the individual actor. Even if the internal reality of each individual will always differ to a certain degree, the explicit internal reality concerning a constrained area might be equal, especially within groups of social actors [9, 19].

With this new framework in place, we have an increased potential for discussing specification quality. The primary goal for semantic quality is a correspondence between the model and the domain, but this correspondence can neither be established nor checked directly: to build the model, one has to go through the audience's knowledge of the domain, and to check the model one has to compare this with the audience's interpretation of the model. Hence, what we do observe at quality control is not the actual semantic quality of the model, but a perceived semantic quality based on comparison of the two imperfect interpretations.

Syntactic quality Syntactic quality is the correspondence between the specification and the language. The goal is syntactic correctness, $\mathcal{M} \setminus \mathcal{L} = \emptyset$, or for a given externalization, $\mathcal{M}_i \setminus \mathcal{L} = \emptyset$. Typical means to ensure syntactic quality is *formal syntax*, i.e., that the language is parsable by a technical actor in the audience, and the modeling activity to perform this is termed syntax checking.

Semantic quality For the semantic quality of the complete model $\mathcal{M}$, no major changes are necessary to the previous version of the framework. [17] defines two goals, feasible validity and feasible completeness.

Discussing perceived semantic quality, we get the following:

- *Perceived validity* of the model projection: $\mathcal{I}_i \setminus \mathcal{K}_i = \emptyset$.
- *Perceived completeness* of the model projection: $\mathcal{K}_i \setminus \mathcal{I}_i = \emptyset$.

The perceived semantic quality can change, for better or for worse, either as a result of changes in (the understanding of) the model, or as a result of changes in the knowledge about the domain. Notice that one way the knowledge of the actor can change, is through the internalization of another sub-model. Internalisation can be expressed crudely as a mapping between the sets of statements, being part of the explicit internal reality of an actor.

$$INT : \mathcal{K}_i \rightarrow (\mathcal{K}_i \cup \mathcal{N}) \subset \mathcal{M}_j \setminus (\mathcal{O} \subset \mathcal{K}_i) \quad (1)$$

$i \neq j, \mathcal{O} \cap \mathcal{N} = \emptyset, \mathcal{K}_i \setminus \mathcal{N} = \mathcal{K}_i$

$\mathcal{N}$ and $\mathcal{O}$ above is sets of statements. $\mathcal{O}$ might be empty giving a monotonous growth of $\mathcal{K}_i$. If $\mathcal{O}$ is not empty there is a non-monotonous growth of $\mathcal{K}_i$.

Pragmatic quality Pragmatic quality can be defined largely the same way as before, the goal being comprehension, i.e. that the model is understood, not its understandability. [17] also defined this on behalf of various participant groups, since each such group will usually only be interested in a part of the model. Similarly, we can define individual comprehension: $\mathcal{I}_i = \mathcal{M}^i$, as the goal that the participant A_i understands the relevant part of the model.

For total comprehension, one must thus have $(\forall i, i \in [1...k])\ \mathcal{I}_i = \mathcal{M}^i$, i.e., that every participant understands the relevant part of $\mathcal{M}$.

Total comprehension is also an unrealistic goal. Hence it is interesting to define feasible comprehension as the situation where comprehension can still be improved, but the drawbacks of doing this exceeds the benefits. This has been done in [17].

That a model is understood from the technical actor's point of view, means that $(\forall i, i \in [n+1...m])\mathcal{I}_i = \mathcal{M}^i$, thus all statements that are relevant to the technical actor to be able to perform code generation, simulation, etc. is comprehended by this actor. In this sense, formality can be looked upon as being a pragmatic goal, formal syntax and formal semantics are means for achieving pragmatic quality. This illustrates that pragmatic quality is dependant on the different actors. This also applies to social actors. Whereas some individuals from the outset are used to formal languages, and a formal specification in fact will be best for them also for comprehension (regardless of execution etc.), other individuals will find a mix of formal and informal statements to be more comprehensive, even if the set of statements in the model is in fact redundant.

Some of the means to achieve pragmatic quality have been identified earlier, namely formality, executability, expressive economy and aesthetics. The corresponding modelling activities are inspection, visualization, filtering, diagram layout, paraphrasing, explanation, execution, animation, and simulation. Another important activity is training the participants in the syntax and semantics of the modelling languages used.

Social quality Inspired by Pohl, we set up the goal for social quality as *agreement.* However, this is not straightforward to define. Four kinds of agreement can be identified, according distinctions along two orthogonal dimensions:

- agreement in knowledge vs. agreement in model interpretation.
- relative agreement vs. absolute agreement

Agreement in model interpretation will usually be a more limited demand than agreement in knowledge, since the former one means that the actors agree about what (they think) is stated in the model, whereas there may still be many issues they disagree about which have not been stated in the model so far, even if it might be regarded as relevant for one of the actors.

Relative agreement means that the various projections are consistent — hence, there may be many statements in the projection of one actor that are not present in that of another, as long as they do not contradict each other. Absolute agreement, on the other hand, means that all projections are the same.

Since different participants often have their expertise in different fields, relative agreement is a more useful concept than absolute agreement. On the other hand, the different actors must have the *possibility* to agree on something, i.e. the parts of the model which are relevant to them have to overlap to some extent.

However, it is not given that all participants will come to agreement. Few decisions are taken in society under complete agreement, and those that are are not necessarily good, due to e.g group-think. To answer this we introduce *feasible agreement*:

Feasible agreement: A situation of feasible comprehension where inconsistencies between statements in the different $\mathcal{I}_i$ are resolved by choosing one of the alternatives when the benefits of doing this is less than the drawbacks of working out agreement.

The pragmatic goal of comprehension is looked upon as a social mean. This because agreement without comprehension is not very useful, at least not when having democratic ideals. Obviously if someone is trying to manipulate a situation, agreement without comprehension is useful. The area of *model monopoly* [3] is related to this.

Some activities for achieving feasible agreement are:

- Viewpoint analysis [15]: This includes techniques for comparing two or more models and find the discrepancies.
- Conflict resolution: Specific techniques for this can be found in the area of computer supported cooperative work, see [4, 11] where argumentation systems are presented.
- Model merging: Merging two potentially inconsistent models into one consistent one.

The above activities can be done either manually, semi-automatically or automatically, for semi-automatic or automatic support, formal syntax and semantics are again useful. In addition is it useful to be able to represent inconcistency and disagreement directly in the model, and not only have to compare separate models.

4 Concluding Remarks

This paper has reviewed and compared two recent frameworks for disussing quality of requirement specifications: the framework of Lindland et al. in [17] and Pohl's framework in [20]. The comparision has shown that the frameworks have different appearences and uses different terminology, but the deeper structures of the frameworks are quite similar.

The main objective of the paper has been to push our understanding of quality aspects in requirements engineering one step further. The comparison of the two frameworks has been useful in that respect. In particular, the concept of agreement in Pohl's framework has inspired us to look deeper into the social process of building a specification.

In contrast to the previous version of the framework of Lindland et al. we are now able to discuss the quality of models where different social actors are developing their submodels based on individual domain knowledge. Furthermore, the process of merging different viewpoints is defined as contributing to social quality. Here, agreement among the actors is the major goal.

Table 1 shows an overview of the goals and means of the extended framework. The overview is based on a similar one in [17], but has been extended as discussed above.

Quality types	*Goals*	*Means*	
		Model properties	Activities
Syntactic q.	Synt. correctness	Formal syntax	Syntax checking
Semantic q.	Feasible validity Feasible compl.	Formal semantics Modifiability	Consistency checking Statement insertion Statement deletion
Perceived sem.q.	Perceived validity Perceived compl.		Statement insertion Statement deletion Audience training
Pragmatic q.	Feasible compr.	Expressive economy Aesthetics	Inspection Visualization Filtering Diagram layout Paraphrasing Explanation Audience training
		Executability	Execution Animation Simulation
Social q.	Feasible agreement	Conflict modelling	Viewpoint analysis Conflict resolution Model merging

Table 1.: Framework for model quality

Although the framework contributes to our understanding of quality issues with respect to requirement engineering, the contribution so far lies on a high level of abstraction. There are several interesting paths for further work by which the framework can be refined to become more directly useful for requirements engineering practitioners. Among others, the follow areas need further exploration:

- *development of further product metrics:* In the current framework quality goals are mainly defined as the degree of correspondence between various sets. Future work should concentrate on developing quantitative metrics so that the quality of the model, audience, and the domain knowledge can be more explicitly assessed. Some initial efforts in this direction are reported in [13].
- *development of process guidelines:* The framework gives an overview of decisions that will have to be made in the requirements engineering phase. Further work should result in guidelines that practitioners may use directly in concrete projects.

Since semantic, pragmatic and social quality are in practice immeasurable, process heuristics may be a more interesting issue to pursue than product metrics.

References

1. P. Berger and T. Luckmann. *The Social Construction of Reality: A Treatise in the Sociology of Knowledge.* Penguin, 1966.
2. B. W. Boehm. Verifying and validating software requirements and design specifications. *IEEE Software*, 1:75–88, 1984.
3. S. Bråten. *Dialogens vilkår i datasamfunnet (In Norwegian).* Universitetsforlaget, 1983.
4. J. Conklin and M. J. Begeman. gIBIS: A hypertext tool for exploratory policy discussion. *ACM Transactions on Office Information Systems*, 6(4):303–331, 1988.
5. B. Dahlbom. The idea that reality is socialy constructed. In Floyd et al. [8], pages 101–126.
6. A. M. Davis. *Software Requirements Analysis & Specification.* Prentice-Hall, 1990.
7. N. E. Fenton, editor. *Software Metrics — A Rigorous Approach.* Chapman & Hall, 1991.
8. C. Floyd, H. Züllighoven, R. Budde, and R. Keil-Slawik, editors. *Software Development and Reality Construction.* Springer Verlag, 1991.
9. R. Gjersvik. *The Construction of Information Systems in Organization: An Action Research Project on Technology, Organizational Closure, Reflection, and Change.* PhD thesis, ORAL, NTH, Trondheim, Norway, 1993.
10. J. Goguen. Requirements engineering: Reconciliation of technical and social issues. Technical report, Centre for Requirementss and Foundations, Oxford University, Cambridge, England, 1992.
11. U. Hahn, M. Jarke, and T. Rose. Group work in software projects: Integrated conceptual models and collaboration tools. In S. Gibbs and A. A. Verrijn-Stuart, editors, *Multi-User Interfaces and Applications: Proceedings of the IFIP WG 8.4 Conference on Multi-User Interfaces and Applications*, pages 83–102. North-Holland, 1990.

12. M. Jarke, J. Bubenko, C. Rolland, A. Sutcliffe, and Y. Vassiliou. Theories underlying requirements engineering: An overview of NATURE at genesis. In *Proceedings of the IEEE International Symposium on Requirements Engineering (RE'93)*, pages 19–31, 1993.
13. J. Krogstie, O. I. Lindland, and G. Sindre. Defining quality aspects for conceptual models. In E. D. Falkenberg et al., editor, *Information Systems Concepts, Proc. ISCO3, Marburg, Germany*. North-Holland, 1995.
14. C. H. Kung. An analysis of three conceptual models with time perspective. In Olle et al., editor, *Information Systems Design Methodologies: A Feature Analysis*, pages 141–168. North-Holland, 1983.
15. J. C. S. P. Leite and P. A. Freeman. Requirements validation through viewpoint resolution. *IEEE Transactions on Software Engineering*, 17(12):1253–1269, December 1991.
16. P. Lindgren ed. A framework of information systems concepts. Technical Report Interrim report, FRISCO, May 1990.
17. O. I. Lindland, G. Sindre, and A. Sølvberg. Understanding quality in conceptual modelling. *IEEE Software*, pages 42–49, April 1994.
18. J. D. McGregor and T. D.. Korson. Integrated object-oriented testing and development processes. *Communications of the ACM*, 37(9), 1994.
19. J. W. Orlikowski and D. C. Gash. Technological frames: Making sense of information technology in organizations. *ACM Transactions on Information Systems*, 12(2):174–207, 1994.
20. K. Pohl. The three dimensions of requirements engineering: A framework and its applications. *Information Systems*, 19(3):243–258, April 1994.
21. H. Rittel. On the planning crisis: Systems analysis of the first and second generations. *Bedriftsøkonomen*, (8), 1972.
22. G. C. Roman. A taxonomy of current issues in requirements engineering. *IEEE Computer*, pages 14–22, April 1985.
23. A. H. Seltveit. An abstraction-based rule approach to large-scale information systems development. In C. Rolland, F. Bodart, and C. Cauvet, editors, *Proceedings of the 5th International Conference on Advanced Information Systems Engineering (CAiSE'93)*, pages 328–351, Paris, France, June 8-11 1993. Springer Verlag.
24. J. Siddiqi. Challenging universal truths of requirements engineering. *IEEE Software*, pages 18–19, March 1994.
25. R. T. Yeh, P. Zave, A. P. Conn, and G. E. Cole Jr. Software requirements: New directions and perspectives. In C. Vick and C. Ramamoorthy, editors, *Handbook of Software Engineering*, pages 519–543. Van Nostrand Reinhold, 1984.

20 Years of Quality of Models

John Krogstie, Guttorm Sindre, and Odd Ivar Lindland

Abstract We are very pleased that our CAiSE'95 paper has been selected to be included in the Springer book that celebrates the 25th anniversary of the CAiSE conferences series. This paper entitled '*Towards a Deeper Understanding of Quality in Requirements Engineering*' presented a development of work started some years earlier in the research group of Arne Sølvberg on the topic of quality of models. This topic has been of interest during the next 20 years by us and a number of other researchers both in the context of IS development and in other areas, and will in our view be a relevant topic for the foreseeable future.

1 Background for the Original Model

Work in our group on quality of models can be traced back to at least 1992. The first manifestation of this work was in the PhD-thesis of Odd Ivar Lindland in 1993 [8]. In one particular group meeting, Odd Ivar described his early ideas on quality of models, and how to differentiate goals and means and relating modelling languages, domain, and actors. Jon Atle Gulla and Guttorm Sindre, also having degrees in linguistics, suggested that he should look at the differentiation between syntax, semantics, and pragmatics found in linguistics and semiotics, which have been a cornerstone in our thinking about quality of models from the start. Guttorm Sindre and Odd Ivar Lindland in particular collaborated on the next step, which ended up in a widely cited article [9] as one of the best papers of the ICRE conference in 1994 being selected to a special issue in IEEE Software.

J. Krogstie (✉) • G. Sindre
IDI, NTNU, Trondheim, Norway
e-mail: krogstie@idi.ntnu.no

O.I. Lindland
Price Waterhouse Coopers, Trondheim, Norway

J. Bubenko et al. (eds.), *Seminal Contributions to Information Systems Engineering*, DOI 10.1007/978-3-642-36926-1_8, © Springer-Verlag Berlin Heidelberg 2013

Although a very elegant framework which was easily applicable for understanding important aspects of quality of models, several other works pointed to the need for extending the framework. Important inspirations in this regard was the three dimensions of RE [14] (also represented and commented in this volume), and the work related to the semiotic ladder presented in early versions of the IFIP 8.1 FRISCO framework [7] and work on social construction of 'reality' (and models thereof) constituting the domain, which is typically not as ideal and objectively given in practice that as the original framework worked with. Specifically the framework of Pohl also pointed to the need for agreement between the stakeholders of the model.

These extension, in addition to a specific focus on requirements specification models resulted in the framework presented in the CAiSE 1995-article, the main addition being the description of perceived semantic quality and social quality.

2 Later Developments

There was not only us working with quality of models and modelling languages in the mid-90s. For instance Moody and Shanks and Moody [10] worked in particular on quality of data models. Becker, Rosemann and Schütte [1] focused on the quality of process models. For us (and the framework later named SEQUAL) on the other hand, the story could have ended here. John Krogstie delivered his PhD-thesis in 1995 and started working in Andersen Consulting; Guttorm Sindre took some years off pursuing a career as a fictional writer, whereas Odd Ivar Lindland had already joined IBM. Both John and Guttorm though kept in contact with academia, and drifted back to more academic positions towards the end of the 90s, taking up work on quality of models.

In hindsight the work done on SEQUAL can be framed as design science research, with the quality framework as the main artefact. Whereas the early validation was primarily analytical, later work e.g. together with Moody [11] has also extended the evaluation with empirical techniques. The framework has been developed through a number of iterations, and has also in some cases been established as part of the knowledge base e.g. in the development of a framework for quality of maps [13]. The current version of the framework is described in [2] where also newer work on language quality is included. The framework has been used for evaluation of modelling and modelling languages of a large number of perspectives, including data [6], process [3, 15], enterprise [5], and goal-oriented [4] approaches. It has been used both for models on the type level and instance level (i.e. data quality [12]). The current framework is illustrated in Fig. 1. Quality has been defined referring to the correspondence between statements belonging to the following sets:

- ***G,*** the set of goals of the modelling task.
- ***L,*** the language extension, i.e., the set of all statements that are possible to make according to the rules of the modelling languages used.

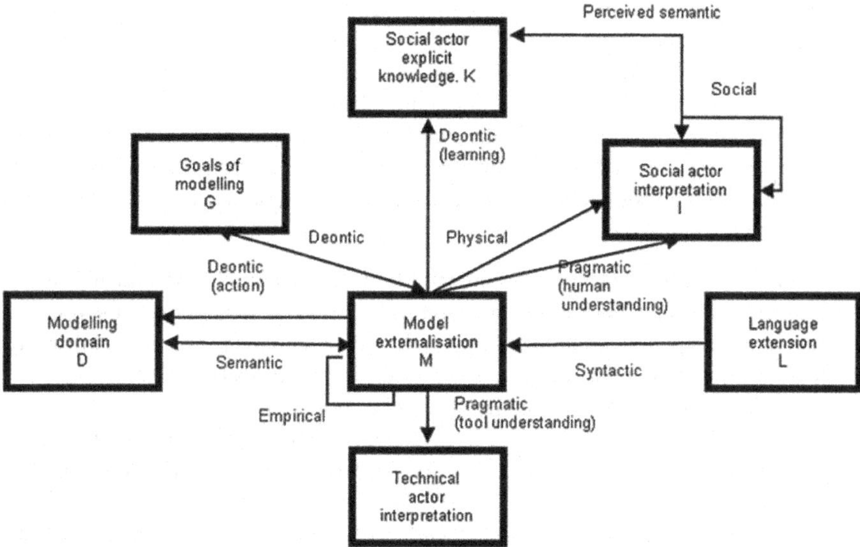

Fig. 1 SEQUAL framework for discussing quality of models

- ***D***, the domain, i.e., the set of all statements that can be stated about the situation.
- ***M***, the externalized model itself.
- ***K***, the explicit knowledge relevant to the domain of the audience.
- ***I***, the social actor interpretation, i.e., the set of all statements that the audience interprets that an externalized model consists of.
- ***T***, the technical actor interpretation, i.e., the statements in the model as 'interpreted' by modelling tools.

The main quality types are:

1. Physical quality: The basic quality goal is that the externalized model ***M*** is available to the relevant actors.
2. Empirical quality deals with comprehension when a visual model ***M*** is read by different social actors. Before evaluating empirical quality, physical quality should be addressed.
3. Syntactic quality is the correspondence between the model ***M*** and the language extension ***L***. Before evaluating syntactic quality, physical quality should be addressed.
4. Semantic quality is the correspondence between the model ***M*** and the domain ***D***. This includes both validity and completeness. Before evaluating semantic quality, syntactic quality should be addressed. Domains can be divided into two parts, exemplified with a software requirements model:
   - Everything the computerized information system (CIS) is supposed to do (for the moment ignoring the different views the stakeholders have on the CIS to be produced).

- Constraints on the model because of earlier baselined models such as system level requirements specifications, enterprise architecture models, statements of work, and earlier versions of the requirement specification to which the new requirement specification model must be compatible.
- Perceived semantic quality is the similar correspondence between the social actor interpretation ***I*** of a model ***M*** and his or hers current knowledge ***K*** of domain ***D***. Before evaluating perceived semantic quality, pragmatic quality should be addressed.

5. Pragmatic quality is the correspondence between the model ***M*** and the actor interpretation (***I*** and ***T***) of it. One differentiates between social pragmatic quality (to what extent people understand the model) and technical pragmatic quality (to what extent tools can be made that can interpret the model). Before evaluating pragmatic quality, empirical quality should be addressed.
6. The goal defined for social quality is agreement among social actor's interpretations (***I***). Before evaluating social quality, perceived semantic quality should be addressed.
7. The deontic quality of the model relates to that all statements in the model ***M*** contribute to fulfilling the goals of modelling ***G***, and that all the goals of modelling ***G*** are addressed through the model ***M***. In particular, one often includes under deontic quality the extent that the participants after interpreting the model learn based on the model (increase ***K***) and that the audience are able to change the domain ***D*** if this is beneficially to achieve the goals of modelling (if the model is prescriptive).

3 Future Directions

More and more modelling methodologies take an active approach to the exploitation of models. In approaches such as Business Process Management (BPM), Model Driven Architecture (MDA), and Domain specific modelling/domain specific modelling languages (DSM/DSL), Enterprise Architecture (EA), and Active Knowledge Modelling (AKM), the models are used directly to form the information system of the organisation. At the same time, similar techniques are used also for sense-making and communication, simulation, quality assurance and requirements specification in connection to more traditional forms of information systems development. Thus we expect the need to judge the quality of models will retain. Although much work has been done on thinking relative to quality of models and modelling languages over the last years, there is still room for developments. Whereas main parts of the framework are supported by empirical evidence some of the later developments should be worked on further. Even if more guidelines for modelling is produced [2, 12], having these put into use in methodologies and tools in an appropriate way are also open for further research and practical exploitation in future model-based development and evolution of information systems such as reported in [16].

References

1. Becker, J., Rosemann, M., Schütte, R.: Guidelines of Modelling (GoM). Wirtschaftsinformatik 37 (1995) 5, 435–445 (in German)
2. Krogstie, J.: Model-based Development and Evolution of Information Systems: A Quality Approach, Springer (2012)
3. Krogstie, J.: Quality of Business Process Models. Proceedings PoEM (2012)
4. Krogstie, J.: Integrated Goal, Data and Process modeling: From TEMPORA to Model-Generated Work-Places. In: Johannesson P, Søderstrøm E (eds) Information Systems Engineering From Data Analysis to Process Networks. IGI, pp 43–65 (2008)
5. Krogstie, J., Arnesen, S.: Assessing Enterprise Modeling Languages using a Generic Quality Framework. In: Krogstie J, Siau K, Halpin T (eds) Information Modeling Methods and Methodologies. Idea Group Publishing (2004)
6. Krogstie, J.: Quality of conceptual data models. Accepted for ICISO 2013 March (2013)
7. Lindgren, P. (ed): A framework for information systems concepts. Interrim report FRISCO (1990)
8. Lindland, O.I.: A Prototyping Approach to Validation of Conceptual Models in Information Systems Engineering. PhD Thesis IDT, NTH (1993)
9. Lindland, O.I., Sindre G. and Sølvberg, A. Understanding Quality in Conceptual Modeling. IEEE Software March (1994)
10. Moody, D. L., Shanks, G. G.: What Makes a Good Data Model? Evaluating the Quality of Entity Relationship Models. In: Proceedings of the 13th International Conference on the Entity-Relationship Approach (ER'94), pages 94–111, Manchester, England (1994)
11. Moody, D.L., Sindre, G., Brasethvik,T. and Sølvberg, A.: Evaluating the Quality of Process Models: Empirical Testing of a Quality Framework. In S. Spaccapietra, S.T. March, and Y. Kambayashi (Eds.): ER 2002, LNCS 2503, pp. 214–231, (2002)
12. Nelson, H.J., Poels, G, Genero M, Piattini, M.: A conceptual modeling quality framework. Software Quality Journal (2011)
13. Nossum, A., Krogstie, J.: Integrated Quality of Models and Quality of Maps. Paper presented at the EMMSAD (2009)
14. Pohl, K.: The Three Dimensions of Requirements Engineering. In: Proceedings of CAiSE'93, Springer, LNCS 685 (1993)
15. Recker, J., Rosemann, M., Krogstie J.: Ontology- versus pattern-based evaluation of process modeling language: A comparison. CAIS 20:774–799 (2007)
16. Wesenberg, H.: Enterprise Modeling in an Agile World. Proceedings of the 4th conference on Practice of Enterprise Modeling, Oslo, Norway, November 2–3 (2011)

From: CAiSE 1996, LNCS 1080 © Springer-Verlag Berlin Heidelberg 1996

MetaEdit+
A Fully Configurable Multi-User and Multi-Tool CASE and CAME Environment

Steven Kelly, Kalle Lyytinen
Matti Rossi
Department of Computer Science and Information Systems
University of Jyväskylä
PL 35
FIN-40351 Jyväskylä
Finland
email: stevek@hyeena.jyu.fi
fax: +358 41 603011

Abstract: Computer Aided Software Engineering (CASE) environments have spread at a lower pace than expected. One reason for this is the immaturity of existing environments in supporting development in-the-large and by-many and their inability to address the varying needs of the software developers. In this paper we report on the development of a next generation CASE environment called MetaEdit+. The environment seeks to overcome all the above deficiencies, but in particular pays attention to catering for the varying needs of the software developers. MetaEdit+ is a multi-method, multi-tool platform for both CASE and Computer Aided Method Engineering (CAME). As a CASE tool it establishes a versatile and powerful multi-tool environment which enables flexible creation, maintenance, manipulation, retrieval and representation of design information among multiple developers. As a CAME environment it offers an easy-to-use yet powerful environment for method specification, integration, management and re-use. The paper explains the motivation for developing MetaEdit+, its design goals and philosophy and discusses the functionality of the CAME tools.

Keywords: CASE, CAME, method, software engineering environments, repository, metamodeling, conceptual modeling, object oriented modeling, tool interoperability, tool integration

1. Introduction

CASE (Computer Aided Systems Engineering) environments have been one of the major technological innovations in systems development during the last decade. Many have claimed that CASE technology will solve the information systems (IS) development problems (Cha86, McC89) that have plagued the community for so long. These include, among others, mediocre productivity (e.g. unrealistic time schedules and cost overruns), and insufficient quality (e.g. low product validity and lack of verifiability) (Bro75, Cha86, Ost87). CASE technologies are expected to provide task related support for software developers in analyzing, designing and implementing a set of information systems (IS) or their components according to a *method.* A method can be defined as a language (vocabulary and grammatical composition rules) which can be used to represent features of the information system to a number of actors (including technical actors such as specific abstract machines like a Smalltalk machine) and a set of rules which define by whom, when, and how such representations are derived and/or used.

The origins of CASE date back to the mid 70's when such well-known software tools as PSL/PSA (Tei77) and SREM (Alf77) were launched. Despite this early start, the breakthrough of these technologies has only occurred during the 90's. One reason for this is the declining cost of computing technologies and its increasing functionality — especially graphical user interfaces. Another is the increased need for disciplining the art of software development and maintenance through standardized process and product models. Finally there is a continuing need to improve the quality and productivity of software production through investments in capital intensive technologies.

In spite of these developments the rate of adopting CASE has been laggard, and the success of adoptions doubtful (Wij90, Aae91). One reason for this is software organizations' lack of the necessary maturity to adopt highly sophisticated technologies such as CASE. Another is the cost of adopting, using and maintaining the technological infrastructure and associated know-how. The third reason is the inadequate technological sophistication of CASE. Most tools in use are stand alone tools that support creation and maintenance of graphical models and can generate code to limited problem domains. Accordingly technologies have not matured for software development in the large and by many. The major deficiencies are thus: insufficient support in integrating methods, inadequate support for alternative representation paradigms, lack of mechanisms to cater for multiple users, rigid method and process support, and focus on task automation (Hen90).

In this paper we report on the development and use experiences of a prototype next generation CASE tool, MetaEdit+. The environment seeks to overcome all the above deficiencies, but pays particular attention to the requirements concerning flexibility, method integration and representational richness. In line with this MetaEdit+ is a multi-method, multi-user, multi-tool platform for both computer aided software engineering (CASE) and computer aided method engineering (CAME). As a CASE tool it establishes a versatile environment for flexible creation, maintenance, manipulation, retrieval and representation of design objects (information) structured and created according to a method. As a CAME tool it provides a flexible and easy-to-use environment for method specification, management, integration and re-use. This paper will explain the motivations for developing MetaEdit+, its design goals and philosophy, its design architecture, its current tool set, and its future development.

2. Related Research

Weaknesses in current CASE tool support can be divided into the following aspects:

1. lack of mechanisms for integrating sets of methods while maintaining consistency between various models (Kel95, Mar95, Kel94a)

2. lack of support for multiple users to create, modify and delete sets of partly overlapping model instances,

3. inadequate catering for multiple representational requirements ranging from fully diagrammatic to fully textual or matrix representations. These are dictated by different method families (Mar95),

4. failure to provide consistent mapping mechanisms between different representational paradigms (Kel95, Mar95),

5. lack of flexibility and evolvability in method support ranging from syntactic variation in methods to crafting totally new method components (Lyy89), and

6. insufficient catering for different information-related needs of a diverse set of stakeholders (Mar95).

2.1 Lack of Method Integration Mechanisms

Several mechanisms are available for method integration or interaction. At the most rudimentary level these deal with mechanisms that enable translations from one representation format to another. Attempts to develop such CASE "EDI" solutions abound, e.g. CDIF (CDI91). Their weakness is that they do not support any inter-model consistency checking, semantic validation and tool interoperability. Accordingly, they can only be used in static model transfer from one environment to another. A more advanced approach has been to develop generic and universal method specification schemata. This "super-schema" would provide a common and universal semantic model onto which all methods used in the environments could be mapped. This can be done directly as in the A/D Cycle information model (Mer90), or through method reference models (Hey92) where the mapping takes place through a reference model. An early solution of this kind was the mapping of system development methods into generic modeling constructs of PSL/PSA (Tei77). The limitation of this approach is its closed nature of method integration which cannot tolerate any flexibility in the mappings. Moreover, it cannot cater for future evolution in the method arena. Finally, it can only support a limited number of method integration solutions which deal solely with object sharing and associated consistency checks.

2.2 Insufficient Multi-User Support

A large body of literature exists on concurrency control and alternative strategies to deal with multiple user operations in software engineering repositories (for a review see Bro91). A number of strategies have emerged recently for achieving varying levels of optimistic concurrency control (Kat84). Despite these advances it is still not known which granularity levels are appropriate for effective concurrency, what are suitable transaction notions, and how much locking and what types of locks are needed. Moreover, it is not clear how much transaction management should be left to users' awareness of others' operations. In this respect, most commercial CASE environments provide solutions that are too crude or inefficient, while advanced mechanisms suggested by researchers can be computationally too demanding (e.g. use of work spaces and merge strategies) or cannot be adapted to the existing CASE architectures. Moreover, a big unsettled issue is how well semantics-driven and dedicated locking strategies operate in such environments and whether we should cater for differences between conceptual and representational objects, or between the different tools that operate on the design data (Kel94a).

2.3 Insufficient Support for Multiple Representation Paradigms

Whilst today's methods contain various representation paradigms — graphical diagrams, matrices, tables, etc. — most existing CASE tools operate on only one: graphical diagrams. If other representation forms are needed they are generated by some user triggered operations such as generating a report. Because of this, CASE tools do not offer the *representation independence* that could make them fully adaptable to differing representation demands. Thus most CASE tools offer only limited syntactic and graphical modifiability in supported methods. Another weakness is the lack of hypertext support for semi-structured and non-structured linking of design objects in different representation formats or model parts. Either the available functionality provides hypertext features *as* the CASE environment (Cyb92), or the support functionality is limited to some model areas (Poh94) or to user interface and user support (Oin93).

2.4 Lack of Method Modifiability and Evolution

The importance of CAME in CASE has been noticed in several studies (Kum92, Che88, Bri90, Wij91, Hey93, Ste93). To this end CASE shells — metaCASE tools, or fully customizable CASE environments — have been developed. Such environments are expected to overcome the inflexibility of method support. According to Bubenko (Bub88) "a CASE shell includes mechanisms to define a CASE tool for an arbitrary technique or a chain of techniques". Yet, metaCASE technology has not yet matured sufficiently to provide adequate method modifiability though the number of CASE products leveraging method modification facilities is increasing. Commercial products offering such features include *Customizer*™ (Ind87), *VSF* (Poc91), *MetaEdit*™ (Smo91a) and *Paradigm+* (Pro94). Research versions of CASE shells include *RAMATIC* (Ber89), *ConceptBase* (Hah91) and *MetaView* (Sor88). Integration of CASE shells and their CASE environments comes in various kinds. A CASE shell can be a separate tool that produces a methodology specification which the CASE environment uses (e.g. *Customizer*), or it can be an integral part of the CASE environment (e.g. *RAMATIC*). *MetaEdit* ™ was one of the first that offered CAME and CASE functionality within the same tool. In MetaEdit methods are specified graphically (Smo91b) and these specifications are converted into a textual form, before compiling and loading the complete method specification into a CASE environment. All these have been steps in the right direction. However, environments that can offer powerful and easy to use modification facilities, method component libraries, method re-use and run-time adaptability are still largely non-existent.

2.5 Lack of Information Retrieval and Computational Facilities

One problem in current CASE tools is their limited information retrieval and reporting capability. Some general and computationally powerful solutions exist in environments that apply a logic programming paradigm (such as ConceptBASE (Hah91)). Though sufficient in their expressive power and generality the use of such query functions is limited by their computational complexity and insufficient user-friendliness. This is due to the lack of data base schema representations and user friendly query formulation. Another problem is that all existing query systems center around retrieving and representing textual information while most of the design information is input and viewed in a graphical format. Finally, few environments provide a means to browse through the repository via hypertext links or various browsing mechanisms.

2.6 Summary

The record of CASE research in each area demonstrates that most concerns have been addressed during the last decade and considerable progress has been made in rendering CASE environments useful. Yet, what seems to be lacking is a comprehensive approach that seeks to tackle most, if not all of, these weaknesses *simultaneously*. Though this may require some compromises and difficult trade-offs in achieving all these goals (like improving multi-user facilities and method flexibility) our contention is that the real impact of future CASE — in the large and by many — will depend on our capability to offer more comprehensive solutions that address most of these concerns within the same environment. Unless such environments emerge the adoption of CASE will in all likelihood continue to be a frustrating experience.

3. The MetaEdit+ Environment

As a meta-CASE environment MetaEdit+ seeks to address most of the above concerns (2.1–2.5) in a comprehensive manner by offering an environment which is:

- **multi-user**, i.e. several users can operate concurrently on the repository (2.2),
- **multi-tool**, i.e. each user can operate several tools simultaneously where each tool provides a different view to the same object (2.3, 2.5),
- **multi-method**, i.e. the environment offers several mechanisms for method integration and consistency checking (2.1),
- **multi-form**, i.e. the environment provides several representation formats for the same design object (2.3), and
- **multi-level**, i.e. the environment is a true metaCASE environment in that both an IS and its design methods can be engineered within the same environment (2.4).

The environment seeks to improve the usability (by multiple users, forms, methods and tools), flexibility (by offering a multi-tool, multi-method approach), and open nature of CASE (i.e. by enabling evolution and plugging of new tools through well defined service protocols). The design goal of the environment has been to base its architecture in principles of *conceptual modeling, layered data base architectures,* and *object orientation.* In this respect, the approach differs to some extent from other metaCASE approaches which focus more on the representation of methods as first order logical theories (Hah91), or on the graphical behavior of design objects (Ber89). From the viewpoint of conceptual modeling the design of a method specification is akin to the development of a conceptual schema for a software repository, and the design of a software tool resembles a design of an external view to a conceptual schema (ANS75). Hence, the method specification language is at the same time the conceptual modeling language for the repository schema, or forms the meta-metamodel level in the IRDS standard (ISO89). The adoption of full object orientation enables flexible organization and re-use of software components in the environment and a high level of interoperability between tools. This is achieved through both data integration (via shared conceptual schemata) and control integration (via object organization) thus making the environment fairly open.

Our motivation in using conceptual modeling and object orientation in the design of MetaEdit+ has suggested three principles for the design: *data independence, representation independence,* and *level independence. Data independence* is defined in a similar way as in traditional data base theory i.e. tools operate on design information without "knowledge" of its physical organization, or logical access structure. *Representation independence* forms a continuum with data independence and it allows conceptual design objects to exist independently of their alternative representations as text, matrix or graphical representations. This principle allows flexible addition of new tools, each one only responsible for its own paradigmatically different view on the same underlying data. *Level independence* means that the environment follows a symmetrical approach in its treatment of data and metadata. Accordingly, the specifications of methods and their behaviors can be managed and manipulated in a similar way to any other object in the environment (therefore the name metaCASE). Moreover, the specifications can be concurrently operated through the same or somewhat specialized tools in the environment.

3.1 General Architecture

The functional architecture of MetaEdit+ is illustrated in Fig. 1. The heart of the environment is the MetaEngine, which handles all operations on the underlying conceptual data through a well-defined service protocol (Smo93a). In other words, the MetaEngine embodies the implementation of the underlying conceptual data model and its operation signature. Accordingly, software tools request services of the MetaEngine in accessing and manipulating repository data. Thereby they avoid the need to duplicate the manipulation code. This design choice allows flexible integration of new tools, each only responsible for its own paradigmatically different view (including operations) on the same underlying repository data. A tool, as the term is used within the MetaEdit+ environment, is a window type with its associated functionality, through which a user can view and possibly alter a design objects in a particular way.

The architecture has similarities with that of the ECMA-PCTE (ECM91) — e.g. common services, separation of components at different levels of integration — but differs from it, most noticeably in the enforcement of no direct communication between components at the same level, or over a common bus between components separated by more than one level: tools communicate only via the MetaEngine.

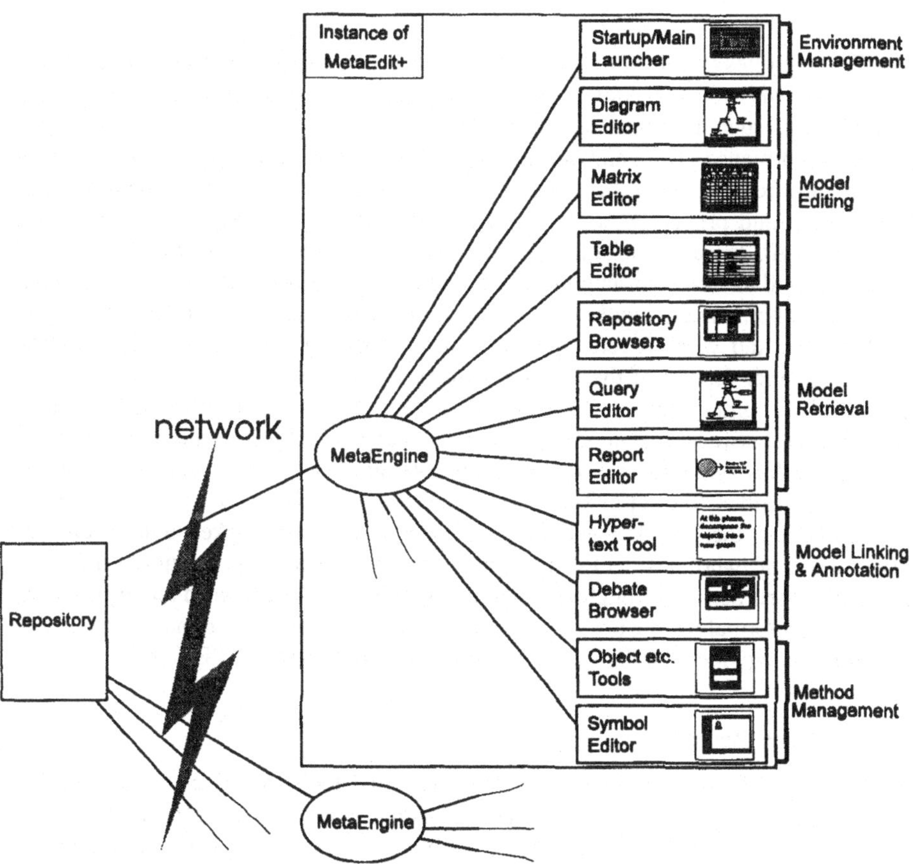

Fig. 1: MetaEdit+ Architecture

MetaEdit+ can run either as a single-user workstation environment, or simultaneously on many workstation clients connected by a network to a server. Each client has a running instance of MetaEdit+, including all its tools and the MetaEngine. The MetaEngine takes care of all issues involved in communicating with the server. Tools communicate with each other only through the MetaEngine, and thereby through the shared data in the repository. Thus the major integration mechanism applied is data integration.

The server forms the software repository holding all the data contained in models, and also in the metamodel(s), in addition to user and locking information. In particular the MetaEdit+ repository includes: *object specification base* containing all the method specifications represented as GOPRR concepts; *symbol specification base* containing all symbols needed to represent Objects, Relationships and Roles; *tool related information base* containing all information needed to represent conceptual objects in different tools (such as spatial coordinates, or size), *user information base* containing all information related to various users such as their passwords, access rights, or current locks held; r*eport specification base* containing all report and other output specifications.

MetaEdit+ applies pessimistic concurrency control in dealing with user and multi-tool interactions with the repository. We have found locks useful despite some of their disadvantages such as stricter user control, interference with users' work, and poorer overall performance. The gains are greater as locks prevent conflicts from occurring between different copies of the repository data, help users to be warned about possible interference, and prevent gaining access to design objects already used in another's transaction. All these are of utmost importance in software repositories. Transactions are understood as long transactions. Their length is defined by a user triggered *commit* operation (automatically requested by the end of the session). The burden of deciding what to lock and when is removed from user's responsibilities and decided by the system. Another feature of the locking strategy is that MetaEdit+ follows more than one level of granularity in locking repository objects. It distinguishes locking granularities between metamodels, graphs, conceptual objects, and representation data. It can thus achieve the following desired features in locking: locks are acquired only when needed, they are well-placed, and are not too small to overburden the system. During their work users can gain information about locked objects and are thus aware of who has locks on which design objects. Accordingly, they can coordinate their actions through negotiating about how locks are freed and transferred. Although no formal testing has been carried out as yet, initial experiences suggest that with this strategy lock conflicts are surprisingly rare in normal CASE work.

3.2 Tool Architecture

In the design of the environment we have classified tools into five distinct families according to their purpose and underlying common functionality. From the viewpoint of conceptual data in the repository each family portrays similar demands in terms of manipulation, locking and retrieval of conceptual design objects, though the different representational paradigms underlying the tools may pose additional demands on retrieval and locking. This has to be dealt with individually in each tool. Each tool family contains one or more tools (Fig. 1). The five tool families are the following:

1. **Environment management tools**: these tools are used to manage features of the environment, its main components and to launch it.
2. **Model editing tools**: these tools are used to create, modify and delete model instances or their parts. In addition, these tools can be used to view the model

instances from different representational viewpoints, and/or to derive new information from existing design information.
3. **Model retrieval tools**: these tools are used for retrieving design objects and their instances from the repository for reuse and review. These tools can operate on both models and metamodels.
4. **Model linking and annotation tools**: these tools are used for linking design objects for traceability and memorization, annotating model instances, finding specific "locations" in the design space, or maintaining conversations about design issues.
5. **Method management tools**: these tools are for method specification, management and retrieval.

4. Conceptual Data Model

Because all method specifications in MetaEdit+ are interpreted as high level conceptual models of method (or methodology) the kernel of the MetaEdit+ functionality and architecture is determined by the underlying conceptual data model called GOPRR. MetaEdit+ uses the GOPRR conceptual data model as a universal and generic meta-metamodel i.e. as a sole language to specify methods. Very little if any method "knowledge" is buried into the code in tools. In addition, GOPRR is primarily intended to model observed, interpreted and recorded development reality *as seen through the methods* (including the world of thought and abstract ideas). In this respect it differs from the ontological IS models (see e.g. Wan93), which attempt to model what actually *is*, rather than just what is perceived and recorded.

4.1 The OPRR Model

Basically, GOPRR (Smo93b) forms an evolutionary extension of the OPRR model which has been successfully used in specifying methods for MetaEdit (Wel92, Smo91b). Whereas the original ER model (Che76) provided only sketchy concepts of attribute: features the object can possess; and of role: the part an object plays in a relationship; the OPRR model has defined these notions in full.

The basic OPRR modeling constructs are:

- Objects, which consist of independent and identifiable design objects. These typically appear as shapes in diagrams, and can have properties such as names. Examples of objects are an Entity in an Entity Relationship Diagram or a Process in a Data Flow Diagram.
- Properties are attributes of objects and can only be accessed as parts of objects or relationships. Properties typically appear as textual labels in diagrams, and they can contain single data entries such as a name, text field or number. An example of a property is the number of a Process in a Data Flow Diagram (Gan79).

- **R**elationships are associations between objects, and can also have properties. Relationships typically appear as lines between shapes in diagrams, or verbs in texts. An example of a relationship is a Data Flow in a Data Flow Diagram.
- **R**oles define the ways in which objects participate in specific relationships. In diagrams roles typically appear as the end points of Relationships (e.g. an arrowhead). Roles too can have properties. An example of a role is the specification by directed arrow which end of a data flow relationship is 'to' and which 'from' part of the flow.

In addition OPRR provides constructs for defining cardinality constraints for relationships (i.e. as properties of relationship meta-objects), and means to determine properties which uniquely identify each object instance. The OPRR model is founded on fixed mapping rules between modeling constructs and their graphical behaviors (Ros92).

OPRR is further designed to be applicable to both the instance (model) and the type (metamodel) levels. Thus an instance object, say a Process '3.1' in a Data Flow Diagram model, has an object type of 'Process' on the metamodel level, while a flow relationship instance 'order info' on the model level is an instance of a relationship type 'Data Flow' on the metamodel level.

4.2 Extensions in the GOPRR Model

GOPRR extends OPRR as a conceptual meta-metamodel in several ways. First, unlike OPRR the GOPRR model allows multiple representations of the same underlying conceptual object (e.g. graphical, matrix, text), and even different graphical representations of the same object in the same representation paradigm. This is achieved by making available mechanisms that can override the default representation. In this sense GOPRR forms a true conceptual "kernel" on which varied representations of data, including not only graphical diagrams but also hypertext, text and matrices, can be built. This allows GOPRR to support a wide range of methodologies including matrix, table or text oriented ones, and gives users the ability to see and manipulate design information in a variety of representations.

Second, the conceptual modeling constructs offered by OPRR have been extended in the GOPRR in several ways which yields a powerful but yet ease-to-use modeling language. These new Graph, object orientation, method integration and rule constructs are described below.

Concept of Graph

The GOPRR model adds the concept of Graph into the modeling constructs. A graph denotes an aggregate concept which contains a certain set of objects and their relationships (with specific roles). Graphs typically appear as windows on whole diagrams which contain objects and their bindings of roles and relationships; a graph also has its own properties. An example of a graph is a whole Data Flow Diagram (as a whole or just one level of it). In use, the Graph concept is fundamentally a generalized decomposition graph: it can be included in a parent graph, attached to an object, role or relationship therein. For instance, in Data Flow Diagrams a top level graph may contain a Process '3', which has a decomposition graph called 'Decomposition of 3', containing Processes '3.1', 3.2' etc. Relationships from '1' and '2' to '3' in the top level graph are actually interface relationships, as we can specify that in the lower-level graph they link to e.g. '3.2' and '3.1' respectively. The interface to the object, and hence to the elements in its decomposition graph, can be shown in the child graph to any degree between 'not at all' and 'show copies of external objects'. The interface is maintained distinct from the elements of the decomposition graph itself, allowing reuse of the decomposition graph in different parent graphs. The interface 'specification' remains the same in all decompositions, but the elements attached to the interface at the higher level can be different in different parent graphs, thus allowing reuse of the graph as a white or black box.

The design of Graph is such that many "representational" graphs can be made for one "conceptual" graph. For instance, a matrix and diagram representation can be made of the same conceptual Data Flow Diagram. In this situation changes in conceptual graphs are propagated between different tools and their "representational" graphs according to their usefulness to the user. Currently, objects added in one graph are immediately available to other graphs, but not automatically added. Changes to properties are made instantly (on transaction commit, if different users are working on different graphs), and additions to or changes of relationships or roles are made instantly in the relationship-oriented Matrix Editor, but buffered in the Diagram Editor, so the user can control their layout when they are added.

The addition of the concept of Graph allows GOPRR to represent multiple methods, and multiple models, whilst still maintaining the contents of each as a coherent distinguishable whole. In this way graph enables modeling and representation of recursive structures such as decompositions, or complex objects as often found in development methods. The graph notion has also been specialized into a modeling unit called *Project,* which can contain other Graphs, and sub-projects. A Project type thus helps manage the allowed linkages between methods used in a particular project.

It is noteworthy that all concepts included in GOPRR are designed for reuse: both types and instances of object, relationship, role, property and graph can be reused within other graph or project types (or instances).

Object Orientation

Another extension, in line with object orientation is the inclusion of *generalization* and *specialization* constructs into the GOPRR language. This extension helps to organize complex method libraries, enhances reuse, and together with the graph notion enables to model in economical way most method components.

In line with object orientation objects a third extension is *polymorphism* of modeling constructs: objects, relationships, roles and properties are polymorphic in the sense that an object seen in one method as an object can be seen in another method as a relationship, or a property. This enables method component re-use and provides a powerful and flexible method integration mechanism. In this way the method specifications can include specifications of a set of interconnections between different IS models.

Method Integration

In addition to decomposition and polymorphism, GOPRR also adds other powerful method integration constructs. Objects, relationships and roles can be reused in many different graphs: a change to the object via one graph is also visible in the other graphs. Similarly, properties can be shared between several objects, with changes affecting all objects referring to that property. These two constructs allow different degrees of saying that two objects in different places are 'the same': an important factor in representing the same 'real world' fact in two different methods. Explosion works similarly to decomposition, but with freer semantics. For instance, each object may have only one decomposition, wherever it occurs, but can have multiple explosion links for every graph in which it takes part.

Integrity Checking Rules

Finally GOPRR provides enhanced rules for checking the model integrity. It is possible to attach rules to properties, in addition to the normal type restrictions. For example, in modeling Data Flow Diagrams, a rule has been added to the property 'DFD Number' which constrains the contents of the string property to be a dot separated sequence of numbers, disallowing combinations like 'Fred', '2.', '3..2.1', '.'. It is also possible to add constraints on the collection of properties for a given object, role, relationship, graph or project type. For example, a rule could be added to specify that a 'start date' must come before an 'end date' in an activity modeling diagram. These rules, too, are inherited by descendant types, but may be overridden.

4.3 Example

Although the improvements in GOPRR are best seen with complicated methods, for ease of understanding we take a simple Data Flow Diagram metamodel as our example. One way to model Data Flow Diagrams with GOPRR is to note the similarities between the various object types (i.e. processes, externals and stores), and how they may be connected. For instance, instances of all three object types must have a name and a description, and they can connect via a Flow relationship with a Process. These similarities motivate the creation of a generalized 'DFDObject' type, which is specialized into 'Process', 'External' and 'Store' types. DFDObject itself is marked so that it can never be instantiated: it is purely an abstract type.

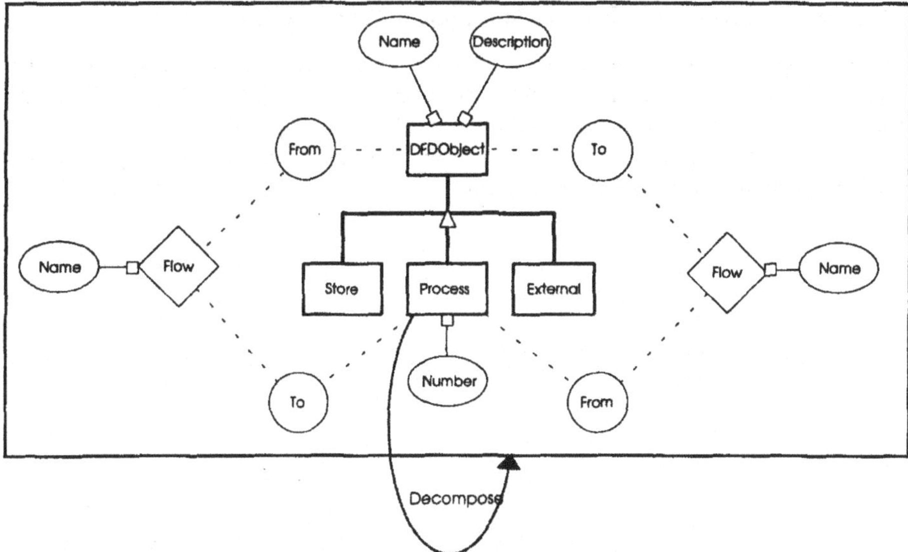

Fig. 2: A GOPRR metamodel of Data Flow Diagrams

This inheritance hierarchy can be seen in the center of Fig. 2, where the rectangles are object types, diamonds are relationship types, circles role types, and ovals property types. DFDObject thus has two properties, Name and Description, and Process inherits these two and adds a third, Number. Objects can be connected by a Flow relationship, with the proviso that one of the objects must always be a Process: on the left, the Process is in the To role, and on the right, in the From role.

The whole figure within the rectangle represents the Graph type of Data Flow Diagrams. The fact that a Process can decompose to a lower-level Data Flow Diagram is represented by the curved gray 'Decompose' relationship between Process and the DFD graph type's rectangle.

5. Method Management Tools

5.1 Motivation and Purpose of the Method Management Tools

In MetaEdit+ the method management tool family has been developed to ease the creation and testing of methods, their management and evaluation support. The primary goal of the tool family is to allow flexibility in method creation and management and ease method construction. Therefore the environment supports alternative ways of method engineering: 1) creation from scratch, where all the parts of the method being defined contain new types, 2) component oriented, where methods are constructed through using prefabricated parts, and 3) reuse oriented, where method engineering seeks to achieve maximal generality of the repository types, and then by specializing these components derive new methods.

5.2 Design Principles of Method Management Tool Family

The development of the MetaEdit+ method management tool family has been influenced by earlier method engineering frameworks (Har93, Hey93, Ros95b, Wel92). These frameworks have sought to consider those aspects that are necessary in a completely functional method engineering environment. Functionally such an environment consists of the following parts:

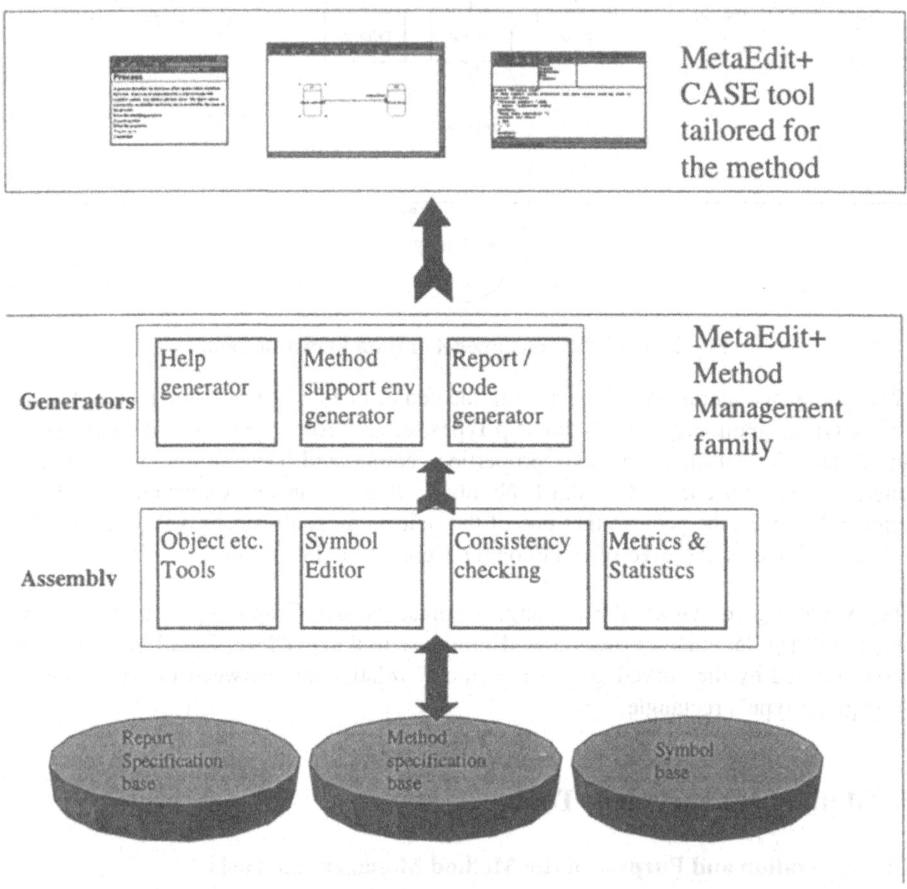

Fig. 3: Method Management Tools in MetaEdit+

Below each subsystem component will be discussed in more detail.

The Method Assembly System

This system part consists of several specialized editors and model retrieval and analysis tools that are needed in method assembly. These tools together allow one to specify a method's objects and relationships and their representations, so that they can be immediately tested within the environment. The most important components are the *metamodel editors* (including object, relationship, role, property and graph editors) by which every method's components and their connections are specified. Due to their different semantics and graphical behaviors Objects, Properties, Relationships and Roles all have their own specification tools. This helps to define their specialized semantics separately, but in particular allows re-use of existing object, relationship and role specifications. These concepts are then collected into complete method specifications using the Graph tool. This also allows the re-use of existing graph "patterns". Each tool also has a dialog definition subsystem, which allows custom definition of dialogs associated with each object type.

The *Symbol Editor* helps specify symbols that are used to distinguish each object type from other object types. Symbols are defined by a specialized drawing tool and are thereafter connected to the appropriate metamodel type. The Symbol Editor also improves re-use as new symbols can be derived by combining or modifying existing symbol patterns and templates retrieved from the repository. The *Consistency checking system* in MetaEdit+ incorporates several rules that ensure the syntactical completeness and consistency of the resulting method specification. Completeness checking covers checking for missing values and missing links between different method components. Consistency checks verify the internal integrity of the method specification by analyzing that the method specification does not include contradictory specifications. The *Metric & statistics system* of the environment offers a number of reports developed using the report generator tool, that analyze the method specification (Ros94, Ros95a). The metrics reports provide a set of computed values, which can be used to review and analyze the properties of the specifications. Examples of metrics are the number of Object, Relationship and Property types in the method (Tei80), and the average number of Properties or Relationships per Object type.

Environment Generation System

This subsystem features several generators that help to deliver a usable and user-friendly CASE tool by using the information contained in the method specifications. The *Method support environment generation system* compiles the method's object specifications into parts of the metamodel repository as soon as they have been defined. As noted above such specifications define the structure of MetaEdit+'s repository data and the symbols to represent and forms to view the object instances. The *Method help generation system* generates an on-line help component associated with each method. This help can then be accessed through a model editing tool interface from the repository. The generation is based on the defined properties of the metamodel types such as a definition what is an External and how it is used in different situations. *Report and transformation generation system* is used for delivering various reports and conducting checking on the models. These reports can be defined using the generic report generator discussed above.

Parts not available in the current MetaEdit+ method management tool family but recognized in the earlier frameworks are: a selection assistant for selecting the right method or its parts for a specific project (Kum92, Har94), and process description and support (Wij91). These needs are not currently addressed in MetaEdit+, but there are ongoing activities in the project that aim at adding these features.

5.3 An Example of a Method Specification

Here we show how to develop part of the Data Flow Diagram metamodel. The example depicts how the defined components of the DFD are connected together to form the actual method. The tools used to manipulate the GOPRR concepts in the concept specification database are form-based.

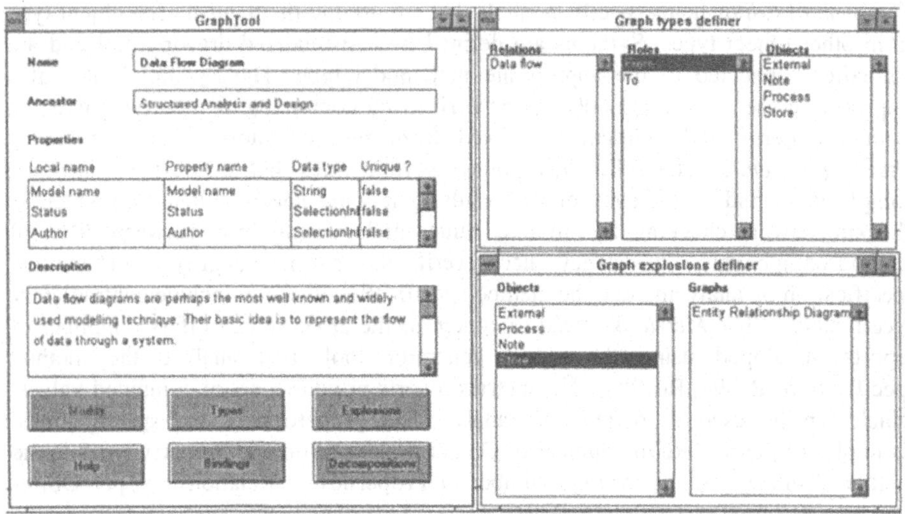

Fig. 4: A Graph Tool

Fig. 4 shows the resulting graph specification of the DFD method. The Graph Tool allows the user to add, remove and edit components of the method (the components, i.e. Objects, Relationships and Roles, are modified with similar tools) and to add and delete method connections. The window on the left shows the definition of the DFD, its properties (i.e. model name and documentation) and related documentation text for method help. The window in the upper right corner of the figure shows the components of the method. The window in the lower right corner shows the possible explosion connections between objects in the DFD and other Graph types: Processes can be exploded into lower level DFD's.

6. Discussion and Conclusions

The limited functionality and rigidity of the current information systems development environments continues to pose a considerable challenge to both academia and practice. In this paper our goal has been to demonstrate how the prototype metaCASE environment called MetaEdit+ deals with these concerns. Overall, we have sought to develop MetaEdit+ as a platform for trying out different tools and tool construction principles, and also to try out the use of object oriented architecture in designing and implementing a metaCASE tool. This is well reflected in its current implementation. MetaEdit+ has been implemented using VisualWorks Smalltalk environment using the ArtBase object repository system and NEDT graphical programming environment, with ENVY as code management system. By doing this, we have been able to re-use about 70% of all code needed to implement the current functionality.

Our goal in developing MetaEdit+ environment has been to develop an environment which:

- Supports high level specification of methods with a powerful yet easy to use method specification language
- Has an open architecture which separates the conceptual specification of the repository and the view (or representation) adopted in different tools and thus conveys a high-level object-oriented API for the tool-repository interactions
- Offers mechanisms for concurrent access of repository data through different tools and users
- Features a comprehensive and well-organized tool set for diverse and complex information handling tasks with some new functionality such as matrices, hypertext tools and the query tool
- Includes flexible, and varying mechanisms for tool integration and both vertical and horizontal method integration support
- Provides symmetrical treatment of IS models and metamodels, and thus enables re-use, metamodel management and utilization within the same environment
- Provides novel support for alternative representational paradigms including matrices, and tables.

We believe that with these features MetaEdit+ addresses many flaws found in current CASE tools. First, through its novel method integration mechanisms it provides innovative ways to organize methods and method families into methodologies, and also to organize methodologies with alternative levels of connectedness and inter-method integrity constraints. Second, through its concurrency management mechanisms MetaEdit+ is able to cater for varying needs and demands for concurrency management for different repository objects. Third, through its open architecture and tool interoperability MetaEdit+ can support the highly diverse representational paradigms and information processing needs which are demanded from software engineering environments. Fourth, through its meta-metamodel MetaEdit+ provides flexibility and evolvability in the method specification and use which is unmatched by any other existing metaCASE tool. Fifth, through the availability of a varied yet uniform (in terms of user accessibility and user interface) tool set the MetaEdit+ environment is able to cater for diverse needs of different system development stakeholders. In this sense MetaEdit+ achieves the design goals of better usability, improved flexibility and a open architecture.

Despite these advances MetaEdit+ is not currently a fully complete environment, suitable for all types of development tasks. First, it does not address the need for multiple distributed repositories which is typical for large scale software development. Second, its concurrency management strategies can be too demanding for large scale software repositories. Third, it does not provide flexible integration mechanisms with other tools (such as electronic publishing or CSCW tools).

Future work in MetaEdit+ will take several directions. First, we want to expand the flexibility and evolvability to cater not only for method representation specifications, but also process and actor models for ISD (Mar94). Second, we will finish the ongoing implementation of the concurrency management system and expand it with the possibility to try out alternative concurrency management strategies which may be applicable in different environments. The third direction is to increase the capabilities to describe integrity constraints within and between method specifications.

On the tool and MetaEngine level the following expansions are currently underway. The applicability of the concept of reusable graphs with 'interface ports', analogous to principles encountered in chip design, will be examined on the model and metamodel levels. The three constructs to represent different levels of 'two things being the same' in a model (multiple representations of the same concept, property sharing, hypertext links) will be examined in the light of current practice in methods. The possibilities of polymorphism based on bindings and metatypes will be examined further in particular as a solution to the problems of metatype polymorphism in existing methods (e.g. objectified associations in NIAM (Nij89), which can be viewed as both objects and relationships). Similarly, the possibilities of the matrix paradigm will be investigated.

To conclude, MetaEdit+ forms a bold attempt to build a versatile platform for implementing flexible design information systems that will form the necessary organizational memory and design resource for knowledge intensive systems and software engineering required in the next millennium. If any improvement has been made in realizing this vision we have achieved our goals.

Acknowledgments. This research was in part funded by the Ministry of Education, University of Jyväskylä, and the Academy of Finland, as the MetaPHOR project (Lyy94). We are also grateful to our colleagues in the MetaPHOR project who have been involved in designing and implementing some parts of the system.

Bibliography

Aae91 Aaen, Ivan, Carsten Sørensen, "*A CASE of Great Expectations,*" Scandinavian Journal of Information Systems 3(**1**) (1991) pp.3–23.

Alf77 Alford, M., "*A Requirements Engineering Methodology for Real Time Processing Requirements,*" IEEE Transactions on Software Engineering 3(**1**) (1977) pp.60–69.

ANS75 ANSI, "*Study Group on Data Base Management Systems: Interim Report 75-02-08,*" ACM SIGMOD Newsletter 7(**2**) (1975).

Ber89 Bergsten, Per, Janis Bubenko jr., Roland Dahl, Mats Gustafsson and Lars-Åke Johansson, "*RAMATIC - A CASE Shell for Implementation of Specific CASE Tools,*" Tempora T6.1 Report, first draft, SISU, Gothenburg (1989).

Bri90 Brinkkemper, Sjaak, "*Formalisation of Information Systems Modelling,*" Ph.D. Thesis, Univ. of Nijmegen, Thesis Publishers, Amsterdam (1990).

Bro75 Brooks, F., "*The Mythical Man Month: Essays on Software Engineering,*" Addison-Wesley, Reading, Mass, USA (1975).

Bro91 Brown, Alan W., "*Object-oriented Databases: their applications to software engineering,*" McGraw-Hill, Maidenhead UK (1991).

Bub88 Bubenko, J. A., "*Selecting a Strategy for Computer-Aided Software Engineering (CASE),*" Report 59, SYSLAB, University of Stockholm, Sweden (1988).

CDI91 CDIF, "*CASE Data Interchange Format Interim Standards vol. 1-3,*" Electronic Industries Association Engineering Department (1991).

Cha86 Charette, R., "*Software Engineering Environments, Concepts and Technology,*" McGraw-Hill, New York, USA (1986).

Che76 Chen, P. P., "*The Entity-Relationship Model: Toward a Unified View of Data,*" ACM Transactions on Database Systems 1(**1**) (1976) pp.9–36.

Che88 Chen, Minder, "*The Integration of Organization and Information Systems Modeling: A Metasystem Approach to the Generation of Group Decision Support Systems and Compute-aided Software Engineering,*" PhD Thesis, University of Arizona, Tuscon, USA (1988).

Cyb92 Cybulski, Jacob L., Karl Reed, "*A Hypertext-Based Software Engineering Environment,*" IEEE Software (March 1992) pp.62–68.

ECM91 ECMA, "*Reference Model for Frameworks of Software Engineering Environments,*" Technical Report ECMA TR/55, 2nd Edition (1991).

Gan79 Gane, C., T. Sarson, "*Structured Systems Analysis: Tools and Techniques,*" Prentice Hall, Englewood Cliffs, NJ (1979).

Hah91 Hahn, U., M. Jarke and T. Rose, "*Teamwork Support in a Knowledge-Based Information Systems Environment,*" IEEE Transactions on Software Engineering 17(**5**) (1991) pp.467–481.

Har93 Harmsen, F., S. Brinkkemper, "Computer Aided Method Engineering based on existing Meta-CASE technology," pp. 125-140 in *Proceedings of the Fourth Workshop on The Next Generation of CASE Tools*, Sjaak Brinkkemper, Frank Harmsen (Ed.)No. 93-32, Univ. of Twente, Enschede, the Netherlands (1993).

Har94 Harmsen, Frank, Sjaak Brinkkemper and Han Oei, "Situational Method Engineering for Information System Project Approaches," pp. 169–194 in *Methods and Associated Tools for the Information Systems Life Cycle (A-55)*, A. A. Verrijn-Stuart and T. W. Olle (Ed.), Elsevier Science B.V. (North-Holland) (1994).

Hen90 Henderson, J., J. Cooprider, "*Dimensions of IS Planning and Design Aids: a functional model of CASE technology,*" Information Systems Research 1(**3**) (1990) pp.227–254.

Hey92 Heym, M., H. Österle, "A Reference Model of Information Systems Development," pp. 215–240 in *The Impact of Computer Supported Technologies on Information Systems Development*, K. E. Kendall, K. Lyytinen, J. L. DeGross (Ed.), North-Holland, Amsterdam (1992).

Hey93 Heym, M., H. Österle, "*Computer-aided methodology engineering,*" Information & Software Technology 35(**6/7**) (1993) pp.345–354.

Ind87 Index Technology Corporation, "*Excelerator Reference Guide,*" Index Technology Corporation, Cambridge, USA (1987).

ISO89 ISO, "*Information processing systems: Information Resource Dictionary System (IRDS) Framework,*" Draft International Standard ISO/IEC DIS 10027 (1989).

Kat84 Katz, Randy H., "Transaction Management in the Design Environment," in *New Applications of Databases*, Georges Garderin and E Ge (Ed.), Academic Press, London UK (1984).

Kel94a Kelly, Steven, Veli-Pekka Tahvanainen, "Support for Incremental Method Engineering and MetaCASE," in *Proceedings of the 5th Workshop on the Next Generation of CASE Tools*, B. Theodoulidis (Ed.) Memoranda Informatica 94-25, Universiteit Twente, Enschede, the Netherlands (1994).

Kel94b Kelly, S., "*A Matrix Editor for a MetaCASE Environment*," Information and Software Technology 36(6) (1994) pp.361–371.

Kel95 Kelly, Steven, Kari Smolander, "*Evolution and Issues in MetaCASE*," Information and Software Technology (to appear) (1995).

Kum92 Kumar, Kuldeep, Richard J. Welke, "Methodology Engineering: A Proposal for Situation Specific Methodology Construction," pp. 257–269 in *Challenges and Strategies for Research in Systems Development*, Kottermann W. W. and Senn J. A. (Ed.), John Wiley & Sons, Washington (1992).

Liu95 Liu, H., "A Visual Interface for Querying a CASE Repository," in *Proc. of the Eleventh IEEE Symposium on Visual Languages (VL'95)*, Darmstadt Germany (1995).

Lyy89 Lyytinen, Kalle, Kari Smolander and Veli-Pekka Tahvanainen, "Modelling CASE Environments in Systems Development," in *Proceedings of the first Nordic Conference on Advanced Systems*, SISU, Stockholm (1989).

Lyy94 Lyytinen, K., P. Kerola, J. Kaipala, S. Kelly, J. Lehto, H. Liu, P. Marttiin, H. Oinas-Kukkonen, J. Pirhonen, M. Rossi, K. Smolander, V.-P. Tahvanainen and J.-P. Tolvanen, "*MetaPHOR: Final report*," University of Jyväskylä, Finland (1994).

Mar94 Marttiin, P., "Towards Flexible Process Support with a CASE shell," pp. 14–27 in *Advanced Information Systems Engineering, Proceedings of the Third International Conference CAiSE'94, Utrecht, The Netherlands, June 1994*, G. Wijers, S. Brinkkemper and T. Wasserman (Ed.), Springer-Verlag, Berlin (1994).

Mar95 Marttiin, Pentti, Kalle Lyytinen, Matti Rossi, Veli-Pekka Tahvanainen and Juha-Pekka Tolvanen, "*Modeling requirements for future CASE: issues and implementation considerations*," Information Resources Management Journal 8(1) (1995) pp.15–25.

McC89 McClure, C., "*CASE is Software Automation*," Prentice Hall, Englewood Cliffs, NJ (1989).

Mer90 Mercurio, V. F., B. F. Meyers, A. M. Nisbet and G. Radin, "*AD/Cycle strategy and architecture*," IBM Systems Journal 29(2) (1990) pp.170-188.

Nij89 Nijssen, G. M., T. A. Halpin, "*Conceptual Schema and Relational Database Design: A fact oriented approach*," Prentice-Hall, Englewood Cliffs, NJ (1989).

Oin93 Oinas-Kukkonen, H., "*Hypertext Functionality in CASE Environments: Preliminary Findings*," Conference on Computers and Hypermedia in Engineering Education, Vaasa, Finland (May 24–26 1993).

Ost87 Osterweil, L. J., "Software processes are software too," pp. 180–188 in *Proceedings of the 9th International Conference on Software Engineering* (1987).

Poc91 Pocock, John N., "VSF and its Relationship to Open Systems and Standard Repositories," pp. 53-68 in *Software Development Environments and CASE Technology*, A. Endres, H. Weber (Ed.), No. 509, Springer-Verlag, Berlin (1991).

Poh94 Pohl, K., R. Dömges and M. Jarke, "PRO-ART: PROcess based Approach to Requirements Traceability," in *Poster Outlines: 6th Conference on Advanced Information Systems Engineering, Utrecht, Netherlands, June 1994* (1994).

Pro94 ProtoSoft Inc., "*Paradigm Plus/ Cadre Edition Reference Manual*," ProtoSoft Inc. (1994).

Ros92 Rossi, M., M. Gustafsson, K. Smolander, L.-Å. Johansson and K. Lyytinen, "Metamodeling editor as a front end tool for a case-shell," pp. 547–567 in *Advanced Information Systems Engineering*, P. Loucopoulos (Ed.), Springer Verlag, Berlin, Germany (1992).

Ros94 Rossi, M., J.-P. Tolvanen, "*Metamodeling approach to method comparison: A survey of a set of ISD methods,*" Working Paper, University of Jyväskylä, Jyväskylä (1994).

Ros95a Rossi, M., S. Brinkkemper, "Metrics in Method Engineering," pp. 200-216 in *Advanced Information Systems Engineering, Proceedings of the 7th International Conference CAiSE'95*, J. Iivari, K. Lyytinen and M. Rossi (Ed.)No. 932, Springer-Verlag, Berlin (1995).

Ros95b Rossi, M., "*The MetaEdit CAME environment,*" Proceedings of the MetaCase 95, University of Sunderland press, Sunderland (1995).

Smo91a Smolander, Kari, Kalle Lyytinen, Veli-Pekka Tahvanainen and Pentti Marttiin, "MetaEdit — A Flexible Graphical Environment for Methodology Modelling," in *Advanced Information Systems Engineering, Proceedings of the Third International Conference CAiSE'91, Trondheim, Norway, May 1991*, R. Andersen, J. A. Bubenko jr. and A. Solvberg (Ed.), Springer-Verlag, Berlin (1991).

Smo91b Smolander, Kari, "OPRR: A Model for Modelling Systems Development Methods," in *Next Generation CASE Tools*, K. Lyytinen and V.-P. Tahvanainen (Ed.), IOS Press, Amsterdam, the Netherlands (1991).

Smo93a Smolander, Kari, "*MetaEdit+ Protocols and standard operations for processing GOPRR information structures: the Application Programmer's Interface,*" Internal Technical Document, MetaPHOR project, Univ. of Jyväskylä, Jyväskylä, Finland (1993).

Smo93b Smolander, Kari, "*GOPRR: a proposal for a meta level model,*" University of Jyväskylä, Finland (1993).

Sor88 Sorenson, Paul G., Jean-Paul Tremblay and Andrew J. McAllister, "*The Metaview System for Many Specification Environments,*" IEEE SOFTWARE (March 1988) pp.30–38.

Ste93 Stegwee, Robert A., Ria M. C. van Waes, "Flexible CASE tools for Information Systems Planning," pp. 248–292 in *Computer-Aided Software Engineering — Issues and Trends for the 1990s and Beyond*, T. Bergin (Ed.), Idea Group Publishing (1993).

Tei77 Teichroew, Daniel, Ernest A. Hershey_III, "*PSL/PSA: A Computer-Aided Technique for Structured Documentation and Analysis of Information Processing Systems,*" IEEE Transactions on Software Engineering (1977).

Tei80 Teichroew, Daniel, Petar Macasovic, III Ernest A. Hershey and Yuzo Yamamoto, "Application of the entity-relationship approach to information processing systems modeling," pp. 15–38 in *Entity-Relationship Approach to Systems Analysis and Design*, P. P. Chen (Ed.), North-Holland (1980).

Wan93 Wand, Yair, Ron Weber, "*On the ontological expressiveness of systems analysis and design grammars,*" Journal of Information Systems (1993).

Wel92 Welke, R. J., "The CASE Repository: More than another database application," in *Challenges and Strategies for Research in Systems Development*, William W. Cotterman and James A. Senn (Eds.) (Ed.), Wiley, Chichester UK (1992).

Wij90 Wijers, G. M., H. E. van Dort, "*Experiences with the use of CASE-tools in the Netherlands,*" Advanced Information Systems Engineering (1990) pp.5–20.

Wij91 Wijers, G. M., "*Modelling Support in Information Systems Development,*" Ph.D. Thesis, Delft University of Technology, Thesis Publishers, Amsterdam (1991).

MetaEdit+ at the Age of 20

Steven Kelly, Kalle Lyytinen, Matti Rossi, and Juha Pekka Tolvanen

Abstract We review the initial vision underlying MetaEdit+, discuss its evolution over the last 20 years, and compare it to the state of the art today. We also note the rise of domain-specific modeling and the value that MetaEdit+ and similar tools have offered in advancing this field. We conclude with a discussion of theoretical and conceptual advances in this field that have taken place since the implementation of the tool, and a review of the future of method engineering.

1 Introduction

In the 1996 CAiSE conference we published a paper called "MetaEdit+: A Fully Configurable Multi-User and Multi-Tool CASE and CAME Environment" [8]. The paper described a state-of-the-art modeling and metamodeling environment that the ongoing project at the University of Jyväskylä had implemented. The main goals of the article were to explain the problems found with existing CASE and method engineering tools, state our vision for the MetaEdit+ environment, and describe the architecture and key principles in its design and implementation.

The MetaEdit+ tool was originally developed in a series of research projects from 1992 until 2001, building on the research behind the earlier, single user and single modeling language MetaEdit tool [22]. A spin-off company, MetaCase, was

S. Kelly (✉) • J.P. Tolvanen
MetaCase, Jyväskylä, Finland
e-mail: stevek@metacase.com; jpt@metacase.com

K. Lyytinen
Case Western Reserve University, Cleveland, USA
e-mail: kjl13@case.edu

M. Rossi
Aalto University, Espoo, Finland
e-mail: matti.rossi@aalto.fi

J. Bubenko et al. (eds.), *Seminal Contributions to Information Systems Engineering*, DOI 10.1007/978-3-642-36926-1_10, © Springer-Verlag Berlin Heidelberg 2013

founded in 1991 and from 1995 research and development associated with the tool progressively shifted there and continues today.[1] The CAiSE article reflects our understanding of the necessary system functionality and its architecture in 1996, at which point most of the initial requirements elicited had been implemented to at least a working beta level.

By reflecting on the implementation and use of MetaEdit+ over the years we have gained a broad and deep appreciation of the challenges of method engineering and its changing nature as the software industry has evolved. In this paper we look at how MetaEdit+ has changed since 1996, and how it has impacted method engineering research and practice. We conclude with a summary of lessons learned and briefly discuss the future of method engineering and method engineering tools.

2 Past and Current Research Issues

In the mid-nineties CASE tools and heavyweight methods were seen as a panacea for most information systems development issues. We observed the need for more versatile tool support and integration and the ability to adapt tools and methods to specific situations. This approach was known as ‘situational’ method engineering, whereby standardized methods were adjusted for varying development tasks and situations [13]. The 1996 article was one of the first to articulate the challenges of situational method engineering and its tool support. That vision was explained and developed further in a series of theses [7, 11, 16, 20, 24, 29] and other publications [6, 21]. In our experience, history has been kind to that vision, and the solutions it presented are still valuable and relevant for software development.

Since CAiSE ’96, large-scale methods for systems development have gradually gone out of fashion. At the same time CASE tools have become standardized work horses which can improve and support specific design and software development tasks. The commercial CASE tool market has also largely vanished whilst many powerful tools have been made open source (Eclipse) or offered for a very low fee (Visual Studio). Comprehensive and integrated methods and workbenches have been replaced with lightweight documentation and agile methods [1].

At the same time method engineering tools have found a new lease of life as language workbenches for Domain-Specific Modeling (DSM) [9]. This fits with the idea of evolutionary ‘method prototyping’, which was described and evaluated in Tolvanen’s thesis [24]. OMG’s MDA and Microsoft’s Software Factories approach [4] have also driven the demand for flexible tools like MetaEdit+. The methods and tools for DSM have been honed in the OOPSLA DSM workshops[2] starting in 2001

[1] http://www.metacase.com

[2] http://www.dsmforum.org/DSMworkshops.html

[25], and the Language Workbench Challenge[3] from 2011. Several special issues have been published on DSM recently [3, 23, 27].

The move towards DSM use of MetaEdit+ emerged from its users, most notably Nokia's Jyrki Okkonen. As is often the case, research can create something interesting, but it takes industrial users to make it truly useful. DSM is however no panacea: most MetaEdit+ users have been concentrated in areas such as embedded systems (automotive, medical), consumer electronics, medical systems and telecommunications. Common themes have often included some kind of product line, a development space defined by use of an in-house platform or framework, or the configuration of complex systems from modular parts.

3 MetaEdit+ at Age 20

Since 1996 MetaEdit+ has evolved through industrial needs as well as innovation. Many of the features included in the 1996 environment have proved their worth, such as visual modeling, WYSIWYG symbol definition, incremental metamodel evolution, reporting and code generation facilities, and repository functions. In contrast, reverse engineering, hypertext, method rationale, and flexible queries and transformations have been used relatively little.

MetaEdit+ contains several browsers allowing flexible method composition from pre-defined parts. This was seen as a key feature of a method development environment at that time [28]. In practice the reuse of method components has rarely proven useful, except for large-grained units such as whole diagram types. The ability to reuse and reference individual elements has, however, proved key for integration between modeling languages. Similarly, method rationale has not been used, but hyperlinking generated code back to the model element that produced it has proved useful in practice.

MetaEdit+ was by no means a finished product in 1996 and many features have been added since then. Here we will just mention a few features we consider most important added between 1996 and the latest 5.0 release in 2012. The ability to represent complex graphical objects has been found to be vital for implementing many modeling languages, and for user acceptance of languages (See Fig. 1). The WYSIWYG Symbol Editor from 1996 has been extended significantly with features such as conditionality, dynamic templates, and SVG support. A new concept of *Port* was introduced, making GOPRR into GOPPRR. In 1996, MetaEdit+ was rather a monolithic, closed environment. Since then, support for a wide array of common image and document formats has been added. Model and metamodel information can be exported and imported as binary files or in an open XML format, and

[3]http://www.languageworkbenches.net

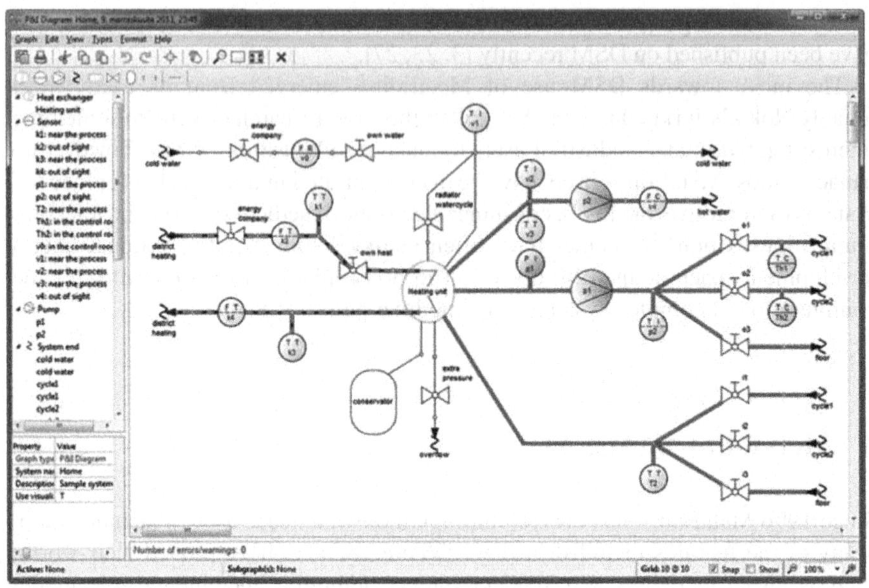

Fig. 1 Example model in MetaEdit+ 5.0 Diagram Editor

accessed and manipulated via an API. Open source plugins integrate MetaEdit+ into Eclipse and Visual Studio IDEs.

3.1 Research Impact

The MetaPHOR research group, from which MetaEdit+ was born, has produced over 10 PhD theses and ca. 50 research papers – most of them after the publication of the paper.[4] MetaEdit+ has been used as a reference tool in several tool comparisons (e.g. [10, 12]). The feature sets envisioned have also formed lists for future tools and MetaEdit+ has been used in many projects as a prototyping and development workbench in developing new software development methods [15, 17–19]. Today more than 50 universities are using MetaEdit+ to support both research and teaching. A 2008 IEEE Software article [5] identified MetaEdit+ as being at the highest level of abstraction for all software development tools, 15 years ahead of the curve. We would include the other early DSM tools such as Vanderbilt's GME [14] and Honeywell's DoME [2] in this category too.

[4] http://metaphor.it.jyu.fi/metapubs.html

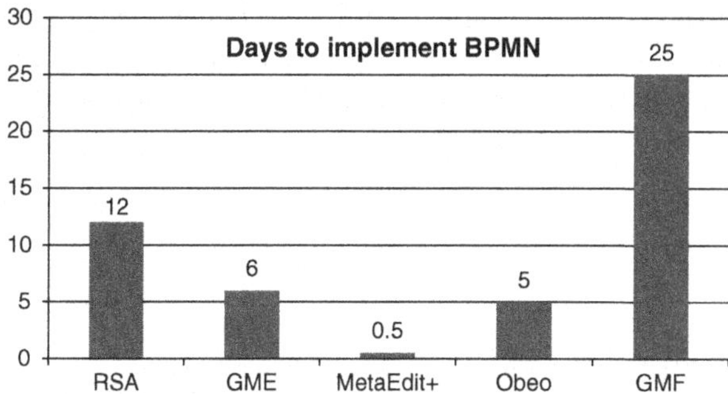

Fig. 2 Comparison of metamodeling time

3.2 *Industry Reception and Practical Impact*

The initial version of MetaEdit+ received recognition from BYTE magazine with a 'Best of CeBIT'95' finalist award, with later versions recognized in the Software Development Magazine Jolt awards (2004, 2005) and SDTimes top 100 (2007, 2008). MetaEdit+ has been used to develop a wide range of both software and hardware solutions. A prime example is Nokia feature phones, which have sold over a billion units running code automatically generated from a DSM language in MetaEdit+. Nokia estimated that applying DSM with MetaEdit+ increased productivity by a factor of ten [26]. Similar results have been achieved in fields as diverse as fish farming, insurance, railway systems, home automation, telecom services, and wearable sports computers. A recent article [12] by committers on the Eclipse Papyrus modeling tool compared MetaEdit+, IBM Rational Software Architect, Obeo Designer, GME and Eclipse GMF. The same language, BPMN, was modeled from scratch with each tool, recording the time taken (Fig. 2).

4 Summary

Advanced information systems engineering has changed technically significantly in the last 25 years. When we started work on metaCASE tools, there were no good graphics or persistency libraries available, so everything had to be developed from scratch. In 2013, creating tool support for modeling language engineering is technically easier, yet still conceptually challenging.

It can be argued that effective adoption and deployment of tools such as MetaEdit+ is no longer limited by the tool capabilities, but by the challenges of organizing the work through (meta)modeling and the intellectual challenges of developing original methods through DSM that can provide the necessary productivity payback. After the divergence to hundreds of languages in the 1980s, the convergence toward the dominance of UML left only a few creating their own languages. There is currently a dearth of knowledge of the principles and benefits of high-level language creation and implementation in industry. Hopefully the recent growth of language development and uptake of DSM tools in universities can seed a new generation of language creators.

References

1. Cockburn A (2002) Agile Software development. Addison-Wesley
2. DoME Users Manual (1996). Honeywell Technology Center, Minneapolis
3. Gray J, Rossi M, Tolvanen J-P (2004) Domain-Specific Modeling with Visual Languages. Journal of Visual Languages & Computing 15 (3-4):207–330
4. Greenfield J, Short K (2004) Software Factories: Assembling Applications with Patterns, Models, Frameworks, and Tools. Wiley, Indianapolis
5. Helsen S, Ryman A, Spinellis D (2008) Where's My Jetpack? IEEE Software 25 (5):18–21
6. Jarke M, Pohl K, Weidenhaupt K, Lyytinen K, Marttiin P, Tolvanen J-P, Papazoglou M (1998) Meta Modeling: A Formal Basis for Interoperability and Adaptability. In: Krämer B, Papazoglou M (eds) Information Systems Interoperability. John Wiley Research Science Press, pp 229–263
7. Kelly S (1997) Towards a Comprehensive MetaCASE and CAME Environment: Conceptual, Architectural, Functional and Usability Advances in MetaEdit+. PhD Thesis, University of Jyväskylä, Jyväskylä
8. Kelly S, Lyytinen K, Rossi M (1996) MetaEdit+: A Fully Configurable Multi-User and Multi-Tool CASE and CAME Environment. In: Constapoulos P, Mylopoulos J, Vassiliou Y (eds) Advanced Information Systems Engineering, proceedings of the 8th International Conference CAISE'96. Lecture Notes in Computer Science. Springer-Verlag, Berlin, pp 1–21
9. Kelly S, Tolvanen J-P (2008) Domain-Specific Modeling: Enabling full code generation. Wiley-IEEE Computer Society Press
10. Kern H, Hummel A, Kühne S Towards a Comparative Analysis of Meta-Metamodels. In: Rossi M, Sprinkle J, Gray J, Tolvanen J-P (eds) Proceedings of the 11th Workshop on Domain-Specific Modeling, 2011.
11. Koskinen M (2000) Process metamodelling - Conceptual foundations and application. Dissertation, University of Jyväskylä
12. Kouhen El A, Dumoulin C, Gérard S, Boulet P (2012) Evaluation of Modeling Tools Adaptation.
13. Kumar K, Welke RJ (1992) Methodology Engineering: A Proposal for Situation Specific Methodology Construction. In: Kottermann WW, Senn JA (eds) Challenges and Strategies for Research in Systems Development. John Wiley & Sons, Washington
14. Ledeczi A, Maroti M, Bakay A, Karsai G, Garrett J, Thomason C, Nordstrom G, Sprinkle J, Volgyesi P The generic modeling environment. In: Workshop on Intelligent Signal Processing, Budapest, Hungary, 2001.
15. Leitner A, Preschern C, Kreiner C (2012) Effective development of automation systems through domain-specific modeling in a small enterprise context. Software & Systems Modeling
16. Marttiin P (1998) Customisable Process Modelling Support and Tools for Design Environment. Dissertation, University of Jyväskylä, Jyväskylä
17. Mewes K (2009) Domain-specific Modelling of Railway Control Systems with Integrated Verication and Validation Disseration
18. Preschern C, Leitner A, Kreiner C (2012) Domain-Specific Language Architecture for Automation Systems: An Industrial Case Study. Paper presented at the Workshop on Graphical Modeling Language Development

19. Qureshi T (2012) Enhancing Model-Based Development of Embedded Systems Dissertation. Disseration
20. Rossi M (1998) Advanced Computer Support for Method Engineering: Implementation of CAME Environment in MetaEdit+. Dissertation, University of Jyväskylä, Jyväskylä
21. Rossi M, Ramesh B, Lyytinen K, Tolvanen J-P (2004) Managing Evolutionary Method Engineering by Method Rationale. Journal of AIS 5 (9 article 12)
22. Smolander K, Lyytinen K, Tahvanainen V-P, Marttiin P (1991) MetaEdit-A Flexible Graphical Environment for Methodology Modelling. In: Andersen R, J. A. Bubenko jr., Solvberg A (eds) Advanced Information Systems Engineering, Proceedings of the Third International Conference CAiSE'91. Lecture Notes in Computer Science. Springer-Verlag, Berlin, pp 168–193
23. Sprinkle J, Mernik M, Tolvanen J-P, Spinellis D (2009) Special issue on Domain-Specific Modeling editorial. IEEE Software 26 (4)
24. Tolvanen J-P (1998) Incremental Method Engineering with Modeling Tools: Theoretical Principles and Empirical Evidence. Dissertation, University of Jyväskylä
25. Tolvanen J-P, Gray J, Lyytinen K, Kelly S Proceedings of 1st OOPSLA Workshop on Domain-Specific Visual Languages. In: Tolvanen J-P, Gray J, Lyytinen K, Kelly S (eds) Proceedings of 1st OOPSLA Workshop on Domain-Specific Visual Languages, 2001. Jyväskylä University Printing House
26. Tolvanen J-P, Kelly S (2000) Benefits of MetaCASE: Nokia Mobile Phones Case Study. MetaCase Consulting plc. http://www.metacase.com/papers/MetaEdit_in_Nokia.pdf. Accessed 1/7 2004
27. Tolvanen J-P, Rossi M, Gray J (2013) Theme Issue on Domain-Specific Modeling in Theory and Applications editorial. Journal of Software and Systems Modeling to appear
28. Zhang Z Defining components in a MetaCASE environment. In: CAiSE'00, Stockholm, Sweden, 2000. Springer-Verlag
29. Zhang Z (2004) Model component reuse : conceptual foundations and application in the metamodeling-based systems analysis and design environment. Dissertation, University of Jyväskylä, Jyväskylä

From: CAiSE 1997, LNCS 1250 © Springer-Verlag Berlin Heidelberg 1997

OO-METHOD: An OO Software Production Environment Combining Conventional and Formal Methods

Oscar Pastor, Emilio Insfrán, Vicente Pelechano, José Romero, José Merseguer
Departament de Sistemes Informàtics i Computació
Universitat Politècnica de València
Camí de Vera s/n
46071 Valencia (Spain)
{opastor | einsfran | pele | jmerse | jromero}@dsic.upv.es

Abstract

OO-Method is an OO Methodology that blends the use of formal specification systems with conventional OO methodologies based on practice. In contrast to other approaches in this field ([Jun95,Esd93]), a set of graphical models provided by the methodology allows analysts to introduce the relevant system information to obtain the conceptual model through a requirements collection phase, so that an OO formal specification in Oasis ([Pas92, Pas95-1]), can be generated at any time. This formal specification acts as a high-level system repository. Furthermore, a software prototype which is functionally equivalent to the Oasis specification is also generated in an automated way. This is achieved by defining an execution model which gives the pattern for obtaining a concrete implementation in a declarative or an imperative software development environment (depending on the user choice). The methodology is supported by a CASE workbench.

1. Introduction

In the context of the object paradigm, several OO methodologies have emerged to deal with the set of OO methods to be used to model and correctly implement an information system. Two main approaches can be distinguished:

- what could be called *conventional* OO methodologies, that come from practical use in industrial software production environments, which do not have a formal basis and which often use classical structured concepts together with the introduction of OO features ([Wir90],[Rum91],[Jac92], [Boo94],[Col94]). Recent proposals are trying to create a unified framework for dealing with all the existing methods (UML [BRJ96]), with the implicit danger of providing users with an excessive set of methods that have an overlapping semantics.
- use of OO *formal specification languages* (Oblog [Ser87,Esd93], Troll [Jun91,Har94], Albert [Dub94], Oasis), which have a solid mathematical background and deducible formal properties such as terms of soundness and completeness.

Our contribution to this state of the art is based on the idea that these two approaches can be mixed. This mixing offers some advantages: the use of such OO formal languages can help designers to detect and eliminate ambiguities and elements of dubious utility. The use of conventional OO methodologies permits us to take advantage of the accumulative experience coming from the industrial context. The research work developed at the DSIC-UPV has been directed towards designing and implementing an OO software production environment that aims to combine the pragmatic aspects attached to the so called conventional methods, with the good formal properties of the OO specification languages.

In contrast to other works in this area ([Wie93,Kus95]), our approach is to use this combination of approaches in a graphic, OO conceptual modeling environment which collects the system properties considered relevant for building a formal, textual OO specification in an automated way. This formal OO specification constitutes a high-level system repository. Furthermore, the definition of a concise execution model and the mapping between the specification language and the execution model notions, makes it possible to build an operational implementation of a software production environment allowing for real automated prototyping, by generating a complete system prototype (including statics and dynamics) in the target software development environment. A CASE workbench which supports this working environment in a unified way is currently available for prototyping purposes.

This blend has produced the OO-Method methodology presented in this paper and is based on OASIS as a formal OO specification language. Our intention is to give a clear description of the most relevant features of the approach, introducing the basic ideas on OO conceptual modeling that are in the basis of the work in section 2, and explaining the main OO-Method features as a methodological approach in section 3. The methods used to capture the system properties in order to produce what we will call a conceptual model will be shown. Subsequently we will show how to represent this model in a particular software development environment according to an abstract execution model, which will fix the operational steps to follow when we want to give a concrete system implementation. A software prototype which is functionally equivalent to a system specification can be obtained in the context of the methodology. We will describe the code generation strategy used. Finally, a view of the CASE tool that has been built to support the methodology will also be introduced.

2. The OO-Method Approach

Nowadays, it is considered mandatory for an OO methodology to cover the following aspects:

- Classes and objects
- Abstraction
- Encapsulation
- Inheritance and Aggregation to deal with complex classes
- Interobjectual Communication

However, the current proposals share a common weakness: the value of the conceptual modeling efforts when the development step is reached is unclear, mainly because it is not possible to produce an accurate code which is functionally equivalent to the system requirements specification. We should be able to produce code in an interactive way from the very beginning of the requirements specification step, and not generate only static templates for the component system classes as most OO CASE tools already do. We should be able to generate a complete programming environment including statics and dynamics. This kind of functional rapid prototyping would allow analysts to show the users a comprehensive image of the application state at any given moment, making it possible to detect analysis errors or misunderstandings as soon as they are originated. Furthermore, system designers would have a validated starting point for their development tasks, avoiding having to start from scratch.

If we work in a declarative environment, the programs generated are theories of a given logic where the three concepts of machine computation, logic deduction and satisfaction in a theory's standard model are equivalent. In this case, a final software product which is *formally equivalent* to the system specification can be obtained using declarative programming languages with a well-defined declarative and operational semantics and with equivalent results between them.

If the target environment is imperative, we lose the quoted declarative properties. However, we can generate a prototype which is *functionally equivalent* to the requirements specification, if we clearly define a mapping between the conceptual and the execution model. This automated prototyping policy (introduced as a code generation strategy later on in this paper) constitutes an important improvement with respect to the current state of the art of the field.

In summary, all these ideas lead us to the OO-Method proposal. OO-Method is an OO methodology, which is intended to overcome these problems and whose contribution is based on the following basic principles:

1. to give support to the OO conceptual modeling notions,
2. to join OO formal method concepts with practical and widely used OO methodologies,
3. to provide an automated prototyping environment, including complete code generation (data and behaviour) in both declarative and imperative programming environments.

3. The Methodology

OO-Method is an Object-Oriented Software Production Methodology whose phases are shown in Figure 1. Basically, we can distinguish two components: the conceptual model and the execution model.

When facing the conceptual modeling step of a given Information System, we have to determine the components of the object society without being worried about any implementation considerations. The problem at this level is to obtain a precise system definition, and this is the conceptual model.

Once we have an appropriate system description, a well-defined execution model will fix the characteristics of the final software product, in terms of user interface, access control, service activation, etc., in short, all the implementation-dependent properties.

In this context, we start with an Analysis step where three models are generated: the Object Model, the Dynamic Model and the Functional Model. They describe the Object Society from three complementary points of view within a well-defined OO framework. For these models we have preserved the names used in many other well-known and widely-used OO methodologies, even if the similarities are purely syntactic as can be seen throughout this paper.

From these analysis models, a corresponding formal and OO Oasis specification (the OO-Method design tool) can be obtained in an automated way.

This is done through an automatic translation process. The resultant Oasis specification acts as a complete system repository, where all the relevant properties of the component classes are included.

According to the execution model, a prototype which is functionally equivalent to the specification is built in an automated way. This may be done in both declarative (Prolog-based) [Can95] and imperative environments (specially those visual OO programming environments that are widely used nowadays). The code generation strategy is independent of any concrete target development environment, even if at the moment our selected environment for automated code generation are Visual C++, Delphi, Java, Visual Basic and PowerBuilder.

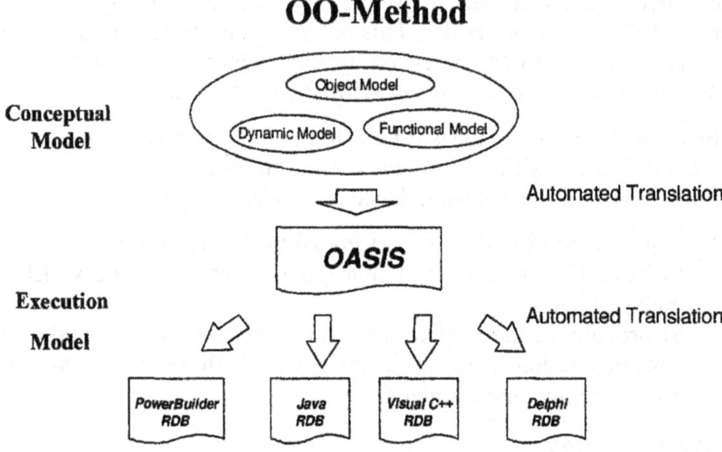

Fig. 1. Phases of OO-Method.

Next, we explain the characteristics of the three models (object, dynamic and functional) that constitute the **conceptual model**, introduce the **execution model** features and explain the conversion strategy from the former to the latter.

3.1 Conceptual model

Object Model

The Object Model is represented by means of a Class Configuration Diagram (CCD), a graphic model where system classes are declared, including their attributes and services. Aggregation and inheritance hierarchies are also graphically depicted representing class relationships. Additionally, agents are introduced to specify who can activate each class service. Classes are the basic modeling units. A class is represented by a rectangle with three areas:

- a header with the class name.
- a static component where attributes are declared.
- a dynamic component where services are introduced, distinguishing among new and destroy events, and among private and shared events.

Shared events are connected by solid lines in the CCD. Client classes (agents) of a given service are represented by dotted lines joining every potential client class with the corresponding server class, capturing the client system view in an easy and intuitive way.

OO-Method deals with complexity by introducing aggregation and inheritance hierarchies.

We represent the aggregation relationship between two classes including its cardinality (minimum and maximum) to determine how many components can be attached to a given container and how many containers a component class can be associated with. See Figure 2.

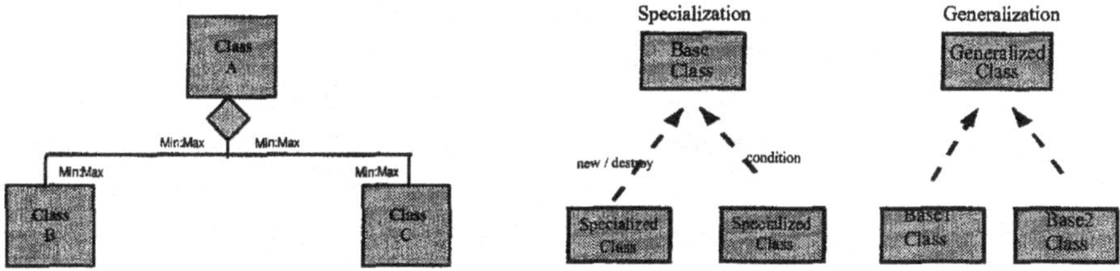

Fig. 2. Aggregation relationship.
Fig. 3. Inheritance relationship.

Inheritance is graphically depicted as an arrow from a given subclass to its superclass. This arrow can be labeled with a condition of specialization, or with the events that activate/cancel the child role, respectively. See Figure 3[1].

Next, the CCD corresponding to a classical Library Information System is shown in the Figure 4. As a basic explanation (for reasons of brevity), we assume that as usual in such a System, there are *readers*, *books* and *loans* relating a book to the reader who orders it. Readers can 'play the role' of *unreliable readers*, if their return dates expire. *Librarian* and *reader* instances are declared as active objects.

---

[1] *This is how inheritance is dealt with in Oasis, distinguishing between permanent and temporal specialization. The permanent case refers to child instances created when the ancestor instance is created, and they need a condition which is built on constant attributes. Temporal specialization (role) appears when a superclass event happens or a condition built on variable attributes holds.*

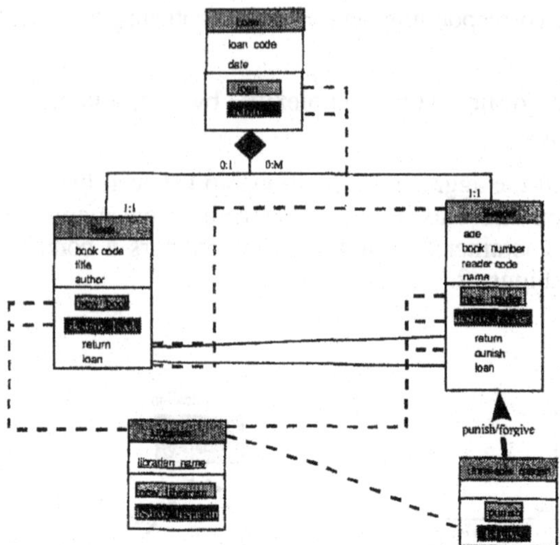

Fig. 4. CCD that represents the Object Model of the Library Information System.

Dynamic Model

The Dynamic Model is used to specify valid object lives and interobjectual interaction. To describe valid object lives, we use State Transition Diagrams (STDs, one for each class). To deal with object interaction, we introduce an Object Interaction Diagram (OID), one for the whole System.

State Transition Diagram

STDs are used to describe correct behaviour by establishing valid object lives. By valid life, we mean a right sequence of states that characterizes the correct behaviour of the objects for every class. In this context states denote the different available situations for class objects, and are depicted using a circle labeled with the state name.

When an object does not exist, a blank circle represents this "state" of non existence, and will be the source of initial transition labeled by the corresponding new event. A bull's eye is used to represent the post-mortem state.

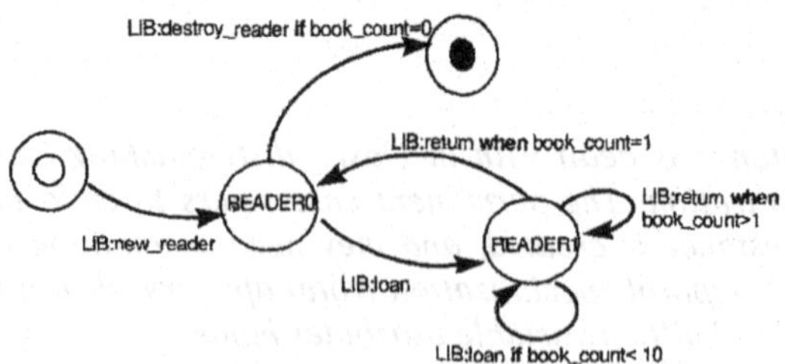

Fig.5 STD for a READER.

Transitions represent valid changes of state that can be constrained by introducing conditions. They follow the syntax shown below:

event | action | transaction [if precondition] [when control condition]

where precondition is a condition defined on the object attributes that must hold for a service to occur and a control condition is a condition that avoids the possible non-determinism for a given action. An example of STD can be seen in Figure 5.

Object Interaction Diagram

The object interactions are represented by diagrams of this kind. We declare two basic interactions:

- *triggers*, which are services of objects which are activated in an automated way when a condition is satisfied by an object of the same or another class.
- *global interactions*, which are transactions involving services of different objects. With these global interactions, interobjectual transactions can be declared. Formally, they can be seen as a local service of the aggregation among the classes providing the services that constitute the global interaction.

Basically, we represent classes in the OID as boxes with a header including the class name. Class services are declared as smaller boxes inside the corresponding class box. The class service boxes are connected when one of the previous types of interactions is defined. Triggers are introduced by starting the corresponding solid line in the header of the class and ending it in the triggered action, and global interactions are introduced by connecting the involved services with a common global interaction identifier (GIid). The general model for an OID can be seen in Figure 6 and 7.

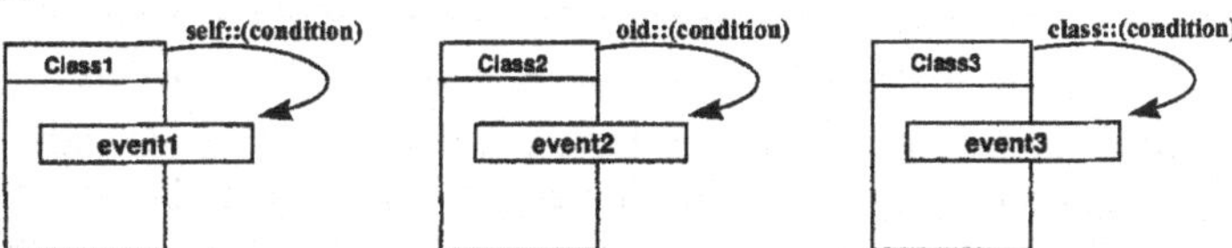

Fig. 6. Trigger Relationships

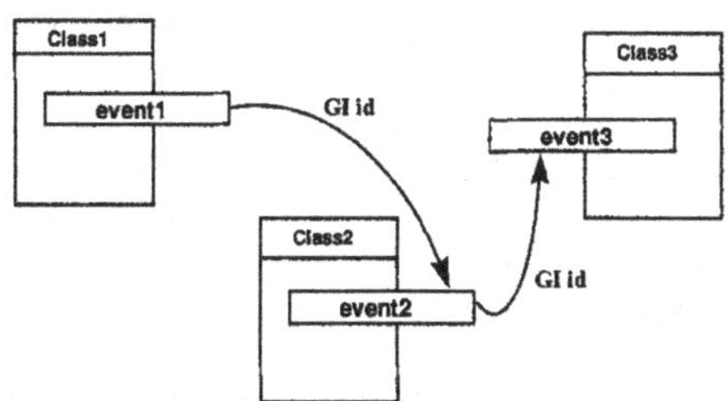

Fig. 7. Global Interaction

Functional Model

After declaring object attributes and services in the Object Model and valid life cycles and object interactions in the Dynamic Model, the aim of the Functional Model is to capture semantics attached to any change of state in an easy and an intuitive way. This model specifies the effect of an event on its relevant attributes through an interactive dialogue. The value of every attribute is modified depending on the action that has been activated, the involved event arguments and the current object state.

The specification of an action effect should be made declaratively, as proposed in Oasis. However, a good specification requires a solid formal basis for any analyst. To solve this situation, the OO-Method provides a model where the Analyst only has to categorize every attribute among a predefined set of three categories and introduce the relevant information depending on the corresponding selected category.

This classification of attributes [Pas96-2] is a contribution of this method and gives a clear and simple strategy for dealing with the task of generating the Execution Model. At the same time, it opens the door to being able to include this information in an Oasis specification in an automated way.

There are three types of attributes: *push-pop*, *state-independent* and *discrete-domain based* attributes.

Push-pop attributes are those whose relevant events increase or decrease their value by a given quantity. Events that reset the attribute to a given value can also exist.

An example of this category is the *book_number* of the *reader* class, with *REA:loan* as increasing action and *REA:return* as decreasing one (*REA* is a variable of type *reader*).

Attribute : book_number *Category* : push-pop

Action Type	Action	Effect	Evaluation Condition
Incr.	REA:loan	+1	
Decr.	REA:return	-1	

Fig. 8. Push-pop attribute *book_number* of the *reader* class.

State-independent attributes have a value that depends only on the latest action that has occurred. Once a relevant action is activated, the new attribute value of the object involved is independent of the previous one. In such a case, we consider that the attribute remains in a given state, having a certain value for the corresponding attribute. We can introduce the attribute *bookshelf* of the *book* class as an example. A *book* has a *bookshelf* assigned when the event *locate*(B) is activated. When this event occurs, *bookshelf* takes the argument value independently of any previous value.

Attribute : bookshelf *Category* : state-independent

Carrier Action	Action Effect	Evaluation Condition
LIB:locate(B)	=B	

Fig. 9. State-independent attribute *bookshelf* of the *book* class.

Discrete-domain valued attributes take their values from a limited domain. The different values of this domain model the valid situations that are possible for objects of the class. Through the activation of carrier actions (that assign a given domain value to the attribute) the object reaches a specific situation. The object abandons this situation when another event occurs (a "liberator" event). As an example, let's consider the *available* attribute of the *book* class. The available value tells us what the current book situation is. The carrier event (*loan*) lets the object into a situation where available has the value false. The situation is abandoned when the event *return* is activated.

Attribute : available *Category* : discrete-domain valued

Actual Value	Action	New Value	Evaluation Condition
TRUE	REA:loan	FALSE	
FALSE	REA:return	TRUE	

Fig. 10. Discrete-valued attribute *available* in the *book* class.

All this information, which constitutes the system description, has a textual representation in Oasis. The specification is obtained at any moment by executing an automated process of translation that converts the collected graphic information into a textual OO specification that constitutes a complete, formal System Repository.

3.2 Execution Model

Once all the relevant system information in the specification that we have called conceptual model is collected , the execution model has to accurately state the implementation-dependent features associated to the selected object society machine representation. More precisely, we have to explain the pattern to be used to implement object properties in any target software development environment.

Our idea at this point is to give an abstract view of an execution model that will set the programming pattern to follow when dealing with the problem of implementing the conceptual model. This execution model has three main steps:

1. *access control:* first, as users are also objects, the object logging in the system has to be identified as a member of the corresponding object society.
2. *object system view:* once the user is connected, he must have a clear representation of which classes he can access. In other words, his object society view must be clearly stated, precising the set of object attributes and services he will be allowed to see or activate, respectively.
3. *service activation:* finally, after being connected and having a clear object system view, the object will be able to activate any available service in the user's world view. Among these services, we will have event or transaction activation served by other objects, or system observations (object queries).

Any service execution is characterized as the following sequence of actions:

1. *object identification*: as a first step, the object acting as server has to be identified. This object existence is an implicit condition for executing any service, except if we are dealing with a *new*[2] event. At this moment, their values (those that characterize its current state) are retrieved.
2. *introduction of event arguments*: the rest of the arguments of the event being activated must be introduced.
3. *state transition correctness*: we have to verify in the STD that a valid state transition exists for the selected service in the current object state.

---

[2] *Formally, a new event is a service of a metaobject representing the class, which acts as object factory for creating individual class instances. This metaobject (one for every class) has as main properties the class population attribute, the next oid and the quoted new event.*

4. *precondition satisfaction*: the precondition associated to the service that is going to be executed must hold. If not, an exception will arise, informing that the service cannot be activated because its precondition has been violated.
5. *valuation fulfilment*: once the precondition has been verified, the induced event modifications are effective in the selected persistent object system.
6. *integrity constraint checking in the new state*: to assure that the service activation leads the object to a valid state, we must verify that the (static and dynamic) integrity constraints hold in this final resulting state.
7. *trigger relationships test*: after a valid change of state, and as a final action, the set of rules condition-action that represent the internal system activity have to be verified. If any of them holds, the corresponding service activation will be triggered. It is the analyst's responsibility to assure the termination and confluence of such triggers.

The previous steps guide the implementation of any program to assure the functional equivalence among the object system description collected in the conceptual model and its reification in a software programming environment according to the execution model.

Next, we are going to present the code generation strategy used in the implementation of the previous execution model in a well-known Windows95 environment, which opens up the possibility of creating a CASE tool that, starting from a set of graphical OO models obtained during the conceptual modeling step (according to OO-Method) can generate a functional software prototype at any time.

3.3 Code generation strategy

Once an abstract execution model has been introduced, we will have different concrete implementations of this execution model for different software development environments. In this paper, we focus on the implementation of the execution model in a Windows95 context, but it must be noted that other concrete and alternative implementations are currently being been developed emphasizing one using Java in an intranet environment. It is important to note that the representation of the conceptual model in the selected execution model is done according to the principles introduced above, thus generating a prototype in an automated way by adapting the code generation strategy that we present to the particularities of the target development environment.

The execution model implementation selected for a Windows95 environment keeps in mind the main principles attached to such a environment. Basically, this means that we have:

- to reproduce the user's mental image of the system, within an OO world view. Users generally expect an application to operate in accordance with its nature, and the OO paradigm provides an operational framework to properly represent a system as a society of interacting objects, where every individual object can access other system component objects and can activate those services it is allowed to. To ensure this consistency, the interfaces built have to resemble the user's environment. They also have to be consistent, complying with the standards in presentation (what the user sees), behaviour (how the application reacts), sequencing (how the dialogs are sequenced) and functionalities (how actions are carried out). Finally they have to be transparent, meaning that the purely technical application mechanisms must be completely transparent to the user.

- to give control to the user. It is the user who must control the application and not the contrary.

To properly implement the set of system classes in a standard Windows95 software development environment, we have to deal with a static and a dynamic point of view. The static one will fix the relational database schema corresponding to the system specification. This automated relational generation is out of the scope of this presentation and is explained in depth in [Pas95-2]. In short, every class is converted into a relation, having the attribute information included in the class specification. Aggregation and inheritance are treated by defining the corresponding foreign keys according to the collected complex class properties. Next, we are going to focus on dynamics explaining the appearence of the prototype which is automatically generated.

The code generation process creates four types of windows as we can see in Figure 11:

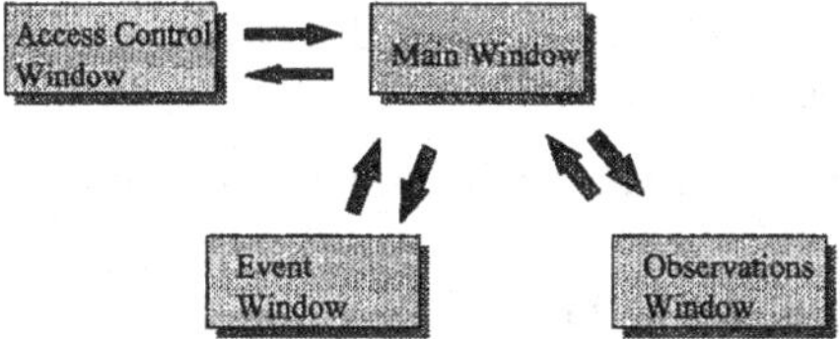

Fig.11 Overview of the generated code structure.

- *Access Control Window*: this is the log-in window, where the corresponding active user has to be identified. This is done by introducing its object identifier, class name and password. The identification is verified on the database to ensure that the object exists. Once the object is incorporated to the system, it will see the available system class services through menu items of the main menu.

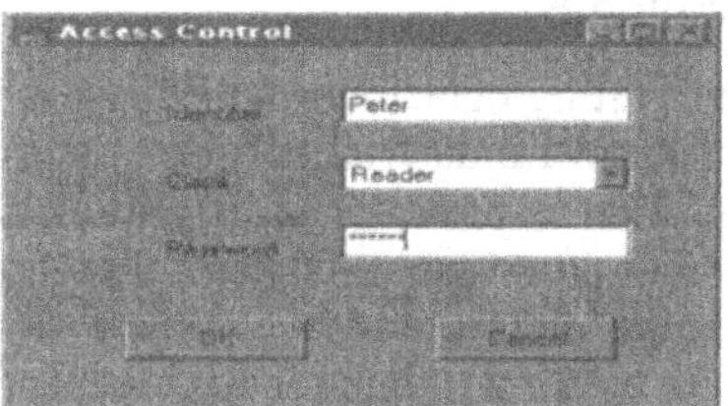

Fig.12 Access Control Window

- *Main Window*; it characterizes the system view that the connected object has. All the services of the classes are requested through it. It has the following options:
  - ◊ the typical File item option of Windows applications.

◊ for every class, a pull-down menu including an item for observations (queries), a section with its descendent classes (if any) and a last section with the available class services.
◊ an interactions item, which allows for the activation of global interactions.

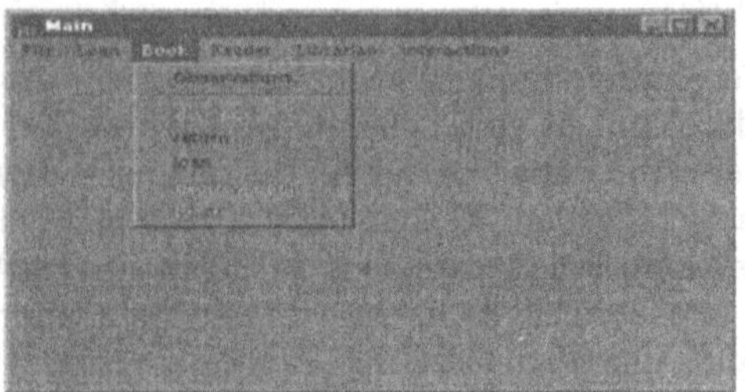

Fig.13 Main Window.

- *Event window*, where the corresponding arguments are introduced and the induced actions are executed through the OK control button.
- *Observations window*; this screen is intended to be a Query By Example pattern where the user can see the results of any query done over the current object state.

Finally, we will give a quick look at the OO-Method CASE tool.

4. The OO-Method CASE Tool

The OO-Method CASE Tool [Pas96-1] provides an operational environment that supports all the methodological aspects of OO-Method. It simplifies the analysis, design and implementation of Information Systems from an object-oriented perspective, providing a comfortable and friendly interface for elaborating the OO-Method models taking advantages of Windows95. The CASE Tool is being used at this moment in the resolution of real complex systems, in the context of a R&D project carried out jointly by the Valencia University of Technology and Consoft S.A.

The most interesting contribution of this CASE environment is its ability to generate code in well-known industrial software development environments from the system specification, what constitutes an operational approach of the ideas of the automated programming paradigm: analysts collect information, and can generate a formal OO system specification, and a complete (including statics and dynamics) software prototype which is functionally equivalent to the quoted system specification whenever the analysts want.

When the CASE Tool is executed, we are placed on a blank blackboard that represents the CCD where we can draw classes and their properties. By selecting one of the classes on the CCD the user can change to the STD dynamic model. The OID completes the dynamic model. In addition to these static and dynamic points of view the user has to fill the functional model information through friendly and interactive dialogs.

The Figure 14 shows a picture of the CASE Tool. The main menu of the tool has the typical items of an editing tool and also allows the user to enter in textual mode the OO-Method models. Two remarkable items are the Project item that includes the options for the Analysis (object, dynamic and functional models), Design (Oasis code, generated in an automated way) and Implementation (Visual C++, Delphi,... code) steps, and the View item which allows the user to manage the complexity of the graphic diagrams.

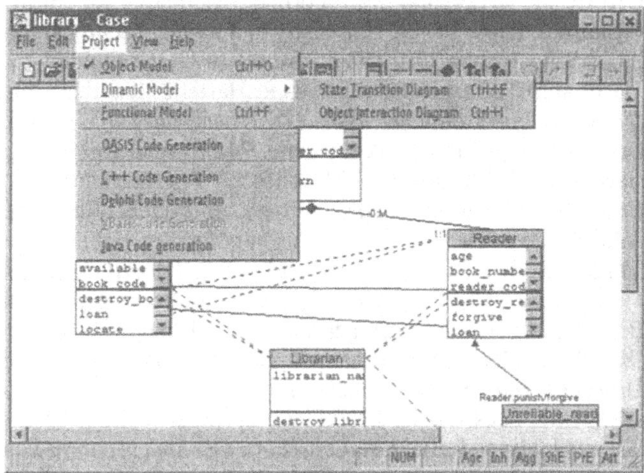

Fig. 14 OO-Method CASE Tool

5. Conclusions

The main aspects of the presented work are the following:

1. A complete OO methodology for dealing with all the Software Production Process phases has been introduced. This methodology uses a formal OO specification language (Oasis) as a central, well-defined repository, from which executable application prototypes can be obtained at any given moment.
2. A CASE tool for Rapid Prototyping is provided. It is embedded in the methodological OO context of OO-Method, having as basic property that the collection of system requirements generates a prototype to be run by final users in order to validate this process of requirements engineering.
3. On the basis of our approach, we find an operational environment blending classical, widely-used OO methods with formal specification languages, complementing their different backgrounds: software development practice on the one hand, and a mathematical theory background on the other hand.

References

[Boo94] Booch,G. *OO Analysis and Design with Applications*. Addison-Wesley, 1994.

[BRJ96] Booch,G.,Rumbaugh,J.,Jacobson,I. *Unified Modeling Language. Version 0.91*. Rational Software Corporation.

[Can95] Canós,J.H.;Penadés,M.C.Ramos,I. *A Knowledge-Based Arquitecture for Object Societies*. Proc. of DEXA-95 (Workshop), pags: 18-25, London, 1995

[Col94] Coleman,D.;Arnold,P.;Bodoff,S.;Dollin,S.;Gilchrist,H.;Hayes,F.;Jeremes,P. *Object-Oriented Development; The Fusion Method*. Prentice-Hall 1994

[Dub94] Dubois,E.;Du Bois,Ph.;Petit,M.;Wu,S. *ALBERT:A Formal Agent-Oriented Requirements Language for Distributed Composite Systems*. In Proc. CAiSE'94 Workshop on Formal Methods for Information System Dynamics, pags: 25-39, University of Twente, Technical Report 1994.

[Esd93] ESDI S.A., Lisboa. OBLOG CASE V1.0- User's Guide

[Har94] Hartmann T.,Saake,G.,Jungclaus,R.,Hartel,P.,Kusch,J. *Revised Version of the Modeling Language Troll (Troll version 2.0)*. Technische Universitat Braunschweig, Informatik-Berichte, 94-03 April 1994.

[Jac92] Jacobson I.,Christerson M.,Jonsson P.,Overgaard G. *OO Software Engineering , a Use Case Driven Approach*. Reading, Massachusetts. Addison -Wesley.

[Jun91] Jungclaus, R., Saake, G., Sernadas, C. *Formal Specification of Object Systems*. Eds. S. Abramsky and T. Mibaum Proceedings of the TapSoft´s 91, Brighton. Lncs. 494, Springer Verlag 1991, pags. 60-82.

[Kus95] Kusch,J.; Hartel,P.;Hartmann,T.;Saake,G. *Gaining a Uniform View of Different Integration Aspects in a Prototyping Environment*. Proc of DEXA-95, pags. 35-42, LNCS 978, Springer-Verlag, 1995

[Pas92] Pastor, O.;Hayes,F.;Bear,S. *OASIS:An OO Specification Language*. Proc. of CAiSE-92 Conference, Lncs (593), Springer-Verlag 1992, pags: 348-363.

[Pas95-1] Pastor,O., Ramos, I. *Oasis 2.1.1: A Class-Definition Language to Model Information Systems Using an Object-Oriented Approach*, October 95 (3 ed).

[Pas95-2] Pastor,O.;Garcia,R.;Cuevas,J. *Implementation of an OO Design in an Oracle7 Development Environment*. Proc. of the European Oracle Users Group Conference, EOUG-95. Vol.4 pags: 35-47, Firenze (Italy).

[Pas96-1] Pastor,O., Barberá, J.M., Merseguer, J., Romero, J., Insfrán, E.: *The CASE OO-METHOD graphic environment description*. Tech. Report, ITI-DT-96.

[Pas96-2] Pastor,O., Pelechano V., Bonet B., Ramos I. : *An OO Methodological Approach for Making Automated Prototyping Feasible*. Proceedings of DEXA96, Springer-Verlag, September 1996.

[Ser87] Sernadas,A.;Sernadas,C.;Ehrich,H.D. *OO Specification of Databases: An Algebraic Approach*. In P.M.Stocker, W.Kent eds., Proc. of VLDB87, pags: 107-116, Morgan Kauffmann, 1987.

[Rum91] Rumbaugh J.,Blaha M., Permerlani W., Eddy F.,Lorensen W. *Object Oriented Modeling and Design*. Englewood Cliffs, Nj. Prentice-Hall.

[Wir90] Wirfs-Brock R., Wilkerson B., Wiener L., *Designing Object Oriented Software*. Englewood Cliffs, Nj. Prentice-Hall.

[Wie93] Wieringa, R.J., Jungclaus, R., Hartel, P., Hartmann, T., Saake, G., *OMTROLL Object Modeling in TROLL*. Proc. of the International Workshop on Information Systems - Correctness and Reusability (IS-CORE'93). Hannover, September 1993. Udo W. Lipeck, G.Koschorrek (eds.).

The Conceptual Model Is The Code. Why Not?

Oscar Pastor and Vicente Pelechano

Abstract The selection of the paper entitled "OO-METHOD: An OO Software Production Environment Combining Conventional and Formal Methods" for this book on Advanced Information Systems Engineering allows us to reflect on the research context where the work was developed and presented (in "CAiSE 1997") and to introduce its main contributions, how they have evolved with time and what influence the approach could have in the emergence of the Model-Driven Engineering domain. As the main goal was to provide a Software Process that should be fully Conceptual Model-based, the central message of this chapter is still the same 16 years later: the Conceptual Model must be the key software artefact of a sound, correct and complete Software Production Process. Novel approaches were required to generate a sound software production process, and they should use conceptual models as the key software artefact. The model should be the code of the application, and a conceptual modelling programming style should become a reality. While historically Software Engineering is in practice focused on programs, we have always tried to provide methods and tools to achieve the objective of make modelling the essential activity of programming. Why not making true the statement that "the model is the code?". This was our point when we published our referred CAiSE paper, and it is still our position now, with many more results and experiences to support it, that we introduce throughout this work.

O. Pastor (✉) • V. Pelechano
Centro de Investigación en Métodos de Producción de Software, Universitat Politècnica de València, Camino de Vera s/n, 46022 Valencia, Spain
e-mail: opastor@pros.upv.es; pele@pros.upv.es

J. Bubenko et al. (eds.), *Seminal Contributions to Information Systems Engineering*, DOI 10.1007/978-3-642-36926-1_12, © Springer-Verlag Berlin Heidelberg 2013

1 Introduction

Among many other significant improvements, last century nineties was the time of CASE methodologies. Providing a complete software process intended to correctly support analysis, design and implementation became a priority. Some proposals that stemmed from Structured Analysis and Design [1, 2] started to apply notions drawn from Object-Oriented (OO) programming to conceptual modelling. A plethora of OO methods were proposed (e.g. [3–6]), with different methodological backgrounds and a diversity of notations, paving the way for the creation of a Unified Modeling Language called UML [7].

Much effort was devoted to investigating and providing a software process capable to guarantee the quality of the final application code. The CASE tools that were constructed constituted a serious attempt to automate, in some degree, the software production process. The strategy was to define a set of models in a conceptual modelling step that should be properly transformed first in a software design, and then in a software code. But unfortunately, too often these CASE tools generated a frustrating experience in practice. Instead of providing a more effective and efficient solution to the software development process, as they were committed to do, users perceived that the tools were adding an additional burden to the problem of programming. Programming was still a big challenge, but additionally now a new method and its modelling language had to be learnt to create models that still had to be converted into code.

In any case, it was becoming clear that the ideas stated already in 1971 in [8] about the automation of systems building were more alive than never: "the size, importance and cost of systems building provides an opportunity for the investigation of ways to improve the process." These new ways had an increasingly conceptual model-oriented perspective, and eventually conceptual models were playing the wished role of essential software artefact.

It was in this historical context where two CAiSE papers [9, 10] were introducing an approach that had the following original and relevant aspects:

- The proposal of a formal, OO specification language –OASIS- that contained the conceptual primitives required for specifying an organizational system, with a precise semantics.
- The definition of an ontology for information systems, based on the FRISCO proposal [11], to characterize those basic concepts that should be present in a modelling language.
- The creation of a methodological background clearly distinguishing between Problem Space (conceptual model-based, focusing on "what" the system is) and Solution Space (final software product, centred on "how" an appropriate support is going to be provided), together with the specification of an Execution Model intended to link the conceptual primitives of the Conceptual Model (Problem Space) with their corresponding software representation in the final software application (Solution Space).

The pair constituted by the OO specification language (OASIS) and its methodological support (called the "OO-Method") conformed a rigorous contribution that will be presented with full historical detail in Sect. 3.

This work did not come alone. In the following years, a set of proposals, methods, and tools were generated following the same direction, creating a family of approaches that shared a common goal. Instead of having a Software Engineering approach based on the principle that "the code is the model", the new conceptual modelling approaches promoted just the contrary: the model should just be the code. All these proposals have made the dream of automating systems development closer to truth than ever. The most relevant works are summarized in Sect. 2.

Finally, projections of the results reported in this work in other challenging domains will be discussed as further work in Sect. 4. Conclusions and a list of references complete the chapter.

2 Model-Driven Development in Practice: The "Model Is the Code" Versus "The Code Is the Model"

Assuming that programs are models of implementations, one may argue that the main challenge of software engineering is to see Conceptual Models as higher-level programs and to provide sound transformations to convert those conceptual models (Problem Space representation) into code (Software Solution representation). Such a full software process should start with the elaboration of a Requirements Model, and continue with its subsequent transformation into its associated Conceptual Schema that should be executable through a Conceptual Model Compilation process.

The essential principles behind the OO-Method proposal [10] were turn into reality by the implementation of the Integranova Conceptual Model Compiler [12], which was developed and used in an industrial environment.

Morgan introduced in [13] the notion of "Extreme Non-Programming (XNP)", opposing Extreme Programming to highlight that XNP programmers should have a conceptual modelling perspective. This means that they should not do programming at all –at least they should not program in the traditional programming sense-. Instead, they should follow the motto "the model is the code".

Olivé proposed in [14] the concept of "Conceptual Schema-Centric Software Development", proposing a precise criteria to support it: to design an Information System, it is necessary and sufficient to create its Conceptual Schema". Not only necessary, but necessary and sufficient.

In the same line of argument, Model-Driven Engineering (MDE), which is also referred to as Model-Driven Development (MDD) or Model-Driven Architecture (MDA) [15], advocates in the recent years the creation of software systems by model specification. This movement has supposed a strong push to all the ideas that are discussed here, and a plethora of methods and tools have started to appear under the common, accepted assumptions that (i) models ought to be used as the key software artefacts, and (ii) models are to be seen as abstract conceptualizations of particular domain concepts, rather than algorithmic specifications written in a high-level language. Conceptual modelling becomes then the primary means of software production.

More recently, the "Conceptual Modelling Programming" manifesto [16] puts together all these principles, focusing on the importance of three basic ideas: (i) conceptual modelling is programming, (ii) the conceptual model, with which modellers program, must be complete and holistic, and conceptual but precise, and (iii) application evolution must occur at the level of the model.

This selection of approaches provides a solid basis to understand the potential of the ideas discussed in [10, 17] to show how effectively they influenced the advances that lead to the existing MDE approaches, and to analyse how fruitful their evolution has been and is still being.

3 The OO-Method Approach: Past, Present and Future

Let us focus now on the most relevant ideas that conformed the contribution presented in the OO-Method Approach [9, 10, 17], how they have evolved, and what is their intended projection for the very next future.

In a context where the terms MD* (Model-Driven Development, Model-Driven Architecture, Model-Driven Engineering, etc.) and Model Transformations did not exist yet, the OO-Method introduced the following remarkable features [10]:

(a) The use of a formal specification language as a support to characterize the modelling primitives that are required for designing Organizational Information Systems. This provided an ontological commitment for the precise conceptual characterization of the building units of a Conceptual Schema. Since that moment, Ontology Engineering, Metamodelling-based approaches and Conceptual Modelling-based techniques have evolved towards the challenge of elaborating a sound and full Software Process based on Conceptual Modelling..

(b) A strategy for executing Conceptual Schemas –so called Execution Model- that basically defined a set of mappings between the conceptual primitives of the Conceptual Model and their corresponding software representation counterpart in the selected target software development environment.

These two contributions together paved the way to the implementation of a Conceptual Model Compiler, as it happened with the design and implementation of Integranova, a Conceptual Modelling Programming tool created by CARE Tech [12] that created an industrial tool to put into practice all the ideas behind the OO-Method approach.

Since then, the approach has had to be adapted to the appearance of new software development environments, which means that the Conceptual Model Compiler must be always ready to evolve in two ways: finding out better software representations and adapting to diverse software architectures that guide the software generation process and that require to extend the Conceptual Model Compiler offer. As the Conceptual Model level is stable, whenever a new development environment (e.g. a new programming language) is targeted, new mappings between the conceptual primitives and their software representation counterpart in the "new" environment are to be properly designed and implemented.

The future of the approach is related to the "Requirements Engineering" (RE) connection that should provide a full Software Process coverage for the method. This will be more detailed in the next section.

4 What Is Next?

Several lines of both, theoretical and applied research, have given a challenging continuity to the results that were originated by the work presented in [10].

Firstly, the ideas originally applied to the context of Organizational Systems were extended to other IS domains. A set of works designed and implemented a similar type of Conceptual Modelling-based Software Process to: (1) Specify and Implement Web Applications (by building the OOWS methodological approach [18]), (2) Specify and Generate code for AmI systems (by providing the PervML methodological approach [19] and (3) Specifying and Generating Business Process Driven Web Applications [20]). New conceptual primitives have conformed new conceptual models, and the subsequent Conceptual Modelling Programming environments have been designed and implemented. Currently, we are providing solutions in the Software Engineering field to tackle with the new technological and engineering challenges such as those introduced by the development of the Internet of Things (integration of the physical and logic worlds) [21] and the Autonomic Computing (reconfiguration, adaptability at run-time of services and user interfaces) [22].

Secondly, once the transformation of a Conceptual Schema (PIM in MDA terms) into code has been defined by constructing a Conceptual Model Compiler (that contains the PSM logic in MDA terms), the process is to be extended with what is was called the Requirements Engineering (RE) connection above. This means that the Conceptual Schema must be seen as the output of a higher-level model –the Requirements Model (RM), the CIM in MDA terms)- This RM must be defined, together with a sound transformation intended to create its corresponding Conceptual Schema with as much automation as possible. This is probably not a fully automated process, because the Conceptual Schema must add some information that is not present yet at the requirements modelling step. But the metaphor of moving from Requirements to Code through a precise, well defined set of models and model transformation is closer than ever to become a reality. Some steps in this direction have been already taken (see [24]), but much work is still to be done to answer the questions (i) what RM should be selected (ii) how to define the corresponding model transformation.

Thirdly, a very interesting perspective is to think about further domains were all these ideas could be used to improve the current software development process and obtain better results. Some challenging candidates can be aircraft control weather prediction, vehicle mobile clouds, digital TV, video-games, etc. But there is one especially appealing that is the modelling of life. Conceptual Modelling of the Human Genome can provide a different perspective of the same problem: considering alive beings "implementations" of a (genetic) code, the problem is to understand the modelling primitives that could make feasible to define models and to understand how these models are converted into the final code (the human being). The clinical projection of this challenge is especially interesting, intended to apply a conceptual modelling-oriented approach to find out and manage the "bugs" (illnesses) that are a consequence of a (genetic) code mistake. Some previous promising results have been reported in [23].

5 Conclusions

Producing a sound information system design and implementing such design into a software product of high quality sounds simple, but it is still a nightmare for Software and Information Systems Engineering. The well-know problems often referred to as the *crisis of software* remain alive. In most of the complex software projects, the design, programming and testing activities still require a substantial manual effort and are keep being error-prone. From the point of view of conceptual modelling and the role of models, we claim that the software development process has not changed much over the past 40 years. We mean that the "program" has been and still is often considered the essential software artefact. Trying to prioritize conceptual modelling over programing,, many attempts have promoted that "the model should be code" instead of insisting that "the code is and will ever be the model". Assuming that looking for a different way for producing software was worth to be explored, we presented in [10] an approach that intended to fulfil that goal. Through a clear separation between Problem Space (Conceptual Schema) and Solution Space (application code), a ontologically well-founded modelling environment was presented, together with an execution strategy to transform the modelling primitives into software components through a process of conceptual-model compilation. This was one of the first works presenting a concrete solution for a domain that a few years later was extensively explored under the model-driven development paradigm, for which it could be argued that it was indeed a very significant contribution.

References

1. DeMarco, T., Structured analysis and system specification. 1979, Englewood Cliffs, New Jersey: Yourdon Press.
2. Ward, P.T, Mellor, S. Structured Development for Real-Time Systems: Essential Modeling Techniques. Prentice Hall.

3. Rumbaugh, J., Blaha. M, Premerlani. W, Eddy. F, Lorensen. W. Object-Oriented Modeling and Design. Prentice Hall. 1999.
4. Booch. G, Maksimchuk. R. A., Engel. M. W., Young. B.J. Object-Oriented Analysis and Design with Applications. Addison-Wesley
5. Jacobson. I., Christerson. M, Jonsson. P, Overgaard. G. Object-Oriented Software Engineering: A Use Case Driven Approach (ACM Press). Addison-Wesley, 1992,
6. Wirfs-Brock. R.J. Designing Object-Oriented Software, with Brian Wilkerson and Lauren Wiener, Prentice-Hall, 1990
7. Booch, G., Rumbaugh, J., Jacobson, I. The Unified Modeling Language User Guide. Addison-Wesley.
8. Teichroew, D., Sayani, H.: Automation of System Building, Datamation (1971).
9. Pastor. O, Hayes. F., Bear. S. OASIS: An Object-Oriented Specification Language. CAiSE 1992: 348–363
10. Pastor. O, Insfrán. E, Pelechano. V., Romero. J.R., Merseguer. J. OO-METHOD: An OO Software Production Environment Combining Conventional and Formal Methods. CAiSE 1997: 145–158.
11. Falkenberg. E.D., Hesse. W., Lindgreen. P., Nilsson. B.E., Oei. J.L.H., Rolland. C., Stamper. R.K., Van Assche. F.J.M., Verrijn-Stuart. A.A., Voss. K. FRISCO : A Framework of Information System Concepts, The IFIP WG 8.1 Task Group FRISCO, December 1996.
12. Integranova Software Soluctions. Available on: http://www.integranova.com/. Last Access: January 19, 2013.
13. Morgan, T.: Business Rules and Information Systems – Aligning IT with Business Goals. Addison-Wesley, Reading (2002).
14. Olivé, À.: Conceptual Schema-Centric Development: A Grand Challenge for Information Systems Research. In: Pastor, Ó., Falcão e Cunha, J. (eds.) CAiSE 2005. LNCS, vol. 3520, pp. 1–15. Springer, Heidelberg (2005).
15. Booch. G, Brown. A., Iyengar. S., Rumbaugh. J., Selic. B. An MDA Manifesto. The MDA Journal: Model Driven Architecture Straight from the Masters, pages 133–143, 2004.
16. Embley. D. W., Liddle. S.W, Pastor, O. Conceptual-Model Programming: A Manifesto. Handbook of Conceptual Modeling, 2011, pp 3–16. Springer.
17. Pastor, O., Gomez, J., Insfrán, E., Pelechano, V.: The OO-Method approach for information systems modeling: from object-oriented conceptual modeling to automated programming. Information Systems 26(7), 507–534 (2001).
18. Fons. J, Pelechano. V, Albert. M, Pastor. O. Development of Web Applications from Web Enhanced Conceptual Schemas. ER 2003: 232–245.
19. Muñoz. J., Pelechano. V. Building a Software Factory for Pervasive Systems Development. CAiSE 2005: 342–356
20. Torres. V., Giner. P., Pelechano. V. Developing BP-driven web applications through the use of MDE techniques. Software and System Modeling 11(4): 609–631 (2012)
21. Giner. P., Cetina. C., Fons. J., Pelechano. V. Developing Mobile Workflow Support in the Internet of Things. IEEE Pervasive Computing 9(2): 18–26 (2010)
22. Cetina. C., Giner. P., Fons. J., Pelechano. V. Vicente Pelechano: Autonomic Computing through Reuse of Variability Models at Runtime: The Case of Smart Homes. IEEE Computer 42(10): 37–43 (2009)
23. Oscar Pastor, Juan Carlos Casamayor, Matilde Celma, Laura Mota, M. Ángeles Pastor, Ana M. Levin: Conceptual Modeling of Human Genome: Integration Challenges. Conceptual Modelling and Its Theoretical Foundations 2012: 231–250
24. Oscar Pastor, Sergio España: Full Model-Driven Practice: From Requirements to Code Generation. CAiSE 2012: 701–702

Architecture and Quality in Data Warehouses[1]

Matthias Jarke[(1)], Manfred A. Jeusfeld[(2)]
Christoph Quix[(1)], Panos Vassiliadis[(3)]

(1) RWTH Aachen, Germany, {jarke,quix}@informatik.rwth--aachen.de

(2) Tilburg University, The Netherlands, jeusfeld@kub.nl

(3) National Technical University of Athens, Greece, pvassil@dbnet.ece.ntua.gr

Abstract. Most database researchers have studied data warehouses (DW) in their role as buffers of materialized views, mediating between update-intensive OLTP systems and query-intensive decision support. This neglects the organizational role of data warehousing as a means of centralized information flow control. As a consequence, a large number of quality aspects relevant for data warehousing cannot be expressed with the current DW meta models. This paper makes two contributions towards solving these problems. Firstly, we enrich the meta data about DW architectures by explicit enterprise models. Secondly, many very different mathematical techniques for measuring or optimizing certain aspects of DW quality are being developed. We adapt the Goal-Question-Metric approach from software quality management to a meta data management environment in order to link these special techniques to a generic conceptual framework of DW quality. Initial feedback from ongoing experiments with a partial implementation of the resulting meta data structure in three industrial case studies provides a partial validation of the approach.

1 Introduction

Data warehouses provide large-scale caches of historic data. They sit between information sources gained externally or through online transaction processing systems (OLTP), and decision support or data mining queries following the vision of

[1] This research was partially supported by the European Commission in ESPRIT Long Term Research Project DWQ (Foundations of Data Warehouse Quality), by the General Secretariat of Research and Technology (Greece) under the PENED program; and by the Deutsche Forschungsgemeinschaft through Graduiertenkolleg "Informatik und Technik".

online analytic processing (OLAP). Three main arguments have been put forward in favor of this caching approach:

1. *Performance and safety considerations*: The concurrency control methods of most DBMSs do not react well to a mix of short update transactions (as in OLTP) and OLAP queries that typically search a large portion of the database. Moreover, the OLTP systems are often critical for the operation of the organization and must not be under danger of corruption of other applications.

2. *Logical interpretability problems*: Inspired by the success of spreadsheet techniques, OLAP users tend to think in terms of highly structured multi-dimensional data models, whereas information sources offer at best relational, often just semi-structured data models.

3. *Temporal and granularity mismatch*: OLTP systems focus on current operational support in great detail, whereas OLAP often considers historical developments at a somewhat less detailed granularity.

Thus, quality considerations have accompanied data warehouse research from the beginning. A large body of literature has evolved over the past few years in addressing the problems introduced by the DW approach, such as the trade-off between freshness of DW data and disturbance of OLTP work during data extraction; the minimization of data transfer through incremental view maintenance; and a theory of computation with multi-dimensional data models.

However, the heavy use of highly qualified consultants in data warehouse applications indicates that we are far from a systematic understanding and usage of the interplay between quality factors and design options in data warehousing. The goal of the European DWQ project [JV97] is to address these issues by developing, prototyping and evaluating comprehensive Foundations for Data Warehouse Quality, delivered through *enriched meta data management facilities* in which specific analysis and optimization techniques are embedded.

This paper develops the DWQ architecture and quality management framework and describes first steps towards its implementation and validation. The main contributions include an extension of the standard DW architecture used in the literature by enterprise modeling aspects, and a strategy for embedding special-purpose mathematical reasoning tools in the architecture which will enable a computationally tractable yet rich quality analysis or quality-driven design process.

Interaction with DW tool vendors, DW application developers and administrators has shown that the standard framework used in the DW literature is insufficient to capture in particular the business role of data warehousing. A DW is a major investment made to satisfy some business goal of the enterprise; quality model and DW design should reflect this business goal as well as its subsequent evolution over time. In section 2, we discuss this problem in detail; our new architectural framework separates (and links) explicitly the concerns of conceptual enterprise perspectives, logical data modeling (the main emphasis of DW research to date), and physical information flow (the main concern of commercial DW products to date).

In section 3, we first build on literature frameworks for data and software quality to come up with a suitable set of DW quality dimensions, as perceived by different groups of stakeholders. We then adapt a variant of the so-called Goal-Question-Metric approach used in software quality management. Through materialized quality views, we link conceptual quality goals to specific analysis techniques developed in DW research and practice, and enable trade-offs between heterogeneous quality goals. Initial experiences with a prototypical implementation of the resulting meta database using the ConceptBase deductive object manager have been gained in cooperation with industrial case studies. Section 4 relates our approach to other work in data warehousing, data and software quality, while section 5 provides a summary and conclusions.

2 The Architecture of a Data Warehouse

Physically, a data warehouse system consists of databases (source databases, materialized views in the distributed data warehouse), data transport agents that ship data from one database to another and a data warehouse repository which stores all kinds of meta data about the system. The content of the repository determines to a large extent how the data warehouse system can be used and evolved. The main goal of our approach is therefore to define a meta database schema which can capture and link all relevant aspects of DW architecture and quality. We shall tackle this very difficult undertaking in several steps.

2.1 Three Perspectives of Data Warehouse Meta Data

Almost all current research and practice understand a data warehouse architecture as a stepwise information flow from information sources through materialized views towards analyst clients, as shown in figure 2.1. Our key observation is that this architecture covers only partially the tasks faced in data warehousing and is therefore unable to even express, let alone support, a large number of important quality problems and management strategies.

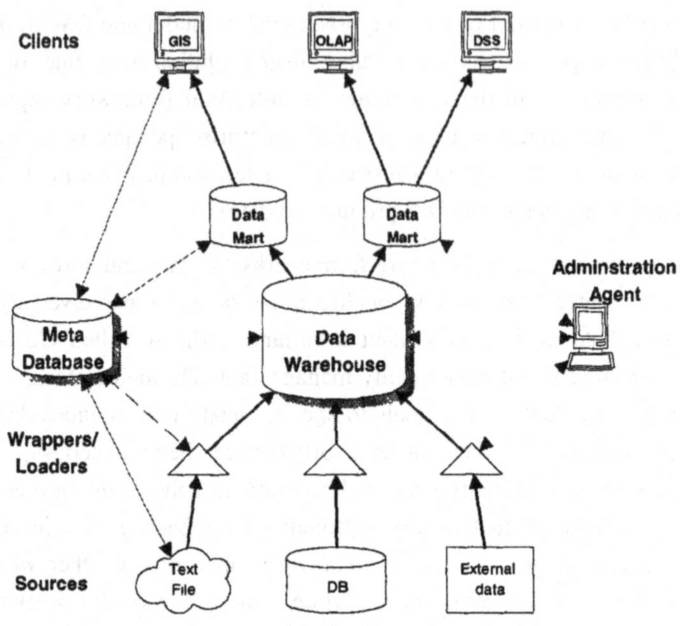

Figure 2.1: Current Understanding of a Data Warehouse

As a consequence, we propose a separation of three perspectives as shown in figure 2.2: a conceptual enterprise perspective, a logical data modeling perspective, and a physical data flow perspective.

The main argument we wish to make is the need for a *conceptual enterprise perspective*. To explain, consider the left two columns of figure 2.2. Suppose an analyst wants to know something about the business -- the question mark in the figure. She does not have the time to observe the business directly but must rely on existing information gained by operational departments, and documented as a side effect of OLTP systems. This way of information gathering implies already a bias which needs to be compensated when selecting OLTP data for uploading and cleaning into a DW where it is then further pre-processed and aggregated in data marts for certain analysis tasks. Considering the long path the data has taken, it is obvious that also the last step, the formulation of conceptually adequate queries and the conceptually adequate interpretation of the answers presents a major problem to the analyst.

The traditional DW literature only covers two of the five steps in figure 2.2. Thus, it has no answers to typical practitioner questions such as "how come my operational departments put so much money in their data quality, and still the quality of my DW is terrible?" (answer: the enterprise views of the operational departments are not easily compatible with each other or with the analysts view), or "what is the effort required to analyze problem X for which the DW currently offers no information?" (could simply be a problem of wrong aggregation in the materialized views, could require access to not-yet-integrated OLTP sources, or even involve setting up new OLTP sensors in the organization).

An adequate answer to such questions requires an explicit model of the conceptual relationships between an enterprise model, the information captured by OLTP departments, and the OLAP clients whose task is the decision analysis. We have argued that a DW is a major investment undertaken for a particular business purpose. We therefore do not just introduce the enterprise model as a minor part of the environment, but demand that *all other models are defined as views on this enterprise model.* Perhaps surprisingly, even information source schemas define views on the enterprise model -- not vice versa as suggested by figure 2.1!

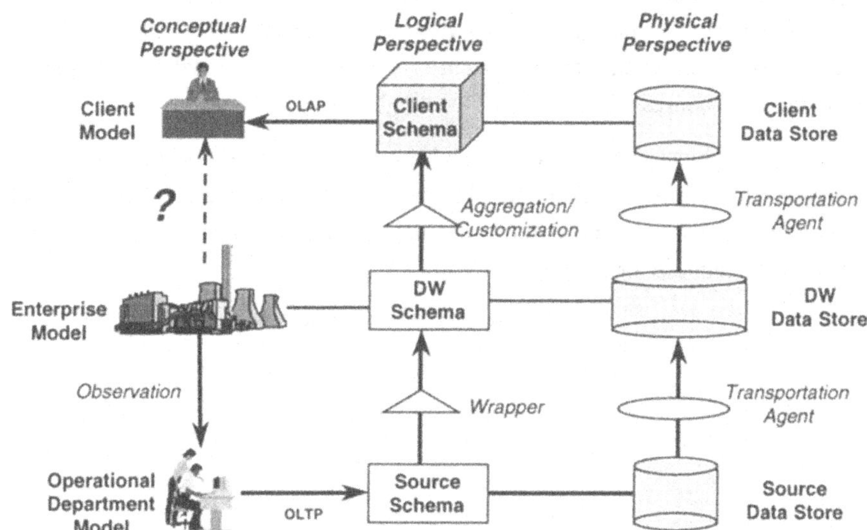

Figure 2.2 The Data Warehouse Meta Data Framework

The wrapping and aggregation transformations performed in the (traditionally discussed) logical perspective can thus be checked for interpretability, consistency or completeness with respect to the enterprise model -- provided an adequately powerful representation and reasoning mechanism is available. At the same time, the logical transformations need to be implemented safely and efficiently by physical storage and transportation -- the third perspective in our approach. It is clear that physical quality aspects require completely different modeling formalisms than the conceptual factors, typical techniques stemming from queuing theory and combinatorial optimization.

There is no single decidable formalism that could handle all of these aspects uniformly in a meta database. We have therefore decided to capture the architectural framework in a deductive object data model in a comprehensive but relatively shallow manner. Special-purpose reasoning mechanisms such as the ones mentioned above can be linked to the architectural framework as discussed in section 3, below.

2.2 A Notation for Data Warehouse Architecture

We use the meta database to store an abstract representation of data warehouse applications in terms of the three-perspective scheme. The architecture and quality models are represented in Telos [MBJK90], a metadata modeling language. Its implementation in the ConceptBase system [JGJ+95] provides query facilities, and definition of constraints and deductive rules. Telos is well suited because it allows to formalize specialized modeling notations by means of meta classes. Preloaded with these metaclasses, the ConceptBase system serves as the meta database for quality-oriented data warehouses.

A condensed graphical overview of the architecture notation is given in Figure 2.3. Bold arrows denote specialization links. The most general meta class is *DW_Object*. It subsumes objects at any perspective (conceptual, logical, or physical) and at any level (source, data warehouse, or client).

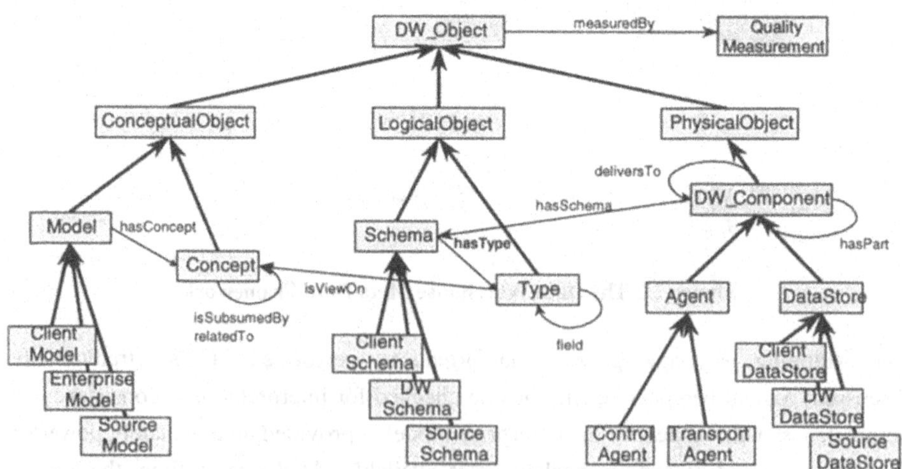

Figure 2.3: Overview of the Architecture Notation

Within each perspective, we distinguish between the modules it offers (e.g. client model) and the kinds of information found within these modules (e.g. concepts and their subsumption relationships). The horizontal links *hasSchema* and *isViewOn* establish the way how the horizontal links in Figure 2.2 are interpreted: the types of a schema (i.e., relational or multidimensional structures) are defined as logical views on the concepts in the conceptual perspectives. On the other hand, the components of the physical perspective get a schema from the logical perspective as their schema.

Each object can have an associated set of materialized views called *QualityMeasurements*. These materialized views (which can also be specialized to the different perspectives -- not shown in the figure) constitute the bridge to the quality model discussed in section 3.

The horizontal levels of the objects are coded by the three subclasses attached to *Model*, *Schema*, and *DataStore*. We found this notation adequate to represent physical data warehouse architectures of commercial applications, such as the SourcePoint tool marketed by Software AG [SAG96] or the DW architecture underlying a data mining project at Swiss Life [SKR97]. The logical perspective currently supports relational schema definitions whereas the conceptual perspective supports the family of extended entity-relationship and similar semantic data modeling languages. Note that all objects in Figure 2.3 are meta classes: actual conceptual models, logical schemas, and data warehouse components are represented as instances of them in the meta database. In the following subsections, we elaborate on the purpose of representing each of the three perspectives.

2.3 Conceptual Perspective

The conceptual perspective describes the business models underlying the information systems of an enterprise. The central role is played by the enterprise model, which gives an integrative overview of the conceptual objects of an enterprise. The models of the client and source information systems are views on the enterprise model, i.e. their contents are described in terms of the enterprise model. One goal of the conceptual perspective is to have a model of the information independent from physical organization of the data, so that relationships between concepts can be analyzed by intelligent tools, e.g. to simplify the integration of the information sources. On the client side, the interests of user groups can also be described as views on the enterprise model.

In the implementation of the conceptual perspective in the meta database, the central class is *Model*. A model is related to a source, a client or the relevant section of the enterprise, and it represents the concepts which are available in the corresponding source, client or enterprise. The classes *ClientModel*, *SourceModel* and *EnterpriseModel* are needed, to distinguish the models of several sources, clients and the enterprise itself. A model consists of *Concepts*, each representing a concept of the real world, i.e. the business world. If the user provides some information about the relationship between concepts in a formal language like description logics, a reasoner can check for subsumption of concepts [CDL97].

The results of the reasoning process are stored in the model as attribute *isSubsumedBy* of the corresponding concepts. Essentially, the repository can serve as a cache for reasoning results. Any tool can ask the repository for containment of concepts. If the result has already been computed, it can directly be answered by the repository. Otherwise, a reasoner is invoked by the repository to compute the result.

2.4 Logical Perspective

The logical perspective conceives a data warehouse from the view point of the actual data models involved, i.e. the data model of the logical schema is given by the corresponding physical component, which implements the logical schema. The central point in the logical perspective is *Schema.* As a model consists of concepts a schema consists of *Types.* We have implemented the relational model as an example for a logical data model; other data models such as the multi-dimensional or the object-oriented data model are also being integrated in this framework.

Like in the conceptual perspective, we distinguish in the logical perspective between *ClientSchema*, *DWSchema* and *SourceSchema* for the schemata of clients, the data warehouse and the sources. For each client or source model, there is one corresponding schema. This restriction is guaranteed by a constraint in the architecture model. The link to the conceptual model is implemented by the relationship between concepts and types: each type is expressed as a view on concepts.

2.5 Physical Perspective

Data warehouse industry has mostly explored the physical perspective, so that many aspects in the physical perspective are taken from the analysis of commercial data warehouse solutions such as Software AG's SourcePoint tool [SAG96], the data warehouse system of RedBrick [RedB97], Informix's MetaCube[Info97], Essbase of Arbor Software [Arbo96] or the product suite of MicroStrategy [MStr97]. We have observed that the basic physical components in a data warehouse architecture are *agents* and *data stores*. *Agents* are programs that control other components or transport data from one physical location to another. *Data stores* are databases which store the data that is delivered by other components.

The basic class in the physical perspective is *DW_Component.* A data warehouse component may be composed out of other components. This fact is expressed by the attribute *hasPart.* Furthermore, a component *deliversTo* another component a *Type,* which is part of the logical perspective. Another link to the logical model is the attribute *hasSchema* of *DW_Component.* Note that a component may have a schema, i.e. a set of several types, but it can only deliver a type to another component. This is due to the observation that agents usually transport only "one tuple at a time" of a source relation rather than a complex object.

One type of component in a data warehousing environment is an *Agent.* There are two types of agents: *ControlAgent* which controls other components and agents, e.g. it *notifies* another agent to start the update process, and *TransportationAgent* which transports data from one component to another component. An *Agent* may also notify other agents about errors or termination of its process.

Another type of component is a *DataStore.* It physically stores the data which is described by models and schemata in the conceptual and logical perspective. As in the other perspectives, we distinguish between *ClientDataStore*, *DW_DataStore* and *SourceDataStore* for data stores of clients, the data warehouse and the sources.

3 Managing Data Warehouse Quality

In this section, we discuss how to extend the DW architecture model by explicit quality models and their support. There are two basic issues to be resolved. On the one hand, quality is a subjective phenomenon so we must organize quality goals according to the stakeholder groups that pursue these goals. On the other hand, quality goals are highly diverse in nature. They can be neither assessed nor achieved directly but require complex measurement, prediction, and design techniques, often in the form of an interactive process. The overall problem of introducing quality models in meta data is therefore to achieve breadth of coverage without giving up the detailed knowledge available for certain criteria. Only if this combination is achieved, systematic quality management becomes possible.

3.1 Stakeholders in Data Warehouse Quality

There exist different roles of users in a data warehouse environment. The *Decision Maker* usually employs an OLAP query tool to get answers interesting to him. A decision maker is usually concerned with the *quality of the stored data*, their *timeliness* and the *ease of querying* them through the OLAP tools. The *Data*

Warehouse Administrator needs facilities like *error reporting, metadata accessibility* and knowledge of the *timeliness* of the data, in order to detect changes and reasons for them, or problems in the stored information. The *Data Warehouse Designer* needs to measure the *quality of the schemata* of the data warehouse environment (both existing or newly produced) and the *quality of the metadata* as well. Furthermore, he needs *software evaluation standards* to test the software packages he considers purchasing. The *Programmers of Data Warehouse Components* can make good use of *software implementation standards* in order to accomplish and evaluate their work. *Metadata reporting* can also facilitate their job, since they can avoid mistakes related to schema information.

Based on this analysis, we can safely argue that different roles imply a different collection of quality dimensions, which a quality model should be able to address in a consistent and meaningful way. In the following, we summarize the quality dimensions of three stakeholders, the data warehouse administrator, the programmer, and the decision maker. A more detailed presentation can be found in [DWQ97b].

Design and Administration Quality. The design and administration quality can be analyzed into more detailed dimensions, as depicted in Figure 3.1. The *schema quality* refers to the ability of a schema or model to represent adequately and efficiently the information. The *correctness* dimension is concerned with the proper comprehension of the entities of the real world, the schemata of the sources (models) and the user needs. The *completeness* dimension is concerned with the preservation of all the crucial knowledge in the data warehouse schema (model). The *minimality* dimension describes the degree up to which undesired redundancy is avoided during the source integration process. The *traceability* dimension is concerned with the fact that all kinds of requirements of users, designers, administrators and managers should be traceable to the data warehouse schema. The *interpretability* dimension ensures that all components of the data warehouse are well described, so as to be administered easily. The *metadata evolution* dimension is concerned with the way the schema evolves during the data warehouse operation.

Software Implementation Quality. Software implementation and/or evaluation is not a task with specific data warehouse characteristics. We are not actually going to propose a new model for this task, but adopt the ISO 9126 standard [ISO91]. The quality dimensions of ISO 9126 are *Functionality* (Suitability, Accuracy, Interoperability, Compliance, Security), *Reliability* (Maturity, Fault tolerance, Recoverability), *Usability* (Understandability, Learnability, Operability), *Software Efficiency* (Time behavior, Resource Behavior), *Maintainability* (Analyzability, Changeability, Stability, Testability), *Portability* (Adaptability, Installability, Conformance, Replaceability).

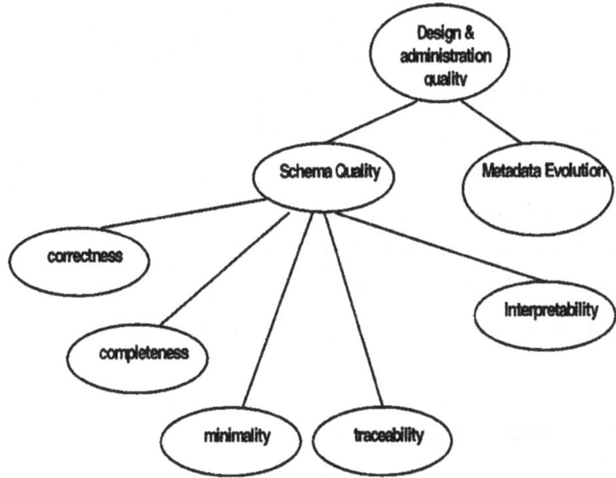

Figure 3.1 Design and administration quality dimensions

Data Usage Quality. Since databases and -in our case- data warehouses are built in order to be queried, the most basic process of the warehouse is the usage and querying of its data. Figure 3.2 shows the hierarchy of quality dimensions related to data usage.

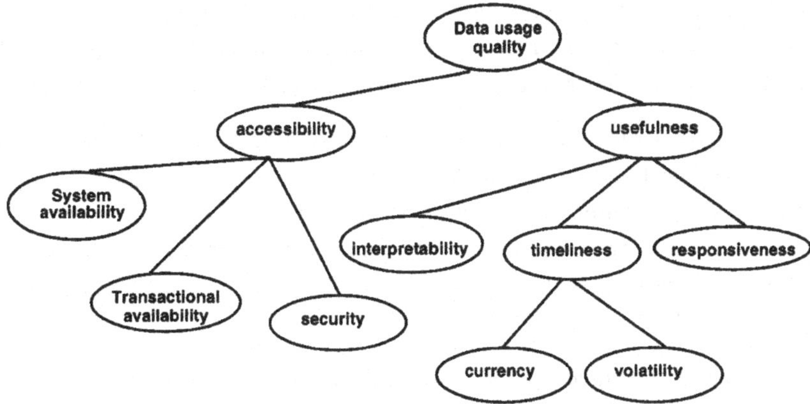

Figure 3.2 Data usage quality dimensions

The *accessibility* dimension is related to the possibility of accessing the data for querying. The *security* dimension describes the authorization policy and the privileges each user has for the querying of the data. *System availability* describes the percentage of time the source or data warehouse system is available (i.e. the system is up and no backups take place, etc.). The *transactional availability* dimension, as already mentioned, describes the percentage of time the information in the warehouse or the source is available due to the absence of update processes which write-lock the data.

The *usefulness* dimension describes the temporal characteristics (*timeliness*) of the data as well as the *responsiveness* of the system. The *responsiveness* is concerned with the interaction of a process with the user (e.g. a query tool which is self reporting on the time a query might take to be answered). The *currency* dimension describes when the information was entered in the sources or/and the data warehouse. The *volatility* dimension describes the time period for which the information is valid in the real world. The *interpretability* dimension, as already mentioned, describes the extent to which the data warehouse is modeled efficiently in the information repository. The better the explanation is, the easier the queries can be posed.

3.2 From Architecture to Quality

We now turn to the formal handling and repository-based management of DW quality goals such as the ones described in the previous section.

A first formalization could be based on a qualitative analysis of relationships between the quality factors themselves, e.g. positive or negative goal-subgoal relationships or goal-means relationships. The stakeholders could then enter their subjective evaluation of individual goals as well as possible weightings of goals and be supported in identifying good trade-offs. The entered as well as computed evaluations could be used as quality measurements in the architecture model of figure 2.3, thus enabling a very simple integration of architecture and quality model.

Such an approach is widely used in industrial engineering under the label of Quality Function Deployment, using a special kind of matrix representation called the House of Quality [Akao90]. Formal reasoning in such a structure has been investigated in works about the handling of non-functional requirements in software engineering, e.g. [MCN92]. Visual tools have shown a potential for negotiation support under multiple quality criteria [GJJ97].

However, while this simple approach certainly has a useful role in cross-criteria decision making, using it alone would throw away the richness of work created by research in measuring, predicting, or optimizing individual DW quality factors. In the DWQ project, such methods are systematically adopted or newly developed for all quality factors found important in the literature or our own empirical work. To give an impression of the richness of techniques to be considered, we use a single quality factor -- responsiveness in the sense of good query performance -- for which the DWQ project has studied three different approaches, one each from the conceptual, logical, and physical perspective.

We start with the logical perspective [TS97]. Here, the quality indicator associated with responsiveness is taken to be a weighted average of query and update "costs" for a given query mix and given information sources. A combinatorial optimization technique is then proposed that selects a collection of materialized views as to minimize the total costs. This can be considered a very simple case of the above Quality Function Deployment approach, but with the advantage of automated design of a solution.

If we include the physical perspective, the definition of query and update "costs" becomes an issue in itself: what do we mean by costs -- response time, throughput, or a combination of both (e.g. minimize query response time and maximize update throughput)? what actually produces these costs -- is database access or the network traffic the bottleneck? A comprehensive queuing model [NJ97] enables the prediction of such detailed metrics from which the designer can choose the right ones as quality measurements for his design process. In addition, completely new design options come into play : instead of materializing more views to improve query response time (at the cost of disturbing the OLTP systems longer at update time), the designer could buy a faster client PC or DBMS, or use an ISDN link rather than using slow modems.

Yet other options come into play, if a rich logic is available for the conceptual perspective. The description logic DWQ uses for formalizing the conceptual perspective [CDL97], allows to state that, e.g., information about all instances of one concept in the enterprise model is maintained in a particular information source, i.e. the source is complete with respect to the domain. This enables the DW designer to drop the materialization of all views on other sources, thus reducing the update effort semantically without any loss in completeness of the answers.

It is clear that there can be no decidable formal framework that even comes close to covering all of these aspects in a uniform language. When designing the meta database extensions for quality management, we therefore had to look for another solution that still maintains the overall picture offered by the shallow quality management techniques discussed at the beginning of this section but is at the same time open for the embedding of specialized techniques.

Our solution to this problem builds on the widely used Goal-Question-Metric (GQM) approach to software quality management [OB92]. The idea of GQM is that quality goals can usually not be assessed directly, but their meaning is circumscribed by questions that need to be answered when evaluating the quality. Such questions again can usually not be answered directly but rely on metrics applied to either the product or process in question; techniques such as statistical process control charts are then applied to derive the answer of a question from the measurements.

Our repository solution uses a similar approach to bridge the gap between quality goal hierarchies on the one hand, and very detailed metrics and reasoning techniques on the other. The bridge is defined through the idea of quality measurements as materialized views over the data warehouse which we already introduced in figure 2.3, and through generic queries over these quality measurements. This implementation strategy provides more technical support than usual GQM implementations. It is enabled through the powerful parameterized query class mechanism offered by the ConceptBase system.

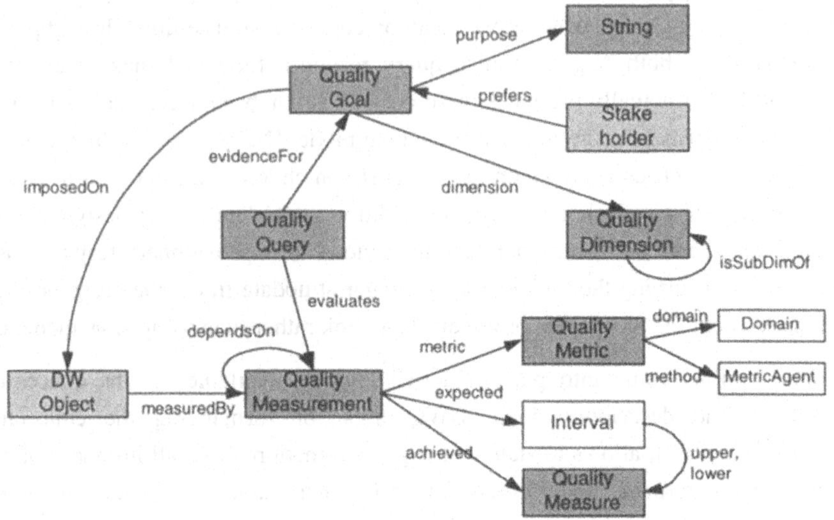

Figure 3.3: A notation for Data Warehouse Quality

The purpose of a quality goal is usually to improve some quality values of the DW or to achieve a certain quality value. Quality goals are associated with types of queries defined over quality measurements. These queries will support the evaluation of a specific quality goal when parameterized with a given (part of a) DW meta database. Such a query usually compares the analysis goal to a certain expected interval in order to assess the level of quality achieved. Furthermore, goals are established by stakeholders, who may have several subjective quality preferences. As a consequence, the quality measurement must contain information about both expected and actual values. Both could be entered into the meta database manually, or computed inductively by a given metric through a specific reasoning mechanism. For example, for a given physical design and some basic measurements of component and network speeds, the queuing model in [NJ97] computes the quality values for response time and throughput, and it could indicate if network or database access is the bottleneck in the given setting. This could then be combined with conceptual or logical quality measurements at the level of optimizing the underlying quality goal.

The interplay of goals, queries, and metrics with the basic concepts of the architecture model is shown in the Telos meta model of figure 3.3. While the development and integration of numerous specific metrics is the goal of ongoing work in the DWQ project, our current implementation just covers the upper levels of the picture, such that only manual entry of quality measurements is supported. A number of quality queries have been implemented, focusing on some that turned out to be relevant when validating the architecture against three case studies: creating a model of Software AG's SourcePoint DW loading environment, modeling data quality problems hindering the application of data mining techniques in Swiss Life, and conceptually re-constructing some design decisions underlying the administrative data warehouses of the City of Cologne, Germany [DWQ97a, DWQ97b].

Quality queries access information recorded in quality measurements. A quality measurement stores the following information about data warehouse components:

1. an interval of expected quality measures
2. the current quality measure
3. the metric used to compute a measure
4. dependencies to other quality measurements

The dependencies between quality measurements can be used to trace quality measurements outside the expected interval to their causes. The following two queries exemplify how quality measurements classify data warehouse components and how the backtracing of quality problems can be done by queries to the meta database:

```
QueryClass BadQualityMeasurement isA QualityMeasurement
 with constraint
   c: $ not (this.expected contains this.current) $
end

GenericQueryClass CauseOfBadQuality isA DW_Object
 with parameter
   badObject : DW_Object
 constraint
   c: $ exists q1,q2/QualityMeasurement
        (badObject measuredBy q1) and
        (q1 in BadQualityMeasurement) and
        (q1 dependsOn q2) and
       (q2 in BadQualityMeasurement) and
       ((this measuredBy q2) or
       (exists o/DW_Object (o measuredBy q2) and
       (this in CauseOfBadQuality[o/badObject]))) $
end
```

4 Related Work

Our approach extends and merges results from data warehouse research and data/software quality research.

Starting with the data warehouse literature, the well-known projects have focused almost exclusively on what we call the logical and physical perspectives of DW architecture. While the majority of early projects have focused on source integration aspects, the recent effort has shifted towards the efficient computation and re-computation of multi-dimensional views. The business perspective is considered at best indirectly in these projects. The *Information Manifold* (IM) developed at AT&T is the only one that employs a rich domain model for information gathering from disparate sources such as databases, SGML documents, unstructured files [LSK95, KLSS95, LRO96] in a manner similar to our approach.

TSIMMIS (*The Stanford-IBM Manager of Multiple Information Sources*) is a project with the goal of providing tools for the integrated access to multiple and diverse information sources and repositories [CGMH+94, Ull97]. Each information source is equipped with a *wrapper* that encapsulates the source, converting the underlying data objects to a common data model - called *Object Exchange Model* (OEM). On top of wrappers, *mediators* [Wie92] can be conceptually seen as views of data found in one or more sources which are suitably integrated and processed.

Similarly, but with slightly different implementation strategies, the *Squirrel* Project [HZ96, ZHK96] provides a framework for data integration based on the notion of *integration mediator*. Integration mediators are active modules that support incrementally maintained integrated views over multiple databases. Moreover, data quality is considered by defining formal properties of *consistency* and *freshness* for integrated views.

The WHIPS (*WareHouse Information Prototype at Stanford*) system [HGMW+95, WGL+96] has the goal of developing algorithms for the collection, integration and maintenance of information from heterogeneous and autonomous sources. The WHIPS architecture consists of a set of independent modules implemented as CORBA objects. The central component of the system is the *integrator*, to which all other modules report.

Turning to data quality analysis, Wang et al. [WSF95] present a framework based on the ISO 9000 standard. They review a significant part of the literature on data quality, yet only the research and development aspects of data quality seem to be relevant to the cause of data warehouse quality design. In [WRK95], an attribute-based model is presented that can be used to incorporate quality aspects of data products. The basis of this approach is the assumption that the quality design of an information system can be incorporated in the overall design of the system. The model proposes the extension of the relational model as well as the annotation of the results of a query with the appropriate quality indicators. Further work on data quality can be found in [BT89], [BWPT93], [Jans88], [LU90], [Hall78], [Krie79], and [AA87].

Variants of the Goal-Question-Metric (GQM) approach are widely adopted in software quality management [OB92]. A structured overview of the issues and strategies, embedded in a repository framework, can be found in [JP92]. Several goal hierarchies of quality factors have been proposed, including the GE Model [MRW78] and [Boeh89]. ISO 9126 [ISO91] suggests six basic factors which are further refined to an overall 21 quality factors. In [HR96] a comparative presentation of these three models is offered and the SATC software quality model is proposed, along with metrics for all their software quality dimensions.

5 Discussion and Conclusions

The goal of our work is to enrich meta data management in data warehouses such that it can serve as a meaningful basis for systematic quality analysis and quality-driven design. To reach this goal, we had to overcome two limitations of current data warehouse research.

Firstly, the basic architecture in which data warehouses are typically described turned out to be too weak to allow a meaningful quality assessment : as quality is usually detected only by its absence, quality-oriented meta data management requires that we address the full sequence of steps from the capture of enterprise reality in operational departments to the interpretation of DW information by the client analyst. This in turn implied the introduction of an explicit enterprise model as a central feature in the architecture. To forestall possible criticism that full enterprise modeling has proven a risky and expensive effort, we point out that our approach to enterprise model formation (including the formal language used in [CDL97]) is fully incremental such that it is perfectly feasible to construct the enterprise model step by step, e.g. as a side effect of source integration or of other business process analysis efforts.

The second major problem is the enormous richness in quality factors, each associated with its own wealth of measurement and design techniques. Our quest for an open quality management environment that can accommodate existing or new such techniques led us to an adaptation and repository integration of the Goal-Question Metric approach where parameterized queries and materialized quality views serve as the missing link between specialized techniques and the general quality framework.

The power of the repository modeling language determines the boundary between precise but narrow metrics and comprehensive but shallow global repository. The deductive object base formalism of the Telos language provides a fairly sophisticated level of global quality analysis in our prototype implementation but is still fully adaptable and general; once the quality framework has sufficiently stabilized, a procedurally object-oriented approach could do even more, by encoding some metrics directly as methods, of course at the expense of flexibility. Conversely, a simple relational meta database could take up some of the present models with less semantics than offered in the ConceptBase system, but with the same flexibility.

As of now, both the framework and its implementation can only be considered partially validated. One strain of current work therefore continues the validation against several major case studies, in order to set priorities among the quality criteria to be explicated in specific metrics and analysis techniques. A second overlapping strain concerns the development of these techniques themselves, and their linkage into the overall framework through suitable quality measurements and extensions to global design and optimization techniques. Especially when progressing from the definition of metrics and prediction techniques to actual design methods, it is expected that these will not be representable as closed algorithms but must take the form of interactive work processes defined over the DW architecture.

As an example, feedback from at least two case studies suggests that, in practice, the widely studied strategy of incremental view maintenance in the logical sense is far less often problematic than the time management at the physical and conceptual level, associated with the question when to refresh DW views such that data are sufficiently fresh for analysis, but neither analysts nor OLTP applications are unduly disturbed in their work due to locks on their data. Our research therefore now focuses on extending the conceptual level by suitable (simple) temporal representation and reasoning mechanisms for representing freshness requirements, complemented by an array of design and implementation methods to accomplish these requirements and the definition of processes at the global level to use these methods in a goal-oriented manner to fulfill the requirements.

While such extensions will certainly refine and in parts revise the approach reported here, the experiences gained so far indicate that it is a promising way towards more systematic and computer-supported quality management in data warehouse design and operation.

Acknowledgements. The authors would like to thanks their project partners in DWQ, especially Maurizio Lenzerini, Mokrane Bouzeghoub and Enrico Franconi, for fruitful discussions of the architecture and quality model.

6 References

[AA87] N. Agmon, N.Ahituv, Assessing data reliability in an information system, *J. Management Information Systems* 4, 2 (1987)

[Akao90] Akao, Y., ed., *Quality Function Deployment*, Productivity Press, Cambridge MA. , 1990

[Arbo96] Arbor Software Corporation. *Arbor Essbase.* http://www.arborsoft.com/essbase.html, 1996.

[Boeh89] Boehm, B., *Software Risk Management,* IEEE Computer Society Press, CA, 1989.

[BT89] D.P. Ballou, K.G. Tayi, Methodology for allocating resources for data quality enhancement, *Comm. ACM*, 32, 3 (1989)

[BWPT93] D.P. Ballou, R.Y. Wang, H.L. Pazer, K.G. Tayi, Modeling Data Manufacturing Systems To Determine Data Product Quality, (No. TDQM-93-09) *Cambridge Mass.: Total Data Quality Management Research Program*, MIT Sloan School of Management, 1993

[CDL97] D. Calvanese, G. De Giacomo, M. Lenzerini. Conjunctive query containment in Description Logics with n-ary relations. *International Workshop on Description Logics*, Paris, 1997.

[CGMH+94] S. Chawathe, H. Garcia-Molina, J. Hammer, K. Ireland, Y. Papakonstantinou, J. Ullman, and J. Widom. The TSIMMIS project: Integration of heterogeneous information sources. In *Proc. of IPSI Conference*, Tokyo (Japan), 1994.

[DWQ97a] DWQ, *Deliverable D1.1, Data Warehouse Quality Requirements and Framework*, NTUA, RWTH, INRIA, DFKI, Uniroma, IRST, DWQ TR DWQ – NTUA - 1001, 1997

[DWQ97b] DWQ, *Deliverable D2.1, Data Warehouse Architecture and Quality Model*, RWTH, NTUA, Uniroma, INRIA, DWQ TR DWQ – RWTH - 002, 1997

[GJJ97] M. Gebhardt, M. Jarke, S. Jacobs, CoDecide -- a toolkit for negotiation support interfaces to multi-dimensional data. *Proc. ACM-SIGMOD Conf. Management of Data*, Tucson, Az, 1997.

[Hall78] Halloran et al., Systems development quality control, *MIS Quarterly*, vol. 2, no.4, 1978

[HGMW+95] J. Hammer, H. Garcia-Molina, J. Widom, W. Labio, Y. Zhuge. The Stanford Data Warehousing Project. *Data Eng., Special Issue Materialized Views on Data Warehousing,* 18(2), 41-48. 1995.

[HR96] L. Hyatt, L. Rosenberg, A Software Quality Model and Metrics for Identifying Project Risks and Assessing Software Quality, *8th Annual Software Technology Conference*, Utah, April, 1996.

[HZ96] R. Hull, G. Zhou. A Framework for supporting data integration using the materialized and virtual approaches. *Proc. ACM SIGMOD Intl. Conf. Management of Data*, 481 - 492, Montreal 1996.

[Info97] Informix, Inc.: *The INFORMIX-MetaCube Product Suite.* http://www.informix.com/informix/products/new_plo/metabro/metabro2.htm, 1997.

[ISO91] ISO/IEC 9126, *Information technology -Software product evaluation- Quality charactyeristics and guidelines for their use, International Organization for Standardization*, http://www.iso.ch

[Jans88] M. Janson, Data quality: The Achilles heel of end-user computing, *Omega J. Management Science*, 16, 5 (1988)

[JGJ+95] M. Jarke, R. Gallersdörfer, M.A. Jeusfeld, M. Staudt, S. Eherer: ConceptBase - a deductive objectbase for meta data management. In *Journal of Intelligent Information Systems*, 4, 2, 167-192, 1995.

[JP92] M.Jarke, K.Pohl. Information systems quality and quality information systems. In Kendall/Lyytinen/DeGross (eds.): *Proc. IFIP 8.2 Working Conf. The Impact of Computer-Supported Technologies on Information Systems Development* (Minneapolis 1992), North-Holland 1992, pp. 345-375.

[JV97] M. Jarke, Y. Vassiliou. Foundations of data warehouse quality -- a review of the DWQ project. *Proc. 2nd Intl. Conf. Information Quality (IQ-97)*, Cambridge, Mass. 1997.

[KLSS95] T. Kirk, A.Y. Levy, Y. Sagiv, and D. Srivastava. The Information Manifold. *Proc. AAAI 1995 Spring Symp. on Information Gathering from Heterogeneous, Distributed Environments*, pp. 85-91, 1995.

[Krie79] C. Kriebel, Evaluating the quality of information system, *Design and Implementation of Computer Based Information Systems*, N. Szyperski/ E.Grochla ,eds. Sijthoff and Noordhoff, 1979

[LRO96] A.Y. Levy, A. Rajaraman, and J. J. Ordille. Query answering algorithms for information agents. *Proc. 13th Nat. Conf. on Artificial Intelligence (AAAI-96)*, pages 40-47, 1996.

[LSK95] A.Y. Levy, D. Srivastava, and T. Kirk. Data model and query evaluation in global information systems. *Journal of Intelligent Information Systems*, 5:121-143, 1995.

[LU90] G.E. Liepins and V.R.R. Uppuluri, Accuracy and Relevance and the Quality of Data, *A.S. Loebl*, ed., vol. 112, Marcel Dekker, 1990

[MBJK90] J. Mylopoulos, A. Borgida, M. Jarke, M. Koubarakis: Telos – a language for representing knowledge about information systems.. In *ACM Trans. Information Systems*, 8, 4, 1990, pp. 325-362.

[MCN92] J. Mylopoulos, L. Chung, B. Nixon. Representing and using non-functional requirements -- a process-oriented approach. *IEEE Trans. Software Eng. 18*, 6 (1992).

[MRW78] J.A. McCall, P.K. Richards, G.F. Walters, Factors in software quality, *Technical Report, Rome Air Development Center*, 1978

[MStr97] MicroStrategy, Inc. *MicroStrategy's 4.0 Product Line*. http://www.strategy.com/launch/ 4_0_arc1.htm, 1997.

[NJ97] M. Nicola, M. Jarke. Integrating Replication and Communication in Performance Models of Distributed Databases. Technical Report, RWTH Aachen, AIB 97-10, 1997.

[OB92] M. Oivo, V. Basili: Representing software engineering models: the TAME goal-oriented approach. *IEEE Trans. Software Eng*. 18, 10 (1992).

[SAG96] Software AG: *SourcePoint White Paper*. Software AG, Uhlandstr 12, 64297 Darmstadt, Germany, 1996.

[SKR97] M. Staudt, J.U. Kietz, U. Reimer. ADLER: An Environment for Mining Insurance Data. *Proc. 4th Workshop KRDB-97*, Athens, 1997.

[TS97] D. Theodoratos, T. Sellis. Data Warehouse Configuration. *Proc. 23th VLDB Conference*, Athens, 1997.

[Ull97] J.D. Ullman. Information integration using logical views. In *Proc. 6th Int. Conf. on Database Theory (ICDT-97)*, Lecture Notes in Computer Science, pages 19-40. Springer-Verlag, 1997

[WGL+96] J. L. Wiener, H. Gupta, W. J. Labio, Y. Zhuge, H. Garcia-Molina, J. Widom. A System Prototype for Warehouse View Maintenance. *Proceedings ACM Workshop on Materialised Views: Techniques and Applications* , Montreal, Canada, June 7, 1996, 26-33.

[Wie92] G. Wiederhold. Mediators in the architecture of future information systems. *IEEE Computer*, pp. 38-49, March 1992.

[WRK95] R.Y. Wang, M.P. Reddy, H.B. Kon, Towards quality data: an attribute-based approach, *Decision Support Systems,* 13(1995)

[WSF95] R.Y. Wang, V.C. Storey, C.P. Firth, A framework for analysis of data quality research, *IEEE Trans. Knowledge and Data Eng.* 7, 4 (1995)

[ZHK96] G. Zhou, R. Hull, R. King. Generating Data Integration Mediators that Use Materialization. *Journal of Intelligent Information Systems*, 6(2), 199-221, 1996.

Data Warehouse Architecture and Quality: Impact and Open Challenges

Matthias Jarke, Manfred A. Jeusfeld, Christoph J. Quix, Panos Vassiliadis, and Yannis Vassiliou

Abstract The CAiSE 98 paper "Architecture and Quality in Data Warehouses" and its expanded journal version [18] was the first to add a Zachman-like [37] explicit *conceptual enterprise modeling perspective* to the architecture of data warehouses. Until then, data warehouses were just seen as collections of – typically multidimensional and historized – materialized views on relational tables, without consideration of modeling of the (business) concepts underlying their structure. The paper pointed out that this additional conceptual perspective was not just necessary for a truly semantic data integration but also a prerequisite for bringing the then very active data warehouse movement together with another topic of quickly growing importance, that of data quality.

We were happy to see the citation and industrial uptake success of this paper as it played a central role in our European IST basic research project "Foundations of Data Warehouse Quality (DWQ)". Indeed, the paper was the first in a series of three CAiSE papers from 1998 to 2000 all three of which were selected as "best" CAiSE papers for expanded journal publication in *Information Systems* and

M. Jarke (✉) • C.J. Quix
Information Systems, RWTH Aachen University & Fraunhofer FIT, Ahornstr. 55, 52074 Aachen, Germany
e-mail: jarke|quix@cs.rwth-aachen.de

M.A. Jeusfeld
Information Management, Tilburg University, Tilburg, Netherlands
e-mail: manfred.jeusfeld@acm.org

P. Vassiliadis
Department Computer Science, University of Ioannina, Ioannina, Greece
e-mail: pvassil@cs.uoi,gr

Y. Vassiliou
DBLab, National Technical University of Athens, Athens, Greece
e-mail: yv@cs.ntua.gr

J. Bubenko et al. (eds.), *Seminal Contributions to Information Systems Engineering*,
DOI 10.1007/978-3-642-36926-1_14, © Springer-Verlag Berlin Heidelberg 2013

collected about 415 citations by end of 2012 according to Google Scholar. The final DWQ results were published in the book [19], still organized around basically the same architecture and quality model.

On a more personal note, it is worth mentioning that for the two junior co-authors (CQ, PV), this was their first major refereed publication, and has strongly influenced their follow-up research over more than a decade.

In this short note, we shall briefly summarize this own follow-up research as well as the impact on research and practice, in the three areas of data quality, data warehouse process engineering, and automated model management. We end with some ongoing research questions and open challenges.

1 Data Quality and Enterprise Integration

In 1998, the time was ripe for a serious treatment of quality as a first-class problem in information system engineering. Few years after the publication of the CAiSE'98 paper, both the necessity of handling data quality as a top-level concern and the idea of injecting quality properties in the metadata started gaining ground, as demonstrated by a proliferation of industrial efforts [2], books [3, 36], papers in top-ranked conferences and journals (e.g. [11]) and workshop series like DMDW, IQIS, and QDB. The CAiSE'98 paper contributed to the establishment of the idea that apart from relieving the operational systems from the query load, data warehouses also conceptually serve Inmon's "single version of the truth" principle for an organization.

A number of our own case studies confirmed this view and developed it further. In [30], we report the enormous impact of introducing DWQ-like semantic data cleaning and integration approaches into the worldwide financial reporting warehouse of Deutsche Bank, then one of the largest and most complex financial data warehouses worldwide. The project reduced the latency of consistent summary data from about 3 months to less than 1 day, at much better data quality. Subsequently, many business IT research groups expanded the conceptual modeling perspective from a management perspective [16], a user perspective [8], or the viewpoint of specific nonfunctional requirements [27].

In science and engineering applications, DW data often reflect project experiences, and our CAiSE'98 model had to be adapted for such knowledge warehouse settings. Already shortly after the CAiSE 98 paper, the Bayer company transferred our architectural concept to what they called their "process data warehouse" [20] for (chemical) process engineering. But this domain requires a richness of facets well beyond business applications, so it took our chemical engineering collaborators a decade to formulate an adequate, widely accepted set of core ontologies for this domain [7]. In a case study with Daimler, we also saw that data quality of long-lived data warehouses is often corrupted by creeping changes in the human interpretation of the schemas, such that data mining techniques had to be developed to reverse-engineer the evolution of schema semantics over time [25]. Query processing over such multiple DW schema versions has been studied by [13].

Last not least, the quality models had to be made more efficiently usable. More than 100 KPI's from the literature were grouped into classes, with mappings to DW schemas. Moreover, it was noticed that quality metrics should not be kept separately but integrated directly into the architecture metamodel and its supporting repository. Manfred Jeusfeld extended ConceptBase, the system in which the CAiSE 98 models were first implemented, to include active rules and recursive functions with optimized execution by tabling prior function calls [17]. This enables natural definition of quality metrics even over hierarchically organized architectural and data elements. A similarly deep integration of quality into quality-aware DW reports has recently also been pursued at IBM [9].

2 Data Warehouse Process Engineering

With the benefit of the hindsight, an interesting omission of the CAiSE'98 paper was the treatment of software processes within a data warehouse. At the time the paper was authored, both the research and the industrial world viewed data warehouses from a static point of view. However, once the core problems of the design of the data architecture (and its contents) had been resolved, the main effort of data warehouse project teams has been devoted to the establishment of the refreshment process [23].

The CAiSE paper was the root of a research agenda that has lasted for more than a decade on the topic, technology, aiming at the establishment of ETL (Extract-Transform-Load) technology as a top-level topic in the data management and information systems engineering research communities [35]. Contributions have been made towards establishing methods that (a) allow administrators to design ETL workflows at conceptual and logical levels (e.g., [34]), (b) implement and tune these workflows at the physical level (e.g., [31]), and, (c) come up with efficient algorithms that can be incorporated in ETL tools to allow the efficient execution of ETL workflows (e.g., [28]). However, the first paper in this line of research came from practically the same team of authors of the CAiSE'98 paper, again in a CAiSE conference [33]. One can safely argue that the two papers should be considered as a pair as the CAiSE'98 paper covers the data architecture aspect and the CAiSE 2000 paper complements it with the management of operational processes for data warehouse metadata and quality.

Nowadays, both tasks are widely accepted in industrial practice – the ETL-based process perspective typically under the label of *Enterprise Application Integration*, the semantic data integration perspective under the label of *Enterprise Data Integration*. For both aspects, the OMG has in the meantime published some metamodel standards, such as the Common Warehouse Metamodel [29].

3 Automated Model Management

CWM also began to address another emerging issue, the growing heterogeneity of data models, by including source modeling packages not just for the relational model but also for XML or direct multidimensional models. But meanwhile, heterogeneity has gone much further. The explosion of IT in business and engineering (cyber-physical systems) has outpaced the possibilities of central data warehouses. Richer information integration architectures such as peer-to-peer networks, data stream management, or personal dataspaces are under investigation. The CAiSE'98 approach of carefully designing a central conceptual model as the basis for integration and quality is becoming infeasible, as a much higher degree of automation even in the handling of schemas/metamodels is required.

The first wave of this so-called *model management* movement [4] focused on introducing a *model algebra* with operators such as the automated generation of formal mappings by *matching* of schema elements, the semantically meaningful *merging* of schemas based on these mappings, and the *composition of mappings* as a basis for distributed query optimization, update propagation, or even schema evolution. In competition to programming solutions attempting to implement such an algebra, research on logic-based approaches continued.

In the end, it turned out that both approaches had to be combined. The key observation in the CLIO project at IBM Research was that the representation of mappings as simple correspondence links between schema elements are far too weak to allow for automated code generation and code optimization e.g. from composed mappings. These mappings needed to be expressed at least as (conjunctive) Datalog queries between any pair of sources to be integrate. For automated data integration, a new variant of so-called tuple-generating dependencies, *second-order tuple-generating dependencies* [12] were shown to allow correct and complete code generation even with composed mappings among relational sources.

In *model management 2.0* [5], model management is reconsidered under such richer mapping representations. In our work, we have aimed to extend the CLIO results to the case of *heterogeneous data models*: conceptual modeling formalisms such as UML or the ER model as well as the different kinds of structured and unstructured database models. A detailed analysis of the richness of these models, combined with the many subtle model variations in the chemical engineering case studies, led us to the conclusion that using the Telos language supporting by the ConceptBase system [26] would lead to a combinatorial explosion of subclass hierarchies which could not be handled with reasonable effort.

The GeRoMe metamodel [21] introduces a role concept at the metalevel which avoids this combinatorial explosion by using role annotations instead of subclassing, However, it maintains the efficient mapping of the conceptual modeling formalism to Datalog. In this way, we could show that query optimization and update propagation as in CLIO is possible even across an open architecture like a peer-to-peer network with heterogeneous data models among the peers [22]; in addition, algorithms can be found to do schema merging in different scenarios not just with preservation of semantics, but also with minimization of the merged schemas [24].

4 Beyond Data Warehouses

In conclusion, we mention two further developments which at first glance seem much more revolutionary but surprisingly also show relationships to this work.

Firstly, we are observing a confluence of database, data warehouse, and search engine technologies. Naïve users expect to ask simple keyword questions also to structured databases, and conversely, many people want to ask structured queries a la SQL or multidimensional versions of it, to databases whose content is text or even multimedia objects. As one well-known example, the YAGO project extracts semantic knowledge in the form of RDF graphs from very large text bases such as Wikipedia [32]. Currently, this is being extended to a kind of RDF warehouse by adding temporal and spatial context [15]. Interestingly, a data quality framework for this web archiving similar to our CAiSE 98 approach has been recently developed [10].

The development of novel column-based main memory databases, such as SAP's HANA system, claims to void the need for separate data warehousing altogether [6, 14]. Other so-called NoSQL databases have also made broad claims, but each approach is typically best suited for particular applications and workload patterns, such that again, it is highly likely than an integration of multiple such non-standard database solutions with each other and with traditional databases will be necessary. At the operational level, a very nice approach to support such integration by a common programming framework has recently been proposed by [1] but it remains open what this implies for the enterprise architecture and for data quality management.

In summary, the field of architecture and quality in information integration appears alive and well for many years to come.

References

1. Atzeni P, Bugiotti B, Rossi L (2012) Uniform access to non-relational database systems. 24th Intl Conf Advanced Information Systems Engineering (CAiSE 2012), Gdansk/Poland, 160–174
2. Barateiro J, Galhardas H (2005) A survey of data quality tools. Datenbank-Spektrum 14: 15–21
3. Batini C, Scannapieco M (2006) Data Quality: Concepts, Methodologies & Techniques. Springer
4. Bernstein PA, Haas LM, Jarke M, Rahm E, Wiederhold G (2000) Is generic metadata management feasible? 26. Intl Conf Very Large Databases (VLDB 2000), Cairo/Egypt, 660–662

5. Bernstein PA, Melnik S (2007) Model management 2.0: manipulating richer mappings. ACM SIGMOD Conf., Beijing, China: 1–12
6. Bog A, Sachs S, Plattner H (2012) Interactive performance monitoring of a composite OLTP and OLAP workload. ACM SIGMOD Intl Conf Mgmt of Data, Scottsdale, Az, 645–648
7. Brandt SC, Morbach J, Miatidis M, Theißen M, Jarke M, Marquardt W (2008) An ontology-based approach to knowledge management in design processes. Computers & Chemical Engineering 32, 1–2: 320–342
8. Cappiello C, Francalanci C, Pernici B (2004) Data quality assessment from the user's perspective. ACM SIGMOD Workshop Information Quality in Information Systems, Paris, 68–73
9. Daniel F, Casati F, Palpanas T, Chayka O, Cappiello C (2008) Enabling better decisions through quality-aware reports. Intl Conf Information Quality (ICIQ), Cambridge/Mass
10. Denev D, Mazeika A, Spaniol M, Weikum G (2011) The SHARC framework for data quality in web archiving. VLDB Journal 20, 2: 183–207
11. Elmagarmid AK, Ipeirotis PG, Verykio VS (2007) Duplicate record detection: a survey. IEEE Trans. Knowl. & Data Eng. 19, 1: 1–16
12. Fagin R, Kolaitis P, Popa L, Tan WC (2005) Composing schema mappings: second-order dependencies to the rescue. ACM Trans. Database Systems 30, 4: 994–1055
13. Golfarelli M, Lechtenbörger J, Rizzi S, Vossen G (2006) Schema versioning in data warehouses: Enabling cross-version querying via schema augmentation. Data Knowl. Eng. 59, 2: 435–459
14. Grund M, Krüger J, Plattner P, Zeier A (2010) Cudré-Mauroux P, Samuel Madden S: HYRISE - A Main Memory Hybrid Storage Engine. PVLDB 4, 2: 105–116
15. Hoffart J, Suchanek FM, Berberich K, Weikum G (2013) YAGO2: A spatially and temporally enhanced knowledge base from Wikipedia. Artif. Intell. 194: 28–61
16. Holten R (2003) Specification of management views in information warehouse projects. Information Systems 28, 7: 709–751
17. Jeusfeld, M.A.; Quix, C.; Jarke, M. (2011) ConceptBase.cc User Manual Version 7.3. Technical Report, Tilburg University, http://arno.uvt.nl/show.cgi?fid=113912
18. Jarke M, Jeusfeld MA, Quix C, Vassiliadis P (1999) Architecture and quality in data warehouses: an extended repository approach. Inform. Systems 24, 3: 131–158.
19. Jarke M, Lenzerini M, Vassiliou Y, Vassiliadis P (2003) Fundamentals of Data Warehouses. 2nd edn., Springer.
20. Jarke M, List T, Köller J (2000) The challenge of process data warehousing. 26. Intl Conf Very Large Databases (VLDB 2000, Cairo/Egypt), 473–483.
21. Kensche D, Quix C, Chatti MA, Jarke M (2007) GeRoMe: a generic role-based metamodel for model management. J. Data Semantics 8: 82–117.
22. Kensche D, Quix C, Li X, Li Y, Jarke M (2009) Generic schema mappings for composition and query answering. Data & Knowledge Engineering 68, 7: 599–621
23. Kimball R, Caserta J (2004) The Data Warehouse ETL Toolkit. Willey
24. Li X, Quix C (2011) Merging relational views: a minimization approach. 30th Intl Conf Conceptual Modeling (ER 2011), Brussels/Belgium, 379–392
25. Lübbers D, Grimmer U, Jarke M (2003) Systematic development of data mining-based data quality tools. 26. Intl Conf Very Large Databases (VLDB 2003, Berlin/Germany), 548–559
26. Mylopoulos J, Borgida A, Jarke M, Koubarakis M (1990) Telos: representing knowledge about information systems. ACM Trans. Information Systems 8, 4: 325–362
27. Pardillo J, Trujillo J: Integrated model-driven development of goal-oriented data warehouses and data marts. 27th Intl Conf Conceptual Modeling (ER 2008), Barcelona, Spain: 426–439
28. Polyzotis N, Skiadopoulos S, Vassiliadis P, Simitsis A, Frantzell N-E (2007) Supporting streaming updates in an active data warehouse. 23rd Intl Conf Data Engineering (ICDE 2007), Constantinople, Turkey, 476–485
29. Poole J, Chang D, Tolbert D, Mellor D: *Common Warehouse Metamodel Developer's Guide*, Wiley Publishing, 2003

30. Schaefer E, Becker J-D, Boehmer A, Jarke M (2000) Controlling data warehouses with know-ledge networks. 26. Intl Conf Very Large Databases (VLDB 2000), Cairo/Egypt, 715–718
31. Simitsis A, Vassiliadis P, Sellis TK (2005) Optimizing ETL processes in data warehouses. 21st Intl Conf Data Engineering (ICDE 2005), Tokyo, Japan, 564–575
32. Suchanek FM,, Kasneci G, Weikum G (2007) Yago: a core of semantic knowledge. 16th Intl Conf World Wide Web (WWW 2007), Banff/Canada, 697–706
33. Vassiliadis P, Quix C, Vassiliou Y, Jarke M (2001) Data warehouse process management. Special Issue on Selected Papers from CAiSE 2000, Information Systems 26, 3: 205–236.
34. Vassiliadis P, Simitsis A, Georgantas PO, Terrovitis M (2003) A framework for the design of ETL scenarios. 15th CAiSE, Klagenfurt/Austria, 520–535
35. Vassiliadis P, Simitsis A (2009) Extraction-Transformation-Loading, In Liu L, Öszu T (eds.): Encyclopedia of Database Systems, Springer
36. Wang RY, Ziad M, Lee YW (2001) Data Quality. Advances in Database Systems 23, Kluwer
37. Zachman JA (1987) A framework for information systems architecture. IBM Systems Journal 26, 3: 276–292

Time Constraints in Workflow Systems

Johann Eder*, Euthimios Panagos, and Michael Rabinovich

AT&T Labs - Research
180 Park Avenue
Florham Park, NJ 07932
eder@acm.org, {thimios, misha}@research.att.com

Abstract. Time management is a critical component of workflow-based process management. Important aspects of time management include planning of workflow process execution in time, estimating workflow execution duration, avoiding deadline violations, and satisfying all external time constraints such as fixed-date constraints and upper and lower bounds for time intervals between activities. In this paper, we present a framework for computing activity deadlines so that the overall process deadline is met and all external time constraints are satisfied.

1 Introduction

Dealing with time and time constraints is crucial in designing and managing business processes. Consequently, time management should be part of the core management functionality provided by workflow systems to control the lifecycle of processes. At build-time, when workflow schemas are developed and defined, workflow modelers need means to represent time-related aspects of business processes (activity durations, time constraints between activities, *etc.*) and check their feasibility (i.e., timing constraints do not contradict each other). At run-time, when workflow instances are instantiated and executed, process managers need pro-active mechanisms for receiving notifications of possible time constraint violations. Workflow participants need information about urgencies of the tasks assigned to them to manage their personal work lists. If a time constraint is violated, the workflow system should be able to trigger exception handling to regain a consistent state of the workflow instance. Business process re-engineers need information about the actual time consumption of workflow executions to improve business processes. Controllers and quality managers need information about activity start times and execution durations.

At present, support for time management in workflow systems is limited to process simulations (to identify process bottlenecks, analyze activity execution durations, *etc.*), assignment of activity deadlines, and triggering of process-specific exception-handling activities (called *escalations*) when deadlines are missed at run time [10,8,7,18,2,3,17]. Furthermore, few research activities about workflow and time management exist in the literature. A comparison with these efforts is presented in Section 7.

Our contributions in this paper include the formulation of richer modeling primitives for expressing time constraints, and the development of techniques for checking

* On leave from the University of Klagenfurt, Austria

M. Jarke, A. Oberweis (Eds.): CAiSE'99, LNCS 1626, pp. 286–300, 1999.

satisfiability of time constraints at process build and instantiation time and enforcing these constraints at run time. The proposed primitives include upper and lower bounds for time intervals between workflow activities, and binding activity execution to certain fixed dates (e.g., first day of the month). Our technique for processing time constraints computes internal activity deadlines in a way that externally given deadlines are met and no time constraints are violated.

In particular, at build time, we check whether for a given workflow schema there exists an execution schedule that does not violate any time constraints. The result is a *timed activity graph* that includes deadline ranges for each activity. At process instantiation time, we modify the the timed activity graph to include the deadlines and date characteristics given when the workflow is started. At run time, we dynamically recompute the timed graph for the remaining activities to monitor satisfiability of the remaining time constraints, given the activity completion times and execution paths taken in the already-executed portion of a workflow instance.

The remainder of the paper is organized as follows. Section 2 describes our workflow model and discusses time constraints. Section 3 presents the workflow representation we assume in this paper. Section 4 presents the calculations that take place during build time. Section 5 shows how these calculations are adjusted at process instantiation to take into account actual date constraints. Section 6 covers run time issues. Section 7 offers a comparison with related work and, finally, Section 8 concludes our presentation.

2 Workflow Model and Time Constraints

A workflow is a collection of *activities, agents,* and *dependencies* between activities. Activities correspond to individual steps in a business process. Agents are responsible for the enactment of activities, and they may be software systems (e.g., database application programs) or humans (e.g., customer representatives). Dependencies determine the execution sequence of activities and the data flow between these activities. Consequently, a workflow can be represented by a workflow graph, where nodes correspond to activities and edges correspond to dependencies between activities.

Here, we assume that execution dependencies between activities form an acyclic directed graph. We should note that we do not propose a new workflow model. Rather, we describe a generic workflow representation for presenting our work. In particular, we assume that workflows are *well structured.* A well-structured workflow consists of m sequential activities, $T_1 \ldots T_m$. Each activity T_i is either a primitive activity, which is not decomposed any further, or a composite activity, which consists of n_i parallel conditional or unconditional sub-activities $T_i^1, \ldots, T_i^{n_i}$. Each sub-activity may be, again, primitive or composite. Typically, well structured workflows are generated by workflow languages that provide the usual control structures and adhere to a structured programming style of workflow definitions (e.g., Panta Rhei [4]).

In addition, we assume that each activity has a duration assigned to it. For simplicity, we assume that activity durations are deterministic. Time is expressed in some basic time units, at build-time relative to the start of the workflow, at run-time in some calendar-time. Some time constraints follow implicitly from control dependencies and activity durations of a workflow schema. They arise from the fact that an activity can only start when its predecessor activities have finished. We call such constraints the *structural time constraints* since they reflect the control structure of the workflow.

In addition, *explicit time constraints* can be specified by workflow designers. These constraints are derived from organizational rules, laws, commitments, and so on. Such explicit constraints are either temporal relations between events or bindings of events to certain sets of calendar dates. In workflow systems, events correspond to start and end of activities. For temporal relationships between events, the following constraints exist:

Lower Bound Constraint: The duration between events A and B must be greater than or equal to δ. We write $lbc(A, B, \delta)$ to express that δ is a lower bound for the time-interval between source event A and destination event B.

Upper Bound Constraint: The distance between events A and B must be smaller than or equal to δ. We write $ubc(A, B, \delta)$ to express that δ is an upper bound for the time-interval between source event A and destination event B.

An example of lower-bound constraint includes a legal workflow with activities of serving a warning and closing a business, with the requirement that a certain time period passes between serving the warning and closing the business. Another example is that the invitation for a meeting has to be mailed to the participants at least one week before the meeting. Upper-bound constraints are even more common. The requirement that a final patent filing is done within a certain time period after the preliminary filing, or time limits for responses to business letters, or guaranteed reaction times after the report of a hardware malfunction provide typical examples of upper-bound constraints.

To express constraints that bind events to sets of particular calendar dates, we first need to provide an abstraction that generalizes a, typically infinite, set of dates such as "every other Monday" or "every fifth workday of a month". Examples of such constraints include: vacant positions are announced at the first Wednesday of each month; loans above USD 1M are approved during scheduled meetings of the board of directors; inventory checks have to be finished on December 31st.

Fixed-Date Type: A fixed-date (type) is a data type F with the following methods: $F.valid(D)$ returns true if the arbitrary date D is valid for F; $F.next(D)$ and $F.prev(D)$ return, respectively, the next and previous valid dates after D; $F.period$ returns the maximum distance between valid dates; and $F.dist(F')$ returns the maximum distance between valid dates of F and F', (with $F.period$ as default value).

Fixed-Date Constraint: Event B can only occur on certain (fixed) dates. We write $fdc(B, T)$, where T is a *fixed-date*, to express the fact that B can only occur on dates which are valid for T.

In the remainder of the paper, we assume that at most one fixed-date constraint can be associated with an activity.

3 Workflow Representation

Our techniques for time constraint management are based on the notion of the *timed activity graph*. This graph is essentially the same as the workflow graph where each

Activity Name	Activity Duration
Earliest Finish Time	Latest Finish Time

Fig. 1. Activity node of a timed workflow graph

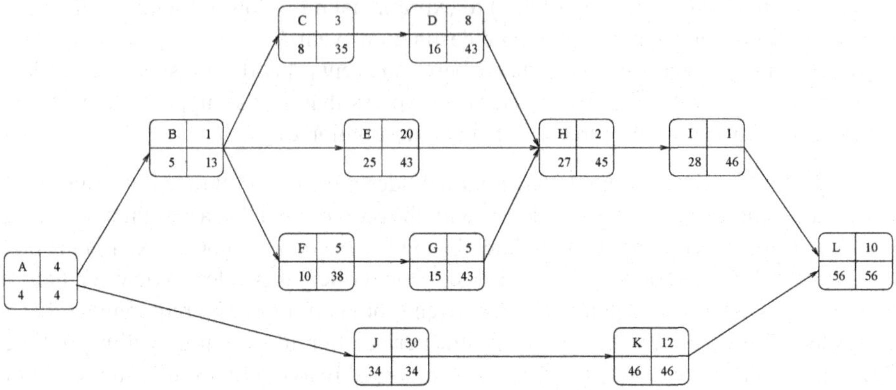

Fig. 2. Example timed workflow graph

activity node n is augmented with two values that represent termination time points for activity executions[1].

- $n.E$: the earliest point in time n can finish execution.
- $n.L$: the latest point in time n has to finish in order to meet the deadline of the entire workflow.

Figure 1 shows the representation of an activity node in the timed workflow graph. Without explicit time constraints, E and L values can be computed using the Critical Path Method (CPM) [14], a well known project planning method that is frequently used in project management software. CPM assumes that activity durations are deterministic. We are aware that this assumption does not hold for many workflows, and that for these workflows a technique dealing with a probability distribution of activity durations like the Project Evaluation and Review Technique (PERT) [14] would be more appropriate. However, we chose CPM because it allows us to present the concept more clearly without the math involved with probability distributions.

Figure 2 shows the timed workflow graph we use in the rest of the paper. The interpretation of E- and L-values is as follows. The earliest point in time for activity F

[1] Since activity durations are assumed to be deterministic, we do not need to represent activity start points. These time points can be computed by subtracting activity durations from activity termination times.

to terminate is 10 time units after the start of the workflow. If F is finished 38 time units after the start of the workflow, the duration of the entire workflow is not extended. Activity L is the last activity of the workflow, and the earliest and latest completion times are the same, 56. This also means that the entire workflow has a duration of 56 time units. The distance between the E-value and the L-value of an activity is called its buffer time. In our example, activity F has a buffer of 28 time units. This buffer, however, is not exclusively available to one activity, but it might be shared with other activities. In our example, the buffer of F is shared with B, G, H, and I. If B uses some buffer-time, then the buffer of F is reduced.

Computing the timed workflow graph delivers the duration of the entire workflow, and deadlines for all activities such that the termination of the entire workflow is not delayed. Incorporating explicit time constraints into the timed activity graph is explained in detail later. For simplicity, we only consider constraints for end events of activities. Therefore, we will use a shortcut and say that an activity (meaning "the end event of the activity") participates in a constraint. The following additional properties are used for representing workflow activities: $n.d$ represents the activity duration; $n.pos$ represents whether the activity n is a start, end, or internal node of the workflow; $n.pred$ represents the predecessors and $n.succ$ the successor activities of n; $n.deadline$ holds the externally assigned deadline of n; $n.tt$ the actual termination time of an activity instance.

For an upper- or lowerbound-constraint c we represent the source activity with $c.s$, the destination activity with $c.d$ and the bound with $c.\delta$. For a fixed-date constraint f, we write $f.a$ for the activity on which f is posed and $f.T$ for the fixed-date.

Since we assume well structured workflows, in the remainder of the paper we assume that for all upper and lower bound constraints the source node is before the destination node according to the ordering implied by the workflow graph.

4 Build-Time Calculations

At build time, our goal is to check if the set of time constraints is satisfiable, i.e., that it is possible to find a workflow execution that satisfies all timing constraints. We start from the original workflow graph and construct a timed workflow graph such that an execution exists that satisfies all constraints. Initially, all fixed-date constraints are transformed into lower-bound constraints. Then, the E- and L-values of all activity nodes in the timed graph are computed from activity durations and lower-bound constraints, using a straightforward modification of the CPM method. Finally, upper-bound constraints are incorporated into the timed graph. The resulting timed graph has at least two (possibly not distinct) valid executions. These executions are obtained if all activities complete at their E-values or all activities complete at their L-values. There may be other valid combinations of activity completion times within (E, L) ranges. We say that a timed graph *satisfies* a constraint if the executions in which all activities complete at their E- or L-values are valid with respect to this constraint.

4.1 Fixed-Date Constraints

The conversion of fixed-date constraints into lower-bound constraints is done using worst-case estimates. This is because at build time we do not have calendar value(s) for the start of the workflow and, thus, we can only use information about the duration between two valid time points for a fixed-date object. At process-instantiation time we will have more information concerning the actual delays due to fixed-date constraints.

Consider a fixed-date constraint $fdc(a, T)$. Assume that activities start instantaneously after all their predecessors finish. In the worst case, activity a may finish at $T.period + a.d$ after its last predecessor activity finishes. Indeed, let t_1 and t_2 be valid dates in T with the maximum time-interval between them. i.e., $t_2 - t_1 = T.period$, and let b be the last predecessor activity to finish. The time-interval between end-events of b and a is the longest if b finishes just after time $t_1 - a.d$, because then a cannot start immediately (it would then not finish at valid date t_1), and would have to wait until time $t_2 - a.d$ before starting. In this case, the distance between b and a is $\delta = (t_2 - t_1) + a.d$ $= T.period + a.d$, assuming b itself does not have a fixed-date constraint associated with it. If b has a fixed-date constraint $fdc(b, T')$, one can use similar reasoning to obtain $\delta = T.dist(T')$ if $a.d \leq T.dist(T')$ and $\delta = a.d + T.period$ otherwise.

To guarantee the satisfiability of all time constraints at build-time, without knowing the start date of the process, the timed graph must allow the distance of at least δ between a and all it's predecessors, where δ is computed for each predecessor as shown above. Consequently, the fixed-date constraint $fdc(a, T)$ is replaced by a lower-bound constraint $lbc(b, a, \delta)$ for every predecessor b of activity a.

4.2 Lower-Bound Constraints

The construction of the timed workflow graph that includes structural and lower-bound constraints is presented below. We should note that due to the way we carry out the computations, the activities in the resulting graph satisfy all lower-bound constraints.

Forward Calculations

```
for all activities a with a.pos = start
    a.E := a.d
endfor
for all activities a with a.pos ≠ start
    in a topological order
    a.E := max({b.E + b.d | b ∈ a.pred},
               {m.s.E + m.δ | m = lbc(s,a,δ)})
endfor
```

Backward Calculations

```
for all activities a with a.pos = end
    a.L := a.E
endfor
for all activities a with a.pos ≠ end
    in a reverse topological order
    a.L := min({s.L - s.d| s ∈ a.succ},
               {m.d.L - m.δ | m = lbc(a,d,δ)})
endfor
```

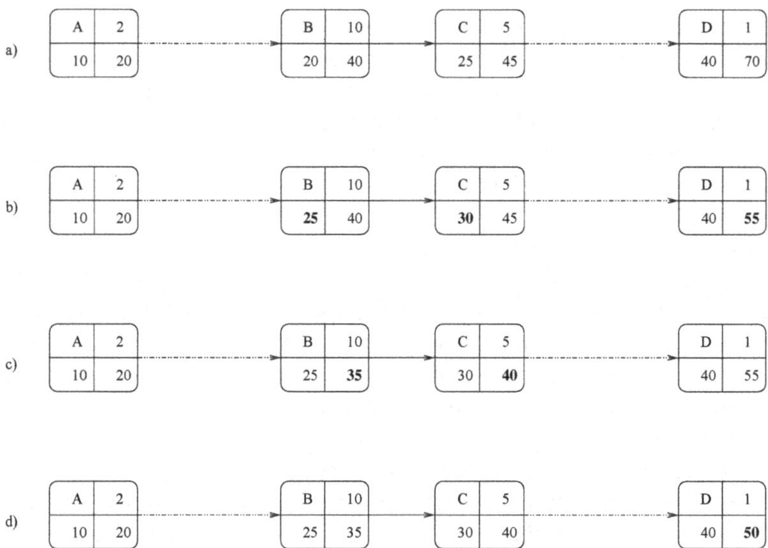

Fig. 3. Incorporating upper-bound constraints

4.3 Upper-Bound Constraints

In the timed workflow graph constructed during the previous step, an upper-bound constraint $ubc(s, d, \delta)$ is violated when either $s.E + \delta < d.E$ or $s.L + \delta < d.L$. In this case, we can use the buffer times of s and d to increase the E-value of s and decrease the L-value of the d in an attempt to satisfy the constraint. However, buffer time availability is a necessary but not sufficient condition for satisfying an upper-bound constraint. For example, in the workflow graph shown in Figure 2, the upper-bound constraint $ubc(B, C, 8)$ cannot be satisfied because the value of $C.E$ is always increased by the same amount as $B.E$.

A necessary condition for constraint $ubc(s, d, \delta)$ to be satisfiable is that the *distance* between s and d is less than δ. The distance is the sum of the durations of the activities on the longest path between s and d, and it can be computed by using the forward or backward calculations presented in the previous section, with s the starting node and d the ending node. We should note that for well structured workflows this distance does not change when the deadline of the entire workflow is relaxed and, therefore, more buffer becomes available for each activity. Consequently, extending the deadline of the whole workflow does not help us in satisfying violated upper-bound constraints.

One can show that if there is a node n between s and d with less buffer than both of them, then the buffer of s and the buffer of d can be reduced without influencing the E-values or L-values of the other node by: $min(buffer(s) - buffer(n), buffer(d) - buffer(n))$. Instead of finding the "safe" value by which the buffer of one end-point of the constraint can be reduced without affecting E and L values of the other end-point, we follow a more constructive approach.

If an upper-bound constraint is violated, we set the E-value of the source node to the value of $d.E - \delta$. If this value is greater than $s.L$, the upper-bound constraint is violated. Otherwise, we recompute the E-values of the timed graph starting at s and if the E-value of d does not change, the constraint is satisfied. In a similar way, we decrease the L-value of the destination node by δ and if this value is not less than $d.E$, we recompute the L-values of all predecessors of d. If the L-value of s does not change, the constraint is satisfied.

While the above can be used for individual upper-bound constraints, it is not enough for handling multiple upper-bound constraints. Figure 3 shows an example that demonstrates this problem. Figure 3a) shows the starting timed graph. Figure 3b) shows the timed graph after the integration of $ubc(B, D, 15)$. When $ubc(A, C, 20)$ is integrated, $ubc(B, D, 15)$ is violated at the L-values, as shown in Figure 3c). Finally, Figure 3d) shows the successful integration of both constraints.

We address this problem by checking whether an already incorporated upper-bound constraint is violated when new upper-bound constraints are incorporated into the timed graph. The following unoptimized algorithm summarizes this procedure. In this algorithm, the re-computation of the timed graph involves the forward and backward computations presented in the previous section.

```
repeat
    error := false
    for each m = ubc(s,d,δ)
          if m.s.E + m.δ < m.d.E              (* violation at E *)
                if m.s.L > m.d.E - m.δ        (* slack  at m.s   *)
                      m.s.E := m.d.E - m.δ
                      recompute timed graph
                      if m.d.E changes
                            error := true
                      endif
                else
                      error := true
                endif
          endif
          if m.s.L + m.δ < m.d.L              (* violation at L *)
                if m.d.E < m.s.L + m.δ        (* slack  at m.d   *)
                      m.d.L := m.s.L + m.δ
                      recompute timed graph
                      if m.s.L changes
                            error := true
                      endif
                else
                      error := true
                endif
          endif
    endfor
until error = true or nothing changed
```

This algorithm for the incorporation of upper-bound constraints has the following properties:

1. *Termination:* The algorithm terminates.
   At each loop there is at least one node `x` for which `x.E` is increased or `x.L` is decreased by at least one unit. Since there is a finite number of nodes, and the E- and L-values are bound, the algorithm must terminate.

2. *Admissibility:* A solution is found if there exists a timed graph satisfying all constraints.
   For an upper-bound constraint $m(s, d, \delta)$, $m.d.E - m.\delta$ is less than or equal to $m.s.E$ and $m.s.L + m.\delta$ is greater than or equal to $m.d.L$ for any timed graph satisfying the constraints. Since we set $m.s.E$ and $m.d.L$ to these values and, moreover, we know that the algorithm terminates, we can conclude that the algorithm will compute a solution, if one exists.
3. *Generality:* The algorithm finds the most general solution, if one exists.
   Let G and G' be timed graphs which differ only in the E- and L-values. We call G more general than G', if for every activity a the following condition holds: $a_G.E \leq a_{G'}.E$ and $a_G.L \geq a_{G'}.L$. Following the discussion of admissibility, it is easy to see that the timed graph generated by the algorithm above is more general than any other timed graph satisfying the constraints.
4. *Complexity:* The worst-case complexity of the algorithm is $O(m * d * n)$, where m is the number of upper-bound constraints, d is the largest buffer, and n is the number of activities.
   We can give an upper bound for number of iterations of this algorithm as follows: in each iteration there is at least one E-value increased or one L-value decreased at least by one unit. If there are m upper-bound constraints, and d is the largest buffer, then the number of iterations is $m * d * 2$ in the worst case. The recalculation is linear with the number of nodes.

5 Calculations at Process Instantiation Time

At process instantiation time, an actual calendar is used in order to transform all time information which was computed relative to the start of the workflow to absolute time points. It is also possible at this procedure to set the $a.deadline$ value for an activity a, and increase or decrease the buffers computed at build time. Based on the calculations performed at build time, a deadline for an activity a is valid if it is greater than or equal to $a.E$. Fixed-date constraints are also resolved at process instantiation time, since they rely on absolute time points. (We used worst case estimates for these constraints during build time).

The computations that take place at process instantiation time are presented below, assuming that the variable $start$ corresponds to the start-time of the workflow instance.

Forward Calculations

```
for all activities a with a.pos = start
    a.E := start + a.d
endfor
for all activities a with a.pos ≠ start
    in a topological order
    a.E := max({b.E + b.d | b ∈ a.pred},
                {m.s + m.δ | m = lbc(s,a,δ)})
    if there exists dc = fdc(a,T)
         a.E := dc.T.next(a.E)
    endif
endfor
```

Backward Calculations

```
for all activities a with a.pos = end
    if a.deadline < a.E
          raise exception
    else
          a.L := a.deadline
endfor
for all activities a with a.pos ≠ end
    in a reverse topological order
    a.L := min({s.L - s.d| s ∈ a.succ},
                 {m.d - m.δ | m = lbc(a,d,δ)})
    if exists a.deadline and a.deadline < a.L
          a.L := a.deadline
    endif
    if there exists dc = fdc(a,T)
          a.L := dc.T.prev(a.L)
    endif
    if a.L < a.E
          raise exception
    endif
endfor
```

Incorporation of Upper-Bound Constraints: **incorporate()**

```
repeat
    error := false
    ok    := true
    for each m = ubc(s,d,δ)
          if m.s.E + m.δ < m.d.E              (* violation at E *)
                m.s.E := m.d.E - m.δ
                ok    := false
                if there exists dc = fdc(m.s,T)
                      m.s.E := dc.T.next(m.s.E)
                endif
                if m.s.E > m.s.L
                      error := true
                endif
          endif
          if m.s.L + m.δ < m.d.L              (* violation at L *)
                 m.d.L := m.s.L + m.δ
                 ok    := false
                 if there exists dc = fdc(m.d,T)
                       m.s.L := dc.T.prev(m.d.L)
                 endif
                 if m.d.E > m.d.L
                       error := true
                 endif
          endif
    endfor
    if ok = false and error = false
          error := recompute();
    endif
until error = true or ok = true
```

Timed Graph Re-computation: **recompute()**

```
for all activities a in topological order
    a.E := max({b.E + b.d | b ∈ a.pred},
                 {m.s + m.δ | m = lbc(s,a,δ)}, a.E)
```

```
        if there exists dc = fdc(a,T)
             a.E := dc.T.next(a.E)
        endif
        if a.L < a.E
              return false
        endif
    endfor
    for all activities a in reverse topological order
        a.L := min({s.L - s.d | s ∈ a.succ},
                   {m.d - m.δ | m = lbc(a,d,δ)}, a.L)
        if there exists dc = fdc(a,T)
              a.L := dc.T.prev(a.L)
        endif
        if a.L < a.E
              return false
        endif
    endfor
    return true
```

There is a possibility of optimizing the re-computation procedure by starting at the first node where an E-value was changed. However, there is additional overhead associated with this. Finally, the algorithm for incorporating upper-bound constraints into the timed graph has the same properties as the corresponding one presented in Section 4.

6 Time Management at Run-Time

6.1 General Computations

During the execution of a given workflow instance, we have to ensure that deadlines are not missed and any time constraints attached to activities are not violated. In order to achieve this, we may have to delay the execution of some of the activities that are either sources of upper-bound constraints or destinations of lower-bound constraints. Figure 4 shows a workflow segment having the upper-bound constraints $ubc(C, I, 18)$ and $ubc(G, H, 7)$. In this example, if F ends at 10 and C ends at 25 and, thus, D will end at 33 and H at 35, G must not start before 28 because the upper-bound constraint will be violated.

Even when we can immediately start the execution of an activity that is the source of some upper-bound constraint, it can be advantageous to delay its enactment so that the remaining activities have more buffer. In the example of Figure 4, if C starts at 7, it will finish at 10 and the buffer for all other activities is reduced. In particular, E, H, and I will have no buffer available since they have to finish at their E-values to satisfy the upper-bound constraints.

Selecting an optimal delay value for an activity is part of on-going work. Furthermore, existing work [11,12,13] can be used for distributing available buffer and slack times to activities and avoid time exceptions – `assign-deadline()` corresponds to this in the algorithm presented below. Buffer distribution addresses the distribution of extra buffer time that results from the assignment of an overall workflow deadline that is greater than the L-values of all activities with no successors. Slack distribution addresses the distribution of slack time that becomes available when activities finish before their L-values.

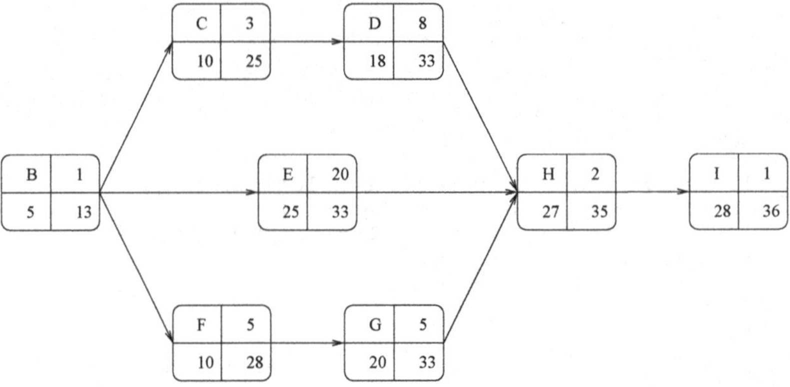

Fig. 4. Workflow segment with $ubc(C, I, 18)$ and $ubc(G, H, 7)$

The algorithm presented below assumes that activities finish within the interval defined by their E- and L-values (this implies that the termination of an activity should be delayed until, at least, its E-value. Allowing activities to finish before their E-values is subject of on-going work). When activity a finishes in the interval $(a.E, a.L)$, we may have to recompute the timed graph and re-incorporate upper-bound constraints before modifying the L-values of the ready activities according to the buffer and slack distribution algorithm. In addition, the re-computation of the timed graph should use the L-values of any active activities for computing E-values in order to avoid upper-bound constraint violations.

```
if a.tt ≤ a.L          (* a.tt = actual termination time *)
    a.L  := a.tt
    a.E  := a.tt
    done := false
    if a is the source of a lower-bound constraint
          recompute()
          incorporate()
          done := true
    endif
    for each b in a.succ that is ready for execution
          if b is source of an upper-bound constraint
                if done = false
                      recompute()
                      incorporate()
                endif
                b.L := assign-deadline(b)
                recompute()
                incorporate()
                done := true
          else
                b.L  := assign-deadline(b)
                done := false
          endif
          launch b for execution
    endfor
else
    invoke escalation process, deadline was missed
endif
```

6.2 Schedules

The execution of a workflow instance according to the procedures above requires re-computation of the timed graph after the completion of an activity that is the source of a lower-bound constraint or has a successor that is the source of an upper-bound constraint. We can avoid these re-computations by sacrificing some flexibility in the timed graph. Recall that the timed graph specifies ranges for activity completion times such that there *exists* a combination of activity completion times that satisfies all timing constraints and in which each completion time is within the range of its activity. Run-time re-computation was required because, once completion time for finished activities has been observed, not all completion times within the ranges of the remaining activities continue to be valid.

We define a *schedule* to be a (more restrictive) timed graph in which *any* combination of activity completion times within $[E, L]$ ranges satisfies all timing constraints. In other words, given a schedule, no violations of time constraints occur as long as each activity a finishes at time within the interval $[a.E, a.L]$. Consequently, as long as activities finish within their ranges, no timed graph re-computation is needed. Only when an activity finishes outside its range must the schedule for the remaining activities be recomputed.

It follows directly from the schedule definition that, for every upper-bound constraint $ubc(s, d, \delta)$, $s.E + \delta \geq d.L$ and for every lower-bound constraint $lbc(s, d, \delta)$, $s.L + \delta \leq d.E$; the reverse is also true, i.e., the timed graph that satisfies these properties is a schedule (compare this property with the two inequalities that are incorporated into the timed graph in Section 4). From the way we compute E- and L-values for the activities in a timed workflow graph, the E- and L-values already qualify as schedules. Consequently, when every workflow activity finishes execution at its E-value, there is no need to check for time constraint violations. The same is true when activities finish execution at L-values.

The development of algorithms for computing schedules with various characteristics is subject of ongoing research.

7 Related Work

The area of handling time-related issues and detecting potential problems at build, instantiation, and run time has not received adequate attention in the workflow literature. Existing workflow systems offer some limited abilities to handle time. For example, they support the assignment of execution durations, and deadlines to business processes and their activities, and they monitor whether deadlines are met.

In [9], an ontology of time is developed for identifying time structures in workflow management systems. They propose the usage of an Event Condition Action (ECA) model of an active database management system (DBMS) to represent time aspects within a workflow environment. They also discuss special scheduling aspects and basic time-failures. We used parts of their definitions as basis of our concept.

In [11,12,13], the authors propose to use static data (e.g., escalation costs), statistical data (e.g., average activity execution time and probability of executing a conditional activity), and run-time information (e.g., agent work-list length) to adjust activity deadlines and estimate the remaining execution time for workflow instances. However, this work can be used only at run-time, and it does not address explicit time constraints.

[1] proposes the integration of workflow systems with project management tools to provide the functionality necessary for time management. However, these project management tools do not allow the modeling of explicit time constraints and, therefore, have no means for their resolution.

In [15], the authors present an extension to the net-diagram technique PERT to compute internal activity deadlines in the presence of sequential, alternative, and concurrent executions of activities. Under this technique, business analysts provide estimates of the best, worst, and median execution times for activities, and the β-distribution is used to compute activity execution times as well as shortest and longest process execution times. Having done that, time constraints are checked at build time and escalations are monitored at run-time. Our work extends this work by providing a technique for handling both structural and explicit time constraints at process build and instantiation times, and enforcing these constraints at run-time.

In [6,16], the notion of explicit time constraints is introduced. Nevertheless, this work focused more on the formulation of time constraints in workflow definitions, the enforcement of time constraints through monitoring of time constraints at run-time and the escalation of time failures within workflow transactions [5]. Our work follows the work described in [6,16] and extends it with the incorporation of explicit time constraints into workflow schedules.

8 Conclusions

Dealing with time and time constraints is crucial in designing and managing business processes.

In this paper, we proposed modeling primitives for expressing time constraints between activities and binding activity executions to certain fixed dates (e.g., first day of the month). Time constraints between activities include lower- and upper-bound constraints. In addition, we presented techniques for checking satisfiability of time constraints at process build and process instantiation time, and enforcing these constraints at run-time. These techniques compute internal activity deadlines in a way that externally assigned deadlines are met and all time constraints are satisfied. Thus the risk of missing an external deadline is recognized early and steps to avoid a time failure can be taken, or escalations are triggered earlier, when their costs are lower.

Our immediate work focuses on: (1) using the PERT-net technique for computing internal deadlines to express deviations from the average execution duration of activities; (2) addressing conditionally and repetitive executed activities by providing execution probabilities to estimate average duration and variance for workflow executions; (3) considering optional activities and pruning the workflow graph when such activities should be eliminated to avoid time exceptions; and (4) addressing the different duration values that could be used at build time: best, average, and worst case execution times and turn-around times, which include the time an activity spends in the work-list and the time between start and end of an activity.

References

1. C. Bussler. Workflow Instance Scheduling with Project Management Tools. In *9th Workshop on Database and Expert Systems Applications DEXA'98*, Vienna, Austria, 1998. IEEE Computer Society Press.
2. CSESystems. *Benutzerhandbuch V 4.1 Workflow*. CSE Systems, Computer & Software Engineering GmbH, Klagenfurt, Austria, 1996.
3. CSE Systems Homepage. http://www.csesys.co.at/, February 1998.
4. J. Eder, H. Groiss, and W. Liebhart. The Workflow Management System Panta Rhei. In A. Dogac et al., editor, *Advances in Workflow Management Systems and Interoperability*. Springer, Istanbul, Turkey, August 1997.
5. J. Eder and W. Liebhart. Workflow Transactions. In P. Lawrence, editor, *Workflow Handbook 1997*. John Wiley, 1997.
6. Johann Eder, Heinz Pozewaunig, and Walter Liebhart. Timing issues in workflow management systems. Technical report, Institut f"ur Informatik-Systeme, Universit"at Klagenfurt, 1997.
7. TeamWare Flow. Collaborative workflow system for the way people work. P.O. Box 780, FIN-00101, Helsinki, Finland.
8. InConcert. Technical product overview. XSoft, a division of xerox. 3400 Hillview Avenue, Palo Alto, CA 94304. http://www.xsoft.com.
9. Heinrich Jasper and Olaf Zukunft. Zeitaspekte bei der Modellierung und Ausführung von Workflows. In S. Jablonski, H. Groiss, R. Kaschek, and W. Liebhart, editors, *Geschäftsprozeßmodellierung und Workflowsysteme*, volume 2 of *Proceedings Reihe der Informatik '96*, pages 109 – 119, Escherweg 2, 26121 Oldenburg, 1996.
10. F. Leymann and D. Roller. Business process management with flowmark. In *Proceedings of the 39th IEEE Computer Society International Conference*, pages 230–233, San Francisco, California, February 1994. http://www.software.ibm.com/workgroup.
11. E. Panagos and M. Rabinovich. Escalations in workflow management systems. In *DART Workshop*, Rockville, Maryland, November 1996.
12. E. Panagos and M. Rabinovich. Predictive workflow management. In *Proceedings of the 3rd International Workshop on Next Generation Information Technologies and Systems*, Neve Ilan, ISRAEL, June 1997.
13. E. Panagos and M. Rabinovich. Reducing escalation-related costs in WFMSs. In A. Dogac et al., editor, *NATO Advanced Study Institue on Workflow Management Systems and Interoperability*. Springer, Istanbul, Turkey, August 1997.
14. Susy Philipose. *Operations Research - A Practical Approach*. Tata McGraw-Hill, New Delhi, New York, 1986.
15. H. Pozewaunig, J. Eder, and W. Liebhart. ePERT: Extending PERT for Workflow Management Systems. In *First EastEuropean Symposium on Advances in Database and Information Systems ADBIS 97*, St. Petersburg, Russia, Sept. 1997.
16. Heinz Pozewaunig. Behandlung von Zeit in Workflow-Managementsystemen - Modellierung und Integration. Master's thesis, University of Klagenfurt, 1996.
17. SAP Walldorf, Germany. *SAP Business Workflow©Online-Help*, 1997. Part of the SAP System.
18. Ultimus. Workflow suite. Business workflow automation. 4915 Waters Edge Dr., Suite 135, Raleigh, NC 27606. http://www.ultimus1.com.

Workflow Time Management Revisited

Johann Eder, Euthimios Panagos, and Michael Rabinovich

Abstract Time is an important aspect of business process management. Here we revisit the following contributions of early workflow time management approaches: representation of temporal information and temporal constraints, analysis of temporal constraint satisfiability, and computation of workflow execution plans that satisfy temporal constraints. In particular, we summarize some of the most important research efforts and results in: (a) modeling temporal aspects of workflows, (b) analysis of temporal properties of workflow models, (c) computation of workflow execution schedules, (d) minimization of exceptions due to violation of temporal constraints, (e) monitoring of temporal workflow aspects, and (f) modeling and calculation of temporal properties for distributed workflows and for guaranteeing Quality of Service in Web-service composition.

1 Introduction

Time is an important component of the management and execution of (business) processes. Processes have to be planned in a temporal dimension for several reasons, e.g., users demand information about process duration, and managers need

J. Eder (✉)
Alpen Adria Universität Klagenfurt, Universitätsstrasse 65, 9020, Klagenfurt, Austria
e-mail: johann.eder@aau.at

E. Panagos
Applied Communication Sciences, 150 Mt Airy Road (2N-021), Basking Ridge, NJ 07920, USA
e-mail: epanagos@appcomsci.com

M. Rabinovich
Electrical Engineering & Computer Science, Case Western Reserve University,
10900 Euclid Avenue, Cleveland, OH 44106-7071, USA
e-mail: michael.rabinovich@case.edu

J. Bubenko et al. (eds.), *Seminal Contributions to Information Systems Engineering*,
DOI 10.1007/978-3-642-36926-1_16,

temporal information for scheduling and organizing work and workforce. Temporal information is necessary for improving business processes, lower cost, and allow timely reactions to external events. Many business processes have restrictions such as limited duration of subprocesses or activities, terms of delivery, dates of re-submission, or activity deadlines. Typically, violations of temporal constraints increase the cost of business processes, may create unnecessary additional work, or lead to the violation of contracts with clients. In summary, poor consideration of temporal aspects reduces the quality of the services offered by an organization and lowers its competitiveness.

Therefore workflow managements systems should care for the following requirements [13, 15]:

- At build-time, when workflow schemas are defined and developed, workflow modelers need means to represent time-related aspects of business processes (activity durations, time constraints between activities, etc.) and check their feasibility.
- Process managers need support to compute schedules for the execution of processes. They need means to be warned about possible violations of temporal constraints as early as possible such that they can react and take measures to avoid time failures, e.g. by extending internal deadlines if possible, assigning overtime, or invoking "emergency" processes.
- Workflow participants need information about urgencies of the tasks assigned to them to manage their personal work lists in accordance with the overall goals.
- Workflow management systems should recognize violations of temporal constraints and trigger exception handling steps to regain a consistent state of active workflow instances.
- Recording temporal information about business process executions helps improving (re-engineering) business processes and allows better planning of process execution.

At the end of the 1990s, the temporal aspects of workflows were taken up by Information Systems Engineering research. Solutions in related areas could not be easily applied to workflows. Production scheduling was an established discipline, but workflows differ from shop floor processes considerably, especially in the information about the individual activities (process steps), the resources they require, the decisions (choices) made during run-time, etc. Project management tools, on the other hand, are tailored towards supporting individual projects rather than the management of multi-instance workflows. While temporal reasoning was helpful for model analysis, it did not address disjunctive constraints (XOR splits) and did not provide support for the other requirements outlined above.

Around 1997–1999 the first papers (e.g. [4, 16, 31, 35, 37]) raising the issues of time management for workflows were published and set the topic on the agenda.

2 Time Constraints in Workflow Systems

In [16], we made contributions to: the formulation of the requirements for workflow time management, the representation of temporal information in workflow models, the temporal analysis of workflow models, and the computation of schedules for workflow execution.

In addition to the definition of the duration of workflow activities and the specification of deadlines for the execution of workflows, we introduced lower- and upper-bound constraints between start and end execution events associated with workflow activities. Furthermore, we allowed events to be bound to fixed dates.

We presented an algorithm that effectively checks whether the set of temporal constraints is satisfiable for a given workflow at build time. The algorithm is constructive in the sense that it computes a time plan specifying the admissible intervals for the start and end events. At process instantiation time, the time plan is mapped to an actual calendar, and the fixed date constraints are resolved and incorporated in the schedule. At run time, execution progress is monitored and the schedule is refined by taking the actual time points of the events into account.

3 Temporal Aspects in Workflows

During the last decade, the management of temporal aspects for workflows has attracted considerable research efforts across different dimensions. We summarize what we consider the most important strands of research in this space and exemplarily reference some relevant papers below.

- *Modeling of temporal aspects and analysis of workflows:* The types of temporal information represented in workflows has been extended by including more complex forms of constraints, such as transport times, and supporting more complex workflow models by considering more complex control structures. The algorithms for computing time plans have been modified accordingly to address these extensions [3, 10, 11, 14, 27, 28].
- *Probabilistic time calculations:* Uncertainty is an integral characteristic of many workflows that can be introduced by many factors, including branching at split points, iterations, and varying activity durations. To better deal with uncertainty, probabilistic temporal workflow models have been developed which allow the computation of probabilistic execution plans [12, 29].
- *Patterns:* The different approaches for representing temporal information and temporal constraints for workflows have been consolidated and documented as temporal workflow patterns [25].
- *Resource constraints:* While temporal constraints are very important, workflow management must also address resource constraints in many scenarios [2, 26].
- *Scheduling:* The information available in timed workflow graphs has been used to support scheduling of workflow activities, computation of individual schedules

for workflow participants to organize their work, and for various attempts to improve the performance of workflow execution [17, 23, 38].

- *Exception handling:* The violation of temporal constraints leads to exceptions in the execution of a workflow. To capture and manage these exceptions in an automatic or an semi-automatic way, various techniques combined approaches from temporal workflow management and exception handling [33, 36, 39].
- *Prediction:* Another approach comes from the confluence of temporal workflow management with workflow mining. While workflow time calculation always relied on empirical data coming from workflow logs, the analysis of these logs with workflow mining techniques provides additional valuable data for scheduling [1].
- *Adaptability, change, flexibility*: In many situations, workflows cannot be executed in their entirety as planned. Rather, they have to be modified at runtime to accommodate unforeseen situations. Adaptable workflows and flexible workflows provide the means for dealing with these situations in an adequate an reliable way. Temporal information is quite important there as changed workflows have to satisfy temporal obligations [9, 24, 32].
- *Grid workflows:* Applications in e-science require the execution of workflows over the grid. The scheduling of these workflows requires temporal information, as well as an efficient way for monitoring execution progress in order to react to different load distributions [6, 7].
- *Distributed workflows:* Business processes do not stop at the perimeter of organizations, but typically transcend organization boundaries. Different approaches for inter-organizational workflows representation and exchange of temporal information between the organizations participating in an inter-organizational workflow have been developed. In addition, various algorithms have been developed to allow time management by exchanging only the permitted temporal information required for balancing the need for temporal workflow management with restrictions associated with passing information between participants [19, 20, 30].
- *QoS for web service composition:* Temporal information is associated with the quality of Web service executions. The techniques of workflow time management have been taken up and adopted for the calculation of Quality-of-Service aspects for the composition of web services [5, 18, 22, 36, 40, 41].
- *Application:* Workflow time management methods have been applied to solve problems in specific application areas like supply chains [21], health care and hospital information systems [8, 34], or scientific workflows [29].

4 Conclusions

Workflow time management was a very productive field of research during the last decade. Enormous progress was made towards providing workflow management systems and workflow applications with sophisticated models and techniques for representing temporal information and temporal constraints and to greatly improve the quality of execution of business processes from a temporal perspective. Developed techniques reduce the number of violations of temporal constraints, and provide better temporal information for workflow managers, workflow participants and the consumers of process executions.

References

1. van der Aalst, W., Schonenberg, M., Song, M.: Time prediction based on process mining. Information Systems **36**(2), 450–475 (2011)
2. Avanes, A.: Adaptive workflow scheduling under resource allocation constraints and network dynamics. In: PVLDB, pp. 1631–1637. VLDB Endowment (2008)
3. Bettini, C., Wang, X., Jajodia, S.: Temporal reasoning in workflow systems. Distributed and Parallel Databases **11**(3), 269–306 (2002)
4. Bussler, C.: Workflow instance scheduling with project management tools. In: Proc. Database and Expert Systems Applications, pp. 753–758. IEEE (1998)
5. Cardoso, J., Sheth, A., Miller, J., Arnold, J., Kochut, K.: Quality of service for workflows and web service processes. Journal of Web Semantics **1**(3), 281–308 (2004)
6. Chen, J., Yang, Y.: Key research issues in grid workflow verification and validation. In: Proceedings of the 2006 Australasian workshops on Grid computing and e-research-Volume 54, pp. 97–104. Australian Computer Society, Inc. (2006)
7. Chen, J., Yang, Y.: Adaptive selection of necessary and sufficient checkpoints for dynamic verification of temporal constraints in grid workflow systems. ACM Transactions on Autonomous and Adaptive Systems (TAAS) **2**(2) (2007). DOI 10.1145/1242060.1242063
8. Combi, C., Gozzi, M., Juarez, J., Oliboni, B., Pozzi, G.: Conceptual modeling of temporal clinical workflows. In: Temporal Representation and Reasoning, 14th International Symposium on, pp. 70–81. IEEE (2007)
9. Combi, C., Gozzi, M., Posenato, R., Pozzi, G.: Conceptual modeling of flexible temporal workflows. ACM Transactions on Autonomous and Adaptive Systems (TAAS) **7**(2) (2012). DOI 10.1145/2240166.2240169
10. Combi, C., Posenato, R.: Controllability in temporal conceptual workflow schemata. In: Business process management (BPM), *LNCS*, vol. 5701, pp. 64–79. Springer (2009)
11. Combi, C., Pozzi, G.: Temporal conceptual modelling of workflows. In: Conceptual Modeling - ER 2003, *LNCS*, vol. 2813, pp. 59–76. Springer (2003)
12. Eder, J., Eichner, H., Pichler, H.: A probabilistic approach to reduce the number of deadline violations and the tardiness of workflows. In: On the Move to Meaningful Internet Systems 2006: OTM 2006 Workshops, *LNCS*, vol. 4277, pp. 5–7. Springer (2006)
13. Eder, J., Gruber, W., Panagos, E.: Temporal modeling of workflows with conditional execution paths. In: Database and Expert Systems Applications, *LNCS*, vol. 1873, pp. 243–253. Springer (2000)
14. Eder, J., Panagos, E.: Managing time in workflow systems, pp. 109–132. Future Strategies Inc. i.a.w. Workflow Management Coalition (2001)
15. Eder, J., Panagos, E., Pozewaunig, H., Rabinovich, M.: Time management in workflow systems. BIS **99**, 265–280 (1999)
16. Eder, J., Panagos, E., Rabinovich, M.: Time constraints in workflow systems. In: Advanced Information Systems Engineering, *LNCS*, vol. 1626, pp. 286–300. Springer (1999)
17. Eder, J., Pichler, H., Gruber, W., Ninaus, M.: Personal schedules for workflow systems. In: Business Process Management, *LNCS*, vol. 2678, pp. 216–231. Springer (2003)

18. Eder, J., Pichler, H., Vielgut, S.: An architecture for proactive timed web service compositions. In: Business Process Management Workshops, *LNCS*, vol. 4103, pp. 323–335. Springer (2006)
19. Eder, J., Pichler, H., Vielgut, S.: Avoidance of deadline-violations for inter-organizational business processes. In: Databases and Information Systems, 2006, pp. 33–40. IEEE (2006)
20. Eder, J., Tahamtan, A.: Temporal conformance of federated choreographies. In: Database and Expert Systems Applications, *LNCS*, vol. 5181, pp. 668–675. Springer (2008)
21. Goel, A., Gupta, S., Srinivasan, S., Jha, B.: Integration of supply chain management using multiagent system & negotiation model. International Journal of Computer and Electrical Engineering **3**(3) (2011)
22. Guermouche, N., Godart, C.: Timed model checking based approach for web services analysis. In: ICWS 2009. IEEE International Conference on Web Services, pp. 213–221. IEEE (2009)
23. Hyun Son, J., Ho Kim, M.: Improving the performance of time-constrained workflow processing. Journal of Systems and Software **58**(3), 211–219 (2001)
24. Klingemann, J.: Controlled flexibility in workflow management. In: Advanced Information Systems Engineering, *LNCS*, vol. 1789, pp. 126–141. Springer (2000)
25. Lanz, A., Weber, B., Reichert, M.: Workflow time patterns for process-aware information systems. In: Enterprise, Business-Process and Information Systems Modeling, Proc., *LNBIP*, vol. 50, pp. 94–107. Springer (2010)
26. Li, H., Yang, Y., Chen, T.: Resource constraints analysis of workflow specifications. Journal of Systems and Software **73**(2), 271–285 (2004)
27. Li, J., Fan, Y., Zhou, M.: Timing constraint workflow nets for workflow analysis. Systems, Man and Cybernetics, Part A: Systems and Humans, IEEE Transactions **33**(2), 179–193 (2003)
28. Li, J., Fan, Y., Zhou, M.: Performance modeling and analysis of workflow. Systems, Man and Cybernetics, Part A: Systems and Humans, IEEE Transactions on **34**(2), 229–242 (2004)
29. Liu, X., Ni, Z., Chen, J., Yang, Y.: A probabilistic strategy for temporal constraint management in scientific workflow systems. Concurrency and Computation: Practice and Experience **23**(16), 1893–1919 (2011)
30. Makni, M., Tata, S., Yeddes, M., Ben Hadj-Alouane, N.: Satisfaction and coherence of deadline constraints in inter-organizational workflows. In: On the Move to Meaningful Internet Systems: OTM 2010, Proc., *LNCS*, vol. 6426, pp. 523–539. Springer (2010)
31. Marjanovic, O., Orlowska, M.: On modeling and verification of temporal constraints in production workflows. Knowledge and Information Systems **1**(2), 157–192 (1999)
32. Müller, R., Greiner, U., Rahm, E.: Agentwork: a workflow system supporting rule-based workflow adaptation. Data & Knowledge Engineering **51**(2), 223–256 (2004)
33. Müller, R., Rahm, E.: Dealing with logical failures for collaborating workflows. In: Cooperative Information Systems, pp. 210–223. Springer (2000)
34. Ouyang, C., Wynn, M.T., Kuhr, J.C., Adams, M.J., Becker, T., ter Hofstede, A.H., Fidge, C.J.: Workflow support for scheduling in surgical care processes. In: The 19th European Conference on Information Systems : ICT and Sustainable Service Development (ECIS 2011). Aalto University School of Economics, Helsinki (2011). URL http://eprints.qut.edu.au/41956/
35. Panagos, E., Rabinovich, M.: Predictive workflow management. In: Proceedings of the 3rd International Workshop on Next Generation Information Technologies and Systems. (1997)
36. Pichler, H., Wenger, M., Eder, J.: Composing time-aware web service orchestrations. In: Advanced Information Systems Engineering, *LNCS*, vol. 5565, pp. 349–363. Springer (2009)
37. Pozewaunig, H., Eder, J., Liebhart, W.: epert: Extending pert for workflow management systems. In: First EastEuropean Symposium on Advances in Database and Information Systems ADBIS, pp. 217–224. Nevsky Dialect (1997)
38. Senkul, P., Kifer, M., Toroslu, I.: A logical framework for scheduling workflows under resource allocation constraints. In: Proc. of the 28th international conference on Very Large Data Bases, pp. 694–705. VLDB Endowment, ACM (2002)
39. Van Der Aalst, W., Rosemann, M., Dumas, M.: Deadline-based escalation in process-aware information systems. Decision Support Systems **43**(2), 492–511 (2007)

40. Wang, M., Cheung, W., Liu, J., Xie, X., Luo, Z.: E-service/process composition through multi-agent constraint management. In: Business Process Management, Proc. BPM 2006, *LNCS*, vol. 4102, pp. 274–289. Springer (2006)
41. Zeng, L., Benatallah, B., Dumas, M., Kalagnanam, J., Sheng, Q.: Quality-driven web services composition. In: Proc. of the 12th International Conference on the World Wide Web, pp. 411–421. ACM Press (2003). DOI 10.1145/775152.775211

Adaptive and Dynamic Service Composition in *eFlow*

Fabio Casati, Ski Ilnicki, LiJie Jin, Vasudev Krishnamoorthy[1], and Ming-Chien Shan

Software Technology Lab
Hewlett-Packard Laboratories, 1U-4A
1501 Page Mill Road
Palo Alto, CA, 94304
{casati,ilnicki,ljjin,shan}@hpl.hp.com

Abstract. E-Services are typically delivered point-to-point. However, the e-service environment creates the opportunity for providing *value-added, integrated services,* which are delivered by composing existing e-services. In order to enable organizations to pursue this business opportunity we have developed *eFlow*, a system that supports the specification, enactment, and management of *composite* e-services, modeled as processes that are enacted by a service process engine. Composite e-services have to cope with a highly dynamic business environment in terms of services and service providers. In addition, the increased competition forces companies to provide customized services to better satisfy the needs of every individual customer. Ideally, service processes should be able to transparently adapt to changes in the environment and to the needs of different customers with minimal or no user intervention. In addition, it should be possible to dynamically modify service process definitions in a simple and effective way to manage cases where user intervention is indeed required. In this paper we show how *eFlow* achieves these goals.

1 Introduction and Motivations

In recent years the Web has become the platform through which many companies communicate with their partners, interact with their back-end systems, and perform electronic commerce transactions. Today, organizations use the Web not only as an efficient and cost-effective way to sell products and deliver information, but also as a platform for providing *services* to businesses and individual customers. Examples of e-services include bill payment, customized on-line newspapers, or stock trading services. As Web technologies continue to improve, allowing for smaller and more powerful web servers, and as more and more appliances become web-enabled, the number and type of services that can be made available through the Internet is likely to increase at an exponential rate.

---

[1] Now with Rightworks corp., 31 N. Second St., suite 400, San Jose, CA, USA. email: vasu@rightworks.com

B. Wangler, L. Bergman (Eds.): CAiSE 2000, LNCS 1789, pp. 13-31, 2000

Today, services are typically delivered point-to-point. However, the e-service environment creates the business opportunity for providing *value-added, integrated services,* which are delivered by composing existing e-services, possibly offered by different companies. For instance, an *eMove* composite service could support customers that need to relocate, by composing truck rental, furniture shipments, address change, and airline reservation services, according to the customer's requirements.

In order to support organizations in pursuing this business opportunity we have developed *eFlow*, a platform for specifying, enacting, and monitoring composite e-services. Composite services are modeled as business processes, enacted by a service process engine. *eFlow* provides a number of features that support service process specification and management, including a powerful yet simple service composition language, events and exception handling, ACID service-level transactions, security management, and monitoring tools.

Unlike "traditional" business processes, which are mostly executed in a predictable and repetitive way, composite services delivered through the Internet have to cope with a highly dynamic environment, where new services become available on a daily basis and the number of service providers is constantly growing. In addition, the availability of many service providers from different countries increases the competition and forces companies to provide customized services to better satisfy the need of every individual customer. These two characteristics of the e-service environment impose demanding requirements on a system that supports the development and delivery of composite services.

In order to stay competitive, service providers should offer the best available service in every given moment to every specific customer. Clearly, it is unfeasible to continuously change the process to reflect changes in the business environment, since these occur too frequently and modifying a process definition is a delicate and time-consuming activity. Ideally, service processes should be able to transparently adapt to changes in the environment and to the needs of different customers with minimal or no user intervention. Furthermore, it should be possible to dynamically modify service process definition in a simple and effective way to manage cases where user intervention is required, for instance to handle major changes in the environment or to cope with unexpected exceptional situations.

This paper shows how *eFlow* supports the definition and enactment of *adaptive* and *dynamic* service processes. We illustrate how the *eFlow* model enables the specification of processes that can automatically configure themselves at run-time according to the nature and type of services available on the Internet and to the requests and needs of each individual customer. We then present the dynamic change features provided by *eFlow*, that allow a great flexibility in modifying service process instances and service process definitions, enabling changes to every aspect of a process. Since dynamic process modification is a very powerful but delicate operation, one of our main goal has been to define very simple modification semantics, so that users can have a clear understanding of the effects of a modification. Prior to applying the changes, *eFlow* will enforce *consistency rules*, to avoid run-time errors resulting from the modifications, as well as *authorization rules*, to guarantee that only authorized users perform the modifications.

2 Overview of *eFlow*

This section presents an overview of the *eFlow* process model. We only present basic concepts that are needed in order to illustrate its adaptive and dynamic features. The interested reader is referred to [5] for details about the model and the implementation.

In *eFlow,* a composite service is described as a process schema that composes other basic or composite services. A composite service is modeled by a graph (the flow structure), which defines the order of execution among the nodes in the process. The graph may include *service, decision,* and *event* nodes. Service nodes represent the invocation of a basic or composite service; decision nodes specify the alternatives and rules controlling the execution flow, while event nodes enable service processes to send and receive several types of events. Arcs in the graph may be labeled with transition predicates defined over process data, meaning that as a node is completed, nodes connected to outgoing arcs are executed only if the corresponding transition predicate evaluates to true. A *service process instance* is an enactment of a process schema. The same service process may be instantiated several times, and several instances may be concurrently running.

Fig. 1 shows a simple graph describing a composite service that helps customers in organizing an award ceremony. In the figures, rounded boxes represent invocations of basic or composite services, filled-in circles represent the starting and ending point of the process, while horizontal bars are one of *eFlow* decision node types, and are used to specify parallel invocation of services and synchronization after parallel service executions.

The semantics of the schema is the following: when a new instance is started, service node *Data Collection* gathers information regarding the customer and his/her preferences and needs. Then, the *Restaurant Reservation* service is invoked, in order to book the restaurant and select the meals for the banquet. This node is executed first, since the characteristics of the selected restaurant (e.g., its location and the number of seats) affect the remainder of the service execution, i.e., the organization of the ceremony. Then, several services are invoked in parallel: the *Advertisement* service prepares a marketing campaign to advertise the ceremony, the *Invitation* service proposes a choice of several types of invitation cards and delivers them to the specified special guests, while the *Registration* service handles guest registrations and payments. Finally, the *Billing* service is invoked in order to present a unified bill to the organizing customer. All services can be either basic services (possibly provided by different organizations) or composite services, specified by *eFlow* processes.

Service nodes can access and modify data included in a *case packet*. Each process instance has a local copy of the case packet, and the *eFlow* engine controls access to these data. The specification of each service node includes the definition of which data the node is authorized to read or to modify.

The *eFlow* model also includes the notion of *transactional regions*. A transactional region identifies a portion of the process graph that should be executed in an atomic fashion. If for any reason the part of the process identified by the transactional region cannot be successfully completed, then all running services in the region are aborted and completed ones are compensated, by executing a service-specific compensating action. Compensating actions may be defined for each service or may be defined at the region level. For instance, by enclosing the Advertisement, Registration, and Invitation services in a transactional region, and by providing compensating actions for each of these services (or one compensating action at the region level), we are guaranteed that either all of the services are executed, or none is.

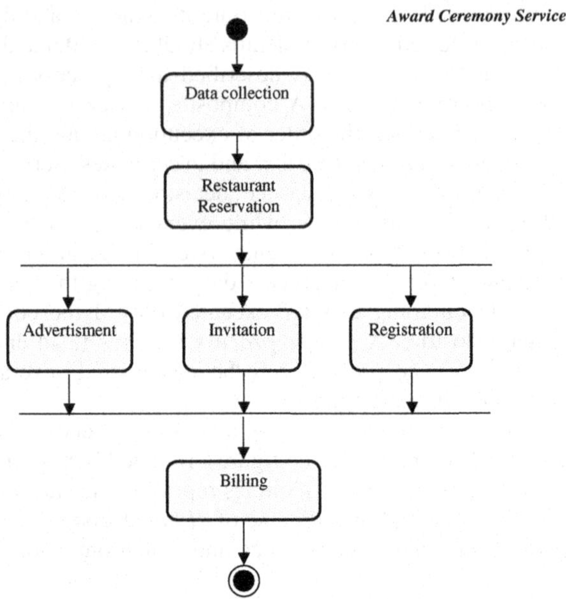

Fig. 1. Ceremony service process definition

Transactional regions may also include the specification of different isolation modes, that prevent data read or modified by nodes in the regions to be accessed by services that are outside the transactional region.

Process instances are enacted by the *eFlow engine*. The main function of the engine is to process messages notifying completion status of service nodes, by updating the value of case packet variables accessed by the service node and by subsequently scheduling the next node to be activated in the instance, according to the process definition. The engine then contacts the service broker in order to discover the actual service (and service provider) that can fulfill the requests specified in the service node definition, and eventually contacts the provider in order to execute the service.

The engine also processes *events* (either detected by the *eFlow* event monitor or notified by external event managers), by delivering them to the requesting event nodes. Notifications of occurred events and of service node completions are inserted into two separate transactional, First-in-First-Out queues (see Fig. 2). The engine extracts elements from the queues and processes them one by one. *eFlow* does not specifies any priority between the queues, but it does guarantee that every element in the queues is eventually processed. Finally, the engine logs every event related to process instance executions (to enable process monitoring, compensation, and to support dynamic process modifications) and ensures process integrity by enforcing transactional semantics and by compensating nodes executed within transactional regions in case of failures.

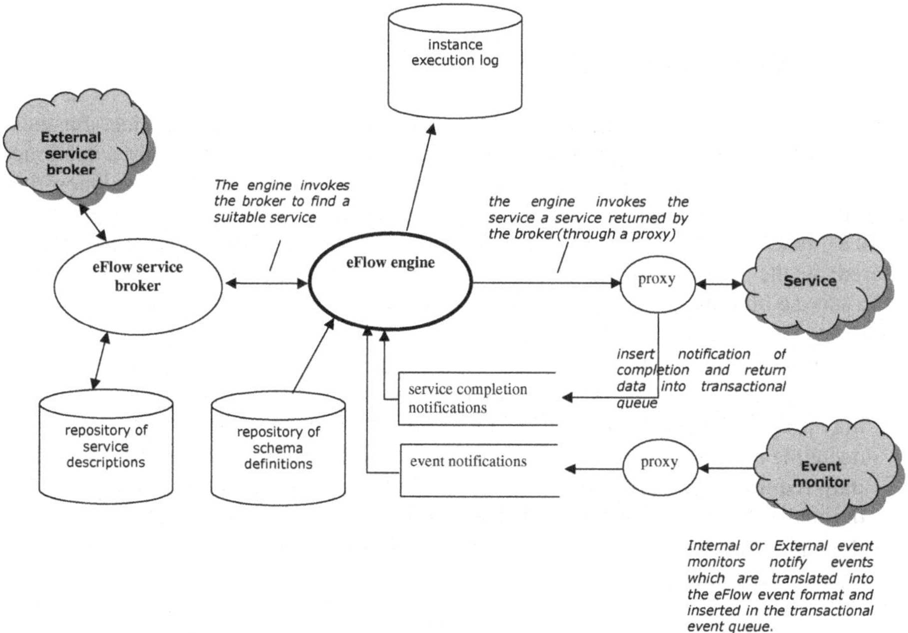

Fig. 2. The eFlow engine processes events and notifications of service completions in order to schedule service node executions

Like most Internet-based services, the *Award Ceremony* service provided by the *OneStopShop* company is executed in a highly dynamic environment. For instance, providers will continue to improve their e-services, and new providers may enter the market while some of the existing ones may cease their business. In addition, new types of e-services that can support the organization of an award ceremony may become available, such as renting of mega-screens and cameras, live broadcast of the ceremony over the Internet, or selection of trained personnel such as an anchorman. In the remainder of the paper we will show how *eFlow* addresses these challenges in order to allow service designer to provide composite services that naturally adapt to changes in the environment with minimal user intervention, that can be customized to fit the needs of every customer, and that are able to cope with unexpected exceptional situations.

3 Adaptive Service Processes

In order to manage and even take advantage of the frequent changes in the environment, service processes need to be *adaptive*, i.e., capable of adjusting themselves to changes in the environmental conditions with minimal or no manual intervention. *eFlow* provides several features and constructs to achieve this goal.

These include *dynamic service discovery*, *multiservice nodes*, and *generic nodes*. In the following we present an overview of these features.

3.1 Dynamic Service Discovery

A service node represents the invocation of a basic or composite service. Besides defining the data that the node is allowed to read and modify, and possibly a deadline to manage delays in service execution, a service node specification includes the description of the service to be invoked. For instance, within the *Advertisement* service node, we may specify that *eFlow* should invoke the *e-campaign* service offered by the *GreatAdvert.com* provider. While useful in some situations, such a static service binding is often too rigid, since it does not allow to:

- select the appropriate service depending on the customer's requirements: for instance, some customers may prefer a low-cost e-mail campaign, while other may prefer advertisements via TV, radio stations, or web sites;
- decouple service selection from the process definition: different service processes may require an advertisement service, and the selection criteria may need to be defined at the company level rather than at the composite service level;
- dynamically discover the best currently available service that fits the need of a specific customer.

To cope with the characteristics of the Internet environment, *eFlow* provides an open and dynamic approach to service selection. The service node includes the specification of a *service selection rule,* which can have several input parameters (defined by references to workflow variables). When a service node is started, the *eFlow* engine invokes a *service broker* that will execute the specified rule and return the appropriate service. Service selection rules are defined in a service broker-specific language, such as XQL if e"speak [4] is used as the service broker.

eFlow only requires that the rule returns an XML document which includes the definition of input and output data, the URI used to contact the service, billing and payment information, and a priority value used to select a specific service when several services are returned by the rule (choice among services with the same priority is non deterministic). Mapping between service node input/output data and the parameters of the invoked service is performed by a *mapping function*, specified as a set of string pairs `<case packet variable name, service variable name>`. A mapping function must be defined for a <service node, service description> pair before the service can be invoked in the context of the service node.

eFlow users can replace the default broker and plug-in the service broker that best fits their needs. Plugged-in brokers are not even required to access the service repository: they can dynamically discover services by contacting other external brokers or service advertisement facility, in order to get the most up to date information about available services and their characteristics.

Service selection rules will be then defined in the language supported by that broker, and can include arbitrary service selection policies. Plugged-in brokers must either present to the engine the same (simple) interface of the default one, or an adapter must be interposed between the engine and the broker to map requests and responses. In addition, if service brokers dynamically discover services not stored in the service description repository, they must also return a mapping function that allows the mapping of service node input/output data to service parameters.

3.2 Multiservice Nodes

In some composite service processes there is the need of invoking multiple, parallel instances of the same type of service. For instance, a restaurant reservation brokering service may request rates and availability to several restaurants that provide on-line access to these information.

In order to allow the specification of these kinds of process semantics, *eFlow* includes the notion of *multiservice* node. The multiservice node is a particular kind of node that allows for multiple, parallel activation of the same service node.

The number of service nodes to be activated is determined at run time in one of the following ways:

1. It can be determined by the number of service providers able to provide a given service. For instance, for the award ceremony service, we may want to contact all restaurant in the San Francisco Bay Area that can host a specified number of guests.
2. It can be equal to the number of elements in a case packet variable of type list. In this case each service node instance receives one and only one of the list items as input parameter. The value of such item will affect service selection and execution. For instance, a list may include a set of customers of different nationalities for which we want to check their credit history. The number of service nodes that will be instantiated within the multiservice node will be equal to the number of customers, and each node will focus on one customer. A service selection rule will be executed for each service node to be activated; the rule can have the customer's data as input parameter, in order to select the appropriate credit check service for each customer, for instance depending on the customer's nationality.

An important part of a multiservice is the specification of when the multiservice can be considered completed and the flow can proceed with the successor service node. In most cases, the flow can proceed only when all invoked services have been completed. However, in other cases, there is no need to wait for all service instances to be completed, since the multiservice goal may have already been achieved before. For instance, suppose that we want to verify a customer's credit with several agencies: if our acceptance criteria is that all agencies must give a positive judgment for the customer to be accepted, then as soon as one agency gives a negative opinion we can proceed with service execution, without waiting for the completion of the other services, which may be canceled. The multiservice termination is specified by a condition, checked every time one of its service nodes terminate. If the condition holds, then the successor of the multiservice is activated and services in execution are canceled. An example of termination condition for the credit check example could be `Rejections.length>0`, where Rejections is a variable of type `ListOf (String)`, and length is an attribute common to every list variable that contains the number of elements in the list. Fig. 3 shows a sample specification of a multiservice node in *eFlow*. The specification includes the reference to the service node to be instantiated (multiple times) as part of the multiservice node, as well as the activation and termination conditions.

```
<MULTISERVICE_NODE id="check_customers_credit">
        <NAME> Check Customers' credit </NAME>
        <SERVICE_NODE id="check_single_customer_credit" />
        <DESCRIPTION>  Multiservice node that checks the credit
                       history of several customers in parallel
        </DESCRIPTION>
        <ACTIVATION mode="by_variable" varref="customers_list" />
        <TERMINATION> rejections.length>0 </TERMINATION>
</MULTISERVICE_NODE>
```

Fig. 3. Specification of a multiservice node in *eFlow*

3.3 Dynamic Service Node Creation

An important requirement for providers of Internet-based services is the ability of providing personalized services, to better satisfy the needs of every individual customer.

While the service process depicted in Fig. 1 may be suited for some customer, other customers might need additional services, such as rental of video/audio equipment or the hiring of trained personnel to work with such equipment. At the same time, some customers may not need the services offered by the *Award Ceremony* service process. For instance, they may not need an advertisement service or they may provide for it by themselves. Clearly, it is practically unfeasible to foresee all possible combinations of services which may be needed by each customer and to define a process for each potential type of customer. Besides, this would imply a very high maintenance cost, especially in the e-service environment where new types of services become available on a daily basis.

To cope with these demanding needs, *eFlow* supports the dynamic creation of service process definitions by including in its model the notion of *generic service node*. Unlike ordinary service nodes, generic nodes are not statically bound or limited to a specific set of services. Instead, they include a configuration parameter that can be set with a list of actual service nodes either at process instantiation time (through the process instance input parameters) or at runtime. The parameter is a variable of type `ListOf(Service_Node)`. The specified services will be executed in parallel or sequentially depending on an *executionMode* attribute of the generic service node.

Generic nodes are resolved each time they are activated, in order to allow maximum flexibility and to cope with processes executed in highly dynamic environments. For instance, if the generic node is within a loop, then its configuration parameters can be modified within the loop, and the node can be resolved into different ordinary service nodes for each loop of the execution. Notice that generic nodes are different from multiservice nodes: multiservice nodes model the activation of a dynamically determined number of instances of the *same* service node, while generic nodes allow the dynamic selection of different service nodes.


```
<GENERIC_NODE id="award_ceremony_services">
   <NAME> Award Ceremony Services </NAME>
   <SERVICE_NODE_POOL> Ceremony Service Pool </SERVICE_NODE_POOL>
  <DESCRIPTION> Placeholder for service nodes related
                to a ceremony service,to be executed in parallel
  </DESCRIPTION>
   <SERVICE_SELECTION_VAR> SelectedServices</SERVICE_SELECTION_VAR>
  <EXECUTION_MODE mode="parallel" />
</GENERIC NODE>
```

Fig. 4. Sample XML description of a generic service node in *eFlow*

4 Dynamic Service Process Modifications

While adaptive processes considerably reduce the need for human intervention in managing and maintaining process definitions, there may still be cases in which process schemas need to be modified, or in which actions need to be taken on running process instances to modify their course. Process modifications may be needed to handle unexpected exceptional situations, to incorporate new laws or new business policies, to improve the process, or to correct errors or deficiencies in the current definition. We distinguish between two types of service process modifications:

- *Ad-hoc changes* are modifications applied to a single running service process instance. They are typically needed to manage exceptional situations that are not expected to occur again, such as the unavailability of a restaurant that had been booked for a ceremony.
- *Bulk changes* refer to modifications collectively applied to a subset (or to all) the running instances of a service process. For instance, suppose that an advertisement company on which many ceremony advertisement campaigns relied upon goes out of business. This situation can affect many instances, and it is practically unfeasible to separately modify each single instance. Bulk changes may also be needed when a new, improved version of a process is defined. If, for instance, a new law forces a modification of a process, then running instances will need to respect the new constraints as well.

4.1 Ad-hoc Changes

Ad-hoc changes are modifications applied to a single, running process instance. *eFlow* allows two types of ad-hoc changes: modifications of the process schema and modifications of the process instance *state*. In the remainder of this section we show how *eFlow* supports both type of changes.

Ad-hoc Changes to the Process Schema

eFlow allows authorized users to modify the schema followed by a given service process instance. The modifications are applied by first defining a new schema (usually by modifying the current one) and by then *migrating* the instance from its current schema (called *source* schema) to the newly defined one (called *destination*

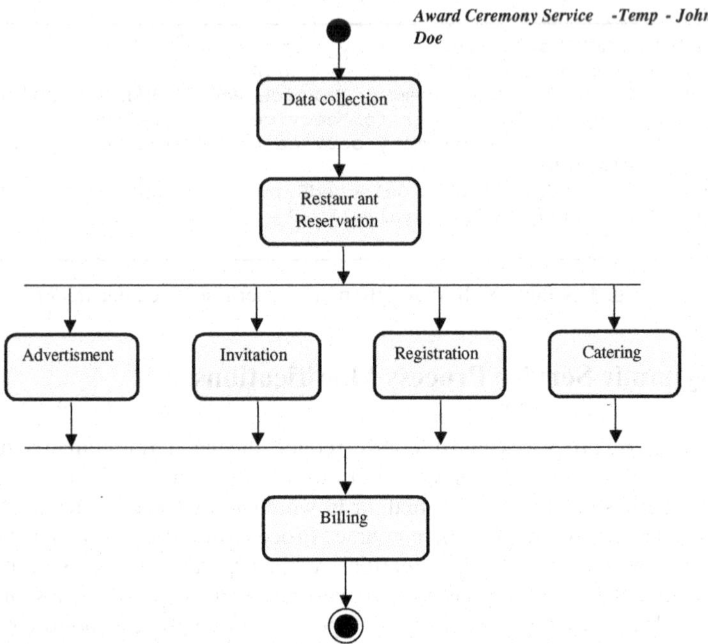

Fig. 5. Ad-hoc process definition to handle the request by customer John Doe

schema). For instance, suppose that a customer of *OneStopShop*, John Doe, is accessing a restaurant reservation service within an Award Ceremony process; John found a restaurant, *Chez Jaques,* that fully satisfies his needs in terms of number of seats, location, and atmosphere, but that does not serve food of satisfactory quality. John then asks *OneStopShop* to provide him a catering service, so that he can rent only the place and separately arrange for the food. Since John is a good customer and the company wants to keep his business, the process responsible decides to satisfy his request and modify the process definition (for this particular instance only) by adding a catering service, as depicted in Fig. 5.

Authorized users can modify every aspect of a schema, including the flow structure, the definition of service, decision, and event nodes, process data, and even transactional regions. *eFlow* only verifies that *behavioral consistency* is respected when migrating an instance to a destination schema (i.e., that instance migration does not generate run-time errors and that transactional semantics can be enforced).

Case migration is a very delicate operation, since it allows changing the rules of the game while it is in progress. Hence, our main design goal has been to define a very simple migration semantics, so that users can easily and clearly understand the behavior of the instance after the modifications have been applied, and avoid the risk of unexpected and undesired effects. In the following we describe how *eFlow* manages and performs instance migrations.

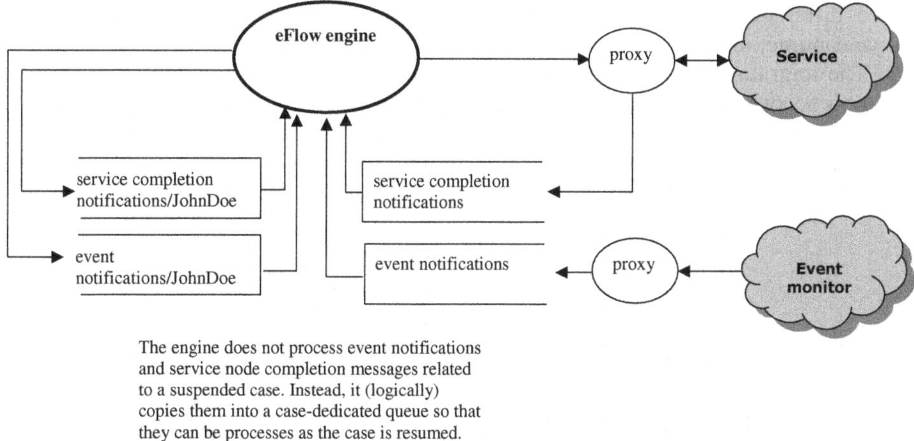
eFlow engine
proxy
Service
service completion notifications/JohnDoe
service completion notifications
event notifications/JohnDoe
event notifications
proxy
Event monitor
The engine does not process event notifications and service node completion messages related to a suspended case. Instead, it (logically) copies them into a case-dedicated queue so that they can be processes as the case is resumed.

Fig. 6. Events and notifications related to suspended instances are not processed, but are placed in a separate queue

Case migration operations

Case migrations are performed by a suitable *eFlow* module, called *migration manager*. The following operations are performed in order to migrate an instance from a schema to another:

1. An authorized user accesses the migration manager and identifies the instance to be migrated as well as the destination schema (details on user authorizations are provided in section 4.3). The destination schema must have been previously defined, either from scratch or by modifying the one being followed by the instance to be migrated.
2. The migration manager notifies to the *eFlow* engine that instance execution (for the process instance to be migrated) should be suspended. When a process instance is suspended, running services are allowed to complete. However, the engine does not schedule any new service and does not deliver events. When the engine processes a service completion notification related to a service node of the suspended instance, it puts this notification into an ad-hoc, temporary queue maintained for the suspended instance. The notification will be processed when instance execution is resumed. Similarly, events to be delivered to the suspended instance are also placed in a different logical queue (see Fig. 6), and will be delivered as instance execution is resumed. An instance can only be suspended when the engine is not processing messages related to it: in fact, the sequence of operations performed by the engine to process events or service node completion messages and to activate subsequent nodes is atomic.
3. The migration manager verifies that the migration preserves behavioral consistency.

4a. If behavioral consistency is preserved, then the migration manager builds an execution state for the instance in the new schema (details are provided below).

4b. If the instance cannot be migrated, the user is notified of the reason that does not allow the migration and is asked to modify the destination schema (or to indicate a different destination schema). Steps 1 to 4 will then be repeated. In the meantime, instance execution remains suspended.

5. The migration manager informs *eFlow* that instance execution can be resumed, now according to the destination schema.

At any time during this sequence of operations the user can abort the migration, and instance execution will be resumed according to the old process schema. The operations performed by the migration manager are summarized in Fig. 7.

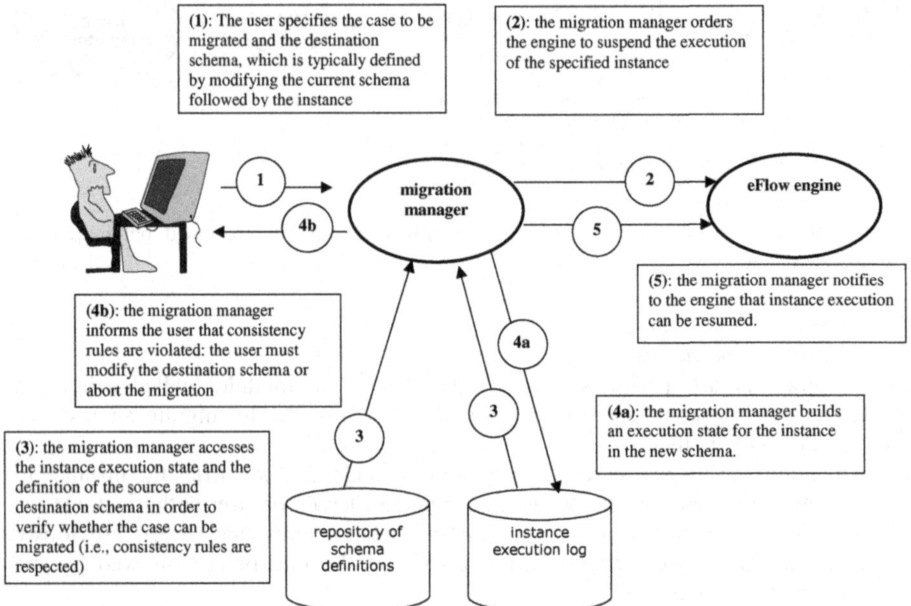

Fig. 7. Sequence of operations performed by the migration manager when migrating an instance

Consistency rules

An instance can be migrated from a version to another only if *behavioral consistency* is preserved. Behavioral consistency implies that the migration does not result in run-time errors or non-deterministic behaviors. In order to guarantee behavioral consistency, *eFlow* enforces the following rules:

1. Each service or event node that is active when the instance is suspended must be present in the destination schema. This rule is necessary since it allows the definition of an execution state for the instance in the new schema, and in particular the definition of which nodes should be set to the *active* state when execution is resumed, as explained below. In addition, it allows the engine to know how to correctly process completion messages related to those running services that will eventually be received. While the definition of active service nodes can differ from the one in the source schema (e.g., they may have different input data or different deadlines), their *write list* must be the same, since it is

expected that the running nodes will actually try to modify the value of those variables.

2. If a variable in the destination schema is also present in the source schema, then it must be of the same type. This rule is needed since variables will keep their current value after migration, and therefore the types in the source and destination schema must be the same.
3. Transactional regions not present in the source schema must not include any node which is part of the source schema and which is active or completed.
4. If a transactional region with the same identifier is present both in the source and destination schema, and the region was active at migration time, then:
   a. The isolation properties of these transactional regions must be the same.
   b. No node in the region of the destination schema should read (write) variables which are not also read (written) by at least one node of the same transactional region in the source schema. The only allowed exception is when the newly introduced variable is only used within the region.
   c. The region should not be extended "in the past", i.e., it should not include nodes that are also in the source schema, that have already been executed, and that are not part of the region in the source schema.

   Rules related to transactional regions are necessary since *eFlow* acquires the read and write locks necessary for enforcing the specified isolation mode at the start of the transactional region.

Migration semantics

The essence of the migration process consists in building an *execution state* for the instance in the new schema, and then in resuming instance execution. An execution state is formed by the value of the case packet variables and by the execution state of all service and event nodes in the instance. The values of case packet variables are set as follows:

- Variables in the destination schema that are also present in the source schema keep the value they had in the case packet of the migrated instance.
- Variables in the destination schema that are not present in the source schema are initialized with their default value (or are left undefined if no default value was provided).

The execution state of service and event nodes is defined as follows:

- Nodes of the destination schema that are also present in the source schema are initialized with the same execution state they had in the migrated instance (e.g., not started, active, completed, failed, canceled, timed out).
- Nodes of the destination schema that are not present in the source schema are initialized to the *not started* state.

After the instance state has been reconstructed, the migration is completed. The migration manager will then inform the engine that instance execution can be resumed. The *eFlow* engine then processes all events and all service completion messages included in the event and service completion queues that were created to manage instance suspension. Elements in these queues are processed with the same semantics used to process elements in the standard queues. After all elements included in both queues have been processed, the engine discards these queues and resume normal operations, that is, it resumes processing of the standard queues.

Modifications to the Process State

Besides changes to the process schema, authorized users can perform the following operations on an instance in execution:

- Change the value of case packet variables.
- Initiate the rollback of a process region or of the entire process.
- Terminate the process.
- Reassign a node to a different service: the running service is canceled, and the one specified by the user is invoked.

These actions are performed through the *service operation monitor* component of *eFlow*, and do not require instance suspension.

4.2 Bulk Changes

Bulk changes handle exceptional situations that affect many instances of the same process. Instead of handling running instances on a case-by-case basis, *eFlow* allows authorized users to apply changes to sets of instances that have common properties. Modifications are introduced by specifying one or more destination schemas and by defining which set of instances should be migrated to each schema. For instance, suppose that *OneStopShop* decides to provide, as a bonus, a security service for all ceremonies that involve more than 100 guests. To perform this, a new service process is defined, by modifying the *Award Ceremony* one, in order to include a security personnel service, as shown in Fig. 8.

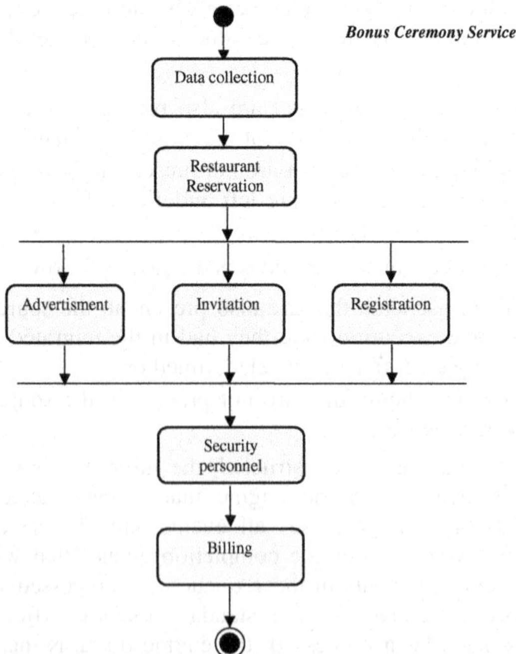

Fig. 8. Modified Award Ceremony service, now including a security service

Next, the service process responsible can migrate all running instances (related to a Ceremony service that involves more than 100 guests) to the newly defined one. Migrations are defined by means of a simple, rule-based language. A migration rule identifies a subset of the running instances of a given process and specifies the schema to which instances in this subset should be migrated. Rules have the form `IF <condition> THEN MIGRATE TO <schema>`. The condition is a predicate over service process data and service process execution state that identifies a subset of the running instances, while `<schema>` denotes the destination schema. Instances whose state does not fulfill the migration condition will proceed with the same schema. An example of migration rule is: `IF (guests>100) THEN MIGRATE TO "Bonus_Ceremony_Service"`.

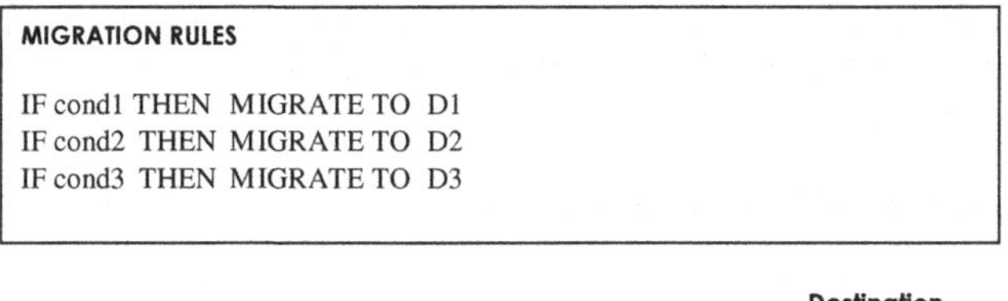

MIGRATION RULES

IF cond1 THEN MIGRATE TO D1
IF cond2 THEN MIGRATE TO D2
IF cond3 THEN MIGRATE TO D3

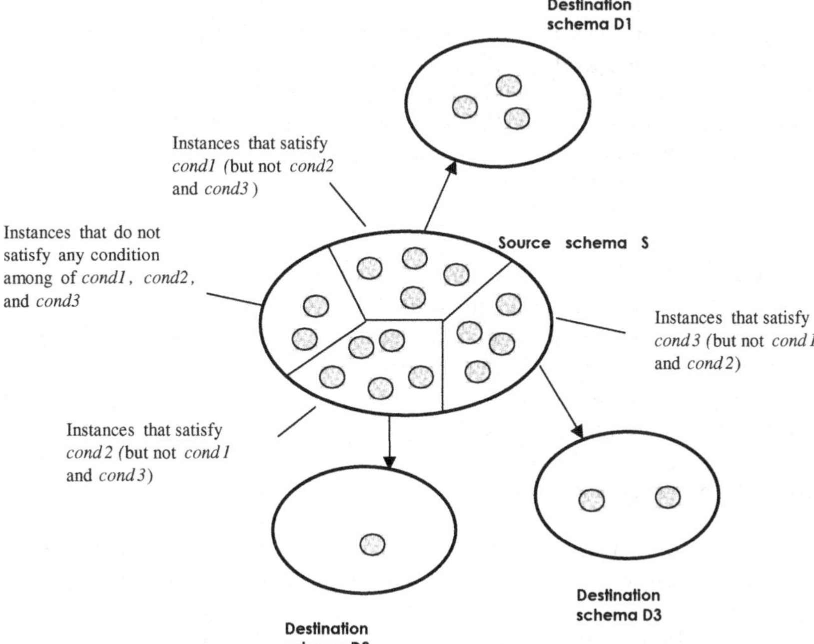

Fig. 9. Bulk migration: instances are migrated to different destination schemas depending on migration rules

The set of rules must define a partitioning over the set of active instances, so that each instance is migrated to one schema at most. Instances that do not satisfy any rule condition are not migrated. Fig. 9 exemplifies bulk migration. The sequence of operations performed in bulk migration is as follows:

1. The user defines, compiles, and checks in the migration rules. All destination schemas referred to by migration rules must have been previously defined.
2. *eFlow* suspends *all* running instances of the process.
3. *eFlow* verifies that the migration rules actually define a partition over the set of running instances. If the state of an instance satisfies more that one migration condition, the user is asked to revise the rules or abort the migration.
4. *eFlow* verifies that each instance can be migrated to the specified destination version of the process schema, i.e., it checks that behavioral consistency is preserved. In addition, it checks that the user who started the migration has the required authorizations to migrate each of the selected instances. Due to the delicacy of a bulk migration operation, *eFlow* does not perform any migration until all instances can be safely migrated to their destination schema.
5. If all migrations can preserve behavioral consistency, then instances are migrated to their destination schema. Instance executions are then resumed.

4.3 Security in Dynamic Process Modifications

Dynamic service process modifications in *eFlow* are constrained by *authorization rules* that defines which user or application is authorized to perform a given modification. Rules are specified at process definition time, and can include an arbitrary number of input parameters, taken from case packet variable. This enables the definition of security rules that differs according to the particular execution state of the instance. Each process definition includes the following authorization rules with respect to process modifications:

- *Authorized_State_Modifiers*: identifies the users (services) that have write access to case packet variables, i.e., that can perform state changes to the instance.
- *Authorized_Node_Modificators*: identifies the users (services) authorized to modify service nodes in the process instance. This rule can also be specified at the node level, to further constrain authorizations.
- *Authorized_Flow_Modificators*: identifies the users (services) authorized to make any kind of dynamic changes to the process instance.
- *Authorized_Initiators*: identifies the users (services) authorized to start an instance of this process

Each time a state change or a migration is requested, *eFlow* verifies that the requestor has the appropriate authorizations, according to the defined rules and to the differences between source and destination schema. In particular, in case of a bulk migration, authorization rule *Authorized_Node_Modificators* (or *Authorized_Flow_Modificators*, depending on the extent of the changes) defined in the *source* schema are executed for each instance to be migrated, and the migration is performed only if the user has the privileges to migrate *all* of these instances. In addition, since the migration will result in executions of the destination schema, rule *Authorized_Initiators* of the defined *destination* schema will be executed, to verify that the user is authorized to create instance of that schema.

5 Related Work

To the best of our knowledge, there is no commercial process management system that supports adaptive and dynamic features such as those of *eFlow*, neither among traditional workflow management systems (such as *MQ Wor*kflow [11] or *InConcert* [10]), nor among newly developed, open, XML- and web-based systems such as *Forte' Fusion* [9] and *KeyFlow* [6].

A few of these systems, such as InConcert and KeyFlow, provide some support for ad-hoc changes, by allowing simple modifications to the schema followed by a given instance as well as execution state modifications. Recently, some approaches to handle dynamic changes have been presented in the literature by the workflow research community.

One of the first contributions come from [2], that defines a correctness criterion for instance migration, based on the definition of the set of all valid node sequences: a change is correct if the execution sequence could have been obtained with the new schema. The paper, however, introduces a simple workflow model and restricts to a limited set of modifications.

Ad-hoc and bulk changes are discussed in [7]. Workflow changes are specified by *transformation rules* composed of a *source schema fragment*, a *destination schema fragment*, and of a *condition*. The system checks for parts of the process that are isomorphic with the source schema and replaces them with the destination schema for all instances for which the condition is verified. The paper also proposes a migration language for managing instance-specific migrations, conceptually similar to our migration language.

Other contributions to the area of workflow evolution come from [8,12]. In [12], a complete and minimal set of workflow modification operations is presented. Correctness properties are defined in order to determine whether a specific change can be applied to a given instance. If these constraints are violated, the change is either rejected or the correctness must be explicitly restored with exception handling techniques. Liu et al [8] focus instead on a language for workflow evolution, by which the designer can specify which instances should be migrated to which versions, depending on conditions over workflow data. The language is conceptually similar to that of [7] and to ours.

In designing *eFlow*, we took advantage of all these research contributions and extended them as follows:

- We designed a model and system that provides all the flexibility features required for a dynamic environment such as that of the Internet, including a wide range of possible ad-hoc and bulk changes;
- we designed a very simple, yet powerful migration language and a very simple migration semantics, to enable an easy understanding of the instance behavior after migration. This is a fundamental requirement in operational environments;
- we discussed migration in the context of a rich process model, which includes events and transactions. These model features posed us additional challenges in managing migrations;
- we introduced authorization constraints that allows the definition who is authorized to perform a given type of change;

- we defined the process followed by the system when the changes are made, focusing in particular on the delicate issue of instance suspension;
- finally, in addition to dynamic change support, *eFlow* also provides a set of adaptive features in order to strongly reduce the need for dynamic changes.

Adaptive process management is also recently gaining attention. The workflow model proposed in [1] includes a "shoot tip" activity: when a shoot tip activity is executed, the control is transferred to a process modeler that can extend the flow structure with one additional activity, which is inserted before the shoot tip activity. Next, instance execution will proceed by activating the newly inserted task and subsequently another "shoot tip" activity to determine the next step. Another interesting approach, which also allows for automatic adaptation, is proposed in [3]. The presented workflow model includes a *placeholder* activity, which is an abstract activity replaced at runtime with a concrete activity type, which must have the same input and output data of those defined as part of the placeholder. A selection policy can be specified to indicate the activity that should be executed. The model has an expressive power similar to the one allowed by *eFlow* dynamic service discovery mechanism. However, we do not restrict the input and output parameters of the selected activity to be the same of those of the node. In addition, we also provide the notion of generic and multiservice node for further achieving additional flexibility and we provide a set of dynamic modification features to cope with situations in which changes in the flow are needed.

6 Conclusions

In this paper we have shown how *eFlow* supports the dynamic composition, enactment, and management of *composite* e-services, i.e., of e-services built on top of other basic or composite services. In particular, we focused on the adaptive and dynamic features of *eFlow*, which are essential characteristics in order to cope with dynamic environments such as that of e-services. Our future research will be focused on providing effective means for monitoring and analyzing instances that have been modified one or more times during their executions.

In summary, we believe that the *eFlow* platform has the required characteristics and functionality to satisfy the need of Internet-based service providers. *eFlow* is integrated with the Hewlett-Packard e-service strategy; however, it is an open technology: it is based on Java and it is compliant with the workflow and Internet standards, such as XML and the Workflow Management Coalition Interface standards. Hence, it can be integrated and used in virtually any IT environment.

References

1. T. Dirk Meijler, H. Kessels, C. Vuijst and R. le Comte. Realising Run-time Adaptable Workflow by means of Reflection in the Baan Workflow Engine. Proceedings of the CSCW Workshop on Adaptive Workflow Management, Seattle, WA, 1998.

2. S. Ellis, K. Keddara and G. Rozenberg, Dynamic Change within Workflow Systems, Proceedings of (COOCS '95), Milpitas, California, 1995.
3. D. Georgakopoulos, H. Schuster, D. Baker, and A. Cichocki. Managing Escalation of Collaboration Processes in Crisis Mitigation Situations. Proceedings of ICDE 2000, San Diego, CA, USA, 2000.
4. Hewlett-Packard. e"speak Architectural Specifications. 2000.
5. Hewlett-Packard. *eFlow* model and architecture, version 1.0. 2000.
6. Keyflow Corp. Workflow Server and Workflow designer. 1999.
7. G. Joeris and O. Herzog. Managing Evolving Workflow Specifications with Schema Versioning and Migration Rules. TZI Technical Report 15, University of Bremen, 1999.
8. C. Liu, M. Orlowska and H. Li. Automating Handover in Dynamic Workflow Environments. Proceedings of CAiSE '98, Pisa, Italy, 1998.
9. J. Mann. Forte' Fusion. Patricia Seybold Group report, 1999.
10. R. Marshak. InConcert Workflow. Workgroup Computing report, Vol 20, No. 3, Patricia Seybold Group, 1997.
11. IBM. MQ Series Workflow - Concepts and Architectures. 1998.
12. M. Reichert, P. Dadam. ADEPTflex - Supporting Dynamic Changes of Workflows Without Loosing Control. Technical report 97-07, DBIS, University of Ulm, 1997.

Promises and Failures of Research in Dynamic Service Composition

Fabio Casati

Abstract This short articles discusses the evolution of research in composition technologies, from workflows to mashups. It emphasizes the failures of composition technologies and makes the case for domain-specific workflows as a possible successful way to leverage composition technologies.

1 Dynamic Workflows

This short articles discusses the evolution of research in composition technologies, from workflows to mashups. It takes as a starting point the work reported in the paper *Adaptive and dynamic service composition in eFlow*[1], published in CAiSE 2000. The objective of that paper was to discuss how we can make a service composition more flexible, deciding at deployment or at runtime which concrete service or sets of services should be invoked. We had already realized, back then, that human intervention in this adaptation would be needed, and so the goal of the paper was to discuss how we could simplify the adaptation process, rather than automating it. At that point, web services and the research area of service composition was in its infancy. Web services themselves were a rather new concept, and indeed in that year we had organized the first workshop on *Technologies for e-services* in conjunction with the VLDB conference. Back then, research in composition technologies was still mostly in the domain of workflow management.

Workflow technology was born in the late 1980s with the promise to automate office procedures and facilitate the coordination and data flow among employees. Composition and workflows – and the related languages and technologies – seemed to make a lot of sense. We have tasks (and often *business* tasks) which we do need to coordinate and orchestrate to achieve some business value, so why not design a

F. Casati (✉)
University of Trento, Trento, Italy
e-mail: Fabio.Casati@unitn.it

J. Bubenko et al. (eds.), *Seminal Contributions to Information Systems Engineering*, DOI 10.1007/978-3-642-36926-1_18,

simple graphical language to help users specify the coordination logic and manage the data exchange among the activities, thereby also avoiding extra work, data entry errors, and allowing accurate work tracking? It seemed like a no brainer and a sure success.

The equivalent of dynamic composition in the workflow space was called *dynamic resource selection*, consisting of languages, policies, and technologies for defining to which person or role a workflow task should be assigned. Research in this area has been extensive, and produced many languages that allowed the specification of complex assignment policies that consider aspects such as workers' skills, schedule, and even compliance rules such as separation of duties [3].

However, the success of workflow systems has been much lower than anticipated. Nearly all major software companies and many startups had an offering in the workflow space, but sales were very low. As I reported in my book [2], part of the problem was that workflow systems were very expensive and "heavy", that is, complex to install and operate as they included lots of functionality (this was not the *only* problem, but we'll get back to this a bit later). Most of the deployments were done for the purpose of *tracking* work more so than automating it. The implication is that the abundant research results were in fact rarely used and had very little impact in practice, especially research in dynamic resource assignment. In a way, we as researchers were trying to solve an advanced and complex problem without addressing (or even understanding) the basic issues that impeded the success of workflow technology.

2 Dynamic Service Composition

In the mid and late 1990s, *Enterprise Application Integration* (EAI) platforms came about, facilitating the interconnection of enterprise systems. Workflows then evolved from orchestrating the work among humans to orchestrating the information flow across enterprise systems. While EAI platforms were rather successful, workflows still enjoyed limited adoption.

Web services seemed to be a key enabler for composition technologies, overcoming some of the issues that impeded the adoption of workflow systems. What web services and the related middlware bring to the table is (at least in principle) a standard way for describing interfaces and interaction protocols and for transporting data. The thought shared by many researchers and practitioners in the area was that every company would expose their services as web services, following a same standard and publishing their interfaces and protocols, so that it would therefore be easy to write program that access these services. As a result we would have a myriad of services available and with them the opportunity of combining such services to obtain a functionality of interest. A global registry (UDDI[4], you may remember it) would contain pointers to all specifications of all services in the world.

The main point of attraction here was that because of the highly standardized (at least technically) nature of web services, it would be easy to interoperate with them. If we could develop a (graphical) language and a model to enable the composition of services (with a supporting execution engine), we would have a powerful tool to quickly create complex services out of other services. The high degree of standardization would reduce the complexity of the composition engines, thereby making the products lighter and cheaper.

This technological development fueled research in workflows under the hat of service composition. New (or, actually, refurbished) models and languages started to appear to support the specification of various aspects of a composition.

Despite the hopes, however, the situation soon mirrored what happened to workflows: lots of hype on service composition, lots of tools by big and small companies, lots of investment, and very limited adoption. Part of the problem here has nothing to do with service composition: web services themselves had a lot of success as a concept (more and more functionality is now accessible programmatically) but there is no standard really used for interface and protocol description, it all really boils down to http. To a large extent, interfaces are specified in plain English, and structured in arbitrary ways. Formal or semantic specifications of interfaces is something that requires highly skilled (and very careful, very precise) people. It works in theory but not in practice.

A part of the problem however does have to do with service composition. The issue here is that, while most languages claimed to be "easy to use", in practice service composition required professional programmers. And because programmers knew how to program, it was and is just easier to code the composition with a conventional programming language rather than learn yet another language and install and maintain yet another piece of software. Most programmers also prefer to script rather than to use graphical languages. Composition systems did provide some extra features (such as advanced transactional models) but once again programmers resorted to the comfort of databases, which were well known and widely tested, and in most cases that was enough.

In this context, once again research on dynamic service composition was flourishing, and still today we often come across new papers proposing some algorithms that improves the status quo. Most papers assumed the existence of several services with the same interface and similar functionality, and that consequently these services could be easily and seamlessly swapped. An algorithm would then determine which service provided the best quality at the lower cost, based on various criteria. The main flaw I see now in this thread of research is that (i) swapping a service with another is not easy from a business perspective. Service relationships are based on contractual agreements and in general the service provider a company chooses depends on many factors difficult to encode; (ii) Most importantly, even if two services have the same interface, the hope to replace one with another and have the composition continue to work smoothly is vain. This is because interoperability with any non-trivial service must be repeatedly tested and the meaning of the different parameters must be fully understood. In my experience, this is true no matter how well the service interface is described. Different services with the same interface would always behave differently because different implementations interpret and understand parameters differently. The reason why these issues are rarely addressed in papers is that they show up in real settings, but not in lab tests. Composition, including dynamic composition, is intuitively attractive, but it is only when we apply it in a real setting that we see the real issues surfacing. And because there were very few real services out there, it was difficult to have them surface.

Additional thread of research included semantic composition (where algorithms were even trying to understand the service goals and behaviors, going beyond the interface, and take dynamic composition decisions based on that) and goal-oriented planning, where a partial or complete composition is created (semi-)automatically based on a description of the goal of the composition. These approaches suffered and still suffer from issues similar to the one described above, only extended because there are more aspects considered by the algorithms besides the interface.

3 Lessons Learned

So, as we saw, history has been repeating in the field of (dynamic) composition. Interestingly, the same is happening today with mashups.

The interesting aspect is, however, to look at those cases where composition is indeed successful. These cases always have a common aspect: they tackle domain-specific problems. Prominent examples of these are data transformation tools or scientific workflows, but there are many others. These tools are specific enough and limited enough to actually become usable by non-programmers and to provide out of the box features that make them attractive. It is the specificity (and the consequent simplicity), not the generality, that makes these tools useful. Somehow we tend as researchers to drive towards generic solution as we feel that this is the goal of research, but in composition technologies we have learned that flexibility comes at a very high price, that of making the technology difficult to use and, very often, useless. The challenge that lies in front of us is, therefore, that of finding ways to easily create domain-specific composition models that are simple enough (and, necessarily, limited enough) to be applicable to one class of problems and that are amenable to non-programmers, meaning, such that non-programmers can create a complete application from start to finish without the need of writing code outside of the platform, or of specifying composition logic that, although graphical, presents all the difficulties (complex parallelism, data transformation, complex exception handling) of programming languages. Unless we can get empower users at the skill level of the average Excel user to write complete composition (possibly after some training), this technology will remain attractive in theory but ineffective in practice.

Acknowledgements A big thanks to the friends, colleagues, and co-authors of the original CAiSE paper: Ski Ilnicki, LiJie Jin, Vasudev Krishnamoorthy, and Ming-Chien Shan.

References

1. F. Casati, S. Ilnicki, L.J. Jin, V. Krishnamoorthy and M.C. Shan, Adaptive and Dynamic Service Composition in eFlow, Procs of Caise'00, Sweden. Springer.
2. G. Alonso, F. Casati, H. Kuno, and V. Machiraju. *Web Services Concepts, Architectures and Applications*. Springer-Verlag, Berlin, 2004.
3. R. Botha and J.Eloff, Separation of duties for access control enforcement in workflow environments, IBM Systems Journal 40 (3), 2001.
4. Luc Clement, Andrew Hately, Claus von Riegen, and Tony Rogers. *UDDI Version 3*. OASIS UDDI Spec TC, 2004.

On Structured Workflow Modelling*

Bartek Kiepuszewski[1], Arthur Harry Maria ter Hofstede[2], and Christoph J. Bussler[3]

[1] Mincom Limited, GPO Box 1397, Brisbane, Qld 4001, Australia, bartek@mincom.com
[2] Cooperative Information Systems Research Centre, Queensland University of Technology, GPO Box 2434, Brisbane, Qld 4001, Australia, arthur@icis.qut.edu.au
[3] Netfish Technologies Inc., 2350 Mission College Blvd., Santa Clara, CA 95054, USA, cbussler@netfish.com

Abstract. While there are many similarities between the languages of the various workflow management systems, there are also significant differences. One particular area of differences is caused by the fact that different systems impose different syntactic restrictions. In such cases, business analysts have to choose between either conforming to the language in their specifications or transforming these specifications afterwards. The latter option is preferable as this allows for a separation of concerns. In this paper we investigate to what extent such transformations are possible in the context of various syntactical restrictions (the most restrictive of which will be referred to as *structured workflows*). We also provide a deep insight into the consequences, particularly in terms of expressive power, of imposing such restrictions.

1 Introduction

Despite the interest in workflow management, both from academia and industry, there is still little consensus about its conceptual and formal foundations (see e.g. [7]). While there are similarities between the languages of various commercially available workflow management systems, there are also many differences. However, it is often not clear whether these differences are fundamental in nature. For example, as different systems impose different syntactic restrictions, one may wonder whether this affects the expressive power of the resulting languages. In addition to that, such variations result in business analysts being confronted with the question as to whether to conform to the target language right away when they specify their workflows, or to transform their specifications in a later stage.

In this paper focus is on syntactic variations in workflow specification languages. Different workflow management systems impose different syntactical restrictions. The most restrictive types of workflows will be referred to as *structured*

* This research is supported by an ARC SPIRT grant "Component System Architecture for an Open Distributed Enterprise Management System with Configurable Workflow Support" between QUT and Mincom.

B. Wangler, L. Bergman (Eds.): CAiSE 2000, LNCS 1789, pp. 431–445, 2000.

workflows. Systems such as SAP R/3 and Filenet Visual Workflo allow for the specification of structured workflows only. While enforcing restrictions may have certain benefits (e.g. verification and implementation become easier), the price that may have to be paid is that the resulting language is more difficult to use and has less expressive power.

In this paper, it will be shown that some syntactic restrictions will lead to a reduction of expressive power of the language involved, while other restrictions are of a less serious nature and can be overcome by the introduction of equivalence preserving transformation rules. It will be also shown that even though for certain workflow models it is possible to transform them to equivalent structured forms, the resulting models are less suitable than the original ones. Nevertheless, the automation of such rules could potentially lead to tools giving business analysts greater freedom in workflow specification without compromising their realisability in terms of commercially available (and preferred) workflow management systems.

2 Structured Workflows: Definitions

In this section the notion of a structured workflow is formally defined and some elementary properties stated. Workflows as used in this paper will employ concepts used in most commercial workflow management systems. Although the graphical notation used for representing workflows is irrelevant in terms of the results presented in this paper, we have to agree on one in order to provide examples to illustrate our arguments. Process elements will be represented by large circles; or-joins and or-splits will correspond to small, white circles, while and-joins and and-splits will correspond to small, shaded circles (the indegree and outdegree will always make it clear whether we are dealing with a join or a split). There are many examples of languages that support the specification of arbitrary workflows, e.g. Staffware (www.staffware.com), Forte Conductor (www.forte.com) and Verve WorkFlow (www.verveinc.com).

A structured workflow is a workflow that is syntactically restricted in a number of ways. Intuitively a structured workflow is a workflow where each or-split has a corresponding or-join and each and-split has a corresponding and-join. These restrictions will guarantee certain important properties shown later in the paper and in some cases correspond to restrictions imposed by commercial workflow management systems.

Definition 1. *A structured workflow model (SWM) is inductively defined as follows.*

1. *A workflow consisting of a single activity is a SWM. This activity is both* initial *and* final.
2. *Let X and Y be SWMs. The concatenation of these workflows, where the final activity of X has a transition to the initial activity of Y, then also is a SWM. The initial activity of this SWM is the initial activity of X and its final activity is the final activity of Y.*

3. *Let $X_1, \ldots, X_n$ be SWMs and let j be an or-join and s an or-split. The workflow with as initial activity s and final activity j and transitions between s and the initial activities of X_i, and between the final activities of X_i and j, is then also a SWM. Predicates can be assigned to the outgoing transitions of s. The initial activity of this SWM is s and its final activity is j.*
4. *Let $X_1, \ldots, X_n$ be SWMs and let j be an and-join and s an and-split. The workflow with as initial activity s and final activity j and transitions between s and the initial activities of X_i, and between the final activities of X_i and j, is then also a SWM. The initial activity of this SWM is s and its final activity is j.*
5. *Let X and Y be SWMs and let j be an or-join and s an or-split. The workflow with as initial activity j and as final activity s and with transitions between j and the initial activity of X, between the final activity of X and s, between s and the initial activity of Y, and between the final activity of Y and j, is then also a SWM. The initial activity of this SWM is j and its final activity is s.*

All commercial WfMSs known to the authors allow for the specification of workflow models that are equivalent to structured models as defined in definition 1. Some of these WfMSs do not allow for the specification of arbitrary models though and they impose certain levels of structuredness by means of syntactical restrictions typically implemented in the graphical process designer.

The most restricted workflow modelling languages known to the authors with respect to imposing structuredness are the languages of FileNet's Visual WorkFlo (www.filenet.com) (VW) and SAP R/3 Workflow. In both languages it is possible to design structured models only. These models resemble the definition provided earlier very closely with some minor exceptions such as that in VW the loops can only be of the form "WHILE p DO X". In SAP R/3 Workflow no loops are allowed to be modelled in a direct way. An example of syntactical restrictions in the more general area of data and process modelling can be found in UML's activity diagrams where business modellers are forced to exclusively specify structured models.

The definition of SWMs guarantees these types of workflows to have certain properties. Specifically, by the use of structural induction it can easily be shown that SWMs do not deadlock (see [5]). In addition to that, in SWMs it is not possible to have multiple instances of the same activity active at the same time. This situation is easily modelled in an arbitrary workflow if an and-split is followed by an or-join construct. Similarly, an arbitrary workflow will deadlock if an or-split is followed by an and-join.

Since in the following sections we will regularly pay attention to arbitrary workflow models that do not deadlock and do not result in multiple instances, for terminological convenience we introduce the notion of *well-behaved* workflows.

Definition 2. *A workflow model is* well-behaved *if it can never lead to deadlock nor can it result in multiple active instances of the same activity.*

Corollary 1. *Every structured workflow model is well-behaved.*

Instead of requiring workflows to be structured, it is more common for workflow languages to impose restrictions on loops only. For example IBM MQSeries/Workflow (www.ibm.com/software) and InConcert (www.inconcert.com) do not allow the explicit modelling of loops. Instead they have to be modelled by the use of decomposition. This is equivalent to using a "REPEAT X UNTIL p" loop. In case of MQSeries/Workflow, predicate p is specified as the *Exit Condition* of the decomposition. Hence, in between arbitrary workflow models and structured workflow models, we recognise a third class of workflow models, referred to as *restricted loop models.*

Definition 3. *A restricted loop workflow model (RLWFM) is inductively defined as follows:*

1. *An arbitrary workflow model without cycles is an RLWFM.*
2. *Let X and Y be RLWFMs with each one initial and one final node. Let j be an or-join and s an or-split. The workflow with as initial activity j and as final activity s and with transitions between j and the initial activity of X, between the final activity of X and s, between s and the initial activity of Y, and between the final activity of Y and j, is then also a RLWFM.*

Note that languages that support loops through decomposition are a subset of the class defined by the above definition (in those cases, essentially, Y corresponds to the empty workflow). Naturally, every SWF is an RLWFM and every RLWFM is an arbitrary workflow model.

3 Equivalence in the Context of Control Flow

As there exist workflow languages that do not allow for the specification of arbitrary workflows, business analysts are confronted with the option to either restrict their specifications such that they conform to the tool that is used or specify their workflows freely and transform them to the required language in a later stage. From the point of view of separation of concerns, the latter option is preferable. To support such a way of working it would be best to have a set of transformations that could be applied to a workflow specification in order to transform it to a structured workflow in the sense of the previous section. Naturally, these transformations should not alter the semantics of the workflows

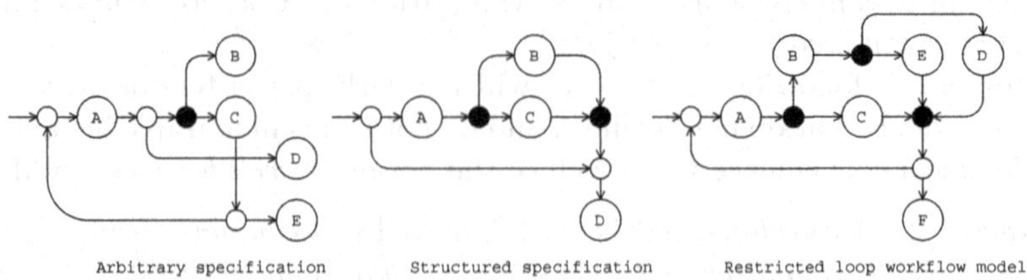

Fig. 1. Illustration of the three different workflow model classes

to which they are applied, they should be *equivalence preserving*. However, this immediately raises the question as to what notion of process equivalence is the most applicable in the context of workflows (for an overview of different notions of process equivalence the reader is referred to [4]).

One of the most commonly used equivalence notions is that of bisimulation. The formal definition of bisimulation between two different workflow systems, given the fact that they would most likely use different syntax and semantics, would have to be defined using some common formalism that can be applied to both systems. One of the most convenient ways to do it is to define bisimulation formally in terms of their Petri-net representation. That immediately leads to the conclusion that *weak bisimulation* has to be considered since Petri-net representations of workflow models may use many, internal, non-labelled places.

In the context of workflow processes with parallelism, the notion of basic weak bisimulation is not strong enough. Bisimulation is defined in terms of execution sequences, i.e. in terms of arbitrary interleaving. As such, however, bisimulation cannot distinguish between a concurrent system and its sequential simulation. For that reason a stronger equivalence notion is needed. Such a notion is provided in [3] where it is referred to as *fully concurrent bisimulation*. Given the fact that the formal definition is relatively complex and the details are not particularly useful for the purpose of this paper, we will present fully concurrent bisimulation in the context of workflow specification in terms of the *bisimulation game* (adapted from [8]):

1. There are two players, Player A and Player B, each of which having a workflow model specification (Workflow A and Workflow B).
2. Player A starts the initial activities in his workflow model specification. Player B responds by starting the initial activities in his workflow model specification (which should exactly correspond to those of player A).
3. Player A may choose to finish any of its activities and start a corresponding subsequent activity. Player B responds accordingly by finishing and starting an activity with the same label (possibly performing some internal, non-labeled, steps first).
4. If Player B cannot imitate the move of Player A, he looses. By imitating we mean that at any point in time the same set of activities in workflow B should be completed and started as in workflow A. Player B wins if he can terminate his workflow once Player A has terminated his workflow. Similarly Player B wins if he can deadlock his workflow once Player A has deadlocked his workflow. The case of an infinite run of the game is considered to be successful for Player B too.

If there is a strategy for defending player (Player B) to always prevent Player A from winning then we say that workflow B can simulate workflow A. If the reverse applies as well (workflow A can simulate workflow B) then we consider the two workflow specifications to be equivalent.

4 From Arbitrary Workflow Models to SWMs

In this section transformations from arbitrary workflow models to SWMs are studied and to what extent such transformations are possible. All transformations presented in this section assume that the workflow patterns they operate on do not contain data dependencies between decisions, in other words for all intents and purposes all decisions can be treated as nondeterministic. This assumption allows us to assume that all possible executions permitted by the control flow specification are possible.

4.1 Simple Workflows without Parallelism

Workflows that do not contain parallelism are simple models indeed. Their semantics is very similar to elementary flow charts that are commonly used for procedural program specification. The or-split corresponds to selection (if-then-else statement) while the activity corresponds to an instruction in the flow chart. It is well known that any unstructured flow chart can be transformed to a structured one. In this section we will revisit these transformation techniques and present and analyse them in the context of workflow models.

Following [11] we will say that the process of *reducing* a workflow model consists of replacing each occurrence of a base model. within the workflow model by a single activity box. This is repeated until no further replacement is possible. A process that can be reduced to a single activity box represents a structured workflow model. Each transformation of an irreducible workflow model should allow us to reduce the model further and in effect reduce the number of activities in the model.

The strong similarity of simple workflow models and flow diagrams suggests that if we do not consider parallelism, there are only four basic causes of unstructuredness (see e.g. [11,9]): 1) Entry into a decision structure, 2) Exit from a decision structure, 3) Entry into a loop structure, and 4) Exit from a loop structure. Entry to any structure is modelled in a workflow environment by an or-join construct. Similarly, an exit is modelled by an or-split. Once parallelism is introduced we will also consider synchronised entry and parallel exit modelled by and-join and and-split constructs respectively.

The first transformation (all transformations in this section are based on [9]), depicted in figure 2, can be performed when transforming a diagram containing an exit from a decision structure. It is important to observe that variable Φ is needed since activity D can potentially change the value of β or, if β is a complex expression, it could change the value of one of its components. This transformation is achieved through the use of auxiliary variables.

The transformations as depicted in figure 3 are used when a workflow model contains an entry to a decision structure. Here workflow $B2$ is a transformation of $B1$ achieved through *node duplication*, whereas workflow $B3$ is a transformation of $B1$ achieved through the use of auxiliary variables. The following two diagrams, depicted in figures 4 and 5, capture transformations to be used when

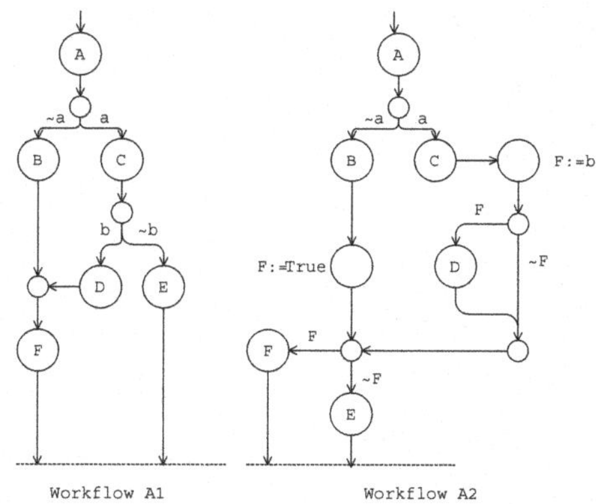

Fig. 2. Exit from a decision structure

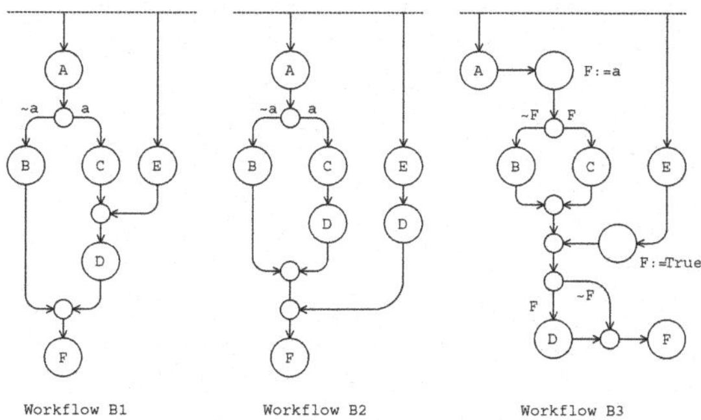

Fig. 3. Entry into a decision structure

a model contains an entry to, or an exit from a loop structure, respectively. Repeated application of the transformations discussed in this section can remove all forms of unstructuredness from a workflow. Hence the following theorem.

Theorem 1. *All unstructured workflows without parallelism have an equivalent structured form.*

Finally, it should be remarked that in some cases we have presented alternative transformations (not using auxiliary variables) and in some cases we have not. In later sections, we will show that this has a reason: in the cases where no extra transformations (not using auxiliary variables) are presented, such transformations turn out not to exist.

4.2 Workflows with Parallelism but without Loops

Addition of parallelism immediately introduces problems related to deadlock and multiple instances. As noted in section 2, structured workflow models never

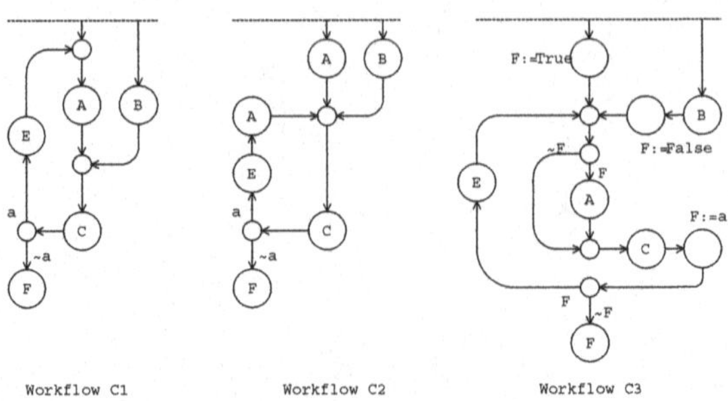

Fig. 4. Entry into a loop structure

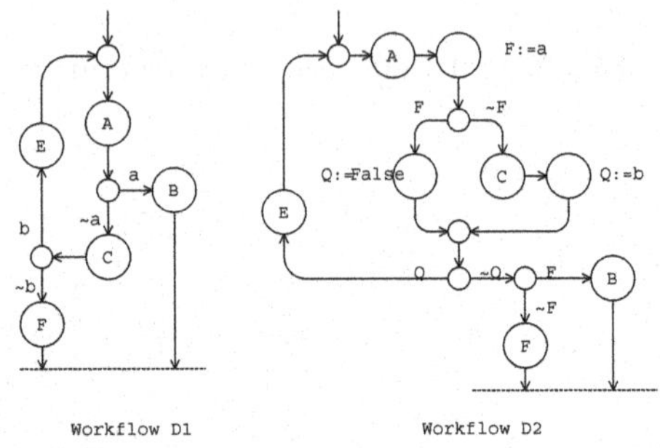

Fig. 5. Exit from a loop structure

result in deadlock nor multiple instances of the same activity at the same time. Hence, structured workflow models are less expressive than arbitrary workflow models. This immediately raises the question as to whether well-behaved workflow models can be transformed to structured workflow models. As the next theorem shows, the answer to this question is negative.

Theorem 2. *There are arbitrary, well-behaved, workflow models that cannot be modelled as structured workflow models.*

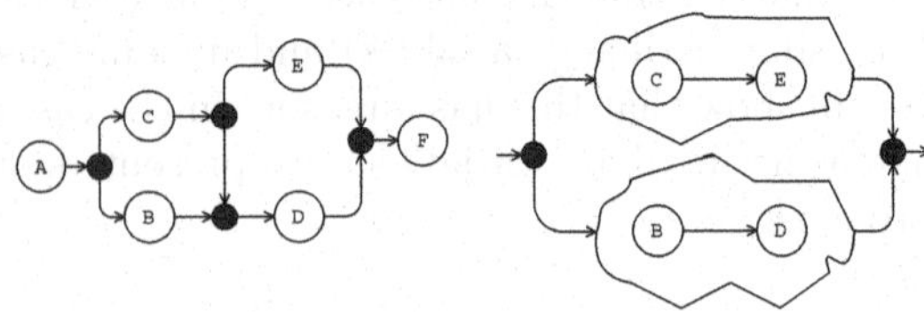

Fig. 6. Arbitrary workflow and illustration of its essential causal dependencies

Proof. Consider the workflow fragment in figure 6. The first observation is that as activities B and C are causally independent (that is, they can be executed concurrently) they have to be in different branches of some parallel structure in a corresponding structured workflow. As activities C and E are causally dependent (E is always performed after C) there must be a path from C to some activity named E. This activity has to be in the same branch as C as it cannot be outside the parallel structure as that would make it causally dependent on B. By applying similar reasoning, an activity named D has to be in the same branch of a parallel structure as B. Now we have that as C and D are in different branches of a parallel structure they are causally independent. However, in the original model they are causally dependent. Contradiction. No corresponding structured workflow exists. □

To find out which workflow models can be effectively transformed into SWMs, let us concentrate on the causes of unstructuredness that can occur when parallelism is added. If loops are not taken into account, these causes are: 1) Entry to a decision structure, 2) Exit from a decision structure, 3) Entry to a parallel structure, 4) Exit from a parallel structure, 5) Synchronised entry to a decision structure, 6) Parallel exit from a decision structure, 7) Synchronised entry to a parallel structure, and 8) Parallel exit from a parallel structure. In the remainder of this section we will concentrate on which of these structures can be transformed to a structure model.

Entries and exits from decision structures are dealt with in section 4.1 and can obviously be transformed to a structured model.

As a synchronised entry to a decision structure and an exit from a parallel structure leads to a potential deadlock (i.e. there are instances of the model that will deadlock), it follows that if the original workflow contains any of these patterns, it cannot be transformed into a SWM.

Parallel exits and synchronised entries to a parallel structure are dealt with in theorem 2. The reasoning of this theorem can be applied to any model that contains these patterns. Hence such models, even though they may be well-behaved, cannot be transformed into SWMs.

Before analysing the two remaining structures let us define a syntactical structure called an *overlapping structure*. This structure has been previously introduced in the context of workflow reduction for verification purposes in [10]. A specific instance of it is shown in figure 7. An overlapping structure consists of an or-split followed by i instances of and-splits, followed by j instances of or-joins and finally by an and-join. The structure of figure 7 has both i and j degrees equal to two. The overlapping structure contains both an entry to a parallel structure and a parallel exit from a decision structure and it never results in a deadlock. It is possible to transform an overlapping structure into a SWM as shown in figure 7.

A thorough analysis of the causes of deadlock and multiple instances in workflow models (see e.g. [10]) leads to the conclusion that workflow models containing a parallel exit from a decision or an entry to a parallel structure will cause a potential deadlock unless they form a part of an overlapping structure or the

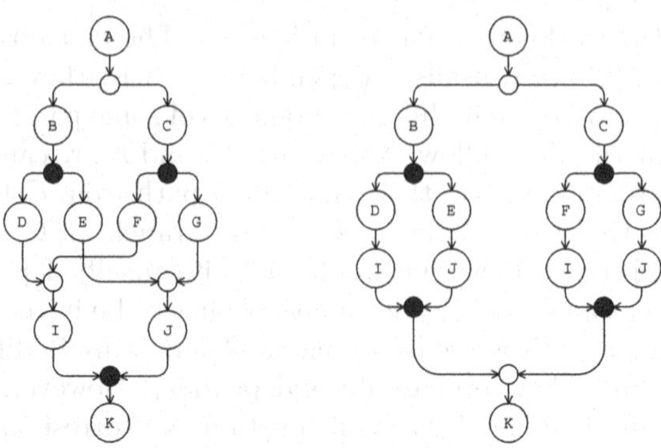

Fig. 7. Overlapping structure

exit path from the decision does not join the main execution path. Hence we conclude:

- An entry to a parallel structure can cause a potential deadlock unless it is part of an overlapping structure (in which case it can be transformed as shown).
- Similarly, a parallel exit from a decision structure can cause a potential deadlock and cannot be transformed into a SWM unless it is part of an overlapping structure or if the exit path does not join the main path (figure 8 illustrates the second case and the corresponding transformation).

The observations in this section have led us to the following conjecture:

Conjecture 1. Any arbitrary well-behaved workflow model that does not have loops, when reduced, does not have a parallel exit from a parallel structure, and, when reduced, does not have a synchronised entry into a parallel structure, can be translated to a SWM.

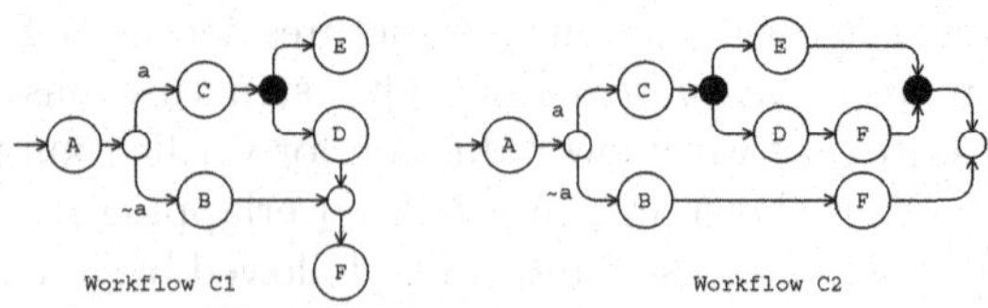

Fig. 8. Exit path not joining main path in parallel exit from decision structure

4.3 Workflows with Parallelism and Loops

Finding out whether a workflow can deadlock or not in the context of loops is much more complex and conjecture 1 cannot be automatically applied. To expose potential difficulties let us concentrate on what kind of loops we can encounter in a workflow model once and-join and and-split constructs are used. Every cycle in a graph has an entry point that can be either an or-join or an and-join and an exit point that can be either an and-split or an or-split. Cycles without an entry point cannot start and cycles without an exit point cannot terminate. The latter case can be represented by a cycle with an exit point where the exit condition on the or-split is set to false.

Most cycles will have an or-joins and or-splits as entry and exit points respectively (note that there may be many exit and entry points in the cycle) provided that the workflow is well-behaved. The transformation of such cycles is straightforward using transformations as presented earlier in this section.

If the cycle has an and-join as an entry point, the workflow will most likely deadlock. Examples of two workflows containing cycles with and-join as an entry-point that do not deadlock are shown in figure 9.

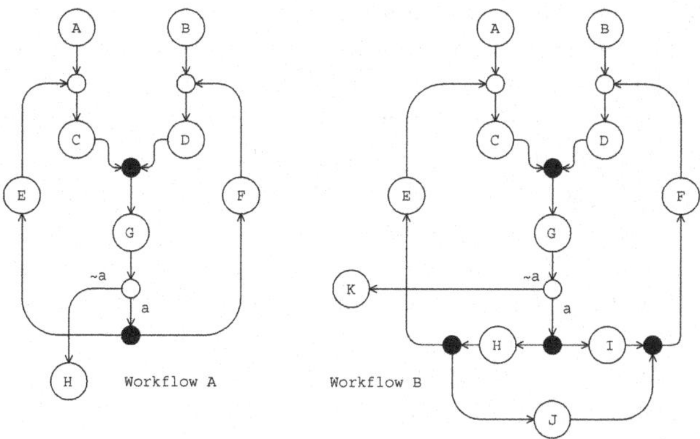

Fig. 9. Two workflow models with arbitrary loops

Conversely, most workflows that have an and-split as an exit point will most likely result in multiple instances. Our previous observation that any workflow resulting in deadlock or multiple instances cannot be modelled as a structured workflow certainly holds whether or not the workflow has loops. The major impact of introducing loops though is that finding out if the workflow deadlocks or results in multiple instances becomes a non-trivial task [6].

In rare cases when a cycle has an and-join as entry and an and-split as exit point and the workflow involved does not deadlock nor result in multiple instances, theorem 2 is helpful when determining if such a workflow can be remodelled as a structured workflow. In figure 9 for example, workflow A can be remodelled as a structured workflow whereas workflow B cannot. The equivalent workflow to workflow A is shown in figure 10.

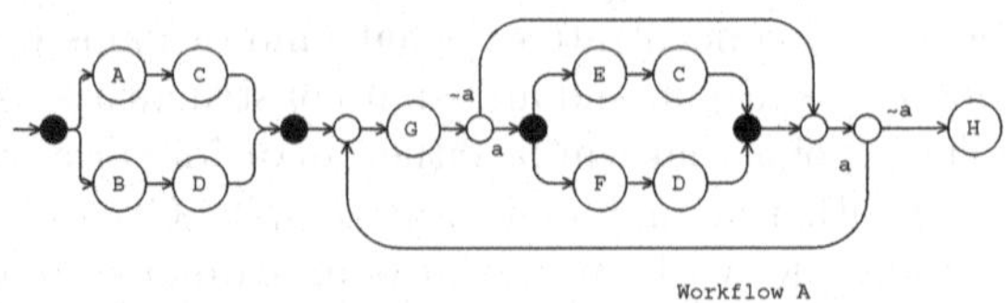

Fig. 10. Structured version of leftmost workflow of figure 9

4.4 Suitability of Transformations

The transformations presented earlier in this section are using two major techniques: 1) node duplication and 2) use of auxiliary variables to control conditions. In this section we will comment on the suitability of these solutions.

Suitability in general refers to the relation between concepts offered in the specification technique and concepts required by the problem domain. There are a number of aspects in a workflow specification, e.g. data and control flow, and there are a number of ways in which the same underlying model can be presented, e.g. data flow and control flow "view". Yet, conceptual models, in general, are required to convey a certain amount of information which should not be split up, if the model is to be effective (this corresponds to the *Cognitive Sufficiency Principle* promulgated by [2]). For example we believe that the model that conveys all control flow interdependencies between activities in a control view is a better model than the model that requires both the control flow view and data flow view to understand relationships between activities. Consider for example the three models from figure 3. In models $B1$ and $B2$ it is clear that activities B and D are exclusive in the sense that they will never be both executed in any process instance. On the other hand, in model $B3$, it seems that activity D can follow the execution of activity B. Only close inspection of the or-splits' predicates as well as implicit knowledge that activity B does not change the value of variable Φ can lead to the conclusion that activities B and D are indeed exclusive.

To retain the suitability of a certain workflow model, transformations should avoid using auxiliary variables to control or-splits through predicates. Unfortunately, this is not always possible.

Theorem 3. *There are forms of unstructuredness that cannot be transformed without the use of auxiliary variables.*

Proof. Consider the workflow model of figure 5. This workflow model contains multiple exits from a loop and as such is unstructured. Now consider another workflow model equivalent to this model, which is structured. The first observation is that as workflow representations are finite, this structured workflow model needs to contain at least one loop as the associated language is infinite. On one such loop there has to be an occurrence of both activities A and C. Activities B and F should be outside any loop (as we cannot use predicates anymore to prevent paths containing these activities to be chosen if they are included in the body of the loop). Playing the bisimulation game yields that after each instance of activity A one should be able to choose to perform either C or B. Since B is outside any loop, there has to be an exit point from the loop sometime after activity A (but before activity C, as one cannot use predicates that guarantee that activity C will be skipped after the decision has been made to exit the loop). Similarly, after each instance of activity C one should be able to choose to perform either activity E or activity F. As F is outside any loop, we also have an exit point from this loop after activity C (but before activity E). Hence, the loop under consideration has at least two exit points and the workflow cannot be structured. Contradiction. Hence a structured workflow equivalent, not using auxiliary variables, to the workflow of figure 5 does not exist. □

An alternative technique to transform arbitrary models into a structured form requires node duplication. As has been proved earlier, it cannot be used for every model, but even when it can be used, it is not without associated problems. Consider once again the model in figure 3. If activity D in the left model is followed by a large workflow specification, the transformation presented in the right model would need to duplicate the whole workflow specification following activity D. The resulting workflow will be almost twice as big as the original and will therefore be more difficult to comprehend.

5 Restricted Loops

In this section we will focus on languages that impose restrictions on loops only. Examples of such languages are MQSeries/Workflow and InConcert. The main reason these languages impose restrictions on loops is that the introduction of cycles in their workflow specifications would result in an immediate deadlock because of their evaluation strategy. MQSeries/Workflow for example propagates true and false tokens and its synchronizing or-join expects tokens from every incoming branch before execution can resume; this results in deadlock if one of these branches is dependent on execution of the or-join itself. Note that the semantics of the synchronising or-join is different from the semantics of the or-join as presented earlier in this paper, but that does not compromise the obtained results. The approach chosen in MQSeries/Workflow and InConcert guarantees that their specifications are well-behaved (for MQSeries/Workflow this is formally proven in [5]).

Even though one may ask the question whether any arbitrary workflow specification can be translated to a specification that uses restricted loops only, the more practical question would be to ask whether any well-behaved arbitrary specification can be translated to a specification using restricted loops only. As the next theorem shows, the answer to this question is negative.

Theorem 4. *There are well-behaved arbitrary workflow specifications that cannot be expressed as RLWFMs.*

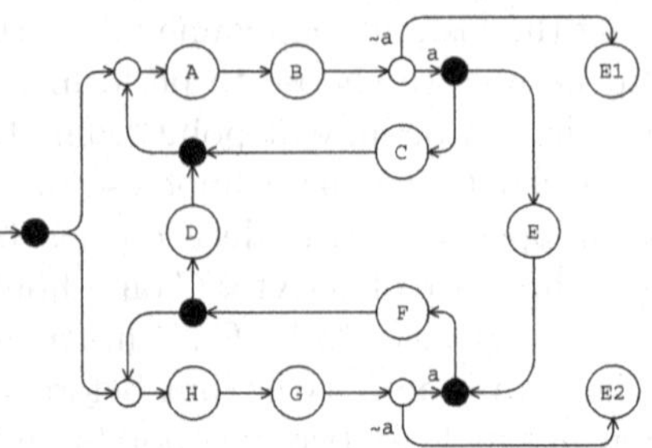

Fig. 11. Well-behaved arbitrary workflow

Proof. By showing that the workflow from figure 11 cannot be modelled as an RLWFM. Observe that after completion of the initial activity and as long as α evaluates to true, there will be at least two tokens in the corresponding Petri-net. That means that in an equivalent workflow specification that has restricted loops only, there have to be two concurrent restricted loops running in parallel (if there was only one loop, the moment the exit condition was evaluated there would be only one token in the corresponding Petri-net). One of the restricted loops would have to contain activities A, B, C, and E, and the other loop would have to contain activities D, F, G, and H. In the original workflow specification A is causally dependent on D. That means that there must be a path between A and D but that is impossible if A belongs to a different restricted loop than D according to the definition of a restricted loop. □

The careful reader may have noticed that in the workflow model of figure 11 data is used to make sure that both loops are exited at the same time (otherwise deadlock would occur). It is an open question as to whether there exist well-behaved arbitrary workflow specifications that do not contain decision dependencies and that can not be transformed into an RLWFM.

6 Conclusions

The transformation of arbitrary workflow models to workflows in a structured form is a necessity typically faced by either an application programmer who has to implement a non-structured workflow specification in an environment supporting structured specifications only (e.g. SAP R/3 workflow or Filenet Visual Workflo), or by a business analyst who is trying to capture real-world requirements in a structured workflow specification technique (e.g. UML's activity diagrams). In this paper we have shown that even simple transformations require the use of auxiliary variables which results in the introduction of dependencies between decisions in a workflow graph. As a result the transformed workflow specification is typically more difficult to understand for end-users. Moreover, some arbitrary specifications cannot be transformed at all to a structured form. Hence in general, structured models are less expressive and less suitable than arbitrary models. For these reasons it is our contention that any high-end workflow management system should support the execution of arbitrary workflow specifications. To some, this might seem to contrast with the common consensus of avoiding GOTO statements (and using WHILE loops instead) in procedural programming languages, but, as shown throughout this paper, the presence of parallelism as well as the nature of workflow specifications provide the essential difference. As a consequence, the good workflow modelling environment should be supported by a powerful verification engine that would help process modellers detect syntactical problems such as potential deadlock or unwanted multiple instances. Using sophisticated verification tools for these purposes (incorporating techniques from state-of-the-art Petri-net theory) seems feasible from a practical perspective (see [1]).

References

1. W.M.P. van der Aalst and A.H.M. ter Hofstede. Verification of Workflow Task Structures: A Petri-net-based Approach. *Information Systems*, 2000. (to appear).
2. A.P. Barros and A.H.M. ter Hofstede. Towards the construction of workflow-suitable conceptual modelling techniques. *Information Systems Journal*, 8(4):313–337, October 1998.
3. E. Best, R. Devillers, A. Kiehn, and L. Pomello. Concurrent bisimulations in Petri nets. *Acta Informatica*, 28:231–254, 1991.
4. R.J. van Glabbeek. The linear time-branching time spectrum. In J.C.M. Baeten and J.W. Klop, editors, *Proceedings of CONCUR'90. Theories of Concurrency: Unification and Extension*, pages 278–297, Berlin, Germany, 1990. Springer-Verlag.
5. A.H.M. ter Hofstede and B. Kiepuszewski. Formal Analysis of Deadlock Behaviour in Workflows. Technical report, Queensland University of Technology/Mincom, Brisbane, Australia, April 1999. (submitted for publication).
6. A.H.M. ter Hofstede and M.E. Orlowska. On the Complexity of Some Verification Problems in Process Control Specifications. *Computer Journal*, 42(5):349–359, 1999.
7. S. Jablonski and C. Bussler. *Workflow Management: Modeling Concepts, Architecture, and Implementation.* International Thomson Computer Press, London, United Kingdom, 1996.
8. P. Jančar. Decidability Questions for Bismilarity of Petri Nets and Some Related Problems. In P. Enjalbert, E.W. Mayr, and K.W. Wagner, editors, *STACS 94, 11th Annual Symposium on Theoretical Aspects of Computer Science*, volume 775 of *Lecture Notes in Computer Science*, pages 581–592, Caen, France, February 1994. Springer-Verlag.
9. G. Oulsnam. Unravelling Unstructured Programs. *Computer Journal*, 25(3):379–387, 1982.
10. W. Sadiq and M.E. Orlowska. Applying Graph Reduction Techniques for Identifying Structural Conflicts in Process Models. In *Proceedings of the 11th Conf on Advanced Information Systems Engineering (CAiSE'99)*, pages 195–209, Hildeberg, Germany, June 1999.
11. M. H. Williams. Generating structured flow diagrams: the nature of unstructuredness. *Computer Journal*, 20(1):45–50, 1977.

The Structured Phase of Concurrency

Artem Polyvyanyy and Christoph Bussler

Abstract This extended abstract summarizes the state-of-the-art solution to the structuring problem for models that describe existing real world or envisioned processes. Special attention is devoted to models that allow for the true concurrency semantics. Given a model of a process, the structuring problem deals with answering the question of whether there exists another model that describes the process and is solely composed of structured patterns, such as sequence, selection, option for simultaneous execution, and iteration. Methods and techniques for structuring developed by academia as well as products and standards proposed by industry are discussed. Expectations and recommendations on the future advancements of the structuring problem are suggested.

1 Introduction to Concurrency

Processes are properties of dynamic systems that are usually defined as series of steps taken to achieve a goal, e.g., chemical or thermodynamic processes. Many scientific disciplines study processes by means of modeling. A model of processes, or a *process model*, is a particular representation of processes of the same nature. The study of processes is predominant to the computer science discipline. Computer programs and workflows are examples of process models.

Concurrency is a property of a process which indicates that steps of the process can be performed simultaneously by several autonomous "workers" that may coordinate their work by means of communication, e.g., instructions of a computer

A. Polyvyanyy (✉)
Queensland University of Technology, Brisbane, QLD, Australia
e-mail: artem.polyvyanyy@qut.edu.au

C. Bussler
Analytica, Inc., Palo Alto, CA, USA
e-mail: chris@real-programmer.com

J. Bubenko et al. (eds.), *Seminal Contributions to Information Systems Engineering*,
DOI 10.1007/978-3-642-36926-1_20, © Springer-Verlag Berlin Heidelberg 2013

program carried out by several processing units within a single or across multiple computers. Usually, concurrent processes are more efficient than processes in which all work is performed by a single worker, where efficiency is the measure of the amount of work accomplished within a given time frame.

There exist several formalisms for describing concurrent processes, cf., [1] for examples and a classification of formalisms. Concurrency can be represented implicitly in a process model as a nondeterministic choice between all possible sequentializations of concurrent steps. Afterwards, an option for a simultaneous execution of steps can be deduced based on the interleaving of these steps. Alternatively, concurrency can be modeled based on partially-ordered sets of steps—an approach that is often referred to as the true concurrency semantics of processes. The true concurrency semantics specifies that unordered steps of a process can be enabled and performed simultaneously. Observe that process models which account for the true concurrency semantics are more informative. They explicitly represent steps that can be performed by different workers, as well as describe all possible sequentializations of steps.

Concurrent processes are *complex*. The complexity is primarily due to the fact that the number of all possible sequentializations of process steps is exponential to the number of concurrent steps in the process. Consequently, concurrent processes are complex to design and analyze because one needs to account for all possible interleavings of steps that can lead to potential flaws.

The next section defines the structured property of process models. Afterwards, Sect. 3 reviews progress achieved in academia and industry that relates to the structuring problem of process models. Finally, expectations and recommendations on the future advancements with respect to structuring are proposed.

2 The Structured Phase

A process can be formalized in many different ways following different modeling styles, i.e., it can take different forms. This reminds of various *states* that a physical matter can take on. For example, H2O is a substance that its gas, liquid, and solid states are widely known, viz. steam, water, and ice, respectively. Often, there exist several phases of the same state of matter, where a *phase* is a region of space (a thermodynamic system), throughout which all physical properties of a material are essentially uniform [2]. For instance, diamond and graphite are both solid carbon with different physical characteristics, e.g., color, crystal shape, etc. Similarly, there can exist several different models of the same process that are captured in the same formal language.

Besides many existing modeling styles, processes are usually formalized by following on the principles of the *imperative* paradigm. Process models that follow the imperative style are described in terms of sequences of statements/commands that change a process state. Intuitively, an imperative process model can be perceived as a directed graph with nodes representing commands and pairs of subsequent commands representing edges.

Process graphs, i.e., graphs induced by imperative process models, can take different forms. However, it is often preferred that process graphs obey some structural rules, like the one that a process graph should be *structured.*

> A process graph is structured, if for every node with multiple outgoing edges (a split) there exists a corresponding node with multiple incoming edges (a join), and vice versa, such that the subgraph between the split and the join forms a single-entry-single-exit fragment; otherwise the graph is unstructured.

Consequently, a process model is *structured* if and only if a process graph induced by the model is structured. The reader can refer to [3] for a detailed motivation of structured process modeling. In summary, most of the benefits of using structured process models boil down to the observation that it is often straightforward to modularize handling of structured process graphs at various stages of their life cycles. For example, it is evident that structured computer programs are easier to understand and maintain as opposed to unstructured ones, which contain arbitrary "jump" constructs leading to programs that induce "spaghetti" process graphs. Nevertheless, unstructured modeling is often praised for the *freedom* it offers when designing a process model. Indeed, there are no restrictions on which form a process graph can take. Considering modeling to be a highly creative activity, the freedom of expressing concepts and ideas in models is of significant importance.

When proposing a process modeling methodology, one faces a dilemma of whether to allow or forbid unstructuredness. Allowing for unstructuredness supports creativity of process designers, while forbidding it comes with a continuous and seamless ability to enjoy benefits of structured models. The problem of *structuring* a process model deals with the automated construction of a structured model that represents the process described in the given model, i.e., finding the *structured phase* of the process.

3 State of the Art

In this section, we review the progress achieved by the research community on a solution to the structuring problem for process models that account for the true concurrency semantics (Sect. 3.1), as well as analyze the support of structured and unstructured process modeling by the software industry sector (Sect. 3.2).

3.1 Research: Methods and Techniques

In this section, we discuss scientific results on methods for structuring process models. Special attention is paid to techniques that address structuring of models that account for the true concurrency semantics.

Results on structuring sequential process models, i.e., models that describe non-concurrent processes, are mainly due to results on elimination of goto constructs in computer programs. The *structured program theorem* [4] provides the theoretical foundation of structured programming. It states that every program can be expressed with three patterns: sequence, selection, and iteration. Moreover, it is well-known that a sequential process model, e.g., a program, can be formalized as a flowchart and structured, e.g., by using the techniques proposed in [5, 6].

The concurrent world is a bit more complex. In this world, the results on structuring of sequential process models cease to hold. In [7], Kiepuszewski et al. showed that not all acyclic concurrent process models, i.e., models of concurrent processes that induce acyclic process graphs, can be structured. The above fact has been proven by means of a counter-example—a *Z-structure* pattern (the name is due to the constellation of causal relations between the concurrent steps). The authors demonstrated that under the true concurrency semantics there exists no structured model that captures the process described by the Z-structure pattern.

In [8, 9], the authors proposed a solution to the structuring problem of acyclic concurrent process models. The technique is capable of recognizing inherently unstructured process models, i.e., models that have no equivalent structured representations. The theoretical basis of the approach builds on interplay of two parsing techniques: a technique for discovering the structure of process graphs [10] and a technique for decomposing causal, conflict, and concurrency relations [11, 12] between process steps by means of the modular decomposition [13].

The work in [14] addresses structuring of acyclic concurrent process models that have no equivalent structured versions but which, nevertheless, can be partially structured into their *maximally-structured* representations. Intuitively, a process model M of a concurrent process P is maximally-structured if and only if there exists no process model that describes P and is composed of more structured modeling patterns (single-entry-single-exit fragments) than M. A maximally-structured process model is a mixture of structured and unstructured phases of the process, similar to an ice-water mixture which has ice cubes as one phase and water as a second phase of the same substance.

The cyclic case of the structuring problem is addressed in [3]. This work proposes a structuring technique and argues about the rationality of its individual stages (by means of proof-sketching). The technique can be seen as a two-stage approach. First, an input process model is transformed into an equivalent one in which all the concurrency is kept encapsulated in single-entry-single-exit fragments. Second, the obtained model is structured by iteratively applying the approach from [9] to its parts.

3.2 Industry: Products and Standards

The software industry has a long tradition in implementing workflow or process management systems that are based on explicit control flow. Early publications show quite a variety of systems that were available [15]. Based on the variety and sheer number of systems, standards were developed in context of process modeling and process execution: Web Services Business Process Execution Language (BPEL) [16] and Business Process Model and Notation (BPMN) [17].

By its nature, BPEL is a structured language. It does not propose native support for unstructured control flow patterns. Whenever an inherently unstructured process needs to be specified in BPEL, one has to rely on the means in BPEL for implicit control flow definition, e.g., the event handler construct [18] or a combination of flow and link constructs [19]. For example, an *event handler* can be used to orchestrate a subset of concurrent process steps via *event-action* rules, which essentially are preconditions for execution of concurrent steps. In contrast, BPMN allows unstructured process modeling. This means that BPMN as the process definition language supports unstructured process specifications. Systems that implement their execution model and semantics based on BPMN can support unstructured process execution.

In the following, we give some examples of process management systems proposed by the software industry (the list is by no means exhaustive). Examples of systems that support BPEL are: Oracle BPEL Process Manager [20] and IBM Business Process Manager Advanced [21]. Those supporting BPMN are: TIBCO ActiveMatrix BPM [22], IBM Business Process Manager [21], Appian BPM Suite [23] and Pegasystems [24]. The system from IBM appears to be a hybrid system that supports both, BPMN and BPEL. Yet, there are process management systems that follow neither BPEL nor BPMN, and those might very well support unstructured processes. For instance, a system not based on standards is Microsoft Workflow Manager [25, 26]; note that the documentation of this product suggests that the control flow model is supporting only structured modeling. Finally, the web site www.workflowpatterns.com [27] discusses some details of unstructured support and compares a few industry products.

Constructs for concurrency are natively supported in several programming languages, e.g., Java and C#. The Windows Workflow Foundation (WWF) has been introduced as a part of the .NET Framework and is a means of implementing long-running processes. It is a common requirement for programming languages that fragments of control flow that include concurrency must be structured. For instance, the WWF does not support arbitrary cycles with parallel branching [28].

4 Expectations and Recommendations

Concurrent process modeling/programming has been practiced for years. However, recently, one can observe a remarkable growth of interest in concurrent processes; mainly, for the purpose of *automation*. One of the reasons for this is physical constraints that forbid frequency scaling in modern computer processors. Nowadays, parallel computing is the dominant paradigm in computer architectures. It gets harder to rely on hardware when getting performance improvements out of good old sequential processes [29]. Rather, sequential processes should be redesigned to allow for simultaneous execution of their parts. We expect that this trend will remain for years to come leading to new requirements on the way processes are modeled.

A formal language that includes constructs for representing process steps and arbitrary jumps between steps can be employed to describe any process (with respect to control flow). Nevertheless, for considerations like clarity, quality, maintainability, modularity, etc., of process models, formal process languages often include high level constructs. Advantages of the structured process modeling style over the unstructured one (and vice versa) have been a topic of active debates for decades. Structured process modeling confines itself to constructs that map to single-entry-single-exit patterns. If the structured process modeling methodology is enforced, one has to accept that certain concurrent processes cannot be modeled.

Results reported in [3, 7–9, 14] provide a basis for structured modeling of concurrent processes, most of which are implemented in a tool called bpstruct; the tool is publicly available at http://code.google.com/p/bpstruct/. Evaluations conducted in [9, 14] report on small average times required to structure real world process models taken from industry. However, in theory, the structuring techniques are inherently complex. For instance, for certain inputs, these techniques subsume a problem for which finding a solution is NP-complete. Future studies must show if the theoretic complexity of structuring algorithms can be improved. Other directions for future work on structuring are outlined in [3].

In terms of products and standards, our expectation is that over time more and more products will support structured as well as unstructured modeling in order to cater for more and wider use cases. Our recommendation is that standards and companies explicitly discuss their support for unstructured processes and extend their modeling tools to incorporate automated transformation from unstructured to structured processes where possible.

Acknowledgments The first author is supported by the ARC Linkage Project LP110100252 "Facilitating Business Process Standardisation and Reuse".

References

1. Sassone, V., Nielsen, M., Winskel, G.: Models for concurrency: Towards a classification. Theoretical Computer Science (TCS) **170**(1–2) (1996) 297–348
2. Modell, M., Reid, R.: Thermodynamics and Its Applications. International Series in the Physical and Chemical Engineering Sciences. Prentice-Hall (1974)
3. Polyvyanyy, A.: Structuring Process Models. PhD thesis, University of Potsdam (2012)
4. Böhm, C., Jacopini, G.: Flow diagrams, Turing machines and languages with only two formation rules. Communications of the ACM (CACM) **9**(5) (1966) 366–371
5. Williams, M.H., Ossher, H.L.: Conversion of unstructured flow diagrams to structured form. The Computer Journal (CJ) **21**(2) (1978) 161–167
6. Oulsnam, G.: Unravelling unstructured programs. The Computer Journal (CJ) **25**(3) (1982) 379–387

7. Kiepuszewski, B., ter Hofstede, A.H.M., Bussler, C.: On structured workflow modelling. In: Conference on Advanced Information Systems Engineering (CAiSE). Volume 1789 of Lecture Notes in Computer Science., Springer (2000) 431–445
8. Polyvyanyy, A., García-Bañuelos, L., Dumas, M.: Structuring acyclic process models. In: Business Process Management (BPM). Volume 6336 of Lecture Notes in Computer Science., Springer (2010) 276–293
9. Polyvyanyy, A., García-Bañuelos, L., Dumas, M.: Structuring acyclic process models. Information Systems (IS) **37**(6) (2012) 518–538
10. Polyvyanyy, A., Vanhatalo, J., Völzer, H.: Simplified computation and generalization of the refined process structure tree. In: Web Services and Formal Methods (WS-FM). Volume 6551 of Lecture Notes in Computer Science., Springer (2010) 25–41
11. McMillan, K.L.: A technique of state space search based on unfolding. Formal Methods in System Design (FMSD) **6**(1) (1995) 45–65
12. Esparza, J., Römer, S., Vogler, W.: An improvement of McMillan's unfolding algorithm. Formal Methods in System Design (FMSD) **20**(3) (2002) 285–310
13. McConnell, R.M., de Montgolfier, F.: Linear-time modular decomposition of directed graphs. Discrete Applied Mathematics (DAM) **145**(2) (2005) 198–209
14. Polyvyanyy, A., García-Bañuelos, L., Fahland, D., Weske, M.: Maximal structuring of acyclic process models. The Computer Journal (CJ). (first published online September 19, 2012) doi:10.1093/comjnl/bxs126.
15. Jablonski, S., Bussler, C.: Workflow Management — Modeling Concepts, Architecture and Implementation. International Thomson (1996)
16. OASIS: Web Services Business Process Execution Language Version 2.0. OASIS Standard. (April 2007) http://docs.oasis-open.org/wsbpel/2.0/wsbpel-v2.0.pdf.
17. Object Management Group (OMG): Business Process Model and Notation (BPMN) Version 2.0. OMG Standard. (January 2011) http://www.omg.org/spec/BPMN/2.0.
18. Ouyang, C., Dumas, M., ter Hofstede, A.H.M., van der Aalst, W.M.P., Mendling, J.: From business process models to process-oriented software systems. ACM Transactions on Software Engineering and Methodology (TOSEM) **19**(1) (2009)
19. Lohmann, N., Kleine, J.: Fully-automatic translation of open workflow net models into simple abstract BPEL processes. In: Modellierung. Volume 127 of Lecture Notes in Informatics., GI (2008) 57–72
20. Oracle BPEL Process Manager: http://www.oracle.com/technetwork/middleware/bpel/overview/index.html.
21. IBM Business Process Manager and IBM Business Process Manager Advanced: ftp://ftp.software.ibm.com/software/integration/business-process-manager/library/pdf801/ibpmoverviewpdfen.pdf.
22. TIBCO ActiveMatrix BPM: http://www.tibco.com/multimedia/ds-amx-bpmtcm8-11546.pdf.
23. Appian BPM Suite: http://www.appian.com/bpm-software/bpm-for-designers/process-management.jsp.
24. Craggs, S.: Comparing BPM from Pegasystems, IBM and TIBCO. (August 2011) http://soapower.com/IBMBPM/Whitepapers/IBM-BPM-Analyst-Report-on-IBM-vs-Pega.pdf.
25. Microsoft Workflow Manager: http://msdn.microsoft.com/en-us/library/windowsazure/jj193528%28v=azure.10%29.aspx.
26. Control Flow Activity Designers: http://msdn.microsoft.com/en-us/library/ee829560.aspx.
27. www.workflowpatterns.com: Pattern 10 (Arbitrary Cycles). http://www.workflowpatterns.com/patterns/control/structural/wcp10.php.
28. Zapletal, M., van der Aalst, W.M.P., Russell, N., Liegl, P., Werthner, H.: An analysis of Windows workflow's control-flow expressiveness. In: European Conference on Web Services (ECOWS), IEEE Computer Society (2009) 200–209
29. Sutter, H.: The free lunch is over: A fundamental turn toward concurrency in software. Dr. Dobb's Journal **30**(3) (2005) 202–210

A Requirements-Driven Development Methodology*

Jaelson Castro[1], Manuel Kolp[2],and John Mylopoulos[2]

[1] Centro de Informática, Universidade Federal de Pernambuco, Av. Prof. Luiz Freire S/N, Recife PE, Brazil 50732-970**
jbc@cin.ufpe.br

[2] Department of Computer Science, University of Toronto, 10 King's College Road, Toronto M5S3G4, Canada
{mkolp,jm}@cs.toronto.edu

Abstract. Information systems of the future will have to better match their operational organizational environment. Unfortunately, development methodologies have traditionally been inspired by programming concepts, not organizational ones, leading to a semantic gap between the system and its environment. To reduce as much as possible this gap, this paper proposes a development methodology named *Tropos* which is founded on concepts used to model early requirements. Our proposal adopts the *i** organizational modeling framework [18], which offers the notions of *actor*, *goal* and (actor) *dependency*, and uses these as a foundation to model early and late requirements, architectural and detailed design. The paper outlines *Tropos* phases through an e-business example. The methodology seems to complement well proposals for agent-oriented programming platforms.

1 Introduction

Information systems have traditionally suffered from an impedance mismatch. Their operational environment is understood in terms of actors, responsibilities, objectives, tasks and resources, while the information system itself is conceived as a collection of (software) modules, entities (e.g., objects, agents), data structures and interfaces. This mismatch is one of the main factors for the poor quality of information systems, also the frequent failure of system development projects.

One cause of this mismatch is that development methodologies have traditionally been inspired and driven by the programming paradigm of the day. This means that the concepts, methods and tools used during all phases of development were based on those offered by the pre-eminent programming paradigm. So, during the era of structured programming, structured analysis and design techniques were proposed [9,17], while object-oriented programming has given rise more recently to object-

* The Tropos project has been partially funded by the Natural Sciences and Engineering Research Council (NSERC) of Canada, and Communications and Information Technology Ontario (CITO), a centre of excellence, funded by the province of Ontario.

** This work was carried out during a visit to the Department of Computer Science, University of Toronto. Partially supported by the CNPq – Brazil under grant 203262/86-7.

K.R. Dittrich, A. Geppert, M.C. Norrie (Eds.): CaiSE 2001, LNCS 2068, pp. 108–123, 2001

oriented design and analysis [1,15]. For structured development techniques this meant that throughout software development, the developer can conceptualize the system in terms of functions and processes, inputs and outputs. For object-oriented development, on the other hand, the developer thinks throughout in terms of objects, classes, methods, inheritance and the like.

Using the same concepts to align requirements analysis with system design and implementation makes perfect sense. For one thing, such an alignment reduces impedance mismatches between different development phases. Moreover, such an alignment can lead to coherent toolsets and techniques for developing system (and it has!) as well, it can streamline the development process itself.

But, why base such an alignment on implementation concepts? Requirements analysis is arguably the most important stage of information system development. This is the phase where technical considerations have to be balanced against social and organizational ones and where the operational environment of the system is modeled. Not surprisingly, this is also the phase where the most and costliest errors are introduced to a system. Even if (or rather, when) the importance of design and implementation phases wanes sometime in the future, requirements analysis will remain a critical phase for the development of any information system, answering the most fundamental of all design questions: "what is the system intended for?"

Information systems of the future like ERP, Knowledge Management or e-business systems should be designed to match their operational environment. For instance, ERP systems have to implement a process view of the enterprise to meet business goals, tightly integrating all functions from the operational environment. To reduce as much as possible this impedance mismatch between the system and its environment, we outline in this paper a development framework, named *Tropos*, which is requirements-driven in the sense that it is based on concepts used during early requirements analysis. To this end, we adopt the concepts offered by *i** [18], a modeling framework offering concepts such as *actor* (actors can be *agents*, *positions* or *roles*), as well as social dependencies among actors, including *goal*, *softgoal*, *task* and *resource* dependencies. These concepts are used for an e-commerce example[1] to model not just early requirements, but also late requirements, as well as architectural and detailed design. The proposed methodology spans four phases:

- Early requirements, concerned with the understanding of a problem by studying an organizational setting; the output of this phase is an organizational model which includes relevant actors, their respective goals and their inter-dependencies.
- Late requirements, where the system-to-be is described within its operational environment, along with relevant functions and qualities.
- Architectural design, where the system's global architecture is defined in terms of subsystems, interconnected through data, control and other dependencies.
- Detailed design, where behaviour of each architectural component is defined in further detail.

The proposed methodology includes techniques for generating an implementation from a *Tropos* detailed design. Using an agent-oriented programming platform for the implementation seems natural, given that the detailed design is defined in terms of

---

[1] Although, we could have included a simpler (toy) example, we decided to present a realistic e-commerce system development exercise of moderate complexity [6].

(system) actors, goals and inter-dependencies among them. For this paper, we have adopted JACK as programming platform to study the generation of an implementation from a detailed design. JACK is a commercial product based on the BDI (Beliefs-Desires-Intentions) agent architecture. Early previews of the *Tropos* methodology appeared in [2, 13].

Section 2 of the paper describes a case study for a B2C (business to consumer) e-commerce application. Section 3 introduces the primitive concepts offered by *i** and illustrates their use with an example. Sections 4, 5, and 6 illustrate how the technique works for late requirements, architectural design and detailed design respectively. Section 7 sketches the implementation of the case study using the JACK agent development environment. Finally, Section 8 summarizes the contributions of the paper, and relates it to the literature.

2 A Case Study

Media Shop is a store selling and shipping different kinds of media items such as books, newspapers, magazines, audio CDs, videotapes, and the like. *Media Shop* customers (on-site or remote) can use a periodically updated catalogue describing available media items to specify their order. *Media Shop* is supplied with the latest releases and in-catalogue items by *Media Supplier*. To increase market share, *Media Shop* has decided to open up a B2C retail sales front on the internet. With the new setup, a customer can order *Media Shop* items in person, by phone, or through the internet. The system has been named *Medi@* and is available on the world-wide-web using communication facilities provided by *Telecom Cpy*. It also uses financial services supplied by *Bank Cpy*, which specializes on on-line transactions.

The basic objective for the new system is to allow an on-line customer to examine the items in the *Medi@* internet catalogue, and place orders.

There are no registration restrictions, or identification procedures for *Medi@* users. Potential customers can search the on-line store by either browsing the catalogue or querying the item database. The catalogue groups media items of the same type into (sub)hierarchies and genres (e.g., audio CDs are classified into pop, rock, jazz, opera, world, classical music, soundtrack, ...) so that customers can browse only (sub)categories of interest.

An on-line search engine allows customers with particular items in mind to search title, author/artist and description fields through keywords or full-text search. If the item is not available in the catalogue, the customer has the option of asking *Media Shop* to order it, provided the customer has editor/publisher references (e.g., ISBN, ISSN), and identifies herself (in terms of name and credit card number).

3 Early Requirements with *i**

During early requirements analysis, the requirements engineer captures and analyzes the intentions of stakeholders. These are modeled as goals which, through some form of a goal-oriented analysis, eventually lead to the functional and non-functional requirements of the system-to-be [7]. In *i** (which stands for "distributed intentionality''), early requirements are assumed to involve social actors who depend on each other for goals to be achieved, tasks to be performed, and resources to be furnished. The *i** framework includes the *strategic dependency model* for describing the network of relationships among actors, as well as the *strategic rationale model* for describing and supporting the reasoning that each actor goes through concerning its relationships with other actors. These models have been formalized using intentional concepts from AI, such as goal, belief, ability, and commitment (e.g., [5]). The framework has been presented in detail in [18] and has been related to different application areas, including requirements engineering, software processes and business process reengineering.

A strategic dependency model is a graph, where each node represents an *actor*, and each link between two actors indicates that one actor depends on another for something in order that the former may attain some goal. We call the depending actor the *depender* and the actor who is depended upon the *dependee*. The object around which the dependency centers is called the *dependum*. Figure 1 shows the beginning of an *i** model.

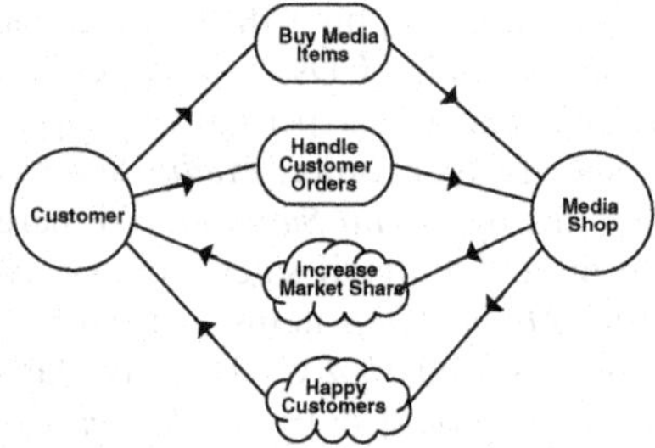

Fig. 1. "*Customers* want to buy media items, while the *Media Shop* wants to increase market share, handle orders and keep customers happy"

The two main stakeholders for a B2C application are the consumer and the business actors named respectively in our case *Customer* and *Media Shop*. The customer has one relevant goal *Buy Media Items* (represented as an oval-shaped icon), while the media store has goals *Handle Customer Orders, Happy Customers,* and *Increase Market Share*. Since the last two goals are not well-defined, they are represented as softgoals (shown as cloudy shapes).

Once the relevant stakeholders and their goals have been identified, a strategic rationale model determines through a means-ends analysis how these goals (including softgoals) can actually be fulfilled through the contributions of other actors. A strategic rationale model is a graph with four types of nodes – *goal*, *task*, *resource*, and *softgoal* – and two types of links – means-ends links and process decomposition links. A strategic rationale graph captures the relationship between the goals of each actor and the dependencies through which the actor expects these dependencies to be fulfilled.

Figure 2 focuses on one of the (soft)goal identified for *Media Shop,* namely *Increase Market Share*. The analysis postulates a task *Run Shop* (represented in terms of a hexagonal icon) through which *Increase Market Share* can be fulfilled. Tasks are partially ordered sequences of steps intended to accomplish some (soft)goal. Tasks can be decomposed into goals and/or subtasks, whose collective fulfillment completes the task. In the figure, *Run Shop* is decomposed into goals *Handle Billing* and *Handle Customer Orders*, tasks *Manage Staff* and *Manage Inventory,* and softgoal *Improve Service* which together accomplish the top-level task. Sub-goals and subtasks can be specified more precisely through refinement. For instance, the goal *Handle Customer Orders* is fulfilled either through tasks *OrderByPhone, OrderInPerson* or *OrderByInternet* while the task *Manage Inventory* would be collectively accomplished by tasks *Sell Stock* and *Enhance Catalogue.*

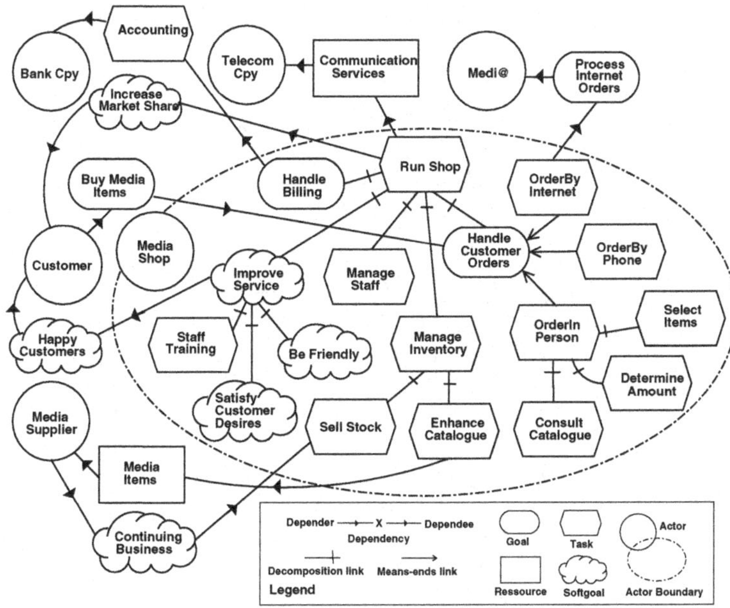

Fig. 2. Means-ends analysis for the softgoal *Increase Market Share*

4 Late Requirements Analysis

Late requirements analysis results in a requirements specification which describes all functional and non-functional requirements for the system-to-be. In *Tropos*, the information system is represented as one or more actors which participate in a strategic dependency model, along with other actors from the system's operational environment. In other words, the system comes into the picture as one or more actors who contribute to the fulfillment of stakeholder goals. For our example, the *Medi@* system is introduced as an actor in the strategic dependency model depicted in Figure 3.

With respect to the actors identified in Figure 2, *Customer* depends on *Media Shop* to buy media items while *Media Shop* depends on *Customer* to increase market share and remain happy (with *Media Shop* service). *Media Supplier* is expected to provide

Media Shop with media items while depending on the latter for continuing long-term business. He can also use *Medi@* to determine new needs from customers, such as media items not available in the catalogue. As indicated earlier, *Media Shop* depends on *Medi@* for processing internet orders and on *Bank Cpy* to process business transactions. *Customer*, in turn, depends on *Medi@* to place orders through the internet, to search the database for keywords, or simply to browse the on-line catalogue. With respect to relevant qualities, *Customer* requires that transaction services be secure and usable, while *Media Shop* expects *Medi@* to be easily maintainable (e.g., catalogue enhancing, item database evolution, user interface update, ...). The other dependencies have already been described in Figure 2.

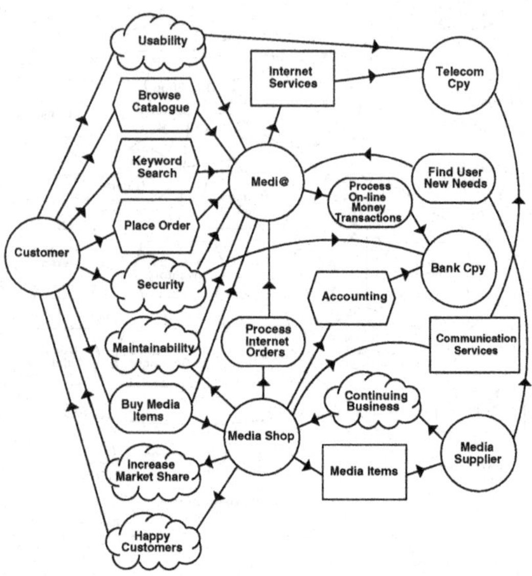

Fig. 3. Strategic dependency model for a media shop

As late requirements analysis proceeds, *Medi@* is given additional responsibilities, and ends up as the depender of several dependencies. Moreover, the system is decomposed into several sub-actors which take on some of these responsibilities. This decomposition and responsibility assignment is realized using the same kind of means-ends analysis along with the strategic rationale analysis illustrated in Figure 2. Hence, the analysis in Figure 4 focuses on the system itself, instead of a external stakeholder.

The figure postulates a root task *Internet Shop Managed* providing sufficient support (++) [3] to the softgoal *Increase Market Share*. That task is firstly refined into goals *Internet Order Handled* and *Item Searching Handled*, softgoals *Attract New Customer*, *Secure* and *Usable* and tasks *Produce Statistics* and *Maintenance*. To manage internet orders, *Internet Order Handled* is achieved through the task *Shopping Cart* which is decomposed into subtasks *Select Item*, *Add Item*, Check *Out,* and *Get Identification Detail*. These are the main process activities required to design an operational on-line shopping cart [6]. The latter (goal) is achieved either through sub-goal *Classic Communication Handled* dealing with phone and fax orders or *Internet Handled* managing secure or standard form orderings. To allow for the ordering of new items not listed in the catalogue, *Select Item* is also further refined into two alternative subtasks, one dedicated to select catalogued items, the other to preorder unavailable products.

To provide sufficient support (++) to the *Maintainable* softgoal, *Maintenance* is refined into four subtasks dealing with catalogue updates, system evolution, interface updates and system monitoring.

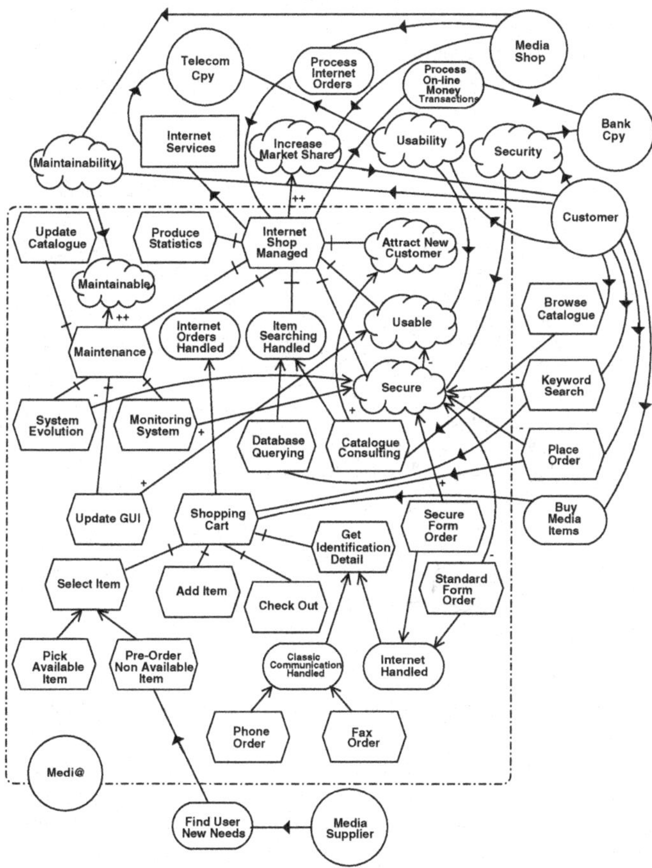

Fig. 4. Strategic rationale model for *Medi@*

The goal *Item Searching Handled* might alternatively be fulfilled through tasks *Database Querying* or *Catalogue Consulting* with respect to customers' navigating desiderata, i.e., searching with particular items in mind by using search functions or simply browsing the catalogued products.

In addition, as already pointed, Figure 4 introduces softgoal contributions to model sufficient/partial positive (respectively ++ and +) or negative (respectively - - and -) support to softgoals *Secure*, *Usable*, *Maintainable*, *Attract New Customers* and

Increase Market Share. The result of this means-ends analysis is a set of (system and human) actors who are dependees for some of the dependencies that have been postulated.

Figure 5 suggests one possible assignment of responsibilities identified for *Medi@*. The *Medi@* system is decomposed into four sub-actors: *Store Front*, *Billing Processor*, *Service Quality Manager* and *Back Store*.

Store Front interacts primarily with *Customer* and provides her with a usable front-end web application. *Back Store* keeps track of all web information about customers, products, sales, bills and other data of strategic importance to *Media Shop. Billing Processor* is in charge of the secure management of orders and bills, and other financial data; also of interactions to *Bank Cpy. Service Quality Manager* is introduced in order to look for *security* gaps, *usability* bottlenecks and *maintainability* issues.

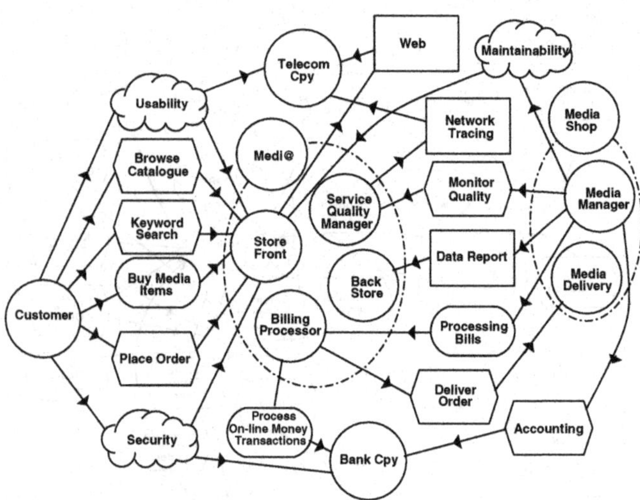

Fig. 5. The web system consists of four inside actors, each with external dependencies

All four sub-actors need to communicate and collaborate. For instance, *Store Front* communicates to *Billing Processor* relevant customer information required to process bills. For the rest of the section, we focus on *Store Front*. This actor is in charge of catalogue browsing and item database searching, also provides on-line customers with detailed information about media items. We assume that different media shops working with *Medi@* may want to provide their customers with various forms of information retrieval (Boolean, keyword, thesaurus, lexicon, full text, indexed list, simple browsing, hypertext browsing, SQL queries, etc.).

Store Front is also responsible for supplying a customer with a web shopping cart to keep track of selected items. We assume that different media shops using the *Medi@* system may want to provide customers with different kinds of shopping carts with respect to their internet browser, plug-ins configuration or platform or simply personal wishes (e.g., Java mode, simple browser, frame-based, CGI shopping cart,…)

Finally, *Store Front* initializes the kind of processing that will be done (by *Billing Processor*) for a given order (phone/fax, internet standard form or secure encrypted form). We assume that different media shop managers using *Medi@* may be processing various types of orders differently, and that customers may be selecting the kind of delivery system they would like to use (UPS, FedEx, ...).

Resource, task and softgoal dependencies correspond naturally to functional and non-functional requirements. Leaving (some) goal dependencies between system actors and other actors is a novelty. Traditionally, functional goals are "operationalized" during late requirements [7], while quality softgoals are either operationalized or "metricized" [8]. For example, *Billing Processor* may be operationalized during late requirements analysis into particular business processes for processing bills and orders. Likewise, a security softgoal might be operationalized by defining interfaces which minimize input/output between the system and its environment, or by limiting access to sensitive information. Alternatively, the security requirement may be metricized into something like "No more than X unauthorized operations in the system-to-be per year".

Leaving goal dependencies with system actors as dependees makes sense whenever there is a foreseeable need for flexibility in the performance of a task on the part of the system. For example, consider a communication goal "communicate X to Y". According to conventional development techniques, such a goal needs to be operationalized before the end of late requirements analysis, perhaps into some sort of a user interface through which user Y will receive message X from the system. The problem with this approach is that the steps through which this goal is to be fulfilled (along with a host of background assumptions) are frozen into the requirements of the system-to-be. This early translation of goals into concrete plans for their fulfillment makes systems fragile and less reusable.

In our example, we have left three goals in the late requirements model. The first goal is *Usability* because we propose to implement *Store Front* and *Service Quality Manager* as agents able to automatically decide at run-time which catalogue browser, shopping cart and order processor architecture fit best customer needs or navigator/platform specifications. Moreover, we would like to include different search engines, reflecting different search techniques, and let the system dynamically choose the most appropriate. The second key softgoal in the late requirements specification is *Security*. To fulfil it, we propose to support in the system's architecture a number of security strategies and let the system decide at run-time which one is the most appropriate, taking into account environment configurations, web browser specifications and network protocols used. The third goal is *Maintainability,* meaning that catalogue content, database schema, and architectural model can be dynamically extended to integrate new and future web-related technologies.

5 Architectural Design

A system architecture constitutes a relatively small, intellectually manageable model of system structure, which describes how system components work together. For our case study, the task is to define (or choose) a web-based application architecture. The canonical web architecture consists of a web server, a network connection, HTML/XML documents on one or more clients communicating with a Web server via HTTP, and an application server which enables the system to manage business logic and state. This architecture is not intended to preclude the use of distributed objects or Java applets; nor does it imply that the web server and application server cannot be located on the same machine.

By now, software architects have developed catalogues of web architectural styles (e.g., [6]). The three most common styles are the *Thin Web Client*, *Thick Web Client* and *Web Delivery. Thin Web Client* is most appropriate for applications where the client has minimal computing power, or no control over its configuration. The client requires only a standard forms-capable web browser. *Thick Web Client* extends the *Thin Web Client* style with the use of client-side scripting and custom objects, such as ActiveX controls and Java applets. Finally, *Web Delivery* offers a traditional client/server system with a web-based delivery mechanism. Here the client communicates directly with object servers, bypassing HTTP. This style is appropriate when there is significant control over client and network configuration.

The first task during architectural design is to select among alternative architectural styles using as criteria the desired qualities identified earlier. The analysis involves refining these qualities, represented as softgoals, to sub-goals that are more specific and more precise and then evaluating alternative architectural styles against them, as shown in Figure 6. The styles are represented as operationalized softgoals (saying, roughly, "make the architecture of the new system *Web Delivery-/Thin Web-/Thick Web*-based") and are evaluated with respect to the alternative non-functional softgoals as shown in Figure 6. Design rationale is represented by claim softgoals drawn as dashed clouds. These can represent contextual information (such as priorities) to be considered and properly reflected into the decision making process. Exclamation marks (! and !!) are used to mark priority softgoals while a check-mark "✔" indicates a fulfilled softgoal, while a cross "✗" labels a unfulfillable one.

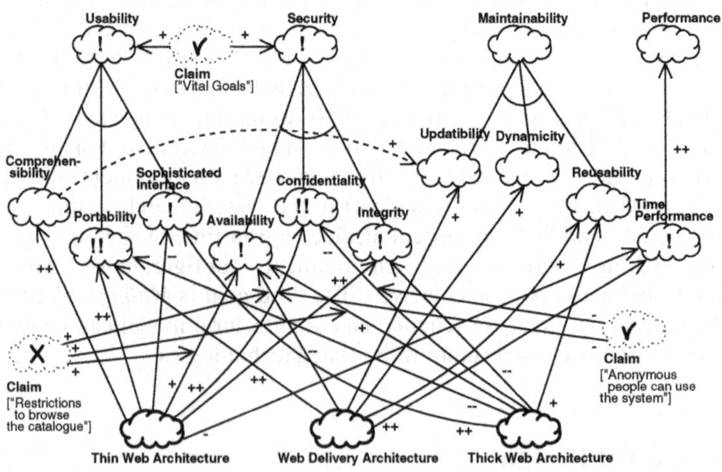

Fig. 6. Refining softgoals in architectural design

The *Usability* softgoal has been AND-decomposed into sub-goals *Comprehensibility*, *Portability* and *Sophisticated Interface.* From a customer perspective, it is important for *Medi@* to be intuitive and ergonomic. The look-and-feel of the interface must naturally guides customer actions with minimal computer knowledge. Equally strategic is the portability of the application across browser implementations and the quality of the interface. Note that not all HTML browsers support scripting, applets, controls and plug-ins. These technologies make the client itself more dynamic, and capable of animation, fly-over help, and sophisticated input controls. When only minimal business logic needs to be run on the client, scripting is often an easy and powerful mechanism to use. When truly sophisticated logic needs to run on the client, building Java applets, Java beans, or ActiveX controls is probably a better approach. A comparable analysis is carried out for *Security* and *Maintainability.*

As shown in Figure 6, each of the three web architectural styles contributes positively or negatively to the qualities of interest. For instance, *Thin Web Client* is useful for applications where only the most basic client configuration can be guaranteed. Hence, this architecture does well with respect to *Portability*. However, it has a limited capacity to support *Sophisticated User Interfaces.* Moreover, this architecture relies on a connectionless protocol such as HTTP, which contributes positively to system availability.

On the other hand, *Thick Web Client* is generally not portable across browser implementations, but can more readily support sophisticated interfaces. As with *Thin Web Client*, all communication between client and server is done with HTTP, hence its positive contribution to *Availability*. On the negative side, client-side scripting and custom objects, such as ActiveX controls and Java applets, may pose risks to client confidentiality. Last but not least, *Web Delivery* is highly portable, since the browser has some built-in capabilities to automatically download the needed components from the server. However, this architecture requires a reliable network.

This phase also involves the introduction of new system actors and dependencies, as well as the decomposition of existing actors and dependencies into sub-actors and sub-dependencies which are delegated some of the responsibilities of the key system actors introduced earlier.

Figure 7 focuses on the latter kind of refinement. To accommodate the responsibilities of *Store Front*, we introduce *Item Browser* to manage catalogue navigation, *Shopping Cart* to select and custom items, *Customer Profiler* to track customer data and produce client profiles, and *On-line Catalogue* to deal with digital library obligations. To cope with the non-functional requirement decomposition proposed in Figure 6, *Service Quality Manager* is further refined into four new system sub-actors *Usability Manager*, *Security Checker*, *Maintainability Manager* and *Performance Monitor*, each of them assuming one of the top main softgoals explained previously. Further refinements are shown on Figure 7.

An interesting decision that comes up during architectural design is whether fulfillment of an actor's obligations will be accomplished through assistance from other actors, through delegation ("outsourcing"), or through decomposition of the actor into component actors. Going back to our running example, the introduction of other actors described in the previous paragraph amounts to a form of delegation in the sense that *Store Front* retains its obligations, but delegates subtasks, sub-goals etc. to other actors. An alternative architectural design would have *Store Front* outsourcing some of its responsibilities to some other actors, so that *Store Front* removes itself from the critical path of obligation fulfilment. Lastly, *StoreFront* may be refined into an aggregate of actors which, by design work together to fulfil *Store Front*'s obligations. This is analogous to a committee being refined into a collection of members who collectively fulfil the committee's mandate. It is not clear, at this point, how the three alternatives compare, nor what are their respective strengths and weaknesses.

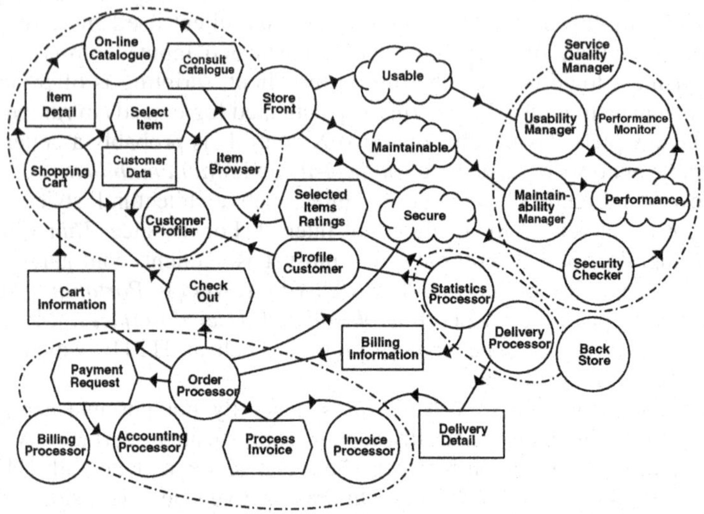

Fig. 7. Strategic Dependency Model for *Medi@* actors

6 Detailed Design

The detailed design phase is intended to introduce additional detail for each architectural component of a system. In our case, this includes actor communication and actor behavior. To support this phase, we propose to adopt existing agent communication languages, message transportation mechanisms and other concepts and tools. One possibility, for example, is to adopt one of the extensions to UML proposed by the FIPA (Foundation for Intelligent Agents) and the OMG Agent Work group [14]. The rest of the section concentrates on the *Shopping cart* actor and the *check out* dependency.

To specify the *checkout* task, for instance, we use AUML - the Agent Unified Modeling Language [14], which supports templates and packages to represent *checkout* as an object, but also in terms of sequence and collaborations diagrams.

Figure 8 focuses on the protocol between *Customer* and *Shopping Cart* which consists of a customization of the FIPA Contract Net protocol [14]. Such a protocol describes a communication pattern among actors, as well as constraints on the contents of the messages they exchange.

When a *Customer* wants to check out, a request-for-proposal message is sent to *Shopping Cart*, which must respond before a given timeout (for network security and integrity reasons). The response may refuse to provide a proposal, submit a proposal, or express miscomprehension. The diamond symbol with an "X" indicates an "exclusive or" decision. If a proposal is offered, *Customer* has a choice of either accepting or canceling the proposal. The internal processing of *Shopping Cart*'s *checkout* plan is described in Figure 9.

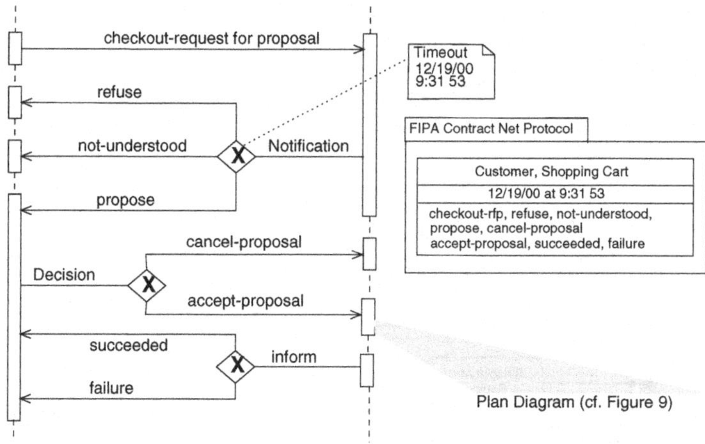

Fig. 8. Agent interaction protocol focusing on a *checkout* dialogue

At the lowest level, we use plan diagrams [12] (See Figure 9), to specify the internal processing of atomic actors. The initial transition of the plan diagram is labeled with an activation event (*Press checkout button*) and activation condition (*[checkout button activated]*) which determine when and in what context the plan should be activated. Transitions from a state automatically occur when exiting the state and no event is associated (e.g., when exiting *Fields Checking*) or when the associated event occurs (e.g., *Press cancel button*), provided in all cases that the associated condition is true (e.g., *[Mandatory fields filled]*). When the transition occurs any associated action is performed (e.g., *verifyCC()*).

An important feature of plan diagrams is their notion of failure. Failure can occur when an action upon a transition fails, when an explicit transition to a fail state (denoted by a small no entry sign) occurs, or when the activity of an active state terminates in failure and no outgoing transition is enabled.

Figure 9 depicts the plan diagram for *checkout*, triggered by pushing the checkout button. Mandatory fields are first checked. If any mandatory fields are not filled, an iteration allows the customer to update them. For security reasons, the loop exits after 5 tries ([i<5]) and causes the plan to fail. Credit Card validity is then checked. Again for security reasons, when not valid, the CC# can only be corrected 3 times. Otherwise, the plan terminates in failure. The customer is then asked to confirm the CC# to allow item registration. If the CC# is not confirmed, the plan fails. Otherwise, the plan continues: each item is iteratively registered, final amounts are calculated, stock records and customer profiles are updated and a report is displayed. When finally the whole plan succeeds, the *ShoppingCart* automatically logs out and asks the *Order Processor* to initialize the order. When, for any reason, the plan fails, the *ShoppingCart* automatically logs out. At anytime, if the cancel button is pressed, or the timeout is more than 90 seconds (e.g., due to a network bottleneck), the plan fails and the *Shopping Cart* is reinitialized.

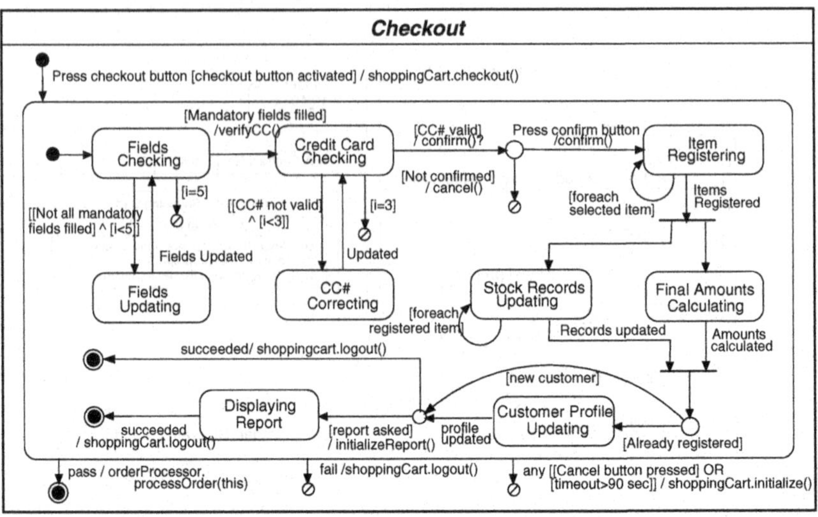

Fig. 9. A plan diagram for *checkout*

7 Generating an Implementation

JACK Intelligent Agents [4] is an agent-oriented development environment designed to provide agent-oriented extensions to Java.

JACK agents can be considered autonomous software components that have explicit *goals* to achieve, or *events* to cope with (desires). To describe how they should go about achieving these desires, agents are programmed with a set of *plans* (intentions).

Each plan describes how to achieve a goal under different circumstances. Set to work, the agent pursues its given goals (desires), adopting the appropriate plans (intentions) according to its current set of data (beliefs) about the state of the world. To support the programming of BDI agents, JACK offers five principal language constructs. These are *agents*, *capabilities*, *database relations*, *events*, and *plans*.

*I** actors, (informational/data) resources, softgoals, goals and tasks will be respectively mapped into BDI agents, beliefs, desires and intentions. In turn, a BDI agent will be mapped as a JACK agent, a belief will be asserted (or retracted) as a database relation, a desire will be posted (sent internally) as a BDIGoalEvent (representing an objective that an agent wishes to achieve) and handled as a plan, and an intention will be implemented as a plan. Finally, an *i** dependency will be directly realized as a BDIMessageEvent (received by agents from other agents).

Figure 10 depicts the JACK layout presenting each of the five JACK constructs as well as the implementation of the first part of the dialogue shown in Figure 8. The request for proposal *checkout-rfp* is a MessageEvent (*extends MessageEvent*) sent by

Customer and handled by the *Shopping Cart*'s *checkout* plan (*extends Plan*) as detailed in Figure 9. Finally, *Timeout* (which we consider a belief) is implemented as a closed world (i.e., true or false) database relation asserting for each *Shopping Cart* one or several timeout delays.

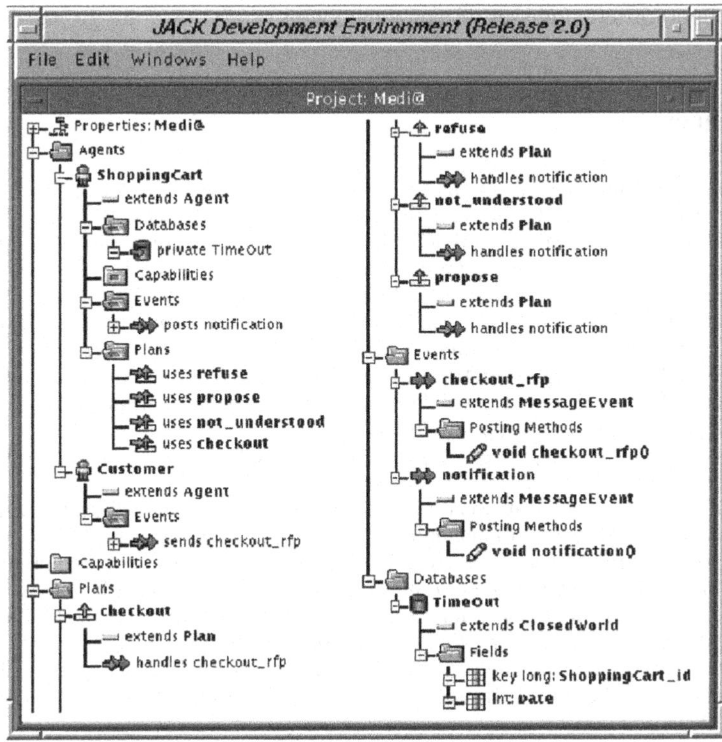

Fig. 10. Partial implementation of Figure 8 in JACK

8 Conclusion and Discussion

We have proposed a development methodology founded on intentional concepts, and inspired by early requirements modeling. We believe that the methodology is particularly appropriate for generic, componentized systems like e-business applications that can be downloaded and used in a variety of operating environments and computing platforms around the world. Preliminary results suggest that the methodology complements well proposals for agent-oriented programming environments.

There already exist some proposals for agent-oriented software development, most notably [10, 11, 14, 16]. Such proposals are mostly extensions to known object-oriented and/or knowledge engineering methodologies. Moreover, all these proposals focus on design – as opposed to requirements analysis – for agent-oriented software and are therefore considerably narrower in scope than *Tropos*.

Of course, much remains to be done to further refine the proposed methodology and validate its usefulness with real case studies. We are currently working on the development of formal analysis techniques for *Tropos*, also the development of tools which support different phases of the methodology.

References

[1] Booch, G., Rumbaugh, J. and Jacobson, I., *The Unified Modeling Language User Guide*, The Addison-Wesley Object Technology Series, Addison-Wesley, 1999.

[2] Castro, J., Kolp, M. and Mylopoulos, J., Developing Agent-Oriented Information Systems for the Enterprise, *Proceedings of the Second International Conference On Enterprise Information Systems* (ICEIS00), Stafford, UK, July 2000.

[3] Chung, L. K., Nixon, B. A., Yu, E. and Mylopoulos, J., *Non-Functional Requirements in Software Engineering*, Kluwer Publishing, 2000.

[4] Coburn, M., *Jack Intelligent Agents: User Guide version 2.0*, AOS Pty Ltd, 2000.

[5] Cohen, P. and Levesque, H., "Intention is Choice with Commitment", *Artificial Intelligence, 32(3)*, 1990, pp. 213-261.

[6] Conallen, J., *Building Web Applications with UML*, The Addison-Wesley Object Technology Series, Addison-Wesley, 2000.

[7] Dardenne, A., van Lamsweerde, A. and Fickas, S., "Goal–directed Requirements Acquisition", *Science of Computer Programming, 20*, 1993, pp. 3-50.

[8] Davis, A., *Software Requirements: Objects, Functions and States*, Prentice Hall, 1993.

[9] DeMarco, T., *Structured Analysis and System Specification*, Yourdon Press, 1978.

[10] Iglesias, C., Garrijo, M. and Gonzalez, J., "A Survey of Agent-Oriented Methodologies", *Proceedings of the 5th International Workshop on Intelligent Agents: Agent Theories, Architectures, and Languages* (ATAL-98), Paris, France, July 1998, pp. 317-330.

[11] Jennings, N. R., "On agent-based software engineering", *Artificial Intelligence, 117*, 2000, pp. 277-296.

[12] Kinny, D. and Georgeff, M., "Modelling and Design of Multi-Agent System", *Proceedings of the Third International Workshop on Agent Theories, Architectures, and Languages* (ATAL-96), Budapest, Hungary, August 1996, pp. 1-20.

[13] Mylopoulos, J. and Castro, J., "Tropos: A Framework for Requirements-Driven Software Development", Brinkkemper, J. and Solvberg, A. (eds.), *Information Systems Engineering: State of the Art and Research Themes*, Springer-Verlag, June 2000, pp. 261-273.

[14] Odell, J., Van Dyke Parunak, H. and Bauer, B., "Extending UML for Agents", *Proceedings of the Agent-Oriented Information System Workshop at the 17 National Conference on Artificial Intelligence*, pp. 3-17, Austin, USA, July 2000.

[15] Wirfs-Brock, R., Wilkerson, B. and Wiener, L., *Designing Object-Oriented Software*, Englewood Cliffs, Prentice-Hall, 1990.

[16] Wooldridge, M., Jennings, N. R. and Kinny D., "The Gaia Methodology for Agent-Oriented Analysis and Design", *Journal of Autonomous Agents and Multi-Agent Systems, 3(3)*, to appear, 2000.

[17] Yourdon, E. and Constantine, L., *Structured Design: Fundamentals of a Discipline of Computer Program and Systems Design*, Prentice-Hall, 1979.

[18] Yu, E., *Modelling Strategic Relationships for Process Reengineering*, Ph.D. thesis, Department of Computer Science, University of Toronto, Canada, 1995.

The Evolution of Tropos

John Mylopoulos, Jaelson Castro, and Manuel Kolp

Abstract The Tropos project was launched in the Fall of 1999 with main objective the development of a methodology for building agent-oriented software systems. The methodology was grounded on i* and was first presented in full at the CAiSE 2001 conference. This short article details some of the directions that were pursued in the project since that time.

1 Introduction

The Tropos project was launched in the Fall of 1999 with main objective the development of a methodology for building agent-oriented software systems. The methodology was grounded on i*, a requirements modeling language founded on intentional and social concepts, such as *actor, goal* and *social dependencies* among actors [18, 19]. Our CAiSE'01 paper was preceded by a couple of preliminary publications, most notably [12]. However, the CAiSE'01 paper constitutes the first comprehensive presentation of the Tropos methodology. Its publication was followed by two journal papers presenting further details on the methodology.

J. Mylopoulos (✉)
Department of Information Engineering and Computer Science, University of Trento, Via Sommarive, 14 – 38122 Povo – Italy
e-mail: jm@disi.unitn.it

J. Castro
Center of Informatics, Federal University of Pernambuco (UFPE), 50740-560 – Recife – PE, Brazil
e-mail: jbc@cin.ufpe.br

M. Kolp
School of Management, Catholic University of Louvain, Place des Doyens, B – 1348 Louvain-la-Neuve, Belgium
e-mail: manuel.kolp@uclouvain.be

J. Bubenko et al. (eds.), *Seminal Contributions to Information Systems Engineering*, DOI 10.1007/978-3-642-36926-1_22, © Springer-Verlag Berlin Heidelberg 2013

Castro et al. [5] is an extended version of the CAiSE'01 paper included in the special issue published for CAiSE'01. Bresciani et al. [3] offers a complementary, more agent-oriented perspective on the modelling language and the accompanying methodology.

In what follows, we present in Sects. 2–4 some of the research questions that were pursued since 2001 at the University of Trento (Italy), the Catholic University of Louvain (Belgium) and the Federal University of Pernambuco (Brazil). The presentation is structured according to topic (Formal analysis, Architectures and Patterns, Methods and Techniques). We conclude with some of the research questions that the project has raised for the research community.

2 Formal Analysis

Much of the research that followed the CAiSE 2001 paper at the University of Trento focused on formal analysis techniques for Tropos models, Formal Tropos [7] extends Tropos by allowing annotations of i* models with Linear Temporal Logic (LTL) constraints. Formal Tropos models can then be translated into specifications for a model checker (in our case, nuSMV) to ensure that they satisfy desired formal properties. Along a parallel path, i* goal models were formalized so that one can check whether a goal model is satisfiable by using a SAT solver [15]. The PhD thesis of Volha Bryl uses an off-the-shelf planner to search among alternative ways of delegating an initial set of requirements among a group of actors and compares these alternatives using a number of local and global metrics for actor dependency networks [4].

Three more PhD theses extend the Tropos framework to address security concerns. Nicola Zannone's PhD thesis extends Tropos with concepts such as *ownership, permission* and *trust* forms of analysis that identify ownership/permission violations [8]. Yudis Asnar's PhD thesis, on the other hand, introduces risk-theoretic concepts to Tropos and looks at the problem of identifying suitable mitigation strategies for identified risks [1]. The thesis of Haralambos Mouratidis also extends Tropos to support secure software designs, but unlike Zannone, focuses on methodological extensions rather than ontological ones [11].

3 Architectures and Patterns

Along a different direction, Tropos has been extended to integrate organizational architectural styles [10] and social design patterns [9] for architectural and detailed design. Architectural styles are manageable abstractions that describe how system components interact and work together while design patterns describe a problem commonly found in software design and prescribe a flexible, reusable solution.

In Tropos, software architectures – be they multi-agent or component-based [13] – are considered social structures composed of autonomous and proactive entities that interact and cooperate with each other to achieve common or private goals. Since the fundamental concepts that drive Tropos are intentional and social, rather than implementation-oriented, theories that study social structures could provide inspiration and insights to define a catalogue of styles and patterns for designing software architectures with Tropos. For this, we turn for guidance to organizational theories, namely *Organization Theory* and *Strategic Alliances*.

Organization Theory describes the structure and design of an organization; *Strategic Alliances* model the strategic collaborations of independent organizational stakeholders who pursue a set of agreed upon business goals. Both disciplines aim to identify and study organizational styles. These are modeling abstractions that can be seen, felt, handled, and operated upon. They have a manifest form and lie in the objective domain of reality as part of the concrete world. A style is however not solely a set of execution behaviors. Rather, it exists in various forms at every stage of crystallization (e.g., specification), and at every level of granularity in the organization. The more manifest is its representation, the more the style emerges and becomes recognizable – whether at a high or low level of granularity.

Taking real-world social structures as metaphor, Tropos has then been extended to propose a set of generic architectural structures:

- At the architectural design level, organizational styles inspired from organization theory and strategic alliances will be used to design the overall system architecture. Styles from organization theory will describe the internal structure and design of the architecture, while styles from strategic alliances will model the cooperation of independent architectural organizational entities that pursue shared goals.
- At the detailed design level, social patterns drawn from research on cooperative and distributed architectures, will offer a more microscopic view of the social architecture description. They will define the software entities and the social dependencies that are necessary for the achievement of goals [9].

Mediation patterns constitute a particular category of social patterns featuring intermediate agents that help other agents reach agreements about an exchange of services. Mediation patterns include ones for monitor, broker, mediator, wrapper, embassy and matchmaker.

Although it is possible to reuse design solutions by using mediation patterns, current practices for instantiating these patterns in multi-agent system (MAS) development makes the application core highly coupled with the patterns' implementation, thereby reducing opportunities of reuse. To address this limitation, we proposed an agent-oriented design pattern description technique, called Agent Pattern Specifications (APS) [16], which takes into account the separation of pattern-related concerns in the MAS design level. A concern is some part of the problem that we want to treat as an integral conceptual unit. In addition, we used aspect-oriented programming to separate pattern-related concerns in the MAS implementation level. To do so, mapping guidelines were defined to guide the implementation of patterns described according to APS by using an integration of JADE and AspectJ. This implementation was evaluated in terms of a suite of metrics for assessing well-known software engineering attributes, such as separation of concerns, coupling, cohesion and size. This assessment showed that aspect-oriented solutions for mediation patterns improved the separation of pattern-related concerns.

4 Methods and Techniques

Another line of research concerns the establishment of a relationship between requirements and architectural descriptions. The SIRA approach constitutes an initial proposal along this direction [2]. Both requirements and architectural designs are described in term of i* as actor dependency diagrams. One such diagram captures the social organization, while another captures a corresponding architectural organization. The organizational model, the main goals are identified by understanding a requirement model as the functionality requested for the system. The organization of the social system consists roles and interactions, as intended by the system and its environment. Additionally, goals and softgoals are used to select an organizational architectural style [10]. In the Assignment Model, roles are clustered into subgroups related to components, based on their similarity with the architectural components. The result is an architectural configuration, which is the allocation of sub-groups to architectural components.

The proliferation of iterative and incremental software development processes as de facto standards for SE practice, suggests a strong integration between requirements engineering and software architecture activities. Such integration can facilitate traceability and the propagation of changes between the models produced within these activities. Recognizing the close relation between architectural design description and requirements specification, we have advocated the use of model transformation approaches as an effective way to generate architectural models from requirements ones, where correlations between requirements and architectural models are accurately specified.

Hence, we have proposed STREAM, a systematic process for generating architectural models from requirements ones, based on horizontal and vertical transformations rules [6]. Horizontal transformations have source and target models at the same level of abstraction, while vertical transformations operate on models at different abstraction levels. In our case, the horizontal transformations are applied to the requirements models resulting in intermediary requirements models closer to architectural concerns. Vertical transformations, on the other hand, map these intermediary models into architectural models. Architectural design activities involve the selection and application of architectural patterns that best satisfy non-functional requirements. In STREAM, requirements models are described in i*, whereas architectural models are described using the Acme ADL.

Some quality attributes, such as adaptivity, are known to have an impact on the overall architecture of a system, so they need to be properly handled since the beginning of the development process. Accordingly, we have proposed a new process called STREAM-A that includes six activities [14]. The first three are related to requirements engineering: (a) requirements refactoring; (b) context annotation and analysis; and (c) identification of sensors and monitors. The last three activities are architecture-related: (d) generate architectural model; (e) define architectural model; and (f) introduce a self-adaptation component.

Also, on the methodological process level, Tropos has been extended to offer iterative and incremental software project management [17]. *"I-Tropos development"* is an extension of the Tropos methodology that supports iterative and agile development.

The notions of *phase* and *discipline* are often presented as synonyms in the software engineering literature. Indeed, Tropos is described as composed of five phases (Early Requirements, Late Requirements, Architectural Design, Detailed Design and Implementation). However, a discipline can be defined as a collection of activities that are all related to a major "area of concern", while phases here are not the traditional sequence of requirements analysis, design, coding, integration, and test. They are completely orthogonal to traditional phases. Each phase is concluded with a major milestone. In order to be compliant with the most generic terminology, traditional Tropos phases are then called disciplines in the I-Tropos process description since "they partition activities under a common theme". In the same way, phases are considered as groups of iterations that are workflows with a minor milestone. In I-Tropos, the Organizational Modeling and Requirements Engineering disciplines respectively correspond to Tropos' Early and Late Requirements disciplines. The Architectural and Detailed Design disciplines correspond to the same stages of the traditional Tropos process.

I-Tropos includes core disciplines, i.e., Organizational Modeling, Requirements Engineering, Architectural Design, Detailed Design, Implementation, Test and Deployment but also supports disciplines to handle Risk Management, Time Management, Quality Management and Software Process Management. For an iterative process, the need to support disciplines to manage the whole software project is of primary importance to precisely understand which project aspect to work on (and through which activity) at a specific time and with the best use of existing resources.

5 Conclusions

The focus of the Tropos project was agent-oriented software for good reasons. To the eyes of many in the Software Engineering and the Multi-Agent System communities, agent-orientation with its promise of autonomous, distributed, open computation seemed like a promising direction. In today's ever-more volatile world, our vision for the software systems of the future has been refined and placed into focus. We don't want just agent-oriented software systems, but rather socio-technical systems consisting of software, human and social actors that work together to fulfill stakeholder requirements. The addition of human and social elements in the design has introduced new uncertainties that can only be addressed through adaptation mechanisms that our systems need to be endowed with. Perhaps more importantly, we don't aspire any more to design systems right from scratch. Rather, we expect to evolve systems continuously and so our methodologies have to be evolution-oriented. Like Darwin, we don't focus anymore on how software species came to be. Rather, we are interested in the ways they can evolve in order to survive.

References

1. Asnar, Y., Giorgini, P., Mylopoulos, J.: Goal-driven risk assessment in requirements engineering. Requirements Engineering Journal **16**(2), 101–116 (2011)
2. Bastos, L.R.D., de Castro, J.B.: Systematic integration between requirements and architecture. In: Springer (ed.) Software Engineering for Multi-Agent Systems III: Research Issues and Practical Applications, no. 3390 in LNCS, pp. 85–103 (2005)
3. Bresciani, P., Perini, A., Giorgini, P., Giunchiglia, F., Mylopoulos, J.: Tropos: An agent-oriented software development methodology. Autonomous Agents and Multi-Agent Systems **8**(3), 203–236 (2004)
4. Bryl, V., Giorgini, P., Mylopoulos, J.: Designing socio-technical systems: From stakeholder goals to social networks. Requirements Engineering Journal **14**(1), 47–70 (2009)
5. Castro, J., Kolp, M., Mylopoulos, J.: Towards requirements-driven information systems engineering: the tropos project. Information Systems **27**(6), 365–389 (2002)
6. Castro, J., Lucena, M., Silva, C.T.L.L., Alencar, F.M.R., Santos, E., Pimentel, J.: Changing attitudes towards the generation of architectural models. Journal of Systems and Software **85**(3), 463–479 (2012)
7. Fuxman, A., Liu, L., Mylopoulos, J., Roveri, M., Traverso, P.: Specifying and analyzing early requirements in tropos. Requirements Engineering Journal **9**(2), 132–150 (2004)
8. Giorgini, P., Massacci, F., Mylopoulos, J., Zannone, N.: Modeling security requirements through ownership, permission and delegation. In: Proceedings of the IEEE International conference on Requirements Engineering (RE'05), pp. 167–176 (2005)
9. Kolp, M., Do, T.T., Faulkner, S.: Social-centric development of multi-agent architectures. Journal of Organizational Computing and E-Commerce **18**(2), 150–175 (2008)
10. Kolp, M., Giorgini, P., Mylopoulos, J.: Multi-agent architectures as organizational structures. Autonomous Agents and Multi-Agent Systems **13**(1), 3–25 (2006)
11. Mouratidis, H., Giorgini, P., Manson, G.: Integrating security and systems engineering: Towards the modelling of secure information systems. In: 15th International Conference on Advanced Information Systems Engineering (CAiSE'03), Klagenfurt, vol. 2681, pp. 63–78. Springer-Verlag (2003)
12. Mylopoulos, J., Castro, J., Kolp, M.: Tropos: A framework for requirements-driven software development. In: Information Systems Engineering: State Of The Art And Research Themes, pp. 261–273. Springer-Verlag (2000)
13. Nguyen, T., Kolp, M., Penserini, L.: A development framework for component-based agent-oriented business services. International Journal of Agent Oriented Systems Engineering **3**(2/3), 328–367 (2009)
14. Pimentel, J.a., Lucena, M., Castro, J., Silva, C., Santos, E., Alencar, F.: Deriving software architectural models from requirements models for adaptive systems: the STREAM-A approach. Requirements Engineering Journal **17**(4), 259–281 (2012)

15. Sebastiani, R., Giorgini, P., Mylopoulos, J.: Simple and minimum-cost satisfiability for goal models. In: 16th International Conference on Advanced Information Systems Engineering (CAiSE '04), Riga, vol. 3084, pp. 20–35. Springer-Verlag (2004)
16. Silva, C., Castro, J., Araujo, J., Moreira, A., Tedesco, P., Mylopoulos, J.: Advanced separation of concerns in agent-oriented design patterns. International Journal of Agent-Oriented Software Engineering **3**(2–3), 306–327 (2009)
17. Wautelet, Y., Kolp, M., Poelmans, S.: Requirements-driven iterative project planning. In: S.B. Escalona Maria Jos Cordeiro Jos (ed.) Communications in Computer and Information Science, *Communications in Computer and Information Science*, vol. 303(6), pp. 121–135. Springer-Verlag (2012)
18. Yu, E.: Towards modeling and reasoning support for early-phase requirements engineering. In: Proceedings of the 3rd IEEE International Symposium on Requirements Engineering, RE '97, pp. 226–235. IEEE Computer Society, Washington, DC, USA (1997)
19. Yu, E., Giorgini, P., Maiden, N., Mylopoulos, J.: Social Modeling for Requirements Engineering. Cooperative Information Systems Series. Mit Press (2011)

The P2P Approach to Interorganizational Workflows

Wil M.P. van der Aalst and Mathias Weske

Department of Technology Management, Eindhoven University of Technology
P.O. Box 513, NL-5600 MB, Eindhoven, The Netherlands
{w.m.p.v.d.aalst, m.weske}@tm.tue.nl

Abstract. This paper describes in an informal way the Public-To-Private (P2P) approach to interorganizational workflows, which is based on a notion of inheritance. The approach consists of three steps: (1) create a common understanding of the interorganizational workflow by specifying a shared public workflow, (2) partition the public workflow over the organizations involved, and (3) for each organization, create a private workflow which is a subclass of the respective part of the public workflow. Using an example, we explain that the P2P approach yields an interorganizational workflow which is guaranteed to realize the behavior specified in the public workflow.

1 Introduction

In today's corporations, products and services are typically created by business processes, and workflow technology can be used for enhancing the flexibility and efficiency of these processes [14,19]. Corporations often operate across organizational boundaries, for example in E-commerce and extended enterprises [11,20,27]. Consequently, workflows between organizations – interorganizational workflows – are becoming increasingly important [21,12]. Interorganizational workflows are typically subject to conflicting constraints of the organizations involved. On the one hand, there is a strong need for coordination to optimize the flow of work in and between organizations. On the other hand, the organizations involved are essentially autonomous and have the freedom to create or modify workflows at any point in time. Some of the issues resulting from these conflicting goals will be tackled in this paper: We introduce the Public-To-Private (P2P) approach to interorganizational workflows which provides the means to specify a common public workflow, to partition it according to the organizations involved and to allow for private refinement of the parts by the organizations, based on a notion of inheritance. The P2P approach guarantees that the private workflows of the participating organizations (or, as we prefer to say, the domains) satisfy the public workflow as agreed upon; it consists of the following steps:

- *Step 1:* The organizations involved agree on a common public workflow, which serves as a contract between these organizations.

K.R. Dittrich, A. Geppert, M.C. Norrie (Eds.): CAiSE 2001, LNCS 2068, pp. 140–156, 2001.

- *Step 2:* Each task of the public workflow is mapped onto one of the domains. Each domain is responsible for a part of the public workflow, referred to as its public part.
- *Step 3:* Each domain can now make use of its autonomy to create a private workflow. To satisfy the correctness of the overall interorganizational workflow, however, each domain may only choose a private workflow which is a subclass of its public part.

This paper introduces the P2P approach in an informal way, guided by an example of an electronic bookstore. The paper is structured according to the steps mentioned, and for each step concepts and notations are introduced when required; the complete definitions and the technical details of the proofs can be found in [4]. Sections 2 through 4 present the phases of the P2P approach, and Section 5 summarizes the main results. A discussion of related work and concluding remarks complete this paper.

2 Designing the Public Workflow (Step 1)

The example used throughout this paper is inspired by electronic bookstores such as Amazon [8] and Barnes and Noble [9]. In this section, we design the public workflow for ordering books. The scope of the workflow process includes the ordering, billing and shipping of books, involving the customer, the bookstore, the publisher, and the shipper.

The P2P approach uses *workflow nets* (WF-nets) [2] for modeling workflows, which are a specific form of Petri nets. In WF-nets, tasks are modeled by transitions, and causal dependencies are modeled by places and arcs. In fact, a place corresponds to a condition which can be used as pre- and/or post-condition for tasks. An AND-split corresponds to a transition with two or more output places, and an AND-join corresponds to a transition with two or more input places. OR-splits/OR-joins correspond to places with multiple outgoing/ingoing arcs. A WF-net has one source place and one sink place because any case (i.e., workflow instance) represented by the WF-net is created when it enters the workflow management system and is deleted once it is completely handled. An additional requirement is that there should be no dangling tasks or conditions, i.e., tasks and conditions which do not contribute to the processing of cases. Therefore, all the nodes of the workflow should be on some path from source to sink. WF-nets with these properties are called *sound* [1,2].

Figure 1 shows the public workflow N^{publ} of the electronic bookstore. This workflow can be regarded as a contract between the domains, i.e., the customer, the bookstore, the publisher, and the shipper. We stress that the public workflow does not necessarily show the way the tasks are actually executed; the real process may be much more detailed, and it may involve much more tasks. The public workflow only contains the tasks which are of interest to all parties. The public workflow shown in Fig. 1 is defined as a WF-net. While the mapping of the tasks to domains is only done in the next step, one can think of the tasks in the left column as performed by the customer, for instance the *place_c_order* task.

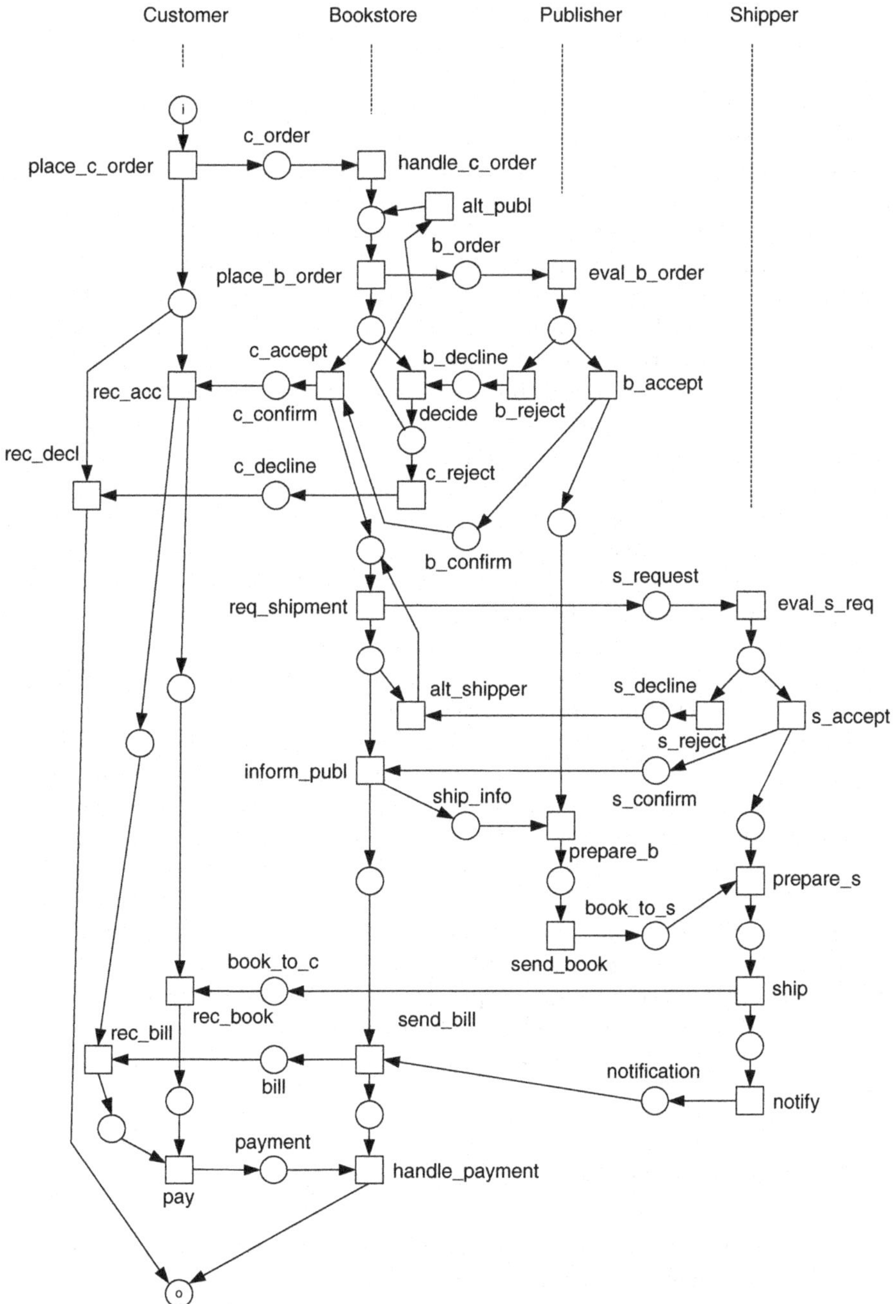

Fig. 1. The public workflow N^{publ}.

The next columns to the right belong to the bookstore (containing, e.g., the *handle_c_order* task to handle the customer order), the publisher (e.g., *eval_b_order*), and the shipper (e.g., *eval_s_req*), respectively.

The workflow process is initiated by a customer placing an order (represented by the task *place_c_order*). This customer order is sent to and is handled by the bookstore (*handle_c_order*). The electronic bookstore is a virtual company which has no books in stock. Therefore, the bookstore transfers the order of the desired book to a publisher (*place_b_order*). The bookstore order is evaluated by the publisher (*eval_b_order*) and either accepted (*b_accept*) or rejected (*b_reject*). In both cases an appropriate signal is sent to the bookstore. If the bookstore receives a negative answer, it decides (*decide*) to either search for an alternative publisher (*alt_publ*) or to reject the customer order (*c_reject*). If the bookstore searches for an alternative publisher, a new bookstore order is sent to another publisher, etc. If the customer receives a negative answer (*rec_decl*), then the workflow terminates. If the bookstore receives a positive answer (*c_accept*), the customer is informed (*rec_acc*), and the bookstore continues processing the customer order.

Once the order is confirmed, the bookstore sends a request to a shipper (*req_shipment*), the shipper evaluates the request (*eval_s_req*) and either accepts (*s_accept*) or rejects (*b_reject*) the shipping request. If the bookstore receives a negative answer, it searches for another shipper. This process is repeated until a shipper accepts. Note that, unlike the unavailability of the book, the unavailability of a shipper can not lead to a cancellation of the order. After a shipper is found, the publisher is informed (*inform_publ*), the publisher prepares the book for shipment (*prepare_b*), and the book is sent from the publisher to the shipper (*send_book*). The shipper prepares the shipment to the customer (*prepare_s*) and actually ships the book to the customer (*ship*). The customer receives the book (*rec_book*) and the shipper notifies the bookstore (*notify*). The bookstore sends the bill to the customer (*send_bill*). After receiving both the book and the bill (*rec_bill*), the customer makes a payment (*pay*). Then the bookstore processes the payment (*handle_payment*) and the interorganizational workflow terminates.

The public workflow shown in Fig. 1 is indeed a sound WF-net, since it has exactly one input place and one output place, at the moment when the workflow reaches the output place, all tasks have completed, and there are no dead transitions, i.e., all tasks of the WF-net are in fact reachable during workflow executions.

3 Partitioning the Public Workflow (Step 2)

In the second step of the P2P approach, the public workflow is partitioned according to the domains, and the public parts are related to each other, making up an interorganizational workflow. An interorganizational workflows is defined by an *interorganizational workflow net* (IOWF-net). An IOWF-net consists of a set of WF-nets, a set of channels, a set of methods, and a channel flow relation.

In our example, the public workflow is partitioned over four domains: the customer domain, the bookstore domain, the publisher domain, and the shipper domain, as shown in Fig. 2. Methods of the domains are represented by shaded boxes, and they are linked to channels by the channel flow relation, which is represented by arrows. In Fig. 2, the public parts of the customer, the bookstore, the publisher and the shipper are represented by boxes N_C^{part}, N_B^{part}, N_P^{part}, and N_S^{part}, respectively. Channels are represented by icons, and the channel flow relation represented by arrows specifies the linkage of the domains. For example, the *c_order* channel and the attached arrows represent the fact that customer order information flows from the customer domain to the bookstore domain, while the confirmation of the order flows in opposite direction, making use of channel *c_confirm*.

Based on this description it is clear how the public workflow needs to be partitioned. The public part of the customer domain is quite simple (cf. Fig. 3): The customer first places an order, using the method *place_c_order*. Then either the order is accepted, the book and the bill are received and the bill is paid, or the order is declined. Notice that for each transition in the WF-net, there is a method linked to it by a dotted line, representing the actual function which is invoked when the task is executed.

The public part of the bookstore workflow is slightly more complex (cf. Fig. 4): After the order arrives, the bookstore checks for a publisher ready for providing the ordered book. If no publisher can be found, the order is rejected. Otherwise, shipment is requested from a shipper, and payment is handled. The public parts of the publisher and shipper workflow are shown in Fig. 5.

The IOWF-net is a high-level representation of the domains and their dependencies; its semantics are given in terms of a labeled P/T net. A IOWF-net is transformed into a labeled P/T net by taking the union of all WF-nets, adding a place for each channel, connecting transitions to these newly added places, and removing superfluous source and sink places. We call this the flattening of the interorganizational workflow. As shown in [4], we can easily make sure that the partitioning is valid, i.e., all public parts are sound WF-nets and there is no multiple activation. We mention that the flattened IOWF-net equals the public workflow. Hence, flattening the interorganizational workflow shown in Fig. 2 results in the public workflow shown in Fig. 1.

4 Designing the Private Workflows (Step 3)

After partitioning the public workflow, each domain can realize the corresponding public part of the interorganizational workflow in any way they want, as long as they make sure that their private workflow is a subclass of their public part.

The subclass relationship between WF-nets is based on a specific notion of inheritance, called *projection inheritance*. Projection inheritance has been defined in [6,10] and uses encapsulation as a mechanism to establish subclass-superclass relationships. The basic idea of projection inheritance can be characterized as follows:

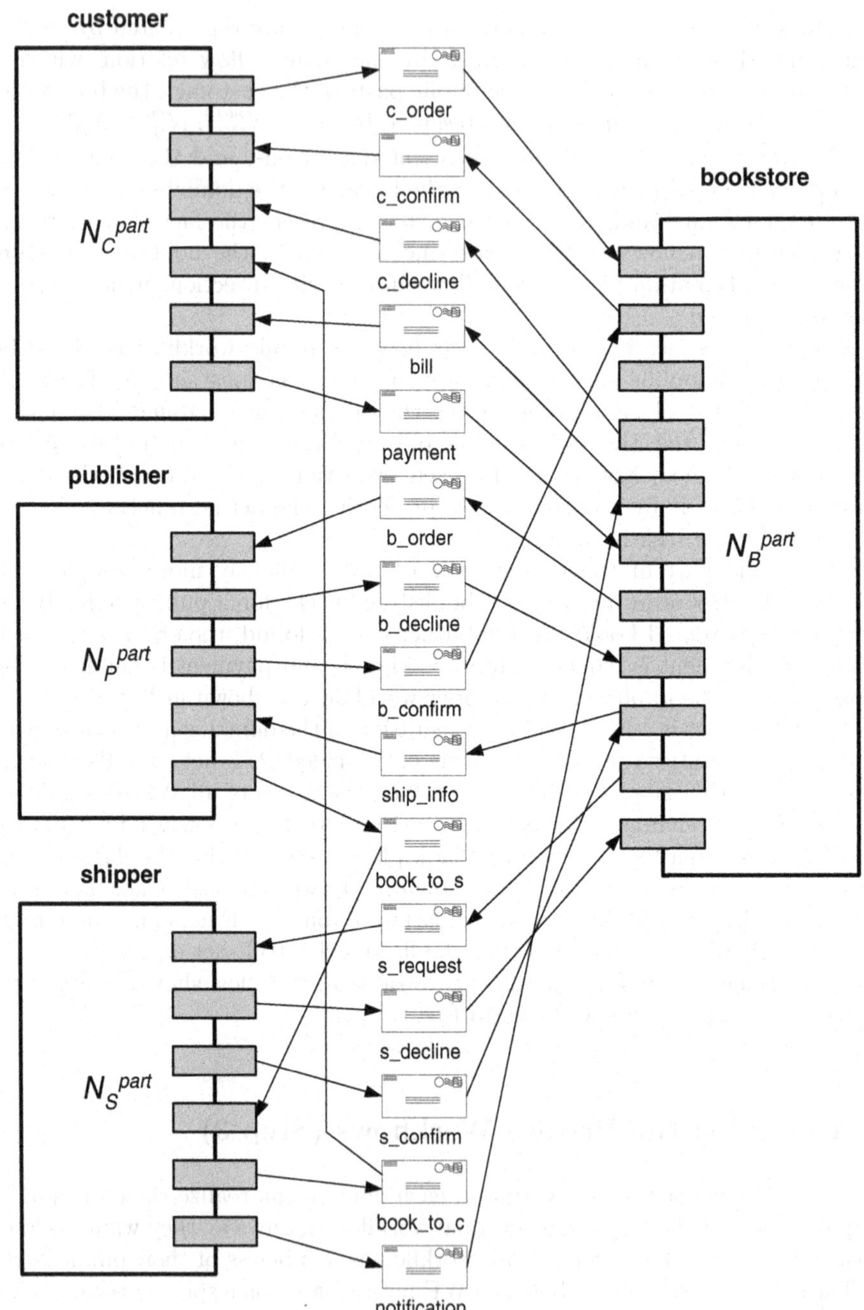

Fig. 2. The interorganizational workflow Q^{part}.

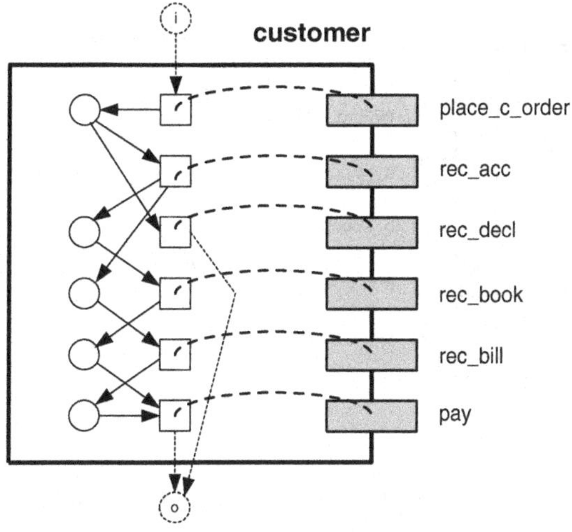

Fig. 3. The WF-net N_C^{part} (public part of the customer domain).

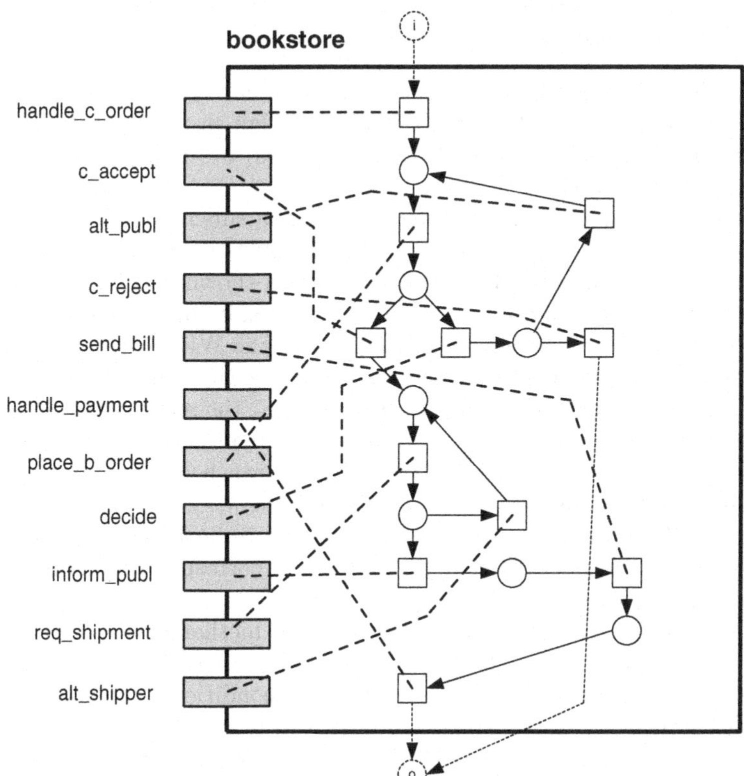

Fig. 4. The WF-net N_B^{part} (public part of the bookstore domain).

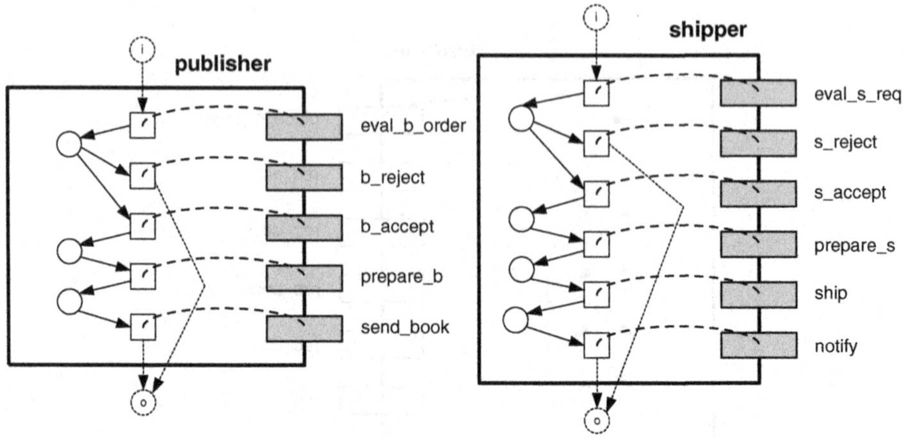

Fig. 5. The WF-net N_P^{part} (public parts of the publisher and shipper domains).

> *If it is not possible to distinguish the behaviors of x and y when arbitrary methods of x are executed, but when only the effects of methods that are also present in y are considered, then x is a subclass of y.*

Projection inheritance is based on branching bisimilarity as the standard equivalence relation on marked, labeled P/T-nets [15]. For projection inheritance, all new methods (i.e., methods added in the subclass) are hidden; an abstraction operator τ is used to hide methods.

For any two sound WF-nets N and N', N' is a subclass of N under projection inheritance if and only if the externally visible behavior of N' is branching bisimilar to N. Let us consider the five WF-nets shown in Fig. 6. N_1 is not a subclass of N_0 because hiding of the new task d results in a potential execution where a is followed by c without executing b, i.e., the WF-net where d is hidden is not branching bisimilar. N_2 is a subclass of N_0 because hiding e in N_2 results in a behavior equivalent to the behavior of N_0, i.e., the addition of e only postpones the execution of b and does not allow for a bypass such as the one in N_1. N_3 is also a subclass of N_0: Hiding the parallel branch containing f yields the original behavior. Finally, N_4 is also a subclass of N_0.

Based on the notion of projection inheritance we have defined three *inheritance-preserving transformation rules.* These rules correspond to design patterns when extending a superclass to incorporate new behavior: (1) adding a loop (rule *PPS*), (2) inserting methods in-between existing methods (rule *PJS*), and (3) putting new methods in parallel with existing methods (rule *PJ3S*). The formal definitions of these transformation rules, their preconditions, and the proofs that these rules actually preserve projection inheritance are given in [6,10].

In the P2P approach, projection inheritance is used as a formal link between the public parts of the domains and the private workflows which are actually executed. Transformation rules are the key mechanism to create specializations of a given WF-net, making use of the fact that applying these rules to a given

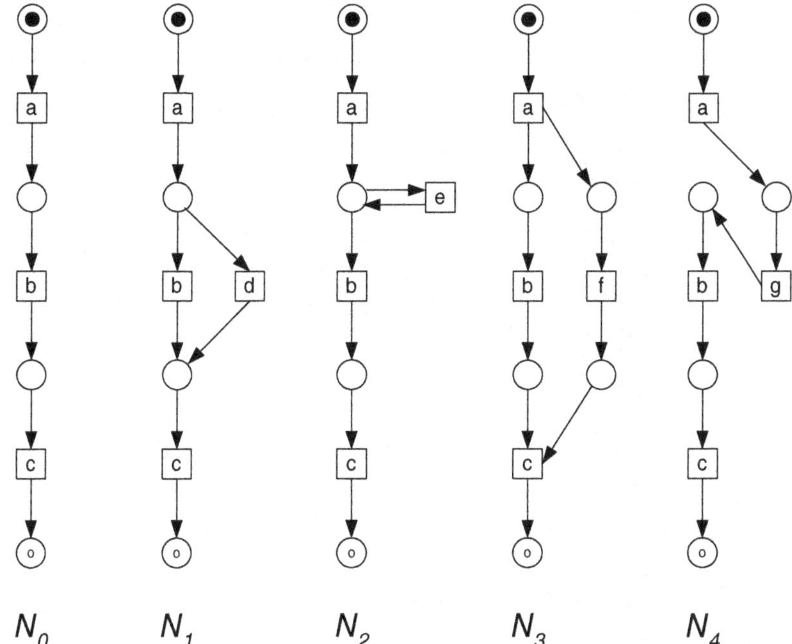

Fig. 6. N_2, N_3, and N_4 are subclasses of N_0 under projection inheritance.

WF-net is guaranteed to create a subclass of that WF-net. Hence, the P2P approach is constructive in the sense that any modification applied to a WF-net via transformation rules *PPS*, *PJS*, and *PJ3S* yields a subclass of the WF-net.

Figure 7 shows the private workflow of the bookstore. Five new tasks, i.e., tasks not present in the public workflow, have been added. After the customer order is handled, the customer profile (information about the interests of the customer) is updated (*update_customer_profile*). This task is executed in parallel with the placement of the bookstore order. After both tasks have been executed, the marketing department is informed (*inform_marketing*). The tasks *monitor_order*, *monitor_shipment*, and *monitor_payment* have been added to monitor the behavior of the publisher, shipper, and customer. The task *monitor_order* can be executed as long as the bookstore is waiting for a response of the publisher. The task *monitor_shipment* can be executed between the moment the publisher is informed and the moment the shipper sends a notification. The task *monitor_payment* can be executed after the bill is sent to the customer. Note that each of the monitor tasks can be executed multiple times. For example, the bookstore checks every week whether the customer has paid and if needed takes action, e.g., sending a bailiff.

We now show by construction that the private workflow N_B^{priv} (Fig. 7) is indeed a subclass of N_B^{part} (Fig. 4): tasks *monitor_order*, *monitor_shipment*, and *monitor_payment* can be added by applying transformation rule *PPS* three times;

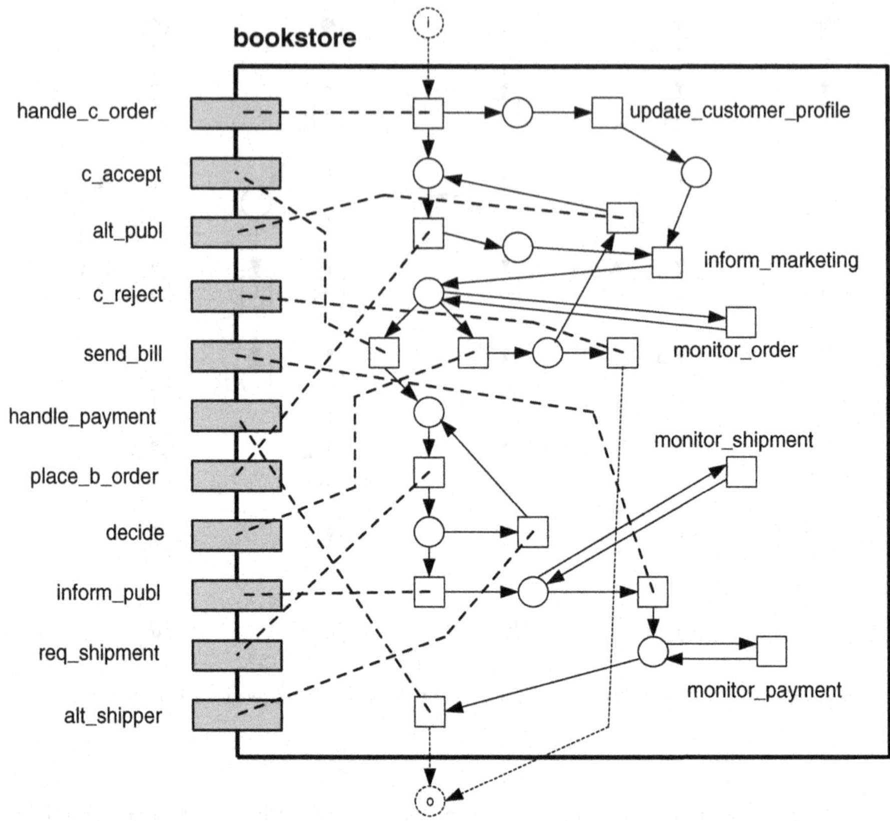

Fig. 7. The WF-net N_B^{priv} (private workflow of the bookstore domain).

task *inform_marketing* can be added using transformation rule *PJS*. To complete the construction, the task *update_customer_profile* can be added using transformation rule *PJ3S*.

Similarly, the private workflow of the publisher (Fig. 8) has been created by applying transformation rule *PJS* to the public part: The task *check_warehouse* has been added in-between the receipt of the order and the decision. In fact, the decision is based on the result of *check_warehouse*. After accepting the order of the bookstore, the corresponding inventory item is locked (*lock_inventory*), the stock is replenished (if possible) (*replenish*), and the book is moved to the part of the warehouse reserved for books which are waiting for shipment (*move_book_to_release_buffer*). It is easy to verify that the private workflow N_P^{priv} is a subclass of N_P^{part}, using the transformation rule *PJS*.

Figure 9 shows the private workflow of the shipper. Using the transformation rules, six new tasks have been added: Task *check_availability_trucks* is executed after the request by the bookstore is received. Based on this task the request is accepted or rejected. Tasks *update_file* and *quality_control* are executed in

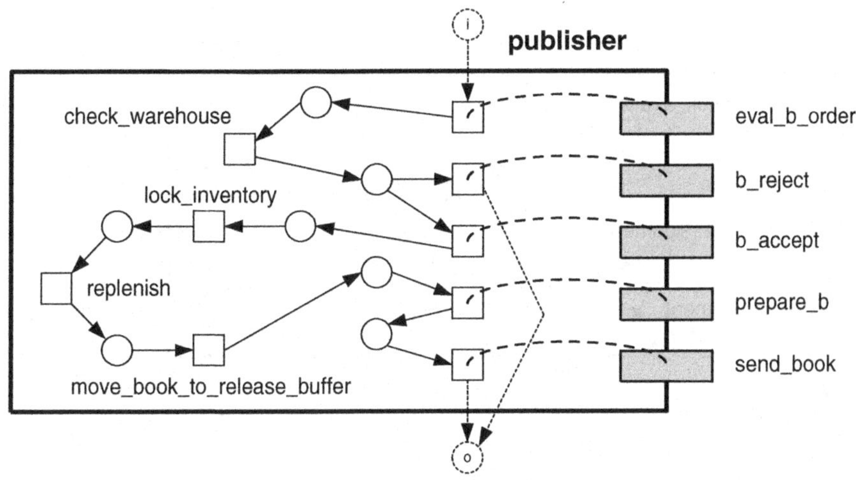

Fig. 8. The WF-net N_P^{priv} (private workflow of the publisher domain).

parallel with the preparation and shipment tasks. After preparation, shipments are assigned to trucks (*assignment*). Based on the assignment, the routing of the truck is determined (*routing*). In-between tasks *assignment* and *routing* the task *re-assignment* can be executed multiple times. Again it is easy to verify that the WF-net shown in Fig. 9 is indeed a subclass of the one shown in Fig. 5. Task *check_availability_trucks* can be added using transformation rule *PJS*. Tasks *update_file* and *quality_control* can be added using transformation rule *PJ3S*. Tasks *assignment*, *re-assignment*, and *routing* can be added using transformation rule *PJS*. Note that it is also possible to first add tasks *assignment* and *routing* using *PJS*, and then add task *re-assignment* using transformation rule *PPS*.

The design of the interorganizational workflow involving a customer, bookstore, publisher, and shipper presented in this paper is a simplification of the real process. In the real process customers can order multiple books at the same time, the customer can return books, the customer can refuse to pay, etc. One can imagine that for realistic interorganizational workflows where the public part consists of more than fifty tasks and the overall workflow consists of hundreds of tasks, a structured approach is needed to avoid all kinds of anomalies. In our opinion, the P2P approach could be used as a starting point for a more comprehensive approach which also deals with other aspects such as data and security.

5 Summary and Main Results

To summarize the P2P approach, in the first step the public workflow is specified in terms of a sound WF-net; it serves as a contract between the business partners involved. In the second step, the public workflow is partitioned over the set of domains. Note that each domain corresponds to an organizational entity. As a

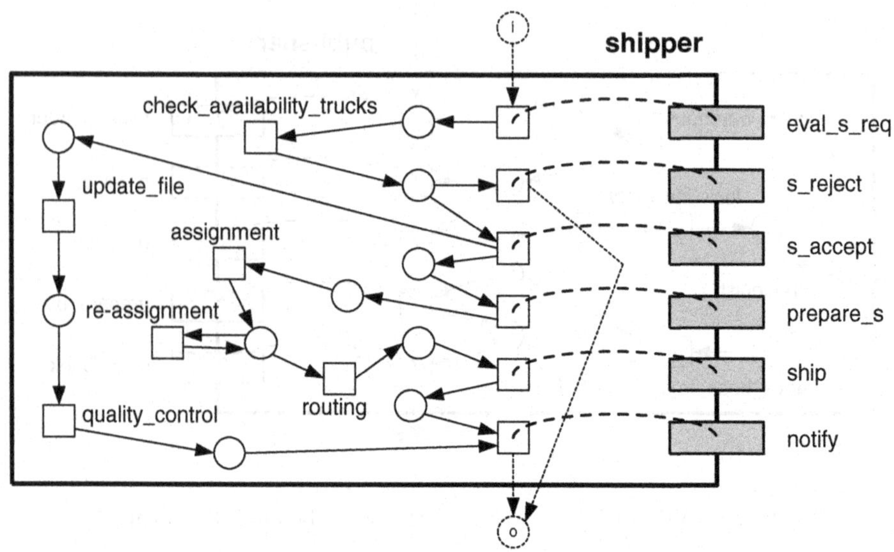

Fig. 9. The WF-net N_S^{priv} (private workflow of the shipper domain).

result of the partitioning, each fragment of the partitioned workflow corresponds to one of the domains and is represented by a sound WF-net, called public part. In the final step, the public parts are replaced by private workflows. Each private workflow corresponds to an actual workflow as it is executed in one of the domains. The P2P approach guarantees that each private workflow is a subclass of the corresponding public part under projection inheritance. It is important to note that the P2P approach is constructive: By applying the three transformation rules introduced above, the design is guaranteed to be correct without the need to check whether each private workflow is actually a subclass of the corresponding public part.

Following the general tone of this paper, we explain the main results informally and introduce concepts if and when required. Please refer to [4] for a detailed theoretical discussion. The first result concerns the *overall workflow*, which consists of all private workflows of the participating domains.

Result 1: The overall workflow is a sound WF-net.

This property is based on the observation that a part of a WF-net (called subflow) can be replaced by a specialization (i.e., a subclass subflow) without endangering soundness of the overall workflow. This result is proven in [4], based on a theorem which shows the compositionality of projection inheritance. From an application point of view, Result 1 makes sure that the P2P approach guarantees that the overall workflow is free of deadlocks and other anomalies.

Result 2: The overall workflow is a subclass of the public workflow.

This result shows that the dynamic behavior of the interorganizational workflow which the business partners agreed upon in the public workflow is in fact guaranteed to be satisfied by the execution of the interorganizational workflow, i.e., the overall workflow. From an application point of view, this is an important result, since it provides the business partners with the ability to perform any private modifications to their public workflow part, as long as the subclass relationship holds. Transformation rules are used for this purpose. Hence, an organization can be sure that its private workflow indeed satisfies the requirements specified in the contract, i.e., the public workflow.

The next result is based on the notion of *local views* of the domains. To introduce local views, we mention that each domain is aware of its private workflow and of the public parts of the other domains. The information which each domain has with respect to the overall workflow is called the local view of that domain. With respect to local views, the following interesting result can be obtained, which stresses the soundness of the P2P approach.

> *Result 3:* The overall workflow is a subclass of the local views of all domains, which in turn are subclasses of the public workflow.

For the final two properties we have to introduce some notation. Since projection inheritance is a partial ordering on the set of WF-nets, the Greatest Common Denominator (GCD) and the Least Common Multiple (LCM) can be defined. GCD and LCM are general concepts that apply to any ordering, and there are different applications of these concepts in the context of WF-nets, as described in more detail in [6]. In essence, the GCD of a set of WF-nets is a WF-net that captures the part these nets have in common, i.e., the part where they agree on. The LCM captures all possible behaviors. Note that projection inheritance is a partial order but not a lattice. Therefore, suitable definitions of GCD and LCM are far from trivial but can be defined as is shown in [6].

For an illustration of these concepts, consider the WF-nets N_0, N_2, N_3, and N_4 shown in Fig. 6. The GCD of these four nets is N_0, i.e., each of the four WF-nets is a subclass of this net and it is not possible to find a different WF-net which is also a superclass of N_2, N_3, and N_4 and at the same time a subclass of N_0. Figure 10 shows $N_{GCD} = N_0$ as the GCD of N_0, N_2, N_3, and N_4. Figure 10 also shows the WF-net N_{LCM}. N_{LCM} is a subclass of each of the four nets considered. Moreover, it is not possible to find a different WF-net which is also a subclass of N_0, N_2, N_3, and N_4 and at the same time a superclass of N_{LCM}. Any execution sequence generated by one of the four nets can also be generated by N_{LCM} after the appropriate abstraction. Based on the characterization of GCD and LCM we are now ready to present the following result:

> *Result 4:* The GCD of all local views is the public workflow.

The application specific interpretation of this result is as follows: The public workflow is the superclass of the local views of all domains, and it is minimal in the sense that no different WF-net can be found, which is a superclass of the local views and at the same time a subclass of the public workflow. This is an interesting, yet not surprising result. It shows that the local views of the domains have exactly the public workflow in common.

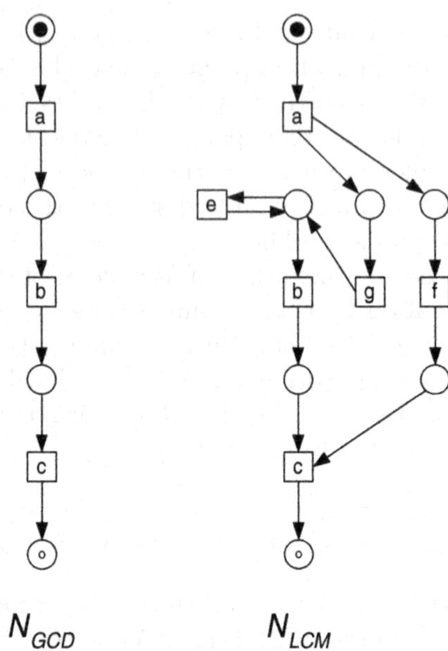

Fig. 10. The greatest common divisor N_{GCD} and least common multiple N_{LCM} of N_0, N_2, N_3, and N_4 shown in Fig. 6.

Analogously to the discussion of Result 4, the final result states a relationship between the local views of the domains and the overall workflow, as it is executed:

Result 5: The LCM of all local views is the overall workflow.

We interpret Result 5 as follows: The overall workflow is a specialization of all local views; conversely, the local views are superclasses of the overall workflow. The overall workflow is minimal in the sense that it is not possible to find a different WF-net which is also a subclass of all local views and which is a superclass of the overall workflow.

6 Related Work and Conclusions

Petri nets have been proposed for modeling workflow process definitions long before the term "workflow management" was coined and workflow management systems became readily available. Consider for example the work on Information Control Nets, a variant of the classical Petri nets, in the late seventies [13].

Only a few papers in the literature focus on the verification of workflow process definitions. In [16] some verification issues have been examined and the complexity of selected correctness issues has been identified, but no concrete verification procedures have been suggested. In [1] and [7] concrete verification procedures based on Petri nets have been proposed. This paper builds upon the work presented in [1] where the concept of a sound WF-net was introduced. The technique presented in [7] has been developed for checking the consistency of transactional workflows including temporal constraints. However, the technique is restricted to acyclic workflows and only gives necessary conditions (i.e., not sufficient conditions) for consistency. In [23] a reduction technique has been proposed. This reduction technique uses a correctness criterion which corresponds to soundness and the class of workflow processes considered are in essence acyclic free-choice Petri nets.

This paper differs from the above approaches because the focus is on interorganizational workflows. Only a few papers explicitly focus on the problem of verifying the correctness of interorganizational workflows [3,17]. In [3] the interaction between domains is specified in terms of message sequence charts and the actual overall workflow is checked with respect to these message sequence charts. A similar, but more formal and complete, approach is presented by Kindler, Martens, and Reisig in [17]. The authors give local criteria, using the concept of scenarios (similar to runs or basic message sequence charts), to guarantee the absence of certain anomalies at the global level. Both approaches [3,17] are not constructive, i.e., they only specify criteria for various notions of correctness but do not provide concrete design rules such as the transformation rules.

In the last decade several researchers explored notions of behavioral inheritance (also named subtyping or substitutability), see [10] for an overview. Researchers in the domain of formal process models (e.g., Petri-nets and process algebras) have tackled similar questions based on the explicit representation of a process by using various notions of (bi)simulation . The inheritance notion used in this paper is characterized by the fact that it is equipped with both *inheritance-preserving transformation rules* to *construct* subclasses [10] and *transfer rules* to *migrate* instances from a superclass to a subclass and vice versa [6]. These features are very relevant for a both constructive and robust approach towards interorganizational workflows.

We have developed a tool named *Woflan* (WOrkFLow ANalyzer [2,28]). Woflan is an analysis tool which can be used to verify the correctness of a workflow process definition. The analysis tool uses state-of-the-art techniques to find potential errors in the definition of a workflow process. Woflan is designed as a workflow management system independent analysis tool. In principle it can interface with many workflow management systems. At the moment, Woflan can interface with the workflow management systems COSA (Software Ley [25]), METEOR (LSDIS [24]), Staffware (Staffware [26]), and with the business process re-engineering tool Protos (Pallas Athena [22]). Woflan has not been designed to analyze interorganizational workflows. However, it can be used to verify the soundness property used throughout this paper, and it can also check whether a given workflow is a subclass of another workflow.

In the future we hope to extend the P2P approach in several directions. First of all, we want to address local dynamic changes. The transfer rules presented in [6] can be used to migrate workflow instances from a superclass to a subclass and vice versa. Therefore, it is possible to change the workflows in each of the domains on the fly, i.e., it is possible to automatically transfer each case to the latest version of the process. Other aspects of future work include the reconfiguration of interorganizational workflows (tasks move from one domain to another), the usage of alternative inheritance notions and the implementation of the concepts in prototypical workflow management systems, e.g., by using METEOR [5,24] or InterProcs [18].

References

1. W.M.P. van der Aalst. Verification of Workflow Nets. In P. Azéma and G. Balbo, editors, *Application and Theory of Petri Nets 1997*, volume 1248 of *Lecture Notes in Computer Science*, pages 407–426. Springer-Verlag, Berlin, 1997.
2. W.M.P. van der Aalst. The Application of Petri Nets to Workflow Management. *The Journal of Circuits, Systems and Computers*, 8(1):21–66, 1998.
3. W.M.P. van der Aalst. Interorganizational Workflows: An Approach based on Message Sequence Charts and Petri Nets. *Systems Analysis - Modelling - Simulation*, 34(3):335–367, 1999.
4. W.M.P. van der Aalst. Inheritance of Interorganizational Workflows: How to Agree to Disagree Without Loosing Control? BETA Working Paper Series, WP 46, Eindhoven University of Technology, Eindhoven, 2000.
5. W.M.P. van der Aalst and K. Anyanwu. Inheritance of Interorganizational Workflows to Enable Business-to-Business E-commerce. In *Proceedings of the Second International Conference on Telecommunications and Electronic Commerce (ICTEC'99)*, pages 141–157, Nashville, Tennessee, October 1999.
6. W.M.P. van der Aalst and T. Basten. Inheritance of Workflows: An approach to tackling problems related to change. *Theoretical Computer Science*, 2001 (to appear).
7. N.R. Adam, V. Atluri, and W. Huang. Modeling and Analysis of Workflows using Petri Nets. *Journal of Intelligent Information Systems*, 10(2):131–158, 1998.
8. Amazon.com, Inc. Amazon.com. http://www.amazon.com, 1999.
9. Barnes and Noble. bn.com. http://www.bn.com, 1999.
10. T. Basten. *In Terms of Nets: System Design with Petri Nets and Process Algebra.* PhD thesis, Eindhoven University of Technology, Eindhoven, The Netherlands, December 1998.
11. R. Benjamin and R. Wigand. Electronic markets and virtual value chains on the information superhighway. *Sloan Management Review*, pages 62–72, 1995.
12. R.W.H. Bons, R.M. Lee, and R.W. Wagenaar. Designing trustworthy interorganizational trade procedures for open electronic commerce. *International Journal of Electronic Commerce*, 2(3):61–83, 1998.
13. C.A. Ellis. Information Control Nets: A Mathematical Model of Office Information Flow. In *Proceedings of the Conference on Simulation, Measurement and Modeling of Computer Systems*, pages 225–240, Boulder, Colorado, 1979. ACM Press.
14. D. Georgakopoulos, M. Hornick, and A. Sheth. An Overview of Workflow Management: From Process Modeling to Workflow Automation Infrastructure. *Distributed and Parallel Databases*, 3:119–153, 1995.
15. R.J. van Glabbeek and W.P. Weijland. Branching Time and Abstraction in Bisimulation Semantics. *Journal of the ACM*, 43(3):555–600, 1996.
16. A.H.M. ter Hofstede, M.E. Orlowska, and J. Rajapakse. Verification Problems in Conceptual Workflow Specifications. *Data and Knowledge Engineering*, 24(3):239–256, 1998.

17. E. Kindler, A. Martens, and W. Reisig. Inter-Operability of Workflow Applications: Local Criteria for Global Soundness. In W.M.P. van der Aalst, J. Desel, and A. Oberweis, editors, *Business Process Management: Models, Techniques, and Empirical Studies*, volume 1806 of *Lecture Notes in Computer Science*, pages 235–253. Springer-Verlag, Berlin, 2000.
18. R.M. Lee. Distributed Electronic Trade Scenarios: Representation, Design, Prototyping. *International Journal of Electronic Commerce*, 3(2):105–120, 1999.
19. F. Leymann and D. Roller. *Production Workflow: Concepts and Techniques.* Prentice-Hall PTR, Upper Saddle River, New Jersey, USA, 1999.
20. T.W. Malone, R.I. Benjamin, and J. Yates. Electronic Markets and Electronic Hierarchies: Effects of Information Technology on Market Structure and Corporate Strategies . *Communications of the ACM*, 30(6):484–497, 1987.
21. M. Merz, B. Liberman, K. Muller-Jones, and W. Lamersdorf. Interorganisational Workflow Management with Mobile Agents in COSM. In *Proceedings of PAAM96 Conference on the Practical Application of Agents and Multiagent Systems*, 1996.
22. Pallas Athena. *Protos User Manual.* Pallas Athena BV, Plasmolen, The Netherlands, 1999.
23. W. Sadiq and M.E. Orlowska. Applying Graph Reduction Techniques for Identifying Structural Conflicts in Process Models. In *Proceedings of the 11th International Conference on Advanced Information Systems Engineering (CAiSE '99)*, volume 1626 of *Lecture Notes in Computer Science*, pages 195–209. Springer-Verlag, Berlin, 1999.
24. A. Sheth, K. Kochut, and J. Miller. Large Scale Distributed Information Systems (LSDIS) laboratory, METEOR project page. http://lsdis.cs.uga.edu/proj/meteor/meteor.html.
25. Software-Ley. *COSA User Manual.* Software-Ley GmbH, Pullheim, Germany, 1998.
26. Staffware. *Staffware 2000 / GWD User Manual.* Staffware plc, Berkshire, United Kingdom, 1999.
27. The White House. A Framework for Global Electronic Commerce. http://www.ecommerce.gov/framewrk.htm, 1997.
28. H.M.W. Verbeek, T. Basten, and W.M.P. van der Aalst. Diagnosing Workflow Processes using Woflan. Computing Science Report 99/02, Eindhoven University of Technology, Eindhoven, 1999.

Reflections on a Decade of Interorganizational Workflow Research

Wil M.P. van der Aalst and Mathias Weske

Abstract The Public-To-Private (P2P) approach presented at CAiSE in 2001 provides a correctness-by-construction approach to realize interorganizational workflows. A behavioral inheritance notion is used to ensure correctness: organizations can alter their private workflows as long as these remain subclasses of the agreed-upon public workflow. The CAiSE'01 paper illustrates the strong relationship between business process management and service-orientation. Since 2001, there is a trend from the investigation of individual process orchestrations to interacting processes, i.e., process choreographies. In this paper, we reflect on the original problem statement and discuss related work.

1 Introduction

In a Service Oriented Architecture (SOA) services are interacting by exchanging messages and by combining services more complex services are created. Choreography is concerned with the composition of such services seen from a global viewpoint focusing on the common and complementary observable behavior.

W.M.P. van der Aalst (✉)
Architecture of Information Systems, Eindhoven University of Technology, NL-5600 MB, Eindhoven, The Netherlands

Business Process Management Discipline, Queensland University of Technology, Brisbane, QLD, Australia

International Laboratory of Process-Aware Information Systems, National Research University Higher School of Economics, Moscow, Russia
e-mail: w.m.p.v.d.aalst@tue.nl

M. Weske
Hasso Plattner Institute at the University of Potsdam, Prof.-Dr.-Helmert-Strasse 2-3, 14482 Potsdam, Germany
e-mail: Mathias.Weske@hpi.uni-potsdam.de

J. Bubenko et al. (eds.), *Seminal Contributions to Information Systems Engineering*, DOI 10.1007/978-3-642-36926-1_24,

Choreography is particularly relevant in a setting where there is not a single coordinator. Orchestration is concerned with the composition of such services seen from the viewpoint of single service. Independent of the viewpoint (choreography or orchestration) there is a need to make sure that the services work together properly to ensure the correct execution of business processes. The resulting system should be free of deadlocks, livelocks, and other anomalies.

The *Public-To-Private* (P2P) approach presented at CAiSE'01 [7] addressed such correctness concerns using a notion of *inheritance* defined for Workflow nets (WF-nets) [3, 4, 9]. The P2P approach consists of three steps: (1) create a common understanding of the interorganizational workflow by specifying a shared public workflow, (2) partition the public workflow over the organizations involved, and (3) for each organization, create a private workflow which is a *subclass* of the respective part of the public workflow. Subsequently, projection inheritance ensures that the resulting interorganizational workflow realizes the behavior specified in the public workflow.

In the remainder, we reflect on a decade of interorganizational workflow research.[1] In Sect. 2 we study the trend in business process management research from process orchestrations to process choreographies, which started about 10 years ago. Two streams of research are highlighted. Formal investigations on how interacting business processes can be analyzed and results related to the modeling of process choreographies and the impact of this research stream on today's standards in business process modeling. In Sect. 3, we challenge the correctness-by-construction approach of [7] and advocate the more active use of event data at run-time.

2 From Process Orchestrations to Process Choreographies

Until about 2001, research in business process management or—at that time—workflow management, centered around individual processes that are enacted within a single organization, i.e., process orchestrations. Process orchestrations consist of activities that are executed in coordination in a technical and organizational environment and are performed to achieve a business goal [22]. Workflow research looked at formal aspects related to process behavior but also at conceptual aspects like the flexibility of processes. In all of these research areas, individual processes were in the center of attention.

After 2001, the scope of research broadened from individual processes performed by single organizations to interactions between several processes performed by different organizations. From today's perspective, this step was quite obvious, since process orchestrations tend to talk to process orchestrations performed by other organizations.

[1]Due to space restrictions, we can only list a tiny fraction of the work on process orchestrations and choreographies and do not suggest being complete in any way.

For instance, when ordering a new laptop computer, we ask several hardware suppliers for quotes. The receipt of such a quote by a supplier spawns a new process orchestration at the supplier's side. Depending on, e.g., the specification of the laptop, the dealer might decide to issue a quote. On receiving a sufficiently large set of quotes, we collect and compare them, and send an purchase order to one of them. In real-world scenarios, the interactions of processes can be much more complex than in this example. However, it shows that process orchestrations are actually interconnected with each other. Studying these types of connections is worthwhile and challenging, both from an academic and from a practical perspective.

2.1 Formal Investigations

A major stream of work relates to the formal investigation of interacting processes. At the beginning of the Millennium, Service Oriented Architectures (SOA) were "en vogue", so many academics started to formalize service notions. After abstracting reality to formal models, such as Petri nets, services and process orchestrations can no longer be distinguished from one another.

One of the earliest results were presented in [15, 16], where the interactions of services were defined by a specific type of Petri nets, called workflow modules, and correctness criteria for interacting services were proposed. Based on this work, [17] looked at the service selection problem, which so far had mostly been discussed from a either a software technology or from a semantics perspective. Operating guidelines for services have been introduced as a powerful behavioral specification of all services that can successfully cooperate with the specific service under consideration. At the same time papers such as [14] related concrete execution languages like the Business Process Execution Language for Web Services (BPEL [8]) to formalisms like Petri nets. The main results of this stream of research are surveyed and partly extended in [23], where controllability of services is in the center of attention by answering the question "Does my service have partners?". Based on this work, a question very similar to that of the original P2P paper was addressed in [6], where multiparty contracts are proposed. These define the overall intended process interactions and the roles of the parties involved. Based on a contract, each party implements its own process orchestration, guided by an accordance criterion.

There is a specific aspect that separates process orchestrations from choreographies; while the former have a static structure, the latter have a dynamic structure. During run-time, a participating organization might select a new partner, so that the structure of the system evolves over time. These aspects can be captured using the pi calculus which provides a mobility notion allowing for communication structures to be changed while the system runs. Decker et al. [10] formally specifies a set of service interaction patterns based on the pi calculus. With interaction soundness, a new criterion for interacting processes was defined in [20]. These results are surveyed and partly extended in [21].

2.2 Modeling and Impact

In addition to the investigation of formal aspects, considerable work on the modeling of process choreographies has been conducted. As of version Version 1 released in 2003, BPMN can be used to model interacting business processes (by drawing a pool for each participant and specifying the interactions between pools by message flow). There were two options to do so. Either the internal processes were hidden or only communication activities were drawn with their local control flow constraints. This modeling technique proves error prone, since the distribution of responsibilities among the participants could not be described properly, which could lead to undesired interaction behavior, such as deadlocks.

In [24, 25], a new modeling technique called Let's Dance was introduced, together with a set of desirable properties of interacting processes, such as local enforceability. The basic idea of this approach is avoiding to connect the communication interfaces of the participants, but to concentrate on the actual interactions and define control flow between them. The term *interaction-based choreography* modeling was coined for this modeling style. In a follow-up paper on interaction BPMN [11], the basic concepts of Let's Dance were maintained, while taking advantage of the BPMN notation. Behavioral consistency of interacting processes was addressed in [12]; the results of this stream of research was surveyed and partly extended in [13].

Based on these insights, BPMN provides dedicated diagram types for modeling process choreographies as of Version 2 [19]. For example, choreography diagrams are directly based on the concepts introduced in the research papers mentioned.

3 Correctness-by-Construction Versus Service Mining

The P2P approach provides a *correctness-by-construction* approach, i.e., parties do not need to know each others' private workflows. However, one needs to assume that the private workflow of another organization is indeed a subclass of the respective part of the public workflow. This assumption seems to be too strong:

- Organizations may implement a non-compliant private workflow (i.e., a workflow that is not a subclass under projection inheritance).
- Private workflows may change over time without an explicit notification and possibly violating earlier agreements.
- There are private workflows that are not a subclass under projection inheritance, but that can never lead to problems. For example, two parallel sending transitions can be made sequential without causing any problems. However, the resulting workflow is not a subclass.

As suggested in [2, 5, 18], it may be better to observe the messages exchanged and use conformance checking instead. Consider for example the public view shown in Fig. 1. Sending payments *sp* before receiving goods *rg* (i.e., effectively removing

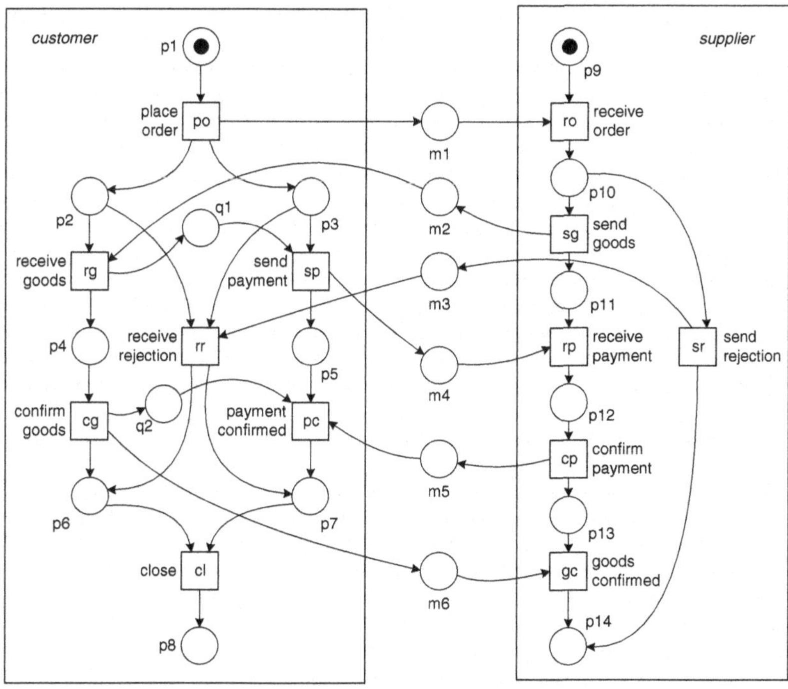

Fig. 1 An interorganizational workflow modeling two interacting processes. Removing place $q1$ may result in deadlock, cf. trace $\langle po, ro, sr, sp \rangle$. Removing place $q2$ changes behavior (payment confirmation may occur before confirming goods) but this cannot jeopardize correctness

place $q1$) may cause deadlocks. This can be observed when message $m4$ precedes message $m2$. Receiving a payment conformation pc before confirming goods cg (i.e., effectively removing place $q2$) is harmless. All suppliers that can cooperate well with the *customer* workflow shown in Fig. 1, can also cooperate with the alternative workflow without place $q2$ (which is not a subclass). This illustrates that the P2P approach may be too strict. Moreover, one needs to monitor the message exchanges to detect violations, because, often, private workflows of other parties cannot be controlled. Therefore, we suggest putting more effort in *service mining* [2], i.e., the application of process mining techniques [1] as a tool for discovering, checking, and improving interorganizational workflows.

References

1. W.M.P. van der Aalst. *Process Mining: Discovery, Conformance and Enhancement of Business Processes*. Springer-Verlag, 2011.
2. W.M.P. van der Aalst. Service Mining: Using Process Mining to Discover, Check, and Improve Service Behavior. *IEEE Transactions on Services Computing*, 2013.

3. W.M.P. van der Aalst and T. Basten. Life-cycle Inheritance: A Petri-net-based Approach. In P. Azéma and G. Balbo, editors, *Application and Theory of Petri Nets 1997*, volume 1248 of *Lecture Notes in Computer Science*, pages 62–81. Springer-Verlag, 1997.
4. W.M.P. van der Aalst and T. Basten. Inheritance of Workflows: An Approach to Tackling Problems Related to Change. *Theoretical Computer Science*, 270(1–2):125–203, 2002.
5. W.M.P. van der Aalst, M. Dumas, C. Ouyang, A. Rozinat, and H.M.W. Verbeek. Conformance Checking of Service Behavior. *ACM Transactions on Internet Technology*, 8(3):29–59, 2008.
6. W.M.P. van der Aalst, N. Lohmann, P. Massuthe, C. Stahl, and K. Wolf. Multiparty Contracts: Agreeing and Implementing Interorganizational Processes. *The Computer Journal*, 53(1):90–106, 2010.
7. W.M.P. van der Aalst and M. Weske. The P2P approach to Interorganizational Workflows. In *International Conference on Advanced Information Systems Engineering (CAiSE'01)*, volume 2068 of *Lecture Notes in Computer Science*, pages 140–156. Springer-Verlag, 2001.
8. A. Alves et al. Web Services Business Process Execution Language Version 2.0 (OASIS Standard). WS-BPEL TC OASIS, http://docs.oasis-open.org/wsbpel/2.0/wsbpel-v2.0.html, 2007.
9. T. Basten and W.M.P. van der Aalst. Inheritance of Behavior. *Journal of Logic and Algebraic Programming*, 47(2):47–145, 2001.
10. G. Decker, F. Puhlmann, and M. Weske. Formalizing Service Interactions. In *International Conference on Business Process Management (BPM 2006)*, volume 4102 of *Lecture Notes in Computer Science*, pages 414–419. Springer-Verlag, 2006.
11. G. Decker and A. Barros. Interaction Modeling Using BPMN. In Arthur H. M. ter Hofstede, Boualem Benatallah, and Hye-Young Paik, editors, *Business Process Management Workshops*, volume 4928 of *Lecture Notes in Computer Science*, pages 208–219. Springer, 2007.
12. G. Decker and M. Weske. Behavioral Consistency for B2B Process Integration. In John Krogstie, Andreas L. Opdahl, and Guttorm Sindre, editors, *CAiSE*, volume 4495 of *Lecture Notes in Computer Science*, pages 81–95. Springer, 2007.
13. G. Decker and M. Weske. Interaction-centric Modeling of Process Choreographies. *Information Systems*, 36(2):292–312, 2011.
14. N. Lohmann, P. Massuthe, C. Stahl, and D. Weinberg. Analyzing Interacting BPEL Processes. In *International Conference on Business Process Management (BPM 2006)*, volume 4102 of *Lecture Notes in Computer Science*, pages 17–32. Springer-Verlag, 2006.
15. A. Martens. On Compatibility of Web Services. In *10th Workshop on Algorithms and Tools for Petri Nets (AWPN 2003), Eichstätt, Germany*, 2003.
16. A. Martens. On Usability of Web Services. In *Fourth International Conference on Web Information Systems Engineering Workshops*, IEEE, 2003.
17. P. Massuthe, W. Reisig, and K. Schmidt. An Operating Guideline Approach to the SOA. In *South-East European Workshop on Formal Methods (SEEFM'05)*, Ohrid, 2005.
18. R. Müller, W.M.P. van der Aalst, and C. Stahl. Conformance Checking of Services Using the Best Matching Private View. In N. Lohmann and M. ter Beek, editors, *WS-FM 2012*, Lecture Notes in Computer Science. Springer-Verlag, 2012.
19. Object Management Group. *Business Process Model and Notation (BPMN) Version 2.0*, formal/2011-01-03 edition, 2011.
20. F. Puhlmann and M. Weske. Interaction Soundness for Service Orchestrations. In *Service-Oriented Computing (ICSOC 2006)*, volume 4294 of *Lecture Notes in Computer Science*, pages 302–313. Springer-Verlag, 2006.
21. F. Puhlmann and M. Weske. A Look Around the Corner: The Pi-Calculus. In *Transactions on Petri Nets and Other Models of Concurrency II*, pages 64–78. Springer-Verlag, 2009.
22. M. Weske. *Business Process Management: Concepts, Languages, Architectures*. Springer-Verlag, second edition, 2012.
23. K. Wolf. Does my Service Have Partners? In *Transactions on Petri Nets and Other Models of Concurrency II*, pages 152–171. Springer-Verlag, 2009.

24. J.M. Zaha, A. Barros, M. Dumas, and A.H.M. ter Hofstede. Let's Dance: A Language for Service Behavior Modeling. In *International Conference on Cooperative Information Systems*, volume 4275 of *Lecture Notes in Computer Science*, pages 145–162. Springer-Verlag, 2006.
25. J.M. Zaha, M. Dumas, A. ter Hofstede, A. Barros, and G. Decker. Service Interaction Modeling: Bridging Global and Local Views. In *International Enterprise Distributed Object Computing Conference (EDOC 2006)*, pages 45–55. IEEE Computer Society, 2006.

Database Schema Matching Using Machine Learning with Feature Selection

Jacob Berlin and Amihai Motro

Information and Software Engineering Department
George Mason University, Fairfax, VA 22030
{jberlin,ami}@gmu.edu

Abstract. Schema matching, the problem of finding mappings between the attributes of two semantically related database schemas, is an important aspect of many database applications such as schema integration, data warehousing, and electronic commerce. Unfortunately, schema matching remains largely a manual, labor-intensive process. Furthermore, the effort required is typically linear in the number of schemas to be matched; the next pair of schemas to match is not any easier than the previous pair. In this paper we describe a system, called Automatch, that uses machine learning techniques to automate schema matching. Based primarily on Bayesian learning, the system acquires probabilistic knowledge from examples that have been provided by domain experts. This knowledge is stored in a knowledge base called the *attribute dictionary*. When presented with a pair of new schemas that need to be matched (and their corresponding database instances), Automatch uses the attribute dictionary to find an optimal matching. We also report initial results from the Automatch project.

1 Introduction

Schema matching is the problem of finding mappings between the attributes of two semantically related database schemas. The schema matching problem is an important, current issue for many database applications such as schema integration, data warehousing, and electronic commerce [12,15]. Unfortunately, schema matching remains largely a manual, labor-intensive process. Furthermore, the effort required is typically linear in the number of schemas to be matched; the next pair of schemas to match is not any easier than the previous pair. Thus, database applications that require schema matching are limited to environments in which the set of member information sources is small and stable. These applications would scale-up to much larger communities of member sources if the schema matching "bottleneck" was broken by automating the matching process.

In this paper we discuss such a system, called Automatch, for automating the schema matching process. Based primarily on Bayesian learning, the system acquires probabilistic knowledge from examples of schemas that have been "mapped" by domain experts into a knowledge base of database attributes called the *attribute dictionary*. Roughly speaking, this dictionary characterizes different

A. Banks Pidduck et al. (Eds.): CAISE 2002, LNCS 2348, pp. 452–466, 2002.

attributes by means of their *possible values* and the *probability estimates* of these values. Furthermore, the dictionary may be extended to contain any attribute metadata that has a probabilistic interpretation (e.g. attribute names or string patterns).

When presented with a pair of "client" schemas that need to be matched (and their corresponding database instances), Automatch matches them "through" its dictionary. Using probabilistic methods, an attempt is made to match every attribute of one client schema with every attribute of the other client schema, resulting in individual "scores." An optimization process based on a Minimum Cost Maximum Flow network algorithm finds the overall optimal matching between the two client schemas, with respect to the sum of the individual attribute matching scores.

To overcome the problem of very large dictionaries caused by very large attribute domains, Automatch employs statistical *feature selection* techniques to learn an efficient representation of the examples. That is, each attribute is represented with a minimal set of most informative values. Thus the attribute dictionary is made human understandable through aggressive reduction in the number of values. Although the example schemas may contain many thousands of values, we are able to focus learning on a very small subset, consisting of as few as 10% of the initial values.

The results of our initial experimentation with Automatch are encouraging as they show performance that exceeds 70% (measured as the harmonic mean of the soundness and the completeness of the matching process). Although the attribute dictionary was built for Automatch, we conjecture that it could be employed as a knowledge asset in other schema matching systems.

The remainder of this paper is organized as follows. Section 3 describes the basic methodology of Automatch; in particular, the probabilistic information in the acquired knowledge base and how it is used to infer optimal matchings between "client" schemas. Section 4 describes alternative methods for reducing the size of the knowledge base through feature selection. Section 5 explains the experiment and its conclusions. Section 6 summarizes the contributions and suggests future research directions. We begin with a brief discussion of other published approaches and how they are related to Automatch.

2 Related Work

A thorough discussion of schema matching techniques and implementations can be found in [6,11,15]. Here we mention two such approaches and compare them to Automatch. Automated schema matching can be classified as rule based and learner based [6].

The Artemis system [5] is a rule-based approach for schema integration. This system determines the *affinity* of attributes from two schemas in a pair-wise fashion. Affinity is based on comparisons of attribute names, structure, and domain types and is scored on a [0,1] interval. The process relies on thesauri to determine semantic relationships. The system uses hierarchical clustering based on affinity values to group together related attributes. Finally, a set of unification rules are employed to interactively guide a user through the construction of an integrated schema. In contrast with Automatch, Artemis considers schema information; Automatch considers instance information. Furthermore, knowledge in Artemis is "pre-coded" in the thesaurus and unification rules; knowledge in Automatch is learned from examples.

SemInt [9,10] is a learner-based system that uses neural networks to identify similar attributes from different schemas. This system uses a combination of schema and instance information. Schema information includes such information as data types, field length, and constraint information. Instance information includes such information as value distributions, character ratios, numeric mean and variance.

For each type of information the system exploits, it determines a numerical value on a $[0, 1]$ interval. A tuple of these numerical values for one attribute is the *signature* of the attribute. The system uses these signatures to cluster similar attributes within the same schema. The system then uses the signatures of the cluster centers to train a neural network to output an attribute category based on the input signatures. Given a new schema, the system determines the signature of each schema attribute using the same type of schema and instance information used for training. These signatures are then applied to the neural network to determine the category of the respective attributes. In contrast with Automatch, SemInt uses a fixed set of features for learning; Automatch combines feature selection with learning to find an optimal set of features for a given problem domain. Furthermore, SemInt discovers matches to attribute clusters; Automatch discovers matches to individual attributes.

3 Methodology

This section describes the basic methodology of Automatch, providing details of its data structures and algorithms. It begins with an intuitive description of the approach and a formal description of the problem.

3.1 The Overall Approach

Automatch is based on a knowledge base about schema attributes which is constructed from examples. When presented with two new "client" schemas that need to be matched (and their corresponding database instances), Automatch checks every client attribute against its attribute dictionary, obtaining individual "matching scores" for each pair of client attribute and dictionary attribute.

These client-dictionary attribute scores are combined to generate client-client attribute scores. To illustrate, assume B is an attribute of one client scheme, C is an attribute of the other client scheme, and A is an attribute of the dictionary, and assume that the matching of B to A is scored w_1 and the matching of C to A is scored w_2; then the matching $B \leftrightarrow C$ receives the score $w_1 + w_2$.[1]

[1] We combine the individual scores by their sum, but other combinations are also possible; for example, their product.

In turn, these individual client-client attribute scores are combined to generate overall schema-schema matching scores. To illustrate, assume schemas $R_1 = \{B_1, B_2\}$ and $R_2 = \{C_1, C_2\}$ and assume the client-client attribute scores: $w_1 : B_1 \leftrightarrow C_1$, $w_2 : B_1 \leftrightarrow C_2$, $w_3 : B_2 \leftrightarrow C_1$, and $w_4 : B_2 \leftrightarrow C_2$. The schema matching $\{B_1 \leftrightarrow C_2, B_2 \leftrightarrow C_1\}$ is then scored $w_2 + w_3$. Other schema matchings are scored similarly.

In a subsequent optimization process, Automatch finds the schema matching with the highest schema-schema score.

3.2 Formalization of the Problem

Our formalization is based on the relational model. However, we are confident that the methods can be extended to other models, such as the object-oriented or the semi-structured models. A *database schema* is simply a finite set of *attributes* $\{A_1, \ldots, A_n\}$. Given two database schemas $R_1 = \{B_1, \ldots, B_p\}$ and $R_2 = \{C_1, \ldots, C_q\}$, a *matching* is a mapping between a subset of R_1 and a subset of R_2.

We assume a knowledge base about database attributes, called the *attribute dictionary* and denoted D. In this knowledge base, each attribute is characterized by a select set of possible values and their probability estimates.

In addition, we assume a *scoring function* f that, given (1) the attribute dictionary D, (2) a pair of database schemas R_1 and R_2, (3) a pair of corresponding database instances r_1 and r_2, and (4) a matching between R_1 and R_2, issues a value (a real number), that indicates the "goodness" of the matching.

The problem is then to find the *best* matching for two given schemas R_1 and R_2. This abstract description leaves two major issues to be discussed in detail:

1. The nature of the attribute dictionary D and the scoring function f.
2. The optimization of f (i.e., finding the best schema matching).

These two issues are discussed in the next two subsections.

3.3 The Attribute Dictionary and the Scoring Function

The attribute dictionary D consists of a finite set of schema *attributes* $\{A_1, \ldots, A_r\}$. Each attribute in the attribute dictionary is characterized by a set of *possible values* and their *probability estimates.* The attribute dictionary serves as a knowledge base that accumulates information about attributes. All attempts to match attributes of client schemas refer to this knowledge base. We use Bayesian learning to populate the attribute dictionary with example values provided by domain experts.

Recall from the intuitive description in Section 3.1 that the first task is to determine client-dictionary attribute scores.

Let X be a client attribute, let A denote a dictionary attribute, and let V denote a set of values that are observed in X (these values are derived from the instance of the client schema to which X belongs).

Let $P(A)$ be the *prior* probability that X maps to A (before observing any values of X), let $P(V)$ represent the unconditional probability of observing values V in X, and let $P(V|A)$ represent the conditional probability of observing the values V, given that X maps to A. Bayes Theorem states that

$$P(A|V) = \frac{P(V|A) \cdot P(A)}{P(V)} . \tag{1}$$

$P(A|V)$ is referred to as the *posterior* probability that X maps to A, because it reflects the probability that a mapping of X to A holds *after* the values V have been observed. This posterior probability serves as the score of the client attribute X and the dictionary attribute A.

Letting V be a sequence of values $(v_1, \ldots, v_n)$, and assuming *conditional independence* of values given the mapping, the client-dictionary attribute score is

$$M(X, A) = \frac{P(A)}{P(V)} \cdot \prod_{k=1}^{n} P(v_k|A) . \tag{2}$$

Although the attribute values may not be conditionally independent, such an assumption has been shown to be an acceptable approach, aimed at reducing the number of probabilities to a tractable amount while not sacrificing optimality [7,8,13].

To build the attribute dictionary for each attribute A we must learn and store the probability estimates $P(A)$, $P(\neg A)$, $P(v|A)$, and $P(v|\neg A)$ for all dictionary attributes A and values v. Note that we do not need to learn $P(V)$ because this term is determined by the requirement that $M(X, A) + M(X, \neg A) = 1$.

$P(A)$, the probability that a client attribute X maps to A, is estimated by the proportion of examples provided by the domain expert that have been mapped to A. $P(v|A)$, the probability that attribute value v occurs given that a mapping to A holds, is estimated by counting the occurrences of v in the set of examples provided by the domain expert. The remaining terms are learned in a similar fashion. For numeric data values, we assume a normal distribution and use the normal probability density function to estimate the conditional probabilities. A thorough discussion of the algorithms for estimating these terms is reported in [4]. A critical selection process that reduces the number of values v that are maintained for each attribute A is discussed in Section 4.

3.4 Optimal Schema Matching

Assume now two given schemas R_1 and R_2 with their corresponding instances r_1 and r_2, and let D denote the attribute dictionary.

The scores $M(X, A)$ from Equation 2 are calculated for each attribute X in the given schema and for each attribute A of the dictionary. A threshold is then adopted, and scores that are below this threshold are interpreted as evidence that X should not be mapped to A. These results may be represented in a weighted tripartite graph in which nodes correspond to attributes, edges correspond to matches, and edge weights correspond to the posterior probabilities.

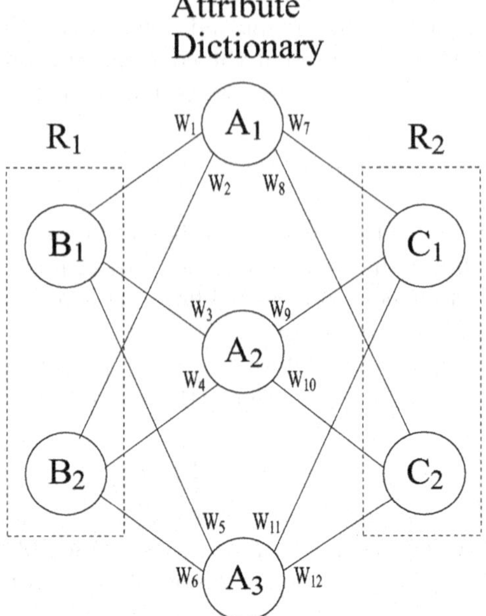

Fig. 1. Weighted tripartite graph for representing individual attribute-attribute scores

Figure 1 shows such a graph for a simple case in which $R_1 = \{B_1, B_2\}$, $R_2 = \{C_1, C_2\}$, and $D = \{A_1, A_2, A_3\}$. This example shows a *full* tripartite graph (every node in the left or right partitions is connected to every node in the center partition), but the use of a threshold implies that in general the graph need not be full.

Recall from the intuitive description in Section 3.1, that the client-dictionary attribute scores w_i are combined to generate client-client attribute scores. Note, however, that every two client attributes may be matched through every dictionary attribute. In the example, B_1 and C_1 may be matched through A_1 (with score $w_1 + w_7$), through A_2 (with score $w_3 + w_9$) and through A_3 (with score $w_5 + w_{11}$). Note that associating a dictionary attribute with every attribute match is like providing a *common type* for the matching attribute pair.

In turn, client-client attribute scores are used in generating overall schema-schema scores. In the example, the schema matching comprising of $B_1 \overset{A_1}{\leftrightarrow} C_2$ and $B_2 \overset{A_3}{\leftrightarrow} C_1$ receives the score $w_1 + w_8 + w_6 + w_{11}$. Obviously, the number of possible matchings between R_1 and R_2 is too high for a simple process that enumerates all the matchings and scores each.

One obvious approach for matching R_1 and R_2 is to choose for each client attribute the most probable dictionary attribute. For instance, in the example, the highest of w_1, w_3 and w_5 will determine whether B_1 is mapped to A_1, A_2 or A_3. Then a mapping can be established between those schema attributes that share a node in the attribute dictionary. In the example, assume that the highest of w_1, w_3 and w_5 is w_3; (i.e., B_1 is best mapped to A_2), and assume that the highest of w_8, w_{10} and w_{12} is w_{10} (i.e., C_2 is best mapped to A_2); the conclusion would then be that B_1 is best matched with C_2. The problem with such an approach is that it easily leads to ambiguity. In the example, if the optimal mappings correspond to the edges with weights w_3, w_4, w_9 and w_{10}, we have established a match between the schemas, but the attribute mapping is ambiguous. Furthermore, the approach easily leads to no match; e.g., if the optimal mappings correspond to the edges with weights w_1, w_6, w_9, and w_{10}.

To avoid these pitfalls, we impose an additional constraint on the matching of R_1 and R_2. Specifically, we limit our search to schema mappings in which the paths between attributes in R_1 and R_2 are free of intersections. That is, two attributes of a client scheme never map to the same dictionary attribute. The resulting problem can then be solved using efficient flow network techniques. Towards this, we must first extend the tripartite graph in several ways.

First, we add two nodes to the graph: a source node S on the left, which is then connected to all the R_1 nodes, and a target node T on the right, which is then connected to all the R_2 nodes. Next, we split each attribute dictionary node A into two nodes, A^{in} and A^{out}. Each A_i^{in} is connected to its corresponding A_i^{out} node. Next, we reconnect the edges from R_1 and R_2 to the appropriate A_{in} or A_{out} node. Finally, each edge is given direction, capacity, and cost. All edges are directed away from the source node S and towards the target node T. The capacity for each edge is 1 (thus, the flow through an edge will be either 0 or 1). The cost of each of the new edges added to the graph is 0. The cost of each of the old edges is the negation of the edge weight. Figure 2 shows the new graph for the example of Figure 1. Edge capacities and costs were omitted for clarity.

The reason for the negation of the weights is that we will be using an algorithm that searches for a minimum when we actually wish to find the maximum (finding a maximum is equivalent to finding the minimum of the negation). With these modifications, we can now find a matching between the schemas R_1 and R_2 that conforms to our constraints by using a Minimum Cost Maximum Flow network algorithm [1]. In the current implementation of Automatch, we use the LEDA software package for this purpose [2].

Specifically for Figure 2, since the source has two outgoing edges of capacity 1 and the target has two incoming edges of capacity 1 (i.e., two attributes are matched on each side), the maximum flow is 2. Thus, we seek to find the edges in the graph that have the minimum cost while supporting a maximum flow of 2. The edges in this set correspond to the optimal mapping of attributes of R_1 to R_2.

Note that when the client schemas do not have the same number of attributes, some of the attributes of the larger schema will be matchless. Moreover, since the tripartite is not necessarily full, the optimal matching may leave attributes

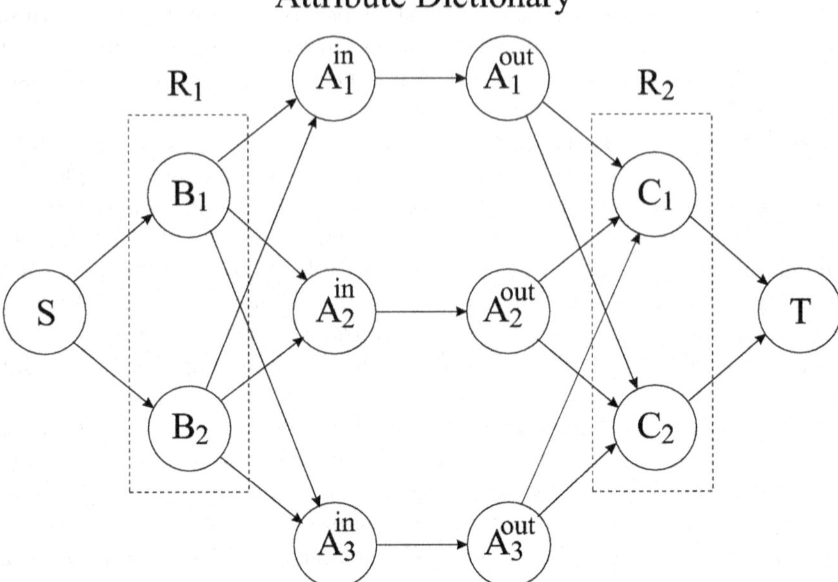

Fig. 2. Minimum-Cost-Maximum-Flow graph for finding optimal schema matching

in the *smaller* schema matchless as well. This is not an undesirable consequence, as it simply indicates that the client schemas include attributes that are unique to their schemas.

4 Optimal Selection of Dictionary Values

Recall that the attribute dictionary of Automatch represents each attribute with a set of possible values and their probability estimates. For schema attributes that contain text, the number of needed probabilities is proportional to the number of unique values of this attribute. An attribute such as *CustomerName* could assume thousands of values, thus imposing considerable space and processing requirements. Furthermore, not all of these probabilities are equally informative. Indeed, many of them are either uninformative (irrelevant) or misleading (noise).

A critical consideration in our methods is to reduce the dictionary representation of attributes while retaining the most informative values. In machine learning terminology these values are called *features* and the reduction process is called *feature selection*. To reduce the size of the Automatch dictionary, we have tested and compared three statistical feature selection strategies: Mutual Information, Information Gain, and Likelihood Ratio. The former two strategies are commonly used for feature selection; to our knowledge the latter strategy has not been used for this purpose.

We will discuss each feature selection strategy in turn. Common to all these approaches is that each feature is assigned a "score." These feature scores can be calculated from the probability estimates in the attribute dictionary. In all of these approaches, higher scores are better. Once these scores have been calculated for a given approach, a percentage of the highest scoring features is retained with ties broken arbitrarily.

Finally, we must normalize the probabilities of the remaining features to sum to unity. Thus, statistical feature selection imposes very little overhead in our approach. In contrast, other machine learning approaches (e.g. neural networks, rule learners, etc.) must execute their respective learning algorithms after feature selection is completed.

4.1 Mutual Information

Mutual information has been used previously as a feature selection strategy in information retrieval tasks such as [16]. The mutual information of a value v and an attribute A is defined as

$$MI(v, A) = \log \frac{P(v \wedge A)}{P(v) \cdot P(A)} . \tag{3}$$

When v and A are independent, the mutual information of v and A is zero. Intuitively, $P(v)$ is a measure of the event that a value v occurs in the client attribute X, and $P(A)$ is a measure of the event the client attribute X is mapped to the dictionary attribute A. Hence, $MI(v, A)$ is a measure of the *co-occurrence* of these two events. For example, if the events are independent (their co-occurrence is unbiased), then the mutual information is 0.

For the purpose of characterizing dictionary attributes, we wish to retain the values that have the greatest score regardless of whether they favor A or $\neg A$. Therefore, we score values in the MI approach using this formula:

$$MI_{max}(v, A) = \max \left\{ \log \frac{P(v \wedge A)}{P(v) \cdot P(A)} , \log \frac{P(v \wedge \neg A)}{P(v) \cdot P(\neg A)} \right\} . \tag{4}$$

The values v with the highest $MI_{max}(v, A)$ are chosen as the characterization of attribute A. The actual number of values chosen is discussed in Section 5.2.

4.2 Information Gain

Information gain is often used in machine learning to determine the value of a particular feature [13]. Given a client attribute X and a dictionary attribute A, the issue is whether X maps to A or not. This issue may be formatted as a binary *message*: 1 if yes, 0 if no.

Denote $P(A)$ the probability that X maps to A. Assume first that our only knowledge is the proportion of attributes that are mapped to A (how "popular" A is as a target of mappings). The entropy (information content) of the message is then

$$H = -(P(A) \cdot \log P(A) + P(\neg A) \cdot \log P(\neg A)) . \tag{5}$$

Assume now that we know a new fact: $v \in X$. The new entropy (information content) of the message is

$$H_1 = -(P(A \mid v) \cdot \log P(A \mid v) + P(\neg A \mid v) \cdot \log P(\neg A \mid v)) . \tag{6}$$

Assume now that we know an alternative fact: $v \notin X$. The new entropy (information content) of the message is

$$H_2 = -(P(A \mid \neg v) \cdot \log P(A \mid \neg v) + P(\neg A \mid \neg v) \cdot \log P(\neg A \mid \neg v)) . \tag{7}$$

H_1 and H_2 may be combined using $P(v)$, the probability that v is in X. Then the entropy (information content) of the message is

$$H' = P(v) \cdot H_1 + p(\neg v) \cdot H_2 . \tag{8}$$

The *information gained* by knowing the presence or absence of v is

$$IG(v, A) = H - H' . \tag{9}$$

4.3 Likelihood Ratio

The likelihood ratio for a value v and attribute A, defined as $P(v|A)/P(v|\neg A)$, measures the *retrospective* support given to A by the occurrence of v [14]. The likelihood ratio produces scores on the interval $(0, \infty)$. It has a value of 1 if the feature provides no support. Likelihood ratios greater than 1 indicate that the feature supports A; likelihood ratios less than 1 indicate that the feature supports $\neg A$.

For the task at hand, we wish to retain the features that provide the most support regardless of whether they favor A or $\neg A$. The features that favor A are on the interval $(1, \infty)$, with higher values indicating stronger support, whereas the features that favor $\neg A$ are on the interval $(0, 1)$, with lower values indicating stronger support. Consequently, it is difficult to use the likelihood ratio as defined, because higher scores are not necessarily better. For this reason, we use an adjustment that inverts the likelihood ratios that support $\neg A$, placing them on the same scale as likelihood ratios that support A, and then choose the stronger of the supports:

$$LR(v, A) = \max \left\{ \frac{P(v|A)}{P(v|\neg A)}, \frac{P(v|\neg A)}{P(v|A)} \right\} . \tag{10}$$

This strategy produces scores on the interval $(1, \infty)$ and higher scores are always better.

5 Experimentation

5.1 Setting Up the Experiment

To experiment with the methods discussed in this paper, we built an attribute dictionary for computer retail information with the following attributes: *DesktopManufacturer, MonitorManufacturer, PrinterManufacturer, DesktopModel, MonitorModel, PrinterModel, DesktopCost, PeripheralCost, Inventory.*

Data for this experiment was taken from the web sites of 15 different computer retailers (e.g. Gateway, Outpost, etc). A total of 22 relations were extracted. The data was collected off-line from HTML web pages and imported into relational database tables accessible through the ODBC protocol.

To experiment with this data, we used a procedure from data mining called *stratified cross-validation* which we briefly describe (see [17] for a complete description). Each of the 22 schemas was manually mapped into our attribute dictionary. We then partitioned these 22 schemas into three *folds* of approximately equal size. Using two folds for learning and one fold for testing, we repeated the experiment for the three possible combinations of folds. For the test fold, we chose two schemas at a time (for all possible combinations) and used Automatch to match the schemas. We used the manually constructed mappings to judge the mappings which Automatch concluded.

5.2 Measuring Performance

To measure performance, each schema-matching result was interpreted as set of mapping decisions for pairs of schema attributes $\langle R_1(B_i), R_2(C_j)\rangle$, where i ranges over all the attributes of R_1 and j ranges over all the attributes of R_2. Each of these attribute mapping decisions falls into one of four sets, A, B, C, and D, where

$A =$ True Positives (decision to map $R_1(B_i)$ to $R_2(C_j)$ is correct).
$B =$ False Negatives (decision to not map $R_1(B_i)$ to $R_2(C_j)$ is incorrect).
$C =$ False Positives (decision to map $R_1(B_i)$ to $R_2(C_j)$ is incorrect).
$D =$ True Negatives (decision to not map $R_1(B_i)$ to $R_2(C_j)$ is correct).

The ratio $|A|/(|A| + |C|)$ is the proportion of true positives among the cases thought to be positive; i.e., it measures the accuracy of Automatch when it decides *True*. The ratio $|A|/(|A| + |B|)$ is the proportion of positives detected by Automatch among the complete set of positives; i.e., it measures the ability to detect positives. Specifically to our application, the former ratio measures the *soundness* of the discovery process, and the latter ratio measures its *completeness*. These two ratios are known from the field of information retrieval as *precision* and *recall*, but we shall refer to them here as the soundness and completeness of the schema matching process.

To simplify the comparison of the three feature selection approaches, we combined soundness and completeness into a single performance measure using their *harmonic mean*. The harmonic mean of precision and recall is often used in information retrieval whenever a single performance measure is preferred [3]. The harmonic mean for our mapping problem is calculated as

$$F(x) = 2 \cdot \frac{S(x) \cdot C(x)}{S(x) + C(x)} \tag{11}$$

where $S(x)$ and $C(x)$ are the soundness and completeness of the discovery process at a given percent reduction x in the feature space. The harmonic mean assumes high values only when both soundness and completeness are high. Thus, maximizing the harmonic mean can be thought of as the best compromise between soundness and completeness.

To measure the performance of each of the feature selection strategies that were discussed in Section 4, we determine the harmonic mean of soundness and completeness for each strategy as we increase the percentage of the feature space that is discarded. We reduce the feature space in increments of 5 percent until 95 percent of the feature space has been discarded.

5.3 Interpreting the Results

First we measured the performance of Automatch without any attempt at optimizing the dictionary through feature selection; that is, we use the Bayesian approach to score matches (Section 3.3) and the flow graph approach to optimize matches (Section 3.4). Using cross validation, we achieved a performance of 66% (measured as the harmonic mean of soundness and completeness). In a separate experiment, we used random guessing to match the same schemas and achieved a performance of 10%.

Next, we compared the three feature selection strategies of Section 4 and assessed their impact on schema matching. Figure 3 shows the performance for schema matching for each of the feature selection strategies. The x-axis is the percentage of low-scoring features that have been discarded, and the y-axis is the performance, measured as the harmonic mean of soundness and completeness. The leftmost point in the graph corresponds to our first experiment with no feature selection.

Initially, with 5% feature reduction, all the feature selection strategies improve performance by at least 6%. The strategies then perform comparably up to 60% reduction. At levels of reduction over 80%, IG and LR continue to produce improved matching performance (relative to no feature selection) while MI falls below performance with no feature selection.

All three feature selection strategies improve performance when compared to the initial performance with no feature selection (though the level to which they sustain this improvement varies). This observation indicates that *all* of these approaches are acceptable for reducing the feature space. Furthermore, if we are seeking the most ambitious reduction in the feature space, LR is preferable to IG which is preferable to MI.

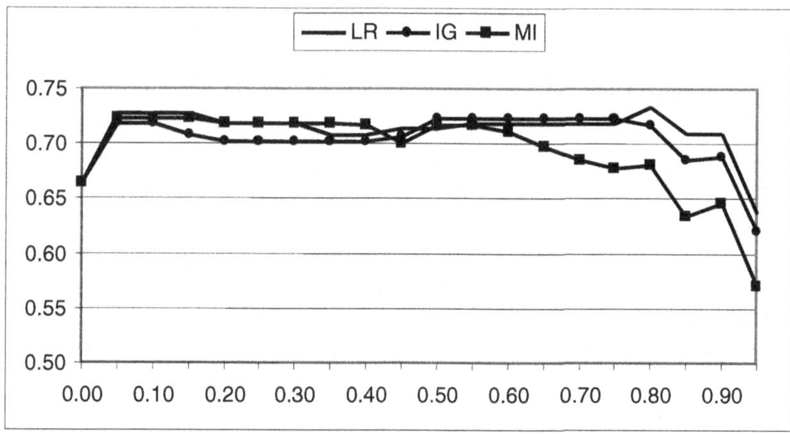

Fig. 3. Harmonic mean of soundness and completeness (y-axis) as the feature set is reduced in increments of 5 percent (x-axis)

6 Conclusion

In this paper we described an automated solution for the well-known problem of database schema matching. Our approach uses Bayesian machine learning, statistical feature selection, and the Minimum Cost Maximum Flow network algorithm to find an optimal matching of attributes between two semantically related schemas.

Our significant findings and contributions in this paper were:

- The Automatch system is a new and viable approach to eliminate the schema-matching bottleneck present in modern database applications. Our results are encouraging as they show performance that exceeds 70% (measured as the harmonic mean of the soundness and the completeness of the attribute matching process).
- Statistical feature selection can be used to improve the performance of Automatch. The improvement is in three areas: (1) in the *storage requirements* for the auxiliary knowledge base, (2) in the *computational costs* of the matching algorithm, and (3) in the *quality* (soundness and completeness) of the results. We estimate that statistical feature selection can be used to improve the performance of other automated schema-matching approaches (such as [6,10]) that must deal with high-dimensional feature spaces.
- Statistical feature selection incurs little overhead in Automatch since we are using a probabilistic learning approach. Learning after feature selection consists simply of normalizing the probabilities of the remaining features. In contrast, other machine learning approaches (e.g. neural networks, rule learners, etc.) must execute their respective learning algorithms after feature selection is completed.

While the performance of 70% in these experiments is promising, user interaction is still necessary to complete the matching process. In our future research, we plan on building a user interface that allows a domain expert to adjust the attribute mappings that have been proposed by Automatch. Furthermore, the interface will allow for iterative adjustment (i.e., after the user adjusts some of the mappings, we can re-apply Automatch for the remaining unmapped attributes).

An important benefit of user interaction in Automatch is that the system will be able to learn continuously. As new matches are provided through the user interface, the learner will be able to combine this information with what has already been learned. Note that this is significantly different than re-executing the entire learning algorithm. Such continuous learning is possible due to the statistical nature of the learning algorithm. As new matches are validated by a user, we can learn from these additional examples by updating the frequency counts of the features.

Finally, while this initial experimentation is encouraging, it is admittedly of a limited scale. Additional experimentation is planned to validate these preliminary conclusions.

Acknowledgement

The authors wish to thank Joseph (Seffi) Naor for his important suggestions in the area of network flows.

References

1. Ravindra K. Ahuja, Thomas L. Magnanti, and James B. Orlin. *Network Flows: Theory, Algorithms, and Applications.* Prentice Hall, 1993. 458
2. Algorithmic Solutions. *The LEDA Users Manual (Version 4.2.1)*, 2001. 458
3. Ricardo Baeza-Yates and Berthier Ribeiro-Neto. *Modern Information Retrieval.* ACM Press, 1999. 463
4. Jacob Berlin and Amihai Motro. Autoplex: Automated discovery of content for virtual databases. In *Proceedings of the Ninth International Conference on Cooperative Information Systems*, pages 108–122, 2001. 456
5. Silvana Castano and Valeria De Antonellis. A schema analysis and reconciliation tool environment for heterogeneous databases. In *Proceedings of the International Database Engineering and Applications Symposium*, pages 53–62, 1999. 453
6. AnHai Doan, Pedro Domingos, and Alon Y. Halevy. Reconciling schemas of disparate data sources: A machine-learning approach. In *Proceedings ACM Special Interest Group for the Management of Data (SIGMOD)*, 2001. 453, 464
7. Pedro Domingos and Michael Pazzani. Conditions for the optimality of the simple bayesian classifier. In *Proceedings of the 13th International Conference on Machine Learning*, pages 105–112, 1996. 456
8. Pat Langley, Wayne Iba, and Kevin Thompson. An analysis of bayesian classifiers. In *Proceedings of the Tenth National Conference on Artificial Intelligence*, pages 223–228, 1992. 456

9. Wen-Syan Li and Chris Clifton. Semantic integration in heterogeneous databases using neural networks. In *Proceedings of 20th International Conference on Very Large Data Bases*, pages 1–12, 1994. 454
10. Wen-Syan Li and Chris Clifton. Semint: A tool for identifying attribute correspondences in heterogeneous databases using neural networks. *Data & Knowledge Engineering*, 33(1):49–84, 2000. 454, 464
11. Jayant Madhavan, Philip A. Bernstein, and Erhard Rahm. Generic schema matching with cupid. In *Proceedings of the 27th International Conferences on Very Large Databases*, pages 49–58, 2001. 453
12. Renée Miller, Laura Haas, and Mauricio Hernández. Schema mapping as query discovery. In *Proceedings of the 26th International Conferences on Very Large Databases*, pages 77–88, 2000. 452
13. Tom Mitchell. *Machine Learning*. McGraw-Hill, 1997. 456, 460
14. Judea Pearl. *Probabilistic Reasoning in Intelligent Systems: Networks of Plausible Inference*. Morgan Kaufmann, 1988. 461
15. Erhard Rahm and Philip Bernstein. On matching schemas automatically. Technical Report MSR-TR-2001-17, Microsoft, Redmond, WA, February 2001. 452, 453
16. Mehran Sahami, Susan Dumais, David Heckerman, and Eric Horvitz. A bayesian approach to filtering junk e-mail. *AAAI-98 Workshop on Learning for Text Categorization*, 1998. 460
17. Ian H. Witten and Eibe Frank. *Data Mining: Practical Machine Learning Tools and Techniques with Java Implementations*. Morgan Kaufmann, 2000. 462

Automatch Revisited

Amihai Motro

Abstract We revisit the Autoplex and Automatch projects from 2001–2005, and in particular the results reported in the paper *Database Schema Matching Using Machine Learning with Feature Selection*, presented in the 14th International Conference on Advanced Information Systems Engineering (2002). We provide the motivation and background for these projects, examine their impact a decade later, and sketch possible research directions.

1 Virtual Databases

The problem of integrating information from multiple, independent and heterogeneous information sources has received considerable attention for almost four decades. The problem has been addressed in different ways [2], but the general approach has been that of creating a *virtual database*, a term originally suggested in [8]. In this approach, illustrated in Fig. 1, a single database schema is created that provides an integrated view of the information included in all the information sources. But whereas a conventional database includes data that correspond to its schema, in a virtual database this content is replaced with a *mapping* that associates the elements of this "global" schema with the corresponding data in the component databases. Users may then present queries to the global schema. Using the mapping, each such query is decomposed by the database system into a set of queries that are presented to the component databases; the answers retrieved are then assembled in a single answer that is returned to the user. Ideally, this entire process should be transparent: that is, users should be unaware that the database they are querying is virtual. The main advantage of this approach is that it can be applied in situations in which *physical* integration (i.e., the construction of a new database that incorporates

A. Motro (✉)
Computer Science Department, George Mason University, Fairfax, VA 22030, USA
e-mail: ami@gmu.edu

J. Bubenko et al. (eds.), *Seminal Contributions to Information Systems Engineering*,
DOI 10.1007/978-3-642-36926-1_26, © Springer-Verlag Berlin Heidelberg 2013

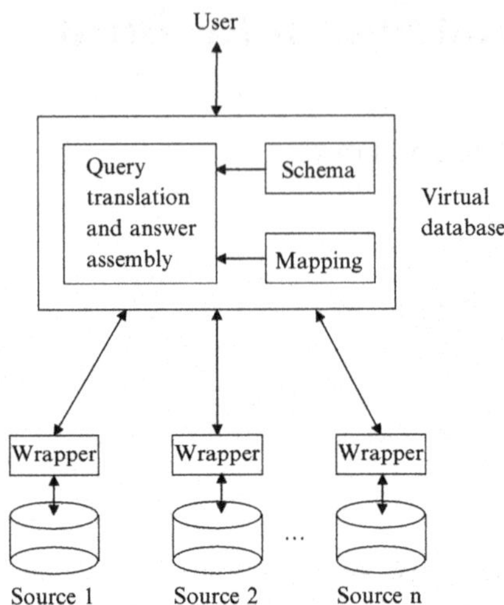

Fig. 1 The architecture of a virtual database system

the information in all the component databases) is impractical—either because it would be too costly or too time-consuming.

This area was continuously evolving during the 1980s, and then enjoyed substantial increase of interest in the 1990s with the decision of DARPA to sponsor research projects in this area. Projects from that period include TSIMMIS [6], Multiplex [10] and Clio [7].

Whereas the original problem assumed mostly a small and static scenario—a small number of databases were to be integrated, and the virtual solution was to endure for an extended period—with the explosion of the Internet in the late 1990s, this scenario has changed dramatically. The set of databases could now be much larger and more dynamic: New relevant databases could become available frequently and would need to be integrated, and old databases might become unavailable and would need to be withdrawn.

Additionally, it has been recognized that the main contributor to the cost of constructing virtual databases was the creation and maintenance of the global schema. This task required comprehending the schemas of the component databases and matching them to the global schema—a laborious task. And when this matching has to be extended and adjusted with each new source, it becomes prohibitively expensive. In brief, a scale-up of the problem needed to be addressed.

2 The Challenge

Given this scenario, it became obvious that one should attempt to automate, at least in part, the process of mapping the global schema to the schemas of the component databases. The intuitive metaphor imagined that one picks up a sheet of paper from the floor and sees a table of some sort; the table is just a grid of values, without any explanations and even without column headings. One then wonders: “What is the meaning of these values?”, and “Can I incorporate them into my accumulated knowledge?” In Internet terms, we envisioned a large collection of sites containing tabular data, possibly discovered with the help of a search engine that was presented with a query comprising global schema terms (e.g., column headings). Each table would then be analyzed to uncover its semantics, and an attempt would be made to match it to the global schema. (This would not only incorporate sources automatically, but would *discover* new sources and thus enrich the virtual database.)

The project was named Autoplex[1] and was described in [3]. It was then observed that a critical part of this automatic resource discovery and global-local schema mapping can be abstracted and generalized to address additional problem domains. Specifically, the problem of matching two independent database schemas (not necessarily global vs. local) has applications, among others, in data warehousing and e-commerce [11]. This sub-project was named Automatch and was the subject of the paper being revisited here.

Automatch applies techniques from machine learning. It assumes a knowledge-base about schema attributes, which has been constructed from examples (in the case of the Autoplex application, these examples would be mappings of the global schema to several component schemas, to be performed manually by experts). This knowledge-base is utilized whenever two new schemas need to be matched. Simply put, the knowledge-base helps score every possible matching of an attribute from one schema with an attribute of the other schema (and eventually, every comprehensive matching of the complete set of attributes of one schema with the complete set of attributes of the other schema).

3 Impact and Future

The work has been well-received and has enjoyed a fair number of bibliographic citations. Arguably, this success is due to the fact that it is part of a trend in the field of information systems to accept solutions that are good but not necessarily perfect. In the pre-Internet years, the focus has been on “critical” applications. Typical domains of interest would be financial, engineering or defense, and there had to be absolute certainty that all solutions are perfect: that data in the database are at all times consistent with the real world, that every answer to a query is precise, and that two databases are integrated flawlessly. While there has been on-going work on information uncertainty and “soft” solutions to information systems tasks (e.g., [1, 9]), with the possible exception of information retrieval, such work has been outside the mainstream, and was generally not awarded center-stage status. The magnitude of the information made available on the Internet has convinced the research community that good but imperfect solutions are sometimes the only available recourse.

---

[1]The name was a reference to earlier virtual database projects called Multiplex and Fusionplex; Retroplex would follow...

Schema matching and database integration deal with data that are *structured*, typically in tables. With most of the information in the public domain being unstructured, the new challenges are to identify correspondence and similarity between information items that are not values in tables (possibly phrases of free text), and to virtually aggregate and integrate non-structured repositories of information. Possibly, this could be approached by imposing some type of structure on the unstructured information items. A related effort was described in [5]. Indeed, information might be encapsulated in *services*, where stored functions deliver information in response to query-like requests. An attempt to find correspondence among such information items and cluster them in repositories was recently described in [4].

Acknowledgements The original paper was co-authored by Jacob Berlin, who was my doctoral student at that time. Jake deserves an equal share of the credit for the work that we have accomplished. Unfortunately, I was unable to contact Jake for the purpose of this article.

References

1. Andreasen, T., Christiansen, H., Larsen, H.L. (Editors). *Flexible Query Answering Systems*. Kluwer Academic Publishers, 1997.
2. Batini, C., Lenzerini, M., Navathe, S.B. A comparative analysis of methodologies for database schema integration. Computing Surveys, 18(4):323–364, 1989.
3. Berlin, J., Motro, A. Autoplex: Automated discovery of contents for virtual databases. In *Proceedings of COOPIS 01, Sixth IFCIS International Conference on Cooperative Information Systems*, Trento, Italy. Lecture Notes in Computer Science No. 2172, pp. 108–122, 1999.
4. Church, J., Motro, A. Learning service behavior with progressive testing. In *Proceedings of SOCA 11, IEEE International Conference on Service-Oriented Computing and Applications*, Irvine, CA, USA. pp. 1–8, 2011.
5. Etzioni, O., Halevy, A., Doan, A., Ives, Z.G, Madhaven, J., McDowell, L., Tatarinov, I. Crossing the structure chasm. In *Proceedings of CIDR-03, First Biennial Conference on Innovative Data Systems Research*, Asilomar, CA, USA., 2003. Available online at http://www-db.cs.wisc.edu/cidr/cidr2003/program/p11.pdf.
6. Garcia-Molina, H., Papakonstantinou, Y., Rajaraman, A., Sagiv, Y., Ullman, J., Vassalos, V., Widom, J. The TSIMMIS approach to mediation: data models and languages. *Journal of Intelligent Information Systems*, 8(2):117–132, 1997.
7. Miller, R.J., Hernandez, M.A., Haas, L.M., Yan, L., Ho, C.T.H., Fagin, R., Popa, L. The Clio project: managing heterogeneity. *SIGMOD Record* 30(1):78–83, 2001.
8. Motro, A. Interrogating superviews. In *Proceedings of ICOD-2, Second International Conference on Databases*, Cambridge, England, pp. 107–126, 1981.
9. Motro, A., Smets, P. *Uncertainty Management in Information Systems: from Needs to Solutions*. Kluwer Academic Publishing, 1996.
10. Motro, A. Multiplex: a formal model for multidatabases and its implementation. In *Proceedings of NGITS 96, Fourth International Workshop on Next Generation Information Tecnologies and Systems*, Zichron Yaacov, Israel. Lecture Notes in Computer Science No. 1649, pp. 138–158, 1999.
11. Rahm, E., Bernstein, P.A. A survey of approaches to automatic schema matching. *The VLDB Journal*, 10(4), pp. 334–350, 2001.

Data Integration under Integrity Constraints

Andrea Calì, Diego Calvanese, Giuseppe De Giacomo, and Maurizio Lenzerini

Dipartimento di Informatica e Sistemistica, Università di Roma "La Sapienza"
Via Salaria 113, I-00198 Roma, Italy
lastname@dis.uniroma1.it,
http://www.dis.uniroma1.it/~*lastname*

Abstract. Data integration systems provide access to a set of heterogeneous, autonomous data sources through a so-called global schema. There are basically two approaches for designing a data integration system. In the global-centric approach, one defines the elements of the global schema as views over the sources, whereas in the local-centric approach, one characterizes the sources as views over the global schema. It is well known that processing queries in the latter approach is similar to query answering with incomplete information, and, therefore, is a complex task. On the other hand, it is a common opinion that query processing is much easier in the former approach. In this paper we show the surprising result that, when the global schema is expressed in the relational model with integrity constraints, even of simple types, the problem of incomplete information implicitly arises, making query processing difficult in the global-centric approach as well. We then focus on global schemas with key and foreign key constraints, which represents a situation which is very common in practice, and we illustrate techniques for effectively answering queries posed to the data integration system in this case.

1 Introduction

Integrating heterogeneous data sources is a fundamental problem in databases, which has been studied extensively in the last two decades both from a formal and from a practical point of view [1,2,3,4,5,6]. Recently, mostly driven by the need to integrate data sources on the Web, much of the research on integration has focussed on so called *data integration* [7,8,6]. Data integration is the problem of combining the data residing at different sources, and providing the user with a unified view of these data. Such a unified view is structured according to a so-called global schema, which represents the intensional level of the integrated and reconciled data, and provides the elements for expressing the queries over the data integration system. It follows that, in formulating the queries, the user is freed from the knowledge on where data are, how data are structured at the sources, and how data are to be merged and reconciled to fit into the global schema.

The interest in this kind of systems has been continuously growing in the last years. Many organizations face the problem of integrating data residing in several sources. Companies that build a Data Warehouse, a Data Mining,

A. Banks Pidduck et al. (Eds.): CAISE 2002, LNCS 2348, pp. 262–279, 2002.

or an Enterprise Resource Planning system must address this problem. Also, integrating data in the World Wide Web is the subject of several investigations and projects nowadays. Finally, applications requiring accessing or re-engineering legacy systems must deal somehow with data integration.

The design of a data integration system is a very complex task, which requires addressing several different issues. Here, we concentrate on two basic issues:

1. specifying the mapping between the global schema and the sources,
2. processing queries expressed on the global schema.

With regard to issue (1), two basic approaches have been used to specify the mapping between the sources and the global schema [7,7,9]. The first approach, called *global-centric* [10,11,12], requires that the global schema is expressed in terms of the data sources. More precisely, to every element of the global schema, a view over the data sources is associated, so that its meaning is specified in terms of the data residing at the sources. In general, the views associated to the elements of the global schema are considered *sound*, i.e., all the data provided by a view satisfies the corresponding element of the global schema, but there may be additional data satisfying the element not provided by the view. The second approach, called *source-centric* [13,14,15], requires the global schema to be specified independently from the sources. In turn, the sources are defined as views over the global schema. Comparisons of the two approaches are reported in [8,16]. In this paper, we study global-centric data integration systems, and, according to the usual approach, we assume that the views associated to the elements of the global schema are sound.

Issue (2) is concerned with one of the most important problems in the design of a data integration system, namely, the choice of the method for computing the answer to queries posed in terms of the global schema. For this purpose, the system should be able to reformulate the query in terms of a suitable set of queries posed to the sources. These queries are then shipped to the sources, and the results are assembled into the final answer. It is well known that processing queries in the source-centric approach is a difficult task [8,17,14,18,19]. Indeed, in this approach the only knowledge we have about the data in the global schema is through the views representing the sources, and such views provide only partial information about the data. Therefore, extracting information from the data integration system is similar to query answering with incomplete information, which is a complex task [20]. On the other hand, query processing is considered much easier in the global-centric approach, where in general it is assumed that answering a query basically means unfolding its atoms according to their definitions in terms of the sources [7]. The reason why unfolding does the job is that the global-centric mapping essentially specifies a single database satisfying the global schema, and evaluating the query over this unique database is equivalent to evaluating its unfolding over the sources.

While this is a common opinion in the literature, we show in this paper that the presence of integrity constraints in the global schema poses new challenges, specially related to the need of taking the semantics of constraints into account during query processing. The importance of allowing integrity constraints in the global schema has been stressed in several work on data integration [15,21,22]. Since the global schema acts as the interface to the user for query formulation, it should mediate among different representations of overlapping worlds, and therefore the schema definition language should incorporate flexible and powerful representation mechanisms, such as the ones based on semantic integrity constraints.

The first contribution in this paper is to show that, when the global schema contains integrity constraints, even of simple forms, the semantics of the data integration system is best described in terms of a set of databases, rather than a single one, and this implies that, even in the global-centric approach, query processing is intimately connected to the notion of querying *incomplete databases*. The fact that the problem of incomplete information is overlooked in current approaches can be explained by observing that traditional data integration systems follow one of the following strategies: they either express the global schema as a set of plain relations without integrity constraints, or consider the sources as exact (see, e.g., [23,24]), as opposed to sound. On the contrary, the goal of our work is to study the more general setting where the global schema contains integrity constraints, and sources are considered sound (but not necessarily complete). The above result demonstrates that, in this case, we have to account for multiple global databases.

The second contribution of the paper is to study the case of global schemas expressed in the relational model with key and foreign key constraints, which represents a situation very common in practice. Although the problem of multiple global databases arises in this case, we have devised techniques for effectively answering queries posed to the data integration system. The resulting algorithm runs in polynomial time with respect to data complexity, i.e., with respect to the size of data at the sources.

The paper is organized as follows. In Section 2 we describe a formal framework for data integration. In Section 3 we show that the presence of integrity constraints in the global schema complicates the task of query processing. In Sections 4 and 5 we present our query processing algorithm for the case of global relational schema with key and foreign key constraints. Section 6 concludes the paper.

2 Framework for Data Integration

In this section we illustrate our formalization of a data integration system, which is based on the relational model with integrity constraints.

In the relational model, predicate symbols are used to denote the relations in the database, whereas constant symbols denote the objects and the values stored in relations. We assume to have a fixed (infinite) alphabet Γ of constants, and, if not specified otherwise, we will consider only databases over such alphabet. We adopt the so-called *unique name assumption*, i.e., we assume that different constants denote different objects. A *relational schema* $\mathcal{C}$ is constituted by:

- An *alphabet* $\mathcal{A}$ of predicate (or relation) symbols, each one with the associated arity, i.e., the number of arguments of the predicate (or, attributes of the relation). We do not use names for referring to attributes, rather, we simply use the numbers corresponding to their positions.
- A set of *integrity constraints*, i.e., assertions on the symbols of the alphabet $\mathcal{A}$ that express conditions that are intended to be satisfied in every database coherent with the schema.

A relational database (or simply, database) $\mathcal{DB}$ for a schema $\mathcal{C}$ is a set of relations with constants as atomic values, and with one relation $r^{\mathcal{DB}}$ of arity n for each predicate symbol r of arity n in the alphabet $\mathcal{A}$. It is well known that a database can be seen as a first-order interpretation for the relation symbols in the schema: the relation $r^{\mathcal{DB}}$ is the interpretation of the predicate symbol r in $\mathcal{DB}$, in the sense that it contains the set of tuples that satisfy the predicate r in $\mathcal{DB}$. A database $\mathcal{DB}$ for a schema $\mathcal{C}$ is said to be *legal* if every constraints of $\mathcal{C}$ is satisfied by $\mathcal{DB}$. The notion of satisfaction depends on the type of constraints.

In our framework we consider the relational model with two kinds of constraints:

- *Key constraints*: given a relation r in the schema, a key constraint over r is expressed in the form $key(r) = \mathbf{A}$, where $\mathbf{A}$ is a set of attributes of r. Such a constraint is satisfied in a database $\mathcal{DB}$ if for each $t_1, t_2 \in r^{\mathcal{DB}}$ we have $t_1[\mathbf{A}] \neq t_2[\mathbf{A}]$, where $t[\mathbf{A}]$ is the projection of the tuple t over $\mathbf{A}$.
- *Foreign key constraints*: a foreign key constraint is a statement of the form $r_1[\mathbf{A}] \subseteq r_2[\mathbf{B}]$, where r_1, r_2 are relations, $\mathbf{A}$ is a sequence of distinct attributes of r_1, and $\mathbf{B}$ is a sequence formed by the distinct attributes forming the key of r_2. Such a constraint is satisfied in a database $\mathcal{DB}$ if for each tuple t_1 in $r_1^{\mathcal{DB}}$ there exists a tuple t_2 in $r_2^{\mathcal{DB}}$ such that $t_1[\mathbf{A}] = t_2[\mathbf{B}]$.

A *relational query* is a formula that specifies a set of tuples to be retrieved from a database. In this work, we restrict our analysis to the class of conjunctive queries. Formally, a *conjunctive query* (CQ) q of *arity* n is written in the form

$$q(x_1, \ldots, x_n) \leftarrow conj(x_1, \ldots, x_n, y_1, \ldots, y_m)$$

where: q belongs to a new alphabet $\mathcal{Q}$ (the alphabet of queries, that is disjoint from both Γ and $\mathcal{A}$); $conj(x_1, \ldots, x_n, y_1, \ldots, y_m)$ is a conjunction of atoms involving the variables $x_1, \ldots, x_n, y_1, \ldots, y_m$, and a set of constants from Γ; and the predicate symbols of the atoms are in $\mathcal{C}$.

The answer to a query q of arity n over a database $\mathcal{DB}$ for $\mathcal{G}$, denoted $q^{\mathcal{DB}}$, is the set of n-tuples of constants $(c_1, \ldots, c_n)$, such that, when substituting each c_i for x_i, the formula $\exists(y_1, \ldots, y_n).conj(x_1, \ldots, x_n, y_1, \ldots, y_m)$ evaluates to true in $\mathcal{DB}$. Note that the answer to q over $\mathcal{DB}$ is a relation whose arity is equal to the arity of the query q.

We now turn our attention to the notion of data integration system.

Definition 1. *A* data integration system $\mathcal{I}$ *is a triple* $\mathcal{I} = \langle \mathcal{G}, \mathcal{S}, \mathcal{M}_{\mathcal{G},\mathcal{S}} \rangle$, *where* $\mathcal{G}$ *is the* global schema, $\mathcal{S}$ *is the* source schema, *and* $\mathcal{M}_{\mathcal{G},\mathcal{S}}$ *is the* mapping *between* $\mathcal{G}$ *and* $\mathcal{S}$.

Now we describe the characteristics of the components of a data integration system in our approach. In particular, we specialize the general framework as follows:

- The *global schema* is expressed in the relational model with both key and foreign key constraints. We assume that in the global schema there is exactly one key constraint for each relation.
- The *source schema* is expressed in the relational model without integrity constraints. In other words, we conceive each source as a relation, and we consider the set of all relations as a unique schema, called source schema.
- The *mapping* $\mathcal{M}_{\mathcal{G},\mathcal{S}}$ is defined in the global-centric approach: to each relation r of $\mathcal{G}$ we associate a query $\rho(r)$ over the source schema. No limitation is posed on the language used to express queries in the mapping $\mathcal{M}_{\mathcal{G},\mathcal{S}}$.
- Queries over the global schema are *conjunctive queries*.

Example 1. An example of data integration system is $\mathcal{I}^1 = \langle \mathcal{G}^1, \mathcal{S}^1, \mathcal{M}^1_{\mathcal{G},\mathcal{S}} \rangle$ where $\mathcal{G}^1$ is constituted by the relation symbols $\mathsf{student}(Scode, Sname, Scity)$, $\mathsf{university}(Ucode, Uname)$, and $\mathsf{enrolled}(Scode, Ucode)$ and the constraints

$$\begin{array}{rl} key(\mathsf{student}) = \{Scode\} & \\ key(\mathsf{university}) = \{Ucode\} & \qquad \mathsf{enrolled}[Scode] \subseteq \mathsf{student}[Scode] \\ key(\mathsf{enrolled}) = \{Scode, Ucode\} & \qquad \mathsf{enrolled}[Ucode] \subseteq \mathsf{university}[Ucode] \end{array}$$

$\mathcal{S}^1$ consists of three sources. Source s_1, of arity 4, contains information about students with their code, name, city, and date of birth. Source s_2, of arity 2, contains codes and names of universities. Finally, Source s_3, of arity 2, contains information about enrollment of students in universities. The mapping $\mathcal{M}^1_{\mathcal{G},\mathcal{S}}$ is defined by

$$\begin{array}{rcl} \rho(\mathsf{student}) & = & \mathsf{st}(X,Y,Z) \leftarrow \mathsf{s}_1(X,Y,Z,W) \\ \rho(\mathsf{university}) & = & \mathsf{un}(X,Y) \leftarrow \mathsf{s}_2(X,Y) \\ \rho(\mathsf{enrolled}) & = & \mathsf{en}(X,W) \leftarrow \mathsf{s}_3(X,W) \end{array}$$

In order to define the semantics of a data integration system $\mathcal{I} = \langle \mathcal{G}, \mathcal{S}, \mathcal{M}_{\mathcal{G},\mathcal{S}} \rangle$, we start from the data at the sources, and specify which are the data that satisfy the global schema. A *source database* $\mathcal{D}$ for $\mathcal{I}$ is constituted by one relation $r^{\mathcal{D}}$ for each source r in $\mathcal{S}$. We call *global database* for $\mathcal{I}$, or simply *database* for $\mathcal{I}$, any database for $\mathcal{G}$. A database $\mathcal{B}$ for $\mathcal{I}$ is said to be *legal* with respect to $\mathcal{D}$ if:

- $\mathcal{B}$ satisfies the integrity constraints of $\mathcal{G}$.
- $\mathcal{B}$ satisfies $\mathcal{M}_{\mathcal{G},\mathcal{S}}$ with respect to $\mathcal{D}$, i.e., for each relation r in $\mathcal{G}$, the set of tuples $r^{\mathcal{B}}$ that $\mathcal{B}$ assigns to r is a subset of the set of tuples $\rho(r)^{\mathcal{D}}$ computed by the associated query $\rho(r)$ over $\mathcal{D}$, i.e., $\rho(r)^{\mathcal{D}} \subseteq r^{\mathcal{B}}$.

Note that the above definition amounts to consider any view $\rho(r)$ as *sound*, which means that the data provided by the sources are not necessarily complete. Other assumptions on views are possible (see [14,18]). In particular, views may be *complete*, i.e., for each r in $\mathcal{G}$, we have $\rho(r)^{\mathcal{D}} \supseteq r^{\mathcal{B}}$, or *exact*, i.e., for each r in $\mathcal{G}$, we have $\rho(r)^{\mathcal{D}} = r^{\mathcal{B}}$. In this paper, we restrict our attention to sound views only, which are typically considered the most natural in a data integration setting.

At this point, we are able to give the semantics of a data integration system, which is formally defined as follows.

Definition 2. *If $\mathcal{I} = \langle \mathcal{G}, \mathcal{S}, \mathcal{M}_{\mathcal{G},\mathcal{S}} \rangle$, and $\mathcal{D}$ is a source database for $\mathcal{I}$, the semantics of $\mathcal{I}$ w.r.t. $\mathcal{D}$, denoted $sem^{\mathcal{D}}(\mathcal{I})$, is the set of databases for $\mathcal{I}$ that are legal w.r.t. $\mathcal{D}$, i.e., that satisfy both the constraints of $\mathcal{G}$, and the mapping $\mathcal{M}_{\mathcal{G},\mathcal{S}}$ with respect to $\mathcal{D}$. If $sem^{\mathcal{D}}(\mathcal{I}) \neq \emptyset$, then $\mathcal{I}$ said to be* consistent *w.r.t. $\mathcal{D}$.*

By the above definition, it is clear that the semantics of a data integration systems is formulated in terms of a *set* of databases, rather than a single one. Indeed, as we will show in the sequel, the cardinality of $sem^{\mathcal{D}}(\mathcal{I})$ is in general greater than one. The impact of this property on query answering will be studied in the next section.

3 Query Answering in the Presence of Constraints

The ultimate goal of a data integration system is to answer queries posed by the user in terms of the global schema. Answering a query posed to a system representing a set of databases, is a complex task, as shown by the following example.

Example 2. Referring to Example 1, suppose to have the following source database $\mathcal{D}^1$:

$s_1^{\mathcal{D}^1}$:

12	*anne*	*florence*	21
15	*bill*	*oslo*	24

$s_2^{\mathcal{D}^1}$:

AF	*bocconi*
BN	*ucla*

$s_3^{\mathcal{D}^1}$:

12	*AF*
16	*BN*

Now, due to the integrity constraints in $\mathcal{G}_1$, 16 is the code of some student. Observe, however, that nothing is said by $\mathcal{D}^1$ about the name and the city of such student. Therefore, we must accept as legal all databases that differ in such attributes of the student with code 16. Note that this is a consequence of the assumption of having sound views. If we had exact or complete views, this situation would have lead to an inconsistency of the data integration system. Instead, when dealing with sound views, we can think of extending the data contained in the sources in order to satisfy the integrity constraint over the global schema. The fact that, in general, there are several possible ways to carry out such extension implies that there are several legal databases for the data integration systems.

Let us now turn our attention to the notion of answer to a query posed to the data integration system. In our setting, a query q to a data integration system $\mathcal{I} = \langle \mathcal{G}, \mathcal{S}, \mathcal{M}_{\mathcal{G},\mathcal{S}} \rangle$ is a conjunctive query, whose atoms have symbols in $\mathcal{G}$ as predicates. Our goal is to specify which are the tuples that form the answer to a certain query posed to $\mathcal{I}$. The task is complicated by the existence of several global databases which are legal for $\mathcal{I}$ with respect to a source database $\mathcal{D}$. In order to address this problem, we adopt the following approach: a tuple $(c_1, \ldots, c_n)$ is considered an answer to the query only if it is a *certain* answer, i.e., it satisfies the query in *every* database that belongs to the semantics of the data integration system.

Definition 3. *Let $\mathcal{I} = \langle \mathcal{G}, \mathcal{S}, \mathcal{M}_{\mathcal{G},\mathcal{S}} \rangle$ be a data integration system, let $\mathcal{D}$ be a source database for $\mathcal{I}$, and let q be a query of arity n to $\mathcal{I}$. The* set of certain answers *$q^{\mathcal{I},\mathcal{D}}$ to q with respect to $\mathcal{I}$ and $\mathcal{D}$ is the set of tuples $(c_1, \ldots, c_n)$ such that $(c_1, \ldots, c_n) \in q^{\mathcal{B}}$, for each $\mathcal{B} \in sem^{\mathcal{D}}(\mathcal{I})$.*

As mentioned, it is generally assumed that query answering is an easy task in the global-centric approach. Indeed, the most common technique for query answering in this approach is based on *unfolding*, i.e. substituting to each relation symbol r in the query its definition $\rho(r)$ in terms of the sources. We now show a simple unfolding strategy is not sufficient for providing all correct answers in the presence of integrity constraints.

Example 3. Referring again to Example 1, consider the query

$$\mathsf{q}(X) \leftarrow \mathsf{student}(X, Y, Z) \wedge \mathsf{enrolled}(X, W)$$

The correct answer to the query is $\{12, 16\}$, because, due to the integrity constraints in $\mathcal{G}_1$, we know that 16 appears in the first attribute of student in all the databases for $\mathcal{I}$ that are legal w.r.t. $\mathcal{D}_1$. However, we do not get this information from $\mathsf{s}_1^{\mathcal{D}_1}$, and, therefore, a simple unfolding strategy retrieves only the answer $\{12\}$ from $\mathcal{D}^1$, thus proving insufficient for query answering in this framework. Notice that, if the query asked for the student name instead of the student code (i.e., the head is $q(Y)$ instead of $q(X)$), then one could *not* make use of the dependencies to infer additional answers.

The above example shows that, in the presence of integrity constraints, even in the global-centric approach we have to deal with incomplete information during query processing.

4 General Description of the Approach

We present the general ideas that are at the basis of our method for query answering in data integration systems.

Let $\mathcal{I} = \langle \mathcal{G}, \mathcal{S}, \mathcal{M}_{\mathcal{G},\mathcal{S}} \rangle$ be a data integration system. In this paper we assume that, for each relation r of the global schema, the query $\rho(r)$ over the source schema that the mapping $\mathcal{M}_{\mathcal{G},\mathcal{S}}$ associates to r preserves the key constraint of r. This may require that $\rho(r)$ implements a suitable duplicate record elimination strategy that ensures that, for every source database $\mathcal{D}$ no pairs of tuples are extracted from $\mathcal{D}$ by $\rho(r)$ with the same value for the key of r. The problem of duplicate record elimination, and, more generally, of data cleaning, is a critical issues in data integration systems, however it is orthogonal to the problem addressed here. We refer to [25,26] for more details.

Let q be a query posed to $\mathcal{I}$, and $\mathcal{D}$ a source database for $\mathcal{I}$. We illustrate a naive method for computing the answer $q^{\mathcal{I},\mathcal{D}}$ to q w.r.t. $\mathcal{I}$ and $\mathcal{D}$. The naive computation of $q^{\mathcal{I},\mathcal{D}}$ proceeds as follows.

1. For each relation r of the global schema, we compute the relation $r^{\mathcal{D}}$ by evaluating the query $\rho(r)$ over the source database $\mathcal{D}$. The various relations so obtained form what we call the *retrieved global database* $ret(\mathcal{I}, \mathcal{D})$. Note

that, since we assume that $\rho(r)$ does not violate the key constraints, it follows that the retrieved global database satisfies all key constraints in $\mathcal{G}$.
2. If, additionally, the retrieved global database satisfies all foreign key constraints in $\mathcal{G}$, then we are basically done: we simply evaluate q over $ret(\mathcal{I}, \mathcal{D})$, and we obtain the answer to the query.
Otherwise, based on the retrieved global database, we can build a database for $\mathcal{I}$ still satisfying the key constraints by suitably adding tuples to the relations of the global schema in such a way that also the foreign key constraints are satisfied.[1] Obviously, there are several possible ways to add tuples to the global relations.
We may try to infer all the legal databases for $\mathcal{I}$ that are coherent with the retrieved global database, and we compute the tuples that satisfy the query q in all such legal databases. However, such a solution is not easy to pursue. Indeed, the direct way to implement it, i.e., building all the legal databases for $\mathcal{I}$ that are coherent with the retrieved global database, is not feasible: in general, there is an infinite number of legal databases that are coherent with the retrieved global database. Fortunately, starting from the retrieved global database, we can build another database, that we call *canonical*, that has the interesting property of faithfully representing all legal databases that are coherent with the retrieved global database.

Let us start by showing how to build the canonical database. First of all, we define the domain of such database, which we denote $HD(\mathcal{D})$, as follows. Based on the global schema $\mathcal{G}$ of $\mathcal{I}$, we introduce the following set of function symbols:

$$HT(\mathcal{G}) = \{f_{r,i} \mid r \in \mathcal{G} \text{ and } i \leq arity(r) \text{ and } i \notin key(r)\}$$

Thus, each $f_{r,i}$ is a function symbol, and such a function symbol has the same arity as the number of attributes of $key(r)$, i.e., $arity(f_{r,i}) = arity(key(r))$. From $\mathcal{D}$, we now define the domain $HD(\mathcal{D})$ as the smallest set satisfying the following conditions:

- $\Gamma \subseteq HD(\mathcal{D})$,
- if $\alpha_1, \ldots, \alpha_k \in HD(\mathcal{D})$, and $f_{R,i} \in HT(\mathcal{G})$, with $arity(f_{R,i}) = k$, then $f_{R,i}(\alpha_1, \ldots, \alpha_k) \in HD(\mathcal{D})$.

Now, given the retrieved global database $ret(\mathcal{I}, \mathcal{D})$, we obtain the canonical database $can(\mathcal{I}, \mathcal{D})$ over the domain $HD(\mathcal{D})$ by repeatedly applying the following rule:

if $(x_1, \ldots, x_h) \in r[\mathbf{A}]$, and the foreign key constraint $r_1[\mathbf{A}] \subseteq r_2[\mathbf{B}]$ is in $\mathcal{G}$,
then insert the tuple t in r_2 such that

[1] Note that, since views are sound, i.e., they return a *subset* of the tuples in a global relation, we cannot conclude that the data integration system violates the foreign key constraints of $\mathcal{G}$. Indeed, it may be the case that the tuples needed to satisfy such constraints are not part of the retrieved subsets.

– $t[\mathbf{B}] = (x_1, \ldots, x_h)$, and
– for each $i \leq arity(r_2)$ not in $\mathbf{B}$, $t[i] = f_{r_2,i}(x_1, \ldots, x_h)$.

Observe that $can(\mathcal{I}, \mathcal{D})$ is indeed a database over the domain $HD(\mathcal{D})$, and that, in general, $can(\mathcal{I}, \mathcal{D})$ is infinite. However, it enjoys important properties, as shown below. The first property is related to the satisfaction of the constraints of $\mathcal{G}$.

Theorem 1. *If $\mathcal{I} = \langle \mathcal{G}, \mathcal{S}, \mathcal{M}_{\mathcal{G},\mathcal{S}} \rangle$, and $\mathcal{D}$ is a source database for $\mathcal{I}$, then $can(\mathcal{I}, \mathcal{D})$ does not violate any foreign key constraint in $\mathcal{G}$.*

Proof. Suppose by contradiction that the foreign key constraint $r_1[\mathbf{A}] \subseteq r_2[\mathbf{B}]$ is violated in $can(\mathcal{I}, \mathcal{D})$. This implies that there is a tuple t in r_1 such that for no tuple t' in r_2 $t'[\mathbf{B}] = t[\mathbf{A}]$. But this would imply that we can apply the rule and insert a new tuple t'' in r_2 such that $t''[\mathbf{B}] = t[\mathbf{A}]$, and for each $i \leq arity(r_2)$ not in $\mathbf{B}$, $t'[i] = f_{r_2,i}(t[\mathbf{A}])$. But this contradicts the assumption.

We now show that there exists a legal database for $\mathcal{I}$ w.r.t. $\mathcal{D}$ (called $can^-(\mathcal{I}, \mathcal{D})$), which implies that $\mathcal{I}$ is consistent w.r.t. $\mathcal{D}$, if and only if $ret(\mathcal{I}, \mathcal{D})$ does not violate any key constraint in $\mathcal{G}$.

Theorem 2. *If $\mathcal{I} = \langle \mathcal{G}, \mathcal{S}, \mathcal{M}_{\mathcal{G},\mathcal{S}} \rangle$, and $\mathcal{D}$ is a source database for $\mathcal{I}$, then there exists a legal database for $\mathcal{I}$ w.r.t. $\mathcal{D}$ if and only if $ret(\mathcal{I}, \mathcal{D})$ does not violate any key constraint in $\mathcal{G}$.*

Proof. It is immediate to see that if $ret(\mathcal{I}, \mathcal{D})$ violates some key constraint in $\mathcal{G}$, then no legal database exists for $\mathcal{I}$ w.r.t. $\mathcal{D}$.

It remains to show that, if $ret(\mathcal{I}, \mathcal{D})$ does not violate any key constraint in $\mathcal{G}$, then there exists a legal database $can^-(\mathcal{I}, \mathcal{D})$ for $\mathcal{I}$ w.r.t. $\mathcal{D}$, which implies that $\mathcal{I}$ is consistent w.r.t. $\mathcal{D}$. We construct $can^-(\mathcal{I}, \mathcal{D})$ from $\mathcal{G}$ and $\mathcal{D}$ similarly to $can(\mathcal{I}, \mathcal{D})$, with the only difference that we use the rule:

If $(x_1, \ldots, x_h) \in r_1[\mathbf{A}]$, $(x_1, \ldots, x_h) \notin r_2[\mathbf{B}]$, and the foreign key constraint $r_1[\mathbf{A}] \subseteq r_2[\mathbf{B}]$ is in $\mathcal{G}$,
then insert the tuple t in r_2 such that
– $t[\mathbf{B}] = (x_1, \ldots, x_h)$, and
– for each $i \leq arity(r_2)$ different from $\mathbf{B}$, $t[i] = f_{r_2,i}(x)$.

It is easy to see that $can^-(\mathcal{I}, \mathcal{D}) \subseteq can(\mathcal{I}, \mathcal{D})$. To show that $can^-(\mathcal{I}, \mathcal{D})$ is indeed a legal database for $\mathcal{I}$ w.r.t. $\mathcal{D}$, we consider key and foreign key constraints separately. As for key constraints, it is easy to see that the tuples inserted during the process of computing $can^-(\mathcal{I}, \mathcal{D})$ cannot violate any key constraints of $\mathcal{G}$. Indeed, in computing $can^-(\mathcal{I}, \mathcal{D})$, we insert a tuple into a relation r only when the key component of that tuple is not already present in r. Since $ret(\mathcal{I}, \mathcal{D})$ does not violate any key constraint in $\mathcal{G}$, it follows that no key constraint of $\mathcal{G}$ is violated in $can^-(\mathcal{I}, \mathcal{D})$. As for foreign key constraints, suppose by contradiction that the foreign key constraint $r_1[\mathbf{A}] \subseteq r_2[\mathbf{B}]$ is violated in $can^-(\mathcal{I}, \mathcal{D})$. This implies that there is a tuple t in r_1 such that for no tuple t' in r_2 $t'[\mathbf{B}] = t[\mathbf{A}]$. But this would imply that we can apply the above rule and insert a new tuple t'' in r_2 such that $t''[\mathbf{B}] = t[\mathbf{A}]$, and for each $i \leq arity(r_2)$ not in $\mathbf{B}$, $t'[i] = f_{r_2,i}(t[\mathbf{A}])$. But this contradicts the assumption.

The canonical database $can(\mathcal{I},\mathcal{D})$ has the interesting property of faithfully representing all legal databases that are coherent with the retrieved global database $ret(\mathcal{I},\mathcal{D})$.

Theorem 3. *Let $\mathcal{I} = \langle \mathcal{G}, \mathcal{S}, \mathcal{M}_{\mathcal{G},\mathcal{S}} \rangle$, let $\mathcal{D}$ be a source database for $\mathcal{I}$, and let $\mathcal{B}$ be a legal database for $\mathcal{I}$ w.r.t. $\mathcal{D}$. There is a total function ψ from $HD(\mathcal{D})$ to Γ such that, for each relation r of arity n in $\mathcal{G}$, and each tuple $(c_1,\ldots,c_n)$ constituted by elements in $HD(\mathcal{D})$, if $(c_1,\ldots,c_n) \in r^{can(\mathcal{I},\mathcal{D})}$, then $(\psi(c_1),\ldots,\psi(c_n)) \in r^{\mathcal{B}}$.*

Proof. We define the function ψ from $HD(\mathcal{D})$ to Γ inductively, and we simultaneously show that for each relation r of arity n in $\mathcal{G}$, and each tuple $(c_1,\ldots,c_n)$ constituted by elements in $HD(\mathcal{D})$, if $(c_1,\ldots,c_n) \in r^{can(\mathcal{I},\mathcal{D})}$, then $(\psi(c_1),\ldots,\psi(c_n)) \in r^{\mathcal{B}}$.

We proceed by induction on the application of the rule used during the construction of $can(\mathcal{I},\mathcal{D})$. As a base step, the function ψ maps each constant in $ret(\mathcal{I},\mathcal{D})$ into itself. It follows that, for each r, if $c_1,\ldots,c_n$ are constants, and $(c_1,\ldots,c_n) \in r^{ret(\mathcal{I},\mathcal{D})}$, then it is obvious that both $(c_1,\ldots,c_n) \in r^{can(\mathcal{I},\mathcal{D})}$, and $(\psi(c_1),\ldots,\psi(c_n)) \in r^{\mathcal{B}}$.

Inductive step. Suppose, without loss of generality, that in the application of the rule, we are inserting the tuple $(\alpha, f_{r,i_1}(\alpha), f_{r,i_2}(\alpha))$ in $r^{can(\mathcal{I},\mathcal{D})}$ where r has arity 3, $key(r) = \{1\}$, and the tuple is inserted in $r^{can(\mathcal{I},\mathcal{D})}$ because of the foreign key constraint $w[j] \subseteq r[1]$. Since we are applying the rule because of the constraint $w[j] \subseteq r[1]$, we have that there is a tuple t in $w^{can(\mathcal{I},\mathcal{D})}$ such that $t[j] = \alpha$. For the induction hypothesis, there is a β in Γ such that $\psi(\alpha) = \beta$, and there is a tuple $t' \in w^{\mathcal{B}}$ such that for each i, $t'[i] = \psi(t[i])$, and $t'[j] = \psi(\alpha) = \beta$. Because of the constraint $w[j] \subseteq r[1]$, and because $\mathcal{B}$ is legal, there is one and only one tuple (β, γ, δ) in $r^{\mathcal{B}}$ (since 1 is a key of r, β appears once in $r^{\mathcal{B}}[1]$). Then, we set $\psi(f_{r,i_1}(\alpha)) = \gamma$, $\psi(f_{r,i_2}(\alpha)) = \delta$, and we can conclude that $(\psi(\alpha), \psi(f_{r,i_1}(\alpha)), \psi(f_{r,i_2}(\alpha))) \in r^{\mathcal{B}}$.

Finally, we show that, if $\mathcal{I}$ is consistent w.r.t. $\mathcal{D}$, then a tuple t of constants is in $q^{\mathcal{I},\mathcal{D}}$ if and only if t is in the answer to q over the database $can(\mathcal{I},\mathcal{D})$.

Theorem 4. *Let $\mathcal{I} = \langle \mathcal{G}, \mathcal{S}, \mathcal{M}_{\mathcal{G},\mathcal{S}} \rangle$, let q be a query posed to $\mathcal{I}$, $\mathcal{D}$ a source database for $\mathcal{I}$, and t a tuple of constants of the same arity as q. If $\mathcal{I}$ is consistent w.r.t. $\mathcal{D}$, then $t \in q^{\mathcal{I},\mathcal{D}}$ if and only if t is in the answer to q over $can(\mathcal{I},\mathcal{D})$.*

Proof. For the "if" direction, we show that if t is in the answer to q over $can(\mathcal{I},\mathcal{D})$, then $t \in q^{\mathcal{I},\mathcal{D}}$. Indeed, consider any $\mathcal{B}$ that is a legal database for $\mathcal{I}$ w.r.t. $\mathcal{D}$. By theorem 3, there is a total function ψ from $HD(\mathcal{D})$ to Γ such that, for each relation r of arity n in $\mathcal{G}$, and each tuple $(c_1,\ldots,c_n)$ constituted by elements in $HD(\mathcal{D})$, if $(c_1,\ldots,c_n) \in r^{can(\mathcal{I},\mathcal{D})}$, then $(\psi(c_1),\ldots,\psi(c_n)) \in r^{\mathcal{B}}$. The fact that t is in the answer to q over $can(\mathcal{I},\mathcal{D})$ means that there is an assignment α from the variables of q to objects in $HD(\mathcal{D})$ such that all atoms of q are true with respect to the assignment. It is easy to see that the assignment $\alpha \cdot \psi$ can be used to show that t is in the answer to q over $\mathcal{B}$.

As for the "only-if" direction, first note that, by hypothesis $\mathcal{I}$ is consistent w.r.t. $\mathcal{D}$, and, therefore, by theorem 2, $ret(\mathcal{I}, \mathcal{D})$ does not violate any key constraint in $\mathcal{G}$, which implies that $can^-(\mathcal{I}, \mathcal{D})$ is a legal database for $\mathcal{I}$ w.r.t. $\mathcal{D}$. Now, since $can^-(\mathcal{I}, \mathcal{D}) \subseteq can(\mathcal{I}, \mathcal{D})$, and since q is a conjunctive query, the fact that t is not in the answer to q over $can(\mathcal{I}, \mathcal{D})$ implies that t is not in the answer of q over $can^-(\mathcal{I}, \mathcal{D})$. Therefore, we can conclude that $t \notin q^{\mathcal{I},\mathcal{D}}$.

Based on the above results, we can conclude that $can(\mathcal{I}, \mathcal{D})$ is the right abstraction for answering queries posed to the data integration system. In the next section we show that, in processing a query q posed to the data integration system, we can find the answers to q over $can(\mathcal{I}, \mathcal{D})$ without actually building $can(\mathcal{I}, \mathcal{D})$.

5 Query Reformulation

The naive computation described in the previous section is impractical, because it requires to build the canonical database, which is in general infinite. In order to overcome the problem, we have devised an algorithm, whose main ideas are as follows.

1. First, as we said in the previous section, we assume that, for each relation r of the global schema, the query $\rho(r)$ over the source schema that the mapping $\mathcal{M}_{\mathcal{G},\mathcal{S}}$ associates to r preserve the key constraint of r.
2. Instead of referring explicitly to the canonical database for query answering, we transform the original query q into a new query $exp_{\mathcal{G}}(q)$ over the global schema, called the *expansion of q w.r.t. $\mathcal{G}$*, such that the answer to $exp_{\mathcal{G}}(q)$ over the retrieved global database is equal to the answer to q over the canonical database.
3. In order to avoid building the retrieved global database, we do not evaluate $exp_{\mathcal{G}}(q)$ on the retrieved global database. Instead, we unfold $exp_{\mathcal{G}}(q)$ to a new query, called $unf_{\mathcal{M}_{\mathcal{G},\mathcal{S}}}(exp_{\mathcal{G}}(q))$, over the source relations on the basis of $\mathcal{M}_{\mathcal{G},\mathcal{S}}$, and we use the unfolded query $unf_{\mathcal{M}_{\mathcal{G},\mathcal{S}}}(exp_{\mathcal{G}}(q))$ to access the sources.

We refer to steps 1 and 2 as the "query reformulation" step. Step 3 is called the "source access". In the rest of the section we discuss the first two steps.

Let $\mathcal{I} = \langle \mathcal{G}, \mathcal{S}, \mathcal{M}_{\mathcal{G},\mathcal{S}} \rangle$ be a data integration system, let $\mathcal{D}$ be a source database, and let q be a query over the global schema $\mathcal{G}$. We show how to reformulate the original query q into a new query $exp_{\mathcal{G}}(q)$ over the global schema, called the expansion of q w.r.t. $\mathcal{G}$, such that the answer to $exp_{\mathcal{G}}(q)$ over the (virtual) retrieved global database is equal to the answer to q over the canonical database.

The basic idea to do so is that the constraints in $\mathcal{G}$ can be captured by a suitable *logic program* $\mathcal{P}_{\mathcal{G}}$. To build $\mathcal{P}_{\mathcal{G}}$, we introduce a new relation p' (called primed relation) for each relation p in $\mathcal{G}$. Then, from the semantics of $\mathcal{G}$ we devise the following rules for $\mathcal{P}_{\mathcal{G}}$ (expressed in Logic Programming notation [27]):

- for each relation r, we have:

$$r'(X_1,\ldots,X_n) \leftarrow r(X_1,\ldots,X_n)$$

- for each foreign key constraint $r_1[\mathbf{A}] \subseteq r_2[\mathbf{B}]$ in $\mathcal{G}$, where $\mathbf{A}$ and $\mathbf{B}$ are sets of attributes and $\mathbf{B}$ is a key for r_2 (assuming for simplicity that the attributes involved in the foreign key are the first h):

$$r_2'(X_1,\ldots,X_h,f_{h+1}(X_1,\ldots,X_h),\ldots,f_n(X_1,\ldots,X_h)) \leftarrow r_1'(X_1,\ldots,X_h,\ldots,X_m)$$

  where f_i are fresh function symbols, called Skolem functions.

We can use the logic program $\mathcal{P}_\mathcal{G}$ to generate the query $exp_\mathcal{G}(q)$ associated to the original query q. This is done as follows.

1. First, we rewrite q by substituting each relation symbol r in the body $body(q)$ of q with a new symbol r'. We denote by q' the resulting query. In the following we call "primed atom" every atom whose relation symbol is primed, i.e., it has the form r' for some r.
2. Then we build a *partial evaluation tree* for q', i.e., a tree having each node labeled by a conjunctive query g, with one of the atoms in $body(g)$ marked as "*selected*", obtained as follows.
   (a) The root is labeled by q', and has one (primed) atom (for example the first in left-to-right order) marked as selected.
   (b) Except if condition (2c) below is satisfied, a node, labeled by a query g having a "selected" atom α, has one child for each rule ϕ in $\mathcal{P}_\mathcal{G}$ such that there exists a most general unifier[2] $mgu(\alpha, head(\phi))$ between the atom α and the head $head(\phi)$ of the rule ϕ, such that the distinguished variables are not assigned to terms involving Skolem functions. Each of such children has the following properties:
      - it is labeled by the query obtained from g by replacing the atom α with $body(\phi)$ and by substituting the variables with $mgu(\alpha, head(\phi))$;
      - it has as marked "selected" one of the primed atoms (for example the first in left-to-right order).
   (c) If a node d is labeled by a query g, and there exist a predecessor d' of d labeled by a query g' and a substitution θ of the variables of g' that makes g' equal to g, then d has a single child, which is labeled by the empty query (a query whose body is false).
3. Finally we return as result the query $exp_\mathcal{G}(q)$ formed as the union of all non-empty queries in the leaves of the partial evaluation tree.

Theorem 5 (Termination). *The algorithm above always terminates.*

[2] We recall that given two atoms α and β the most general unifier $mgu(\alpha,\beta)$ is a most general substitution for the variables in α and β that makes α and β equal [27].

Proof. The termination of the algorithm follows directly from the following observations:

- The queries in all nodes on the tree have exactly the same number of atoms as the original query q. This is an immediate consequence of the fact that for rule ϕ in $\mathcal{P}_\mathcal{G}$, $body(\phi)$ is formed by exactly one atom.
- Condition (2c) guarantees a finite bound on the nesting of Skolem functions in the queries in the nodes.

As a consequence, the number of queries along each branch of the partial evaluation tree must be finite, hence the thesis holds.

Our goal now is to show that if $\mathcal{I}$ is consistent w.r.t. $\mathcal{D}$, then $t \in q^{\mathcal{I},\mathcal{D}}$ if and only if t is in the answer to $unf_{\mathcal{M}_{\mathcal{G},\mathcal{S}}}(exp_\mathcal{G}(q))$ over $\mathcal{D}$. We will prove such result by applying results from the logic programming theory [27] and, in particular, results on the partial evaluation of logic programs [28]. We first observe that $ret(\mathcal{I},\mathcal{D})$ can be seen as a (finite) set of ground facts in logic programming terms. We proceed by proving a series of lemmas, each dealing with a particular aspect of the proof. The relationship between the *logic program* $\mathcal{P}_\mathcal{G}$ and the canonical database of the data integration system $\mathcal{I}$ is characterized by the following lemma.

Lemma 1. *Up to the renaming of each relation symbol r by the corresponding primed symbol r', $can(\mathcal{I},\mathcal{D})$ coincides with the minimal model of $\mathcal{P}_\mathcal{G} \cup ret(\mathcal{I},\mathcal{D})$.*

Proof. The thesis is an immediate consequence of the semantics of $can(\mathcal{I},\mathcal{D})$ and $\mathcal{P}_\mathcal{G} \cup ret(\mathcal{I},\mathcal{D})$ [27].

Next we focus on SLD-refutation. We observe that, since the query q is a conjunctive query, the query q' is a union of conjunctive queries:

$$q'(X_1,\ldots,X_n) \leftarrow disj_1 \vee \cdots \vee disj_k$$

An SLD-refutation for $\mathcal{P}_\mathcal{G} \cup ret(\mathcal{I},\mathcal{D}) \cup \neg q'(t)$ is defined as an SLD-refutation for $\mathcal{P}_\mathcal{G} \cup \mathcal{P}'_q \cup ret(\mathcal{I},\mathcal{D}) \cup \neg q'(t)$, where $\mathcal{P}'_q$ is constituted by the rules:

$$q(X_1,\ldots,X_n) \leftarrow disj_1$$
$$\cdots$$
$$q(X_1,\ldots,X_n) \leftarrow disj_k$$

one for each disjunct $disj_i$ of the query q' (see [27]).

Lemma 2. *$q'(t)$ is true in the minimal model of $\mathcal{P}_\mathcal{G} \cup ret(\mathcal{I},\mathcal{D})$ iff there is an SLD-refutation for $\mathcal{P}_\mathcal{G} \cup ret(\mathcal{I},\mathcal{D}) \cup \{\neg q'(t)\}$.*

Proof. The thesis follows directly from the soundness and completeness of SLD-resolution for definite logic programs, see e.g., [27].

Next, let us consider a slight modification of the algorithm above where Condition (2c) is replaced by the following one:

If a node d that is labeled by a query g and there exists a predecessor d' of d labeled by a query g' and a substitution θ of the variables of g' that makes g' equal to g, then d has a single child, which is labeled by g itself but without any atom marked as selected.

Let us call $exp^-_{\mathcal{G}}(q)$ the query obtained from such a modified algorithm. For $exp^-_{\mathcal{G}}(q)$, we have the following result.

Lemma 3. *$\mathcal{P}_{\mathcal{G}} \cup ret(\mathcal{I},\mathcal{D}) \cup \{\neg q'(t)\}$ has an SLD-refutation iff $ret(\mathcal{I},\mathcal{D}) \cup \{\neg exp^-_{\mathcal{G}}(q)(t)\}$ has an SLD-refutation.*

Proof. It is easy to see that the modified algorithm generates a so-called partial evaluation [28] of the program $\mathcal{P}_{\mathcal{G}}$ w.r.t. the query q'. From the results in [28] on soundness and completeness of partial evaluation of logic programs, the thesis follows.

Lemma 4. *$\mathcal{P}_{\mathcal{G}} \cup ret(\mathcal{I},\mathcal{D}) \cup \{\neg q'(t)\}$ has an SLD-refutation iff $ret(\mathcal{I},\mathcal{D}) \cup \{\neg exp_{\mathcal{G}}(q)(t)\}$ has an SLD-refutation.*

Proof. The difference between $exp^-_{\mathcal{G}}(q)$ and $exp_{\mathcal{G}}(q)$ is that in $exp_{\mathcal{G}}(q)$ we drop the disjuncts coming from those nodes labeled by a query g such that there exists a query g' and a substitution θ of the variables of g' that makes g' equal to g. Next we show that, in doing this we do not loose any potential SLD-refutation of $\mathcal{P}_{\mathcal{G}} \cup ret(\mathcal{I},\mathcal{D}) \cup \{\neg q'(t)\}$.

Suppose that the shortest (possibly the only one) SLD-refutation for $\mathcal{P}_{\mathcal{G}} \cup ret(\mathcal{I},\mathcal{D}) \cup \{\neg q'(t)\}$ goes through a node labeled by one such g. Let us say the length of the SLD-refutation is n, and that node labeled by g is the k-th node along the SLD-refutation. From such SLD-refutation we get an SLD-refutation for $\mathcal{P}_{\mathcal{G}} \cup ret(\mathcal{I},\mathcal{D}) \cup \{\neg g(t)\}$ of length $n-k$. Observe that, by the so called Lifting Lemma [27], such an SLD-refutation is also an SLD-refutation for $\mathcal{P}_{\mathcal{G}} \cup ret(\mathcal{I},\mathcal{D}) \cup \{\neg g'(t)\}$. Hence there exists an SLD-refutation for which occurs in a node of the SLD-refutation for $\mathcal{P}_{\mathcal{G}} \cup ret(\mathcal{I},\mathcal{D}) \cup \{\neg q(t)\}$ that is shorter than n, which leads to contradiction. It follows that for each SLD-refutation for $\mathcal{P}_{\mathcal{G}} \cup ret(\mathcal{I},\mathcal{D}) \cup \{\neg q'(t)\}$ going through a node satisfying Condition (2c) there is also another (a shorter one in fact) that does not go through that node. Hence we may drop from the partial evaluation $exp^-_{\mathcal{G}}(q)$ all the conjuncts involving such nodes, thus getting $exp_{\mathcal{G}}(q)$ without loosing any SLD-refutation for the original query.

Finally, we observe that, since $exp_{\mathcal{G}}(q)$ does not involve any prime atom, the rules in $\mathcal{P}_{\mathcal{G}}$ cannot be applied along an SLD-refutation for $\mathcal{P}_{\mathcal{G}} \cup ret(\mathcal{I},\mathcal{D}) \cup \{\neg exp_{\mathcal{G}}(q)(t)\}$. Hence every SLD-refutation for $\mathcal{P}_{\mathcal{G}} \cup ret(\mathcal{I},\mathcal{D}) \cup \{\neg exp_{\mathcal{G}}(q)(t)\}$ is also an SLD-refutation for $\mathcal{P}_{\mathcal{G}} \cup ret(\mathcal{I},\mathcal{D}) \cup \{\neg exp_{\mathcal{G}}(q)(t)\}$.

With this lemma in place we can finally present our main theorem.

Theorem 6 (Soundness and Completeness). *Let $\mathcal{I} = \langle \mathcal{G}, \mathcal{S}, \mathcal{M}_{\mathcal{G},\mathcal{S}} \rangle$, let q be a query posed to $\mathcal{I}$, $\mathcal{D}$ a source database for $\mathcal{I}$, and t a tuple of constants of the same arity as q. If $\mathcal{I}$ is consistent w.r.t. $\mathcal{D}$, then $t \in q^{\mathcal{I},\mathcal{D}}$ if and only if t is in the answer to $unf_{\mathcal{M}_{\mathcal{G},\mathcal{S}}}(exp_{\mathcal{G}}(q))$ over $\mathcal{D}$.*

Proof. By Lemma 1, Lemma 2, Lemma 4, we have that $q(t)$ is true in $can(\mathcal{I}, \mathcal{D})$ iff $ret(\mathcal{I}, \mathcal{D}) \cup \{\neg exp_{\mathcal{G}}(q)(t)\}$ has an SLD-refutation. That is by, again applying Lemma 2, $q(t)$ is true in $can(\mathcal{I}, \mathcal{D})$ iff t is in the answer to $exp_{\mathcal{G}}(q)$ over $ret(\mathcal{I}, \mathcal{D})$, i.e., by the semantics of $ret(\mathcal{I}, \mathcal{D})$, iff t is in the answer to $unf_{\mathcal{M}_{\mathcal{G},\mathcal{S}}}(exp_{\mathcal{G}}(q))$ over $\mathcal{D}$.

With regard to the characterization of the computational complexity of the algorithm, we observe that the number of disjuncts in $exp_{\mathcal{G}}(q)$ can be exponential in the number of rules in the logic program $\mathcal{P}_{\mathcal{G}}$ (and therefore in the size of the global schema $\mathcal{G}$), and in the number of variables in the original query q. Note, however, that this bound is independent of the size of $\mathcal{D}$, i.e., the size of data at the sources. We remind the reader that the evaluation of a union of conjunctive queries can be done in time polynomial with respect to the size of the data. Since $exp_{\mathcal{G}}(q)$ is a union of conjunctive queries, as the queries associated by $\mathcal{M}_{\mathcal{G},\mathcal{S}}$ to the elements of $\mathcal{G}$ are, then evaluating $unf_{\mathcal{M}_{\mathcal{G},\mathcal{S}}}(exp_{\mathcal{G}}(q))$ over $\mathcal{D}$ is also polynomial in the size of the data at the sources. It follows that our query answering algorithm is polynomial with respect to data complexity.

The following example illustrates the application of the expansion algorithm in a simple case.

Example 4. Suppose we have the following relations in the global schema $\mathcal{G}$ of a data integration system:

$$\mathsf{person}(Pcode, Age, CityOfBirth)$$
$$\mathsf{student}(Scode, University)$$
$$\mathsf{city}(Name, Major)$$

with the following integrity constraints:

$$key(\mathsf{person}) = \{Pcode\} \qquad \mathsf{person}[CityOfBirth] \subseteq \mathsf{city}[Name]$$
$$key(\mathsf{student}) = \{Scode\} \qquad \mathsf{city}[Major] \subseteq \mathsf{person}[PCode]$$
$$key(\mathsf{city}) = \{Name\} \qquad \mathsf{student}[SCode] \subseteq \mathsf{person}[PCode]$$

The logic program $\mathcal{P}_{\mathcal{G}}$ makes use of the predicates $\mathsf{person}'/3$, $\mathsf{student}'/1$, $\mathsf{city}'/2$ and constitutes of the following rules:

$$\mathsf{person}'(X,Y,Z) \leftarrow \mathsf{person}(X,Y,Z) \qquad \mathsf{city}'(X, f_1(X)) \leftarrow \mathsf{person}'(Y,Z,X)$$
$$\mathsf{student}'(X,Y) \leftarrow \mathsf{student}(X,Y) \qquad \mathsf{person}'(Y, f_2(Y), f_3(Y)) \leftarrow \mathsf{city}'(X,Y)$$
$$\mathsf{city}'(X,Y) \leftarrow \mathsf{city}(X,Y) \qquad \mathsf{person}'(X, f_4(X), f_5(X)) \leftarrow \mathsf{student}'(X,Y)$$

Suppose the user query is $\mathsf{q}(X) \leftarrow \mathsf{person}(X,Y,Z)$.

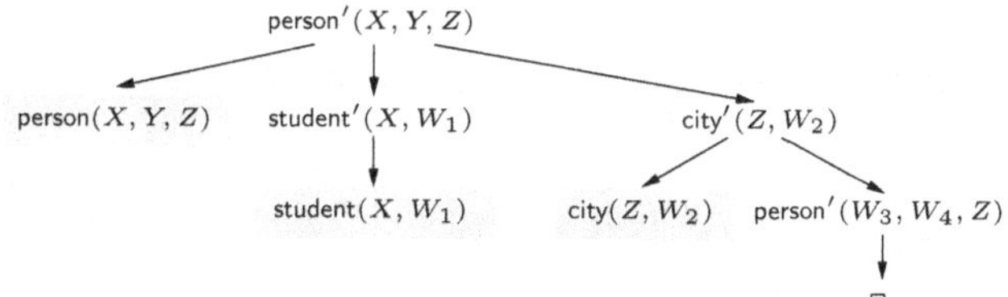

Fig. 1. Partial evaluation tree for the query of Example 4

The partial evaluation tree of q is shown in Figure 1. Note that in the rightmost branch, Condition (2c) is verified and hence the evaluation stops, producing the empty clause □. This prevents the evaluation process to get into an infinite branch. The new variables W_1, W_2, and W_3 are introduced in order to avoid variable clashes when performing unification. The non-empty leaves, shaded in the figure, provide the following expansion $\mathsf{q}' = exp_{\mathcal{G}}(\mathsf{q})$ of the query q:

$$\begin{aligned} \mathsf{q}'(X) &\leftarrow \mathsf{person}(X, Y, Z) \\ \mathsf{q}'(X) &\leftarrow \mathsf{student}(X, W_1) \\ \mathsf{q}'(W_2) &\leftarrow \mathsf{city}(Z, W_2) \end{aligned}$$

Intuitively, we see that the expanded query searches for codes of persons not only in the relation person, but also in student and city, where, due to the integrity constraints, it is known that codes of persons are stored.

6 Conclusions

While it is a common opinion that query processing is an easy task in the global-centric approach to data integration, we have shown the surprising result that, when the global schema contains integrity constraints, even of simple forms, query processing becomes more difficult. The difficulties basically arise because of the need of dealing with incomplete information, similarly to the case of the source-centric approach to data integration. We have studied the case of global schemas expressed in the relational model with key and foreign key constraints, and we have presented techniques for effectively answering queries posed to the data integration system in this case.

As future work, we aim at considering more forms of integrity constraints in the global schema, with the goal of modifying the algorithm described in this paper in order to take into account the new classes of constraints during query processing.

References

1. Batini, C., Lenzerini, M., Navathe, S. B.: A comparative analysis of methodologies for database schema integration. ACM Computing Surveys **18** (1986) 323–364 262
2. Sheth, A. P., Larson, J. A.: Federated database systems for managing distributed, heterogeneous, and autonomous databases. ACM Computing Surveys **22** (1990) 183–236 262
3. Thomas, G., Thompson, G. R., Chung, C. W., Barkmeyer, E., Carter, F., Templeton, M., Fox, S., Hartman, B.: Heterogeneous distributed database systems for production use. ACM Computing Surveys **22** (1990) 237–266 262
4. Litwin, W., Mark, L., Roussopoulos, N.: Interoperability of multiple autonomous databases. ACM Computing Surveys **22** (1990) 267–293 262
5. Catarci, T., Lenzerini, M.: Representing and using interschema knowledge in cooperative information systems. J. of Intelligent and Cooperative Information Systems **2** (1993) 375–398 262
6. Hull, R.: Managing semantic heterogeneity in databases: A theoretical perspective. In: Proc. of PODS'97. (1997) 262

7. Halevy, A. Y.: Answering queries using views: A survey. VLDB Journal **10** (2001) 270–294 262, 263
8. Ullman, J. D.: Information integration using logical views. In: Proc. of ICDT'97. Volume 1186 of LNCS., Springer (1997) 19–40 262, 263
9. Li, C., Chang, E.: Query planning with limited source capabilities. In: Proc. of ICDE 2000. (2000) 401–412 263
10. Garcia-Molina, H., Papakonstantinou, Y., Quass, D., Rajaraman, A., Sagiv, Y., Ullman, J. D., Vassalos, V., Widom, J.: The TSIMMIS approach to mediation: Data models and languages. J. of Intelligent Information Systems **8** (1997) 117–132 263
11. Anthony Tomasic, Louiqa Raschid, P. V.: Scaling access to heterogeneous data sources with DISCO. IEEE Trans. on Knowledge and Data Engineering **10** (1998) 808–823 263
12. Goh, C. H., Bressan, S., Madnick, S. E., Siegel, M. D.: Context interchange: New features and formalisms for the intelligent integration of information. ACM Trans. on Information Systems **17** (1999) 270–293 263
13. Kirk, T., Levy, A. Y., Sagiv, Y., Srivastava, D.: The Information Manifold. In: Proceedings of the AAAI 1995 Spring Symp. on Information Gathering from Heterogeneous, Distributed Enviroments. (1995) 85–91 263
14. Abiteboul, S., Duschka, O.: Complexity of answering queries using materialized views. In: Proc. of PODS'98. (1998) 254–265 263, 266
15. Calvanese, D., De Giacomo, G., Lenzerini, M., Nardi, D., Rosati, R.: Data integration in data warehousing. Int. J. of Cooperative Information Systems **10** (2001) 237–271 263, 264
16. Calì, A., De Giacomo, G., Lenzerini, M.: Models for information integration: Turning local-as-view into global-as-view. In: Proc. of Int. Workshop on Foundations of Models for Information Integration (10th Workshop in the series Foundations of Models and Languages for Data and Objects). (2001) 263
17. Gryz, J.: Query folding with inclusion dependencies. In: Proc. of ICDE'98. (1998) 126–133 263
18. Grahne, G., Mendelzon, A. O.: Tableau techniques for querying information sources through global schemas. In: Proc. of ICDT'99. Volume 1540 of LNCS., Springer (1999) 332–347 263, 266
19. Calvanese, D., De Giacomo, G., Lenzerini, M., Vardi, M. Y.: Query processing using views for regular path queries with inverse. In: Proc. of PODS 2000. (2000) 58–66 263
20. van der Meyden, R.: Logical approaches to incomplete information. In Chomicki, J., Saake, G., eds.: Logics for Databases and Information Systems. Kluwer Academic Publisher (1998) 307–356 263
21. Fernandez, M. F., Florescu, D., Levy, A., Suciu, D.: Verifying integrity constraints on web-sites. In: Proc. of IJCAI'99. (1999) 614–619 264
22. Fernandez, M. F., Florescu, D., Kang, J., Levy, A. Y., Suciu, D.: Catching the boat with strudel: Experiences with a web-site management system. In: Proc. of ACM SIGMOD. (1998) 414–425 264
23. Carey, M. J., Haas, L. M., Schwarz, P. M., Arya, M., Cody, W. F., Fagin, R., Flickner, M., Luniewski, A., Niblack, W., Petkovic, D., Thomas, J., Williams, J. H., Wimmers, E. L.: Towards heterogeneous multimedia information systems: The Garlic approach. In: Proc. of the 5th Int. Workshop on Research Issues in Data Engineering – Distributed Object Management (RIDE-DOM'95), IEEE CS Press (1995) 124–131 264

24. Li, C., Yerneni, R., Vassalos, V., Garcia-Molina, H., Papakonstantinou, Y., Ullman, J. D., Valiveti, M.: Capability based mediation in TSIMMIS. In: Proc. of ACM SIGMOD. (1998) 564–566 264
25. Galhardas, H., Florescu, D., Shasha, D., Simon, E.: An extensible framework for data cleaning. Technical Report 3742, INRIA, Rocquencourt (1999) 268
26. Bouzeghoub, M., Lenzerini, M.: Introduction to the special issue on data extraction, cleaning, and reconciliation. Information Systems **26** (2001) 535–536 268
27. Lloyd, J. W.: Foundations of Logic Programming (Second, Extended Edition). Springer, Berlin, Heidelberg (1987) 272, 273, 274, 275
28. Lloyd, J. W., Shepherdson, J. C.: Partial evaluation in logic programming. J. of Logic Programming **11** (1991) 217–242 274, 275

Rewrite and Conquer: Dealing with Integrity Constraints in Data Integration

Andrea Calì, Diego Calvanese, Giuseppe De Giacomo, and Maurizio Lenzerini

Abstract The work "Data Integration under Integrity Constraints", published at the CAiSE 2002 Conference, proposes a rewriting technique for answering queries in data integration systems, when the global schema contains the classical key and foreign key constraints, and the mapping between the data sources and the global schema is of the global-as-view type. In this addendum, we explain why this research was important and how it gave rise to several results in the following years.

1 Introduction

Our work [3], republished in this volume, considers a data integration setting where a set of data sources is integrated into a global schema by means of *global-as-view* (*GAV*) mappings, and where the global schema contains integrity constraints. In data integration, the mapping establishes the relationship between the data at the sources and the elements of the global schema. While in the *local-as-view* (*LAV*) approach to mappings, every data source is described in terms of a view over the global schema, in the GAV approach the data sources are mapped to the global schema by associating to each element in the global schema a view over the data sources, with the meaning that every tuple satisfying the view at the sources, also satisfies

A. Calì (✉)
University of London, Birkbeck College, UK

University of Oxford, UK
e-mail: andrea@dcs.bbk.ac.uk

D. Calvanese
Free University of Bozen-Bolzano, Bolzano, Italy
e-mail: calvanese@inf.unibz.it

G. De Giacomo · M. Lenzerini
"Sapienza" Università di Roma, Rome, Italy
e-mail: degiacomo@dis.uniroma1.it; lenzerini@dis.uniroma1.it

J. Bubenko et al. (eds.), *Seminal Contributions to Information Systems Engineering*,
DOI 10.1007/978-3-642-36926-1_28,

the element of the global schema in the virtual global database. On the other hand, the global schema provides a common representation for the domain of interest, and including integrity constraints is important if we aim at modeling the domain of interest with reasonable expressive power. Indeed, integrity constraints are the obvious means to express rules corresponding to semantic conditions characterizing the domain.

Referring to the setting described above, the paper addresses one of the most important problems in the design of a data integration system, namely, the definition of the method for computing the answer to queries posed in terms of the global schema. The integrity constraints considered in the paper are key and foreign key constraints, which are very popular mechanisms for adding semantics to a plain relational database schema. The challenge posed by the considered setting derives exactly from the presence of such integrity constraints. The query answering algorithm should compute the answer to queries by taking into account not only the data and the mapping, but also the facts implied by the constraints in the global schema.

The first contribution in the paper was to show that, when the global schema contains key and foreign key constraints, the semantics of the data integration system is best described in terms of a set of databases, rather than a single one, and this implies that query processing is intimately connected to the notion of querying incomplete databases. As a simple example, suppose that a foreign key constraint in the global schema asserts that every value of attribute A of relation r should appear in the (unary) key K of relation s, and assume that the data retrieved from the sources through the mappings do not satisfy this constraints, i.e., there is a value a in $r[A]$ that does not appear in position (attribute) K in any tuple of s. How do we interpret the semantics of the data integration system in this case? One option would be to consider the whole system incorrect, and not even try to answer queries, which is obviously unacceptable. Another option is to interpret the absence of the tuple in s as a form of incompleteness, and consider as possible global databases every global database that has a new tuple $\mathbf{t}$ in s such that $\mathbf{t}[K] = a$. To account for incompleteness, given a query q, we should make sure that we answer q by computing the tuples that satisfy the query in every possible database, i.e, the so-called *certain answers* to q. This is exactly the approach adopted in the paper.

The second contribution of the paper was to propose a specific method to answer conjunctive queries posed to the global schema in the case of GAV mappings, and with key and foreign key constraints in the global schema. The method is based on a rewriting technique. A conjunctive query q is first rewritten into a union of conjunctive queries q' taking into account the integrity constraints in the global schema, and then q' is rewritten, taking into account the mapping, into a query q'' to be evaluated at the sources. The correctness of the method was proved by showing that the algorithm computes exactly the set of certain answers to the original query q. It is important to note that the query q'' is a first-order query over the data sources, and therefore the query answering algorithm runs in polynomial time (actually, in AC^0) with respect to data complexity, i.e., with respect to the size of data at the sources.

In the following, we first place these results in the historical context of research in data integration, and highlight then two lines of research resulting from our work: approaches based on rewriting queries into efficiently evaluable first-order queries, and approaches aiming at tractable query answering by resorting to Datalog.

2 Historical Perspective

At the time of CAiSE 2002, the research on data integration was very active [17]. However, most of the contributions were based on the LAV approach, and only some of them considered the presence of integrity constraints in the global schema [17]. As for the GAV approach, there was the common belief that query answering is somehow trivial, because, at least in principle, a simple unfolding strategy suffices: substitute every atom α of the query with the source query associated to α by the mapping. Obviously, if the views over the sources are first-order queries, the query to be sent to the sources is also first-order, and the complexity of the whole process is AC^0 in data complexity. While this is true for the case of GAV without constraints, our work in [3] demonstrates that the presence of integrity constraints in the global schema, even of a very basic form, may change the picture considerably: key and foreign key constraints introduce a form of incomplete information in the system, and such incompleteness must be reasoned upon during query answering, which cannot be reduced to simple mapping-based unfolding.

A few months after CAiSE 2002, a seminal paper on data exchange, namely [11], was presented at ICDT 2003. *Data exchange* is a form of information integration where the emphasis is on transferring data from a source to a target database according to a set of mappings. Thus, differently from data integration, where the global database can be virtual, in data exchange the main task is to use the mappings to materialize a database starting from the source data. The work in [11] illustrates the importance of the *chase* for data exchange. The chase is a fixpoint algorithm enforcing implication of data dependencies over an incomplete database. Since mappings can be expressed as special dependencies, namely, *tuple-generating dependencies*, the chase turns out to be the right tool to exchange data from the source to the target. Now, if the target schema includes integrity constraints, depending on the form of such constraints, the chase may not terminate. For this reason, [11] introduced a specific form of target constraints, namely, *weakly-acyclic tuple-generating dependencies*, for which the chase terminates, so that a correct target database can be computed by chasing source data with respect to both the mappings and the integrity constraints in the target schema.

Unfortunately, this algorithm does not work in the case of key and foreign key constraints: indeed, in the presence of such constraints, and in particular when the foreign keys are cyclic, the chase might not terminate. We believe that one of the merits of [3] was to show an alternative way to treat integrity constraints in the global schema with respect to a chase-based algorithm, namely via *rewriting*. Our work also indicated that classes of practically relevant integrity constraints, that cannot be treated by the chase, can still be taken into account in data integration.

In the next two sections, we discuss two lines of research following the approach and the methodology presented in [3]. Section 3 describes the efforts to single out new classes of integrity constraints that can be dealt with by means of first-order rewriting algorithms. Section 4 reports on recent research work on incorporating the constraints considered in [3] in Datalog-like languages for expressing the global schema.

3 First-Order Rewritability

One line of research deriving from our work [3] has been concerned with identifying classes of languages to express constraints over the global-schema that allow for computing certain answers with an approach based on rewriting. The key feature of this approach is that the constraints are taken into account by *rewriting*, independently of the underlying data, the given query q into a new query q_r that can be *expressed in first-order logic*. Hence q_r can be unfolded and evaluated by a standard relational database engine. This property of an integrity constraint language is what later became known as *first-order rewritability* of query answering [8], and it has been investigated intensively in the setting of ontology languages.

First-order rewritability imposes strict conditions on the expressive power of the underlying constraint/ontology language. It has led to the development of the *DL-Lite* family of lightweight ontology languages [8]. On the one hand, for the logics of this family conjunctive query answering is first-order rewritable. On the other hand, such logics are tightly connected to conceptual modeling formalisms, and can indeed capture the most important modeling features of UML class diagrams and Entity-Relationship diagrams, as well as constructs that are part of the OWL standard [1, 7]. An exception are covering constraints, which require disjunction to be represented, and lead to query answering that is coNP-hard in data complexity, hence not first-order rewritable [9]. Interestingly, first-order rewritability does not impose any form of acyclicity on the set of constraints. Hence, the logics of the *DL-Lite* family depart from the constraint languages adopted in data-exchange to ensure finiteness of the chase (but see also Sect. 4).

First-order rewritability per se does not guarantee overall efficiency of query answering. In general, rewritings expressed as unions of conjunctive queries [8] may be very large (in the worst case exponential in the size of the original query), and hence not manageable by the DBMS engine. Experiments have shown that such a blowup typically occurs in real-world scenarios. This triggered the development of alternative rewriting techniques [14, 18, 21], whose focus has been on the reduction of the size of generated queries. These techniques produce rewritings that in many cases are polynomial, however the worst-case complexity is still exponential. The technique proposed in [12] produces worst-case polynomial rewritings at the cost of significantly complicating their structure, so that their execution is likely to suffer from poor performance [13]. An alternative, so called *combined*, approach has also been developed [15], in which the original data is first expanded with respect to the constraints/ontology (cf. Sect. 4), and then a rewritten query is executed over this expanded data. This allows for keeping the rewriting both small and efficiently executable, offering good performance at query time. However, it might not be applicable in those settings where no direct control over the data sources is granted, e.g., in data integration scenarios. Current research is investigating approaches in which a holistic view of the query answering/integration system is taken, that considers together with the constraints/ontology expressed at the global level, also the dependencies coming from the data sources and/or induced by the mappings, to optimize the overall query answering process [10, 19, 20].

4 Datalog-Based Approach: Tractable Query Answering

Our work [3], which deals with "traditional" key and foreign key constraints, was the starting point of several studies on more general constraint languages. Datalog, in particular, has been used as a paradigmatic query language for over three decades, and can be naturally adopted in data integration. Datalog has some limits in modeling ontologies, which can be overcome with the introduction of existential quantification in the rule heads; this way, rules become *tuple-generating dependencies (TGDs)*. Unfortunately, checking the entailment of a ground fact by a database (set of ground facts) and a set of TGDs is undecidable. The Datalog$^{\pm}$ family of languages [4] naturally extends [3] by proposing several TGD-based languages based on restrictions on the form of TGD bodies, so as to ensure decidability of query answering, and in some case tractability in data complexity. The two main decidability paradigms in Datalog$^{\pm}$ are *guardedness* and *stickiness*, which we briefly discuss below. Notice that, following the approach of our paper [3], none of the Datalog$^{\pm}$ languages guarantees the finiteness of the chase, which – we believe – is a necessary premise to ensure sufficient expressive power.

Guardedness is a well-known property of first-order theories that guarantees decidability. *Guarded TGDs* [4], or *guarded Datalog*$^{\pm}$, have been inspired by this notion, and offer PTIME data complexity of query answering. *Linear TGDs*, or *linear Datalog*$^{\pm}$, are a less expressive extension of the keys and foreign keys of [3], which enjoys better computational properties that guarded Datalog$^{\pm}$; in particular, linear Datalog$^{\pm}$ is first-order rewritable, with a technique analogous to that of [3]. Extension of guarded Datalog$^{\pm}$ include the addition of stratified negation, and a relaxation of guardedness that defines *weakly-guarded Datalog*$^{\pm}$ [6].

Stickiness is a completely different paradigm from guardedness, and it has been designed with the aim of devising a first-order rewritable Datalog$^{\pm}$ language. *Sticky sets of TGDs*, or *sticky Datalog*$^{\pm}$ [6], are defined by an easily testable syntactic condition, and are obviously first-order rewritable. Extension of sticky Datalog$^{\pm}$ are also studied in [6].

To achieve better expressive power, some works extend Datalog$^{\pm}$ with so-called negative constraints [6] and *equality-generating dependencies* [5], the latter obviously extending the key constraints in our original work [3].

Datalog$^{\pm}$ languages have found several applications; without the restriction of chase termination, their expressive power allows for capturing several ontology languages. Interestingly, the work [16] unites the notions of chase termination and guardedness in a single language.

Other works propose semantic characterizations of sets of TGDs, with emphasis on rewriting. The work [2] defines the notion of *finite unification set*, that is, a set of TGDs that is first-order rewritable by means of a backward-chaining unification algorithm. Rewritability, introduced by us in data integration under integrity constraints in [3], remains a crucial notion for reasons of efficiency of query answering.

Acknowledgements We acknowledge the support of the EU through the large-scale integrating project (IP) Optique (Scalable End-user Access to Big Data), grant agreement n.~FP7-318338.

References

1. A. Artale, D. Calvanese, R. Kontchakov, and M. Zakharyaschev. The *DL-Lite* family and relations. *J. of Artificial Intelligence Research*, 36:1–69, 2009.
2. J.-F. Baget, M. Leclère, M.-L. Mugnier, and E. Salvat. On rules with existential variables: Walking the decidability line. *Artificial Intelligence*, 175(9–10):1620–1654, 2011.
3. A. Calì, D. Calvanese, G. De Giacomo, and M. Lenzerini. Data integration under integrity constraints. In *Proc. of CAiSE 2002*, volume 2348 of *LNCS*, pages 262–279. Springer, 2002.
4. A. Calì, G. Gottlob, T. Lukasiewicz, B. Marnette, and A. Pieris. Datalog+/−: A family of logical knowledge representation and query languages for new applications. In *Proc. of LICS 2010*, pages 228–242, 2010.
5. A. Calì, G. Gottlob, G. Orsi, and A. Pieris. On the interaction of existential rules and equality constraints in ontology querying. In *Correct Reasoning*, pages 117–133, 2012.
6. A. Calì, G. Gottlob, and A. Pieris. Towards more expressive ontology languages: The query answering problem. *Artificial Intelligence*, 193:87–128, 2012.
7. D. Calvanese, G. De Giacomo, D. Lembo, M. Lenzerini, A. Poggi, M. Rodríguez-Muro, and R. Rosati. Ontologies and databases: The *DL-Lite* approach. In S. Tessaris and E. Franconi, editors, *Semantic Technologies for Informations Systems – 5th Int. Reasoning Web Summer School (RW 2009)*, volume 5689 of *LNCS*, pages 255–356. Springer, 2009.
8. D. Calvanese, G. De Giacomo, D. Lembo, M. Lenzerini, and R. Rosati. Tractable reasoning and efficient query answering in description logics: The *DL-Lite* family. *J. of Automated Reasoning*, 39(3):385–429, 2007.
9. D. Calvanese, G. De Giacomo, D. Lembo, M. Lenzerini, and R. Rosati. Data complexity of query answering in description logics. *Artificial Intelligence*, 195:335–360, 2013.
10. F. Di Pinto, D. Lembo, M. Lenzerini, R. Mancini, A. Poggi, R. Rosati, M. Ruzzi, and D. F. Savo. Optimizing query rewriting in ontology-based data access. In *Proc. of EDBT 2013*, 2013.
11. R. Fagin, P. G. Kolaitis, R. J. Miller, and L. Popa. Data exchange: Semantics and query answering. In *Proc. of ICDT 2003*, pages 207–224, 2003.
12. G. Gottlob and T. Schwentick. Rewriting ontological queries into small nonrecursive Datalog programs. In *Proc. of KR 2012*, pages 254–263, 2012.
13. S. Kikot, R. Kontchakov, V. Podolskii, and M. Zakharyaschev. Long rewritings, short rewritings. In *Proc. of DL 2012*, volume 846 of *CEUR*, ceur-ws.org, 2012.

14. S. Kikot, R. Kontchakov, and M. Zakharyaschev. Conjunctive query answering with OWL 2 QL. In *Proc. of KR 2012*, pages 275–285, 2012.
15. R. Kontchakov, C. Lutz, D. Toman, F. Wolter, and M. Zakharyaschev. The combined approach to ontology-based data access. In *Proc. of IJCAI 2011*, pages 2656–2661, 2011.
16. M. Krötzsch and S. Rudolph. Extending decidable existential rules by joining acyclicity and guardedness. In *Proc. of IJCAI 2011*, pages 963–968, 2011.
17. M. Lenzerini. Data integration: A theoretical perspective. In *Proc. of PODS 2002*, pages 233–246, 2002.
18. H. Pérez-Urbina, B. Motik, and I. Horrocks. Tractable query answering and rewriting under description logic constraints. *J. of Applied Logic*, 8(2):186–209, 2010.
19. M. Rodriguez-Muro and D. Calvanese. High performance query answering over *DL-Lite* ontologies. In *Proc. of KR 2012*, pages 308–318, 2012.
20. R. Rosati. Query rewriting under extensional constraints in *DL-Lite*. In *Proc. of DL 2012*, volume 846 of *CEUR*, ceur-ws.org, 2012.
21. R. Rosati and A. Almatelli. Improving query answering over *DL-Lite* ontologies. In *Proc. of KR 2010*, pages 290–300, 2010.

Automated Reasoning on Feature Models*

David Benavides, Pablo Trinidad, and Antonio Ruiz-Cortés

Dpto. de Lenguajes y Sistemas Informáticos,
University of Seville, Av. de la Reina Mercedes S/N, 41012 Seville, Spain
{benavides, trinidad, aruiz}@tdg.lsi.us.es

Abstract. Software Product Line (SPL) Engineering has proved to be an effective method for software production. However, in the SPL community it is well recognized that variability in SPLs is increasing by the thousands. Hence, an automatic support is needed to deal with variability in SPL. Most of the current proposals for automatic reasoning on SPL are not devised to cope with extra–functional features. In this paper we introduce a proposal to model and reason on an SPL using constraint programming. We take into account functional and extra–functional features, improve current proposals and present a running, yet feasible implementation.

1 Introduction and Motivation

Research on SPLs is thriving. Unlike other approaches reuse in SPL has to become systematic instead of ad–hoc. In order to achieve such a goal, SPL practices guide organizations towards the development of products from existing assets rather than the development of separated products one by one from scratch. Thus, features that are shared by all SPL products are reused in every single product. Most of the existing methods [3, 6] for SPL engineering agree that a way for modelling SPL is needed. In this context feature models [7, 9, 11, 13, 22] have been quoted as one of the most important contributions to SPL modelling [7, pag.82]. As in other cases, first applications in routine production are stimulating the development of a supporting science for improving the production methods [17].

Feature models are used to model SPL in terms of features and relations amongst them. In this type of models, the number of potential products of an SPL increases with the number of features. Consequently, a large number of features lead to SPLs with a large number of potential products. In an extremely flexible SPL, where all features may or may not appear in all potential products, the number of potential products is equal to 2^n, being n the number of features. Moreover, current feature models are only focused on modelling functional features and in the most quoted proposals [7, 9, 11, 13, 22] there is a lack of modelling artifacts that deal with extra–functional features (features related to so–called quality or non–functional features). If extra–functional features are taken

* A preliminary version of this paper was presented at [4]. This work was partially funded by the Spanish Ministry of Science and Technology under grant TIC2003-02737-C02-01 (AgilWeb) and PRO-45-2003 (FAMILIES).

O. Pastor and J. Falcão e Cunha (Eds.): CAiSE 2005, LNCS 3520, pp. 491–503, 2005.

into account the number of potential products increases even further. Although it is accepted that in an SPL it is necessary to deal with these extra–functional features [5, 11, 12], there is no consensus about how to deal with them.

Automated reasoning is an ever challenging field in SPL engineering [18, 23]. It should be considered specially when the number of features increases due to the increase in the number of potential products. To the best of our knowledge, there are only a couple of limited attempts by Van Deursen *et al.* and Mannion [8, 14] that treat automatic manipulation of feature models. Although those proposals only consider functional features, leaving out extra–functional features. Van Deursen *et al.* [8] explore automated manipulation of feature descriptions providing an algebra to operate on the feature diagrams proposed in [7]. Mannion's proposal [14] uses first–order logic for product line reasoning. However it only provides a model based on propositional–logic using AND, OR and XOR logical operators to model SPLs. Both attempts have several limitations:

1. They do not allow to deal with extra–functional features (both attempts leave this work pending).
2. They basically answer to the single question of how many products a model has.
3. As far as we know, they have no available an implementation.

In addition, Mannion's model uses the XOR ($\oplus$) operator to model alternative relations, which is either a mistake or a limitation because the model becomes invalid if more than two features are involved in an alternative relation.

The contribution of this paper is threefold. First, we extend existing feature models to deal with extra–functional features. Secondly, we deal with automatic reasoning on extended feature models answering five generic questions, namely i) how many potential products a model has ii) which is the resulting model after applying a filter (e.g. users constraint) to a model, iii) which are the products of a model, iv) is it a valid model, and v) which is the best product of a model according to a criterion and finally giving an accessible, running implementation.

The remainder of this paper is structured as follows. In Section 2, we propose an extension to deal with extra–functional features. In Section 3, we present a mapping to transform an extended feature model into a Constraint Satisfaction Problem (CSP) in order to formalize extended feature models using constraint programming [15]. In Section 4, we improve current reasoning on feature models and we give some definitions to be able to automatically answer several questions on extended feature models. In Section 5, we show how our model can be applied to other important activities such as obtaining commonality and variability information. In Section 6, we briefly present a running prototype implementation. Finally, we summarize our conclusions and describe our future work in Section 7.

2 Extending Feature Models with Extra–Functional Features

2.1 Feature Models

The main goal of feature modelling is to identify commonalities and differences among all products of a SPL. The output of this activity is a compact representation of all po-

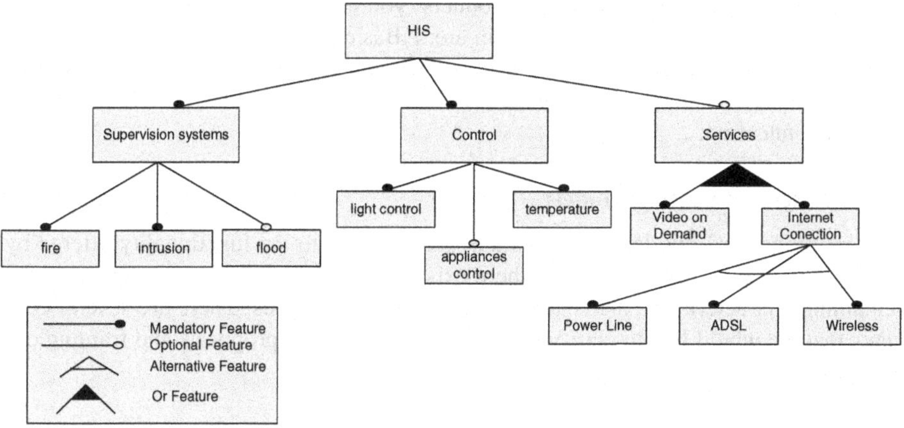

Fig. 1. Feature model of an SPL in the HIS domain

tential products of an SPL, hereinafter called *"feature model"*. Feature models are used to model SPL in terms of features and relations among them. Roughly speaking, a feature is a distinctive characteristic of a product. Depending on the stage of development, it may refer to a requirement [10], a component in an architecture [2] or even to pieces of code [16] (feature oriented programming) of a SPL.

There are several notations to design feature models [7, 9, 11, 13, 22]. We found that the one proposed by Czarnecki is the most comprehensible and flexible as well as being one of the most quoted. Figure 1 depicts a possible feature model of an SPL for the domain of Home Integration Systems (HIS) using Czarneky's notation. This example is partially inspired by [13].

Czarnecki's notation proposes four relations, namely: mandatory, optional, alternative and or–relation. In these relations, there is always a parent feature and one (in the case of mandatory and optional relations) or more (in the case of alternative and or–relation) child features.

- **Mandatory**: the child feature in this relation is always present in the SPL's products when its parent feature is present. For example, Every HIS is equipped with $i)$ fire and intrusion supervision systems and $ii)$ light and temperature control.
- **Optional**: the child feature in an optional relation may or may not be present in a product when its parent feature is present. For Example, there are HISs with services and others without them.
- **Alternative**: a child feature in an alternative relation may be present in a product if its parent feature is included. In this case, only one feature of the set of children is present. For example, in a HIS product if an Internet connection is included, then the customer has to choose between an ADSL, powerline or wireless connection, but only one.
- **Or–relation**: the child feature in an or–relation may be present in a product if its parent feature is included. Then, at least one feature of the set of children may be present. For example, in a HIS the products may have Video or Internet or both at the same time.

This model includes 32 potential products (you can check this on *http://www.tdg-seville.info/topics/spl*). Examples of them are: i)Basic product: consisting of a fire and intrusion supervision systems and light and temperature control. ii)Full product: a product with all supervision and control features as well as a power line, ADSL or wireless Internet connection.

2.2 Extended Feature Models

Current proposals only deal with characteristics related to the functionality offered by an SPL (functional features). Thus, there exists no solid proposal for dealing with the remaining characteristics, also called extra-functional features. There are several concepts that we would like to clarify before analyzing current proposals and framing our contribution:

- Feature: a prominent characteristic of a product. Depending on the stage of development, it may refer to a requirement [10] (if products are requirement documents), a component in an architecture [2] (if products are component architectures) or even to pieces of code [16] (if products are binary code in a feature oriented programming approach) of an SPL.
- Attribute: the attribute of a feature is any characteristic of a feature that can be measured. *Availability* and *cost* are examples of attributes of the *Service* feature of figure 1. *Latency* and *bandwidth* may be examples of attributes of an Internet connection.
- Attribute domain: the space of possible values where the attribute takes its values. Every attribute belongs to a domain. It is possible to have discrete domains (e.g:integers, booleans, enumerated) or continuous domains (e.g.:real).
- Extra–functional feature: a relation between one or more attributes of a feature. For instance: $\mathit{bandwidth} = 256, \mathit{Latency}/\mathit{Availability} > 50$ and so on. These relations are associated to a feature.

In figure 1, every feature refers to functional features of the HIS product line so that every product differs because of its functional features. However, every feature of figure 1 may have associated extra–functional features. For instance, considering the *services* feature, it is possible to identify extra–functional features related to it, such as relations among attributes like *availability,reliability, development time, cost* and so forth. Likewise the *Internet Connection* feature can have extra–functional features such as relations among *latency* or *bandwidth*. Furthermore, the attributes' values of extra–functional features can differ from one product to another. It means, every product not only differs because of its functional features, but because of its extra–functional features too.

Consider the full product of the HIS product line example presented formerly with the same functional features. It is possible to offer several products with the same functional features but different extra–functional features, for instance: i) High quality full product: a product with full functionality and high quality: high *availability* and *reliability* and high *cost* too. ii) Basic quality full product: a product with full functionality but lower quality: lower *availability* and *reliability* and lower *cost* too.

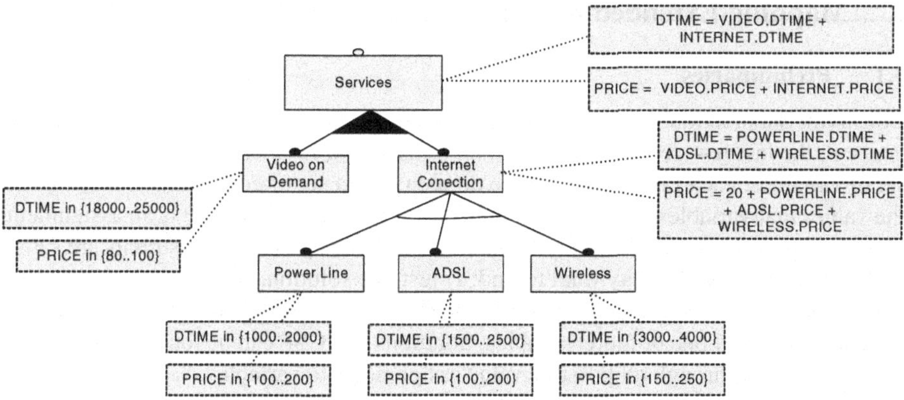

Fig. 2. Extended feature model for an SPL in the HIS domain

To date, we have not found any proposal dealing with functional and extra–functional features in the same model. However, there are some works in the literature that suggest the need of dealing with extra–functional features: Kang *et. al* have been suggesting the need to take into account extra–functional features since 1990 [11, pag. 38] when they depicted a classification of features, although they did not provide a way to do it. Later, in 1998 Kang *et. al* [12] made an explicit reference to what they called 'non–functional' features (a possible type of what we call extra–functional features). However the authors still did not propose a way to solve it. In 2001 Kang *et. al* [5], proposed some guidelines for feature modelling: in [5, pag. 19], the authors once again made the distinction between functional and quality features and pointed out the need of a specific method to include extra–functional features, but they did not provide this specific method on this occasion either.

2.3 A Notation for Extended Feature Models

We propose to extend Czarneki's feature models with extra–functional features and improve previous vague notations proposed in [20] by allowing relations amongst attributes. Using the HIS example, every feature may have one or more attribute relations, for example, the *price* ($PRICE$) and *development time* (expressed in hours) ($DTIME$) taking a range of values in both a discrete or continuous domain (integer or real for example). Thus, it would be possible to decorate the graphical feature model with this kind of information. Figure 2 illustrates a piece of the feature model of figure 1 with extra–functional features with our own notation inspired by [20].

In this example, every sub feature of the *Service* feature has two attributes: $PRICE$ and $DTIME$. Each of the attributes of leaf features are in a domain of values. For instance, the price of an ADSL connection can range from 100 to 200 [1]. In the case of parent features, the values of the attributes are the addition of their children values. For example, the price of an Internet connection is the sum of the prices of the possible Internet connections.

[1] These values are just illustrative, they may have nothing to do with real values.

3 Mapping Extended Feature Models onto CSP

3.1 Preliminaries

Constraint Satisfaction Problems [21] have been object of research in Artificial Intelligence in the last few decades. A Constraint Satisfaction Problem (CSP) is defined as a set of variables, each ranging on a finite domain, and a set of constraints restricting all the values that variables can take simultaneously. A solution to a CSP is an assignment of a value from its domain to every variable, in such a way that all constraints are satisfied simultaneously. We may want to find: i) just one solution, with no preference as to which one, ii) all solutions, iii) an optimal solution by means of an objective function defined in terms of one or more variables. Solutions to a CSP can be found by searching (systematically) through all possible value assignments to variables.

In many real-life applications, we do not want to find any solution but a good solution. The quality of a solution is usually measured by an application dependent function called objective function. The goal is to find a solution that satisfies all the constraints and minimize or maximize the objective function, respectively. Such problems are referred to as Constraint Satisfaction Optimization Problems (CSOP), which consist of a standard CSP and an optimization function that maps every solution (complete labelling of variables) to a numerical value. These are some basic definitions of what a CSP is.

Definition 1 (CSP). *A CSP is a three–tuple of the form (V, D, C) where $V \neq \emptyset$ is a finite set of variables, $D \neq \emptyset$ is a finite set of domains (one for each variable) and C is a constraint defined on V.*

Consider, for instance, the CSP: $(\{a, b\}, \{[0..2], [0..2]\}, \{a + b < 4\})$

Definition 2 (Solution). *Let ψ be a CSP, a solution of ψ is whatever valid assignment of all elements in V as satisfies C.*

In the previous example, a possible solution is $(2, 0)$ since it verifies that $2 + 0 < 4$.

Definition 3 (Solution space). *Let ψ be a CSP of the form (V, D, C), its solution space denoted as $sol(\psi)$ is made up of all its possible solutions. A CSP is satisfiable if its solution space is not empty.*

$$sol(\psi) = \{S \mid \forall s_i \cdot s_i \in S \Rightarrow C(s_i) = true\}$$

In the previous example, there are eight solutions. The only assignment that does not satisfy $a + b < 4$ is $(2, 2)$. Nevertheless, if we replace the constraint with $a + b < -1$, then the CSP is not satisfiable.

Definition 4 (CSOP). *A CSOP is a four–tuple of the form (V, D, C, O) where V, D and C stand for a CSP and O is a real function defined on D.*

Consider, for instance, the CSOP: $(\{a, b\}, \{[0..2], [0..2]\}, \{a + b < 4\}, a)$

Definition 5 (Optimum space). *Let ψ be a CSOP of the form (V, D, C, O), its optimum space denoted as $max/min(\psi, O)$ is made up of all solutions that maximize or minimize O.*

$$max(\psi, O) = \{s \mid \forall s\prime \cdot s\prime \in sol(\psi) \wedge s\prime \neq s \Rightarrow O(s) \geq O(s\prime)\}$$

$$min(\psi, O) = \{s \mid \forall s\prime \cdot s\prime \in sol(\psi) \ \wedge \ s\prime \neq s \ \Rightarrow O(s) \leq O(s\prime)\}$$

In the previous example, $max(\psi, a) = \{(2,0),(2,1)\}$.

3.2 The Mapping

In [1] we presented an algorithm to transform an extended feature model into a CSP. The mapping between a feature model and a CSP has the following general form: $i)$ the features make up the set of variables, $ii)$ the domain of each variable is the same: $\{true, false\}$, $iii)$ extra–functional features are expressed as constraints and $iv)$ every relation of the feature model becomes a constraint among its features in the following way:

- Mandatory relation: Let f be the parent and f_1 the child in a mandatory relation , then the equivalent constraint is: $f_1 = f$
- Optional relation: Let f be the parent and f_1 the child in an optional relation, then the equivalent constraint is: $f_1 \Rightarrow f$
- Or–relation: Let f be the parent in an or–relation and $f_i \mid i \in [1 \ldots n]$ the set of children, then the equivalent constraint is: $f_1 \vee f_2 \vee \ldots f_n \Leftrightarrow f$.
- Alternative relation: Let f be the parent of an alternative relation and and $f_i \mid i \in [1 \ldots n]$ the set of children, then the equivalent constraint is:
  $(f_1 \Leftrightarrow (\neg f_2 \wedge \ldots \wedge \neg f_n \wedge f)) \wedge (f_2 \Leftrightarrow (\neg f_1 \wedge \neg f_3 \ldots \wedge \neg f_n \wedge f)) \wedge$
  $(f_n \Leftrightarrow (\neg f_1 \wedge \ldots \wedge \neg f_{n-1} \wedge f))$

There may be several different algorithms to map extended feature models. The one presented in [1] is a possible one. Hereinafter, we refer to the equivalent CSP resulting from the mapping as ψ_M. Using this mapping, constraints for functional and extra–functional features can be handled together. Thus, table 1 shows the equivalent constraints for figure 1 with the extra–functional features of figure 2. Constraints of extra–functional features are denoted by an asterisk. $POWERLINE, ADSL$ and $WIRELESS$ extra–functional features are not shown for lack of space as they are very similar to the $VIDEO.$ ones.

4 Automated Reasoning on Extended Feature Models

Since we go toward automated reasoning on feature models, a formal model of SPL becomes necessary. We propose to use Constraint Programming to reason on extended features models.

Our model is able to answer the following questions:

4.1 Number of Products

One of the questions to be answered is how many potential products a FM contains. This is a key question in SPL engineering because if the number of products increases the SPL becomes more flexible as well as more complex.

Table 1. A trace of the algorithm presented in [1] for HIS example

Relation	ψ_{HIS}
HIS 1	$(SUPERVISION = HIS)$
HIS 2	$(CONTROL = HIS)$
HIS 3	$(SERVICES \Rightarrow HIS)$
SUPERVISION 1	$(FIRE = SUPERVISION)$
SUPERVISION 2	$(INTRUSION = SUPERVISION)$
SUPERVISION 3	$(FLOOD \Rightarrow SUPERVISION)$
CONTROL 1	$(LIGHT = CONTROL)$
CONTROL 2	$(APPLIANCE \Rightarrow CONTROL)$
CONTROL 3	$(TEMPERATURE = CONTROL)$
SERVICES 1	$((VIDEO \vee INTERNET) \Leftrightarrow SERVICES)$
SERVICES *	$(SERVICES.PRICE = VIDEO.PRICE + INTERNET.PRICE) \wedge$ $(SERVICES.DTIME = VIDEO.DTIME + INTERNET.DTIME)$
VIDEO *	$((VIDEO.PRICE \in [80\ 100]) \Leftrightarrow VIDEO) \wedge$ $((VIDEO.PRICE = 0) \Leftrightarrow \neg VIDEO) \wedge$ $((VIDEO.DTIME \in [18000, 25000]) \Leftrightarrow VIDEO) \wedge$ $((VIDEO.DTIME = 0) \Leftrightarrow \neg VIDEO)$
INTERNET 1	$(POWERLINE \Leftrightarrow (\neg ADSL \wedge \neg WIRELESS \wedge INTERNET)) \wedge$ $(ADSL \Leftrightarrow (\neg POWERLINE \wedge \neg WIRELESS \wedge INTERNET)) \wedge$ $(WIRELESS \Leftrightarrow (\neg POWERLINE \wedge \neg ADSL \wedge INTERNET))$
INTERNET *	$((INTERNET.PRICE = ADSL.PRICE + WIRELESS.PRICE$ $+ POWERLINE.PRICE + 20) \Leftrightarrow INTERNET) \wedge$ $((INTERNET.PRICE = 0) \Leftrightarrow \neg INTERNET) \wedge$ $((INTERNET.DTIME = ADSL.DTIME + WIRELESS.DTIME$ $+ POWERLINE.DTIME) \Leftrightarrow INTERNET) \wedge$ $((INTERNET.DTIME = 0) \Leftrightarrow \neg INTERNET)$

Definition 6 (Cardinal). *Let M be an extended feature model, the number of potential products of M, hereinafter cardinal, is equal to the solution number of its equivalent CSP ψ_M.*

$$cardinal(M) = |sol(\psi_M)|$$

In the HIS example of figure 1 $cardinal(HIS) = 32$, simply by adding for example a new service like *Radio Streaming*, the number of potential products raises to 64. Likewise adding the attributes of figure 2 $cardinal(HIS) = 260$.

4.2 Filter

There should be a way to apply filters to the model. These filters can be imposed by the users. A filter acts as a limitation for the potential products of the model. A typical application of this operation occurs when customers are looking for a product with a specific set of characteristics, that is, they are not interested in all potential products but in some of them only (those passing the filter).

Definition 7 (Filter). *Let M be an extended feature model and F a constraint representing a filter, the filtered model of ψ_M, hereinafter filter, is equal to ψ_M adding the constraint F.*

$$filter(M, F) = (\psi_M \wedge F)$$

A possible filter for the HIS example would be to ask for all products with video on demand, making the number of potential products decrease from 32 to 16. It is also possible to apply filters to attributes. For example, it would be possible to ask for all products whose prices are lower than 200, 12then

$$cardinal(filter(\text{HIS}, \text{SERVICES.PRICE} < 200)) = 44$$
(when any filter is imposed, it decreases from 260 to 44).

4.3 Products

Once ψ_M is defined, there should be a way to get the solutions of the model, that is the products of ψ_M.

Definition 8 (Products). *Let M be an extended feature model, the potential products of the model M, hereinafter products, is equal to the solutions of the equivalent CSP ψ_M.*

$$products(M) = \{s \in sol(\psi_M)\}$$

In the HIS example we would want to get all the possible products of the model or even apply a filter and then get the products. Thus $M = filter($ HIS,VIDEO = true $)$ and $products(M) = \{s \in sol(\psi_{HIS} \wedge$ VIDEO=true $))\}$.

4.4 Validation

A valid extended feature model is a model where at least one product can be selected. That is, a model where ψ_M has at least one solution.

Definition 9 (Valid model). *A feature model M is valid if its equivalent CSP is satisfiable.*

$$valid(M) \iff products(M) \neq \emptyset$$

The HIS model of the example is valid, but there might be situations where the constraints are not satisfiable, making the model invalid. For instance, if the Service's price is lower than 100, and a filter is imposed to have $INTERNET$, then the model is not valid:

$$valid(filter(HIS, INTERNET = \text{true} \wedge SERVICE.PRICE < 100)) = false$$

4.5 Optimum Products

Finding out the best products according to a determinate criterion is an essential task in our model.

Definition 10 (Optimum). *Let M be an extended feature model and O an objective function, then the optimum set of products, hereinafter max and min, is equal to the optimum space of ψ_M.*

$$max(M,O) = max(\psi_M,O)$$
$$min(M,O) = min(\psi_M,O)$$

It is also possible to apply a filter to the HIS example and then ask for an optimal product. Thus, a possible optimum criterion for the HIS example would be to ask for all products with video on demand, and the minimum value for the multiplication of price and development time. In this case selected products P_{opt} are:

The model presented in this section can support current feature models. The only dif-

$$\begin{array}{l|} M = filter(\ HIS, VIDEO = true\ ) \\ O = SERVICE.PRICE * SERVICE.DTIME \\ P_{opt} = min(M,O) \end{array}$$

ference is that current feature models do not support extra–functional features which means that when using our model to reason on current feature models, attributes are not taken into account. Thus, the algorithm presented in [1] and all previous definitions remain valid for current feature models.

5 Realising the Benefits

Compared to others, our approach is very flexible because it is so easy to extend. Below, we show two more definitions based on the previous ones to demonstrate how our approach can be extended and give valuable information to SPL engineers.

5.1 Variability

As mentioned previously, feature models are composed of a set of features and relations among them. If relations restrict the number of products to only one, we are considering the lowest variability while a feature model defining no possible product would be considered a non-valid model. On the other hand, considering no relations, the number of products within the feature model would be the highest. This case would represent the highest variability. Relations restrict the number of potential products, so variability depends on relation types.

Let a leaf feature be a feature that has no child feature. Parent features add no variability to the model, because they are feature aggregates. We define the variability factor as follows.

Definition 11 (Variability Factor(VF)). *Let M be an extended feature model, and ψ_M the equivalent CSP. Let M^V be another extended feature model, considering the leaf features in M and no relation among its features, and ψ_M^V the equivalent CSP.*

$$VF(M) = \frac{cardinal(M)}{cardinal(M^v)} = \frac{|sol(\psi_M)|}{|sol(\psi_M^V)|}$$

The variability factor in the real domain would take values ranging from 0 to 1.

VF can assist decision making. For instance, when many products are going to be developed one of the first decisions to be taken, is whether the SPL approach or traditional approach is going to be applied. A high VF may suggest an SPL approach; a low VF may suggest a traditional approach.

5.2 Commonality

In a feature model, some features will appear in every product, some in only one product and others in some products. When deciding the order in which features are going to be developed, it is very important to know which are the most common features in order to prioritize their building. Obtaining commonality information from the feature model can be feasible by asking questions to our model. We define the feature commonality as the percentage of products containing that feature.

Definition 12 (Commonality). *Let M be an extended feature model and F the feature we want to know its commonality.*

$$commonality(M, F) = \frac{cardinal(filter(M, F = true))}{cardinal(M)}$$

6 Implementation

We have already implemented some of the ideas presented in this paper using OPL Studio, a commercial CSP solver. This implementation is available at *http://www.tdg-seville.info/topics/spl*.

Three modules have been developed in our implementation: first, a feature markup language and XML Schema were agreed on. This language allows to represent the Czarnecki's feature model [7]. Secondly, a parser to transform this XML documents to a CSP following the algorithm described in [1] was developed. Finally, a web–based prototyping interface was made available to allow to test some of the capabilities of the model. In order to test our implementation, we have modeled four problems (two academical and two real product lines) that are available on the web site.

In order to evaluate the implementation, we measured its performance and effectiveness. We implemented the solution using Java. We ran our tests on a WINDOWS XP PROFESSIONAL machine that was equipped with a 1.5Ghz AMD Athlon XP microprocessor, and 496 MB of DDR 266Mhz RAM memory. The test was based on the feature model in Figure 1, adding new features. Several tests were made on each feature model in order to avoid as many exogenous interferences as possible.

We have experimentally inferred that the implementation presented has an exponential behavior while increasing the number of features in the feature model and maintaining a constant variability factor. We have measured the solving time for $products(M)$, which is the most complex to obtain, and have considered it for different values of VF as shown in Figure 3. Our test determines our model has a good performance up to 25 features while the VF is kept constant.

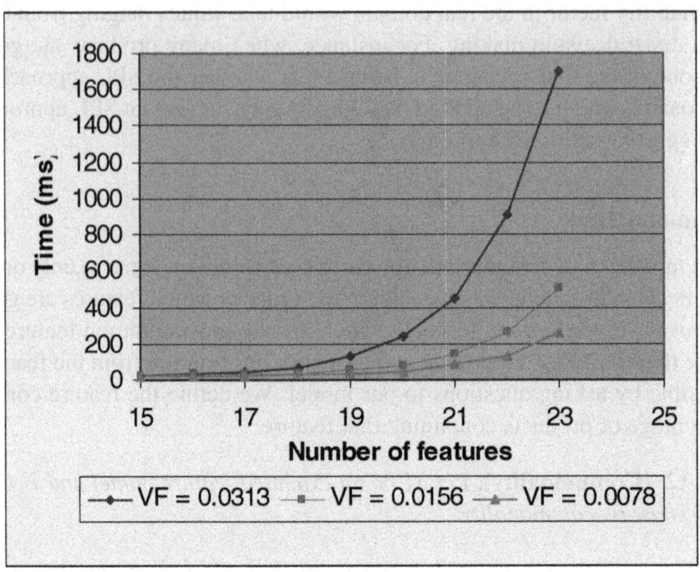

Fig. 3. Empirical performance test for $products(M)$

7 Conclusion and Further Work

In this paper we set the basis for reasoning on SPL with features and attribute relations at the same time and in the same model using constraint programming.

There are some challenges we have to face in the near feature, namely: i) extending our model to support dependencies such as a feature that *requires* or *excludes* another feature (e.g. video on demand requires $ADSL128$) that are also proposed in other feature models ii) extending our current feature markup language to include extra–functional features iii) developing a case tool to validate our model on an industrial context, iv) performing a more rigorous validation of our implementation, studying the influences as well as the number of solutions, the types of relations, the number of features, and so on, v) comparing our work with others in the product configuration field[19].

References

1. D. Benavides, A. Ruiz-Cortés, and P. Trinidad. Coping with automatic reasoning on software product lines. In *Proceedings of the 2nd Groningen Workshop on Software Variability Management*, November 2004.
2. M. Bernardo, P. Ciancarini, and L. Donatiello. Architecting families of software systems with process algebras. *ACM Transactions on Software Engineering and Methodology*, 11(4):386–426, 2002.
3. J. Bosch. *Design and Use of Software Architectures.* Addison-Wesley, 1th edition, 2000.

4. J. Bosch and H. Obbink. Proceedings of the 2nd Groningen Workshop on Software Variability Management. Technical Report to be published, University of Groningen, November 2004.
5. G. Chastek, P. Donohoe, K.C. Kang, and S. Thiel. Product Line Analysis: A Practical Introduction. Technical Report CMU/SEI-2001-TR-001, Software Engineering Institute, Carnegie Mellon University, June 2001.
6. P.C. Clements and L. Northrop. *Software Product Lines: Practices and Patterns.* SEI Series in Software Engineering. Addison–Wesley, August 2001.
7. K. Czarnecki and U.W. Eisenecker. *Generative Programming: Methods, Techniques, and Applications.* Addison–Wesley, may 2000. ISBN 0–201–30977–7.
8. A. van Deursen and P. Klint. Domain–specific language design requires feature descriptions. *Journal of Computing and Information Technology*, 10(1):1–17, 2002.
9. M. Griss, J. Favaro, and M. d'Alessandro. Integrating feature modeling with the RSEB. In *Proceedings of theFifthInternational Conference on Software Reuse*, pages 76–85, Canada, 1998.
10. S. Jarzabek, Wai Chun Ong, and Hongyu Zhang. Handling variant requirements in domain modeling. *The Journal of Systems and Software*, 68(3):171–182, 2003.
11. K. Kang, S. Cohen, J. Hess, W. Novak, and S. Peterson. Feature–Oriented Domain Analysis (FODA) Feasibility Study. Technical Report CMU/SEI-90-TR-21, Software Engineering Institute, Carnegie Mellon University, November 1990.
12. K.C. Kang, S. Kim, J. Lee, K. Kim, E. Shin, and M. Huh. FORM: A feature–oriented reuse method with domain–specific reference architectures. *Annals of Software Engineering*, 5:143–168, 1998.
13. K.C. Kang, J. Lee, and P. Donohoe. Feature–Oriented Product Line Engineering. *IEEE Software*, 19(4):58–65, July/August 2002.
14. M. Mannion. Using First-Order Logic for Product Line Model Validation. In *Proceedings of the Second Software Product Line Conference (SPLC2)*, LNCS 2379, pages 176–187, San Diego, CA, 2002. Springer.
15. K. Marriot and P.J. Stuckey. *Programming with Constraints: An Introduction.* The MIT Press, 1998.
16. Christian Prehofer. Feature-oriented programming: A new way of object composition. *Concurrency and Computation: Practice and Experience*, 13(6):465–501, 2001.
17. M. Shaw. Prospects for an engineering discipline of software. *IEEE Softw.*, 7(6):15–24, 1990.
18. M. Sinnema, S. Deelstra, J. Nijhuis, and J. Bosch. COVAMOF: A Framework for Modeling Variability in Software Product Families. In *Proceedings of the Third Software Product Line Conference (SPLC04)*, San Diego, CA, 2004.
19. T. Soininen, J. Tiihonen, T. Männistö, and R. Sulonen. Towards a general ontology of configuration. *AI EDAM*, 12(4):357–72, 1998.
20. D. Streitferdt, M. Riebisch, and I. Philippow. Details of formalized relations in feature models using ocl. In *Proceedings of 10th IEEE International Conference on Engineering of Computer–Based Systems (ECBS 2003), Huntsville, USA. IEEE Computer Society*, pages 45–54, 2003.
21. Edward Tsang. *Foundations of Constraint Satisfaction.* Academic Press, 1995.
22. J. van Gurp, J. Bosch, and M. Svahnberg. On the notion of variability in software product lines. In *Proceedings of the Working IEEE/IFIP Conference on Software Architecture (WICSA'01), IEEE Computer Society*, pages 45–54, 2001.
23. A. Wasowski. Automatic Generation of Program Families by Model Restrictions. In *Proceedings of the Third Software Product Line Conference (SPLC04)*, San Diego, CA, 2004.

Automated Analysis of Stateful Feature Models

Pablo Trinidad, Antonio Ruiz-Cortés, and David Benavides

Abstract In CAiSE 2005, we interpreted the extraction of relevant information from extended feature models as an automated reasoning problem based on constraint programming. Such extraction is driven by a catalogue of basic and compound operations. Much has been done since, renaming the problem as the automated analysis of feature models, a widely accepted problem in the *Software Product Line (SPL)* community. In this chapter, we review this seminal contribution and its impact in the community, highlighting the key milestones up to a more complete problem formulation that we coin as the *Automated Analysis of Stateful Feature Models (AASFM)*. Finally, we envision some breakthroughs and challenges in the AASFM.

1 Original Contribution

SPL engineering [1] is an emerging paradigm to build families of software products in a given domain considering systematic reuse as a must since very early stages of development. *Feature Models (FMs)* are one of the most widely used models to manage variability and compactly represent the set of products in a SPL [2]. These products are defined as a set of features, each of which describe an increment in product functionality. Besides features, FMs can use attributes to model certain properties of products in so-called *Extended Feature Models (EFMs)*. The automated analysis of FM defined as the automated extraction of information from FMs is an important task to support decision making such as product configuration or model debugging.

In CAiSE 2005 [3] we interpreted the automated analysis of FM and EFMs as an automated reasoning problem based on *Constraint Satisfaction Problems (CSPs)*.

P. Trinidad (✉) · A. Ruiz-Cortés · D. Benavides
University of Seville, Seville, Spain
e-mail: ptrinidad@us.es; aruiz@us.es; benavides@us.es

J. Bubenko et al. (eds.), *Seminal Contributions to Information Systems Engineering*, DOI 10.1007/978-3-642-36926-1_30, © Springer-Verlag Berlin Heidelberg 2013

Our main contribution was supporting the automated analysis as a catalogue of five basic operations (cardinal, filter, products, valid model and optimum product) and two derived operations (commonality and variability factor), giving a semantics to these operations in terms of a unique semantics domain: constraint programming. The main advantage of CSPs over other automated reasoning techniques was its high declarativity and the wide offer of off-the-shelf solvers to build a reference implementation of the operations by the catalogue.

2 Impact and Evolution

An analysis on the references to our work inclines us to think that its main attraction lies in four factors: (i) we pioneered the use of off-the-shelf solvers for the automated analysis. (ii) despite EFMs had already been used for modelling purposes, it was the first approach that enabled their automated analysis. (iii) the proposal of the optimum product operation, which was the first specific analysis operation of EFMs. (iv) we envisioned the composability of the analysis operations, opening the door to the future addition of new analysis operations.

This work has been a reference for many authors [4] who (i) have extended the operations catalogue up to more than 30 operations [5], and (ii) have proposed new techniques which offer a better performance for certain operations. For the authors of the paper, it has been the base of Benavides' and Trinidad's doctoral dissertations [6, 7]. Benavides's work formalises a catalogue of operations for the *Automated Analysis of Feature Models (AAFM)*. The more recent Trinidad's work proposes *Stateful Feature Models (SFMs)* as a kind of fully-configurable FM, and a catalogue of analysis operations on them, which subsumes the AAFM adding a full support for explanatory operations in the so-called *Automated Analysis of Stateful Feature Models (AASFM)*. In Sect. 3 and 4 we provide an overview on the AAFM and the AASFM respectively.

3 Automated Analysis of Feature Models

The AAFM can be seen as a black-box process that takes an FM (with maybe some additional information) as an input and outputs a result which depends on an analysis operation (see Fig. 1). For some analysis operations, additional information is needed such as a minimality criterion to find an optimum product, a feature to calculate its commonality, or a *Configuration Model (CM)*, which collects the decisions made by users along a configuration process, to check if there exists at least one product in the FM that fits into their decisions.

The use of declarative approaches is a trend in the AAFM. In [3] we proposed the first interpretation of FMs in terms of CSPs. The seven analysis operations were defined in terms of CSP operations. So for example, searching for all the solutions in a CSP provides the list of products in a FM; or counting all the solutions it is possible

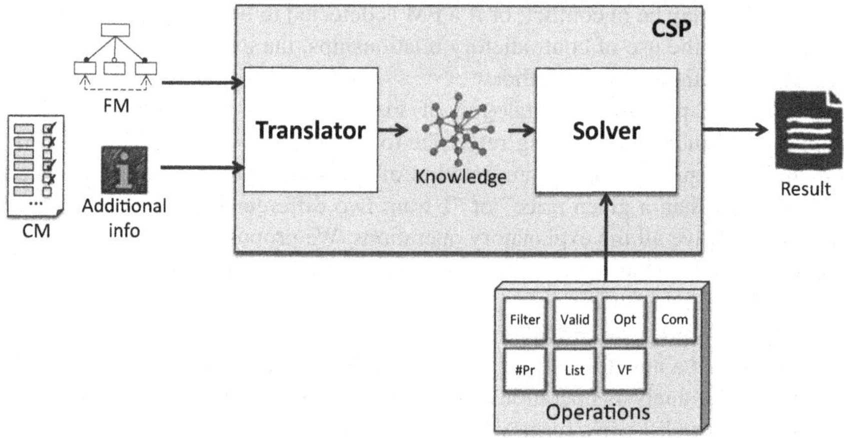

Fig. 1 Schema of the automated reasoning of feature models proposed in [3]

to obtain the number of products defined within a FM. This was the first proposal to date that were able use attributes for analysis purposes, enabling an optimisation operation that searches for the best product according to a given criterion.

Since our work, other authors have proposed the use of other declarative paradigms such as binary decision diagrams, satisfiability problems or description logics. All these works interpret one or more analysis operations in terms of reasoning problems under these declarative paradigms, generally improving the performance or the expressiveness of previous approaches. In 2010, we counted up to 30 analysis operations [5] using up to 10 different solvers or techniques. Nowadays, the AAFM keeps on being an ongoing discipline in the SPL community with more than 40 proposed operations.

The homogeneity of the AAFM proposals allowed us to develop the FAMA Framework [8], an open-source tool for the AAFM widely used by several research institutions and companies. This tool offers an easy-to-use interface with the most updated catalogue of analysis operations, each of them implemented in several off-the-shelf solvers.

The verification of AAFM tools, i.e. the detection of inconsistencies between AAFM implementation and specification, is an important task in our research. Testing techniques have been developed to verify any AAFM tool in general and FAMA Framework in particular [9].

4 Automated Analysis of Stateful Feature Models

Since 2006, one of the open issues in the AAFM was the explanatory analysis [10], i.e. a set of analysis operations to obtain the reasons why another analysis operation has provided a certain result. So for example, if a filter operation detects that there exist no product for a given CM, the explanatory analysis provides for the user decisions that may be in conflict; or if a FM is detected to be void, i.e. it defines no product due to the use of contradictory relationships, the explanatory analysis can suggest the relationships in conflict.

In [11], we proposed a catalogue of 11 explanatory operations. In [7] we establish the inability of making reference to cardinalities and attributes in CMs. This limitation prevents the representation of decisions such as "I want a system that costs less than a given price" or "I want two different Internet connections", necessary to solve all the explanatory operations. We propose SFMs as a new kind of model that (i) enables user decisions on cardinalities and attributes. (ii) joins FMs and CMs in a single model.

Thanks to SFMs, we provided a semantics for all the explanatory operations but also enabled a new formal specification framework for analysis operations. We interpret all the analysis operations as particular cases of deductive and abductive reasoning, two well-known forms of reasoning in the Artificial Intelligence community. With this approach, we propose a reasoner-independent semantics for all the analysis operations on SFMs in the so-called AASFM.

Besides improving the expressiveness, SFMs aim to improve the analysis capabilities of the AAFM in two aspects: (i) giving a semantics to all the explanatory operations defined in [11], and (ii) as formal specification frameworks are as difficult to build and taking into account that currently there are more than 40 analysis operations, which 11 of them are explanatory operations, we aim to provide a formal specification framework that overcomes these drawbacks.

With this two main goals in mind, the AASFM provides a simple, configurable and expressive semantics to all the explanatory operations, even for those that remained undiscovered in the AAFM. It enables the definition of the following minimal set of core analysis operations whose semantics is given in terms of deductive and abductive operations:

- Validation: this operation determines if a SFM is valid, i.e. it checks if the decisions within the SFM satisfy all the relationships.
- Product listing: this operation obtains a list of all the products in a SFM that satisfy all the user decisions and relationships.
- Propagation: this operation calculates a new SFM where user decisions are automatically suggested from previous user decisions.
- Relationship explanation: this operation explains the possible causes why an SFM is invalid in terms of the relationships that can be causing it [12].
- Configuration explanation: this operation explains the possible causes why an SFM is invalid in terms of the user decisions that must be repaired to reach a valid configuration [13].

Besides these core operations, we provide the composition mechanisms that enables the definition of a set of compound operations inspired in the catalogue of analysis operations proposed for the AAFM, while we open the door for the definition of new operations. Figure 2 shows an overview of the AASFM where we can see the differences with respect to AAFM.

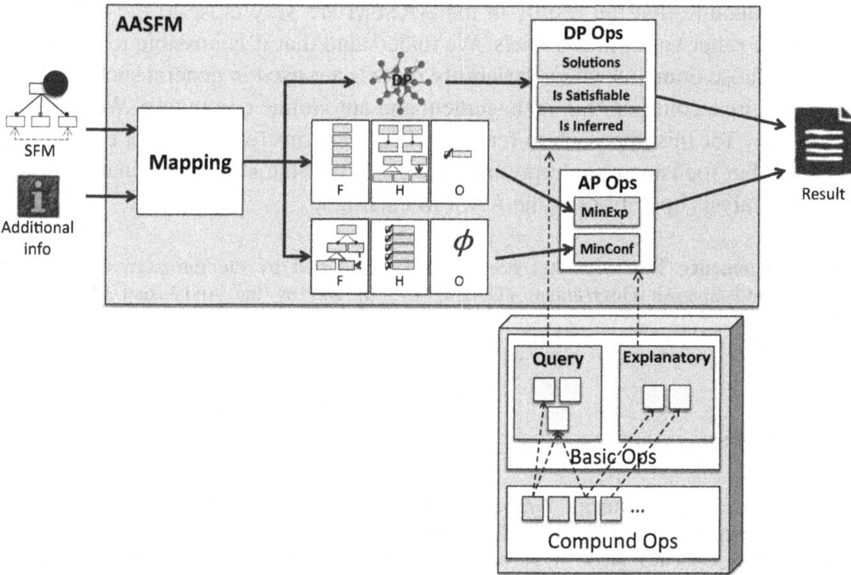

Fig. 2 General schema of the automated analysis of stateful feature models

As a last contribution, we have explored the use of *Model-driven Engineering (MDE)* approaches to build engines for the AASFM. The large number of solvers and analysis operations in FAMA Framework becomes its maintenance in a time consuming task. With MDE, models are transformed into other models in a chain of transformations until a suitable representation is obtained. The AAFM and the AASFM can be seen as a chain of transformations, what makes the MDE a natural approach to implement them that reduces the maintenance costs.

5 Breakthroughs, Challenges and Applications

The AASFM subsumes the AAFM, providing new analysis operations and covering some important gaps in the AAFM, such as the lack of expressiveness of CMs and an incomplete support of explanatory operations. The extensibility of the new catalogue of operations lets the users define their own analysis operations in terms of basic operations, even reducing the efforts to build AASFM engines.

One of the main challenges in the AASFM is the verification of all the operations in the catalogue, adapting existing proposals from the AAFM to the AASFM. Besides verification, obtaining a good performance for AASFM engines in order to incorporate them to the most widespread SPL tools is another challenge in the AASFM.

We conjecture that the results in the AASFM are very close to the automated analysis of other variability models. We understand that it is possible to apply our results to those domains where variability models are used in general such as cloud infrastructures, configuration management and autonomic computing. We envision that the key for this approach to real-world applications resides in not reinventing the wheel but focusing on interpreting real-world problems as a combination of the existing analysis operations in the AASFM catalogue.

Acknowledgements This work has been partially supported by the European Commission (FEDER) and Spanish Government (TIN2009-07366) and by the Andalusian Government (TIC-5906).

References

1. P. Clements and L. Northrop. *Software Product Lines: Practices and Patterns*. SEI Series in Software Engineering. Addison–Wesley, 2001.
2. K. Kang, S. Cohen, J. Hess, W. Novak, and S. Peterson. Feature–Oriented Domain Analysis (FODA) Feasibility Study. Technical Report CMU/SEI-90-TR-21, Software Engineering Institute, Carnegie Mellon University, nov 1990.
3. D. Benavides, A. Ruiz-Cortés, and P. Trinidad. Automated reasoning on feature models. *LNCS, Advanced Information Systems Engineering: 17th International Conference, CAiSE 2005*, 3520:491–503, 2005.
4. Microsoft Academic Research. Automating reasoning of feature models references. http://goo.gl/Yj5iL, 2012.
5. D. Benavides, S. Segura, and A. Ruiz Cortés. Automated analysis of feature models 20 years later: A literature review. *Information Systems*, 35(6):615–636, 9 2010.
6. D. Benavides. *On the Automated Analysis of Software Product Lines Using Feature Models. A framework for developing automated tool support.* PhD thesis, University of Seville, 2007.
7. P. Trinidad. *Automating the Analysis of Stateful Feature Models*. PhD thesis, University of Seville, http://www.lsi.us.es/~trinidad, 2012.
8. P. Trinidad, D. Benavides, A. Ruiz-Cortés, S. Segura, and A.Jimenez. Fama framework. In S. Thiel and K. Pohl, editors, *Software Product Lines, 12th International Conference, SPLC 2008, Limerick, Ireland, September 8–12, 2008, Proceedings. Second Volume (Workshops)*. Lero Int. Science Centre, University of Limerick, Ireland, 2008.
9. Sergio Segura, Robert M. Hierons, David Benavides, and Antonio Ruiz-Cortés. Automated metamorphic testing on the analyses of feature models. *Information and Software Technology*, 53(3):245–258, 2011.
10. D. Batory, D. Benavides, and A. Ruiz-Cortés. Automated analysis of feature models: Challenges ahead. *Communications of the ACM*, 49(12):45–47, December 2006.
11. P. Trinidad and A. Ruiz-Cortés. Abductive reasoning and automated analysis of feature models: How are they connected? In *3rd. International Workshop VAMOS'09*, pages 145–153, Sevilla, Spain, Jan 2009. ICB Research Report N. 29.
12. P. Trinidad, D. Benavides, A. Durán, A. Ruiz-Cortés, and M. Toro. Automated error analysis for the agilization of feature modeling. *Journal of Systems and Software*, 81(6):883–896, 2008.
13. J. White, D. Benavides, D.C. Schmidt, P. Trinidad, B. Dougherty, and A. Ruiz-Cortes. Automated diagnosis of feature model configurations. *Journal of Systems and Software*, 83(7):1094–1107, 2010.

Change Patterns and Change Support Features in Process-Aware Information Systems

Barbara Weber[1,⋆], Stefanie Rinderle[2], and Manfred Reichert[3]

[1] Quality Engineering Research Group, University of Innsbruck, Austria
Barbara.Weber@uibk.ac.at
[2] Inst. Databases and Information Systems, Ulm University, Germany
stefanie.rinderle@uni-ulm.de
[3] Information Systems Group, University of Twente, The Netherlands
m.u.reichert@cs.utwente.nl

Abstract. In order to provide effective support, the introduction of process-aware information systems (PAIS) must not freeze existing business processes. Instead PAIS should allow authorized users to flexibly deviate from the predefined processes if required and to evolve business processes in a controlled manner over time. Many software vendors promise flexible system solutions for realizing such adaptive PAIS, but are often unable to cope with fundamental issues related to process change (e.g., correctness and robustness). The existence of different process support paradigms and the lack of methods for comparing existing change approaches makes it difficult for PAIS engineers to choose the adequate technology. In this paper we suggest a set of changes patterns and change support features to foster systematic comparison of existing process management technology with respect to change support. Based on these change patterns and features, we provide an evaluation of selected systems.

1 Introduction

Contemporary information systems (IS) more and more have to be aligned in a process-oriented way. This new generation of IS is often referred to as Process-Aware IS (PAIS) [1]. In order to provide effective process support, PAIS should capture real-world processes adequately, i.e., there should be no mismatch between the computerized processes and those in reality. In order to achieve this, the introduction of PAIS must not lead to rigidity and freeze existing business processes. Instead PAIS should allow authorized users to flexibly deviate from the predefined processes as required (e.g., to deal with exceptions) and to evolve PAIS implementations over time (e.g., due to process optimizations or legal changes). Such process changes should be enabled at a high level of abstraction and without affecting the robustness of the PAIS [2].

The increasing demand for process change support poses new challenges for IS engineers and requires the use of change enabling technologies. Contemporary

⋆ This work was done during a postdoctoral fellowship at the University of Twente.

J. Krogstie, A.L. Opdahl, and G. Sindre (Eds.): CAiSE 2007, LNCS 4495, pp. 574–588, 2007.

PAIS, in combination with service-oriented computing, offer promising perspectives in this context. Many vendors promise flexible software solutions for realizing adaptive PAIS, but are often unable to cope with fundamental issues related to process change (e.g., correctness and robustness). This problem is further aggravated by the fact that several competing process support paradigms exist, all trying to tackle the need for more process flexibility (e.g., adaptive processes [3,4,5] or case handling [6]). Furthermore, there exists no method for systematically comparing the change frameworks provided by existing process-support technologies. This, in turn, makes it difficult for PAIS engineers to assess the maturity and change capabilities of those technologies. Consequently, this often leads to wrong decisions and misinvestments.

During the last years we have studied processes from different application domains and elaborated the flexibility and change support features of numerous tools and approaches. Based on these experiences, in this paper we suggest a set of *changes patterns* and *change support features* to foster the comparison of existing approaches with respect to process change support. Change patterns allow for high-level process adaptations at the process type as well as the process instance level. Change support features ensure that changes are performed in a correct and consistent way, traceability is provided, and changes are facilitated for users. Both change patterns and change support features are fundamental to make changes applicable in practice. Finally, another contribution of this paper is the evaluation of selected approaches/systems based on the presented change patterns and change support features.

Section 2 summarizes background information needed for the understanding of this paper. Section 3 describes 17 change patterns and Section 4 deals with 6 crucial change support features. Based on this, Section 5 evaluates different approaches from both academia and industry. Section 6 discusses related work and Section 7 concludes with a summary.

2 Backgrounds

A PAIS is a specific type of information system which allows for the separation of process logic and application code. At run-time the PAIS orchestrates the processes according to their defined logic. Workflow Management Systems (e.g., Staffware [1], ADEPT [3], WASA [5]) and Case-Handling Systems (e.g., Flower [1,6]) are typical technologies enabling PAIS.

For each business process to be supported a process type represented by a *process schema* S has to be defined. In the following, a process schema is represented by a directed graph, which defines a set of *activities* – the process steps – and control connections between them (i.e., the precedence relations between these activities). Activities can either be atomic or contain a sub process (i.e., a reference to a process schema S') allowing for the hierarchical decomposition of a process schema. In Fig. 1a, for example, process schema $S1$ consists of six activities: Activity `A` is followed by activity `B` in the flow of control, whereas `C` and `D` can be processed in parallel. Activities `A` to `E` are atomic, and activity `F` constitutes a sub process with own process schema $S2$. Based on a process schema S, at run-time new *process instances* $I_1, \ldots, I_n$ can be created and executed. Regarding process instance I_1 from Fig. 1a, for example, activity A is completed and activity B is activated (i.e., offered in user worklists). Generally, a large number of process instances might run on a particular process schema.

PAIS must be able to cope with change. In general, changes can be triggered and performed at two levels – the process type and the process instance level (cf. Fig. 1b) [2]. Schema changes at the type level become necessary to deal with the evolving nature of real-world processes (e.g., to adapt to legal changes). Ad-hoc changes of single instances are usually performed to deal with exceptions, resulting in an adapted *instance-specific* process schema.

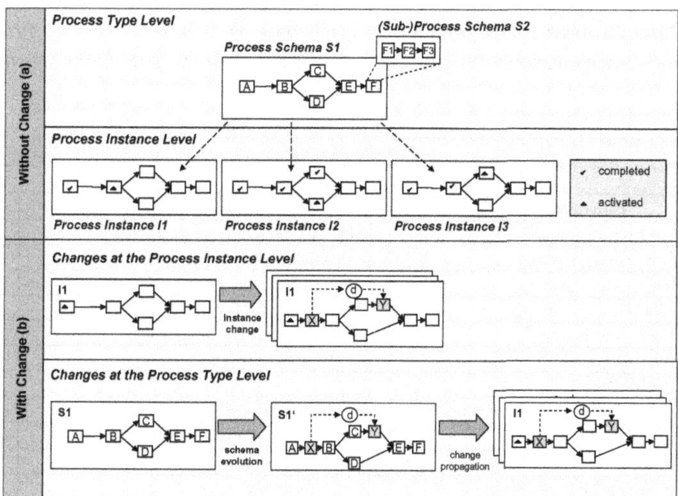

Fig. 1. Core Concepts

3 Change Patterns

In this section we describe 17 characteristic patterns we identified as relevant for *control flow changes* (cf. Fig. 2). Adaptations of other process aspects (e.g., data or resources) are outside the scope of this paper. Change patterns reduce the complexity of process change (like design patterns in software engineering reduce system complexity [7]) and raise the level for expressing changes by providing abstractions which are above the level of single node and edge operations. Consequently, due to their lack of abstraction, low level change primitives (add node, delete edge, etc.) are not considered to be change patterns and thus are not covered in this section.

As illustrated in Fig. 2, we divide our change patterns into *adaptation patterns* and *patterns for predefined changes*. Adaptation patterns allow modifying the schema of a process type (type level) or a process instance (instance level) using high-level change operations. Generally, adaptation patterns can be applied to the whole process schema or process instance schema respectively; they do not have to be pre-planned, i.e., the region to which the adaptation pattern is applied can be chosen dynamically. By contrast, for predefined changes, at build-time, the process engineer defines regions in the process schema where potential changes may be performed during run-time.

For each pattern we provide a name, a brief description, an illustrating example, a description of the problem it addresses, a couple of design choices, remarks regarding its implementation, and a reference to related patterns. *Design Choices* allow for parametrization of patterns keeping the number of distinct patterns manageable. Design choices which are not only relevant for particular patterns, but for a whole pattern category, are described only once at the category level. Typically, existing approaches only support a subset of the design choices in the context of a particular pattern. We denote the combination of design choices supported by a particular approach as a *pattern variant.*

CHANGE PATTERNS			
ADAPTATION PATTERNS (AP)			
Pattern Name	**Scope**	**Pattern Name**	**Scope**
AP1: Insert Process Fragment(*)	I / T	**AP8:** Embed Process Fragment in Loop	I / T
AP2: Delete Process Fragment	I / T	**AP9:** Parallelize Process Fragment	I / T
AP3: Move Process Fragment	I / T	**AP10:** Embed Process Fragment in Conditional Branch	I / T
AP4: Replace Process Fragment	I / T	**AP11:** Add Control Dependency	I / T
AP5: Swap Process Fragment	I / T	**AP12:** Remove Control Dependency	I / T
AP6: Extract Sub Process	I / T	**AP13:** Update Condition	I / T
AP7: Inline Sub Process	I / T		
PATTERNS FOR PREDEFINED CHANGES (PP)			
Pattern Name	**Scope**	**Pattern Name**	**Scope**
PP1: Late Selection of Process Fragments	I / T	**PP3:** Late Composition of Process Fragments	I / T
PP2: Late Modeling of Process Fragments	I / T	**PP4:** Multi-Instance Activity	I / T

I... Instance Level, T ... Type Level
(*) A process fragment can either be an atomic activity, an encapsulated sub process or a process (sub) graph

Fig. 2. Change Patterns Overview

3.1 Adaptation Patterns

Adaptation patterns allow to structurally change process schemes. Examples include the insertion, deletion and re-ordering of activities (cf. Fig. 2). Fig. 3 describes general design choices valid for all adaptation patterns. First, each adaptation pattern can be applied at the process type or process instance level (cf. Fig. 1b). Second, adaptation patterns can operate on an atomic activity, an encapsulated sub process or a process (sub-)graph (cf. Fig. 3). We abstract from this distinction and use the generic concept *process fragment* instead. Third, the effects resulting from the use of an adaptation pattern at the instance level can be permanent or temporary. A *permanent instance change* remains valid until completion of the instance (unless it is undone by a user). By contrast, a *temporary instance change* is only valid for a certain period of time (e.g., one loop iteration) (cf. Fig. 3).

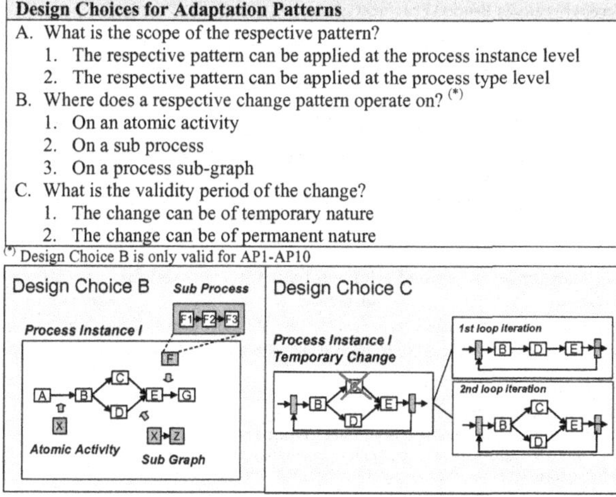

Design Choices for Adaptation Patterns

A. What is the scope of the respective pattern?
   1. The respective pattern can be applied at the process instance level
   2. The respective pattern can be applied at the process type level

B. Where does a respective change pattern operate on? (*)
   1. On an atomic activity
   2. On a sub process
   3. On a process sub-graph

C. What is the validity period of the change?
   1. The change can be of temporary nature
   2. The change can be of permanent nature

(*) Design Choice B is only valid for AP1-AP10

Fig. 3. Design Choices for Adaptation Patterns

We describe four selected adaptation patterns in more detail. These four patterns allow for the insertion, deletion, movement, and replacement of process fragments in a given process schema. The *Insert Process Fragment* pattern (cf. Fig. 4a) can be used to add process fragments to a process schema. In addition to the general options described in Fig. 3, one major design choice for this pattern (Design Choice D) describes the way the new process fragment is embedded in the respective schema. There are systems which only allow to serially insert a fragment between two directly succeeding activities. By contrast, other systems follow a more general approach allowing the user to insert new fragments between two arbitrary sets of activities [3]. Special cases of the latter variant include the insertion of a fragment in parallel to another one or the association of the newly added fragment with an execution condition (*conditional insert*). The *Delete Process Fragment* pattern, in turn, can be used to remove a process fragment (cf. Fig 4b). No additional design choices exist for this pattern. Fig. 4b depicts alternative ways in which this pattern can be implemented.

The *Move Process Fragment* pattern (cf. Fig. 5a) allows to shift a process fragment from its current position to a new one. Like for the *Insert Process Fragment* pattern, an additional design choice specifies the way the fragment can be embedded in the process schema afterwards. Though the *Move Process Fragment* pattern could be realized by the combined use of AP1 and AP2 (*Insert/Delete Process Fragment*), we introduce it as separate pattern as it provides a higher level of abstraction to users. The latter also applies when a process fragment has to be replaced by another one. This change is captured by the *Replace Process Fragment* pattern (cf. Fig. 5b).

We have only described the most relevant adaptation patterns. Additional patterns we identified are: swapping of activities (AP5), extraction of a sub process from a process schema (AP6), inclusion of a sub process into a process schema (AP7), embedding of an existing process fragment in a loop (AP8),

a) Pattern AP1: Insert Process Fragment

Description: A process fragment is added to a process schema.
Example: For a particular patient an allergy test has to be added due to a drug incompatibility.
Problem: In a real world process a task has to be accomplished which has not been modeled in the process schema so far.
Design Choices (in addition to the ones in Fig. 3):

D. How is the additional process fragment X embedded in the process schema?
   1. X is inserted between 2 directly succeeding activities (serial insert)
   2. X is inserted between 2 activity sets (insert between node sets)
      a) Without additional condition (parallel insert)
      b) With additional condition (conditional insert)

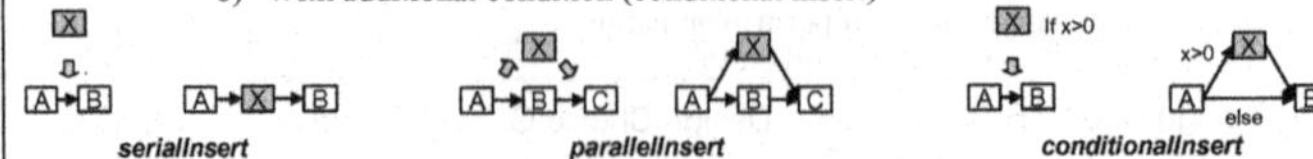

Implementation: The *insert* adaptation pattern can be realized by transforming the high level insertion operation into a sequence of low level change primitives (e.g., add node, add control dependency).

b) Pattern AP2: Delete Process Fragment

Description: A process fragment is deleted from a process schema.
Example: For a particular patient no computer tomography is performed due to the fact that he has a cardiac pacemaker (i.e., the computer tomography activity is deleted).
Problem: In a real world process a task has to be skipped or deleted.

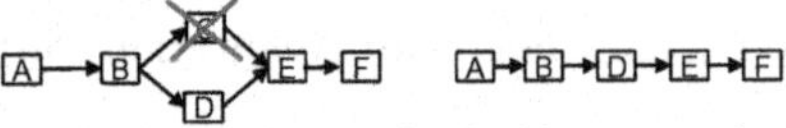

Implementation: Several options for implementing the *delete* pattern exist: (1) The fragment is physically deleted (i.e., corresponding activities and control edges are removed from the process schema), (2) the fragment is replaced by one or more null activities (i.e., activities without associated activity program) or (3) the fragment is embedded in a conditional branch with condition *false* (i.e., the fragment remains part of the schema, but is not executed).

Fig. 4. Insert (AP1) and Delete (AP2) Process Fragment patterns

a) Pattern AP3: Move Process Fragment

Description: A process fragment is moved from its current position in the process schema to another position.
Example: Usually employees are only allowed to book a flight, after getting approval from the manager. For a particular process instance the booking of a flight is exceptionally done in parallel to the approval activity (i.e., the book flight activity is moved from its current position to a position parallel to the approval activity).
Problem: Predefined ordering constraints cannot be completely satisfied for a set of activities.

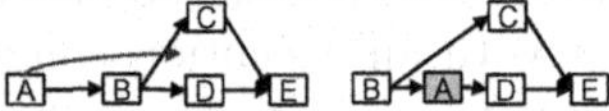

Design Choices:

D. How is the process fragment X embedded in the process schema?
   1. X is inserted between 2 directly succeeding activities (serial move)
   2. X is inserted between 2 activity sets (move between node sets)
      a) Without additional condition (parallel move)
      b) With additional condition (conditional move)

Implementation: This adaptation pattern can be implemented based on Pattern AP1 and AP2 (insert / delete process fragment).
Related Patterns: *Swap* adaptation pattern (AP5) (not detailed in the paper)

b) Pattern AP4: Replace Process Fragment

Description: A process fragment is replaced by another process fragment.
Example: Instead of the computer tomography activity, the X-ray activity shall be performed for a particular patient.
Problem: A process fragment is no longer adequate, but can be replaced by another one.

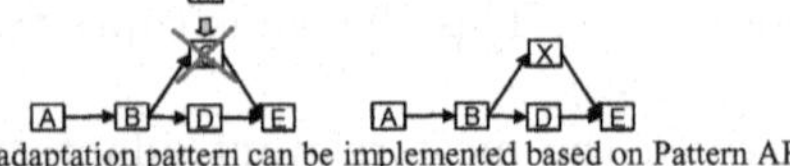

Implementation: This adaptation pattern can be implemented based on Pattern AP1 and AP2 (insert / delete process fragment).

Fig. 5. Move (AP3) and Replace (AP4) Process Fragment patterns

parallelization of process fragments (AP9), embedding of a process fragment in a conditional branch (AP10), addition of control dependencies (AP11), removal of control dependencies (AP12), and update of transition conditions (AP13). A description of these patterns can be found in [8].

3.2 Patterns for Predefined Changes

The applicability of adaptation patterns is not restricted to a particular process part a priori. By contrast, the following patterns predefine constraints concerning the parts that can be changed. At run-time changes are only permitted within these parts. In this category we have identified 4 patterns, *Late Selection of Proces Fragments* (PP1), *Late Modeling of Process Fragments* (PP2), *Late Composition of Process Fragments* (PP3) and *Multi-Instance Activity* (PP4) (cf. Fig. 6). The *Late Selection of Process Fragments* pattern (cf. Fig. 7) allows to select the implementation for a particular process step at run-time either based on predefined rules or user decisions. The *Late Modeling of Process Fragments* pattern (cf. Fig. 8a) offers more freedom and allows to model selected parts of the process schema at run-time. Furthermore the *Late Composition of Process Fragments* pattern (cf. Fig. 8b) enables the on-the fly composition of process fragments (e.g., by dynamically introducing control dependencies between a set of fragments).

In case of *Multi-Instance Activities* the number of instances created for a particular activity is determined at run-time. We do not consider multi-instance activity patterns in detail as they constitute some of the workflow patterns described in [9]. Multi-instance activities enable the creation of a particular process activity during run-time. The decision how many activity instances are created can be based either on knowledge available at build-time or on some run-time knowledge. We do not consider multi-instances of the former kind as change pattern since their use does not lead to change. For all other types of multi-instance activities the number of instances is determined based on run-time knowledge which can or cannot be available a-priori to the execution of the multi-instance activity. While in the former case the number of instances can be determined at some point during run-time, this is not possible for the latter case. We consider multi-instance activities as change patterns too, since their dynamic creation works like a dynamic schema expansion.

4 Change Support Features

So far, we have introduced a set of change patterns, which can be used to accomplish changes at the process type and/or process instance level. However, simply counting the number of supported patterns is not sufficient to analyze how well a system can deal with process change. In addition, change support features must be considered to make change patterns useful in practice (cf. Fig. 9). Relevant change support features include *process schema evolution* and *version control*,

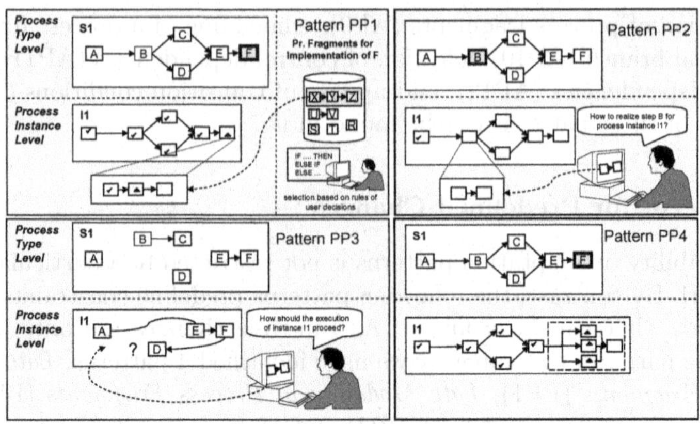

Fig. 6. Patterns for Predefined Changes (Overview)

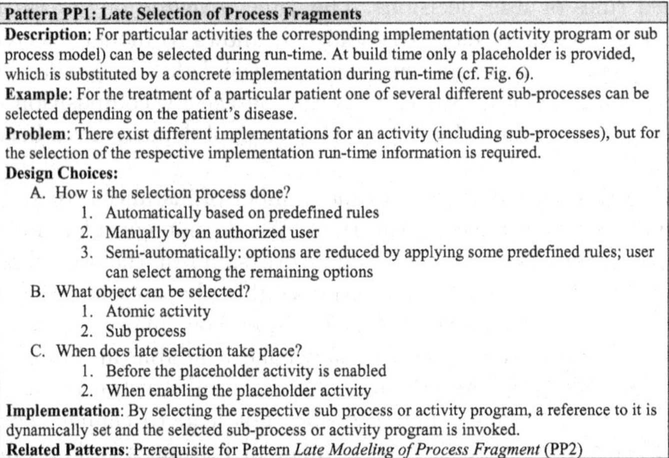

Pattern PP1: Late Selection of Process Fragments

Description: For particular activities the corresponding implementation (activity program or sub process model) can be selected during run-time. At build time only a placeholder is provided, which is substituted by a concrete implementation during run-time (cf. Fig. 6).

Example: For the treatment of a particular patient one of several different sub-processes can be selected depending on the patient's disease.

Problem: There exist different implementations for an activity (including sub-processes), but for the selection of the respective implementation run-time information is required.

Design Choices:

A. How is the selection process done?
   1. Automatically based on predefined rules
   2. Manually by an authorized user
   3. Semi-automatically: options are reduced by applying some predefined rules; user can select among the remaining options

B. What object can be selected?
   1. Atomic activity
   2. Sub process

C. When does late selection take place?
   1. Before the placeholder activity is enabled
   2. When enabling the placeholder activity

Implementation: By selecting the respective sub process or activity program, a reference to it is dynamically set and the selected sub-process or activity program is invoked.

Related Patterns: Prerequisite for Pattern *Late Modeling of Process Fragment* (PP2)

Fig. 7. Late Selection of Process Fragments (PP1)

change correctness, change traceability, access control and change reuse[1]. As illustrated in Fig. 9 the described change support features are not equally important for both process type level and process instance level changes. Version control, for instance, is primarily relevant for changes at the type level, while change reuse is particularly useful at the instance level [10].

4.1 Schema Evolution, Version Control and Instance Migration

In order to support changes at the process type level, version control for process schemes should be supported (cf. Fig. 9). In case of long-running processes, in

[1] Again we restrict ourselves to the most relevant change support features. Additional change support features not covered in this paper are change concurrency control and change visualization.

a) Pattern PP2: Late Modeling of Process Fragments

Description: Parts of the process schema have not been defined at build-time, but are modeled during run-time for each process instance (cf. Fig. 6). For this purpose, placeholder activities are provided, which are modeled and executed during run-time. The modeling of the placeholder activity must be completed before the modeled process fragment can be executed.
Example: The exact treatment process of a particular patient is composed out of existing process fragments at run-time.
Problem: Not all parts of the process schema can be completely specified at build time.
Design Choices:

A. What are the basic building blocks for late modeling?
   1. All process fragments (including activities) from the repository can be chosen
   2. A constraint-based subset of the process fragments from the repository can be chosen
   3. New activities or process fragments can be defined

B. What is the degree of freedom regarding late modeling?
   1. Same modeling constructs and change patterns can be applied as for modeling at the process type level [(*)]
   2. More restrictions apply for late modeling than for modeling at the process type level

C. When does late modeling take place?
   1. When a new process instance is created
   2. When the placeholder activity is instantiated
   3. When a particular state in the process is reached (which must precede the instantiation of the placeholder activity)

D. Does the modeling start from scratch?
   1. Late modeling may start with an empty template
   2. Late modeling may start with a predefined template which can then be adapted

Implementation: After having modeled the placeholder activity with the editor, the fragment is stored in the repository and deployed. Finally, the process fragment is dynamically invoked as an encapsulated sub-process. The assignment of the respective process fragment to the placeholder activity is done through late binding.
Related Patterns: necessitates *Late Selection of Process Fragments* (PP1) of the dynamically modified fragment

[(*)] Which of the adaptation patterns are supported within the placeholder activity is determined by the expressiveness of the used modeling language.

b) Pattern PP3: Late Composition of Process Fragments

Description: At build time a set of process fragments is defined out of which a concrete process instance can be composed at run time. This can be achieved by dynamically selecting fragments and adding control dependencies on the fly (cf. Fig. 6).
Example: Several medical examinations can be applied for a particular patient. The exact examinations and the order in which they are performed are defined for each patient individually.
Problem: There exist several variants of how process fragments can be composed. In order to reduce the number of process variants to be specified by the process engineer during build time, process instances are dynamically composed out of fragments.

Fig. 8. Late Modeling (PP2) and Late Composition of Process Fragments (PP3)

Change Support Features			
Change Support Feature	**Scope**	**Change Support Feature**	**Scope**
F1: Schema Evolution, Version Control and Instance Migration	T	2. By change primitives	
		F3: Correct Behavior of Instances After Change	I + T
No version control – Old schema is overwritten		**F4: Traceability & Analysis**	I + T
1. Running instances are canceled		1. Traceability of changes	
2. Running instances remain in the system		2. Annotation of changes	
Version control		3. Change Mining	
3. Co-existence of old/new instances, no instance migration		**F5: Access Control for Changes**	I+T
4. Uncontrolled migration of all process instances		1. Changes in general can be restricted to authorized users	
5. Controlled migration of compliant process instances		2. Application of single change patterns can be restricted	
F2: Support for Ad-hoc Changes	I	3. Authorizations can depend on the object to be changed	
1. By change patterns		**F6: Change Reuse**	I

T ... Type Level, I ... Instance Level

Fig. 9. Change Support Features

addition, controlled migration of already running instances, from the old process schema version to the new one, might be required. In this subsection we describe different existing options in this context (cf. Fig. 10).

If a PAIS provides no version control feature, either the process designer can manually create a copy of the process schema (to be changed) or this schema is overwritten (cf. Fig. 10a). In the latter case running process instances can either be withdrawn from the run-time environment or, as illustrated in Fig. 10a, they remain associated with the modified schema. Depending on the execution state of the instances and depending on how changes are propagated to instances which have already progressed too far, this missing version control can lead to inconsistent states and, in a worst case scenario, to deadlocks or other errors [2]. As illustrated in Fig. 10a process schema $S1$ has been modified by inserting activities X and Y with a data dependency between them. For instance $I1$ the change is uncritical, as $I1$ has not yet entered the change region. However, $I2$ and $I3$ would be both in an inconsistent state afterwards as instance schema and execution history do not match (see [2]). Regarding $I2$, worst case, deadlocks or activity invocations with missing input data might occur.

By contrast, if a PAIS provides explicit version control two support features can be differentiated: running process instances remain associated with the old schema version, while new instances will be created on the new schema version. This approach leads to the co-existence of process instances of different schema versions (cf. Fig. 10b). Alternatively a migration of a selected collection of process instances to the new process schema version is supported (in a controlled way) (cf. Fig. 10c). The first option is shown in Fig. 10b where the already running instances $I1$, $I2$ and $I3$ remain associated with schema S1, while new instances ($I4$-$I5$) are created from schema $S1'$ (co-existence of process instances of different schema versions). By contrast, Fig. 10c illustrates the controlled migration of process instances. Only those instances are migrated which are *compliant*[2] with $S1'$ ($I1$). All other instances ($I2$ and $I3$) remain running according to $S1$. If instance migration is uncontrolled (as it is not restricted to *compliant* process instances) this will lead to inconsistencies or errors. Nevertheless, we treat the uncontrolled migration of process instances as a separate design choice since this functionality can be found in several existing systems (cf. Section 5).

4.2 Other Change Support Features

Support for Ad-hoc Changes: In order to deal with exceptions PAIS must support changes at the process instance level either through high level changes in the form of patterns (cf. Section 3) or through low level primitives. Although changes can be expressed in both ways, change patterns allow to define changes at a higher level of abstraction making change definition easier.

Correctness of Change: The application of change patterns must not lead to run-time errors (e.g., activity program crashes due to missing input data, deadlocks, or inconsistencies due to lost updates or vanishing of instances).

[2] A process instance I is compliant with process schema S, if the current execution history of I can be created based on S (for details see [2]).

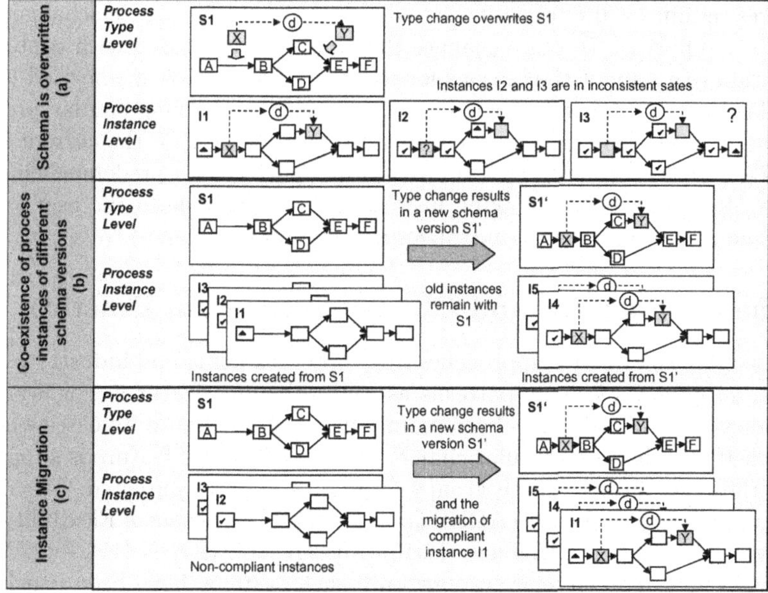

Fig. 10. Version Control

Different criteria (see [2]) have been introduced to ensure that instances can only be updated to a new schema if they are compliant with it.

Traceability and Analysis: To ensure traceability of changes, they have to be logged. For adaptation patterns the applied changes have to be stored in a change log as change patterns and/or change primitives. While both options allow for traceability, change mining [11] becomes easier when the change log contains high-level information about the changes as well. Regarding patterns for predefined changes, an execution log is usually sufficient to enable traceability. In addition, logs can be enriched with more semantical information, e.g., about the reasons and context of the changes [10]. Finally, change mining allows for the analysis of changes (e.g., to support continuous process improvement) [11].

Access Control for Changes: The support of change patterns leads to increased PAIS flexibility. This, in turn, imposes security issues as the PAIS becomes more vulnerable to misuse. Therefore, the application of changes at the process type and the process instance level must be restricted to authorized users. Access control features differ significantly in their degree of granularity. In the simplest case, changes are restricted to a particular group of people (e.g., to process engineers). More advanced access control components allow to define restrictions at the level of single change patterns (e.g., a certain user is only allowed to insert additional activities, but not to delete activities). In addition, authorizations can depend on the object to be changed, e.g., the process schema.

Change Reuse: In the context of ad-hoc changes "similar" deviations (i.e., combination of one or more adaptation patterns) can occur more than once. As it requires significant user experience to define changes from scratch change reuse should be supported. To reuse changes they must be annotated with contextual information (e.g., about the reasons for the deviation) and be memorized by the PAIS. This contextual information can be used for retrieving similar problem situations and therefore ensures that only changes relevant for the current situation are presented to the user [12,10]. Regarding patterns for predefined changes, reuse can be supported by making historical cases available to the user and by saving frequently re-occurring instances as templates.

5 Change Patterns and Change Support in Practice

In this section we evaluate approaches from both academia and industry regarding their support for change patterns as well as change features. For academic approaches the evaluation has been mainly based on literature. In cases where it was unclear whether a particular change pattern or change feature is supported or not, the respective research groups were additionally contacted. The evaluated academic approaches are ADEPT[3], WIDE [13], Pockets of Flexibility [14], Worklets/Exlets [4,15], CBRFlow [12,10], MOVE [16], HOON [17], and WASA [5]. In respect to commercial systems only such systems have been considered for which we have hands on experience as well as a running system installed. This allowed us to test the change patterns and change features. As commercial systems Staffware [1] and Flower [6] were considered. Evaluation results are summarized in Fig. 11. A detailed description of the evaluated approaches can be found in [8].

If a change pattern or change support feature is not supported at all, the respective table entry will be labeled with "-". Otherwise, it describes the exact pattern variants as supported by listing all available design choices. In case no design choices exist for a particular change pattern, which is supported, the respective table entry is simply labeled with "+". Partial support is labeled with "o". As an example take change pattern PP1 of the Worklet/Exlet approach [4,15]. The string "A[1,2], B[1,2], C[2]" indicates that design choices A, B and C are supported. Further, it shows for every design choice the exact options available (e.g., for design choice A, Options 1 and 2 are supported).

In particular an adaptation pattern will be only considered as being provided, if the respective system supports the pattern directly, i.e., based on one high-level change operation. Of course, adaptation patterns can be always expressed by means of a set of basic change primitives (like add node, delete node, add edge, etc.). However, this is not the idea behind adaptation patterns. Since process schema changes (at the type level) based on these modification primitives are supported by almost each process editor, this is not sufficient to qualify for pattern support. By contrast, the support of high-level change operations allows introducing changes at a higher level of abstraction and consequently hides a lot of the complexity from the user. Therefore changes can be performed in a more efficient and less error prone way. In addition, in order to qualify as an adaptation pattern the application of the respective change operations must not be restricted to predefined regions in the process.

Several of the adaptation patterns (e.g., AP3 or AP4) can be implemented by applying a combination of the more basic patterns AP1, AP2, AP10 and AP11. However, a given approach will only qualify for a particular adaptation pattern, if it supports this pattern directly (i.e., it offers one respective change operation).

Note that missing support for adaptation patterns does not necessarily mean that no run-time changes can be performed. As long as feature F2 is supported ad-hoc changes to running process instances are possible (for details see [8]). In general, if a respective approach provides support for predefined change patterns like for instance late modeling of process fragments (PP1) or late selection of process fragments (PP2) the need for structural changes of the process schema can be decreased making feature F3 less crucial.

The evaluation of selected approaches shows that there exists no single system which supports all change patterns and features (cf. Table 11). In particular, none of the approaches provides both adaptation patterns and predefined change patterns, which would allow addressing a much broader process spectrum. While predefined change patterns allow to reduce the need for structural changes during run-time by providing more flexible models, adaptation patterns allow for structural changes which cannot be pre-planned. In addition, they make changes more efficient, less complex and less error-prone through providing high-level change operations.

Change Patterns and Change Support									
Pattern/ Feature	Academic							Commercial	
	ADEPT / CBRFlow	WIDE	Pockets of Flexibility	Worklets / Exlets	MOVE	HOON	WASA	Staffware	Flower
Change Patterns									
Adaptation Patterns									
AP1	A[1, 2], B[1,2,3], C[1,2], D[1, 2]	A[2], B[1], C[2], D[1,2]	–	–	–	–	–	–	–
AP2	A[1, 2], B[1,2,3], C[1,2]	A[2], B[1], C[2]	–	–	–	–	–	–	A[2], B[1], C[2]
AP3	A[1, 2], B[1,2,3], C[1,2], D[1, 2]	–	–	–	–	–	–	–	–
AP4	–	A[2], B[1], C[2]	–	A[1], B[2], C[1,2]	–	–	–	–	–
Preplanned Change Patterns									
PP1	–	–	–	A[1,2], B[1,2], C[2]	–	A[1,2], B[1,2], C[2]	–	A[1,2], B[1,2], C[2]	–
PP2	–	–	A[1,2], B[2], C[2], D[1,2]	–	A[1], B[1], C[3], D[1,2]	–	–	–	–
PP3	–	–	–	–	–	–	–	–	–
PP4	–	+	–	–	–	–	–	+	+
Change Features									
F1	3, 5	3, 5	–	3	–	–	3, 5	3, 4	1, 2, 3
F2	1	–	2	2	2	2	2	2	1
F3	+	+	+	○	+	+	+	–	–
F4	1, 2, 3	1	1	1	1	1	1	1	1
F5	1, 2, 3	1, 3	1, 2, 3	1, 2, 3	1, 3	1, 2, 3	1	1, 2, 3	1, 2, 3*
F6	+	–	+	+	–	–	–	–	–

(*) Flower supports Option 2 and 3 of feature F4 only for process instance changes, but not for process type changes

Fig. 11. Change Patterns and Change Support Features in Practice

6 Related Work

Patterns were first used to describe solutions to recurring problems by Ch. Alexander, who applied patterns to descibe best practices in architecture [18]. Patterns also have a long tradition in computer science. Gamma et al. applied the same concepts to software engineering and described 23 patterns in [7].

In the area of workflow management, patterns have been introduced for analyzing the expressiveness of process modeling languages (i.e., control flow patterns [9]). In addition, workflow data patterns [19] describe different ways for modeling the data aspect in PAIS and workflow resource patterns [20] describe how resources can be represented and utilized in workflows. The introduction of workflow patterns has significant impact on the design of PAIS and has contributed to the systematic evaluation of PAIS and process modeling standards. However, to evaluate the powerfulness of a PAIS regarding its ability to deal with changes, the existing patterns are important, but not sufficient. In addition, a set of patterns for the aspect of workflow change is needed. Further, the degree to which control flow patterns are supported provides an indication of how complex the change framework under evaluation is. In general, the more expressive the process modeling language is (i.e., the more control flow and data patterns are supported), the more difficult and complex changes become.

In [21] exception handling patterns which describe different ways for coping with exceptions are proposed. In contrast to change patterns, exception handling patterns like *Rollback* only change the state of a process instance (i.e., its behavior), but not its schema. The patterns described in this paper do not only change the observable behavior of a process instance, but additionally adapt the process structure. For a complete evaluation of flexibility, both change patterns and exception handling patterns must be evaluated.

7 Summary and Outlook

In this paper we proposed 17 change patterns (and described 8 of them in detail) and 6 change support features, which in combination allow to assess the power of a particular change framework. In addition, we evaluated selected approaches and systems regarding their ability to deal with process changes. We believe that the introduction of change patterns complements existing workflow patterns and allows for more meaningful evaluations of existing systems and approaches. In combination with workflow patterns the presented change framework will enable (PA)IS engineers to choose process management technologies

Future work will include change patterns for aspects other than control flow (e.g., data or resources) and patterns for more advanced adaptation policies (e.g., the accompanying adaptation of the data flow when introducing control flow changes) as well as the evaluation of additional systems and approaches.

Acknowledgements. We would like to thank S. Shadiq, M. Adams, M. Weske and Y. Han for their valuable feedback and the many fruitful discussions, which helped us to significantly improve this paper.

References

1. Dumas, M., ter Hofstede, A., van der Aalst, W. (eds.): Process Aware Information Systems. Wiley Publishing, Chichester (2005)
2. Rinderle, S., Reichert, M., Dadam, P.: Correctness criteria for dynamic changes in workflow systems – a survey. Data and Knowledge Engineering 50, 9–34 (2004)
3. Reichert, M., Dadam, P.: ADEPT$_{flex}$ – supporting dynamic changes of workflows without losing control. JIIS 10, 93–129 (1998)
4. Adams, M., ter Hofstede, A.H.M., Edmond, D., v.d.Aalst, W.M.: A service-oriented implementation of dynamic flexibility in workflows. In: Coopis'06 (2006)
5. Weske, M.: Workflow management systems: Formal foundation, conceptual design, implementation aspects. University of Münster, Germany, Habil Thesis (2000)
6. van der Aalst, W., Weske, M., Grünbauer, D.: Case handling: A new paradigm for business process support. Data and Knowledge Engineering. 53, 129–162 (2005)
7. Gamma, E., Helm, R., Johnson, R., Vlissides, J.: Design Patterns: Elements of Reusable Object-Oriented Software. Addison-Wesley, New York (1995)
8. Weber, B., Rinderle, S., Reichert, M.: Identifying and evaluating change patterns and change support features in process-aware information systems. Technical Report Report No. TR-CTIT-07-22, CTIT, Univ. of Twente, The Netherlands (2007)
9. van der Aalst, W.M.P., ter Hofstede, A.H.M., Kiepuszewski, B., Barros, A.P.: Workflow patterns. Distributed and Parallel Databases 14, 5–51 (2003)
10. Rinderle, S., Weber, B., Reichert, M., Wild, W.: Integrating process learning and process evolution - a semantics based approach. In: BPM 2005, pp. 252–267 (2005)
11. Günther, C., Rinderle, S., Reichert, M., van der Aalst, W.: Change mining in adaptive process management systems. In: CoopIS'06, pp. 309–326 (2006)
12. Weber, B., Wild, W., Breu, R.: CBRFlow: Enabling adaptive workflow management through conversational cbr. In: ECCBR'04, Madrid, pp. 434–448 (2004)
13. Casati, F.: Models, Semantics, and Formal Methods for the design of Workflows and their Exceptions. PhD thesis, Milano (1998)
14. Sadiq, S., Sadiq, W., Orlowska, M.: A framework for constraint specification and validation in flexible workflows. Information Systems 30, 349–378 (2005)
15. Adams, M., ter Hofstede, A.H.M., Edmond, D., v. d. Aalst, W.M.: Dynamic and extensible exception handling for workflows: A service-oriented implementation. Technical Report BPM Center Report BPM-07-03, BPMcenter.org (2007)
16. Th. Herrmann, A.-W., Scheer, H.W. (eds.): Verbesserung von Geschftsprozessen mit flexiblen Workflow-Management-Systemen - Verffentlichungen des Forschungsprojektes MOVE. Bd. 1 - 4. Physica Verlag, Heidelberg (1998)
17. Han, Y.: Software Infrastructure for Configurable Workflow Systems. PhD thesis, Univ. of Berlin (1997)
18. Alexander, C., Ishikawa, S., Silverstein, M. (eds.): A Pattern Language. Oxford University Press, New York (1977)
19. Russell, N., ter Hofstede, A., Edmond, D., van der Aalst, W.: Workflow data patterns. Technical Report FIT-TR-2004-01, Queensland Univ. of Techn. (2004)
20. Russell, N., ter Hofstede, A., Edmond, D., van der Aalst, W.: Workflow resource patterns. Technical Report WP 127, Eindhoven Univ. of Technology (2004)
21. Russell, N., van der Aalst, W.M., ter Hofstede, A.H.: Exception handling patterns in process-aware information systems. In: CAiSE'06 (2006)

Process Change Patterns: Recent Research, Use Cases, Research Directions

Manfred Reichert and Barbara Weber

Abstract In previous work, we introduced change patterns to foster a systematic comparison of process-aware information systems with respect to change support. This paper revisits change patterns and shows how our research activities have evolved. Further, it presents characteristic use cases and gives insights into current research directions.

1 Introduction

Information systems (IS) are increasingly aligned in a process-oriented way. This emerging generation of IS is referred to as process-aware information systems (PAIS) [1]. A PAIS should support real-world processes properly, i.e., there should be no mismatch between the processes implemented by it and those existing in reality. Hence, advanced support is needed for customizing a PAIS to its application environment as well as for quickly adapting implemented processes to changing needs. The increasing demand for process change support poses new challenges for IS engineers and requires the use of change enabling technologies.

Accordingly, a method is required that allows PAIS engineers to systematically assess the change capabilities of available technologies. In [2], we introduced change patterns as well as change support features to enable such a systematic assessment of PAIS with respect to process change support. In particular, change patterns allow for high-level process adaptations. In turn, change support features

M. Reichert (✉)
University of Ulm, Ulm, Germany
e-mail: manfred.reichert@uni-ulm.de

B. Weber
University of Innsbruck, Innsbruck, Austria
e-mail: barbara.weber@uibk.ac.at

J. Bubenko et al. (eds.), *Seminal Contributions to Information Systems Engineering*,
DOI 10.1007/978-3-642-36926-1_32, © Springer-Verlag Berlin Heidelberg 2013

summarize fundamental features to be provided by a PAIS in order to change and evolve implemented processes in a correct, robust and secure way.

This paper discusses how our research on change patterns has evolved, how they have been used in theory and practice, and what research directions are.

2 Background: Process Change Patterns

Originally, in [2] we introduced 17 patterns for realizing control flow changes. These patterns reduce the complexity of process changes and raise the level for expressing changes by providing abstractions above the level of primitive change operations. To structure the change patterns, we divided them into *adaptation patterns* and *change patterns for predefined changes* (cf. Fig. 2 in [2]). While the former enable structural changes of a process schema, the latter allow process participants to add information regarding unspecified parts of a process schema during run-time.

An *adaptation pattern (AP)* enables structural changes of process schemes. AP1 (AP2) allows inserting (deleting) a process fragment. Moving and replacing fragments is supported by AP3 (Move Process Fragment), AP4 (Replace Process Fragment), AP5 (Swap Process Fragment), and AP14 (Copy Process Fragment). AP6 and AP7 allow adding or removing levels of hierarchy: the extraction of a sub-process from a process schema is supported by AP6, whereas the inclusion of a sub-process into a process schema is supported by AP7. Patterns AP8–AP12 support adaptations of control dependencies: embedding a process fragment in a loop (AP8), parallelizing a process fragment (AP9), embedding a process fragment in a conditional branch (AP10), and adding/removing control dependencies (AP11, AP12). Finally, AP13 allows changing transition conditions. Generally, the region to which an adaptation pattern is applied may be chosen dynamically. Hence, adaptation patterns are well suited for realizing ad-hoc changes and coping with the evolving nature of business processes [1]. For each adaptation pattern, we have provided a name, a description, an illustrating example, a description of the problem it addresses, a couple of design choices, remarks regarding its implementation, and references to related patterns. In this context, design choices allow parameterizing change patterns keeping the number of distinct patterns manageable.

Patterns for changes in pre-defined regions allow for better dealing with uncertainty by deferring decisions regarding the exact control-flow to the run-time. Instead of requiring a process model to be fully specified prior to execution, parts of the model may remain unspecified. As opposed to adaptation patterns, whose application is not restricted a priori to a particular process part, the parts of a process schema that may be changed or expanded are constrained. In this category, we identified four patterns: Late Selection (PP1), Late Modeling (PP2) and Late Composition of Process Fragments (PP3), and Multi-Instance Activity (PP4). These four patterns differ regarding the parts that may remain unspecified resulting in a different degree of freedom during run-time.

3 Recent Research on Process Change Patterns

In recent work we have detailed the change patterns and provided empirical evidence for them. Further, we have formalized and implemented them. In detail:

Detailing change patterns and empirical evidence. We extended our original work in [3], which provides an in-depth description of all change patterns; it describes the pattern selection criteria, the data sources used, and the procedure applied for pattern identification. Further, it discusses how the patterns were identified based on the analysis of large process model collections from the healthcare and automotive domains. Finally, Weber et al. [3] introduces additional patterns and provides an extended pattern-based evaluation of selected approaches from industry as well as academia.

Change pattern formalization. To obtain unambiguous pattern descriptions and ground pattern implementation as well as pattern-based analyses on a sound basis, we provided a formal semantics for change patterns in [4]. For each change pattern, its formal semantics is specified by comparing the execution traces producible on a process schema before and after applying the pattern to it. The formalization is independent from any process meta model and thus allows implementing the patterns in a variety of process support tools.

Pattern implementation. The change patterns were implemented in an adaptive PAIS – the AristaFlow BPM Suite [5]. The adaptation patterns are realized in terms of high-level change operations, which can be used for creating and changing process schemes. Hence, flexible exception handling and controlled process evolution become possible. Further, adaptation patterns are associated with pre-/post-conditions to ensure structural and behavioral soundness of a process schema after pattern application; i.e., correctness by construction is ensured.

Recently, we complemented the existing workflow patterns by a set of time patterns to make PAIS comparable with respect to their ability to deal with temporal constraints [6].

4 Characteristic Use Cases for Change Patterns

On one hand, change patterns provide the basis for realizing changes in different stages of the process life cycle [7]. On the other, they serve as benchmark for evaluating change support in existing languages and tools.

4.1 Supporting Process Changes Along the Process Life Cycle

We first discuss fundamental use cases for realizing changes in different stages of the process life cycle:

Process schema creation. Change patterns have been used for intelligent process schema creation [8]. For example, AristaFlow allows modeling a sound process schema based on an extensible set of adaptation patterns [5]. Only those patterns may be applied in a given context, which do not violate the soundness of the process schema. In turn, Gschwind et al. [9] describes a set of pattern compounds, similar to the adaptation patterns, allowing for the context-sensitive selection and composition of workflow patterns during process modeling. Finally, adaptation patterns have been used for the model-based integration of services into business applications at later stages during the process life cycle [10].

Process schema configuration. The configuration of a reference process schema constitutes another use case for adaptation patterns. Provop, for example, allows creating a process variant by applying a sequence of adaptation patterns (e.g., AP1, AP2 or AP3) to the given reference schema [11]. By utilizing the semantics of the adaptation patterns applied in a given configuration setting, it is further ensured that the resulting process variant schema is sound [12].

Process instance change. An important use case is to enable actors to deviate from a pre-specified process schema at run-time, e.g., to cope with exceptions. For this purpose, AristaFlow supports instance-specific changes based on the same adaptation patterns as used for process modeling [5]. Further, it utilizes the semantics of the applied adaptation patterns to ensure correctness of the resulting process instance schema. Recently, approaches aiming at automated instance changes have emerged. Usually, they only consider a subset of the adaptation patterns. For example, Q-Advice uses AP1 and its variants to automatically inject quality measure activities into the workflows of software engineers at run-time. The activities to be added are determined situationally using contextual knowledge and quality goal tracking [13]. A more generic approach to automate instance adaptations, which is based on declarative processes and planning, is described in [14]. Regarding ad-hoc changes, Kumar et al. [15] additionally ensures compliance of process instance adaptations with defined semantic constraints. For this, integer programming formulation is used to validate the applied adaptation patterns against the given set of semantic constraints (AP1–AP5 are considered). An approach for the flexible support of product development processes is presented in [16]; the sub-processes of such a process, which refine analysis, synthesis, and verification activities, may be dynamically selected to allow for a flexible process execution without need for structural adaptations. Thereby, a subset of the patterns for changes in pre-defined regions is considered (i.e., PP1–PP3).

Process schema evolution. Adaptive PAIS allow for schema evolution considering version management and the migration of already running process instances to the new schema version. Gerth et al. [17] presents techniques for detecting and resolving conflicting change operations, which rely on selected adaptation patterns and their semantics. In turn, Küster et al. [18] shows how to compute a sequence of adaptation patterns required to transform a given schema version into another one.

Both scenarios consider AP1, AP2, and AP3. Particularly, adaptation patterns play a crucial role for ensuring the correctness of schema changes and instance migrations. In AristaFlow, schema evolution is based on the same adaptation patterns as used for process modeling and ad-hoc changes [5]. Thereby, pattern semantics is utilized to cope with conflicting changes at the type and instance level, to increase the number of migratable process instances, and to efficiently represent applied changes [19–21]. Note that similar concepts exist for evolving service compositions [22]. Furthermore, continuous process improvement, relying on case-based reasoning and adaptation patterns, is considered in [23]. Finally, Jamshidi and Pahl [24] introduces patterns for co-evolving processes and software architectures. These patterns are based on selected adaptation patterns and allow describing the impact a business process change has on corresponding software architectures.

Process schema refactoring. A specific kind of schema evolution is provided by process schema refactorings; i.e., syntactical transformations of a process schema not changing its behavior. Examples of such refactorings and their relation to adaptation patterns (e.g., AP6 and AP7) are discussed in [25].

Process change reuse. When handling exceptions, it might be useful to reuse changes applied in similar problem contexts earlier [26]. For example, ProCycle fosters change reuse based on case-based reasoning and semantic change annotations [7]. Further, it supports AP1–AP5 and utilizes their specific semantics to adjust parameter settings of recorded changes when reusing them.

Process schema comparison. Comparing two process schemes is crucial to decide how similar the schemes are or how to derive the one from the other. In this context, adaptation patterns can be used to describe the structural difference (i.e., edit distance) between schemes in terms of high-level changes. Based on specific variants of patterns AP1–AP3, Li et al. [27] presents a technique that allows determining this difference. A similar approach is presented in [28].

Process change analysis. Adaptive PAIS capture process changes in *change logs*, which record applied adaptation patterns and their parameter settings. For change analysis, different techniques exist. Based on AP1–AP3, Günther et al. [29] applies process mining to change logs to discover *change processes* providing an aggregated visualization of all changes. In turn, MinAdept does not presume the existence of a change log, but allows analyzing a collection of process variants derived from the same schema [30]; algorithms are provided discovering a reference process schema whose average edit distance to the process variants is minimal.

In summary, process change patterns are relevant for a variety of use cases in the process life cycle. As shown, the patterns have served as basis for the design and implementation of techniques supporting these use cases. While tools like AristaFlow enable a broad support of most use cases and adaptation patterns, other proposals only consider a specific use case and a subset of the adaptation patterns.

4.2 *Assessing and Designing Process Change Frameworks*

Change patterns have been used for realizing pattern catalogs for specific modeling languages, assessing existing PAIS, and enabling user-friendly changes. Examples of corresponding approaches are presented in the following.

Realizing a pattern catalog for a specific modeling language. Döhring et al. [31] combines change, exception and time patterns into a BPMN pattern catalog. Change patterns are referred to as generic patterns, which are tailored and extended to be applicable to BPMN. In turn, Tragatschnig and Zdun [32] uses the adaptation patterns for designing a pattern catalog for BPEL schema changes.

Assessing existing approaches. A measure for a pattern-based assessment of service orchestration languages is defined in [33]. In particular, the designed pattern catalog includes the patterns for changes in predefined regions (i.e., PP1–PP4) and discusses how they are supported in existing BPEL dialects.

Enabling user-friendly changes. Kolb et al. [34] presents an approach enabling end users to change large process schemes based on personalized process views; AP1, AP2, and AP8–AP10 may be applied to a process view, followed by the propagation of the defined changes to the underlying process schema. In turn, Kolb et al. [35] introduces a user-centric approach for creating, changing and visualizing process schemes based on the Concurrent Task Tree (CTT) – a task modeling language known from end-user programming. Thereby, the described adaptation patterns are mapped to CTT change operations. Finally, Kolb et al. [36] presents a controlled experiment that investigates the way users create and change process schemes on multi-touch devices. Based on this, a gesture set for realizing adaptation patterns AP1, AP2, AP6, AP7, AP8, AP10, and AP11 on multi-touch devices is designed.

5 Research Directions

When using change patterns for modeling, the quality of process schemes might increase. Particularly appealing in this context is the mentioned correctness by construction. However, the use of change patterns implies a different way of creating process schemes compared to the use of change primitives. First of all, the correctness-by-construction principle imposes a rather structured way of modeling and hence constraints on change pattern combinations. In addition, the exact set of change patterns (e.g., presence vs. non-presence of the move pattern) might determine how patterns have to be combined to create a process fragment. While the creation of process schemes based on change primitives has caused attention in recent years [37], only little is known about the process of process modeling when utilizing change patterns. To obtain an in-depth understanding of it, we are currently working on empirical studies on the use of change patterns.

References

1. Reichert, M., Weber, B.: Enabling Flexibility in Process-Aware Information Systems - Challenges, Methods, Technologies. Springer (2012)
2. Weber, B., Rinderle, S., Reichert, M.: Change patterns and change support features in process-aware information systems. In: Proc. CAiSE'07. (2007) 574–588
3. Weber, B., Reichert, M., Rinderle-Ma, S.: Change patterns and change support features - enhancing flexibility in process-aware information systems. Data and Knoweldge Engineering **66** (2008) 438–466
4. Rinderle-Ma, S., Reichert, M., Weber, B.: On the formal semantics of change patterns in process-aware information systems. In: Proc. ER'08. (2008) 279–293
5. Dadam, P., Reichert, M.: The ADEPT project: a decade of research and development for robust and flexible process support. Comp Scie - R&D **23** (2009) 81–97
6. Lanz, A., Weber, B., Reichert, M.: Time patterns for process-aware information systems. Requirements Engineering (2013)
7. Weber, B., Reichert, M., Wild, W., Rinderle-Ma, S.: Providing integrated life cycle support in process-aware information systems. Int'l Journal of Cooperative Information Systems **18** (2009) 115–165
8. Smirnov, S., Weidlich, M., Mendling, J., Weske, M.: Object-sensitive action patterns in process model repositories. In: Proc. BPM'10 Workshops. (2010) 251–263
9. Gschwind, T., Koehler, J., Wong, J.: Applying patterns during business process modeling. In: Proc BPM'08. (2008) 4–19
10. Heller, M., Allgaier, M.: Model-based service integration for extensible enterprise systems with adaptation patterns. In: ICE-B. (2010) 163–168
11. Hallerbach, A., Bauer, T., Reichert, M.: Capturing variability in business process models: The Provop approach. Journal of Software Maintenance and Evolution: Research and Practice **22** (2010) 519–546
12. Hallerbach, A., Bauer, T., Reichert, M.: Guaranteeing soundness of configurable process variants in Provop. In: Proc. CEC'09. (2009) 98–105
13. Grambow, G., Oberhauser, R., Reichert, M.: Contextual injection of quality measures into software engineering processes. Int'l J Adv in Software **4** (2011) 76–99
14. Marrella, A., Mecella, M., Russo, A.: Featuring automatic adaptivity through workflow enactment and planning. In: Proc CollaborateCom'11. (2011) 372–381
15. Kumar, A., Yao, W., Chu, C.H., Li, Z.: Ensuring compliance with semantic constraints in process adaptation with rule-based event processing. In: Proc RuleML'10. (2010) 50–65
16. Reichel, T., Rünger, G., Steger, D.: Flexible workflows for an energy-oriented product development process. In: Proc ISSS/BPSC'10. (2010) 243–254
17. Gerth, C., Küster, J., Luckey, M., Engels, G.: Detection and resolution of conflicting change operations in version management of process models. SOSYM (2011) 1–19
18. Küster, J., Gerth, C., Engels, G.: Dynamic computation of change operations in version management of business process models. In: ECMFA'10. (2010) 201–216
19. Rinderle, S., Reichert, M., Dadam, P.: On dealing with structural conflicts between process type and instance changes. In: Proc. BPM'04, Potsdam (2004) 274–289
20. Rinderle-Ma, S., Reichert, M., Weber, B.: Relaxed compliance notions in adaptive process management systems. In: Proc. ER'08. (2008) 232–247
21. Rinderle, S., Reichert, M., Jurisch, M., Kreher, U.: On representing, purging, and utilizing change logs in process management systems. In: BPM'06. (2006) 241–256
22. Andrikopoulos, V., Benbernou, S., Papazoglou, M.P.: Managing the evolution of service specifications. In: Proc. CAiSE'08. (2008) 359–374
23. Kim, D., Lee, N., Kang, S.H.: An approach to continuous process improvement based on case-based reasoning and process change patterns. IJICIC **8** (2011)
24. Jamshidi, P., Pahl, C.: Business process and software architecture model co-evolution patterns. In: Proc. MISE'12. (2012) 91–97

25. Weber, B., Reichert, M., Mendling, J., Reijers, H.A.: Refactoring large process model repositories. Computers in Industry **62** (2011) 467–486
26. Aghakasiri, Z., Mirian-Hosseinabadi, S.H.: Workflow change patterns: Opportunities for extension and reuse. In: Proc. SERA'09. (2009) 265–275
27. Li, C., Reichert, M., Wombacher, A.: On measuring process model similarity based on high-level change operations. In: Proc. ER'08. (2008) 248–264
28. Küster, J.M., Gerth, C., Förster, A., Engels, G.: Detecting and resolving process model differences in the absence of a change log. In: BPM'08. (2008) 244–260
29. Günther, C.W., Rinderle, S., Reichert, M., van der Aalst, W.M.P.: Change mining in adaptive process management systems. In: Proc. CoopIS'06. (2006) 309–326
30. Li, C., Reichert, M., Wombacher, A.: Mining business process variants: Challenges, scenarios, algorithms. Data & Knowledge Engineering **70** (2011) 409–434
31. Döhring, M., Zimmermann, B., Karg, L.: Flexible workflows at design- and runtime using bpmn2 adaptation patterns. In: Proc. BIS. (2011) 25–36
32. Tragatschnig, S., Zdun, U.: Runtime process adaptation for bpel process execution engines. In: EDOCW, IEEE Computer Society (2011) 155–163
33. Lenhard, J., Schönberger, A., Wirtz, G.: Edit distance-based pattern support assessment of orchestration languages. In: OTM Conferences (1). (2011) 137–154
34. Kolb, J., Kammerer, K., Reichert, M.: Updatable process views for user-centered adaption of large process models. In: Proc. ICSOC'12. (2012) 484–498
35. Kolb, J., Reichert, M., Weber, B.: Using concurrent task trees for stakeholder-centered modeling and visualization of business processes. In: S-BPM ONE. (2012)
36. Kolb, J., Rudner, B., Reichert, M.: Towards gesture-based process modeling on multi-touch devices. In: Proc. CAiSE Workshops. (2012) 280–293
37. Pinggera, J., et al: Modeling styles in business process modeling. In: BMMDS/EMMSAD. (2012) 151–166

Measuring Similarity between Business Process Models

Boudewijn van Dongen[1], Remco Dijkman[1], and Jan Mendling[2]

[1] Eindhoven University of Technology, The Netherlands
{b.f.v.dongen,r.m.dijkman}@tue.nl
[2] Queensland University of Technology, Brisbane, Australia
j.mendling@qut.edu.au

Abstract. Quality aspects become increasingly important when business process modeling is used in a large-scale enterprise setting. In order to facilitate a storage without redundancy and an efficient retrieval of relevant process models in model databases it is required to develop a theoretical understanding of how a degree of behavioral similarity can be defined. In this paper we address this challenge in a novel way. We use *causal footprints* as an abstract representation of the behavior captured by a process model, since they allow us to compare models defined in both formal modeling languages like Petri nets and informal ones like EPCs. Based on the causal footprint derived from two models we calculate their similarity based on the established vector space model from information retrieval. We validate this concept with an experiment using the SAP Reference Model and an implementation in the ProM framework.

Keywords: Business Process Modeling, Event-driven Process Chains, Similarity, Equivalence.

1 Introduction

Many multi-national companies use tools such as ARIS Toolset for documenting their business processes. Due to the operational diversity of such large enterprises, there are often several thousands of processes modeled and stored in the database of the modeling tool [26]. The sheer number causes serious problems for the management and maintenance of these model: It is difficult to see the forest because there are too many trees, as a German proverb puts it. While quality aspects of process models (e.g. [15]) and process modeling languages (e.g. [10]) are quite well understood, there is a notable research gap on quality issues across models.

The similarity between business process models can be related to several of these cross-model quality issues. Consider a large organization that wants to identify redundancies in the operations of different divisions. Models are indeed helpful to discuss the overlap of two processes and the potential for integration, yet it is difficult and time-consuming to identify similarities in a process database with several thousands of models. Clearly, there is a need for automatic detection of similarities between process models to facilitate certain model management activities. There are several model management activities that would benefit from good tool support. Firstly, similar models as well as the corresponding business operations can be integrated into one process. This is interesting not only for refactoring the model database, but also to facilitate the

Z. Bellahsène and M. Léonard (Eds.): CAiSE 2008, LNCS 5074, pp. 450–464, 2008.

integration of business operations in a merger scenario. Secondly, the reference models of an ERP system vendor could be automatically compared to company processes. This way, organizations could more easily decide which packages match their current operations best. Thirdly, multi-national enterprises can identify specialized processes of some national branch which no longer comply with the procedures defined in the company-wide reference model using a similarity measurement.

In this paper, we discuss the foundations of detecting and measuring similarity between business process models. In particular, our contribution is an approach considering linguistic and behavioral aspects of process models to calculate a degree of similarity. We validate the approach using the SAP reference model. The results highlight which benefits organizations can have from tool support for similarity detection.

The remainder of the paper is organized as follows. Section 2 introduces Event-driven Process Chains (EPCs), a popular process modeling language that we use to illustrate our approach. Furthermore, we discuss one particular redundancy problem that was identified in the SAP reference model in prior research. Section 3 then presents our approach to calculate the degree of similarity between two processes based on their causal footprint. A causal footprint covers extensive behavioral information about a process without calculating its state space, but requires the identification of matching functions in the EPCs being compared. Section 4 addresses the problem of matching functions across different processes, with an emphasis on EPCs. We discuss an approach to identify matches between functions automatically. In Section 5, the presented techniques are combined, applied to a large portion of the SAP reference model, and empirically validated against human interpretations of similarity. Then, Section 6 discusses related work to our approach before Section 7 concludes the paper.

2 Background on EPCs

In this paper, we will illustrate our argument using Event-driven Process Chains (EPCs). The EPC is a popular business process modeling language that was introduced in [13]. EPCs are used by most companies that manage their process models with ARIS Toolset. This way, our results are directly applicable for these organizations.

EPCs capture the control flow of a process in terms of the temporal and logical dependencies of activities [13]. EPCs offer *function type* elements to represent these activities, *event type* elements describing pre- and post-conditions of functions, and three kinds of *connector types* including AND, OR, and XOR. Control flow arcs are used to link these elements. Connectors have either multiple incoming and one outgoing arc (join connectors) or one incoming and multiple outgoing arcs (split connectors). As a syntax rule, functions and events have to alternate on each path through the EPC, either directly or indirectly when they are linked via one or more connectors.

The informal (or intended) semantics of an EPC can be described as follows. The AND-split activates all subsequent branches in a concurrent manner. The XOR-split represents a choice between one of several alternative branches. The OR-split triggers one, two or up to all of multiple branches based on conditions. For both XOR-splits and OR-splits, the activation conditions are given in events subsequent to the connector. The AND-join waits for all incoming branches to complete, then it propagates control to the subsequent EPC element. The XOR-join merges alternative branches. The OR-join synchronizes all active incoming branches. This feature is called non-locality since the state of all transitive predecessor nodes has to be considered. For a recent discussion of formal semantics of EPCs refer to [18].

The following definition formalizes EPC. We need this definition in the section on behavioral similarity. Furthermore, we define a notion of syntactical correctness that we check before applying our approach to the SAP reference model.

Definition 2.1. (EPC)
An $EPC = (E, F, C, l, A)$ consists of three pairwise disjoint and finite sets E, F, C, a mapping $l : C \rightarrow \{and, or, xor\}$, and a binary relation $A \subseteq (E \cup F \cup C) \times (E \cup F \cup C)$ such that

- An element of E is called *event*. $E \neq \emptyset$.
- An element of F is called *function*. $F \neq \emptyset$.
- An element of C is called *connector*.
- The mapping l specifies the type of a connector $c \in C$ as *and*, *or*, or *xor*.
- The relation A defines the control flow as a coherent, directed graph. An element of A is called an *arc*. An element of the union $N = E \cup F \cup C$ is called a *node*.

In order to be able to discuss the events surrounding a function, or the functions surrounding an event, notations are introduced for paths and connector chains.

Definition 2.2. (Paths and Connector Chains)
Let N be a set of *nodes* and $A \subseteq N \times N$ a binary relation over N defining the arcs. For each *node* $n \in N$, we define *path* $a \hookrightarrow b$ refers to the existence of a sequence of EPC nodes $n_1, \ldots, n_k \in N$ with $a = n_1$ and $b = n_k$ such that for all $i \in 1, \ldots, k$ holds: $(n_1, n_2), (n_2, n_3), \ldots, (n_{k-1}, n_k) \in A$. This includes the empty path of length zero, i.e., for any node $a : a \hookrightarrow a$. If $a \neq b \in N$ and $n_2, \ldots, n_{k-1} \in C$, the path $a \stackrel{c}{\hookrightarrow} b$ is called *connector chain*. This includes the empty connector chain, i.e., $a \stackrel{c}{\hookrightarrow} b$ if $(a, b) \in A$.

In this paper, we focus on syntactically correct EPCs, i.e. EPCs with at least one initial and final events, at least one function and strict alternation of functions and events on all paths. According to this definition, both example EPCs of Figure 1 are syntactically correct. Therefore, we can apply the techniques for matching functions that are discussed later in Section 4. Out of the 604 EPCs in the SAP reference model mentioned before, 556 are syntactically correct. Please note that we demand a strict alternation of functions and events, which is not included in all EPC syntax definitions.

Figure 1 gives an example of two EPCs that captures similar processes (cf. [19]). Both are taken from the aforementioned SAP Reference Model. The EPC on the left-hand side of Figure 1 stems from the Sales and Distribution branch and its name is *Customer Inquiry*. In essence, when a customer inquires about a product (denoted by the event "Customer inquires about products"), this inquiry is processed and a quotation is created which results in the fact that a customer project is needed. As an alternative, the need for a customer project can arise based on plan data which triggers a resource related quotation. The EPC on the right-hand side of Figure 1 is taken from the Project Management branch and it is called *Customer Inquiry and Quotation Processing*. It

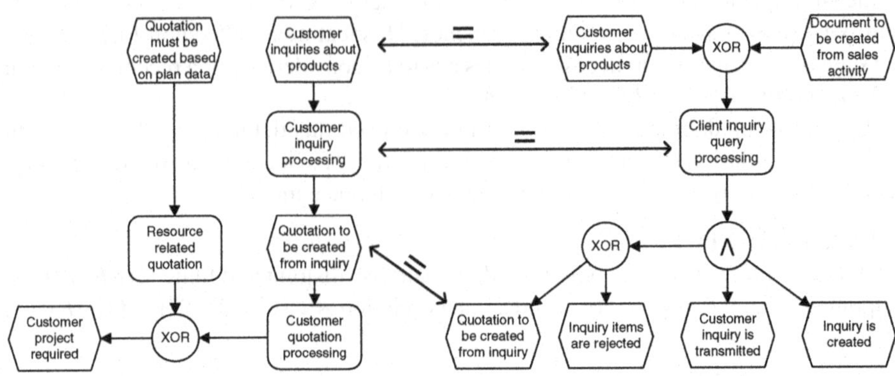

Fig. 1. *Customer Inquiry* and *Customer Inquiry and Quotation Processing* EPCs

identifies a sales activity as alternative reason to process a customer inquiry. As a result the inquiry is created and transmitted. Furthermore, either a quotation is created or the inquiry is rejected. The processes share two equivalent events and one equivalent function as depicted in Figure 1 . Since the overlapping part of the models, i.e. the sequence "customer inquiry", "inquiry processing", and "quotation to be created", can be handled by both processes, they could easily be integrated into one model, for instance using the approach defined in [19].

In Section 3, we provide a metric for determining how similar two business processes are, given that it is known which functions (or activities in the more general sense) in one model correspond to functions in the other model. In Section 4, we show how to automatically find the relations between functions of different models.

3 Similarity of Behavior

Comparing the behavior of processes using traditional notions such as bisimulation is problematic for different reasons. Firstly, most of these notions are defined as a verification property which yield as yes or no, but no degree of similarity. Secondly, process models with concurrency suffer from a state explosion problem. For some process modeling languages a formalization of the reachability graph as a transition system is even missing. Thirdly, if there are deadlocks or dead transitions in the process model, these parts are not captured in the behavioral comparison. Motivated by these problems, we defined the concept of a causal footprint [7] which is a collection of the essential behavioral constraints imposed by a process model.[1] We will use the causal footprints of two processes as a basis to calculate their similarity. Section 3.1 describes the derivation of a causal footprint, then Section 3.2 defines the degree of similarity for causal footprints.

[1] Note that this paper adopts the concept of a causal footprint from [7] where we use it for verification purposes. In contrast to [7] we use this concept for measuring similarity.

3.1 Deriving the Causal Footprint of an EPC

Before defining a causal footprint of an EPC, we first need to introduce the notion of a case as well as the semantics of look-back and look-ahead links.

A case basically captures the behavior of one particular execution sequence of functions according to the rules of a process model. Consider N as the set of nodes of an EPC. The behavior of the process Φ_{EPC} is defined as the set $W \subseteq N^*$, where N^* is the set of all sequences that are composed of zero of more nodes from N. A $\sigma \in W$ is called a *case*, i.e. a possible execution of the EPC. To denote a function at a specific index in σ, we use $\sigma[i]$, where i is the index ranging from 1 to $|\sigma|$.

The causal footprint identifies two relationships between nodes in N that are called look-back and look-ahead links. For each *look-ahead link*, we say that the execution of the source of that link leads to the execution of at least one of the targets of that link, i.e., if $(a, B) \in L_{la}$, then any execution of a is followed by the execution of some $b \in B$. A look-ahead link is denoted as a bullet with one or more outgoing arrows. Furthermore, for each *look-back link*, the execution of the target is preceded by at least one of the sources of that link, i.e., if $(A, b) \in L_{lb}$, then any execution of b is preceded by the execution of some $a \in A$. The notation of a look-back link is a bullet with one or more incoming arrows. Note that we do not give any information about when in the future or past executions took place, but only that they are there. This way of describing a process is related to work on dominance and control dependence in program analysis (see e.g. [12]), and similar to the work presented in [8]. However, by splitting up the semantics in the two different directions (i.e. forward and backward), causal footprints are more expressive. With footprints you can for example express the fact that task `A` is always succeeded by `B`, but that `B` can also occur before `A`, which is typically hard to express in other languages.

Definition 3.1. (Causal Footprint)
We define a causal footprint $G = (N, L_{lb}, L_{la})$ as a graph where, where:

- N is a finite set of *nodes* (activities),
- $L_{lb} \subseteq (\mathcal{P}(N) \times N)$ is a set of *look-back links*[2]
- $L_{la} \subseteq (N \times \mathcal{P}(N))$ is a set of *look-ahead links*.

For relating the definition of a causal footprint to the behavior of an EPC we define a notion of consistency based on the cases implied by the EPC process model.

Definition 3.2. (Consistency of Causal Footprint with EPC)
Let N be a set of nodes and $EPC = (E, F, C, l, A)$ be an EPC with behavior W. Furthermore, let $G = (N, L_{lb}, L_{la})$ be a causal footprint. We say that $G = (N, L_{lb}, L_{la})$ is consistent with the behavior of EPC, denoted by $G \in \mathcal{F}_{EPC}$, if and only if:

1. $N = F$, i.e. the nodes of the footprint represent the functions of the EPC,
2. For all $(a, B) \in L_{la}$ holds that for each $\sigma \in W$ with $n = |\sigma|$, such that there is a $0 \leq i \leq n-1$ with $\sigma[i] = a$, there is a $j : i < j \leq -1$, such that $\sigma[j] \in B$,
3. For all $(A, b) \in L_{lb}$ holds that for each $\sigma \in W$ with $n = |\sigma|$, such that there is a $0 \leq i \leq n-1$ with $\sigma[i] = b$, there is a $j : 0 \leq j < i$, such that $\sigma[j] \in A$,

[2] With $\mathcal{P}(N)$, we denote the powerset of N, where $\emptyset \notin \mathcal{P}(N)$.

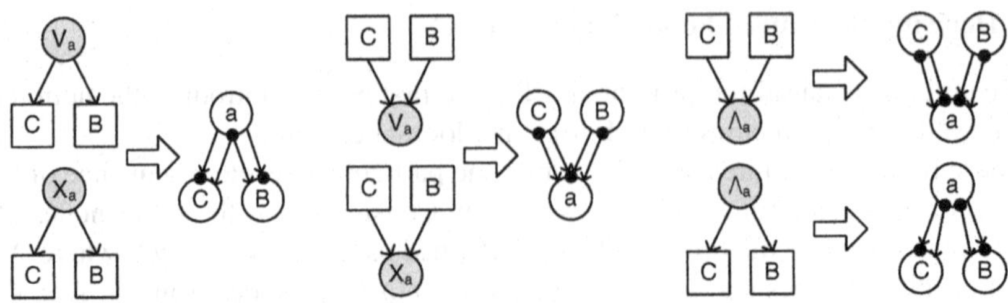

Fig. 2. Mapping of EPCs to causal footprints

While the different cases of an EPC can explicitly be generated using the semantics formalization defined in [18], there is a more efficient way. The mapping defined in [7] and depicted in Figure 2 yields a consistent causal footprint for an EPC under the assumption that no AND-join or OR-join deadlocks. Furthermore, it is clear from Definition 3.2 that a causal footprint is not unique, i.e., different processes can have common footprints. For example, $G = (N, \emptyset, \emptyset)$ is the causal footprint of any process having activities F. Therefore, we aim at footprints that are more informative without trying to capture detailed semantics. In [7] a set of rules for calculating the transitive closure of a causal footprint are introduced such that the closure is still a causal footprint that is consistent with the EPC. In Section 5, where we present the application to the SAP reference model, we used the rules of Figure 2 in combination with the transitive closure rules of [7] to obtain a causal footprint for all EPCs.

3.2 Similarity of Causal Footprints

In information retrieval the degree of similarity between a document and a query plays a very important role for ranking the returned documents according to their relevance. For calculating similarity, we use the well-known *vector model* [2, 28] which is one of the basic techniques used for information filtering, information retrieval, and the indexing of web pages. Its classical application is to determine the similarity between a query and a document. The original vector space model proposed by Salton, Wong, and Yang in [28] attaches weights based on term frequency to the so-called "document vector". We use a more liberal interpretation, where other weights are possible. However, to explain the basic mechanism we use terms originating from the domain of information retrieval, i.e., terms like "document collection", a set of "terms", and a set of "weights" relating to the terms. Later we will provide a mapping of these terms to causal footprints.

The *document collection* contains a set of documents. Each of these documents is considered to be a list of *terms* which are basically the words of the document. The union of all terms of all documents is then used to describe each document as a vector. For one specific document an entry in the vector represents that the term associated with the vector position of this entry is included in the document. In a simple case the occurrence of a term can be indicated by a one and the non-occurrence with a zero, however there is also the option to assign *weights* to terms in order to address the fact that they differ in relevance. A common choice is to use one divided by the number of occurrences of a term throughout all documents of the document collection as a weight which has the effect that scarcely used terms get a higher weight. A query can also be considered as a document, i.e., a list of terms.

The similarity between a query and a document is then calculated based on their vector representation as the cosine of the angle between the two vectors [2, 28]. Calculating this degree of similarity for each document provides a mechanism to rank them according to their relevance for the query.

Our proposal for determining the similarity of two business process models builds on the vector model and causal footprints. We consider causal footprints of two processes $G_1 = (N_1, L_{1,lb}, L_{1,la})$ and $G_2 = (N_2, L_{2,lb}, L_{2,la})$ as input for the calculation. In order to apply the vector model, we have to define (1) the document collection, (2) the set of terms, and (3) the set of weights.

The document collection includes two entries, namely the two causal footprints that need to be compared. We will refer to the first and the second causal footprint as $G_1 = (N_1, L_{1,lb}, L_{1,la})$ and $G_2 = (N_2, L_{2,lb}, L_{2,la})$).

The set of terms is build from the union over nodes, look back, and look ahead links of the two causal footprints. We define $\Theta = N_1 \cup L_{1,lb} \cup L_{1,la} \cup N_2 \cup L_{2,lb} \cup L_{2,la}$ as the set of terms and $\lambda : \Theta \rightarrow \{1, 2, \ldots |\Theta|\}$ as an indexing function that assigns a running number to each term, i.e., the set of all elements appearing in the two footprints are enumerated. (Note that we implicitly assume all sets of nodes and links to be disjoint in a single model.)

The relevance of each term is closely related to the number of tasks from which it is built. Consider for example two look ahead links $x_{la} = (a, \{g\}) \in L_{la}$ and $y_{la} = (a, \{b, c, d, e, f\}) \in L_{la}$. x_{la} refers to only two tasks: a and g. y_{la} refers to six tasks (a through f). It seems obvious that the look ahead links with fewer tasks are more informative and therefore more important. To address this we use weights depending on the number of tasks involved in a look-ahead/back link.

The weights are determined using the size of the relations. If $\theta \in \Theta$ is a single node (i.e. $\theta \in N_1 \cup N_2$), then we define the weight of θ as $w_\theta = 1$. Furthermore, since the number of potential look ahead and look back links depends upon the powerset of nodes, is seems natural to use exponentially decreasing weights. Therefore, for all links $\theta \in \Theta$, we define the weight of a link $w_\theta = 1/(2^{|\theta|-1})$, where $|\theta|$ denotes the number of tasks in the link.

For the two look ahead links $x_{la} = (a, \{g\})$ and $y_{la} = (a, \{b, c, d, e, f\})$, we get $w_{x_{la}} = 1/(2^{2-1}) = 0.5$ and $w_{y_{la}} = 1/(2^{6-1}) = 0.03125$ as their weights.

Using the document collection, the set of terms and the weights presented above, we define the document vectors, which we call *footprint vectors*.

Definition 3.3. (Footprint vectors)
Let $G_1 = (N_1, L_{1,lb}, L_{1,la})$ and $G_2 = (N_2, L_{2,lb}, L_{2,la})$ be two causal footprints, with Θ the set of terms and $\lambda : \Theta \rightarrow \mathbb{N}$ an indexing function. We define two footprint vectors, $\overrightarrow{g_1} = (g_{1,1}, g_{1,2}, \ldots g_{1,|\Theta|})$ and $\overrightarrow{g_2} = (g_{2,1}, g_{2,2}, \ldots g_{2,|\Theta|})$ for the two models as follows. For each element $\theta \in \Theta$, we say that for each $i \in \{1, 2\}$ holds that

$$g_{i,\lambda(\theta)} = \begin{cases} 0 & \text{if } \theta \notin (N_i \cup L_{i,lb} \cup L_{i,la}) \\ w_\theta = \frac{1}{2^{|\theta|-1}} & \text{if } \theta \in (L_{i,lb} \cup L_{i,la}) \\ w_\theta = 1 & \text{if } \theta \in N_i \end{cases}$$

Using the two footprint vectors, we can define the similarity between two footprints as the cosine of the angle between these two vectors.

Definition 3.4. (Footprint similarity)
Let $G_1 = (N_1, L_{1,lb}, L_{1,la})$ and $G_2 = (N_2, L_{2,lb}, L_{2,la})$ be two causal footprints, with Θ the set of terms and $\lambda : \Theta \to \mathbb{N}$ an indexing function. Furthermore, let $\overrightarrow{g_1}$ and $\overrightarrow{g_2}$ be the corresponding footprint vectors. We say that the similarity between G_1 and G_2, denoted by $sim(G_1, G_2)$ is the cosine of the angle between those vectors, i.e.

$$sim(G_1, G_2) = \frac{\overrightarrow{g_1} \times \overrightarrow{g_2}}{|\overrightarrow{g_1}| \cdot |\overrightarrow{g_2}|} = \frac{\sum_{j=1}^{|\Theta|} g_{1,j} \cdot g_{2,j}}{\sqrt{\sum_{j=1}^{|\Theta|} g_{1,j}^2} \cdot \sqrt{\sum_{j=1}^{|\Theta|} g_{2,j}^2}}$$

The value of $sim(G_1, G_2)$ ranges from 0 (no similarity) to 1 (equivalence). In this paper, we do not elaborate on this formula. If one accepts the weights that we associate to the "terms" in a causal footprint, then the cosine of the angle between these two vectors provides a generally accepted way to quantify similarity [2, 28].

The similarity $sim(G_1, G_2)$ between footprints can be calculated for any two footprints G_1 and G_2. However, for the similarity to exceed 0, there should be at least one node $n \in N_1 \cap N_2$.

Property 3.5. (Disjoint footprints have similarity 0)
Let $G_1 = (N_1, L_{1,lb}, L_{1,la})$ and $G_2 = (N_2, L_{2,lb}, L_{2,la})$ be two causal footprints, with Θ the set of terms and $\lambda : \Theta \to \mathbb{N}$ an indexing function. Furthermore, let $\overrightarrow{g_1}$ and $\overrightarrow{g_2}$ be the corresponding footprint vectors. If $N_1 \cap N_2 = \emptyset$ then $sim(G_1, G_2) = 0$.

Proof. It is sufficient to show that $\overrightarrow{g_1} \times \overrightarrow{g_2} = 0$, i.e. that $\sum_{j=1}^{|\Theta|} g_{1,j} \cdot g_{2,j} = 0$. Assume that for some $1 \leq j \leq |\Theta|$ holds that $g_{1,j} > 0$. Then, from Definition 3.3, we know that $\lambda(\theta) = j$ with either $\theta \in N_1$, or $\theta \in (L_{1,lb} \cup L_{1,la})$. Assume $\theta \in N_1$. Then we know that $g_{2,j} = 0$, since $\theta \notin N_i$. Hence $g_{1,j} \cdot g_{2,j} = 0$. Assume $\theta \in (L_{1,lb} \cup L_{1,la})$. Since Definition 3.1 shows that $L_{1,lb} \subseteq (\mathcal{P}(N_1) \times N_1)$ and $L_{1,la} \subseteq (N_1 \times \mathcal{P}(N_1))$, we know that $\theta \notin (L_{2,lb} \cup L_{2,la})$ and hence that $g_{1,j} \cdot g_{2,j} = 0$. Therefore, $\sum_{j=1}^{|\Theta|} g_{1,j} \cdot g_{2,j} = 0$ and hence $sim(G_1, G_2) = 0$. □

Property 3.5 shows that for two footprints to be considered similar, we need to identify nodes that appear in both footprints. For this, we use the notion of an equivalence mapping defined in Section 4.

4 Matching Functions

When comparing EPCs it is not realistic to assume that equivalent functions and events have labels that are the same to the letter. Figure 1 illustrates this: the functions "Customer inquiry processing" and "Client inquiry query processing" are similar from a human perspective, but they have different labels.

To determine the match between functions from different EPCs, we:

1. determine how similar pairs of functions are on a 0 to 1 scale, based on the equivalence of words in their labels (we call this the semantic similarity score);
2. determine whether a function matches another function on a true/false scale, based on the semantic similarity score;
3. determine what the best mapping is between all functions from one EPC and all functions from another, based on the semantic similarity score; and
4. extend this technique by determining the best match by not only looking at the semantic similarity score of the functions themselves, but also at the semantic similarity scores of the events that surround these functions (we call this the contextual similarity score).

These techniques are explained successively in the following subsections.

We experimented with other techniques for determining function mappings, inspired by the work of Ehrig, Koschmider and Oberweis [9]. We also experimented with different parameters for these techniques. However, we obtained the best results for the techniques and parameters explained below. A comparison is presented in the technical report that accompanies this paper [6].

4.1 Determine the Semantic Similarity Score between Two Functions

Given two functions, their semantic similarity score is the degree of similarity, based on equivalence between words in their labels. Words that are identical are given an equivalence score of 1, while words that are synonymous are given an equivalence score of 0.75, a value that was determined experimentally. We assume an exact match is preferred over a match on synonyms. Hence, the semantic similarity score is defined as follows.

Definition 4.1. (Semantic similarity)
Let $(E_1, F_1, C_1, l_1, A_1)$ and $(E_2, F_2, C_2, l_2, A_2)$ be two disjoint EPCs. Let $f_1 \in F_1$ and $f_2 \in F_2$ be two functions (and assume that f_1 and f_2 are sets of words, i.e. we denote the number of words by $|f_1|$). We define the *semantic similarity* as follows:

$$\text{sem}(f_1, f_2) = \frac{1.0 \cdot |f1 \cap f2| + 0.75 \cdot \sum_{(s,l) \in f_1 \setminus f_2 \times f_2 \setminus f_1} \text{synonym}(s, l)}{\max(|f_1|, |f_2|)}$$

Where $synonym$ is a function that returns 1 if the given words are synonyms and 0 if they aren't.

For example, consider the functions "Customer inquiry processing" and "Client inquiry query processing" from figure 1, which consist of the collections of words $f1 =$ ["Customer","inquiry","processing"] and $f2 =$["Client", "inquiry", "query", "processing"], respectively. We only need to consider a synonym mapping between $f_1 \setminus f_2$ and $f_2 \setminus f_1$, i.e. between ["Customer"] and ["Client","query"]. Therefore, the semantic similarity between f_1 and f_2 equals
$sem(f_1, f_2) = \frac{1.0 \cdot 2 + 0.75 \cdot (1+0)}{4} \approx 0.69.$

When determining equivalence between words, we disregard special symbols, and we change all characters to lower-case. Furthermore, we skip frequently occurring words, such as "a", "an" and "for". Also we *stem* words using Porter's stemming algorithm [23]. Stemming reduces words to their stem form. For example, "stemming", "stemmed" and "stemmer" are stemmed into "stem".

4.2 Determine a Semantic Match between Two Functions

The semantic similarity score of two functions is a value between 0 and 1. However, when determining equivalence, we require a boolean result stating whether or not two functions are equivalent, i.e. we need cut-off values that state when the similarity score exceeds this value then the functions are equivalent. The optimal cut-off value is the cut-off value for which the syntactic similarity degree most accurately reflects the equivalence judgements of a human.

We conducted experiments to optimize these cut-off values for use in the context of the SAP Reference Models. In particular, we compared the semantic similarity scores with human judgement for 210 function pairs from the SAP Reference Model. Their similarity degrees were evenly distributed over the 0 to 1 range and they were compared against human judgement as to whether these function pairs are equivalent of not. Based on this experiment, we determined an optimal cut-off for the similarity scores to decide whether functions match or not. We expect that these cut-off values and correctness score are typical for the SAP reference model, since other data-sets yield different values [9].

Our experiments determined that for semantic similarity, a cut-off value of 0.89 while giving synonyms a similarity score higher than 0.75 is optimal. It leads to a prediction of whether functions are a match according to humans, with a 90% accuracy.

4.3 Determine a Semantic Mapping between All Functions

So far, we only considered the similarity between two functions. However, the behavioral comparison presented in Section 3 requires a symmetric mapping between functions of two process models, i.e. we have to select pairs of functions that we consider a match, where each pair consists of a function from one model and a function from the other model.

Definition 4.2. (Equivalence mapping)
Let F_1, F_2 be two disjoint sets. Furthermore, let $s : F_1 \times F_2 \rightarrow \{0..1\}$ be a symmetric similarity function and let $c \in \{0..1\}$ be a cut-off value. A function $m : F_1 \rightarrow F_2$ is an *equivalence mapping*, if and only if:

- m is invertible ($m(f_1) = f_2$ implies that $m(f_2) = f_1$), and
- $m(f_1) = f_2$ implies that $s(f1, f2) \geq c$.

In the following section, we evaluate the degree of similarity calculation for the SAP Reference Model with different approaches to matching functions.
An *optimal equivalence mapping* $m^{opt} : F_1 \rightarrow F_2$ is an equivalence mapping, such that for all other equivalence mappings m holds that

$\sum_{(f1,f2)\in m^{opt}} s(f1,f2) \geq \sum_{(f1,f2)\in m} s(f1,f2)$.

When determining an equivalence mapping between the functions of two EPCs, each mapping satisfying Definition 4.2 is a good mapping, i.e. each element of the mapping satisfies the criterium that the similarity between the two functions exceeds the cut-off value. However, many equivalence mappings are possible. Therefore, we define the concept of an optimal equivalence mapping m^{opt}, i.e. the sum of the similarities expressed by m^{opt} is greater than the sum of the similarities of all other possible equivalence mappings[3]. An optimal equivalence mapping can be calculated in a straightforward way using integer linear programming techniques with binary variables.

4.4 Contextual Similarity

The techniques that we provided so far can be applied when comparing any two business process models. However, we are specifically considering EPCs, where each function has a preset and a postset of events. We define a second similarity metric based on this pre- and postset, which we call the contextual similarity metric. This metric produces better results than the semantic similarity metric.

Given two functions the contextual similarity technique returns the degree of similarity, based on the similarity of the events that precede and succeed them. We call these input and output events the input and output context of a function, respectively.

Definition 4.3. (Input and output context)
Let (E, F, C, l, A) be an EPC. For a function $f \in F$, we define the input context $f^{in} = \{e \in E \mid e \overset{C}{\hookrightarrow} f\}$ and the output context $f^{out} = \{e \in E \mid f \overset{C}{\hookrightarrow} e\}$

Now, we use the concept of equivalence mappings to determine the contextual similarity between functions.

Definition 4.4. (Contextual similarity)
Let $(E_1, F_1, C_1, l_1, A_1)$ and $(E_2, F_2, C_2, l_2, A_2)$ be two disjoint EPCs. Let $f_1 \in F_1$ and $f_2 \in F_2$ be two functions. Furthermore, let $m_{in}^{opt} : f_1^{in} \to f_2^{in}$ and $m_{out}^{opt} : f_1^{out} \to f_2^{out}$ be equivalence mappings between the input and output contexts of f_1 and f_2 respectively. We define the contextual similarity as follows:

$$con(f_1, f_2) = \frac{|\{m_{in}^{opt}\}|}{2 \cdot \sqrt{|f_1^{in}|} \cdot \sqrt{|f_2^{in}|}} + \frac{|\{m_{out}^{opt}\}|}{2 \cdot \sqrt{|f_1^{out}|} \cdot \sqrt{|f_2^{out}|}}$$

A full implementation of the function matching and the similarity degree calculation is available in the Process Mining framework ProM, which can freely be downloaded from www.processmining.org. In the following section we evaluate our approach using the data generated by this tool.

[3] Note that there might be more optimal equivalence mappings, however they all express a good mapping and we have no way of distinguishing between them, so any optimal equivalence mapping will suffice.

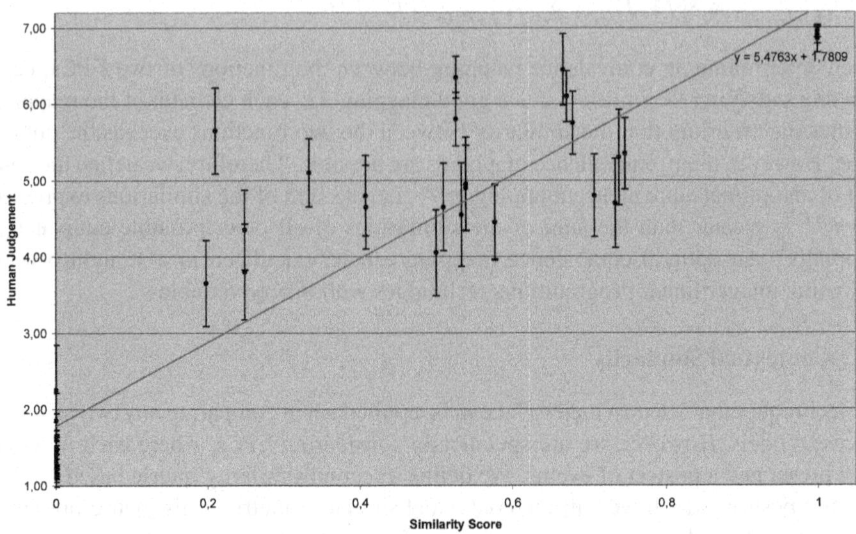

Fig. 3. Correlation between Similarity Score and Human Judgement.

5 Empirical Validation

We validated our approach to calculate the degree of similarity by computing its correlation with a similarity assessment of process modelers.

We obtained the similarity assessment using an online questionnaire that was distributed among academic process modelers. This questionnaire consisted of 48 pairs of process models from the SAP reference model database. For each pair of models, we asked the participants whether they agreed or disagreed (on a 1 to 7 Likert scale) with the proposition: 'These processes are similar.' To obtain a representative collection of model pairs, we selected the model pairs to be evenly distributed over the 0 to 1 similarity degree range. More details on how a representative collection of processes was obtained is described in the technical report that accompanies this paper [6].

We computed the correlation of the human assessment with various similarity degree metrics, which we obtained by varying cut-off values and relative importance of the syntactic, semantic and contextual similarity. We observed the best correlation for a similarity score metric that:

- does not consider syntactic similarity,
- uses a cut-off value of 0.89 for semantic similarity of events,
- uses a relative importance of semantic:contextual similarity of 1:2 and a cut-off value of 0.90 for similarity of functions.

Figure 3 shows the correlation between the similarity degree (computed using the settings described above) and the similarity assessment as obtained from the questionnaire. Each point in the graph represent a pair of processes, with a similarity degree as indicated by its x-value and a human similarity assessment as indicated by its y-value. The confidence intervals are also plotted (with a 90% confidence). For this metric we got a high (Pearson) correlation coefficient of 0.84 with the human judgement. The correlation is represented as a straight line in the graph. The correlation for two other metrics that we investigated was lower, i.e. the metric presented here was the best one. Details on all similarity degree metrics are given in the technical report that accompanies this paper [6].

An important observation is that, within the 'sales and distribution' branch of the SAP reference model (which contains 74 models), there are 124 process pairs with a similarity score of 1 (this is 50 more than the expected 74 pairs that represent comparison of a process with itself). In addition to that there are 52 process pairs with a similarity score s, such that $0.5 \leq s < 1.0$. These figures show the overlap between processes in 'sales and distribution' branch. This information can be used by people that are searching the SAP reference model for a suitable process; they can find overlapping processes based on this information. It can also be used to maintain consistency when updating a process for which there exists an overlapping process.

6 Related Work

This paper mainly relates to two streams of research, namely (1) similarity of business process models and (2) quality of business process models.

Existing work in the context of determining *similarity* between process models can be assigned to three categories: verification, behavioral similarity, and textual similarity. There are different notions of equivalence of process models that are subject to *verification* such as trace equivalence and bisimulation. While trace equivalence is based on a comparison of the sets of completed execution traces, bisimulation also considers at which point of time which decisions are taken, i.e., bisimulation is a stricter notion of equivalence. Details on different equivalence notions are given e.g. in [1]. A general problem of such verification approaches is that it provides a true-false answer to the question whether two models are similar. While some work has been done on determining a degree of behavioral similarity that measures the fitness of a set of event logs relative to a process model [1], we compare causal footprints [7] of two process models. Since causal footprints capture constraints instead of the state space, this approach relates to declarative approaches to process modeling and verification [8,17,22]. Beyond that, there are some works on textual or metadata similarity of process models (e.g. [9,14,20]). In this paper we adapt some concepts from this area for matching function labels, and we combine this approach with the calculation of behavioral similarity.

While there has been intensive research into quality aspects of process models and process modeling languages [3, 10, 15], there is little work on quality issues across models. The guidelines of modeling [3] touch this area by stressing the importance of a systematic design. The novelty of our approach is that systematic design in terms of non-overlapping models can now be checked automatically. This might prove valuable for providing tool support for process model normalization as defined in [21]. Beyond that, the quantification of a degree of behavioral similarity between process models could be a useful contribution for the area of process model *integration*. While there are several approaches reported on integration issues [5] and regarding *how* two models are integrated (e.g. [11,19,24]) the similarity degree gives an answer to the question *which* two process models might be good candidates for integration, e.g. in a merger situation. The redundancies that we identified in the SAP reference model underline the need for techniques and tools to manage process model variants such as defined in [25, 27]. Furthermore, there is clearly a need for a view concept on business process models in order to avoid anomalies [4] as they were identified in database research before.

7 Conclusion

In this paper, we presented a novel approach for measuring the degree of similarity of business process models. This approach builds on the vector model from information retrieval, an abstract representation of process behavior as causal footprints, and an automatic matching of functions across process models. While quality aspects of single process models and process modeling languages are well understood, this work contributes to a better foundation of those quality aspects across models that relate to similarity. Our approach has been validated using the SAP Reference Model, and a respective implementation is available as part of the ProM framework.

The results that we obtained for the SAP Reference Model clearly highlight the need for an automatic detection of similarity for supporting refactoring activities of a process model database. In future research we will investigate the benefits of our approach in various case studies. In particular, we aim to use the degree of similarity to detect operational overlap between companies that engage in a merger. While the application for the SAP Reference Model could build on a presumably homogeneous vocabulary of function labels, we assume that synonyms in function labels might play a more important role in a merger. Furthermore, there are some practical issues with reading the similarity matrix for a large set of models that need to be addressed. Once there is commercial tool support available, companies will find it easier to maintain large databases of process models.

References

1. van der Aalst, W.M.P., Alves de Medeiros, A.K., Weijters, A.J.M.M.: Process Equivalence: Comparing two process models based on observed behavior. In: Dustdar, S., Fiadeiro, J.L., Sheth, A. (eds.) BPM 2006. LNCS, vol. 4102, pp. 129–144. Springer, Heidelberg (2006)
2. Baeza-Yates, R.A., Ribeiro-Neto, B.A.: Modern Information Retrieval. ACM Press, New York (1999)
3. Becker, J., Rosemann, M., von Uthmann, C.: Guidelines of Business Process Modeling. In: van der Aalst, W.M.P., Desel, J., Oberweis, A. (eds.) Business Process Management. Models, Techniques, and Empirical Studies, pp. 30–49. Springer, Berlin (2000)
4. Biskup, J.: Achievements of relational database schema design theory revisited. In: Libkin, L., Thalheim, B. (eds.) Semantics in Databases 1995. LNCS, vol. 1358, pp. 29–54. Springer, Heidelberg (1998)
5. Dijkman, R.: A Classification of Differences between Similar Business Processes. In: Proceedings of the 11th IEEE EDOC Conference (EDOC 2007), pp. 37–50 (2007)
6. van Dongen, B.F., Dijkman, R.M., Mendling, J.: Detection of similarity between business process models. BETA Working Paper 233, Eindhoven University of Technology (2007)
7. van Dongen, B.F., Mendling, J., van der Aalst, W.M.P.: Structural Patterns for Soundness of Business Process Models. In: Proceedings of the 10th IEEE International EDOC Conference (EDOC 2006), pp. 116–128. IEEE, Los Alamitos (2006)

8. Eertink, H., Janssen, W., Oude Luttighuis, P., Teeuw, W.B., Vissers, C.A.: A business process design language. In: Wing, J.M., Woodcock, J.C.P., Davies, J. (eds.) FM 1999. LNCS, vol. 1708, pp. 76–95. Springer, Heidelberg (1999)
9. Ehrig, M., Koschmider, A., Oberweis, A.: Measuring similarity between semantic business process models. In: Roddick, J.F., Hinze, A. (eds.) Proceedings of the Fourth Asia-Pacific Conference on Conceptual Modelling (APCCM 2007), pp. 71–80 (2007)
10. Green, P., Rosemann, M.: Integrated Process Modeling. An Ontological Evaluation. Information Systems 25(2), 73–87 (2000)
11. Grossmann, G., Ren, Y., Schrefl, M., Stumptner, M.: Behavior based integration of composite business processes. In: van der Aalst, W.M.P., Benatallah, B., Casati, F., Curbera, F. (eds.) BPM 2005. LNCS, vol. 3649, pp. 186–204. Springer, Heidelberg (2005)
12. Johnson, R., Pearson, D., Pingali, K.: The program structure tree: Computing control regions in linear time. In: Proceedings of the ACM SIGPLAN'94 Conference on Programming Language Design and Implementation. SIGPLAN Notices, vol. 29(6), pp. 171–185 (1994)
13. Keller, G., Nüttgens, M., Scheer, A.-W.: Semantische Prozessmodellierung auf der Grundlage Ereignisgesteuerter Prozessketten (EPK). Heft 89, Institut für Wirtschaftsinformatik, Saarbrücken, Germany (1992)
14. Klein, M., Bernstein, A.: Toward high-precision service retrieval. IEEE Internet Computing 8(1), 30–36 (2004)
15. Krogstie, J., Sindre, G., Jørgensen, H.D.: Process models representing knowledge for action: a revised quality framework. Europ. J. of Information Systems 15(1), 91–102 (2006)
16. Levenshtein, I.: Binary code capable of correcting deletions, insertions and reversals. Cybernetics and Control Theory 10(8), 707–710 (1966)
17. Manna, Z., Pnueli, A.: The Temporal Logic of Reactive and Concurrent Systems: Specification. Springer, New York (1991)
18. Mendling, J., van der Aalst, W.M.P.: Formalization and Verification of EPCs with OR-Joins Based on State and Context. In: Krogstie, J., Opdahl, A., Sindre, G. (eds.) CAiSE 2007 and WES 2007. LNCS, vol. 4495, pp. 439–453. Springer, Heidelberg (2007)
19. Mendling, J., Simon, C.: Business Process Design by View Integration. In: Eder, J., Dustdar, S. (eds.) BPM Workshops 2006. LNCS, vol. 4103, pp. 55–64. Springer, Heidelberg (2006)
20. Momotko, M., Subieta, K.: Process query language: A way to make workflow processes more flexible. In: Benczúr, A.A., Demetrovics, J., Gottlob, G. (eds.) ADBIS 2004. LNCS, vol. 3255, pp. 306–321. Springer, Heidelberg (2004)
21. Pankratius, V., Stucky, W.: A formal foundation for workflow composition, workflow view definition, and workflow normalization based on petri nets (2005)
22. Pesic, M., Schonenberg, M.H., Sidorova, N., van der Aalst, W.M.P.: Constraint-based workflow models: Change made easy, pp. 77–94 (2007)
23. Porter, M.F.: An algorithm for suffix stripping. Program 14(3), 130–137 (1980)
24. Preuner, G., Conrad, S., Schrefl, M.: View integration of behavior in object-oriented databases. Data & Knowledge Engineering 36(2), 153–183 (2001)
25. Recker, J., Mendling, J., Rosemann, M., van der Aalst, W.M.P.: Model-driven Enterprise Systems Configuration. In: Dubois, E., Pohl, K. (eds.) CAiSE 2006. LNCS, vol. 4001, pp. 369–383. Springer, Heidelberg (2006)
26. Rosemann, M.: Potential pitfalls of process modeling: part b. Business Process Management Journal 12(3), 377–384 (2006)
27. Rosemann, M., van der Aalst, W.: A Configurable Reference Modelling Language. Information Systems 32, 1–23 (2007)
28. Salton, G., Wong, A., Yang, C.S.: A Vector Space Model for Automatic Indexing. Communications of the ACM 18(11), 613–620 (1975)

A Short Survey on Process Model Similarity

Remco M. Dijkman, Boudewijn F. van Dongen, Marlon Dumas, Luciano García-Bañuelos, Matthias Kunze, Henrik Leopold, Jan Mendling, Reina Uba, Matthias Weidlich, Mathias Weske, and Zhiqiang Yan

Abstract Process model similarity has developed into a prolific field of investigation. This paper summarizes the research after the CAISE 2008 paper on this topic. We identify categories of problems and provide an outlook on future directions.

1 Introduction

Analysing the similarity of process models has become a dynamic field of research in business process management. This short paper serves as commentary to the CAISE 2008 paper on "Measuring Similarity between Business Process Models" [1] – one of the first major conference papers on this topic after early

R.M. Dijkman (✉) · B.F. van Dongen · Z. Yan
TU Eindhoven, 5600 MB Eindhoven, The Netherlands
e-mail: R.M.Dijkman@tue.nl; b.f.v.dongen@tue.nl; zhiqiang.yan.1983@gmail.com

M. Dumas · L. García-Bañuelos · R. Uba
University of Tartu, 50409 Tartu, Estonia
e-mail: marlon.dumas@ut.ee; luciano.garcia@ut.ee; reinak@ut.ee

M. Kunze · M. Weske
HPI – University of Potsdam, 14482 Potsdam, Germany
e-mail: matthias.kunze@hpi.uni-potsdam.de; mathias.weske@hpi.uni-potsdam.de

H. Leopold
Humboldt-University Berlin, 10099 Berlin, Germany
e-mail: henrik.leopold@wiwi.hu-berlin.de

J. Mendling
Wirtschaftsuniversität Wien, 1090 Wien, Austria
e-mail: jan.mendling@wu.ac.at

M. Weidlich
Technion – Israel Institute of Technology, 32000 Haifa, Israel
e-mail: weidlich@tx.technion.ac.il

J. Bubenko et al. (eds.), *Seminal Contributions to Information Systems Engineering*,
DOI 10.1007/978-3-642-36926-1_34, © Springer-Verlag Berlin Heidelberg 2013

papers by Mendling, van Dongen and van der Aalst [2], Ehrig, Koschmider and Oberweis [3], Eshuis and Grefen [4], and Corrales, Grigori and Bouzeghoub [5] were published before. The article by Dijkman et al. [6] summarizes contributions before 2011.

The aim of this paper is to summarize the essential directions that emerged from these initial papers. Section 2 discusses the similarity problem in a very general way. Section 3 reviews alternative notions for calculating the similarity of process models. Section 4 turns to the problem of finding matching activities in a pair of process models. Section 5 highlights how the calculation of similarity between process models can help in search and indexing. Section 6 identifies directions of future research as a conclusion of this commentary.

2 The Challenge of Process Model Similarity

Process model similarity calculation is hindered by multiple inherent sources of heterogeneity. Even if two process models define exactly the same behaviour at the same level of granularity and with the same projection on the real-world process, the process models might still look quite different. We might encounter heterogeneity of behavioural representation, labelling styles, and terminology [7].

The first reason for this observation is that the representation of the same behaviour can be achieved with different structures. Partially, this phenomenon relates to the option to "multiply out" different choices in the process. Indeed, corresponding techniques are defined in [8] for making an unstructured process model structured. Therefore, we cannot assume that a different structure of process models does actually imply a difference in behaviour. Second, it has been observed that the labels can be formulated in different grammatical ways. Activities like "Send Invoice" (verb plus object) and "Sending of Invoice" (gerund plus preposition plus object) clearly point to the same type of activity. However, we cannot assume that a difference in the grammatical structure implies a difference in the activity. Techniques for automatically transforming activity labels to a canonical verb-object style are presented in [9]. Third, we can use syntactically different terms to defer to the same matter. For instance, two activity labels in verb-object style like "Check Invoice" and "Evaluate Bill" might use synonymous terms to refer to the same matter. Here again, we cannot assume that a difference in terms always implies a difference in meaning. Calculating the similarity of process models becomes much easier in a setting where we can assume that these heterogeneities are resolved.

These issues of heterogeneous representation can be present even if two models capture one process at the same level of granularity and using the same projections. Yet, even projections and granularity may differ. In the first case, we have to deal with problems that parts of a first process model might simply be left out in a second process model. The question then becomes to which extent the calculation of similarity should punish such a difference in projection. Technically this question relates to the properties of underlying notions for similarity calculation. For the second case, we have to consider questions of granularity. In terms of similarity, it has to be decided in how far a sequence of activities in one model shall be punished when it is shown as a single abstracted activity in the second model.

3 Underlying Notions for Process Model Similarity Calculation

Most approaches for process similarity are based on either the process model's graph structure or the behaviour captured in the model [10]. Similarity is typically quantified by symmetric and non-negative distance functions that capture the amount of differences a pair of process models exposes. Accordingly, two process models are identical if their distance equals 0.

The process model graph plus the execution semantics of its elements prescribe the allowed behaviour of the process, which is typically analysed by means of reachability graphs or the set of allowed execution traces. The problem of calculating the similarity of two process models based on both these options is that both approaches suffer from exponential complexity due to concurrency and loops in the process model [11]. Hence, abstractions have been proposed that only consider the order in which two activities can be executed in any process instance [12]. Two variants are (1) the transition adjacency relation [13, 14] that consider pairs of activities that can be executed directly after each other (non-transitive) and (2) weak order relations [4, 15] which consider any pair of activities that can be executed after each other eventually (transitive). An extension of the latter are behavioural profiles, which distinguish these relations by mutual exclusion, strict, and interleaving order [16, 17]. Although these relations abstract from certain behavioural aspects, e.g., causality and cardinality, they have been shown to support the human assessment of process model similarity [18]. Higher precision can be achieved based on event structures which yield a matrix of relations that fully characterizes a model in terms of a strong notion of behavioral equivalence [19].

An alternative to a notion of distance based on behavioural relations is graph edit distance [20]. The graph edit distance is the minimum number of basic graph operations that is needed to transform one graph into another. The basic operations are: add node, remove node, add edge and remove edge. In labelled graphs, node substitution can also be used as an operation, in which one node is substituted by another node with a different label. The graph edit distance can be transformed into a similarity metric in different ways, e.g., by dividing the distance by the number of nodes and edges of the largest graph and using one minus the result of that.

4 Process Model Matching

A basic technique required for many approaches to process model similarity is matching, the construction of correspondences between the process model activities. Process model matching is inspired by schema and ontology matching [21, 22] and adopts techniques for syntactic or semantic matching proposed in these fields. Despite the conceptual similarities, the problem of matching process models differs from the one of matching data schemas. For instance, the distinguished labelling styles observed for activities and the execution semantics of a process model may be leveraged for matching process models. On other hand, unlike in schema matching, instance data is typically not available for matching.

Recently, several approaches for process model matching have been presented. Most of them combine concepts for textual comparison of activity labels with the aforementioned similarity measures. A generic architecture for process model matching is defined by the ICoP framework [23]. Following this architecture, a matcher may rely on the string edit distance for comparing activity labels and a structural similarity measure for process model graphs, as presented in [24]. Activity labels have also been compared based on semantic annotations derived by part of speech tagging. Leopold et al. [25] derive match hypotheses from these annotations and rely on probabilistic inference for the construction of correspondences.

A major challenge for process model matching are differences in modelling granularity. The construction of complex 1:n or even n:m correspondences between activities is hindered by a combinatorial problem: there are exponentially many activity subsets in either process model that form possible candidate correspondences. Heuristics to select candidate correspondences are based on the graph distance [23] or structural decomposition of the process model graph [23,26]. Then, sets of activities (potentially including their descriptions) are textually compared using coefficients over terms or bigrams [26] or vector space scoring [23].

5 Process Model Search and Indexing

One of the applications of process similarity lies in finding all process models in a process model collection that are sufficiently similar to a so-called "search process model". Indexing techniques are required for implementing such a search efficiently. Pairwise computation of the distance of process models allows comparing a given query with models from a process repository, and thus, to find similar models. They also need to be ranked [27]. However, traditional indexes cannot be applied as the notion of pairwise similarity does not yield any ordering of process models. There are two competing approaches to indexing process models: (1) indexing process model elements [28, 29]; and (2) indexing complete process models, provided a similarity metric is used that satisfied the triangle inequality property [30].

The first approach is based on breaking each process model up into parts on which existing indexing techniques can be applied. In particular MTree [28] and B+ tree [29] indexing techniques have been used. The types of parts that have been used include: the labels of the tasks in the process models, paths of subsequent tasks and more complex constructs such as choices between tasks or parallel tasks. Using these indexing techniques, the search for similar models is executed by breaking the search model up into parts (e.g. only selecting the task labels) and then using the index to find the process models that have sufficiently many similar parts (e.g. similar task labels). The work on process model search and indexing is related to general graph search and its application to e.g. face recognition and fingerprint search.

The second approach uses metric spaces [31] to tackle this problem, as they facilitate efficient search in the absence of coordinates and ordering of elements if the distance function, beside the properties mentioned above, satisfies the triangle inequality. This property allows determining minimum and maximum distance of two process models without computing the distance function, if their pairwise distance to a third model is given. Such transitivity improves search efficiency and can be applied to both structural [32] and behavioural [18] process model similarities.

6 Future Research on Process Model Similarity

Though we have seen exciting advancements in research on process model similarity, several challenges still await solutions. While behavioural and label styles can be homogenized with recent techniques, we are missing approaches to harmonize terminology and the level of granularity. These challenges are specifically important for process model matching. Another open issue is the lack of reference samples to perform thorough evaluations of different approaches. Dijkman et al. [6] conducted a survey and let process model experts judge on the similarity of 1,000 pairs of process models, which helped to refine techniques. More such datasets are required in order to increase the degree of repeatability and reproducibility in this field of research. This will provide a good basis for further comparative studies such as [33]. Related application scenarios such as clustering process models [34], detection of clones [35] and behavioural patterns [36] are expected to further benefit from research into process model similarity.

References

1. van Dongen, B.F., Dijkman, R.M., Mendling, J.: Measuring similarity between business process models. In Bellahsene, Z., Léonard, M., eds.: CAiSE 2008. LNCS 5074 (2008) 450–464
2. Mendling, J., van Dongen, B.F., van der Aalst, W.M.P.: On the degree of behavioral similarity between business process models. In Nüttgens, M., Rump, F.J., Gadatsch, A., eds.: EPK Workshop 2007. Volume 303 of CEUR Workshop Proceedings, CEUR-WS.org (2007) 39–58
3. Ehrig, M., Koschmider, A., Oberweis, A.: Measuring similarity between semantic business process models. In Roddick, J.F., Hinze, A., eds.: APCCM 2007. CRPIT 67 (2007) 71–80
4. Eshuis, R., Grefen, P.W.P.J.: Structural matching of bpel processes. In: ECOWS 2007, IEEE Computer Society (2007) 171–180
5. Corrales, J.C., Grigori, D. Bouzeghoub, M.: BPEL Processes Matchmaking for Service Discovery. In: OTM 2006, Part I, LNCS 4275 (2006) 237–254

6. Dijkman, R.M., Dumas, M., van Dongen, B.F., Käärik, R., Mendling, J.: Similarity of business process models: Metrics and evaluation. Inf. Syst. **36**(2) (2011) 498–516
7. Mendling, J.: Three challenges for process model reuse. In Daniel, F., Barkaoui, K., Dustdar, S., eds.: BPM Workshops (2). LNBIP 100 (2011) 285–288
8. Polyvyanyy, A., García-Bañuelos, L., Dumas, M.: Structuring acyclic process models. Inf. Syst. **37**(6) (2012) 518–538
9. Leopold, H., Smirnov, S., Mendling, J.: On the refactoring of activity labels in business process models. Inf. Syst. **37**(5) (2012) 443–459
10. Dumas, M., García-Bañuelos, L., Dijkman, R.M.: Similarity search of business process models. IEEE Data Eng. Bull. **32**(3) (2009) 23–28
11. Valmari, A.: The state explosion problem. In Reisig, W., Rozenberg, G., eds.: Petri Nets. LNCS 1491 (1996) 429–528
12. van der Aalst, W.M.P., Weijters, T., Maruster, L.: Workflow mining: Discovering process models from event logs. IEEE Trans. Knowl. Data Eng. **16**(9) (2004) 1128–1142
13. Bae, J., Liu, L., Caverlee, J., Zhang, L.J., Bae, H.: Development of distance measures for process mining, discovery and integration. Int. J. Web Service Res. **4**(4) (2007) 1–17
14. Zha, H., Wang, J., Wen, L., Wang, C., Sun, J.: A workflow net similarity measure based on transition adjacency relations. Computers in Industry **61**(5) (2010) 463–471
15. Weidlich, M., Mendling, J., Weske, M.: A foundational approach for managing process variability. In Mouratidis, H., Rolland, C., eds.: CAiSE 2011. LNCS 6741 (2011) 267–282
16. Weidlich, M., Mendling, J., Weske, M.: Efficient consistency measurement based on behavioral profiles of process models. IEEE Trans. Software Eng. **37**(3) (2011) 410–429
17. Weidlich, M., Polyvyanyy, A., Mendling, J., Weske, M.: Causal behavioural profiles - efficient computation, applications, and evaluation. Fundam. Inform. **113**(3–4) (2011) 399–435
18. Kunze, M., Weidlich, M., Weske, M.: Behavioral similarity - a proper metric. In Rinderle-Ma, S., Toumani, F., Wolf, K., eds.: BPM 2011. LNCS 6896 (2011) 166–181
19. Armas-Cervantes, A., García-Bañuelos, L., Dumas, M.: Event structures as a foundation for process model differencing, part 1: acyclic processes, In: WS-FM 2012. (to appear)
20. Dijkman, R.M., Dumas, M., García-Bañuelos, L.: Graph matching algorithms for business process model similarity search. In Dayal, U., Eder, J., Koehler, J., Reijers, H.A., eds.: BPM 2009. LNCS 5701 (2009) 48–63
21. Bellahsene, Z., Bonifati, A., Rahm, E., eds.: Schema Matching and Mapping. Springer (2011)
22. Euzenat, J., Shvaiko, P.: Ontology matching. Springer (2007)
23. Weidlich, M., Dijkman, R.M., Mendling, J.: The ICoP framework: Identification of correspondences between process models. In CAiSE 2010. LNCS 6051 (2010) 483–498
24. Dijkman, R.M., Dumas, M., García-Bañuelos, L., Käärik, R.: Aligning business process models. In: EDOC 2009, IEEE Computer Society (2009) 45–53
25. Leopold, H., Niepert, M., Weidlich, M., Mendling, J., Dijkman, R.M., Stuckenschmidt, H.: Probabilistic optimization of semantic process model matching. In Barros, A.P., Gal, A., Kindler, E., eds.: BPM 2012. LNCS 7481 (2012) 319–334
26. Branco, M.C., Troya, J., Czarnecki, K., Küster, J.M., Völzer, H.: Matching business process workflows across abstraction levels. In France, R.B., Kazmeier, J., Breu, R., Atkinson, C., eds.: MoDELS 2012. LNCS 7590 (2012) 626–641
27. Grigori, D., Corrales, J.C., Bouzeghoub, M., Gater, A.: Ranking bpel processes for service discovery. IEEE T. Services Computing **3**(3) (2010) 178–192
28. Yan, Z., Dijkman, R., Grefen, P.: Fast business process similarity search. Distributed and Parallel Databases **30** (2012) 105–144
29. Jin, T., Wang, J., Wu, N., La Rosa, M., ter Hofstede, A.: Efficient and accurate retrieval of business process models through indexing. In: OTM, Part I. LNCS 6426 (2010) 402–409
30. Kunze, M., Weidlich, M., Weske, M.: Behavioral similarity – a proper metric. In: BPM 2011. LNCS 7481 (2011) 166–181
31. Zezula, P., Amato, G., Dohnal, V., Batko, M.: Similarity Search - The Metric Space Approach. Volume 32 of Advances in Database Systems. Kluwer (2006)

32. Kunze, M., Weske, M.: Metric trees for efficient similarity search in large process model repositories. In zur Muehlen, M., Su, J., eds.: BPM Workshops. LNBIP 66 (2010) 535–546
33. Becker, M., Laue, R.: A comparative survey of business process similarity measures. Computers in Industry **63**(2) (2012) 148–167
34. Niemann, M., Siebenhaar, M., Schulte, S., Steinmetz, R.: Comparison and retrieval of process models using related cluster pairs. Computers in Industry **63**(2) (2012) 168–180
35. Ekanayake, C.C., Dumas, M., García-Bañuelos, L., Rosa, M.L., ter Hofstede, A.H.M.: Approximate clone detection in repositories of business process models. In Barros, A.P., Gal, A., Kindler, E., eds.: BPM 2012. LNCS 7481 (2012) 302–318
36. Smirnov, S., Weidlich, M., Mendling, J., Weske, M.: Action patterns in business process model repositories. Computers in Industry **63**(2) (2012) 98–111

How Much Language Is Enough? Theoretical and Practical Use of the Business Process Modeling Notation

Michael zur Muehlen[1] and Jan Recker[2]

[1] Stevens Institute of Technology, Howe School of Technology Management, Castle Point on Hudson, Hoboken, NJ 07030 USA
Michael.zurMuehlen@stevens.edu
[2] Queensland University of Technology, Faculty of Information Technology, 126 Margaret Street, Brisbane QLD 4000, Australia
j.recker@qut.edu.au

Abstract. The Business Process Modeling Notation (BPMN) is an increasingly important industry standard for the graphical representation of business processes. BPMN offers a wide range of modeling constructs, significantly more than other popular languages. However, not all of these constructs are equally important in practice as business analysts frequently use arbitrary subsets of BPMN. In this paper we investigate what these subsets are, and how they differ between academic, consulting, and general use of the language. We analyzed 120 BPMN diagrams using mathematical and statistical techniques. Our findings indicate that BPMN is used in groups of several, well-defined construct clusters, but less than 20% of its vocabulary is regularly used and some constructs did not occur in any of the models we analyzed. While the average model contains just 9 different BPMN constructs, models of this complexity have typically just 4-5 constructs in common, which means that only a small agreed subset of BPMN has emerged. Our findings have implications for the entire ecosystems of analysts and modelers in that they provide guidance on how to reduce language complexity, which should increase the ease and speed of process modeling.

Keywords: BPMN, Language Analysis, Process Modeling.

1 Introduction

The Business Process Modeling Notation (BPMN) [1] is emerging as a standard language for capturing business processes, especially at the level of domain analysis and high-level systems design. A growing number of process design, enterprise architecture, and workflow automation tools provide modeling environments for BPMN. The development of BPMN was influenced by the demand for a graphical notation that complements the BPEL standard for executable business processes. Although this development gives BPMN a technical focus, the intention of the BPMN designers was to develop a modeling language that can equally well be applied to typical business modeling activities. This is clearly visible in the specification document, which

Z. Bellahsène and M. Léonard (Eds.): CAiSE 2008, LNCS 5074, pp. 465–479, 2008.

separates the BPMN constructs into a set of core graphical elements and an extended, more specialized set. BPMN's developers envisaged the core set to be used by business analysts for the essential, intuitive articulation of business processes in very easy terms. The full set of constructs would then enable users to specify even complex process scenarios with a level of detail that facilitates process simulation, evaluation or even execution. This separation mirrors an emerging tendency in industry to separate business-focused process modeling from implementation-oriented workflow implementation.

The evolution of BPMN closely mirrors the emergence of another modeling standard, UML [2]. Both have been ratified by the standardization body OMG. Both contain a larger set of constructs in contrast to competing languages, and offer a multitude of options for conceptual modeling. Both have been found in analytical studies to be not only semantically richer but also theoretically more complex than other modeling languages, [e.g., 3, 4]. And, in UML's case, this complexity motivated users to deliberately reduce the set of constructs for system analysis and design tasks. Related studies found that frequently not even 20% of the constructs are used in practice [5, 6].

The apparent complexity of the BPMN standard seems to be similar to the UML standard, which raises a number of questions: Are BPMN users able – and willing – to cope with the complexity of the language? Does the separation into core and extended constructs provided by the specification hold in modeling practice? And – really – how exactly is BPMN used in practice?

While BPMN has been receiving significant attention not only in practice but also in academia, virtually all contributions have been made on an analytical or conceptual level, [7, 8]. There are only few empirical insights into how BPMN is used in practice – exceptions are reported in [9] and [10].

Accordingly, our research imperative has been to provide empirical evidence on the usage of BPMN in real-life process modeling practice. The *aim of this paper* is to examine, using statistical techniques, which elements of BPMN are used in practice. We collected a large set of BPMN diagrams from three different application areas (i.e., consulting, education, process re-engineering) and analyzed the models regarding their construct usage. This study is a first step to determine the most commonly used set of BPMN constructs and to provide the ecosystem of process modelers with specific advice which elements of BPMN to use when. BPMN training programs could benefit from a structure that introduces students to the most commonly used subset first before moving on to advanced modeling concepts.

We proceed as follows: The next section briefly introduces the background of our research, viz., BPMN and our data sources, and presents our research design. Section 3 presents the analysis results and discusses them. Section 4 concludes this paper with a discussion of contributions, implications and limitations, and provides an outlook to future research.

2 Background

2.1 Introduction to BPMN

The Business Process Modeling Notation [1] is a recently published notation standard for business processes. Its development has been based on the revision of other notations including UML, IDEF, ebXML, RosettaNet, LOVeM and Event-driven Process Chains.

BPMN was developed by an industry consortium (BPMI.org), whose constituents represented a wide range of BPM tool vendors but no end users. The standardization process took six years and more than 140 meetings, both physical and virtual. The BPMN working group developed a specification document that differentiates the BPMN constructs into a set of core graphical elements and an extended specialized set. The complete BPMN specification defines 50 constructs plus attributes, grouped into four basic categories of elements, viz., Flow Objects, Connecting Objects, Swimlanes and Artefacts. *Flow Objects*, such as events, activities and gateways, are the most basic elements used to create BPMN models. *Connecting Objects* are used to inter-connect Flow Objects through different types of arrows. *Swimlanes* are used to group activities into separate categories for different functional capabilities or responsibilities (e.g., different roles or organizational departments). *Artefacts* may be added to a model where deemed appropriate in order to display further related information such as processed data or other comments. For further information on BPMN refer to [1].

Existing research related to BPMN includes, *inter alia*, analyses and evaluations, [e.g., 9, 11], use in combination with other grammars, especially BPEL [7], or its support for workflow concepts and technologies [8]. This and other research is mostly analytical in nature. Few insights exist into the practical use of BPMN, which has motivated our study.

2.2 Data Sources

In order to arrive at an informed opinion about the use of BPMN in practice we collected BPMN models from three types of sources: A search using Internet search engines for "BPMN model" resulted in 57 BPMN diagrams, obtained from organizations' web sites, from practitioner forums and similar sites. These diagrams were labeled in a variety of languages, but since our study focuses on the modeling constructs and not their content this was no hindrance. We collected an additional 37 BPMN diagrams from consulting projects to which we had access. These diagrams depicted as-is and to-be processes from business improvement projects or software deployment projects. An additional 26 diagrams were collected through BPMN education seminars taught by the authors. These diagrams were created by seminar participants and depicted business processes from the participants' organization. Overall, our data set consists of 126 BPMN models approximating the use of BPMN for a variety of purposes including process (re-) design, education, consulting, and software and workflow engineering. 6 models were excluded from the analysis because they explicitly illustrated nonsensical diagrams or were duplicates.

While by no means do we claim our data set to be statistically representative of the overall use of BPMN in practice, it nevertheless gives us an informed opinion about the *real* use of BPMN beyond the examples typically given by developers or tool vendors.

2.3 Research Design

Having obtained a large set of BPMN models, our next step was to prepare these models for analysis. We created an Excel spread sheet counting the type of BPMN constructs in use per model. Each occurrence of a BPMN construct was marked as 1, otherwise 0. This coding allowed us to treat the individual models as binary strings for further analysis. In our coding effort, we kept track of the data sources for each model, which, for analysis purposes, we labeled 'web' (those models that we obtained from Internet search engines), 'consulting' (those that we obtained from consulting engagements) and 'seminar' (those obtained from educational seminars).

The resulting tables provided the basis for the application of statistical techniques such as cluster analysis, frequency analysis, covariance analysis and distribution analysis. We employed analysis techniques available in Excel (frequency counts), Mathematica (covariance matrices, Hamming distances) and R (cluster analysis). The following sections provide further details about the exact application of the various techniques used, and discuss the results we obtained.

3 Analysis and Discussion

3.1 Overall Use of BPMN Constructs

BPMN offers 50 modeling constructs, ranging from Task and Sequence Flow to Compensation Associations and Transaction Boundaries. Our first question was: Which of these symbols are used in practice and how frequently?

Fig. 1 shows the frequency distribution of the individual BPMN constructs, separated by the three sample sets and ranked by overall frequency. Generally speaking, the distribution of constructs follows a power-law distribution, with only four constructs being common to more than 50% of the diagrams: Sequence Flow, Task, End Event, and Start Event. Notably, these constructs all belong to the originally specified BPMN core set [1].

Fig. 1 shows that every model contained the Sequence Flow construct, and nearly every model contained the basic Task construct (the diagrams that did not contain the Task construct used the Subprocess construct). The majority of Web and Seminar models contained Start and End Events, while the Consulting models replaced these with more specific event types (e.g., Message or Timer Events for Start Events, Terminate, Message, or Link, for End Events). The other BPMN constructs were unevenly distributed. A visual inspection of Fig. 1 leads to a number of interesting observations:

While the majority of consulting models contained Data-based XOR Gateways (77%), Pools (81%) and Lanes (69%), these constructs were much less frequent in the other two sample sets (57%, 30%, 21% and 23%, 56%, 16% respectively for web and seminar models). This indicates that the consulting models depict organizational structure in more detail than the random web sample. The majority of consulting models contained detailed Gateway constructs, whereas only ¼ of the seminar models did not used them. This implies that beginning modelers tend to create diagrams with few alternative or parallel flows.

The Web diagrams use (non-specific) Gateways frequently (observed in 55% of the models), whereas the consulting and seminar sets make much less use of this symbol (5% and 12%, respectively). Models in the web sample express the control flow logic of the diagrams in plain text (which can be inserted into the basic Gateways), rather than the more formal XOR, AND, and Inclusive OR constructs.

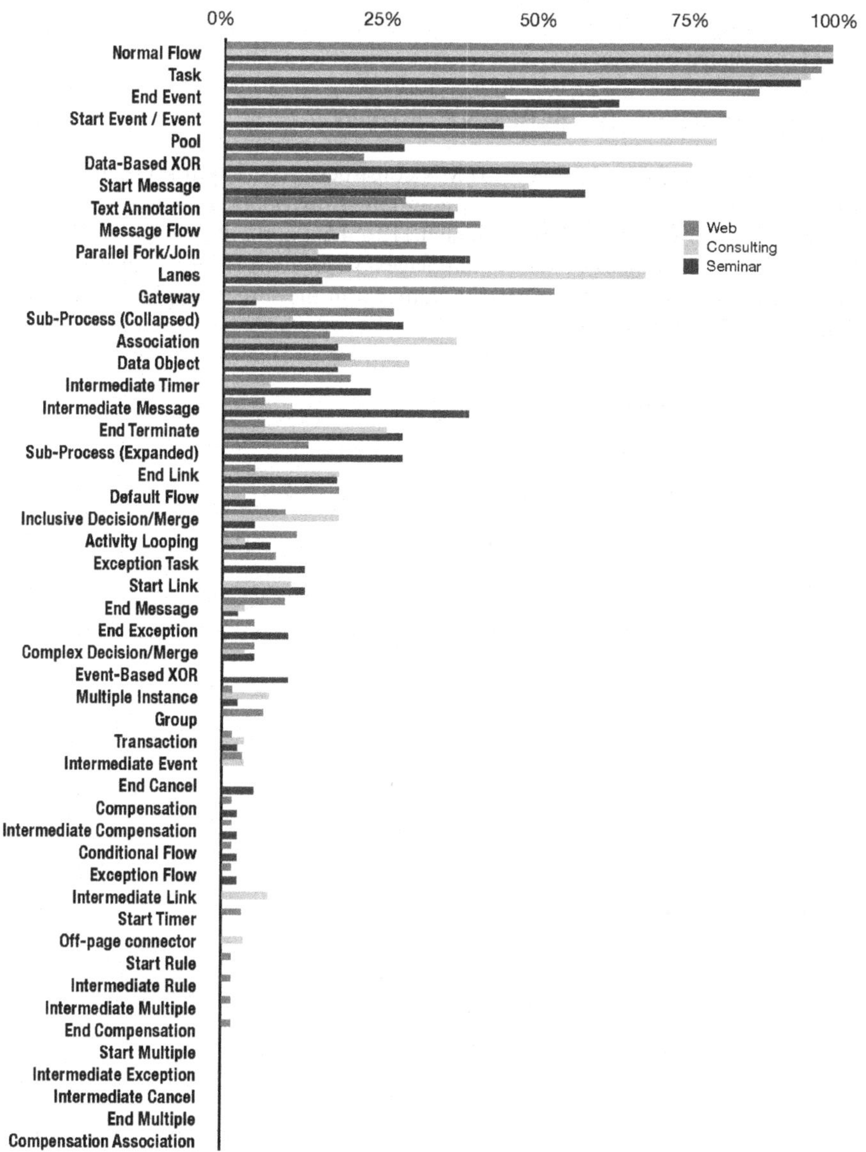

Fig. 1. Occurrence Frequency of BPMN Constructs

A sizable fraction of seminar models contain Intermediate Message constructs (41%) whereas only 7% of web models and 12% of consulting models contain this construct. This indicates that this construct is emphasized in BPMN classes but not very common in practice. A potential explanation may stem from the underlying design paradigm for process choreography in BPMN, which typically requires a lot of time to explain in classrooms. Practitioners in general may not be fully confident in the use of these choreography concepts, which could be explain the less frequent usage of the related constructs.

3.2 Frequency Distribution of BPMN Constructs

The ranked frequency distribution of BPMN constructs generally follows an exponential (power-law) distribution, similar to long-tailed distributions that have been observed as a result of preferential attachment [12]. This particular shape has been observed previously in studies of natural languages, [e.g., 13, 14]. Fig. 2 shows a plot of the frequency distribution of the BPMN elements in the three sample sets compared with the Zipfian distribution [14].

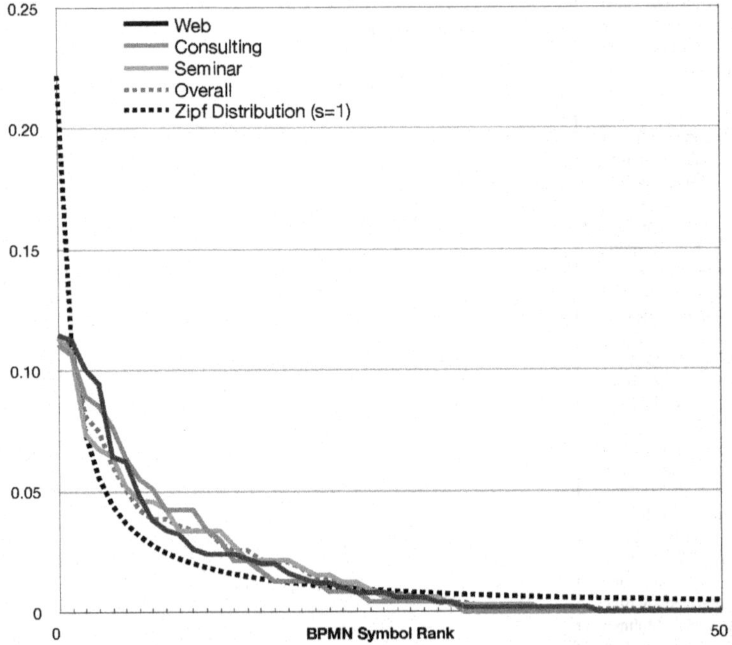

Fig. 2. Frequency Plot of BPMN Constructs by Rank

Zipf's Law states that the frequency of words in natural languages is inverse to their rank (in other words, the second most frequent word is used 1/2 the time of the first, the third most frequent word 1/3 of the time, and so on) and has been observed in numerous contexts [see, for instance, 13]. While not a perfect fit, the BPMN subsets exhibit a distribution that is very close to the distribution of word usage in natural languages. This suggests that the use of BPMN constructs to design (graphical) statements about organizational or system processes mirrors the use of natural languages.

This finding is of importance for future research on the way users learn, retain, and use BPMN constructs, and – really – any other graphical modeling language. For instance, linguistics research could be used to formulate conjectures about appropriate modeling training programs – a still under-researched aspect of modeling research in

IS. In general terms, the distribution of BPMN constructs shows that BPMN – as many natural languages – has a few essential constructs, a wide range of constructs commonly used, and an abundance of constructs virtually unused. Based on this observation, training and usage guidelines can be designed to reduce the complexity of the language to inexperienced analysts and to deliberately build such models that can safely be assumed to depict the core essence of a process without adding too much complexity.

3.3 BPMN Construct Correlations

Having determined the most frequent set of BPMN constructs in use, we turn to some related questions: Which of the BPMN constructs are typically used in combination? Which are used in alternation? In order to answer these questions, we used Mathematica to generate covariance matrices, which allowed us to examine pairs of BPMN constructs with regard to their combined or alternative use. Those pairs of constructs with negative covariance ($p < -0.05$) indicate alternatively used constructs while those with positive covariance ($p > 0.05$) indicate constructs used in combination. Table 1 summarizes the results.

Table 1. Combined and alternative use of BPMN constructs

Constructs with p > 0.05	Constructs with p < -0.05
Data Object → Association	Start Event → Start Message
Pool → Message Flow	Gateway → Data-based XOR
Start Event → End Event	Text Annotation → Message Flow
Start Message → Data-based XOR	Start Message→ End Event
Start Message → Intermediate Message	Start Message → Gateway
Start Message → End Terminate	Start Event → Data-based XOR
Pool → Lane	End Event → Data-based XOR
Lane → Message Flow	

Our findings present some interesting implications regarding BPMN modeling practice. Looking at the combined use of BPMN constructs (left column in Table 1), most correlations confirm that BPMN modeling practice obeys the grammatical rules of BPMN. For instance, Data Objects need to be linked to flow objects via the Association constructs, Pools can only communicate with other Pools via message flow, Lanes require Pools, and BPMN models require both Start and End Event. However, at least two interesting observations emerge. First, the positive correlation of Start Message events with End Terminate events indicates a more sophisticated level of BPMN modeling, suggesting that when users start using the differentiated event constructs, they tend to use a variety of these. Similarly, the combined use of Start Message events with the Data-based XOR constructs indicates an advanced use of the language for models in which different types of messages lead to different variants of a process, depending on the actual content of the arriving message.

Looking at the alternative use of BPMN constructs (right column in Table 1), we can identify additional interesting patterns of BPMN use. For instance, the negative correlation between Gateway and Data-based XOR suggests that when modelers refine the semantics of their models they choose the data-based XOR over the unspecific

Gateway in order to clarify the control flow semantics of their models. The negative correlation between Text Annotation and Message Flow suggests that at initial stages, modelers avoid choreography concepts and instead use free-form text to indicate message exchange. More advanced modeling relies on the provided semantic constructs instead of simple textual additions. Similarly, the negative correlations between Start Message event and the Gateway construct, and the Start/End Event and the Data-based XOR imply that modelers who refine the event constructs have achieved a level of sophistication of language use at which they avoid the use of the non-descriptive gateways altogether and instead rely on the more differentiated gateway and event subtypes.

3.4 BPMN Construct Clusters

In addition to identifying pairs of constructs that are used alternatively or in combination, we were also interested in uncovering whether clusters of BPMN constructs can be found in practice. To that end, we performed a hierarchical cluster analysis using the Euclidian distance measure in order to classify the set of BPMN constructs into distinct subsets. Fig. 3 shows the resulting dendrogram.

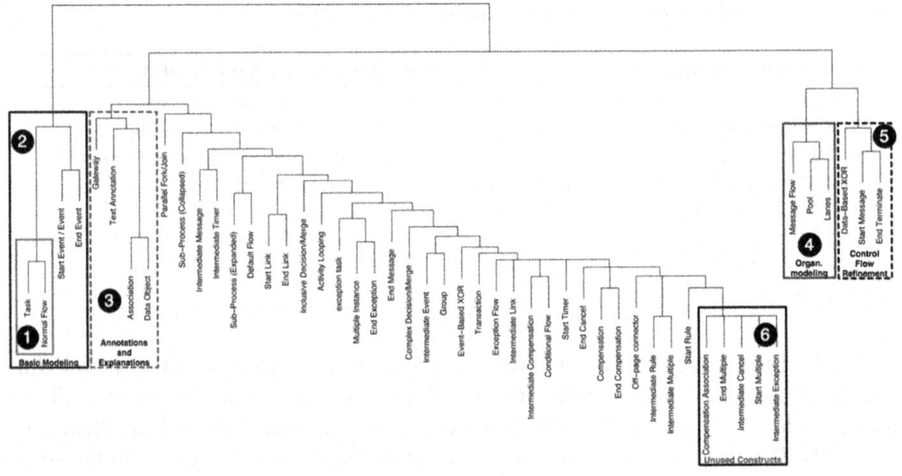

Fig. 3. Cluster Dendrogram of BPMN Constructs

In Fig. 3 six construct clusters are highlighted. First, the Task and Normal Flow cluster depicts the core of process modeling – the orchestration of activities that constitute a business process. Together with start and event conditions (through the use of events), these clusters indicate the simplest form of depicting the essence of a process in a graphical model. A third cluster is comprised of elements that are used to embellish and explain such process models through the use of text annotations, gateways (that specify control flow conditions of sequences of tasks) and data processing information. Clusters four and five essentially denote additions to these core modeling concepts by adding information about the organizational task allocation schemes, required roles and responsibilities as well as choreography information in collaborative scenarios, or refinements to the orchestration of the flow of the process through different types of event and gateway constructs. The sixth cluster we found denotes the set of constructs that are very simply not used at all (e.g., compensation association, end message, etc).

The clustering of BPMN constructs provides a promising starting point for a complete ecosystem of BPMN users – vendors, consultants, coaches and end users alike. These users can be guided in their efforts to learn and apply BPMN in an effective and efficient manner. Training programs, for instance, could focus on the 'basic modeling' clusters first before teaching advanced concepts such as organizational modeling and control flow orchestration. Coaches and consultants in charge of modeling conventions are guided by delineating the most common – and most frequently avoided – BPMN constructs.

3.5 Core or Extended Set?

According to the BPMN specification, BPMN modelers are envisaged to choose either the core set of ten BPMN constructs, or an extended set in which these core constructs are modified (i.e., revised and extended). Our questions are: Do modelers use core or extended constructs? Do they comply with the differentiation?
In order to answer these questions we split the modeling constructs into 10 sets:

- Tasks are split into Basic Tasks and an extended task set which contains the constructs for Subprocesses (collapsed and expanded) as well as Tasks with additional semantics, such as Multiple Instance Tasks, Compensations, or Transactions.
- Sequence flow constructs are split into a basic set (the Normal Flow) and an extended set (consisting of Default Flow, Conditional, and Exception flow).
- Gateways are split into the Basic (blank) XOR Gateway, and an extended Gateway set, which comprises Data- (X-labeled) and Event-based XOR, Inclusive-OR, and Parallel Gateways. We contrast these two sets with the representation of routing information through the Conditional Sequence Flow construct.
- Events are split into the Basic Events, and an extended Event set including constructs such as Messages, Rule Events, Links, etc.
- In addition we distinguished from these constructs Layout elements such as off-page connectors and the Grouping construct.

For these sets, we performed three separate frequency counts, for each of the three data sets. The results are shown in Fig. 4.

The usage patterns exhibited in Fig. 4 shed some light on when users turn to elements from the extended set of BPMN constructs. First, while users tend to employ basic task and sequence flow constructs, they mostly employ an extended set of gateway constructs. Especially the sequence flow extensions are rarely used in practice. In terms of event constructs, basic and extended sets appear to be equally utilized. The following additional observations can be made from the frequency analysis:

- Consultants especially avoid extended task constructs and use mainly basic tasks. On the other hand, they largely utilize the set of specialized gateway constructs.

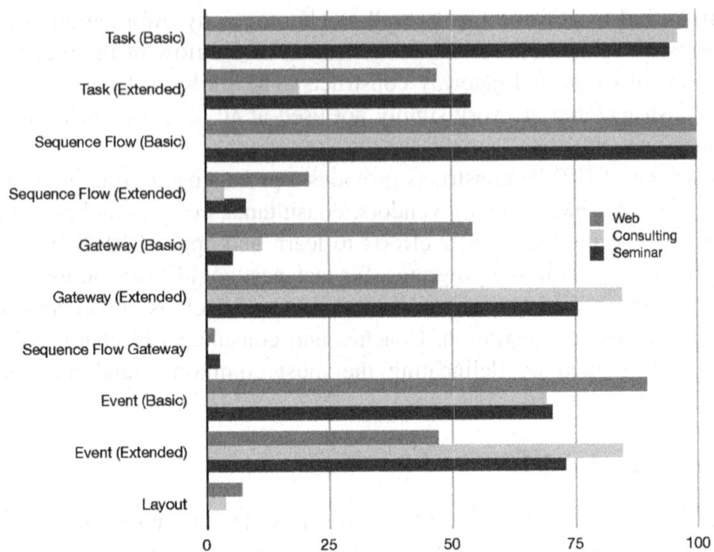

Fig. 4. Use of Core and Extended BPMN Constructs

- Decision Sequence Flow constructs are very rarely used. This would suggest that BPMN users prefer the explicit decision routing representation capacity of Gateways over the alternative, rather implicit way of annotating sequence flows.
- Basic Gateways are dominant on the web. However, neither consulting nor seminar models use them in large numbers. This suggests that formal training (as exercised through seminar courses or trained consultants) leads to the use of precise semantics for articulating process orchestration.
- Layout constructs are very rarely used. This suggests two things. First, language users often use tool functionality to annotate diagrams (e.g., meta-tags, free form tags, navigation capacity). Second, it may be worthwhile externalizing such constructs from a modeling language in order to reduce their complexity.

3.6 Complexity of BPMN Models

Previous studies on the usage of UML [5, 6] uncovered that the theoretical complexity of a language (as measured by the number of constructs originally specified) often considerably differs from the practical complexity (the number of constructs actually used in a model). We are interested in whether a similar situation exists in the case of BPMN. In other words, while the theoretical complexity of BPMN is standardized by its specification [1], we wanted to measure the practical complexity of BPMN (i.e., the vocabulary used in practice). To that end, we contrasted the semantic complexity of the BPMN models we obtained (i.e., the size of the models) with their syntactic complexity (i.e., the number of semantically different BPMN constructs used in these models). Fig. 5 illustrates the results of this analysis.

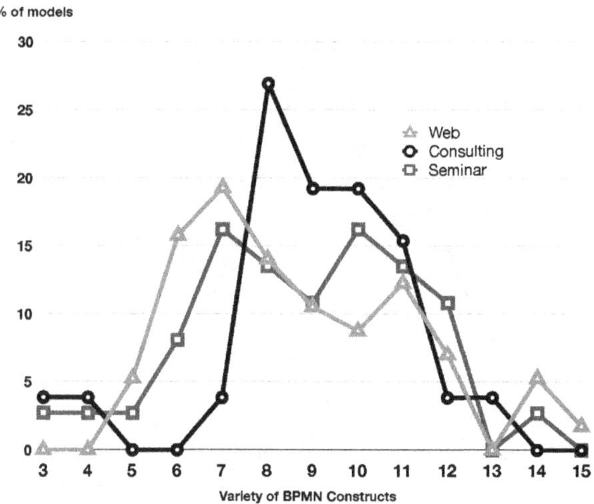

Fig. 5. Syntactic Complexity of BPMN Models

While the 50 BPMN constructs theoretically allow for 2^{50} permutations, the actual number of usable subsets is much smaller. All BPMN models obviously require the use of Tasks and Sequence Flow. Since the majority of models we observed used a BPMN vocabulary of between 6 and 12 constructs, the number of possible BPMN vocabulary subsets in practice is between $\binom{48}{4}$ =194,580 and $\binom{48}{10}$ = 6,540,715,896. Given that 9 constructs in our sample were used by fewer than two models we can exclude these from the search space and arrive at a theoretical range from $\binom{39}{10}$ = 82,251 to $\binom{39}{4}$ = 635,745,396. On average, we found the average number of semantically different BPMN constructs to be 9 (consulting), 8.78 (web), and 8.7 (seminar), respectively. However, while this finding indicates the size of the average BPMN vocabulary used in practice, it does not mean that every model with 9 BPMN constructs uses the exact same BPMN subset. In fact, a pair wise comparison of the 120 models revealed only 6 pairs of models that shared the same BPMN subset between each pair (i.e., there were 6 identical pairs of construct sets).

3.7 Variety of BPMN Subsets

In order to determine the variety of BPMN subsets, we computed the Hamming Distance [15] for each model vocabulary. Originally, the Hamming distance between two strings of equal length is the number of positions for which the corresponding symbols are different. In other words, it measures the minimum number of substitutions required to change one into the other. In the case of BPMN, we treated each model vocabulary as a 50-bit binary string, where a positive bit at position *i* signals the usage of BPMN construct [*i*]. The Hamming Distance between two model vocabularies then indicates the number of bits that differ between the two vocabularies, in other words the discrepancy between the BPMN constructs used in the creation of two models. The results are visualized in Fig. 6.

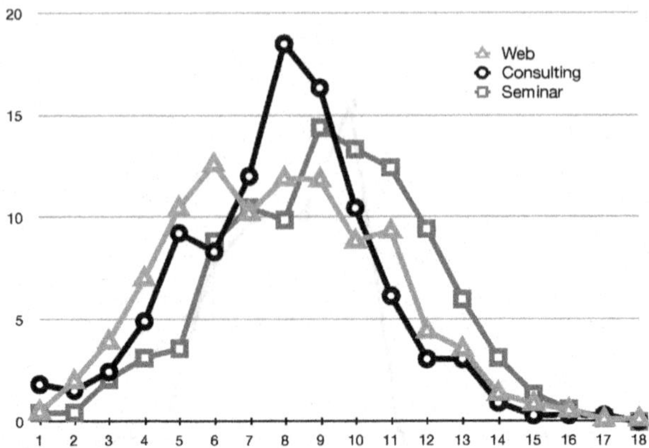

Fig. 6. Hamming Distance of BPMN Vocabularies

The average Hamming distance for the three subsets was 7.6 (web), 7.5 (consulting), and 8.8 (seminar), indicating a slightly more diverse use of BPMN constructs by novice modelers, whereas the web and consulting sets were slightly more homogeneous (but not by much). These metrics indicate that the average dissimilarity between two BPMN subsets is 7-8 constructs. A common scenario would be that one model uses 4 BPMN constructs that the other model does not exhibit and vice versa. As BPMN becomes more prevalent we plan on observing this metric over time, to see whether the commonly used vocabularies become more homogeneous over time. Annotating these BPMN subsets with context information (e.g., the process modeling purpose), in turn, could provide a starting point for deriving the most suitable BPMN subsets for a variety of application areas.

3.8 The Common Core of BPMN

Our evaluation thus far has focused on the individual elements and their grouping into core and extended constructs. However, one of our questions relates to the subset of BPMN constructs that are shared by different models. While we found six pairs of models that each share a complete set of constructs, there are subsets that are shared by more than two models. Figure Fig. 7 shows a Venn diagram of different BPMN construct combinations. The number in the corner of each grouping indicates the number of models that contained this specific subset of the language. We included combinations of constructs that were shared by more than 10 models.

The most apparent subset is the combination of Tasks and Sequence Flow – 97% of the models we analyzed shared this subset, and those that did not used a representation for tasks from the extended BPMN set (e.g., Subprocess). The addition of Start and End Events is the next most common subset – used by more than half of the models we analyzed. The following subsets show an interesting pattern: Either modelers focus on *process orchestration* through by adding gateways and their refinement to their models, or they focus on *process choreography* and add related organizational constructs, such as Pools and Lanes. While the addition of Pools leads to a subset that is common in nearly 30% of all models, the addition of Lanes halves this fraction.

Adding Basic Gateways or Parallel Gateways to the core set leads to a subset that is shared by 20% of all models. The popularity of the Data-based XOR Gateway and the Parallel Gateway construct indicate that they are a core element in many modeler vocabularies, even though the BPMN specification places them in the extended set of the language. The same situation holds for Message and Timer Events (both Start Events and Intermediate Events). While other event types were used very infrequently, these two event types were the most popular addition to the core modeling set in lieu of unspecified events.

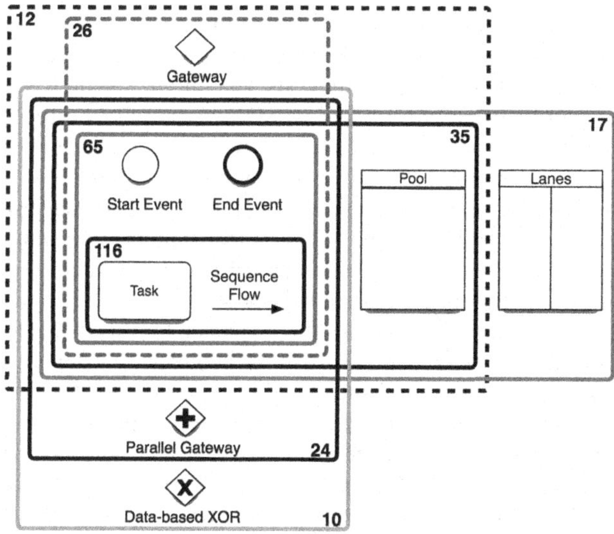

Fig. 7. Most popular BPMN Vocabulary Subsets

Overall, BPMN models appear to fall into two main sets (indicated in Fig. 7 by horizontal versus vertical grouping). The horizontal groups contain tasks, basic events plus constructs for separating organizational duties and responsibilities (Pools and Lanes). Consultants will use these types of models will most likely for organizational (re-)engineering and process improvement. The vertical groups add to this set of constructs refined constructs for specifying the exact control flow of processes (through various gateway types) as well as the exact event conditions pertaining to a process (i.e., various event construct types). This is not shown in Fig. 7 in the interest of clarity. Overall, this set of BPMN construct combinations can be expected to be favored by designers and analysts seeking to articulate the precise flow conditions, for instance, in the context of workflow engineering or process simulation rather than the organizational responsibilities (depicted by Lanes or Pools).

An interesting property of the BPMN subsets is their frequency distribution. The ranked frequency distribution again follows an exponential distribution, mirroring the behavior of individual BPMN constructs. This suggests that modelers use blocks or subsets of BPMN constructs in a similar fashion as they use individual constructs.

Combinations of BPMN constructs can thus be treated as metawords and be analyzed as such.

4 Contributions, Limitations, and Outlook

In this paper we studied the use of BPMN in actual process modeling practice. We obtained 126 (120 considered) BPMN models and used a wide range of statistical techniques to shed light onto the practical complexity afforded by the use of BPMN. Our paper makes a key contribution to the growing area of process modeling by reflecting on empirical data about the use of a rising industry standard. The most important finding is that the complexity of BPMN in practice differs considerably from its theoretical complexity. This, in turn, suggests that future research should take this distinction into account when considering BPMN's expressive power, complexity or other features or characteristics. Our study shows that the frequency of BPMN constructs follows an exponential distribution, both at the elementary level and the subset level. This means that the practical use of a formal modeling language shows similarities to the use of natural language, and suggests that linguistic techniques can be applied to better understand the formation and use of languages in conceptual modeling overall. We see an opportunity for replicating our study with other standardized modeling approaches (e.g., UML) to obtain further evidence for this conjecture.

Our findings have major implications, both for language developers and the organizational ecosystems in which modeling languages are used. Our findings point to some areas of concern in current language standardization practices, which appear to prefer language extensions (more expressive languages) to language revision (more lean languages). Our findings indicate that this may be to some extent contradictory to practical usage. Also, our findings motivate organizations to invest resources into *conventions management* in order to be able to manage and limit the complexity brought to bear by the languages employed for process modeling.

The presented research findings have to be contextualized in light of some *limitations*. First, the source of empirical evidence is limited to three sets of data sources and 126 BPMN models overall. We also did not consider any longitudinal data (e.g., the evolution of BPMN models through various iterations). However, we made an effort to collect data from multiple application areas and to consider these in our analysis. While we grouped the models by origin, we did not have sufficient information about the model content to analyze the models based on their intended use. We performed a hierarchical cluster analysis on the models themselves, but did not identify significant clusters. While this supports the random nature of our sample, it contradicts one of our expectations – that there is a clear differentiation between BPMN models depending on their intended use.

In future research, we will continue our data collection and extend it with more context-related information, e.g., for what purpose were the models created, what types of modelers created the models etc. This will allow us to triangulate our findings with contextual variables so as to arrive at informed opinions about BPMN usage across a wide range of application areas. In a related stream of research, we will apply a number of complexity metrics [e.g., 16] to the identified BPMN clusters to make a statement about how complex the frequently used BPMN constructs subsets are.

References

1. BPMI.org, OMG: Business Process Modeling Notation Specification. Final Adopted Specification. Object Management Group (2006), `http://www.bpmn.org`
2. Fowler, M.: UML Distilled: A Brief Guide To The Standard Object Modelling Language, 3rd edn. Addison-Wesley Longman, Boston, Massachusetts (2004)
3. Siau, K., Cao, Q.: Unified Modeling Language: A Complexity Analysis. Journal of Database Management 12, 26–34 (2001)
4. Rosemann, M., Recker, J., Indulska, M., Green, P.: A Study of the Evolution of the Representational Capabilities of Process Modeling Grammars. In: Dubois, E., Pohl, K. (eds.) CAiSE 2006. LNCS, vol. 4001, pp. 447–461. Springer, Heidelberg (2006)
5. Siau, K., Erickson, J., Lee, L.Y.: Theoretical vs. Practical Complexity: The Case of UML. Journal of Database Management 16, 40–57 (2005)
6. Kobryn, C.: UML 2001: A Standardization Odyssey. Communications of the ACM 42, 29–37 (1999)
7. Ouyang, C., Dumas, M., ter Hofstede, A.H.M., van der Aalst, W.M.P.: Pattern-based Translation of BPMN Process Models to BPEL Web Services. International Journal of Web Services Research 5, 42–61 (2008)
8. Recker, J., Rosemann, M., Krogstie, J.: Ontology- versus Pattern-based Evaluation of Process Modeling Languages: A Comparison. Communications of the Association for Information Systems 20, 774–799 (2007)
9. Recker, J., Indulska, M., Rosemann, M., Green, P.: How Good is BPMN Really? Insights from Theory and Practice. In: Ljungberg, J., Andersson, M. (eds.) Proceedings of the 14th European Conference on Information Systems. Association for Information Systems, Goeteborg, Sweden, pp. 1582–1593 (2006)
10. zur Muehlen, M., Ho, D.T.-Y.: Service Process Innovation: A Case Study of BPMN in Practice. In: Sprague Jr., R.H. (ed.) Proceedings of the 41th Annual Hawaii International Conference on System Sciences, Waikoloa, Hawaii (2008)
11. Wahl, T., Sindre, G.: An Analytical Evaluation of BPMN Using a Semiotic Quality Framework. In: Siau, K. (ed.) Advanced Topics in Database Research, vol. 5, pp. 102–113. Idea Group, Hershey, Pennsylvania (2006)
12. Barabási, A.-L., Bonabeau, E.: Scale-Free Networks. Scientific American 288, 50–59 (2003)
13. Li, W.: Random Texts Exhibit Zipf's-Law-Like Word Frequency Distribution. IEEE Transactions on Information Theory 38, 1842–1845 (1992)
14. Zipf, G.K.: On the Dynamic Structure of Concert Programs. Journal of Abnormal and Social Psychology 41, 25–36 (1946)
15. Hamming, R.W.: Error Detecting and Error Correcting Codes. Bell System Technical Journal 26, 147–160 (1950)
16. Rossi, M., Brinkkemper, S.: Complexity Metrics for Systems Development Methods and Techniques. Information Systems 21, 209–227 (1996)

We Still Don't Know How Much BPMN Is Enough, But We Are Getting Closer

Michael zur Muehlen and Jan Recker

Abstract Process models expressed in BPMN typically rely on a small subset of all available symbols. In our 2008 study, we examined the composition of these subsets, and found that the distribution of BPMN symbols in practice closely resembles the frequency distribution of words in natural language. We offered some suggestions based on our findings, how to make the use of BPMN more manageable and also outlined ideas for further development of BPMN. Since this paper was published it has provoked spirited debate in the BPM practitioner community, prompted the definition of a modeling standard in US government, and helped shape the next generation of the BPMN standard.

1 Motivation and Genesis of Paper

Process modeling is not a new phenomenon, but the notations for mapping out process diagrams seem to be in constant state of flux. Established notations are applied, refined, evolve, and are replaced with new notations. Like natural languages, process representations and their associated grammars seem to evolve. The Business Process Model & Notation (BPMN) has evolved since its inception in 2001 and has found its fair share of adopters in both modeling tool vendors, and industrial applications. Since the BPMN notation contains a large number of constructs (compared to older process notations such as Flow Charts, Petri Nets,

M. zur Muehlen (✉)
Howe School of Technology Management, Stevens Institute of Technology, Castle Point on Hudson, Hoboken NJ 07030, USA
e-mail: Michael.zurMuehlen@stevens.edu

J. Recker
Information Systems School, Queensland University of Technology, Brisbane QLD 4000, Australia
e-mail: j.recker@qut.edu.au

J. Bubenko et al. (eds.), *Seminal Contributions to Information Systems Engineering*,
DOI 10.1007/978-3-642-36926-1_36,

or Event-driven Process Chains), we were interested in the question which subset of BPMN elements modelers would choose to represent models. Was the language mature? Was there a defined subset that modelers naturally gravitated toward? Both authors approached this topic from different starting points – one (Recker) from the empirical use of modeling notations, the other (zur Muehlen) from the evolution of standards over time. Both of us expected modelers to use a problem-specific subset of the notation, but neither of us knew how large this subset would be, nor which symbols it would contain.

To address the research question, we began collecting BPMN diagrams. Both authors had worked in process modeling projects in industry, so the models generated as part of consulting engagements became a seed data set. This was complemented with models generated by students in process modeling courses, and models that were collected through Internet searches. Once we felt that we had obtained a sufficient number of models we began counting symbols, and tallied our results in a statistical software package. The results confirmed our hunch: Most models contained a small fraction of BPMN symbols, and the overall frequency distribution of symbols followed closely the exponential Zipf-curve that is indicative of the word distribution in natural languages. We concluded from this study that we can learn much about how we could and should use BPMN from our use of natural languages in different settings such as informal conversations, tech talks, essays and so forth.

2 Impact on Industry

2.1 Reception in Practice: Feedback by Practitioners

> *If you have even a passing interest in BPMN, you're probably aware of the great debate happening amongst a few of the BPM bloggers in the past week. [. . .] It's worth taking the time to work your way through this debate, and keep and eye on Bruce and Michael's blogs for any further commentary.* (Sandy Kemsley, Column 2, blog post 13 March 2008, http://www.column2.com/2008/03/the-great-bpmn-debate/).

One of the interesting phenomena that emerged around our paper was its reception by the BPM community of practitioners. To aid the transfer of research into practice, we decided to blog about what we believed to be main findings and implications (http://www.workflow-research.com/2008/03/03/how-much-bpmn-do-you-need/). This post led to some spirited comments and related blog posts. We were surprised by the number of commentaries and the critical feedback we received from the community, starting with Bruce Silver's challenge of the implications we laid out in our post (http://www.brsilver.com/wordpress/2008/03/09/on-how-much-bpmn-do-you-need/), and with the views of other participants that responded to this debate (e.g., http://processdevelopments.blogspot.com/2008/03/hottest-bpmn-process-modelling-debate.html).

Much of this debate was dedicated to interpreting the findings in a set of actionable implications for the community. While we had originally set out to study how BPMN *was* being used, it became clear that practitioners were interested in how BPMN *should* be used. We aspired to formulate recommendations especially for vendors and training providers; and obviously some of our arguments were deliberately challenging and provocative, in an effort to inspire certain changes around standard making, method and tool design and training development.

Some, but not all, of our recommendations and interpretations were lauded by respondents to the blogs; some responses were equally challenging and provocative, and also criticized the scientific method applied. In hindsight, we very much welcomed all the feedback we received and we still see this debate as a prime example of a healthy and fertile debate between industry and academia – especially because such conversations more often than not are absent [8].

What we learned from this episode are two things: First, making research insights more relevant requires a thorough re-write and re-publication in more accessible and readable forums, and proves to be a very worthwhile activity for academics. Second, sparking (and not necessarily winning) a debate is in itself an extremely useful activity as it sparks imagination, critical analysis and reflection – both on the side of the contributors and the recipients. We have certainly learned from this episode and continue to attempt as often as possible to convey our research not only within our scientific forums but also decisively outside of this community.

2.2 Practical Impact: The US Department of Defense

After the paper generated some interest in the BPM practitioner community, we were invited to speak at industry conferences, including the 2007 Transformation + Innovation conference in Washington, DC. The CTO and Chief Architect of the US Department of Defense's Business Mission Area was the keynote speaker at this event and talked about a practical issue: The several hundred information systems in the department were documented in various proprietary languages and notations, making systems integration challenging and training onerous. Was there a way to design and implement a standard-based notation to describe the department's processes? The conference chairman facilitated a behind-the-scenes meeting, which led to an invitation to present our findings in Washington.

The brief presentation led to the initiation of a project to define the smallest usable set of BPMN constructs for the DoD's Business Mission Area, accompanied by a style guide that would help modelers develop process models in a uniform fashion. The main driver for this style guide was the disambiguation of process fragments that could be represented in BPMN in more than one way, for example branching moments that could be represented either by using a gateway or by using conditional sequence flows. The findings from our original paper guided the selection of modeling constructs, while the design of the style guide was driven by the work on workflow patterns [14].

Once the BPMN subset and patterns had been field-tested, a question arose: The available process modeling tools did not enforce the reduced symbol pallet, much less the design patterns that had been established. What would it take to get the BPM vendor community to support the effort? We began talking to the Object Management Group's BPMN Finalization Task Force.

2.3 *Method Impact: Shaping BPMN 2.0 Conformance Classes*

The original study of BPMN models was based on version 1.2 of the BPMN standard. As our work with stakeholders in industry progressed, the Object Management Group began finalizing version 2.0 of the BPMN specification. In talking to some key stakeholders in the finalization task force, namely Robert Shapiro, Bruce Silver, and Denis Gagne, it became clear that there was appetite to group BPMN constructs into subsets to facilitate process modeling at different levels of sophistication. Bruce Silver had proposed three levels of BPMN modeling in his book [11], Robert Shapiro was representing the interests of the Workflow Management Coalition, which needed a defined subset to tailor the XPDL model interchange format to [13], and the Department of Defense had a vital interest in anchoring the newly formulated BPMN primitives in the official standard. Through a series of meetings, the elements for three BPMN conformance classes were defined: Descriptive for simple, flowchart-like diagrams; Analytic for more sophisticated models that include event handling and messaging; and Common Executable with a focus on the model attributes that a Business Process Management System would expect. The three conformance classes became part of the official BPMN 2.0 specification [12].

2.4 *Application: Conformance Classes in Practice*

Now that the conformance classes were defined, they could be designated a mandatory feature of process modeling tools that could be procured by the U.S. government. Vendor briefings were held, policy was written, and after a development period of more than 3 years, the BPMN Analytic Conformance class was officially adopted as the process modeling standard for the Business Mission Area. Today, an increasing number of BPMN tools support the conformance classes defined by the Object Management Group. But simply providing a defined subset of symbols in software was not sufficient to ensure its proper use in practice. Training classes needed to be developed, and style guides had to be written. This work is still ongoing today.

3 Academic Research on the Use of Process Modeling Notations

We have always been proud of the impact that the paper generated in industry. Still, as academics we also envisaged to leave a footprint in the body of knowledge. How do you gauge the impact of a paper on the trajectory of research in the community? A standard way of measuring impact is by means of scientometric analysis, e.g., by examining citation statistics [e.g., 1].

The 2008 CAiSE paper ranks as the third-most cited research paper on BPMN, as per Harzing's Publish or Perish (behind a paper on the semantics of the BPMN specification [2] and Steven White's guide to modeling with BPMN [10]). The paper attracted over 130 citations in the 5 years since its publication.

Exploring the types of research that perused our findings, we find that the research inspired research across empirical, analytical and formal dimensions, on BPMN [6], other process modeling notations [3, 7] and even other research domains such as web services [9], process mining [4] or software development, amongst others [5].

Two themes have dominated the research building on our work:

(a) How suitable is BPMN for modeling certain kinds of processes? One way that our research was continued by our colleagues was to adopt the key finding of our study (that modelers use specialized and limited subsets of the BPMN vocabulary) and examine dedicated application scenarios – which part of BPMN do we need when we model web service interfaces? How much BPMN do we need for software development?
(b) How do modelers learn to use BPMN? Another vein of research has started to explore another implication of our work: if modelers use different subsets of BPMN only, how could a staged approach to learning BPMN look like? Which (sets of) symbols are easier or harder to apply, and which of the symbol characteristics are more likely to introduce modeling errors or understandability problems?

The true impact of papers on the ever-evolving body of knowledge remains to be seen in the long term. There might be studies still at the planning stage that build on, extend, challenge or dispute the findings from the 2008 paper. In whatever format this work is extended, we are hoping that the study remains a fertile ground for other academics to start thinking about BPM research, even if this means that at some stage our findings will be disconfirmed and replaced with much better theory and explanation of how much language is enough.

4 Insights

In looking back at our 2008 paper, we believe there are a number of properties of the paper – and the research it describes – that offer insights to the next 25 years of advanced information systems engineering and the wider IS community.

First, at the time of writing the content of the paper – an empirical study of the use of a notation that was predominantly subject to formal and analytical research so far – was clearly a niche topic in a densely populated subject area. Both authors continue to look for such niche topics, hoping to contribute to popular debates with a different view.

Second, we learned about the importance of complementing the scientific work with other reporting styles and formats that make the findings available to and accessible for other communities that may have an interest. Means such as blogging, essaying or presenting allow academics to deliberately and decisively address different audiences beyond academia – even if that means further work. To create practical impact from a research study may take much longer than the next publishing cycle, but it can fuel the next round of inquiry.

Last but not least, one of the most important lessons is the value of feedback, and the virtue of welcoming and working with such feedback – especially the critical type. Only this way a true debate is emerging, and only through debate can we continue to identify topics that are (a) challenging (otherwise there would be no debate) and (b) relevant (otherwise debates would not become intense and fierce).

We look forward to the next 25 years of advanced information systems engineering research and the lessons and challenges that this era will bring.

References

1. Chen, C., Song, I.-Y., Yuan, X., Zhang, J.: The Thematic and Citation Landscape of Data and Knowledge Engineering (1985–2007). Data & Knowledge Engineering 67 (2008) 234–259
2. Dijkman, R.M., Dumas, M., Ouyang, C.: Semantics and Analysis of Business Process Models in BPMN. Information and Software Technology 50 (2008) 1281–1294
3. Lassen, K.B., van der Aalst, W.M.P.: Complexity Metrics for Workflow Nets Information and Software Technology 51 (2009) 610–626
4. Li, C., Reichert, M., Wombacher, A.: Mining Business Process Variants: Challenges, Scenarios, Algorithms. Data & Knowledge Engineering 70 (2011) 409–434
5. Monsalve, C., Abran, A., April, A.: Measuring Software Functional Size from Business Process Models. International Journal of Software Engineering and Knowledge Engineering 21 (2011) 311–338
6. Recker, J.: Opportunities and Constraints: The Current Struggle with BPMN. Business Process Management Journal 16 (2010) 181–201
7. Recker, J., Rosemann, M., Indulska, M., Green, P.: Business Process Modeling: A Comparative Analysis. Journal of the Association for Information Systems 10 (2009) 333–363
8. Robey, D., Markus, M.L.: Beyond Rigor and Relevance: Producing Consumable Research about Information Systems. Information Resource Management Journal 11 (1998) 7–15
9. Swanson, E.B.: Information System Implementation: Bridging the Gap Between Design and Utilization. Irwin, Homewood, Illinois (1988)
10. White, S.A., Miers, D.: BPMN Modeling and Reference Guide. Lighthouse Point, Florida, Future Strategies (2008)
11. Silver, B.: BPMN Method and Style, 2nd Edition, with BPMN Implementer's Guide: A structured approach for business process modeling and implementation using BPMN 2.0. Cody-Cassidy Press, Aptos, CA (2011).

12. Object Management Group: Business Process Model and Notation (BPMN 2.0). OMG Specification dtc/11-01-03. Framingham, MA (2011)
13. WfMC: XML Process Definition Language (XPDL), WfMC Standards. WFMC-TC-1025, http://www.wfmc.org, 2001.
14. van Der Aalst, W. M., Ter Hofstede, A. H., Kiepuszewski, B., & Barros, A. P.: Workflow Patterns. Distributed and Parallel Databases, 14 (2003) 1, 5–51.

The Future of CAiSE

John Krogstie, Oscar Pastor, and Barbara Pernici

Abstract In this chapter an analysis of the current goals and positioning of CAiSE is provided and aims and goals for future years are discussed. First, the conference role in the Information Systems community is considered, then we focus on how the goal of maintaining the conference at top level could be achieved, in a world in which new communication venues and practices are changing established scientific practices.

1 The CAiSE Experience and the Changing World of Publications

Most of the editors and authors of this book have participated in many CAiSE conferences and have considered it a place where attending regularly would not only provide an excellent publication forum, but also a place where ideas could be exchanged with other researchers in the field, and, for the youngest ones, an opportunity was given to discuss new ideas with established researchers in the field.

In contrast to many other scientific disciplines, computer science considers conference publications, and as illustrated in [1] one can show formally that a few computer science conferences are equally important in terms of impact as the top journals in the field. In the last few years, a debate has started in the Computer

J. Krogstie (✉)
Department of Computer and Information Science, NTNU- The Norwegian University of Science and Technology, Trondheim, Norway
e-mail: krogstie@idi.ntnu.no

O. Pastor
Centro de Investigación ProS, DSIC – Edificio 1 F, Universidad Politécnica de Valenci, Camino de Vera S/N, Valencia 46022, Spain

B. Pernici
Politecnico di Milano, piazza Leonardo da Vinci, 32, Milan, Italy

J. Bubenko et al. (eds.), *Seminal Contributions to Information Systems Engineering*, DOI 10.1007/978-3-642-36926-1_37, © Springer-Verlag Berlin Heidelberg 2013

Science field on publication venues and on the role of conferences and journals in the field. It has been claimed that the focus on publications through conferences is a sign that the fields of Computer Science/Information Systems is not mature, and it is indicated also CS/IS should shift to have journals as the main publication channel, and that "Computer science should refocus the conference system on its primary purpose of bringing researchers together" [2]. We think that this is to a large degree happening already (e.g. in most countries, it is the best journals that are the most prestigious publication outlets, in particular when research evaluations and selections for positions are performed) although the set of focused workshops and conferences is very important, especially for PhD candidates to get feedback from the research community quickly enough for it to be useful towards their PhD thesis. It is also useful for a discipline like Information Systems and Information Systems Engineering, which deals with designed (and not natural) artifacts in interaction with human reality to have robust mechanism to build arenas for bringing people together to bring the research ahead. In particular for new research directions it is not sufficient to only read each other works in scientific journals; discussion and interaction are needed.

The paper published in CACM also lists a number of reasons for having conferences [2]:

1. To rate publications and researchers.
2. To disseminate new research results and ideas.
3. To network, gossip, and recruit.
4. To discuss controversial issues in the community.

In most fields, items 2, 3 and partly 4 are most important, although also the first is relevant as we have seen.

On the other hand, an increasing number of conferences in the Information Systems area are emerging, focusing either on general topics or on more specialized issues. The challenge therefore is not only to have a conference to provide an interesting discussion environment, but also a conference that is considered a high quality forum for exchanging ideas and meeting other researchers.

In an attempt to compare conferences in the Computer Science domain, the position of the conference in international rankings can be taken into consideration. Ranking also give criteria for such evaluations that can be considered as goals for a top level conference. For instance, in his web site,[1] Osmar R. Zaïane lists the following criteria: "based on general reputation of the conference in the field, the citation of the papers published in the conference, reputation of program committee members and reputation of the review process. ... Top conferences are known for their impact history and their rigorous review process. They should be equivalent, if not superior in impact and prestige, to reputable journals".

[1] http://webdocs.cs.ualberta.ca/~zaiane/htmldocs/ConfRanking.html

In the most comprehensive list of relevant conferences,[2] published by The Computing Research and Education Association of Australasia (CORE), CAiSE is rated as a top conference, a position which we should work to keep.

As indicated above there are several indicators that can be taken into consideration in the evaluation of a conference. For community-building, one possible metric is the ratio attendants/papers. Another important point here is that the conference is relatively focused as for topics. A conference accepting papers across a large number of areas will seldom be central to a specific community. As for value for researchers, the review process is also important, with a well managed reviewing process that provides constructive feedback to the authors, both for accepted and rejected papers. One can also look at impacts (as for citations). Although not on the same level as for the top journals, the best conferences have an H-index on the same level as the second-best journals (the numbers below are from 'Journal Impact on Publish or Parish (based on google scholar)'. The data quality might differ between different events, based on how consistently they are referenced though. Here also some SE-outlets are included (the best computing journals have an H-index in the area of 200–300):

- EJIS-journal: 81
- IST-journal: 80
- ICSE-conference: 73
- CAiSE-conference: 66 based on conference papers (73 if you include papers in special issues)
- JAIS-journal: 66
- ICIS-conference: 58
- CAIS-journal: 57

Apart from noticeable impact as indicated above, how is CAiSE doing so far?

- *Community gathering*: In total the number of participants to the conference has been around 200 with around 40 papers to the main conference. Many of the those not having a role in the conference do have other roles though, e.g., in the Forum or in Workshops, thus we should work to make the conference even more attractive as a community event (e.g. have possibilities to arrange meetings for related activities, as in the case of the IFIP 8.1 Working Group, which since many years has had its business meeting at the conference). On mix of focus and development, [3] writes: "Over time, CAiSE manages to not only retain authors who are working on the established ideas of the conference, but also to attract new authors who would bring fresh ideas to the community. A comparison of the returning rating of CAiSE authors and their contributions to other conferences shows that CAiSE now retains a healthy fraction of recurring authors in order to keep the community open." Thus we can argue that there is a logical place for

[2] http://core.edu.au/index.php/categories/conference%20rankings/1

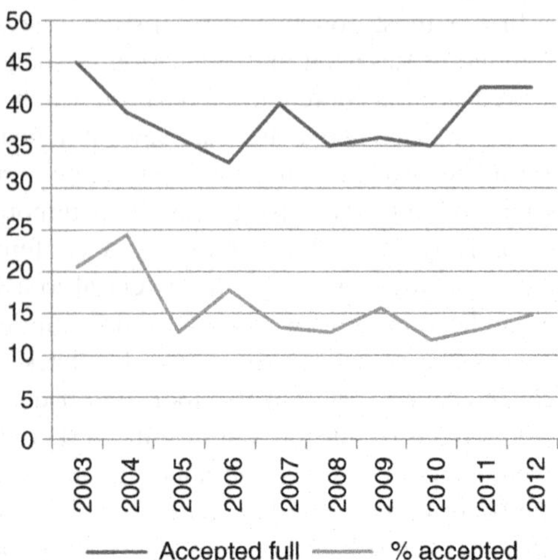

Fig. 1 Submission and acceptance rates

ISE, merging the more technical SE area with the more business oriented SE area as also concluded by [3].

- A top conference should have good possibilities for *interaction* (e.g., long discussions, special interactive sessions, doctoral consortium etc.). This should also have a positive impact for conferences and workshop that would be less prestigious as independent events: for instance, whereas the main paper sessions in CAiSE has been relatively traditional, the workshops such as EMMSAD are organized with a format where each paper is discussed over a 45 min slot in which the main presentation is only half of this time, thus providing more interaction. So does the forum, both types of events being able to also support the dissemination of more novel ideas. Controversial issues for the community are openly addressed in panel sessions in the main conference.
- A top conference should have a rigorous *review process* that ensures fair review and detailed review comments to all authors. In CAiSE for instance, three usually quite comprehensive reviews are provided from members of the international program committee. A member of the program board then looks on the reviews, and supports a discussion among the reviewers where there are differences in the ratings. Based on the reviews and further discussions, the program board and program committee members select the papers to be accepted in a program board meeting going over 2 days. Papers with novel ideas that are not thoroughly validated yet to be accepted for the main conference might be proposed for either the forum or one of the workshops.
- *Impact*: A top level conference typically has a 20 year + history, and it is also cited quite a lot. A top level conference would thus be expected to have a H-index above 50. As we mentioned above, this is valid for e.g. CAiSE (and other top IS and SE conferences).
- A top level conference should have low *acceptance rate* (<20). Figure 1 shows an illustration of the development of acceptance figures for CAiSE over the years.

Whereas acceptance rate until 2004 was around 25 %, over the last years it has been below 15 % (which some might argue is even a bit too low).

2 Future Plans

In terms of the future, the CAiSE environment provides a set of significant features that show a promising, successful future. Modern IT requirements recognize more than ever the importance of Engineering Information Systems correctly. It is not just a matter of "Software". Information Systems design and implementation cover all the facets of our society, and new challenges appear continuously. CAiSE is intended to be the natural forum where past, present and future of Information Systems Engineering should be properly discussed and explored.

While keeping a top quality level – including both an academic perspective and the practical applications – is already a must for CAiSE, it is also remarkable the friendly atmosphere that has been created during this 25-years old trip. When a sound and rigorous scientific environment is linked to a friendly and pleasant working environment, centered around a relatively well-defined topic area the working context as a whole becomes much richer. This is happening year after year with CAiSE, and this is part of the conference idiosyncrasy that every organizer is committed to preserve and reinforce.

Incorporating young, brilliant researchers to the community is another "must" for the CAiSE community. It is well recognized how important it is to balance the experience of seniors with the enthusiasm of juniors. The quality required by the Scientific Committees of the conference requires also to open the community to different countries. From its initially European conception, the very next future will continue broadening the CAiSE influence to the rest of the world, reinforcing continuously the already relevant participation of scientists from America, Asia, Australia, and Africa.

There are many other tasks to accomplish. Improving and adapting the conference format with the new times, using extensively the capabilities of social networks, exploring advance channels of publication of papers, providing a journal-based style for the CAiSE audience... Many new ideas to explore to show to the community the sound compromise of fitting the requirements of our modern IT-oriented society. Our CAiSE community has a real potential to make all these goals come true, through the accumulated amount of people and knowledge that is ready to explore new ways being fully respectful with all the experience accumulated in the past. This is by far the most important legacy of these 25 years of history. We have a very strong basis to face new challenges.

Summarizing, from the hard and brilliant work that so many people have done in this 25 exciting years, CAiSE has the exciting challenge of becoming the most top-ranked international conference of Information Systems Engineering. We are all committed to this task, and you are all invited to share the CAiSE adventure with us for – at the very least – the next 25 years.

References

1. Pham, M.C., Klamma, R., and Jarke, M. (2011) Development of computer science disciplines: a social network analysis approach. Social Netw. Analys. Mining, 1(4):321–340.
2. Fortnow L. (2011) CACM Viewpoint: Time for computer science to grow up, Communications of the ACM, Vol. 52 No. 8, Pages 33–35
3. Jarke, M., Pham, M.C., and Klamma, R. (2013) Evolution of the CAiSE Author Community: A Social Network Analysis. This book, Chapter 2, Springer.